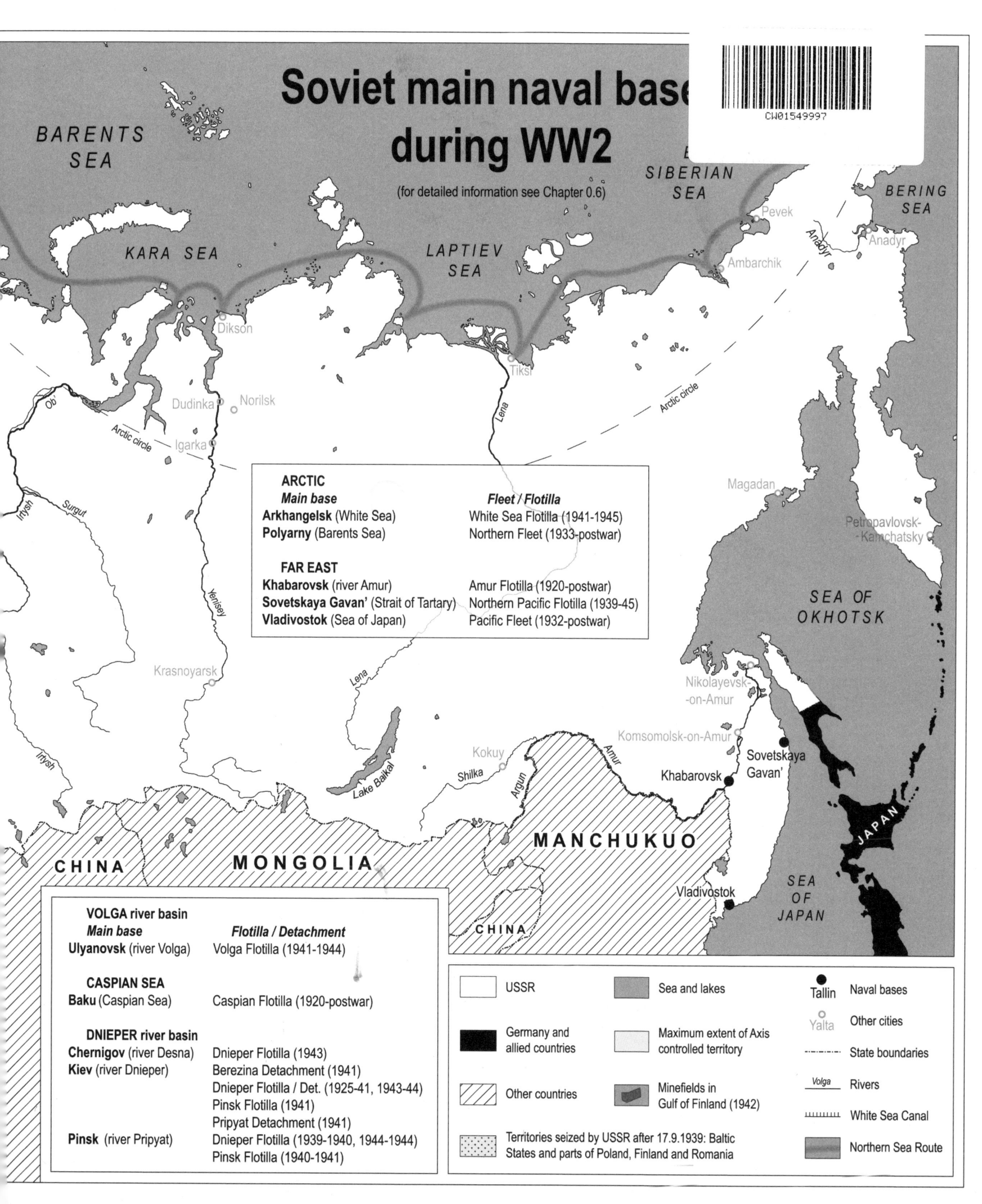

Warships of the Soviet Fleets
1939–1945

Warships of the Soviet Fleets 1939–1945

Volume II: Escorts and Smaller Fighting Ships

Przemysław Budzbon • Jan Radziemski • Marek Twardowski

Line drawings by:
Jerzy Lewandowski • Tomasz Grotnik
Jarosław Dzierżawski

Seaforth
PUBLISHING

Dedication

The book is dedicated to our grandchildren (listed in order of appearance)
as some form of compensation for the time we didn't spend with them:
Tymoteusz, Zofia and Jędrzej of Przemek
Nicole, and Karina of Jan
Olaf and Helena of Marek

Frontispiece:
Tros (T-2) during transfer from Baltic to Vladivostok, approaching Panama Canal in July 1939.
Naval History and Heritage Command NH 79334

Copyright © Przemysław Budzbon, Jan Radziemski & Marek Twardowski 2022
Line drawings © Jerzy Lewandowski, Tomasz Grotnik & Jarosław Dzierżawski 2022

First published in Great Britain in 2022 by
Seaforth Publishing
An imprint of Pen & Sword Books Ltd
47 Church Street, Barnsley
S Yorkshire S70 2AS

www.seaforthpublishing.com
Email info@seaforthpublishing.com

British Library Cataloguing in Publication Data
A CIP data record for this book is available from the British Library

ISBN 978-1-3990-2277-4 (Hardback)
ISBN 978-1-3990-2278-1 (ePub)
ISBN 978-1-3990-2279-8 (Kindle)

All rights reserved. No part of this publication may be reproduced or transmitted in any form or by any means, electronic or mechanical, including photocopying, recording, or any information storage and retrieval system, without prior permission in writing of both the copyright owner and the above publisher.

The rights of the authors of this work have been asserted in accordance with the
Copyright, Designs and Patents Act 1988

Pen & Sword Books Limited incorporates the imprints of Atlas, Archaeology, Aviation, Discovery, Family History, Fiction, History, Maritime, Military, Military Classics, Politics, Select, Transport, True Crime, Air World, Frontline Publishing, Leo Cooper, Remember When, Seaforth Publishing, The Praetorian Press, Wharncliffe Local History, Wharncliffe Transport, Wharncliffe True Crime and White Owl.

Typeset and designed by Mousemat Design Limited
Printed and bound in India Replika Press Pvt Ltd

Contents

Vol II. Escorts and Smaller Fighting Ships

Alphabetical acronyms carried by Soviet warships   6

11. Escort ships   11
11.1. Standard Soviet-built types   11
11.2. NKVD patrol ships   19
11.3. Lend-Lease ships   22
11.4. War prizes   24
   11.4.1. Baltic States, 1940   24
   11.4.2. Romania, 1944   24
   11.4.3. Manchukuo, 1945   25
11.5. Conversions   25
   11.5.1. Seagoing escorts   25
      11.5.1.1. Mobilised trawlers   27
   11.5.2. Coastal escorts   35
   11.5.3. River escorts   38

12. Large submarine hunters   40
12.1. Standard Soviet-built   40
12.2. Lend-Lease   47
12.3. War prizes – Southeast Europe, 1944   50

13. Small submarine hunters   51
13.1. The 'unitary' MO types   51
13.2. The war-built standard types   80
13.3. Miscellaneous   91
13.4. War prizes – Southeast Europe   92

14. Patrol boats   93
14.1. Standard types   93
14.2. Lend-Lease boats   115
14.3. Miscellaneous NKVD patrol boats   118
14.4. Army conversions   123
14.5. Civilian conversions   124
   14.5.1. Mobilised passenger vessels   124
   14.5.2. NKVD Border Guard fishing vessel types   124
   14.5.3. Mobilised fishing vessels   127
   14.5.4. Tugs   137
   14.5.5. Naval auxiliaries   137
14.6. War prizes   137
   14.6.1. Poland, 1939   137
   14.6.2. Finland, 1940   138
   14.6.3. Lithuania, 1940   138
   14.6.4. Iran, 1941   139
   14.6.5. Southeast Europe, 1944   139
   14.6.6. Manchukuo, 1945   140
14.7. Motor launches   140

15. Floating artillery batteries   144

16. AA defence ships   145
16.1. Floating AA batteries   145
16.2. Air warning service ships   148
16.3. Air warning & AA defence boats   151

17. Minelayers   154
17.1. Naval constructions   154
17.2. Conversions   155
   17.2.2. Naval conversions   155
   17.2.3. Civilian conversions   157

18. Netlayers   163
18.1. Conversions   165

19. Minesweepers   166
19.1. Russian-built   166
19.2. Standard Soviet-built types   166
19.3. Lend-Lease ships   181
19.4. War prizes   188
   19.4.1. Poland, 1939   188
   19.4.2. Baltic States, 1940   189
   19.4.3. Southeast Europe, 1944–1945   191
19.5. Conversions   193
   19.5.1. Mobilised trawlers   193
   19.5.2. Mobilised tugs   200
      19.5.2.1. Seagoing and coastal tugs   200
      19.5.2.2. River tugs   213
      19.5.2.2.3. Volga tugs for minesweeping rafts   218
   19.5.3. Naval & Army conversion   221
   19.5.4. Civilian conversions   222
   19.5.5. War prizes – Southeast Europe, 1944-1945   227

20. Minesweeping boats   228
20.1. Standard types   228
20.2. War prizes – Bulgaria, 1944   241
20.3. Conversions   241
   20.3.1. Naval conversions   241
   20.3.2. Civilian conversions   244
      20.3.2.1. Passenger, cargo and service motorboats   244
      20.3.2.2. Fishing boats   248
         20.3.2.2.1. Motorboats   248
         20.3.2.2.2. Seiners   255
         20.3.2.2.3. Drifters   262
         20.3.2.2.4. Sail-motor schooners   263
      20.3.2.3. Tugs   265
   20.3.3 War prizes –1944–1945   272

21. Landing vessels and craft   275
21.1. Soviet-built standard types   275
21.2. Lend-lease ships   291
21.3. War prizes 1943-45   294

Index   297

Warships of the Soviet Fleets, 1939–1945

Alphabetical acronyms carried by Soviet warships.

Numerous smaller or auxiliary ships carried identifiers instead of or as well as names. The alphanumerical identifiers consisted of alphabetical acronym followed by connector or character (No) and followed by the number.

Only general acronyms (not related to individual ships' classes or types) are listed here.

Acronym	Full meaning	English equivalent
A	**A**rkhangel'skij	Arkhangelsk (harbour craft)
AK	**K**ater **A**kademii	Boat of Naval Academy
AKA	**A**rtillerijskij **k**ater	Artillery (Rocket) boat
AMB	**A**rkhangel'skij **m**oto**b**ot	Motorboat of Arkhangelsk harbour
AO	**A**rtillerijskij **o**tdel	Artillery department (boat of)
AS	**A**varijno-**s**pasatel'nyj	Salvage-rescue
ASVB	**A**varijno-**s**pasatel'nyj **v**odolaznyj **b**ot	Salvage-rescue diving tender
B	**B**ol'shaia	Large (submarine)
B	**B**uksirovshchik	Tug
BAD	**B**arzha **a**rtillerijskaia **d**esantnaia	Fire support landing craft
BAMT	**B**arzha **a**rtillerijsko-**m**inno-**t**orpednaia	Artillery-mine-torpedo barge
BD	**B**arzha **d**esantnaia	Landing ship
BDB	**B**ystrokhodnaia **d**esantnaia **b**arzha	Fast landing ship
BG	**B**uksir **g**avanskij	Harbour tug
BK	**B**ronirovannyj **k**ater	AMGB
BK	**B**uksirnyj **k**ater	Tugboat
BKA	**B**ronirovannyj **k**ater	AMGB
BM	**B**uksir **m**orskoj	Seagoing tug
BMK	**B**ol'shoj **m**orskoj **k**ater	Large seagoing boat
BO	**B**ol'shoj **o**khotnik	Large submarine hunter
BP	**B**uksirnyj **p**arokhod	Steam tug
BPL	**B**rigada **p**odvodnykh **l**odok	Auxiliary boat of submarine brigade
BR	**B**uksir **r**ejdovyj	Coastal tug
BRN	**Br**andvakhtennoe sud**n**o	Guard vessel
BS	**B**randvakhtennoe **s**udno	Guard vessel
BSh	**B**lok**sh**iv	Hulk
BSN	**B**arzha **s**ukhogruznaia **n**esamokhodnaia	Dry cargo dumb barge
BSS	**B**arzha **s**ukhogruznaia **s**amokhodnaia	Dry cargo propelled barge
BTP	**B**uksirovshchik **t**ral**p**lotika	Tug of minesweeping raft
BTShch	**B**uksir-**t**ral'**shch**ik	Tug-minesweeper
BTShch	**B**ystrokhodnyj **t**ral'**shch**ik	Fast minesweeper
BVB	**B**eregovyj **v**odolaznyj **b**ot	Shore diving tender
ChF	**Ch**ernomorskij **F**lot	Auxiliary boat of the Black Sea Fleet
ChFBK	**Ch**ernomorskij **F**lot **b**uksirnyj **k**ater	Towboat of the Black Sea Fleet
ChFMP	**Ch**ernomorskij **F**lot **m**otorno **p**arusnyj	Sail-motor boat of the Black Sea Fleet
ChFMSh	**Ch**ernomorskij **F**lot **m**otornaia **sh**khuna	Motor-schooner of the Black Sea Fleet
ChTZ	**Ch**eliabinskij **T**raktornyj **Z**avod	Boat of the Chelyabinsk Tractor Factory (Civilian)
DB	**D**esantnaia **b**arzha	Landing craft
DB	**D**esantnyj **b**ot	Landing motorboat
DF	**D**neprovskaia **F**lotilla	Auxiliary boat of the Dnieper Flotilla
DFMB	**D**neprovskaia **F**lotilla **m**oto**b**ot	Motorboat of the Dnieper Flotilla
DFPD	**D**neprovskaia **F**lotilla **p**lavuchij **d**ok	Floating dock of the Dnieper Flotilla
DG	**D**e**g**azatsionnoe sudno	Gas cleansing vessel
DK	**D**esantnyj **k**orabl'	Landing ship
DMB	**D**esantnyj **m**oto**b**ot	Landing motorboat
DPB	**D**egazatsionnaia **p**lav**b**aza	Gas cleansing depot ship
DS	**D**esantnoe **s**udno	Landing craft

DT	**D**esantnyj **t**ransport	Landing ship transport
DZ	**D**ym**z**aveshchik	Smoke-screen layer
EBR	**E**lektromagneticheskaia stantsiia **b**ezobmotochnogo **r**azmagnichivaniia	Electromagnetic windless degaussing station
EK	**E**skortnyj **k**orabl'	Escort ship
EL	**EL**sportles	Boat of the Eksportles trust (Civilian)
EMKATShch	**E**lektro**m**agnitnyj **kat**er-tral'**shch**ik	Electromagnetic minesweeping boat
EMT	**E**lektro**m**agneticheskij **t**ral'shchik	Electromagnetic minesweeper
EMTSchch	**E**lektro**m**agnitnyj **t**ral'**shch**ik	Electromagnetic minesweeper
GB	**G**avanskij **b**uksir	Harbour tug
GE	**G**idrograficheskaia **e**kspeditsiia	Surveying expedition (boat of)
GK	**G**idrograficheskij **k**ater	Surveying boat
GM	**G**lavnyj **m**iner	Chief miner (department boat)
GO	**G**idrograficheskij **o**triad	Surveying branch (boat of)
GOK	**G**idrograficheskij **o**triad **k**ater	Surveying branch boat
GOLB	**G**idrograficheskij **o**triad **l**otsmeisterskij **b**ot	Surveying branch pilot boat
GP	**G**lavnyj voennyj **p**ort (Vladovostok)	Auxiliary boat of the main naval base (Vladivostok)
GRS	**G**runtoraz**m**yvochnoe **s**udno	Ground abrasion vessel
GS	**G**ospital'nyj **t**ransport	Hospital transport
I	**I**strebitel'	Hunter (submarine)
I	**I**talskaia	Italian (war-booty submarine)
Ia	**Ia**roslavets	Boat from Iaroslavl Yd
IOK	**I**nzhenernyj **o**triad **k**orabl'	Ship of engineering branch
IP	**I**zmailskij **p**ort	Izmail harbour (boat of)
IS	**I**nstitiut (NIMIST)	Institut = Naval scientific-research institute of communications and tele-mechanics (boat of)
IU	**I**ugo-Baltijskij Flot	Auxiliary boat of the Southern Baltic Fleet (post-war)
K	**K**rejserskaia	Cruiser (submarine)
K	**K**ronshtadskij port	Kronshtadt harbour (boat of)
K-Zis	**K**ater-**Zis**	Launch powered by ZiS engine
KATShch	**K**ater-**t**ral'**shch**ik	Minesweeping boat
KB	**K**illektornaia **b**arzha	Mooring lighter
KBP	**K**abinet **b**oevoj **p**odgotovki	Combat training cabinet
KBZ	**K**ater **b**eno**z**apravshchik	Petrol tanker boat
KD	**K**ater **d**esantnyj	Landing boat
KEMTSchch	**K**ater-**e**lektro**m**agnitnyj **t**ral'**shch**ik	Boat-electromagnetic minesweeper
Kh	**Kh**abarovskij port	Khabarovsk harbour (boat of)
KhP	**Kh**ankovskij **p**ort	Hanko harbour (boat of)
KL	**K**anonerskaia **l**odka	Gunboat
KMB	**K**ater **m**oto**b**ot	Motorboat
KMSh	**K**ater **m**otornaia **sh**khuna	Motor schooner boat
KP	**K**ievskij **p**ort	Kiev harbour (boat of)
KP	**K**ronshtadskij **p**ort	Kronshtadt harbour (boat of)
KS	**K**abel'noe **s**udno	Cable layer
KS	**K**ater **s**viazi	Communication boat
KT	**K**ater-**t**ral'shchik	Minesweeping boat
KVN	**K**orabl' **v**ozdushnogo **n**abliudeniia	Air surveillance ship
L	**L**eningradskij (port)	Leningrad harbour (boat of)
LD	**L**edoko**l**	Icebreaker
LED	**L**e**d**okol	Icebreaker
LF	**L**adozhskaia **f**lotilla	Auxiliary boat of the Ladoga Flotilla
LK	**L**inejnyj **k**orabl'	Auxiliary ship of the Squadron
LOTs	**Lot**smejsterskoe **s**udno	Pilot boat
LP	**L**eningradskij **p**ort	Leningrad harbour (boat of)

Warships of the Soviet Fleets, 1939–1945

Acronym	Full meaning	English equivalent
LVR	**L**eningradskij **v**odnyj **r**ajon	Leningrad water area
M	**M**alaia	Small (submarine)
M	**M**urmanskij port	Murmansk harbour (boat of)
MA	**M**orskaia **A**kademiia	Naval academy (boat of)
MB	**M**orskoj **b**uksir	Seagoing tug
MB	**M**oto**b**ot	Motorboat
MBTShch	**B**uksirovshch**ik EMT**	Tug of electromagnetic sweep
MI	**M**otobot **i**nzhenernyj	Motorboat of engineering branch
MK	**M**innyj **k**ater	Armed (rocket) boat
MKhTshch	Tral'**shch**ik-buksirovshchik **MKhT**	Minesweeper-tug of magnetic tail sweep
MKL	**M**orskaia **k**anonerskaia **l**odka	Seagoing gunboat
MMB	**M**urmansk **m**oto**b**ot	Murmansk harbour motorboat
MO	**M**alyj **o**khotnik	Small submarine hunter
MO-L	**M**alyj **o**khotnik - **L**eningrad	Small submarine hunter - Leningrad
MP	**M**urmanskij **p**ort	Murmansk harbour (boat of)
MPK	**M**alyj **p**rotivolodochnyj **k**orabl'	Small antisubmarine ship
MRT	**M**alyj **R**ybolovnyj **T**rauler	Civilian
MS	**M**otornyj **s**ejner	Civilian
MSh	**M**otornaia **sh**khuna	Motor schooner
MSK	**M**orskoj **s**anitarnyj **k**ater	Seagoing sanitary boat
MSO	**M**orskoj **s**anitarnyj **o**bvod	Seagoing sanitary region (boat of)
MT	**M**inno-**t**orpednaia	Mine-torpedo (barge)
MTO	**M**inno-**to**rpednaia	Mine-torpedo (barge)
MU	**M**orskoe **u**chilishche	Naval high school (boat of)
N	**N**emetskaia	German (submarine)
N	**N**ikolaevsk-on-Amur	Nikolaevsk-on-Amur harbour (boat of)
NAMB	**Na**khodka **m**oto**b**ot	Nakhodka harbour motorboat
NK	**N**ovozemel'skij **k**ater	Novaya Zemlya base boat
NMB	**N**ovozemel'skiaia baza **m**oto**b**ot	Novaya Zemlya base motorboat
NP	**N**ikolaevskij **p**ort	Nikolaev harbour (boat of)
NS	**S**luzhba **n**abliudeniia i **s**viazi	Surveillance and communication service (boat)
O	**S**udno **o**tmetchik	Target practice recorders
OK	**O**pytovoj **k**orabl'	Experimental vessel
OO	**O**sobovoj **o**tdel'	NKVD special branch (boat of)
OP	**O**desskij **p**ort	Odessa harbour (boat of)
OPS	**Op**ytovoe **s**udno	Experimental vessel
OS	**O**pytovoe **s**udno	Experimental vessel
OShK	**K**ater **ob**"edinyonnoj **sh**koly	Boat of union of naval schools
OT	**S**udno-**ot**opitel'	Heater
OV	**O**khrana **v**odnogo rajona	Protection of water area
OVR	**O**khrana **v**odnogo **r**ajona	Protection of water area
PAB	**P**lavuchaia **a**rtillerijskaia **b**atereia	Floating artillery battery
PB	**P**lavuchaia **b**aza	Depot ship
PBN	**P**lavuchaia **b**aza **n**esamokhodnaia	Dumb depot ship
PBS	**P**lavuchaia **b**aza **s**amokhodnaia	Propelled depot ship
PD	**P**lavuchij **d**ok	Floating dock
PG	**P**olu**g**lisser	Half-hydroplane launch
PK	**P**lavuchij **k**ran	Floating crane
PK	**P**ogranichnyj **k**ater	Border guard boat
PKDS	**P**lavuchaia **k**ontrol'no-**d**ozimetricheskaia **s**tantsiia	Floating radiation monitoring station
PKZ	**P**lavuchaia **k**azarma	Accommodation hulk
PL	**P**odvodnaia **l**odka	Auxiliary boat of submarine brigade

PM	**P**lavuchaia **m**asterskaia	Floating workshop
PMB	**M**oto**b**ot **p**odvodnykh rabot	Diving motor tender
PMB	**P**lavuchaia **m**asterskaia moto**b**ot	Floating workshop boat
PMR	**P**lavuchaia **r**emontno-**m**asterskaia	Floating repair-workshop
PMSh	**P**arusno-**m**otornaia **sh**khuna	Sail-motor schooner
POK	**Po**syl'nyj **k**ater	Dispatch boat
PP	**P**odvodnoe **p**lavanie	Submarine department (boat of)
PPK	**P**echorskij port **p**lavuchij **k**ran	Floating crane of the Pechora harbour
PPR	**P**lavuchij **pr**ichal	Floating berth
PS	**P**ogranichnoe **s**udno	Border guard vessel
PS	**P**osyl'noe **s**udno	Dispatch vessel
PSh	**P**ogranichnaia **sh**khuna	Border guard schooner
PSK	**P**ogranichnyj **s**torozhevoj **k**orabl'	Patrol ship of border guard
PSKL	**P**lavuchij **skl**ad	Floating warehouse
PSKR	**P**ogranichnyj **s**torozhevoj **ka**ter	Border guard patrol ship
PSZHT	**P**lavuchij **S**klad **Z**hidkogo **T**opliva	Floating Storage of Liquid Fuel
PT		Army designation
PU	**P**olit**u**pravlenie	Political authority (boat of)
PVO	**P**roti**v**ovozdushnaia **o**borona	AA defence (boat)
PZB	**P**lavuchaia **z**enitnaia **b**atreia	Floating AA battery
PZS	**P**lavuchaia **z**ariadovaia **s**tantsiia	Floating charging plant
RB	**R**abochij **b**ot	Launch
RB	**R**ejdovyj **b**uksir	Coastal tug
RBZ	**R**ejdovyj **b**arkas	Coastal longboat
RK	**R**abochij **k**ater	Service craft
RK	**R**az"ezdnoj **k**ater	Communication boat
RMB	**R**echnoj **m**oto**b**ot	River motorboat
RT	**R**ybolovnyj **t**rauler	Fishing trawler (Civilian designation)
RTShch	**R**echnoj **t**ral'**shch**ik	River minesweeper
RZS	**R**ezervnaia **z**ariadovaia **s**tantsiia	Reserve charging station
S	**S**redniaia	Medium (submarine)
SB	**S**amokhodnaia **b**arzha	Propelled barge
SB	**S**amokhodnaia desantnaia **b**arzha	Propelled landing craft
SB	**S**pasatel'nyj **b**uksir	Salvage tug
SBR	**S**tantsiia **b**ezobmotochnogo **r**azmagnichivaniia	Windless degaussing station
SDK	**S**pasatel'no-**d**eaktivatsionnyj **k**orabl'	Salvage-deactivation ship
SF	**S**evernyj **F**lot (sudno)	Auxiliary ship of the Northern Fleet
Sh	**Sh**tabnoj	Staff (vessel)
ShK	**Sh**tabnoj **k**orabl'	Staff ship
SK	**S**torozhevoj **k**ater	Patrol boat
SKA	**S**torozhevoj **ka**ter	Patrol boat
SKh	**S**udno-**kh**ranilishche	Storage-ship
SKR	**S**torozhevoj **k**orabl'	Escort ship
SM	**S**udno-**m**ishen'	Target ship
SP	**S**evastopol'skij **p**ort	Sevastopol harbour (boat of)
SP	**S**udno **p**arusnoe	Sailing vessel
SPK	**Sp**asatel'nyj **k**ater	Salvage boat
SS	**S**pasatel'noe **s**udno	Salvage vessel
SS*	**S**torozhevoe **s**udno	Guard vessel
SSV	**S**udno **s**oedinenia i **v**iazi	Communication ship
STR	**S**anitarnyj **tr**ansport	Sanitary transport
STZh	**S**tantsiia **t**renirovki **zh**ivuchesti	Survivability training station
SZ	**S**etevoj **z**agraditel'	Netlayer

Acronym	Full meaning	English equivalent
T	**T**ral'shchik	Minesweeper
TDS	**T**anko-**d**esantnoe **s**udno	Tank landing ship
TK	**T**orpednyj **k**ater	MTB
TKA	**T**orpednyj **ka**ter	MTB
TKL	**T**orpednyj **k**ater **L**evkova	Levkov's MTB
TKM	**T**orpednyj **k**ater-**m**ishen'	MTB target
TL	**T**orpedo**l**ov	Torpedo recovery (vessel)
TM	**T**rofejnaia **m**alaja	War-booty small (submarine)
TN	**T**a**n**ker	Oiler
TR	**Tr**ansport	Transport
TS	**T**rofejnaia **s**redniaia	War-booty medium (submarine)
TSB	**T**orpednaia **s**amokhodnaia **b**arzha	Propelled torpedo barge
TShch	**T**ral'**shch**ik	Minesweeper
TsL	Sudno **ts**e**l**'	Target ship
TV	**T**orpedolo**v**	Torpedo recovery vessel
TZ	**T**ral'shchik-**z**agraditel'	Minesweeper-minelayer
U	**U**chyobnyj	Training (ship)
UBO	**U**chyobnyj **m**orskoj **o**khotnik	Training small submarine hunter
UBPL	**U**chyobnyj **b**rigady **p**odvodnykh **l**odok	Training vessel of Submarine Brigade
UK	**U**chyobnyj **k**ater	Training boat
UK	**U**chyobnyj **k**orabl'	Training ship
UO	**U**chyobnyj **o**triad	Training branch (boat of)
US	**U**chyobnoe **s**udno	Training vessel
UTs	Korabl' **u**pravleniia **ts**elami	Target control ship
UTS	**U**chyobno-**t**renirovochnaia **s**tantsia	School-training station
V	**V**ladivostoyskij port	Vladivostok harbour (ship)
VLB	**V**oenno-**l**otsmanskij **b**ot	Naval-pilot boat
VM	**M**orskoj **v**odolaznyj bot	Seagoing diving tender
VMB	**V**odolaznyj **m**oto**b**ot	Motor diving tender
VN	**V**ozdushnoe **n**abliudenie	Air observation (ship)
VNOS	**V**ozdushnoe **n**abliudenie, **o**poveshchenie i **s**viaz'	Air observation, surveillance and communication (ship)
VP	**V**entspils **p**ort	Venspils harbour (boat of)
VP	**V**ladivostotskij **p**ort	Vladivostok harbour (boat of)
VP*	**V**ooruzyonnyj **p**arokhod	Armed steamer
VR	**V**odolaznyj **r**ejdovyj bot	Coastal diving tender
VRD	**V**odolaznyj **r**ejdovyj **d**vizhushchijsia bot	Coastal propelled diving tender
VS	**V**ozdushnye **s**ily	Air force (boat of)
VTR	**V**oennyj **t**ranspo**r**t	War transport
VU	**V**olnovoe **U**pravlenie	Wave (Remote) Controlled (boat)
VVS	**V**oenno-**v**ozdushnye **s**ily	Air Force (boat of)
ZAS	**Z**ariadovaia **a**kkumulatornaia **s**tantsiia	Battery charging station
ZBS	**Z**agraditel' **b**onovo-**s**etovoj	Boom-netlaying vessel
ZG	**Z**a**g**raditel'	Minelayer
ZM	**Z**agraditel' **m**innyj	Minelayer
ZS	**Z**agraditel' **s**etovoj	Netlayer

* These acronyms are used only in tables in this book to save space. In fact, a full wording was used as identifier of the ship.

11. Escort ships

Сторожевые корабли (СКР)

11.1. Standard Soviet-built types

Uragan class (*Project 2, 4, 39*)

Escort ships

Displacement: 490t standard, 562t normal, 633t full load; *Series II* 450t standard, 530t normal, 619t full load; *Series III* and *Series IV*: 443t standard, 599t normal, 635t full load

Dimensions: 71.5 x 7.4 x 2.95m

Machinery: 2-shaft Parsons turbines, 2 boilers (21kg/cm^2, 270°C), 5700 (Shtorm and Shkval 4620)hp = 21 (Shtorm and Shkval 18)kts. Oil fuel 116–119t; range 850nm (Shtorm and Shkval 900nm) at 16kts (see notes for later Series)

Armament: 2-4in/60 (*Series IV* 100mm/56 B-24 BM), 4-45mm/46 21-K, 2-0.3in Maxim MGs, 3-450mm TTs M1913 (*Series III* and *Series IV* 3-N), 2 DC chutes, 20–30 B-1 DCs, (20 KB mines *Series I* only) 32 M1926 mines (see notes for war modifications)

Complement: 107–114 (wartime)

Smerch in 1942 in early type of Arctic camouflage.
Przemysław Budzbon Collection

Pt No	Name	Builder	YN	Laid down	Launched	Comp	Comm	Fleet	Fate
	Series I (Project 2)								
10	GROZA	Zhdanov Yd (190), Leningrad	324	13.8.1927	28.9.1930	22.7.1932	22.7.1932	N	Hulked 25.2.1953
	SHKVAL	A. Marti (198), Nikolaev	187	24.10.1927	Sum 1930	5.3.1933	11.1.1935	BS	Deleted 12.11.1952
	SHTORM	A. Marti (198), Nikolaev	186	24.10.1927	4.4.1930	1.10.1932	31.10.1932	BS	Deleted 30.1.1946
15	SMERCH	Zhdanov Yd (190), Leningrad	322	13.8.1927	22.7.1929	13.9.1932	13.9.1933	N	BU late 1960s
	TAJFUN	Zhdanov Yd (190), Leningrad	321	13.8.1927	1.6.1929	14.9.1931	18.9.1931	B	Training ship 30.11.1954
	TSIKLON	Zhdanov Yd (190), Leningrad	323	13.8.1927	27.11.1929	3.7.1932	3.7.1932	B	Lost 28.8.1941
16	URAGAN	Zhdanov Yd (190), Leningrad	320	13.8.1927	4.9.1928	16.12.1930	16.12.1930	N	Deleted 5.6.1949
	VIKHR'	Zhdanov Yd (190), Leningrad	325	13.8.1927	12.10.1930	12.9.1932	12.9.1932	B	Deleted 30.11.1954
	Series II (Project 4)								
	BURUN	A. Marti (198), Nikolaev Dalzavod (202), Vladivostok	221	22.4.1932	27.9.1934	7.10.1935	7.10.1935	P	Deleted 30.11.1954
	GROM	A. Marti (198), Nikolaev Dalzavod (202), Vladivostok	220	17.6.1932	22.9.1934	22.7.1935	6.11.1935	P	Deleted 30.11.1954
	METEL'	A. Marti (198), Nikolaev Dalzavod (202), Vladivostok	423	18.12.1931	15.6.1934	18.11.1934	5.3.1935	P	Deleted 30.11.1954
	V'IUGA	A. Marti (198), Nikolaev Dalzavod (202), Vladivostok	424	26.12.1931	5.7.1934	18.11.1934	5.3.1935	P	Deleted 30.11.1954
	Series III (Project 39)								
	BURIA	Zhdanov Yd (190), Leningrad	481	06.1934	11.1935	27.10.1936	6.11.1936	B	Sunk 24.8.1942
	MOLNIIA	Zhdanov Yd (190), Leningrad Dalzavod (202), Vladivostok	478	23.3.1934	24.11.1934	20.9.1936	20.9.1936	P	Deleted 30.11.1954
	PURGA	Zhdanov Yd (190), Leningrad	480	6.1934	11.1935	4.9.1936	4.9.1936	B La	Sunk 1.9.1942
	ZARNITSA	Zhdanov Yd (190), Leningrad Dalzavod (202), Vladivostok	479	21.3.1934	6.11.1934	6.11.1936	6.11.1936	P	Deleted 30.11.1954
	Series IV (Project 39)								
	SNEG	Zhdanov Yd (190), Leningrad	495	27.04.1935	14.7.1936	25.9.1938	25.9.1938	B	Sunk 28.8.1941.
	TUCHA	Zhdanov Yd (190), Leningrad	496	27.4.1935	20.10.1936	25.9.1938	18.9.1938	B	Deleted 9.6.1956

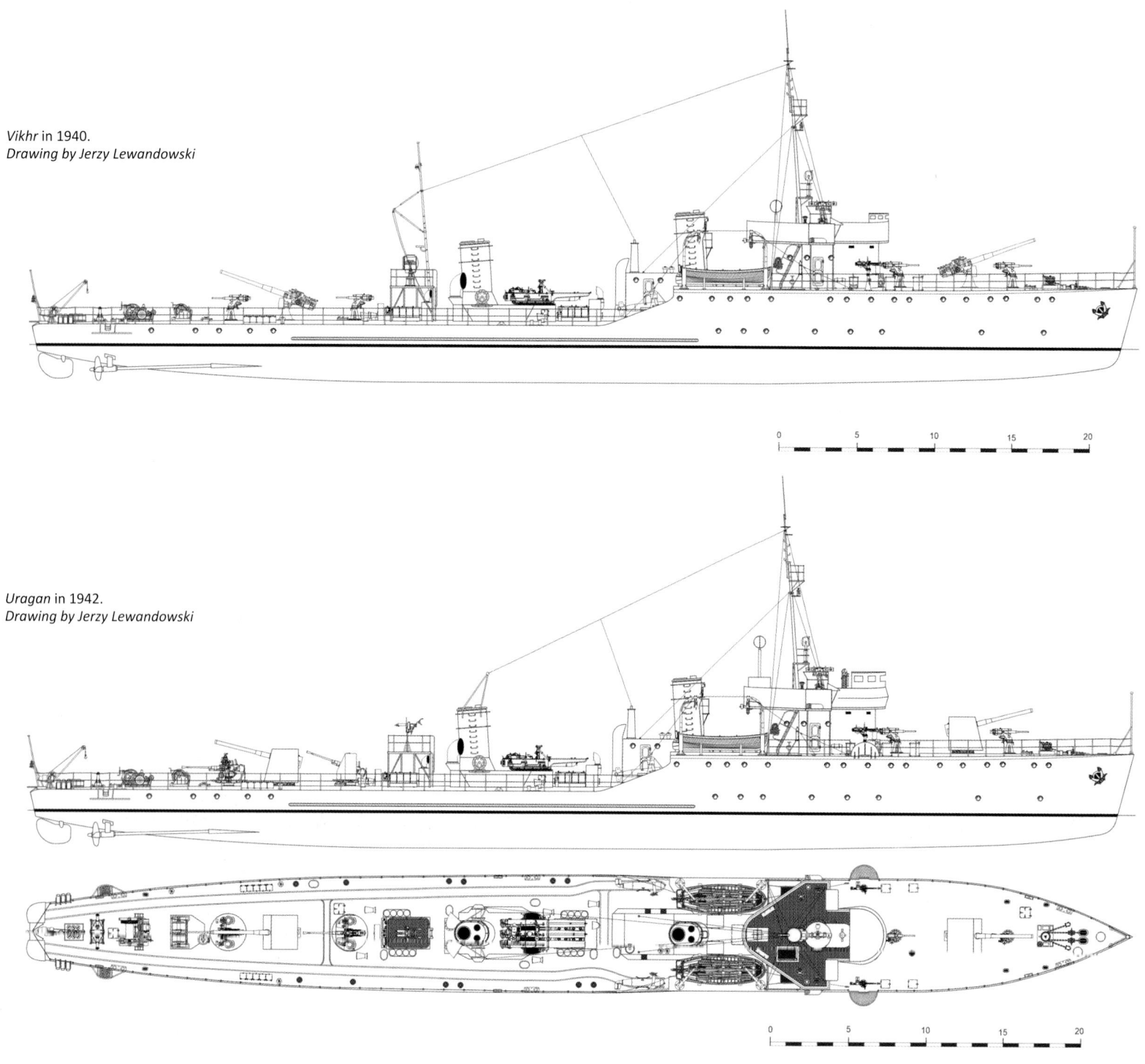

Vikhr in 1940.
Drawing by Jerzy Lewandowski

Uragan in 1942.
Drawing by Jerzy Lewandowski

Authorised under the 1926 Programme. The first seagoing warships designed and built in the Soviet Union, intended as dual-purpose escorts (for the *Marat* class battleships) and torpedo boats (able to launch torpedo attacks on the enemy battle line). To provide enough range diesel propulsion was contemplated for a while but abandoned because there was no possibility of procuring engines abroad. They were in fact to compensate for the lack of modern destroyers and the design was modelled on the German World War 1 *A* class torpedo boat. The whole concept made sense considering the intended 6-knot speed margin over the Soviet battleline and operational conditions in the Gulf of Finland and the Black Sea.

The design was allocated the code *Project 1* but proved to be a failure. The prototype *Uragan* reached only 26kts on trials which destroyed most of her tactical applications as the battleline escort or torpedo boat, while lack of depth charge handling equipment and echo-sounder devices eliminated her as anti-submarine ship. On completion the AA armament consisted only of a few 0.3in Maxim MGs, as the planned four AA 37mm/67.5 11-K guns (remodelled Vickers 2pdrs) did not enter production. Only in the late 1930s was the gap filled by 45mm/46 guns distributed on the weather decks forward and aft of the main guns.

The boat proved to be top-heavy while her machinery was not reliable and prone to faults. Therefore, her code was quietly changed to *Project 2*, while the honour of first place in Soviet warship design history was awarded to the second project in the queue – the *Leningrad* class flotilla leaders. With no other project at hand the production of these ships lasted until the late 1930s, in a consecutive series with some improvements (mostly increases in horsepower) but without significant results.

11.0 Escort Ships

Tucha in 1943.
Drawing by Jerzy Lewandowski

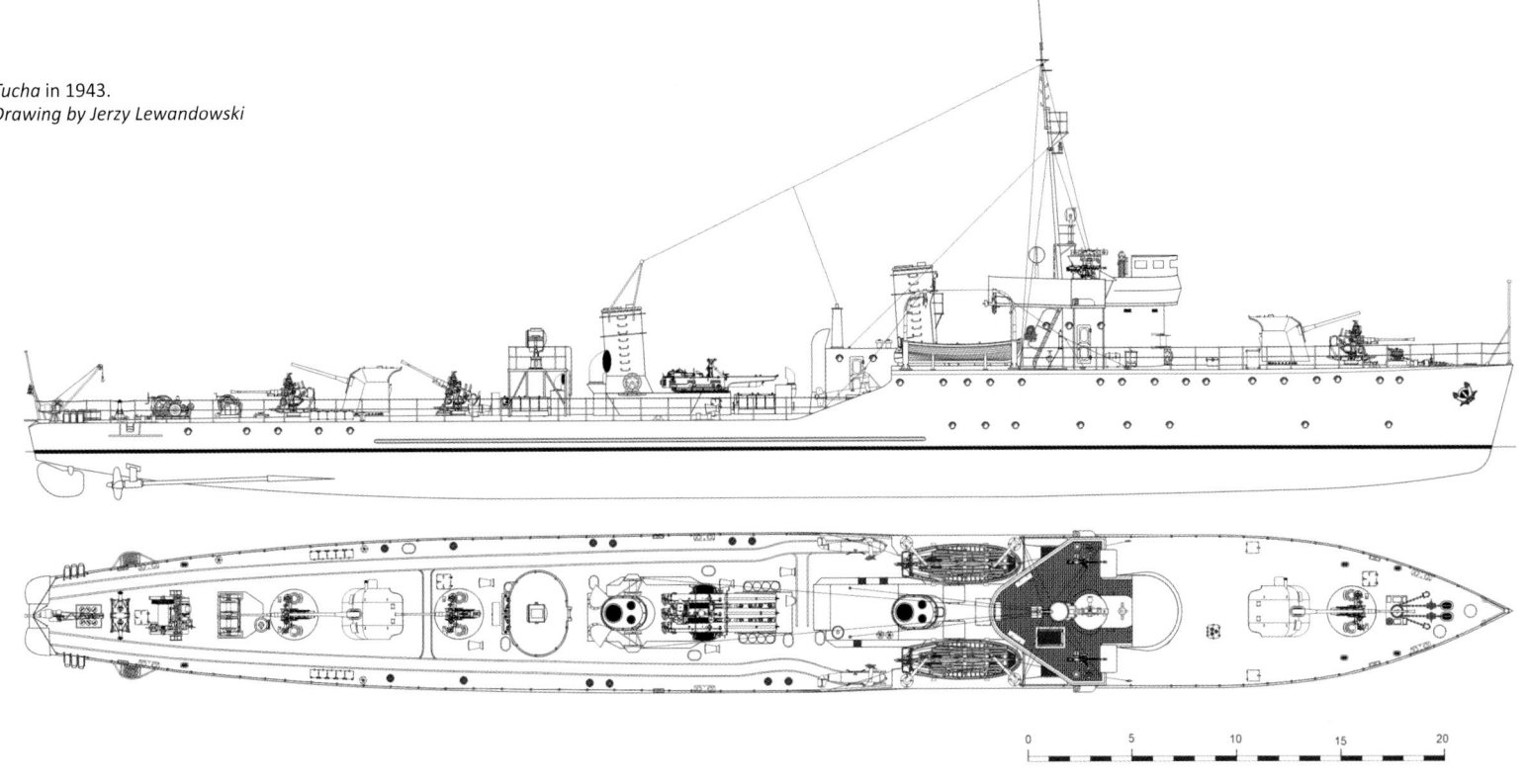

Uragan in Sept 1942 after refit. Note 45mm 21-K guns forward and aft of the B-24-BM 100mm forward gun, twin 0.5in Colt MGs on a platform abaft the second funnel and 37mm 70-K guns forward and aft of her 100mm aft mounting.
Boris Lemachko Collection

Machinery note

Series	Total power	Speed (max)	Range
II	6290hp	23kts	1200nm at 14kts
III & IV	6800hp	24kts	960nm at 18kts

In 1933 three ships of the *Series I* were trfd to the Arctic while the whole *Series II* and two of the *Series III* were transported in sections to the Far East and assembled there. In both cases they were to face severe conditions for which they were not designed.

Wartime armament changes: **main guns**: 4in/60 changed to 100mm/56 B-24 BM on *Uragan*, *Taifun* and *Vikhr* during 1942-1944; **AA guns**: 45mm/46 21-K gradually replaced by 37mm/67.5 70-K (*Shtorm* in 1943 carried 2-45mm/46 and 3-37mm/67.5; the fifth light gun mounting was placed right aft instead of the DCTs); **MGs**: Maxim mountings were gradually replaced by 0.5in DShK ones and 0.5in twin Colt-Brownings; the number increased to max 6 barrels in up to four mountings; **DCTs**: two BMB-1 fitted on survived ships late in 1941, these on *Shtorm* were replaced by additional 45mm/46 21-K gun mounting; **radars**: British Type 291 were fitted by 1945 on *Burun*, *Metel'*, *Shkval*, *Smerch*, *Taifun* and *Vikhr'*; **ASDIC**: various British Asdic types (128c on *Groza*) fitted on some by 1945; **sweeps**: *Taifun* and *Tucha* conv 1944 to fleet minesweepers with the TTs removed and replaced by electromagnetic and acoustic minesweeping devices.

Close up of *Groza* in June 1942 in her original as-built configuration. Note MG on the forecastle deck abreast the bridge.
Przemysław Budzbon Collection

Groza in Dec 1944 after refit. Her main mast was removed and AA armament augmented; the 37mm 70-K gun is visible in front of the bridge. Note a new camouflage scheme.
Vitalij Kostrichenko Collection

Series I

Groza: fire support and escort duties 1939-1940 and 1941-1945, including support to Allied convoys to Kola Bay (PQ.9 to PQ.11, PQ.17, JW.64, RA.65) and Soviet Arctic convoys, modernised from 25.11.1943 up to December 1944, conv 12.11.1952 to target ship, conv 25.2.1953 to accomodation hulk *PKZ-51*.

Shkval: under repair at the Yd No 201 at Sevastopol from 5.3.1939, 4.11.1941 damaged during trials by a gale, trfd to the repair yard at Poti until recomm 24.5.1942. In escort service during defence of Sevastopol and Novorossisk, numerous support actions off Caucasian shores. After the loss of three destroyers in October 1943, together with *Shtorm* she remained the biggest ship of the Black Sea Fleet which could put so sea without direct order of Stavka.

Shtorm: under repair at the Yd No 201 at Sevastopol from 5.3.1939, trfd 4.11.1941 to repair yard at Poti, recomm 24.6.1942. Carried out escort duties during defence of Sevastopol and Novorossisk, and numerous support actions off Caucasian shores. Following the loss of three destroyers in October 1943, together with *Shkval* she remained the biggest ship of the Black Sea Fleet which could put so sea without direct order of Stavka. Torpedoed 11.5.1944 by *U-9* off Tuapse and lost stern, towed to harbour, considered constructive total loss and deleted after the war.

Smerch: escort duties 1939-1940, modernised July 1940 to May 1941, fire support and escort duties from 1941 including support to Allied convoys to Kola Bay (PQ.8 to PQ.11, QP.9, JW.64, JW.65, RA.65) and Soviet Arctic convoys, under repairs from 27.8.1942, sunk 8.12.1942 by aircraft at shipyard in Murmansk, raised 24.12.1942 and repaired during 22.5.1943 to 8.9.1944, but damaged 13.10.1944 by a mine and repaired by 23.2.1945. Damaged in a gale end of March 1945, under repair until 5.5.1945. Arrived 12.7.1948 in Moscov *via* inland waterways, trfd 8.2.1949 to the DOSFLOT as training ship.

Tajfun: under repair at the Yd No 190 from 1939, damaged 23.9.1941 by aircraft, raised and repaired by 29.12.1943 with parts cannibalised from *Vikhr'*. Escort and support duties in the Gulf of Finland, conv during winter 1944 to 31.3.1945 as fleet minesweeper, conv 30.11.1954 to training ship.

Tsiklon: under repair 1938/9, 3.12.1939 support to landing at Suursaaari, sunk by a mine off Cape Juminda.

Uragan: refurbished and rearmed during October 1938 to 13.9.1942 with two 100mm B-24-BM, 2-45mm 21-K, 2-37mm 70-K guns, 2-0.5in DShK, 2-0.5in (1x2) Colt-Browning MGs, 2 BMB-1 DCTs, escort duties for Allied (JW.53, JW.57, JW.59, RA.57) and Soviet Arctic convoys, trfd 5.6.1949 to the DOSFLOT.

Vikhr': pennant No *VKh* in 1939, 30.12.1939 in support of landing at Laavansaari, under repair at Kronshtadt from 1940, sunk 22.9.1941 by aircraft. Raised 23.7.1942, buyoancy restored in October 1943 and towed to the Yd No 190 for repairs. Partially cannibalised to repair damaged *Tajfun*, but refitted herself with boilers and turbines removed from sunken *Purga* in 1943. Renamed *Purga* in 1943, name reverted to *Vikhr'* 8.7.1944, recomm December 1945, conv 24.4.1948 to target ship.

Series II
Burun: overhauled during 1943–1945.

Close up of an *Uragan* class ship with the 0.5in twin Colt MGs and 37mm 70-K gun. Breach of the aft 4in/60 gun is visible at left and B-1 depth charges.
Boris Lemachko Collection

Grom: overhauled during 1944–1945.

Metel': overhauled 1941–1942, 15.8.1945 landing at Seishin (Korea), 18.8.1945 landing at Jōshin (Korea), conv 5.10.1945 to training ship.

V'iuga: overhauled 1939–1942, 15.8.1945 landing at Seishin (Korea), conv 5.10.1945 to training ship.

Series III
Buria: 30.11.1939 support to landing at Laavansaari, 3.12.1939 to landing at Suursaari, under repair 1940. Damaged 27.9.1941 by artillery fire at Kronshtadt, repaired and recomm 15.5.1942. Escort and support duties in the Gulf of Finland, sunk by mine off Lavansaari.

Molniia: conv 5.10.1945 to training ship, overhauled 1945–1947.

Purga: 3.12.1939 covered landing at Suursaari, trfd 20.7.1941 to the Ladoga Flotilla, escort duties on Lake Ladoga, sunk by aircraft off Shlisselburg. Raised 9.9.1943, turbines and boilers were removed to fit at *Vikhr'*.

Zarnitsa: 16–17.8.1945 landing at Sakhalin.

Shkval after being rearmed with 100mm B-24-BM guns. Note the band on her forward funnel. *Przemysław Budzbon Collection*

Series IV
Sneg: escort and support duties in December 1939, sunk by mine off Cape Juminda.

Tucha: 3.12.1939 in cover of landing at Suursaari, under repair during winter 1940 to 25.6.1941, damaged 18.7.1941 by own mine during mining operation off Riga, towed to Kronshtadt for repairs which lasted until July 1943, later on escort and support duties at the Gulf of Finland. Conv during winter 1944 to 31.3.1945 to fleet minesweeper, conv 30.12.1952 to training electro-magnetic station.

Shtorm in 1943 with additional AA armament: 37mm 70-K guns in front of the bridge and forward and aft of her aft 4in/60 gun, 45mm 21-K gun forward of the bow 4in/60 gun, and forecastle deck 0.5in DShK MG alongside the bridge. Note funnel bands. *Przemysław Budzbon Collection*

Iastreb class (*Project 29*) — *Escort ships*

Displacement: 842 standard, 920t normal, 995t full load
Dimensions: 85.7 x 8.4 x 3.2m
Machinery: 2-shaft geared turbines, 2 boilers (28kg/cm^2, 340°C), 23,000hp = 34kts. Oil fuel 300t, range 2700nm at 15kts
Armament: 3-100mm/56 B-34, 8-0.5in DShKM-2 (4x2) MGs, 3-450mm 3-N (1x3) TTs, 2 DC chutes, 20 B-1 DCs, 40 M-1 DCs, 24 M1931 mines
Complement: 112

Data for 1939 specification. See note.

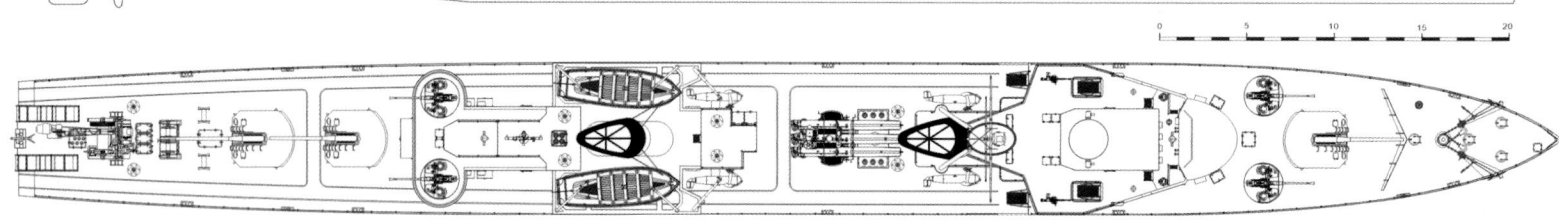

Iastreb as completed.
Drawing by Jerzy Lewandowski

Name	Builder	YN	Laid down	Launched	Comp	Comm	Fleet	Fate
AL'BATROS	198, Nikolaev					7.10.1945	P	Deleted 28.2.1961
	199, Komsomolsk-on-Amur	2	4.12.1939	2.6.1942	29.9.1945			
BERKUT	190, Leningrad	553	Aug 1940	-	-	-	B	BU on slipway
BUREVIESTNIK ex-*Chajka* (Sept 1940)	198, Nikolaev					15.7.1947	P	Deleted 28.1.1958
	199, Komsomolsk-on-Amur	1	4.12.1939	17.7.1943	14.2.1947			
FREGAT	199, Komsomolsk-on-Amur	6	-	-	-	-	P	Cancelled
GRIF	190, Leningrad	537	25.5.1940	-	-	-	B	BU on slipway
GRIF (ii)	190, Leningrad	555	May 1941	-	-	-		BU on slipway
IAGUAR	198, Nikolaev					-	BS	Hull destroyed 1942
	201, Sevastopol	1098368	1941	-	-			
IASTREB	190, Leningrad	533	16.5.1939	19.6.1940	23.2.1945	29.9.1945	B	Deleted 12.9.1959
KONDOR	190, Leningrad	563	-				B	Cancelled 19.7.1941
KORSHUN	190, Leningrad	535	25.10.1939	28.5.1941		21.1.1951	B	Deleted 31.1.1964
	194, Leningrad				3.5.1947			
KUGUAR	198, Nikolaev	1099				-	BS	Hull destroyed 1942
	201, Sevastopol	369	1941	-	-			
LEOPARD	198, Nikolaev	1092				-	BS	Hull destroyed 1942
	201, Sevastopol	366	1940	-	-			
ORYOL	190, Leningrad	534	28.5.1939	12.2.1941		20.2.1951	B	Deleted 18.9.1965
	820, Kaliningrad				21.12.1950			
ORLAN	199, Komsomolsk-on-Amur	9	-	-	-	-	P	Cancelled
PANTERA	198, Nikolaev	110				-	BS	Material expended
	201, Sevastopol	0370	-	-	-			
RYS'	198, Nikolaev	1097				-	BS	Hull destroyed 1942
	201, Sevastopol	367	1941	-	-			
SOKOL'	190, Leningrad	554	Oct 1940	-	-	-	B	BU on slipway
TIGR	198, Nikolaev	1091				-	BS	Hull destroyed 1942 on slipway
	201, Sevastopol	365	1940	-	-			
VORON	190, Leningrad	536	23.5.1940	31.10.1940		-	B	Discarded 1960
	820, Kaliningrad				21.2.1950			
VORON (ii)	190, Leningrad	556	-	-	-	-	B	Cancelled 19.7.1941

11.0 Escort Ships

Iastreb in 1945. Note the Type 291 radar antenna at the masthead. Przemysław Budzbon Collection

Construction of 30 escort ships was authorised under the Third Five-Year Programme, with delivery of the first five planned for 1941. The requirements aimed at a multipurpose escort ship designed as a screen for the battleline and coastal convoys as well as Border Guard patrol ships. The purpose of their TTs was to be different from the ill-considered offensive concept of the *Uragan* class – instead, they were to provide self-defence against cruisers attacking convoys. Interesting, the naming theme for the new escorts repeated the German convention for torpedo-boats – predators and birds. The outline project was accepted in August 1938 and work started in three shipyards before the technical project was finally approved, which reflected the usual approach at the time.

The leading Zhdanov shipyard in Leningrad laid down six hulls with an additional two for the NKVD Border Guard, while the A. Marti yard at Nikolaev, having a surplus of prefabrication resources, became the supplier of hull construction elements for the Sevmorzavod at Sevastopol and the Far Eastern yard at Komsomolsk-on-Amur. The whole programme became delayed from the start by late delivery of the turbines and issues with the fledgling technology of tin sheet welding. In total 15 ships were laid down before the German invasion with six hulls already launched. The construction of the remaining ships was suspended; those laid down in the Black Sea area were captured in-situ by the Germans, while those on the slipways at Leningrad were damaged by aircraft or artillery fire. Of the four hulls launched in Leningrad, construction was resumed in summer 1942 only on the prototype *Iastreb*, which was ready for sea trials in September 1944. Excessive vibrations and cracks were experienced at the stern which has to be strengthened. She was completed without the *Soiuz-29* type fire control system, nor the asdic, while the unavailable twin turret DShKM-2 MG mountings were replaced by 4-37mm/67.5 70-K guns, which improved AA defence, and two single 0.5in DShK MGs. Incidentally, the unavailability of the planned 100mm/56 B-34 guns required the modification of the gun bases for the 85mm/52 90-K mountings, which was changed back when the 100mm ones became available. The wartime complement was increased to 177. The ship was substantially overweight by 9% as compared with the original project (920t standard, 998t normal, 1073t full load) at a cost of at least 2kts if not 3kts of her speed and range reduced by 20%. Apart from the prototype, the only one completed before end of the war was *Al'batros*, fitted with three 85mm/52 90-K mountings, 4-37mm/67.5 70-K, 3-0.5in DShK MGs, and TTs but lacking the asdic.

Iastreb class in the 1950s with Soviet radar types. Przemysław Budzbon Collection

Korshun on Lake Ladoga in the 1950s.
Boris Lemachko Collection

Al'batros: conv 17.2.1956 to training ship, conv 11.3.1958 to stationary training ship *UTS-82*

Berkut: construction suspended 19.7.1941

Burevestnik: comp to the *Project 29K*, conv May 1957 to stationary training ship *UTS-84*

Fregat: construction cancelled during the war

Grif: trfd to the NKVD Border Guard after laid down, renamed *Izumurd*, then *Bditel'nyj*

Grif (ii): construction suspended 19.7.1941

Iaguar: hull demolished on the slipway before surrender of Sevastopol to avoid capture by the Germans

Iasterb: conv 17.2.1956 to training ship, conv 31.8.1956 to target ship

Kondor: construction cancelled before laying down

Korshun: comp to the *Project 29K*, conv 1958 to experimental ship *OS-28*

Kuguar: hull demolished on the slipway before surrender of Sevastopol to avoid capture by the Germans

Leopard: hull demolished on the slipway before surrender of Sevastopol to avoid capture by the Germans

Oryol: comp to the *Project 29K*, conv 18.8.1958 to experimental ship *OS-27*, conv Mar 1964 to accommodation hulk *PKZ-17*

Orlan: construction cancelled during the war

Pantera: not laid down before capture of Sevastopol by the Germans, material expended

Rys': hull demolished on the slipway before surrender of Sevastopol to avoid capture by the Germans

Sokol': construction suspended 19.7.1941

Tigr: hull demolished on the slipway before surrender of Sevastopol to avoid capture by the Germans

Voron: trfd to the NKVD Border Guard after laid down, renamed *Almaz*, then *Zorkij*. Comp to the *Project 29K*. Relegated to stationary training ship UTS-9, trfd 1960 to the DOSAAF at Kiev, discarded 4.11.1975

Voron (ii): construction cancelled before laying down

Zorkij as the stationary training ship *UTS-9*. *Sergej Berezhnoj Collection*

11.2. NKVD patrol ships

Brilliant class (*Project 43*) *Escort ships*

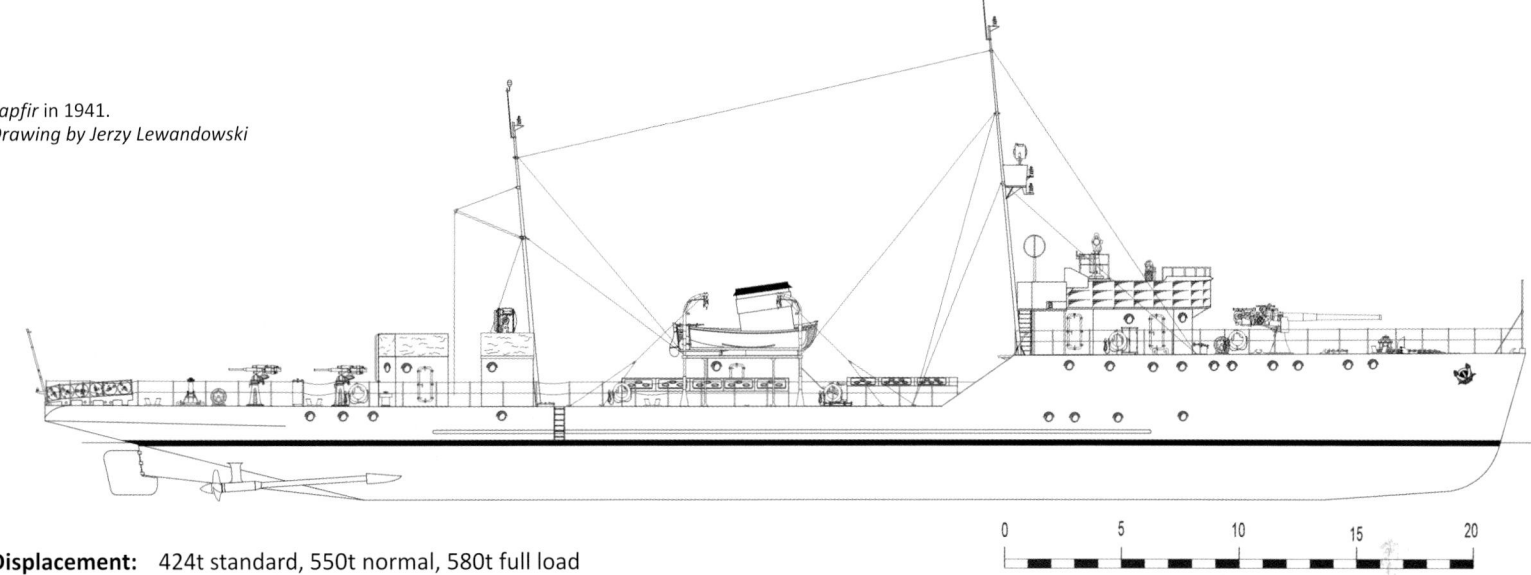

Sapfir in 1941.
Drawing by Jerzy Lewandowski

Displacement: 424t standard, 550t normal, 580t full load
Dimensions: 62.0 x 7.2 x 3.0m
Machinery: 2-shaft, two 42 BMRN-6 diesels, 2200hp = 17.2. Oil fuel 75t, range 3500nm at 13kts
Armament: 1-4in/60, 2-45mm/46 21-K (replaced 1943/4 by 2-37mm/67.5 70-K), (added 1942 1-37mm/67.5 70-K), 2(6 from 1944) -0.5in DShK MGs, (added 1941 2 BMB-1 DCTs), 20 B-1 DCs, 20 M-1 DCs, 31 M 1926 mines
Complement: 61

Built for the NKVD Border Guard, design based on the *Project 3* minesweepers but without the minesweeping gear and some fittings adapted for Arctic conditions. The design which inherited the stability issues received the code *Project 43*; all four trfd to the Arctic *via* the Baltic-White Sea Canal. An additional six were ordered at the Yard 201, Sevastopol but the order was cancelled in 1936 and the material gathered was used for construction of the *Fugas* class *Series IV* minesweepers. All four were operationally detached to the Northern Fleet on 22.6.1941 and comm next day.

Brilliant: damaged 12.5.1942 by aircraft in roadstead of Iokanga, sank after explosion of DCs. Raised 12.9.1942, recomm 20.6.1944. Sunk by *U-957* at the Kara Sea

Rubin: under repair from June 1944 until after end of the war. Trfd 16.2.1945 to the Northern Fleet, returned 25.1.1946 to the NKVD, recomm 2.3.1955 with the Northern Fleet as dispatch ship, renamed 31.5.1955 *Kushum*

Sapfir: damaged 6.7.1942 by aircraft, repaired by November 1942. Rebuilt from June 1944 until after end of the war. Trfd 16.2.1945 to the Northern Fleet, returned 25.1.1946 to the NKVD, recomm 2.3.1955 with the Northern Fleet as dispatch ship, renamed 31.5.1955 *Vizim*

Zhemchug: sunk by *U-451* at the White Sea

Rubin during the war. Przemysław Budzbon Collection

Sapfir as completed. Boris Lemachko Collection

Pt No	Name	YN	Laid down	Launched	Comp	Comm	Fleet	Fate
	Builder: 190, Leningrad							
29	BRILLIANT ex-*PSK-303* (5.1.1941)	484	Oct 1934	5.11.1935	6.6.1937	23.6.1941	Wh	Sunk 23.9.1944
28	RUBIN ex-*PSK-302* (5.1.1941)	485	3.11.1934	18.8.1935	18.12.1936	23.6.1941	Wh N	Deleted 1960
30	SAPFIR ex-*PSK-304* (5.1.1941)	486	26.12.1934	20.12.1935	12.12.1937	23.6.1941	Wh N	Deleted 1960
27	ZHEMCHUG ex-*PSK-301* (5.1.1941)	483	June 1934	Nov 1935	Dec 1937	23.6.1941	Wh N	Sunk 11.8.1941

Kirov class (*Project 19*) — *NKVD patrol ships*

Displacement: 951.37t standard, 1025t normal, 1161t full load
Dimensions: 80 x 8.3 x 3.75m
Machinery: 3-shaft E-6 Franco-Tossi diesels, 4500hp =18.5kts. Oil fuel 140t, range 5975nm at 16.5kts
Armament: 3-4in/60 (3x1), 4-45mm/46 21-K, 3-0.5in DShK MGs, (*Dzerzhinskij* only 4-0.3in (1x4) Maxim MGs), 2 BMB-1 DCTs, 10 B-1 DCs, 35 M-1 DCs, 24 M1926 mines
Complement: 121

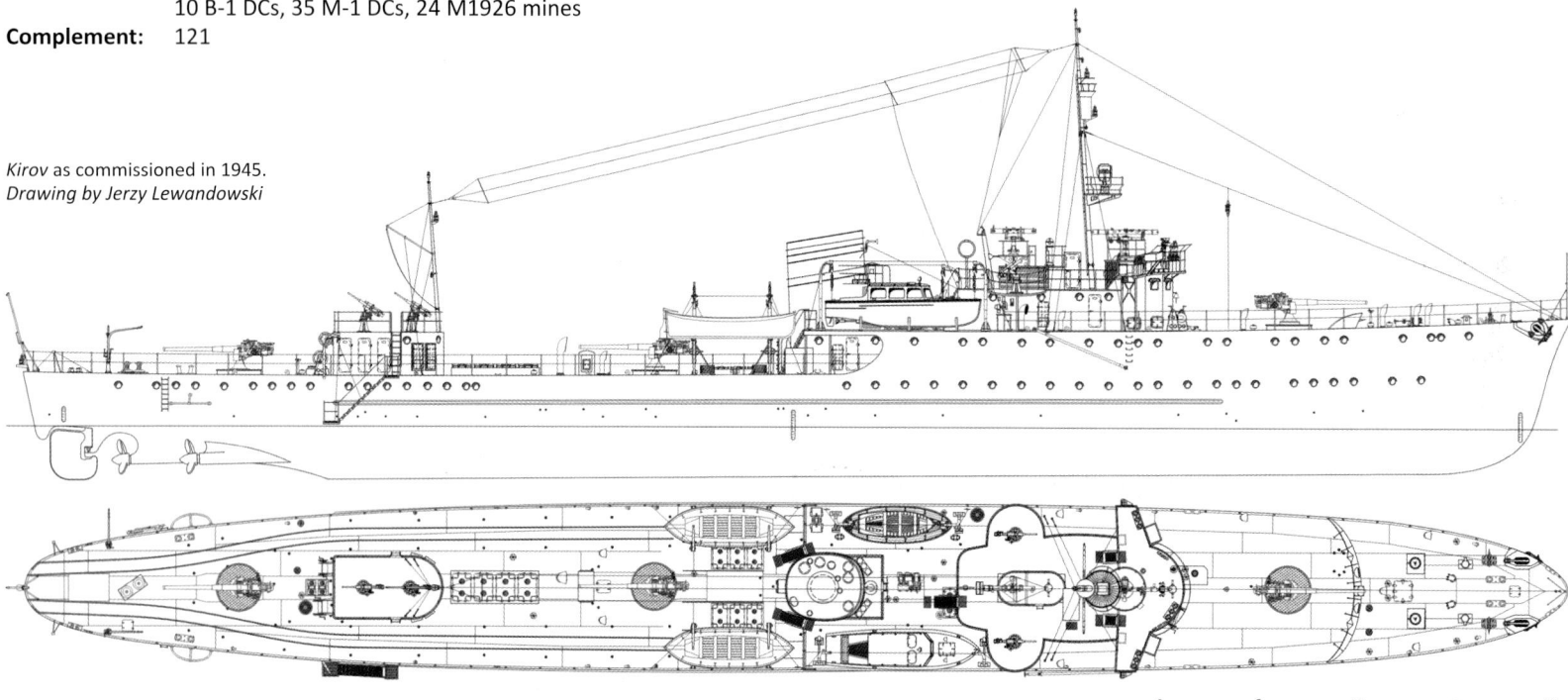

Kirov as commissioned in 1945. Drawing by Jerzy Lewandowski

The NKVD Border Guard ships ordered in Italy, completed without armament. They left Genoa 27.10.1934 with Italian crews and arrived Vladivostok 11.12.1934 to be taken over by the Soviets next day and armed with Soviet weaponry. Because of stability issues the planned triple bank of 450mm TTs was replaced by the additional 4in/60 gun. Both were operationally subordinated to the Petropavlovsk-Kamchatski naval base and were actually comm 9.8.1945 according to some recent Russian sources; both took part in the landing on Kuril. Returned to the NKVD after the Soviet-Japanese War.

Dzerzhinskij: renumbered PS-28 from 18.5.1957, discarded 11.6.1957, conv 27.6.1960 to stationary staff ship of the Border Guard at the Shikotan at the Kuril archipelago. Beached 1961 in a gale, abandoned

Kirov: discarded 23.9.1959, conv to civilian accommodation hulk *PKZ-89*

Kirov with her designed armament. Boris Lemachko Collection

Name	Laid down	Launched	Comp	Comm	Fleet	Fate
Builder: Ansaldo, Sestri Ponente						
DZERZHINSKIJ ex-*PSK-1* (26.3.1935) ex-*PS.26* (Feb 1935)	8.2.1933	16.9.1934	27.10.1934	9.8.1945	P	Stranded 1961
KIROV ex-*PSK-2* (26.3.1935) ex-*PS.08* (Feb 1935)	8.2.1933	19.8.1933	27.10.1934	9.8.1945	P	BU mid-1960s

Dzerzhinskij as completed without armament.
Przemysław Budzbon Collection

Kirov during 1950s with 85mm 90-K guns, two twin 1in *2M-3* guns on the poop, and Soviet radar outfit.
Vitalij Kostrichenko Collection

Kirov during trials under Italian colours.
Marek Twardowski Collection

Purga class
NKVD patrol ships

Displacement: 3165t standard, 3819t full load
Dimensions: 95.3 x 15.2 x 5.7m
Machinery: 3-shaft diesels, 12,000hp = 17.5kts, range 12,588nm at 10kts
Armament: 3-130mm/50 B-13, 4-45mm/46 21-K, 30 mines
Complement: 219

Ordered for the Border Guard of the NKVD and designed for patrol service in heavily iced Arctic areas. A large series was planned, but construction was given a low priority and the second ship was cancelled to made slipways free for a pair of *S* class submarines. Construction was suspended 19.7.1941 when 28% complete, to be resumed after the war at the Marti Yd yard to the modified *Project 52* engined with the new type 37-D diesels (used for the *Project 613* postwar submarines) and armed with 4-100mm B-24 guns, 6 twin 37mm/67.5 V-11 mountings, 4 BMB-2 DCTs, 70 DCs, 30 mines. Following completion *Purga* was trfd *via* the Northern Sea Route to the Pacific station of the Border Guard.

Purga as completed in 1957. Vitalij Kostrichenko Collection

She was never in naval commission, but was nominally dispatched under naval command on commencement of hostilities with Germany.

Name	Builder	YN	Laid down	Launched	Comp	Comm	Fleet	Fate
PURGA	196, Leningrad	116630	17.12.1938	24.4.1941		-	N	Discarded Apr 1990
	194, Leningrad				31.3.1957			
-	196, Leningrad	117	-	-	-	-	N	Cancelled 19.10.1940

11.3. Lend-Lease ships

US Tacoma class
Patrol frigates

Displacement: 1770t standard, 2199t normal, 2277t full load
Dimensions: 92.6 x 11.35 x 4.4m
Machinery: 2-shaft VTE, 2 boilers, 5500hp = 19.5kts. Oil fuel 750t, range 7300nm at 15kts
Armament: 3-3in/50, 2-40mm/60, 9-20mm Oerlikon, (9x1), 1 Hedgehog Mk 10, 8 Mk-6 DCTs, 2 DC chutes, 280 DCs
Complement: 195

Data in Russian service.

Transferred to the Soviet Union as part of Project Hula in which the United States transferred naval vessels in anticipation of the Soviets eventually joining the war against Japan, specifically in preparation for planned Soviet invasions of southern Sakhalin and the Kurils. There was a plan to transfer 30 frigates in total, but on 5.9.1945 a few hours after the Soviet army completed the seizure of Kuril the project was closed and transfer of PF-15 *Annapolis* and PF-16 *Bangor* (apparently designated to carry numbers *EK-23* and *EK-24*) was cancelled. The transfer included training a nucleus of Soviet crews, which together with the electronic technology on these ships, was of tremendous value to the Soviets. They did not fit with Soviet classification at that time, so instead of the traditional SKR (*Storozhevoj Korabl'*) they were given the unique designation EK (*Eskortnyi Korabl'*) which was never to be repeated.

Twenty-seven ships, except *EK-3* (stranded 17.11.1948 at the Port of Korsakov at Sakhalin and relegated to non-propelled depot ship) were returned to the US at Maizuru (Japan) and laid up there until the outbreak of the Korean War a few months later. They were recomm for the US and Korean navies on commencement of hostilities, and others went to Japan in 1953. The majority were BU in the early 1970s.

USS *Pasco* (PF-6), the future *EK-12*, shortly after completion on 25.5.1944.
Naval History and Heritage Command NH 93245

11.0 Escort Ships

No	US No	US Name	Builder	Laid down	Launched	Comp	Tansferred	Comm	Fleet	Fate
EK-1	PF-25	CHARLOTTENVILLE	Walter Butler	1943	30.7.1943	10.4.1944	12.7.1945	23.7.1945	P	Returned 17.10.1949
EK-2	PF-34	LONG-BEACH	Consolidated, San Pedro	21.4.1943	5.5.1943	8.9.1943	12.7.1945	23.7.1945	P	Returned 17.2.1950
EK-3	PF-35	BELFAST	Consolidated, San Pedro	1943	20.5.1943	24.11.1943	12.7.1945	23.7.1945	P	Deleted 29.4.1960
EK-4	PF-53	MACHIAS	Froemming	8.5.1943	22.8.1943	23.12.1943	12.7.1945	23.7.1945	P	Returned 17.2.1950
EK-5	PF-37	SAN PEDRO	Consolidated, San Pedro	17.4.1943	11.6.1943	23.10.1943	12.7.1945	23.7.1945	P	Returned 17.2.1950
EK-6	PF-36	GLENDYLE	Consolidated, San Pedro	1943	25.8.1943	1.10.1943	12.7.1945	23.7.1945	P	Returned 17.2.1950
EK-7	PF-54	SANDUSKY	Froemming	8.7.1943	5.10.1943	18.4.1944	12.7.1945	23.7.1945	P	Returned 17.10.1949
EK-8	PF-38	CORONADO	Consolidated, San Pedro	1943	17.6.1943	17.11.1943	12.7.1945	23.7.1945	P	Returned 16.10.1949
EK-9	PF-52	ALLENTOWN	Froemming	1943	13.7.1943	24.3.1944	12.7.1945	23.7.1945	P	Returned 15.10.1949
EK-10	PF-39	OGDEN	Consolidated, San Pedro	21.5.1943	23.6.1943	20.12.1943	12.7.1945	23.7.1945	P	Returned 15.11.1949
EK-11	PF-3	TACOMA	Kaiser Richmond #4	10.3.1943	7.7.1943	6.11.1943	16.8.1945	26.8.1945	P	Returned 16.10.1949
EK-12	PF-6	PASCO	Kaiser Richmond #4	10.3.1943	17.8.1943	15.4.1944	16.8.1945	26.8.1945	P	Returned 16.10.1949
EK-13	PF-5	HOQUIAM	Kaiser Richmond #4	10.4.1943	31.7.1943	6.5.1944	16.8.1945	26.8.1945	P	Returned 1.11.1948
EK-14	PF-7	ALBUQUERQUE	Kaiser Richmond #4	1943	14.9.1943	20.12.1943	16.8.1945	26.8.1945	P	Returned 15.11.1949
EK-15	PF-8	EVERETT	Kaiser Richmond #4	1943	29.9.1943	22.1.1944	16.8.1945	26.8.1945	P	Returned 15.11.1949
EK-16	PF-4	SAUSALITO	Kaiser Richmond #4	7.4.1943	20.7.1943	4.3.1944	16.8.1945	26.8.1945	P	Returned 1.11.1949
EK-17	PF-46	BISBEE	Consolidated, San Pedro	7.8.1943	7.9.1943	15.2.1944	26.8.1945	5.9.1945	P	Returned 1.11.1949
EK-18	PF-48	ROCKFORD	Consolidated, San Pedro	28.8.1943	27.9.1943	6.3.1944	26.8.1945	5.9.1945	P	Returned 17.2.1950
EK-19	PF-49	MUSKOGEE	Consolidated, San Pedro	18.9.1943	18.10.1943	16.3.1944	26.8.1945	5.9.1945	P	Returned 1.11.1949
EK-20	PF-50	CARSON CITY	Consolidated, San Pedro	1943	13.11.1943	24.3.1944	26.8.1945	5.9.1945	P	Returned 31.10.1949
EK-21	PF-51	BURLINGTON	Consolidated, San Pedro	19.10.1943	7.12.1943	3.4.1944	26.8.1945	5.9.1945	P	Returned 14.11.1949
EK-22	PF-47	GALLUP	Consolidated, San Pedro	18.8.1943	17.9.1943	19.2.1944	26.8.1945	5.9.1945	P	Returned 17.2.1950
EK-25	PF-21	BAYONNE	American, Cleveland	1943	11.9.1943	14.2.1944	2.9.1945	9.9.1945	P	Returned 14.11.1949
EK-26	PF-22	GLOUCESTER	Walter Butler	1943	12.7.1943	10.12.1944	9.9.1945	25.9.1945	P	Returned 31.10.1949
EK-27	PF-26	POUGHKEEPSIE	Walter Butler	3.6.1943	12.8.1943	8.9.1944	2.9.1945	25.9.1945	P	Returned 31.10.1949
EK-28	PF-27	NEVPORT	Walter Butler	5.6.1943	15.8.1943	8.9.1944	9.9.1945	25.9.1945	P	Returned 14.11.1949
EK-29	PF55	BATH	Froemming	1943	14.11.1943	8.9.1944	9.9.1945	25.9.1945	P	Returned 15.11.1949
EK-30	PF-70	EVANSVILLE	Leathem	1943	27.11.1943	Nov 1944	9.9.1945	25.9.1945	P	Returned 17.2.1950

Above: *EK-2* (ex-USS *Long-Beach*, PF-34) in Soviet service.
Przemysław Budzbon Collection

Right above: *EK-5* (ex-USS *San Pedro*, PF-37).
Boris Lemachko Collection

Right below: *EK-1* (ex-USS *Carlottenville*, PF-25).
Boris Lemachko Collection

11.4. War prizes

11.4.1. Baltic states, 1940

German A II type — *Coastal torpedo boat*

Displacement:	275t normal, 286t full load
Dimensions:	52.0 x 5.3 x 2.9m
Machinery:	1-shaft, 2 Parsons geared turbines, 1 Normand boiler (18.5 kg/cm^2), 3500hp =24kts. Oil fuel 58t, range 600nm at 12kts
Armament:	2-75mm replaced by 1941 with 3-45mm/46 21-K, (3-0.5in DShK MGs added 1942/3), 2-450mm TTs (removed by 1941), 16 M-1 DCs, 31 M1926 mines
Complement:	46

German torpedo boat stranded 25.10.1917 off Saaremaa, raised 13.10.1923 by the Estonians and 1.11.1923 comm in the Estonian Navy. Seized on Soviet annexation of Estonia and comm with the Baltic Fleet. Trfd 17.10.1940 to the Border Guard of the NKVD, conv 9.1.1941 to NKVD training ship of the Border Guard Naval Academy, renamed *Ametist*. Returned 22.6.1941 to the Baltic Fleet, comm as escort ship *Ametist*. Returned 15.6.1945 to the Border Guard with the power plant out of order. Conv to NKVD stationary training and accommodation ship.

Name	Builder	Laid down	Launched	Comp	Comm	Fleet	Fate
SULEV ex-*Sulev* (Est, 18.8.1940) ex-*A-32* (Ger, 3.6.1924)	Schichau, Elbing	1916	15.7.1916	14.10.1916	18.8.1940	B	Discared 4.1.1952

Cross reference: Rated as escort ships.

Name	Details	Type	From	To	Fate
Korall	M1916	Minesweeper	19.8.1941	25.11.1943	Conv to minesweeper
Virsajtis	M1916	Minesweeper	25.7.1941	3.12.1941	Lost

11.4.2. Romania, 1944

Austro-Hungarian 250-tonners — *Torpedo boats*

Displacement:	262t standard, 320t full load (Toros 266t standard, 330t full load)
Dimensions:	58.2 (Toros 58.5) x 5.7 (Toros 5.8) x 1.5m
Machinery:	2-shaft Parsons turbines, 2 Yarrow (Toros AEG) boilers, 5000hp = 24kts
Armament:	2-66mm/30, 2-20mm Oerlikon, (Musson only 2-450mm TTs (2x2)), (Toros only 1 DTC)
Complement:	30–38

Former Austro-Hungarian high-seas torpedo boats, allocated to Romania in 1920 under the terms of the Saint-Germain-en-Laye Treaty. *Smeul* was converted to escort ship before the war with her twin TTs replaced by the 400mm DCT. Both were captured 29.8.1944 at Constanța and taken over by the Soviet navy on 5.9.1944. Both returned 12.10.1945 to Romania. Served as escort ships *E-1* and *E-2* until late 1950s.

Name	Builder	Laid down	Launched	Comp	Comm	Fleet	Fate
MUSSON ex-*Sborul* (Rom, 20.11.1944) ex-*81* T (A-H, 1920)	STT	6.2.1914	6.8.1914	2.12.1914	14.9.1944	BS	BU 1958
TOROS (*do 20.10.1944*) ex-*Smeul* (Rom, 20.11.1944) ex-*83* F (A-H, 1920)	Ganz Danubius	17.11.1913	7.11.1914	21.7.1915	14.9.1944	BS	BU 1960

11.0 Escort Ships

11.4.3. Manchukuo, 1945

Manchukuo **Hai Feng** class — *Border patrol boats*

Displacement: 184t standard, 220t full load
Dimensions: 43.6 x 6.1 x 1.5m
Machinery: 2-shaft 2 diesels, 800hp = 14kts
Armament: 2-37mm/67.5 70-K, 2-0.5in MGs

Name	YN	Laid down	Launched	Comp	Comm	Fleet	Fate
Builder: Kawasaki DY, Kobe							
VETER	577	14.3.1933	12.6.1933	4.7.1933	13.9.1945	P	Discarded 20.4.1963
ex-*Hai Feng* (Man, 13.9.1945)							
ex-*Kaiho* (Jap, 1935)							
SHTIL'	578	14.3.1933	12.7.1933	30.7.1933	13.9.1945	P	Discarded 27.5.1966
ex-*Hai Lung* (Man, 13.9.1945)							
ex-*Koirun* (Jap, 1935)							

Patrol craft of Border Police of Manchukuo captured 22.8.1945 at Port Arthur and comm with the Pacific Fleet. Trfd 28.2.1948 to Border Guard, decomm 1950s to civilian service as training ships.

Veter: renamed *PS-428* on 28.2.1948.

Shtil': renamed *PS-•* on 28.2.1948.

11.5. Conversions

11.5.1. Seagoing escorts

FYODOR LITKE — *Icebreaker*

Displacement: 5500t normal
Tonnage: 2216grt
Dimensions: 83.2 x 14.6 x 8.6m
Machinery: 2-shaft, VTE, 4 boilers, 7000hp = 14kts; range 3900nm at 11kts
Armament: 3-100mm, 2-0.3in MGs, from 1943: 4-3in/56, 4-45mm/46 21-K, 2-20mm Oerlikon, 6-0.5in MGs
Complement: 136

Fyodor Litke in September 1947.
Boris Lemachko Collection

Pt No 1941	Name	YN	Built	Comm	Fleet	Remarks
	Builder: Vickers					
18	FYODOR LITKE	385	1909	8.1.1940	N	Purchased 1914, mobilised 1917 with Northern Ocean Flotilla as naval icebreaker, captured 1918 by White Russians; recovered 1920, mobilised, conv to auxiliary cruiser, 1921 to civilian service. Mobilised 1940, conv to escort ship, decomm 8.4.1940 to civilian service. Mobilised 26.6.1941, conv to escort ship, comm 2.7.1941. Trfd 13.8.1941 to the White Sea Flotilla. Decomm 14.5.1944 to civilian service. Discarded 14.11.1958
	ex-*Tretij Internatsional* (1921)					
	ex-*Kanada* (1920)					
	ex-*Earl Grey* (Can, 1914)					

Severmorput'-1 type *(Project 53)* — *Cargo steamers*

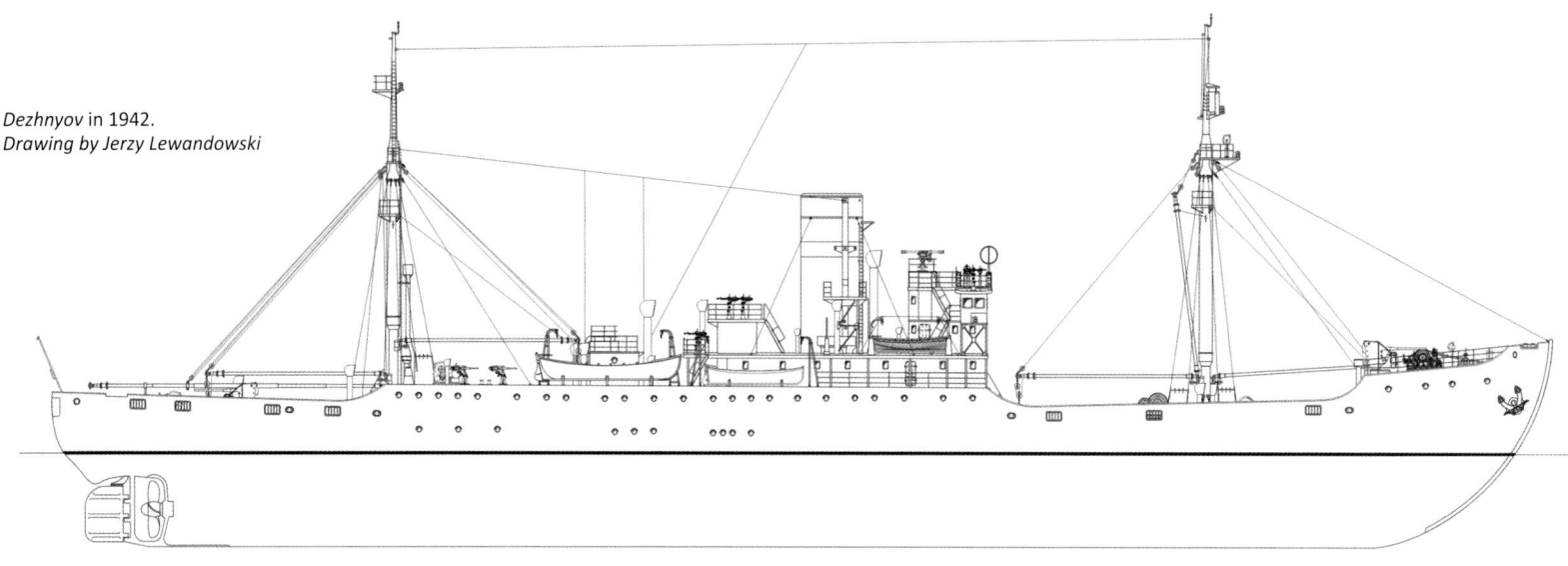

Dezhnyov in 1942. Drawing by Jerzy Lewandowski

Displacement: 6530t standard, 7330t full load
Tonnage: 3591grt
Dimensions: 104.0 x 15.0 x 6.3m
Machinery: 1-shaft VTE, 3 boilers, 2500hp = 12.6kts; range 4700 miles
Armament: *Dezhnyov* 4-3in/55, 4-45mm/46 21-K, 6-0.5in MGs
Complement: *Dezhnyov* 122, *Levanevskij* 45

Two decked, general cargo vessels designed for supply of polar bases and fitted with four motorboats onboard for unloading on a bare shore. Ordered as a result of experience from loss of the steamer *Cheliuskin* (Chelyuskin) in 1934. Design by Sudoproekt, based on the *Anadyr'* type with an icebreaking bow, ice strengthening of scantlings, 32-35mm thick ice belt and caisson for replacement of propeller blades. Equipped with cabins for 7 passengers and additional berths for 66 on the tween deck. It was planned to convert both vessels into seaplane tenders in time of war under the *Project 2393* armed with 4-3in and 4-45mm/46 and able to carry 2 *MBR-2* or four *KOR-1* seaplanes.

Dezhnyov during the war. Vitalij Kostrichenko Collection

Pt No 1941	Transport No 1941	Name	YN	Built	Comm	Fleet	Remarks
		Builder: 198, Leningrad					
19		DEZHNYOV ex-*Severmorput'*-1 (1937?)	365	1939	Dec 1939	N	Mobilised 19.12.1939, conv to escort ship; decomm 19.7.1940 to civilian service. Mobilised 25.6.1941, conv to escort ship. Stranded off the Dickson 27.8.1942 after shelling by the German cruiser Admiral Scheer. After temporary repairs floated off the shallows next day and sailed to Dudinka, recomm 11.9.1942. Decomm summer 1945 to civilian service, discarded by 1969
	582	S. A. LEVANEVSKIJ ex-*Severmorput'*-2 (1937?)	366	1940	22.6.1941	B	Mobilised as transport, taken in hand Aug 1941 at Kronshtad Harbour to conv to auxiliary cruiser. Sunk 21.9.1941 by German aircraft, raised 26.11.1941, recomm as a naval tanker, renamed *Levanevskij*. Decomm 1947 to civilian service, reverted to general cargo trfd to the Arctic. Discarded 1968

11.0 Escort Ships

Cargo-passenger steamer

Sevastopol' in passenger service at the mid-1930s.
Boris Lemachko Collection

Name	Details	Comm	Fleet	Remarks
SEVASTOPOL'	1433grt; 79.4 x 10.5 x 5.1m; 1000hp = 11kts; 1941: 1-45mm/46 21-K, 2-0.3in MGs; 1942: 4-45 mm, 6-0.3in; 51 men	10.8.1941	AzBS	Built 1896 Laing. Mobilised 20.7.1941, conv to escort ship-minesweeper, conv 15.5.1942 to transport, trdf to the Black Sea Fleet. Sunk 10.8.1942 by the German MTB S-102 off Tuapse

Cross reference: Rated as escort ships.

Name	Details	Type	From	To	Fate
PARTIZAN	*Kamchadal* class	Surveying ship	28.10.1941	20.8.1945	Lost
VETER	*Aleksei Rykov* type	Transport	23.11.1939	29.12.1940	Decomm to civilian service
			30.6.1941	29.7.1941	Conv 29.7.1941 to depot ship
INZHENER	*Inzhener*	Experimental ship	22.11.1939	12.12.1939	Reverted to experimental ship

11.5.1.1. Mobilised trawlers

The surviving 16 ships of the Russian ocean trawler fleet, depleted by World War 1 and the Civil War, were insufficient by the mid-1920s to satisfy both food needs and, more importantly, the demand for hard currency. Russian lack of experience in the construction of this type of vessel prompted the Soviet authorities to order 66 trawlers from German and Italian shipyards. At the same time, based on the experience gained in foreign shipyards, it was planned – as usual on a grandiose scale – to build a fleet of 70 trawlers in Russia within five years.

The escort ship conversion project – its designation is not known – provided for the installation of two 45mm/46 guns (one each on forecastle and poop), and two single 0.3in MGs on M-1 type mounts on the wheelhouse deck. To clear firing angles of the aft 45mm/46 gun, the boat davits were moved to amidships, and DC rails were installed on the poop. They were not equipped with any submarine detection devices.

During the war, the armament was increased by replacing 45mm/46 guns with 3in weapons, installing 20mm Oerlikons and replacing Maxim MGs with 0.5in DShK ones. The anti-submarine armament was supplemented by the installation of DCTs and increasing the number of DCs.

PS-1 in 1930s.
Boris Lemachko Collection

Steam trawler

No 18.8.1941	Name	Details	Comm	Type	Fleet	Remarks
SKR-20	NEPTUN ex-*PS-1* (1941) ex-*T-15* (1928)	550t; 35.0 x 7.0 x 3.0m; 550hp =7.5kts; 2-45mm/46 21-K, (added 1943: 2-20mm Oerlikon), 2-0.3in MGs, 2 DC rails, 63 men	13.8.1941	Minesweeper	Wh	Built 1916 Smith's Dock. Purchased 1916 for the Arctic Ocean Flotilla, conv to minesweeper. Sank 2.8.1918, raised by White Russians, recovered 1920. Trfd 1921 to the OGPU Border Guard. Mobilised 23.6.1941, comm with the White Sea Flotilla as escort ship, numbered 18.8.1941 SKR-20. Decomm 15.1.1946, returned to the Border Guard. Discarded 3.1.1957

Smena type — *Steam trawlers*

Displacement: *Series 1*: 1200t
Dimensions: *Series 1*: 53.4 x 9.05 x 4.3m; *Series 2*: 55.1 x 9.0 x 4.35m
Machinery: 1-shaft compound, 1 boiler, 650hp = 11kts (*Series 2*: 10.5kts). Coal 270t (*Series 2*: 275t), range 4100nm
Armament: escort ships 1939-1942: 2-45mm/3in, 2-0.3in Maxim MGs, 2 DC rails, 18 DCs
minesweepers 1939-1942: 2-45mm/3in, 2-0.3in Maxim MGs, 1 MTSh sweep, 1 MZT sweep
both types 1943: added 1-37mm/67.5 and 1 or 2-20mm Oerlikon, Maxim type MGs replaced by 0.5in DShK
escort ships 1943: some received DCTs
minesweepers 1943: had number of sweeps increased, some received AT sweeps (see notes)
Complement: 43–54 (see notes)

Pt No 1941	No on Comm	No	FN	Name	YN	Built	Comm	Type	Fleet	Remarks
				Series 1						
				Builder: Severnaia, Leningrad						
79	SKR-24[3]		RT-64	AJSBERG ex-*Severnyj polius* ex-*Ian Gamarnik* (1937)	379	1933	29.7.1941	Escort ship	N Wh	Mobilised 25.6.1941. Trfd 23.8.1941 to the White Sea Flotilla. Decomm 9.7.1943 to civilian service (29.7.1941)
25			RT-58	BRIZ ex-*Spartak* (29.7.1941)	373	1933	29.7.1941	Escort ship	N Wh	Mobilised 25.6.1941. Trfd 23.8.1941 to the White Sea Flotilla. Converted 25.12.1944 to salvage depot ship
	BS-3	SKR-32[4] SKR-84[5]	RT-59	KOLKHOZNIK	374	1931	1941 15.10.1943	Guard ship Escort ship	N Wh	Mobilised 29.7.1941, conv to guard ship, conv 1.9.1942 to escort ship. Decomm 30.1.1943 to civilian service. Recomm 15.10.1943 as escort ship to the White Sea Flotilla, decomm 19.11.1943 to civilian service
11	DK-60		RT-60	RABOCHIJ	375	1932	1939	Escort ship	N	Mobilised 2.12.1939, renamed *Toros* on 4.3.1940, decomm 15.5.1944 to civilian service
21			RT-82	GRAD ex-*Dimitrov* (1941)	397	1935	29.7.1941	Escort ship	N	Mobilised 25.6.1941, decomm 15.5.1944 to civilian service. Discarded 1960s
				ODESSKIJ GORSOVET		1931	12.5.1944	Transport	BS	Conv 1940 to freighter. Mobilised 1944, sunk by mine off Odessa 1946
70	PS-70		RT-70	KAPITAN VORONIN	385	1932	29.7.1941	Dispatch ship	N	Mobilised June 1941, conv to dispatch ship. Sunk 6.8.1941 by German submarine *U-652* seven miles off Cape Teriberka near Murmansk
75	PS-75		RT-75	SARATOV	390	1932	29.7.1941	Dispatch ship	N	Mobilised June 1941, conv to dispatch ship. Decomm postwar to civilian service
			RT-63	POLIARNYJ	378	1932	10.11.1941	Heater	N	Mobilised 1941, conv to heater. Decomm 4.5.1943 to civilian service
			RT-65	REVOLIUTSIIA	380	1932	10.11.1941	Heater	N	Mobilised 1941, conv to heater. Decomm 9.2.1943 to civilian service, recomm 4.5.1943. Decomiss. 31.12.1943 to civilian service
			RT-67	MOLOTOV	382	1931	-	Salvage ship	N	Mobilised 4.7.1941 but sunk 13.7.1941 before commissioning by German 6th Destroyer Flotilla near Cape Teriberski, the Kola Peninsula
70	SKR-11	SKR-62[3]	RT-66	URAL	381	1932	16.7.1941	Escort ship	N Wh	Mobilised 14.7.1941. Trfd 13.8.1941 to the White Sea Flotilla. Lost 26.10.1941 on mines E of Tersko-Orlovsky Mayak (Kola Peninsula)
71	SKR-12		RT-77	CHELIUSKINETS PAVLOV	392	1933	16.7.1941	Escort ship	N Wh	Mobilised 14.7.1941. Trfd 13.8.1941 to White Sea Flotilla, decomm 18.3.1945 to civilian service
75	SKR-16		RT-78	GROZNYJ	393	1933	23.9.1841	Escort ship	Wh	Mobilised 15.8.1941. Decomm 18.3.1945 to civilian service
76	SKR-21		RT-73	KUJBYSHEV ex-*Filipp Medved'* (1939)	388	1932	20.9.1941	Escort ship	Wh	Mobilised 13.8.1941. Sunk 17.5.1942 by German aircraft in roads of Ostrovnoy (Yokanga) at the Kola Peninsula. Wreck raised 3.7.1944

11.0 Escort Ships

Pt No 1941	No on Comm	No	FN	Name	YN	Built	Comm	Type	Fleet	Remarks
77	SKR-22		RT-79	TBILISI ex-*Otto Shmidt* (1939)	394	1933	1.10.1941	Escort ship	Wh	Mobilised 20.9.1941. Decomm 2.3.1945 to civilian service. Discarded 1960s
78	SKR-23		RT-57	SMENA	375	1931	Oct 1941	Escort ship	Wh	Mobilised 20.9.1941. Sunk 7.11.1942 by German cruiser *Admiral Hipper* and destroyers, SE of Novaya Zemlya
81	SKR-26		RT-74	OSOAVIAKHIM	389	1933	31.12.1941	Escort ship	Wh	Mobilised 11.9.1941. Decomm 18.3.1945 to civilian service, renamed Nogin
72	SKR-64	SKR-13[3]	RT-80	BATUMI ex-*Batum* (1936)	395	1934	16.7.1941	Escort ship	N Wh	Mobilised 14.7.1941. Trfd 13.8.1941 to the White Sea Flotilla. Decomm 15.5.1944 to civilian service. Discarded 1960s
40	T-1 T-899[1]	T-894[2]	RT-83	SEVERNYJ	398	1935	Oct 1939 29.7.1941	Minesweeper	N	Mobilised 19.10.1939. Decomm 29.3.1940 to civilian service. Mobilised 25.6.1941, comm 29.7.1941. Decomm 15.5.1944 to civilian service. Discarded 1960s
41	T-2 T-898[1]	T-895[2]	RT-84	GOL'FSTRIM	399	1935	19.10.1939 29.7.1941	Minesweeper	N Wh	Mobilised 19.10.1939. Decomm 29.3.1940 to civilian service. Mobilised 25.6.1941, comm 29.7.1941, trfd 23.8.1941 to the White Sea Flotilla. Decomm 1.2.1943 to civilian service. Discarded 1960s
36	T-882	SKR-83[5]	RT-72	LENINGRAD	387*	1933	29.7.1941 15.10.1943	Minesweeper Escort ship	N	Mobilised 25.6.1941, conv to minesweeper, decomm 30.1.1943 to civilian service. Recomm 15.10.1943 as escort ship. Decomm after the war to civilian service
64	T-910		RT-81	KOLOMNA	396	1933	23.10.1941	Minesweeper	Wh	Mobilised 13.8.1941. Decomm after the war to civilian service
65	T-911		RT-76	ASTRAKHAN'	391	1933	26.11.1941	Minesweeper	Wh	Mobilised 13.11.1941. Sunk 30.7.1943 by *U-703* off Belushya Bay, Novaya Zemlya
			Builder: Sevmorzavod, Sevastopol							
42	T-2 T-894[1]	T-896[5]	RT-308	KRASNYJ ONEZHANIN	47?	1933	Nov 1939 29.7.1941	Minesweeper	N	Mobilised 9.11.1939. Decomm 29.3.1940 to civilian service. Mobilised 25.6.1941, comm 29.7.1941. Sunk 1.10.1943 by *U-960* at the Kara Sea off the Izvestiy TSIK Islands
43	T-4 T-897[1]	T-897[2] SKR-82[5]	RT-309	MUD'IUZHANIN	48	1933	1939[3] 29.7.1941 15.10.1943	Minesweeper Escort ship	N Wh	Mobilised 19.10.1939, conv to minesweeper. Decomm 29.3.1940 to civilian service. Mobilised 25.6.1941, conv to minesweeper, comm 29.7.1941. Decomm 30.1.1943 to civilian service. Recomm 15.10.1943 with the White Sea Flotilla conv to escort ship. Decomm after the war
44	T-5 T-896[1]	T-898[2]	RT-411	NENETS	49	1933	1939 29.7.1941	Minesweeper	N Wh	Mobilised 19.10.1939. Decomm 29.3.1940 to civilian service. Mobilised 25.6.1941, comm 29.7.1941. Trfd 23.8.1941 to the White Sea Flotilla, sunk 25.8.1941 by *U-752* off Cape Sviatoy Nos at Barents Sea
45	T-6 T-895[1]	T-899[2]	RT-412	KOLGUEVETS	50	1933	1939 29.7.1941	Minesweeper	N	Mobilised 19.10.1939. Decomm 29.3.1940 to civilian service. Mobilised 25.6.1941, comm 29.7.1941. Decomm 8.3.1945 to civilian service
				Series 2						
				Builder: Severnaia, Leningrad						
22			RT-102	PASSAT ex-*V. Chkalov* (1941)	•**	1931	2.7.1941	Escort ship	N	Mobilised 25.6.1941. Sunk 13.7.1941 by German 6th Destroyer Flotilla near Cape Teriberski, the Kola Peninsula

Pt No 1941	No on Comm	No	FN	Name	YN	Built	Comm	Type	Fleet	Remarks
73	SKR-14		RT-86	INDIGA	401	1937	12.9.1941	Escort ship	Wh	Mobilised Aug 1941. Beached 2.12.1941 in Pechora Bay, salvaged 8.8.1942 and repaired, stranded 17.10.1943 at Kara Sea, total loss
74	SKR-15		RT-85	SERGO ORDZHONIKIDZE ex-*Timanets* (1938)	400	1937	11.9.1941	Escort ship	Wh	Mobilised 15.8.1941. Decomm 2.3.1945, to civilian service
80	SKR-25		RT-88	PECHORETS ex-*Pechora* (1938)	363*	1933	1941	Escort ship	Wh	Mobilised 20.9.1941. Decomm 2.3.1945 to civilian service
54 57[3]	SKR-65	T-903[3] PS-89[6]	RT-89	BELOMORETS	383*	1936	1941	Escort ship Minesweeper	N Wh	Mobilised 3.7.1941, conv to escort ship, trfd 13.8.1941 to the White Sea Flotilla. Conv 20.9.1941 to minesweeper. Conv 2.2.1944 to dispatch ship, renamed. Decomm 15.5.1944 to civilian service
55 58[3]	SKR-66	T-904[3]	RT-94	ZHDANOV	409	1935	July 1941	Escort ship Minesweeper	N Wh	Mobilised 3.7.1941, conv to escort ship. Trfd 13.8.1941 to the White Sea Flotilla, conv 20.9.1941 to minesweeper. Lost 25.7.1943 in Pechora Bay on a mine laid by German submarine *U-625*
35	T-881		RT-101	I. PAPANIN	416**	1940	29.7.1941	Minesweeper	N	Mobilised 25.6.1941. Decomm after the war to civilian service, renamed 1957 *Kapitan Poriadin*. Discarded 1964

* Completed by the Sudomekh Works. ** Completed by the Murmansk Yard.

Exceptions noted in the main table.

No	Year	Date
1	1939	23.11.1939
2	1941	29.7.1941
3		20.9.1941
4	1942	1.9.1942
5	1943	15.10.1943
6	1944	15.5.1944

The design of the first Soviet-built trawlers was ordered from Deutsche Werft. The 'mass' construction of the trawlers was entrusted to the Severnaia Verf' shipyard at Leningrad, where the construction of 28 slipways on adjacent land was started in the spring of 1929; keels for the first hulls were laid even before the completion of the works. In a manner typical for the time, seventy ships were planned, with the first batch of fifty to be completed by the end of 1931. As the construction of the slipways was protracted, the first four trawlers were laid down on temporary wooden slipways, and four more on the main slipways of the shipyard. In 1933 the design was modified, and the trawlers built according to it were designated *Series 2*, while those previously built were retrospectively named *Series 1*.

Delays in an unrealistic construction schedule meant that several hulls were handed over to the Sudomekh shipyard for completion, which did not help much as the plant was undergoing a major overhaul in preparation for the naval construction programme. Moving construction to the repair shipyard in Murmansk also did little, as the plant was not ready until 1937. In total, 41 trawlers (including those built on the Black Sea) were completed before the outbreak of the war with Germany, *ie* about 60% of the planned seventy in twice the planned time – a result typical of those times in the Soviet Union.

Of the *Series 1 RT-69 Irtysh, RT-61 Vodnik, RT-62 Voroshilov, RT-68 Enisej* (sunk 17.1.1942 by *U-454*), *RT-71 Moskva* and *Series 2 RT-103 Pobeda* (sunk 4.4.1942 by German aircraft) remained in civilian service during the war. *RT-105 Fillofora* was completed after the war.

T-910 back in a fishing role in the 1960s.
Boris Lemachko Collection

T-881 during the war. Note acoustic hammer at the bow and camouflage scheme.
Przemysław Budzbon Collection

11.0 ESCORT SHIPS

T-894 of the *Series 1* in the minesweeper configuration.
Drawing by Jerzy Lewandowski

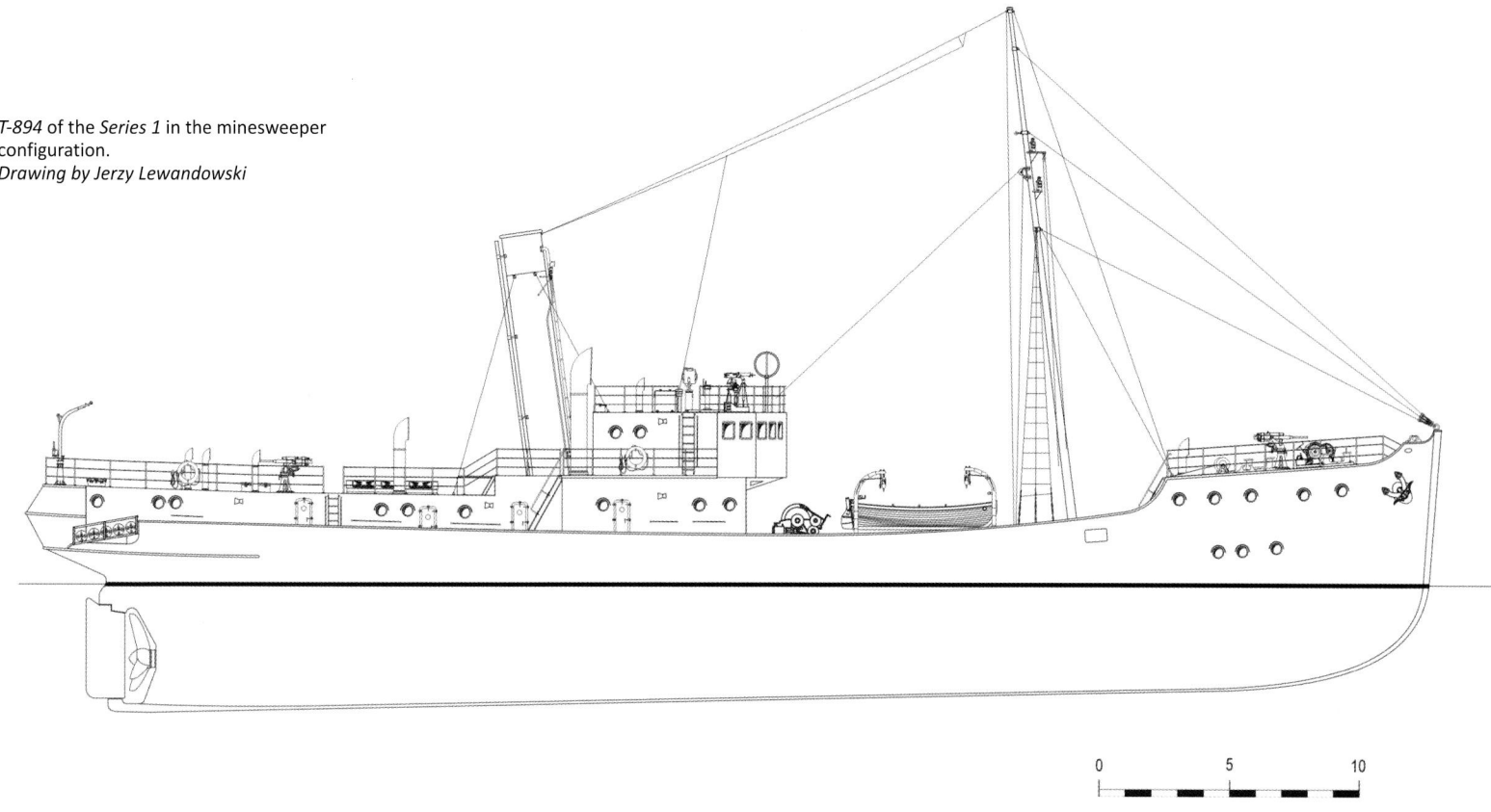

Series 2 trawler in the patrol ship configuration.
Drawing by Jerzy Lewandowski

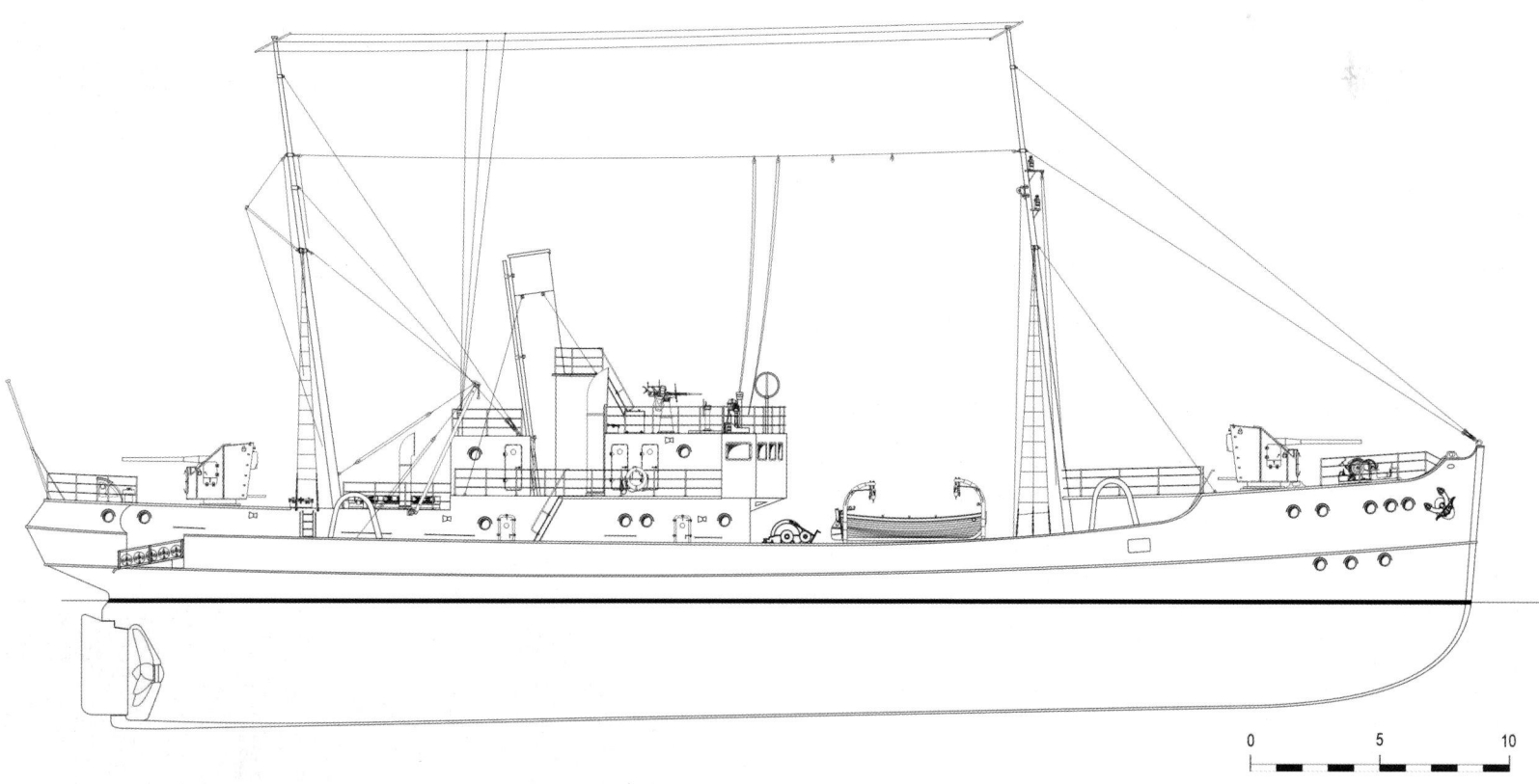

Note on armament and complement. Information on complement is not related to any specific period of service.

Name	Complement	1939-1942		1943-1945
Series 1				
Aisberg	43	2-3in/55, 2-0.3in Maxim MGs		-
Briz	43	2-3in/55, 2-0.3in Maxim MGs	added	2-20mm Oerlikon
BS-3	43	2-45mm/46 21-K, 2-0.3in Maxim MGs	changed to	-
DK-60	43	2-45mm/46 21-K, 2-0.3in Maxim MGs	changed to	37mm/67.5, 2-0.5in DShK MGs
Grad	43	2-45mm/46 21-K, 2-0.3in Maxim MGs	changed to	2-37mm/67.5, 1-20mm Oerlikon, 3-0.5in DShK MGs
Odesskij Gorsovet	43	-		not armed
PS-70	43	not armed		-
PS-75	43	not armed		not armed
RT-63 Poliarnyi	43	not armed		-
RT-65 Revoliutsiia	43	not armed		-
RT-67 Molotov	43	not armed		-
SKR-11, SKR-21	42	2-3in/55, 2-0.3in Maxim MGs		-
SKR-12	49	2-3in/55, 2-0.3in Maxim MGs	changed to	3-3in/55, 3-20mm Oerlikon, 2-0.3in MGs, 2 DCTs
SKR-16	49	2-3in/30 Lender, 2-0.3in Maxim MGs	changed to	2-85mm/52, 3-20mm Oerlikon, 1-0.5in DShK MG, 2 DCTs
SKR-22	42	2-75mm/50, 2-0.3in Maxim MGs	changed to	2-3in/55, 2-20mm Oerlikon 2-0.3in Maxim MGs
SKR-23	42	2-75mm/50, 2-0.5in Maxim MGs	changed to	2-3in/55, 2-20mm Oerlikon, 2-0.3in Maxim
SKR-26	42	2-3in/30 Lender, 2-0.3in Maxim MGs	replaced by	2-85mm/52, 2-37mm/67.5, 1-20mm Oerlikon, 3-0.3in MGs, 2 DCTs
SKR-64	49	2-3in/55, 2-0.3in Maxim MGs	replaced by	3-3in/55, 2-20mm Oerlikon, 1-0.3in MG, 2 DCTs
T-1	44	2-45mm/46 21-K, 2-0.3in MGs, 1 MTSh sweep, 1 MZT sweep	added	1-20mm Oerlikon, 1 AT sweep
T-2	43	2-45mm/46 21-K, 3-0.3in MGs, 1 MTSh sweep, 1 MZT sweep		-
T-882	54	2-3in, 2-0.3in MGs, 1 MTSh sweep, 1 MZT sweep		•
T-910	43	2-3in/55, 2-0.3in MGs, 1 MTSh sweep, 2 MZT sweeps	added	2-20mm Oerlikon, 1 AT sweep
T-911	43	2-45mm/46 21-K, 2-0.3in MGs, 1 MTSh sweep, 2 MZT sweeps		-
T-3, T-4, T-5	43	2-45mm/46 21-K, 3-0.3in MGs, 1 MTSh sweep, 1 MZT sweep		-
T-6	43	2-45mm/46 21-K, 2-0.3in MGs, 1 MTSh sweep, 1 MZT sweep	added	4-0.5in Vickers MG (4x1)
Series 2				
Passat	43	2-45mm/46 21-K, 2-0.3in Maxim MGs		-
SKR-14	42	2-3in/55, 2-0.3in Maxim MGs		-
SKR-15	42	2-3in/55, 2-0.3in Maxim MGs	changed to	1-3in/55, 2-20mm Oerlikon
SKR-25	42	2-3in/30 Lender, 2-0.3in Maxim MGs	replaced by	2-85mm/52, 2-20mm Oerlikon, 2-0.3in MGs
SKR-65	43	3-45mm/46 21-K, 3-0.3in MGs, 1 MTSh sweep, 2 MZT sweeps	added	2-20mm Oerlikon
SKR-66	43	3-45mm/46 21-K, 3-0.3in MGs, 1 MTSh sweep, 2 MZT sweeps		no changes
T-881	52	2-3in/55, 2-0.3in MGs, 1 MTSh sweep, 1 MZT sweep	changed to	2-3in/55, 1-37mm/67.5, 1-20mm Oerlikon, 2-0.5in DShK MGs, 1-0.3in MG, 1 MTSh sweep, 1 MZT sweep, 2 DCTs

Odesskij Gorsovet before the war. *Boris Lemachko Collection*

T-899 during the war wearing camouflage scheme. *Przemysław Budzbon Collection*

Soiuzryba type
Motor trawlers

Displacement: 800t
Dimensions: 43.6 x 7.9 x 4.12m
Machinery: 1-shaft Deutz diesel, 560hp = 11kts. Oil 75t, range 8500nm
Armament: 2-45mm/46 21-K, (*PS-48:* 1943 added 1-20mm Oerlikon), 2-0.3in Maxim MGs, 2 DC rails
Complement: 42

PS-48 in 1943 wearing camouflage.
Boris Lemachko Collection

Pt No 1941	No 1939	No 1941	FN	Name	YN	Built	Comm	Type	Fleet	Remarks
				Builder: Howaldswerke						
48		PS-48	RT-48	SEVGOSRYBTREST	715	1931	29.7.1941	Dispatch ship	N	Mobilised 1941, conv to dispatch ship. Decomm 2.3.1945 to civilian service. Discarded mid-1950s
	AD		RT-49	BRIZ ex-*Skumbriia* (23.11.1939)	716	1931	Oct 1939	Escort ship	N	Mobilised 19.10.1939. Stranded 25.1.1940, total loss
20	BD		RT-51	SHTIL' ex-*Leshch* (23.11.1939)	718	1931	Oct 1939 2.7.1941	Escort ship	N	Mobilised 19.10.1939. Decomm 28.1.1941 to civilian service, name reverted. Mobilised 25.6.1941, recomm 2.7.1941, name reverted Sunk 19.7.1941 by German aircraft at the Ura Bay
	DK-52		RT-52	PASSAT ex-*Som* (4.3.1940)	719	1931	Dec 1939	Escort ship	N	Mobilised 2.12.1939. Decomm 29.3.1940 to civilian service, name reverted. Sunk 26.12.1944 by *U-995*.
23	DK-54		RT-54	MUSSON ex-*Sudak* (4.3.1940)	721	1931	Dec 1939 2.7.1941	Escort ship	N	Mobilised 2.12.1939. Decomm 29.3.1940 to civilian service, name reverted. Mobilised 25.6.1941, recomm 2.7.1941, name reverted. Sunk 11.10.1942 by mine laid by *U-589* in the Matochkin Strait
	DK-55		RT-55	GRAD ex-*Keta* (4.3.1940)	722	1931	Dec 1939	Escort ship	N	Mobilised 2.12.1939. Decomm 29.3.1940 to civilian service, name reverted
	DK-56		RT-56	BURAN ex-*Beluga* (4.3.1940)	723	1931	Dec 1939	Escort ship	N	Mobilised 2.12.1939. Decomm 29.3.1940 to civilian service, name reverted

RT-50 Moiva in civilian service during the war. *RT-53 Osyotr* lost 31.1.1932, *RT-47 Soiuzryba* lost 31.2.1932.

Ussuriets type — *Steam trawlers*

Displacement: 1255t
Dimensions: 54.8 x 9.0 x 4.6m
Machinery: 1-shaft VTE, 1 boiler, 675hp = 10kts. Coal fuel, range 3600nm.
Armament: *DK-30:* 2-45mm/46 21-K, 2-0.3in MGs, 2 DC racks, (from 1943: 3-37mm/67.5, 2-20mm Oerlikon, 2-0.5in DShK MGs, 2 DC racks)
Complement: 43

Zaria during the war.
Boris Lemachko Collection

Pt No 1941	No 1939	FN	Name	YN	Built	Comm	Type	Fleet	Remarks
			Builder: Partenopei						
13	DK-30	RT-30	ZARIA ex-*Ussuriets* (4.3.1940) ex-*RT-310 Ussuriets* (1934)	82	1931	Dec 1939	Escort ship Salvage depot ship	N	Mobilised 2.12.1939, conv to escort ship. Conv 21.4.1944 to salvage depot ship. Decomm 18.3.1947 to civilian service. Discarded 1960s
		RT-311	PESHKOV ex-*Amurets* (1934)	83	1932	July 1934	Surveying ship	P	Mobilised 1934, conv to surveying ship. Deleted mid-1960s

RT-312 Abrek in civilian service during the war.

Vostok type
Steam trawlers

Displacement: 1255t
Dimensions: 54.8 x 9.0 x 4.2m
Machinery: 1-shaft Christiansen-Meyer double expansion, 1 boiler, 650hp = 10kts. Coal fuel, range 3600nm
Armament: *Askol'd*: not armed
DK-38: 2-45mm/46, 2-0.3in MGs, 2 DC rails
Complement: 43

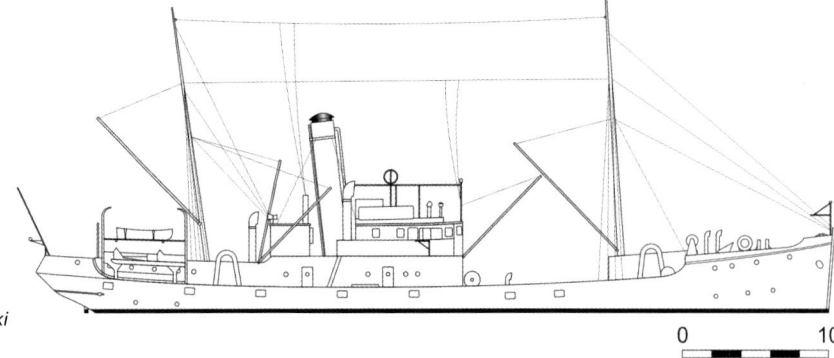

RT-314 Askol'd as built.
Drawing by Jaroslaw Dzierżawski

Pt No 1941	No 1939	FN	Name	YN	Built	Comm	Type	Fleet	Remarks
			Builder: Quarnaro						
		RT-42	ASKOL'D ex-RT-314 Askol'd (1934)	135	1931	10.11.1941	Heater	N	Mobilised 1941, conv to heater, decomiss.13.7.1942 to civilian service. Stranded 2.10.1960
26	DK-38	RT-38	MGLA ex-*Strelok* (4.3.1940) ex-RT-315 *Strelok* (1934)	136	1932	Dec 1939 29.7.1941	Escort ship	N	Mobilised 2.12.1939. Decomm 29.3.1940 to civilian service, name reverted. Stranded 8.3.1942

RT-313 Vostok in civilian service during the war, lost 1952

Cross reference: Rated as escort ships.

No	Name	Details	Type	From	To	Fate
DK-5	PRILIV	*Lenin* type	Minesweeper	2.12.1939	3.8.1943	Lost
DK-10	TUMAN	*Rolik* type		19.12.1939	10.8.1941	Lost
SKR-31	RYBETS	*Dnepr* type	Minesweeper	1.9.1942	12.5.1943	Lost
SKR-61	NEVA	*Neva* type	Minesweeper	4.7.1941	20.9.1941	Conv to minesweeper

11.5.2. Coastal escorts

Russian Barsuk class
Tugs

Displacement: 202t normal
Dimensions: 30.5 x 5.85 x 2.5m
Machinery: 1-shaft VTE, 1 Scotch boiler (11 kg/cm^2), 350hp = 9.5kts. Oil fuel 24t, 1200nm at 11kts
Armament: (1-3in 34-K Leninets only), 1 (Sobol' 3)-45mmm 21-K, 2-0.3in MGs
Complement: 37

Name	YN	Laid down	Launched	Comp	Comm	Type	Fleet	Fate
Builder: Lehtoniemi, Varkaus								
GORNOSTAJ ex-*O-4* (17.12.1916)		1915	1915	1.4.1916	14.8.1941	Guardship	Cs	Decomm 25.11.1943 to civilian service
LENINETS ex-*Vydra* (1930s)ex-*O-7* (17.12.1916)	165	1915	1915	1.4.1916	2.7.1941	Escort ship	Cs	Discarded 1960s
MOGILEVSKIJ ex-*Khoryok* (25.4.1925) ex-*O-6* (17.12.1916)	168	1915	1915	1.4.1916	22.6.1941	Escort ship	Cs	Discarded 1.6.1957
SOBOL' ex-*O-3* (17.12.1916)		1915	1915	1.4.1916	July 1941	Escort ship	Cs	Deleted 25.11.1943

Displacement:	273t normal, 286t full load
Dimensions:	39.2 x 5.85 x 2.4m
Machinery:	2-shaft, 2 38-KR-8 diesels, 16,000hp = 14kts. Oil fuel 25t, 2800nm at 11kts
Armament:	2-3in/55 34-K, 2-0.5in DShK MGs
Complement:	51

Originally a series of seven tugs designated as recorders for artillery and torpedo practice built for the Baltic Fleet of the Imperial Russian Navy. *Barsuk* (ex-*O-1*) lost 1917, *Laska* (ex-*O-5*) 1927 to civilian service, fate unknown. Trfd during Civil War to the Caspian Sea, they were unable to return to the Baltic because of damage and neglect of the Marijnsky Canal System connecting the Baltic Sea with the Volga. Comm with the Caspian Flotilla, trdf in 1920s to the Border Guard of the GPU or to civilian service.

Gronostai: trfd 1922 to civilian service, mobilised 22.6.1941 and comm as guardship. Deleted and returned to civilian service, fate unknown

Leninets: trfd 30.101926 to civilian service, mobilised 22.6.1941, conv to escort ship. Because of poor condition returned 21.5.1942 to civilian service. Foundered in Sum 1948, raised 20.7.1948 and repaired

Mogilevskij: trfd 27.12.1922 to the Border Guard of the OGPU, rebuilt 1939/40, mobilised 22.6.1941. Returned 27.7.1944 to the Border Guard, deleted 11.6.1954 to civilian service

Sobol': trfd 12.8.1922 to civilian service, mobilised 22.6.1941, decomm to civilian service

Atarbekov: trfd 27.12.1922 to the Border Guard of the OGPU, during 1938/9 completely rebuilt, lengthened, re-engined with diesels and rearmed. Mobilised 22.6.1941, detached to the civilian service during 30.10.1943–28.4.1944 as tug. Returned 27.7.1944 to the Border Guard, recomm 6.10.1954 with the Caspian Flotilla as surveying ship *Geliograf*.

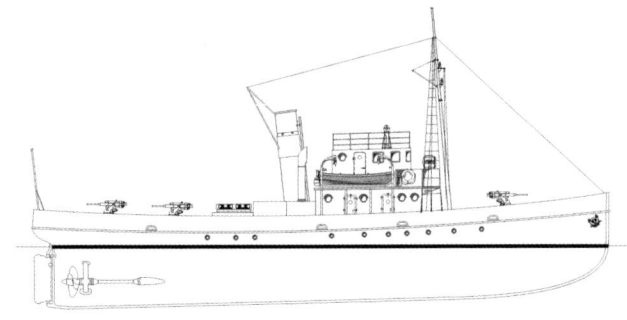
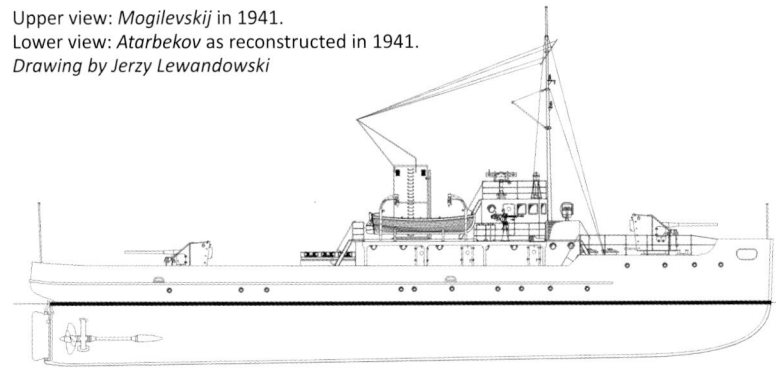
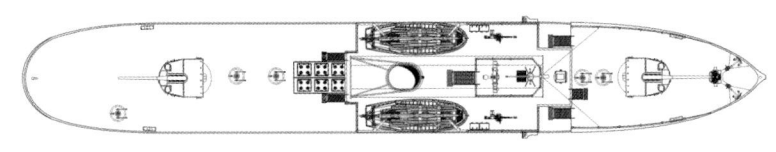

Upper view: *Mogilevskij* in 1941.
Lower view: *Atarbekov* as reconstructed in 1941.
Drawing by Jerzy Lewandowski

Right: The OGPU Border Guard patrol ship *G. Atarbekov* in her original configuration in 1929. *Boris Lemachko Collection*
Below: *Atarbekov* showing extent of her conversion in 1941. *Boris Lemachko Collection*

Name	YN	Laid down	Launched	Comp	Comm	Fleet	Fate
Builder: Lehtoniemi, Varkaus							
ATARBEKOV ex-*Kunitsa* (25.4.1925) ex-*O-2* (17.12.1916)	163	1915	1915	1.4.1916	22.6.1941	Cs	Deleted 7.7.1956

11.0 Escort Ships

Steam tugs

Pt No 1941	Name	Details	Comm	Fleet	Remarks
	KASATKA	332hp	28.6.1941	B	Built 1913. Mobilised 23.6.1941, conv to escort ship. Laid up 8.8.1942, 17.4.1944 reverted to tug, renumbered *F-16*. Decomm after the war to civilian service. Discarded June 1959
	URAN	247t; 31.0 x 6.5 x 4.0m; 400hp = 7.2kts; 666nm at 6kts; 2-45mm/46 21-K, 6 DCs; 31 men	7.9.1941	B	NKVD Border Guard patrol ship detached 22.6.1941 to the Baltic Fleet. Decomm 25.8.1942, laid up 1.7.1943
	OST ex-*Chernomorskij № 3* (1923)	230t; 28.9 x 6.3 x 3.0m; 450hp = 9kts, 500nm at 8kts; 1-45mm/46 21-K, 2-0.5in MGs, 1-0.3in MG	27.6.1941	B	Built 1915 Sandvikens. Comm 1915 the Baltic Fleet, decomm 1922 to civilian service. Mobilised 23.6.1941 conv to escort ship; decomm 9.7.1942 reverted to tug. Further fate unknown
102	PETRASH ex-*Kashalot* (1935) ex-*Ruslan* (1924) ex-*Dobrynia* (1916)	560t; 42.0 x 7.2 x 4.7m; 700hp = 12kts; 1300nm at 9kts; 1-3in, 2-45 mm, 2-0.3in MGs; 1943: 2-45mm/46 21-K, 1-20mm Oerlikon, 2-0.5in MGs, 2-0.3in MGs; 47 men	15.7.1941	BS	Built 1914. Harbour icebreaker of the War Ministry. Mobilised 1916 in Baltic Fleet, dispatch ship. Trfd 1922 to the OGPU Border Guard, 1924 to civilian service. Trfd 1926 to the Black Sea. Mobilised 13.7.1941, conv to escort ship. Reverted 11.11.1942 to tug of the Tuapse Naval Base, numbered *T-11* on 17.5.1943. Sunk 7.8.1943 by MTBs

Harbour vessel

TShch No 25.7.1941	Name	Details	Comm	Fleet	Remarks
№ 49	LAJNE ex-*Laine* (Est, 1940) ex-*Lauterbach* (Ger, 1918) ex-*Sputnik* (Rus, 1918)	400t; 39.0 x 6.1 x 2.8m; 400hp = 12kts, 800nm at 8kts; 1-3in, 2-45mm/46 21-K, 5-0.5in (1x2, 3x1) MGs, 10 DCs; 34	19.12.1941	B	Built 1913 Crichton. Conv 1915 to dispatch ship, seized 1918 by the Germans, comm as tender. Trfd 1918 to Estonia, comm as gunboat. Seized 1940, comm 6.8.1940 as dispatch ship. Conv 25.7.1941 to minesweeper; conv 19.12.1941 to escort ship, renamed 20.2.1942 *Gangutets*. Conv 5.11.1945 to surveying ship, deleted 3.1.1954.

Petrash after conversion to dispatch vessel in 1916.
Sergej Berezhnoj Collection

Cross reference: Rated as escort ships.

Name	Details	Type	From	To	Fate
BUG	*Bug* class	Hopper barge	7.7.1941	13.8.1941	Conv to gunboat
CHAPAEV	*Severoles* type	Tug (minesweeper conversion)	25.6.1941	8.8.1942	Laid up
DNESTR	*Bug* class	Hopper barge	15.7.1941	13.8.1941	Conv to gunboat
DON	*Bug* class	Hopper barge	7.7.1941	13.8.1941	Conv to gunboat
DOZORNYJ	*Dozornyj* class	Experimental ships	9.12.1939	28.6.1940	Reverted to experimental ship
KONSTRUKTOR	*Konstruktor*	Experimental ship	3.8.1941	4.11.1941	Sunk, raised and conv 1943 to gunboat.
KUBAN'	*Bug* class	Hopper barge	12.7.1941	25.6.1943	Conv to gunboat
LK-1	*Udalets* class	Tug	2.7.1941	22.8.1942	Laid up
LK-2	*Severoles* type	Minesweeper	2.7.1941	15.7.1942	Lost
PERVANSH	*SP-26*	Tug	22.7.1941	10.4.1942	Reverted to tug
RADUGA	№ 5 *Ejna*	Patrol boat (drifter conversion)	4.3.1940	4.3.1941	Decomm to civilian service
RAZVEDCHIK	*Dozornyj* class	Experimental ship	9.12.1939	28.6.1940	Reverted to experimental ship
			22.6.1941	8.7.1942	Conv to minesweeper
RION	*Bug* class	Hopper barge	7.7.1941	13.8.1941	Conv to gunboat
SILIN	*Silin*	Transport	-	-	Planned conversion
SHCHORS	*Severoles* type	Tug (minesweeper conversion)	25.6.1941	29.8.1941	Lost
SKR-14	*Martiets* type	Gunboat (tug conversion)	10.5.1944	10.7.1944	Decomm to civilian service
SKR-15	*Martiets* type	Gunboat (tug conversion)	10.5.1944	10.7.1944	Decomm to civilian service
STEPAN RAZIN	*Stepan Razin*	Minesweeper (tug conversion)	7.9.1941	24.2.1942	Reverted to tug

11.5.3. River escorts

TEKHNIK (*Project SB-6*) — *Paddle steam tug*

Displacement: 180t
Dimensions: 43.4 x 11.5/6.0 x 1.1m
Machinery: 2 side wheels, compound, 1 boiler (12kg/cm^2), 175hp = 7kts
Armament: 1-75mm/50, 2-0.3in Maxim MGs, 1-0.3in DP MG

No	Name	Built	Comm	Fleet	Remarks
July 1941					
Builder: Leninskaia Kuznitsa, Kiev					
SK-4	TEKHNIK	1931	July 1941	Pn	Mobilised 23.6.1941, conv to escort ship. Sunk 26.8.1941 by artillery fire on the Dnieper off Domantovo. Raised after the war, repaired, to civilian service

Vodop'ianov class (*Project SB-20*) — *Paddle steam tugs*

Displacement: 200t
Dimensions: 45.0 x 12.85/6.0 x 1.1m
Machinery: 2 side wheels, compound, 1 boiler (12kg/cm^2), 175hp = 7kts. Oil: 20t
Armament: SK-1, SK-5: 2-3in/30 M1902 field guns, 2-0.3in Maxim MGs, 1-0.3in DP MG
SK-2, SK-3: 2-3in/55, 2-0.3in Maxim MGs, 1-0.3in DP MG
Complement: 65

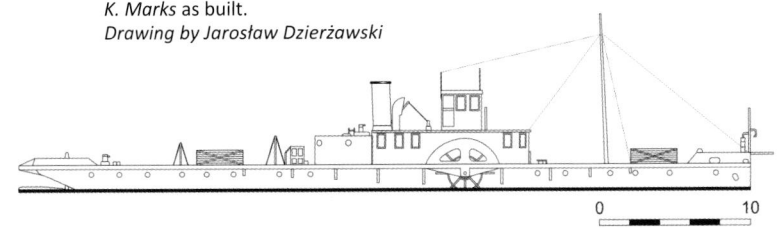

K. Marks as built.
Drawing by Jarosław Dzierżawski

No	Name	YN	Built	Comm	Fleet	Remarks
22.6.1941						
Builder: Leninskaia Kuznitsa, Kiev			1934	22.7.1941	Pn	Mobilised 22.6.1941. Sunk 26.8.1941 by artillery fire on the Dnieper
SK-1	VODOP'IANOV ex-*Tukhachevskij* (1937)					off Domantovo. Raised after the war, repaired, to civilian service
SK-2	PUSHKIN ex-*Ian Gamarnik* (1936)		1934	6.7.1941	Pn	Mobilised 23.6.1941. Stranded 9.9.1941 and sunk by artillery fire on the Desna off Karpilovka
SK-3	PARIZHSKAJA KOMMUNA		1935	July 1941	Pn	Mobilised 23.6.1941. Damaged 26.8.1941 by artillery fire and stranded on the Dnieper off Okuninivski bridge. Wreck blown up by the Soviets next day. Raised 1948 and BU
SK-5	BOL'SHEVIK		1935	July 1941	Pn	Mobilised 23.6.1941. Sunk 26.8.1941 by artillery fire on the Dnieper off Domantovo. Raised 1947 and BU
SK-7	F. ENGEL'S		1935	-	Pn	Mobilised 22.6.1941, planned conv to escort ship but abandoned, comm as tug. Replaced by *Rulevoj*. Sunk 30.8.1941 by artillery fire on the Dnieper north of Kiev
SK-8	K. MARKS		1935	-	Pn	Mobilised 22.6.1941, planned conv to escort ship but abandoned, comm as tug. Replaced by *Reka*. Scuttled 10.9.1941 on the Desna off Chernigov

VOROSHILOV (*Project SB-39*) — *Paddle steam tug*

Displacement: 130t
Dimensions: 41.7 x 6.0/13.45 x 0.7m
Machinery: 2 side wheels, compound, 1 boiler (12kg/cm^2), 150hp = 10.2kts
Armament: 2-3in/30 Lender, 2-0.3in Maxim MGs, 1-0.3in DP MG
Complement: 50

No	Name	Built	Comm	Fleet	Remarks
22.6.1941					
	Builder: 300, Kiev				
SK-6	VOROSHILOV ex-*Marshal Voroshilov* (1941)	1937	July 1941	Pn	Mobilised 23.6.1941, conv to escort ship. Sunk 26.8.1941 by artillery fire on the Dnieper off Domantovo. Raised after the war, repaired, to civilian service

Paddle cargo-passenger steamers

Name	Details	Comm	Fleet	Remarks
MARIUPOL' ex-*Pobeda* (1922)	256t; 55.4 x 6.4 x 1.8m; 700hp = 8kts; 3-45 mm, 3-0.5in MGs	1.8.1941	Az BS Da	Built 1905. Mobilised 22.7.1941, conv to escort ship-minesweeper. Conv 7.10.1942 to transport, trfd to the Black Sea Fleet, conv 13.4.1944 to depot ship, trfd to the Danube Flotilla. Deleted 26.9.1944
SHTURMAN ex-*Pavel Kotsebu* (1922) ex-*Rostov* (1883)	196grt; 41.2 x 7.2 x 1.5m; 300hp = 9kts; 470nm; 1941: 2-45mm/46 21-K, 2-0.3in MGs; 1942: 4-45 mm, 6-0.3in MGs	8.8.1941	Az	Built 1868, Mitchell. Mobilised 1920 dispatch ship for Azov Flotilla, conv to depot ship 1921. Decomm 1922 to civilian service. Mobilised 29.7.1941 conv to escort ship-minesweeper. Damaged 15.8.1942 by German aircraft at Temriuk, blown up 24.8.1942 by the Soviets

Shturman in civilian service in the mid-1920s. *Boris Lemachko Collection*

Paddle steam tugs

No 22.6.1941	Name	Details	Comm	Fleet	Remarks
SK-7	RULEVOJ ex-*Gerojskij* (1924) ex-*KL № 9* (1919) ex-*Apollon* (1919)	200t; 42.9 x 12.9/5.85 x 1.1m; 165hp = 7.5kts; 2-75mm/50, 2-0.3in Maxim MGs, 1-0.3in DP MG; 50 men	11.7.1941	Pn	Built 1912, Kondzerski. Mobilised 1919, conv to gunboat, decomm 1919 to civilian service. Mobilised 22.6.1941 as replacement of *K. Marks* of the *Vodop'ianov* class, conv to escort ship. Sunk 26.8.1941 by artillery fire on the Dnieper off Okuninivski bridge. Raised after the war, repaired, to civilian service
SK-8	REKA ex-*Neva* (1923)	225t; 43.0 x 5.85 x 1.1m; 210hp = 8kts; 2-75mm/50, 1-45mm/46 21-K, 2-0.3in Maxim MGs, 1-0.3in DP MG; 75 men	11.7.1941	Pn	Mobilised 22.6.1941 as replacement of *F. Engel's* of the *Vodop'ianov* class, conv to escort ship. Sunk 26.8.1941 by artillery fire on the Dnieper off Okuninivski bridge. Raised after the war, planned to repair. Fate unknown
	VOJKOV ex-*TShch № 13* (1926) ex-*Saki* (1924) ex-*Test'* (1922) ex-*T-1* (1921) ex-*Test'* (1921) ex-*T-382* (1920) ex-*T-282* (1918) ex-*Test'* (1916)	173t; 34.8 x 6.1 x 2.7m; 350hp = 7kts; 520nm at 5kts; 2-45 mm, 4-0.3in MGs	10.8.1941	Az	Built 1883. Mobilised 1916 the Black Sea Fleet, conv to minesweeper. Seized 1918 by the Germans, trfd to the White Russians, recovered 1920, to civilian service. Mobilised 1920, conv to minesweeper, decomm 1926 to civilian service. Mobilised 22.7.1941, conv to escort ship-minesweeper. Sunk 20.8.1942 by artillery fire in the Kerch Strait.

12. Large submarine hunters

Большие охотники за подводными лодками

12.1. Standard Soviet-built

Artillerist class (*Project 122, 122a, 122-bis*)

Project	Project 122	Project 122a			Project 122-bis
Series		Series I	Series II		Series I
Year	1939	1941	1942	1943	1947
Displacement (standard):	•	220.4t	•		•
Displacement (normal):	225t	229.3t	227t	233t	307t
Displacement (full):	238.4t	238.3t	249.8t	257t	325t
Length:	48.5m	48.5m	50.35m	50.6m	51.8m
Beam:	5.45m	5.75m	5.75m	5.7m	6.2m
Draught:	1.9m	1.9m	2.1m	2.0m	2.2m
Diesel engines (3-shaft):	MAN ?	9D (38-K-8)	General Motors 12-278-A	General Motors 12-278-A	General Motors 12-278-A
Total power:	12	3300hp	3600hp	3600hp	3600hp
Speed (max):	24kts	23.2kts	21.4kts	22.4kts	18.7kts
Fuel (petrol):		18t	17t	17t	•
Range:	2500nm	2410nm at 9kts	1000nm	1900nm at 9kts	4100nm
Main armament:	1-3in/55 34-K	1-3in/55 34-K	1-3in/55 34-K	1-85mm/52 90-K	1-85mm/52 90-K
AA armament:	-	-	2-37mm/67.5 70-K	2-37mm/67.5 70-K	2-37mm/67.5 70-K
MGs:	2-0.5in DShK	2-0.5in DShK	2-0.5in	5-0.5in	5-0.5in Colt-Browning
Sensors:	hydrophone Posejdon	sonar Tamir-1	sonar Tamir-1	-	sonar Tamir 9
DCTs / DC chutes:	- / 2	- / 2	- / 2	2 BMB-1 / 1	2 BMB-1
DCs:	24 B-1, 48 M-1	24 B-1, 48 M-1	24 B-1, 48 M-1	30 B-1, 32 M-1	30 B-1, 30 M-1
Complement:	49	49	49	50	50

Name / No *NKVD Name	No 4.1.1945	Builder	YN	Laid down	Launched	Comp	Comm	Fleet *Station	Remarks
Project 122									
TOPAZ* ex-*OKhT-1* (9.1.1941)		340, Zelenodolsk		1939		Jan 1941	-	Baltic*	NKVD Border Guard. Trfd end 1940 to the Baltic. Detached 26.11.1941 to the Baltic Fleet. Sunk 28.8.1941 before commissioning by mine in the Gulf of Finland
KORALL* ex-*OKhT-2* (9.1.1941)		340, Zelenodolsk		1939		1940	-	Baltic*	NKVD Border Guard. Trfd end 1940 to the Baltic. Detached 26.11.1941 to the Baltic Fleet, returned 1944
ARTILLERIST ex-*Almaz* (1941) ex-*OKhT-3* (9.1.1941)	BO-101	340, Zelenodolsk	306	1939	21.4.1940	1941	15.11.1941	Cs BS	Laid down for the NKVD Border Guard. Trfd June 1941 to the Baltic for sea trials. Taken over June 1941 by the Navy, returned to the Caspian Sea. Comm in the Caspian Flotilla after completion. Trfd 30.6.1944 to the Black Sea Fleet. Trfd Sept 1948 to Bulgaria
MINER ex-*Iakhont* (1941) ex-*OKhT-4* (9.1.1941)	BO-102	340, Zelenodolsk	307	1939	1940	1941	15.11.1941	Cs BS	Laid down for the NKVD Border Guard. Taken over June 1941 by the Navy, ran sea trials in the Caspian Sea, comm in the Caspian Flotilla. Trfd 30.6.1944 to the Black Sea Fleet
TORPEDIST	BO-103	340, Zelenodolsk	343	1939	1941	1942	24.6.1942	Cs BS	Trfd 30.6.1944 to the Black Sea Fleet
ZENITCHIK	BO-104	340, Zelenodolsk	345	1939	1941	1942	17.9.1942	Cs BS	Trfd 30.6.1944 to the Black Sea Fleet. Trfd 1948 to Bulgaria

BO-105 *Botsman* of the *Project 122a Series I* at the Caspian Sea.
Vitalij Kostrichenko Collection

A *Project 122a Series II* boat after the war.
Boris Lemachko Collection

		300, Kiev		1939	June 1941	-	-		Emergency launched. Hull evacuated from Kiev, scuttled summer 1941 off Kherson
		300, Kiev		1939	June 1941	-	-		Emergency launched. Hull evacuated from Kiev, scuttled summer 1941 off Kherson
		300, Kiev		1939	June 1941	-	-		Emergency launched. Hull evacuated from Kiev, scuttled summer 1941 off Kherson
		300, Kiev		1939	June 1941	-	-		Emergency launching. Hull evacuated from Kiev, scuttled summer 1941 off Kherson
Project 122a Series I									
		300, Kiev		1940	-	-	-		Hull destroyed on the slipway
		300, Kiev		1940	-	-	-		Hull destroyed on the slipway
		300, Kiev		1940	-	-	-		Hull destroyed on the slipway
		300, Kiev		1940	-	-	-		Hull destroyed on the slipway
BOTSMAN	BO-105	340, Zelenodolsk	338	1940	1941	1942	17.9.1942	Cs BS	Trfd 30.6.1944 to the Black Sea Fleet
DAL'NOMERSHCHIK	BO-106	340, Zelenodolsk	337	15.10.1941	27.4.1942	1942	25.11.1942	Cs BS	Trfd 30.6.1944 to the Black Sea Fleet
MARSOVYJ	BO-107	340, Zelenodolsk	344	1940	1941	4.7.1943	1943	On BS	Trfd 16.7.1944 to the Black Sea Fleet. Discarded 16.4.1951, trfd to the DOSAAF. BU 1969
PROZHEKTORIST	BO-108	340, Zelenodolsk	354	1940	1941	1944	28.1.1945	Cs	Survived the war
NAVODCHIK	BO-109	340, Zelenodolsk	355	1940	1941	1945	13.8.1945	Cs	Survived the war
OGNEMETCHIK	BO-110	340, Zelenodolsk	356	1940	1941	1945	13.8.1945	Cs	Survived the war
Project 122a Series II									
SVIAZIST	BO-122	199, Komsomolsk-on-Amur	31	1943	8.1.1944	1945	5.12.1945	P	Trfd 18.3.1954 to North Korea
SIGNAL'SHCHIK	BO-123	199, Komsomolsk-on-Amur	32	1943	25.1.1944	1946	1946	P	Trfd 18.3.1954 to North Korea
RADIST	BO-124	199, Komsomolsk-on-Amur	33	1943	25.4.1944	1946	1946	P	Trfd 18.3.1954 to North Korea
TELEGRAFIST	BO-125	199, Komsomolsk-on-Amur	34	1943	1945	5.12.1946	1946/7	P	Trfd 18.3.1954 to North Korea
AKUSTIK	BO-126	199, Komsomolsk-on-Amur	35	1943	1945	5.12.1946	1946/7	P	Trfd 18.3.1954 to North Korea

Warships of the Soviet Fleets, 1939–1945

Project 122a Series II boat armed with 3in/55 34-K gun.
Drawing by Jerzy Lewandowski

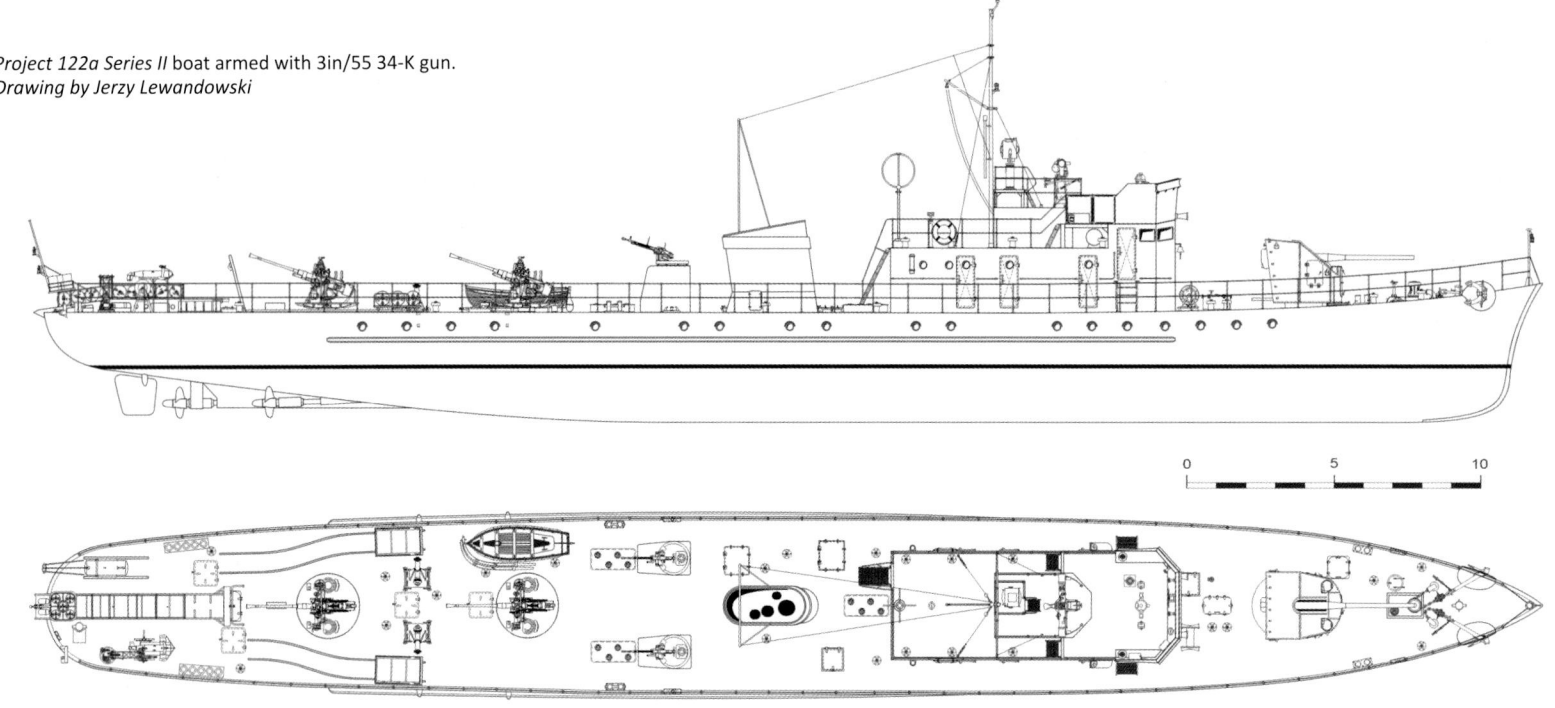

Name / No	No 4.1.1945	Builder	YN	Laid down	Launched	Comp	Comm	Fleet	Remarks
GIDROAKUSTIK	BO-127	199, Komsomolsk-on-Amur	36	1943	1945	5.12.1946	1946/7	P	
		199, Komsomolsk-on-Amur	37	1943	-	-			Cancelled 26.11.1945
		199, Komsomolsk-on-Amur	38	1943	-	-			Cancelled 26.11.1945
		199, Komsomolsk-on-Amur	39	1943	-	-			Cancelled 26.11.1945
		199, Komsomolsk-on-Amur	40	1943	-	-			Cancelled 26.11.1945
		199, Komsomolsk-on-Amur	41	1943	-	-			Cancelled 26.11.1945
		199, Komsomolsk-on-Amur	42	1943	-	-			Cancelled 26.11.1945
SHTURMAN	BO-131	402, Molotovsk	140	Oct 1941	25.9.1943	14.4.1944	25.5.1944	N Wh	Trfd 30.1.1945 to the White Sea Flotilla. Deleted 16.10.1956
KIROVETS ex-*Rulevoj* (24.4.1944)	BO-132	402, Molotovsk	141	Oct 1941	5.10.1943	1.6.1944	30.7.1944	N Wh	Trfd 30.1.1945 to the White Sea Flotilla. Rated 27.12.1956 as Small Antisubmarine Ship, renumbered *MPK-132*. Deleted 28.1.1958
MEKHANIK	BO-133	402, Molotovsk	142	Oct 1941	20.5.1944	23.6.1944	30.7.1944	N Wh	Trfd 30.1.1945 to the White Sea Flotilla. Rated 27.12.1956 as Small Antisubmarine Ship, renumbered *MPK-133*. Conv 25.11.1957 to non-propelled training station *UTS-52*. Deleted 6.10.1958

12.0 LARGE SUBMARINES HUNTERS

BO-134 Mashinist of the *Project 122a Series II* during trials. Note 85mm 90-K gun and camouflage. *Przemysław Budzbon Collection*

A *Project 122a Series II* boat in profile. *Boris Lemachko Collection*

MASHINIST	BO-134	402, Molotovsk	143	Oct 1941	26.5.1944	26.6.1944	30.7.1944	N Wh	Trfd 30.1.1945 to the White Sea Flotilla. Trfd 24.6.1949 to the Border Guard. Discarded mid-1950s
MOTORIST	BO-135	402, Molotovsk	150	Sum 1942	19.8.1944	19.11.1944	1944	N Wh	Trfd 16.2.1945 to the White Sea Flotilla. Trfd 24.6.1949 to the Border Guard. Trfd 7.3.1955 to the DOSAAF
TURBINIST	BO-136	402, Molotovsk	151	Sum 1942	19.8.1944	19.11.1944	1944	N Wh	Trfd 30.1.1945 to the White Sea Flotilla. Trfd 24.6.1949 to the Border Guard, returned 7.3.1955 and conv to experimental vessel *V'iun*. Deleted 10.7.1956
ELEKTRIK	BO-137	402, Molotovsk	152	1942	30.9.1944	20.11.1944	10.12.1944	N Wh	Trfd 30.1.1945 to the White Sea Flotilla. Rated 27.12.1956 as Small Antisubmarine Ship, renumbered *MPK-137*. Conv 31.3.1958 to guard ship *BRN-42*. Deleted 28.3.1961
TRIUMNYJ	BO-138	402, Molotovsk	153	1942	28.9.1944	20.11.1944	10.12.1944	N Wh	Trfd 30.1.1945 to the White Sea Flotilla. Rated 27.12.1956 as Small Antisubmarine Ship, renumbered *MPK-138*. Conv 31.3.1958 to guard ship *BRN-43*. Deleted 2.2.1959
INZHENER	BO-139	402, Molotovsk	154	25.2.1944	18.5.1945	24.6.1945	10.8.1945	N	Deleted 1.9.1955
KOCHEGAR	BO-140	402, Molotovsk	155	06.2.1944	21.5.1945	25.7.1945	10.8.1945	N	Rated 27.12.1956 as Small Antisubmarine Ship, renumbered *MPK-140*. Conv 31.3.1958 to guard ship *BRN-44*. Converted 30.6.1961 to target ship, renumbered *SM-22* on 27.3.1965. Deleted 7.10.1969
LYOTCHIK	BO-141	402, Molotovsk	158	30.11.1944	8.10.1945	23.11.1946	5.12.1946	N	Rated 27.12.1956 as Small Antisubmarine Ship, renumbered MPK-143. Deleted 3.4.1958
PILOT	BO-142	402, Molotovsk	157	21.12.1943	15.1.1945	18.6.1945	24.6.1945	N	Deleted 16.10.1956
TEKHNIK	BO-143	402, Molotovsk	158	30.11.1944	8.10.1945	23.11.1946	5.12.1946	N	Rated 27.12.1956 as Small Antisubmarine Ship, renumbered *MPK-143*. Deleted 3.4.1958
STRELOK	BO-144	402, Molotovsk	159	30.11.1944	13.10.1945	30.11.1946	5.12.1946	N	Rated 27.12.1956 as Small Antisubmarine Ship, renumbered *MPK-144*. Conv 21.8.1958 to guard ship *BRN-45*. Deleted 28.2.1961
KHIMIK	BO-145	402, Molotovsk	160	30.11.1944	16.6.1946	31.10.1946	1946	N	Rated 27.12.1956 as Small Antisubmarine Ship, renumbered *MPK-145*. Conv 21.8.1958 to guard ship *BRN-46*. Deleted 28.2.1961
STROEVOI	BO-146	402, Molotovsk	161	30.11.1944	18.6.1946	5.11.1946	1946	N	Deleted 20.12.1948, to civilian service as fishery protection vessel

Fitting out two *Project 122a Series II* boats at the Yard No 402 at Molotovsk. The one on the left looks more advanced. *Przemysław Budzbon Collection*

A *Project 122a Series II* boat after the war. *Przemysław Budzbon Collection*

Name / No	No 4.1.1945	Builder	YN	Laid down	Launched	Comp	Comm	Fleet *Station	Remarks
BO-147		402, Molotovsk	162	30.12.1944	Aug 1946	25.11.1946	-	Arctic*	Trfd 17.3.1946 to the Border Guard when under construction. Launched and completed as patrol ship. Discarded 7.3.1955, trfd to the DOSAAF
BO-148		402, Molotovsk	163	30.12.1944	30.11.1944	1946	12.8.1946	N	Rated 27.12.1956 as Small Antisubmarine Ship, renumbered *MPK-148*(?). Deleted 28.1.1958
BO-149		402, Molotovsk	164	30.12.1944	28.9.1946	27.9.1947	1947	N	Trfd 31.12.1946 to the Border Guard when under fitting. Reverted 31.3.1947 to naval service, completed as large submarine hunter. Deleted 16.10.1956
BO-150		402, Molotovsk	165	30.12.1944	21.5.1947	1947	6.11.1947	N	Deleted 20.12.1948, to civilian service as fishery protection vessel
BO-151		402, Molotovsk	166	30.7.1945	21.6.1947	6.11.1947	23.11.1947	N	Deleted 20.12.1948
BO-152		402, Molotovsk	167	31.7.1945	22.7.1947	10.12.1947	29.12.1947	N	Rated 27.12.1956 as Small Antisubmarine Ship, renumbered *MPK-152*. Deleted 3.4.1958
BO-153		402, Molotovsk	168	31.7.1945	Aug 1947	1948	-	Arctic*	Construction suspended 23.7.1946, resumed 7.10.1946. Trfd 31.12.1946 to the Border Guard when under construction, renamed *BO-168*. Launched and completed as patrol ship. Discarded 7.3.1955, trfd to the DOSAAF
Project 122-bis Series I									
BO-270		340, Zelenodolsk	367	30.6.1945	27.4.1946	27.9.1947	23.10.1947	Cs N	Trfd 13.8.1951 to the Northern Fleet. Conv 16.10.1956 to dispatch vessel *PS-6*, deleted 21.1.1960
BO-171		340, Zelenodolsk	368	30.6.1945	28.4.1946	4.11.1947	27.11.1947	B	Detached 7.7.1950 to the Naval Command. Rated 27.12.1956 as Small Antisubmarine Ship, renumbered *MPK-171*. Deleted 18.6.1959

12.0 Large submarines hunters

*Project 122bis Series I boat.
Drawing by Jerzy Lewandowski*

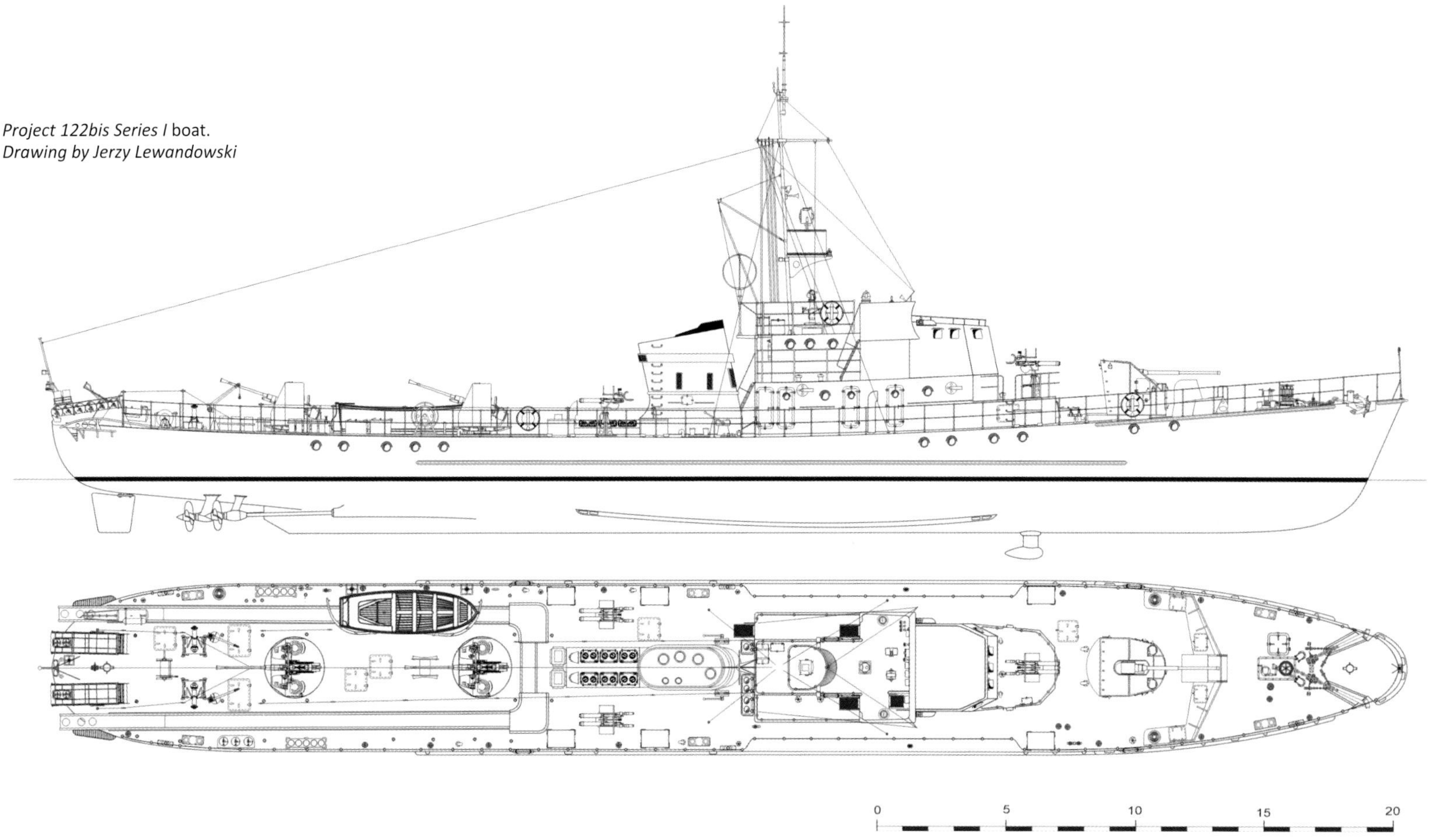

Close up of the midships area of a *Project 122a Series II* boat. *Vitalij Kostrichenko Collection*

Name / No *NKVD Name	No 4.1.1945	Builder	YN	Laid down	Launched	Comp	Comm	Fleet *Station	Remarks
BO-172		340, Zelenodolsk	379	29.9.1945	28.4.1946	30.11.1947	11.12.1947	B	Rated 27.12.1956 as Small Antisubmarine Ship, renumbered *MPK-172*. Conv 31.3.1958 to guard ship *BRN-47*. Deleted 18.6.1959
BO-173		340, Zelenodolsk	380	29.11.1945	27.4.1946	10.1.1948	29.1.1948	B	Rated 27.12.1956 as Small Antisubmarine Ship, renumbered *MPK-173*. Conv 31.3.1958 to guard ship *BRN-48*. Deleted 21.5.1959
BO-174		340, Zelenodolsk	381	-					Listed 28.7.1945, cancelled 23.7.1946
BO-175		340, Zelenodolsk	382	-					Listed 28.7.1945, cancelled 23.7.1946
BO-176		340, Zelenodolsk	383	-					Listed 28.7.1945, cancelled 23.7.1946
BO-177		340, Zelenodolsk	384	-					Listed 28.7.1945, cancelled 23.7.1946
BO-178		340, Zelenodolsk	385	-					Listed 28.7.1945, cancelled 23.7.1946
BO-179		340, Zelenodolsk	386	-					Listed 28.7.1945, cancelled 23.7.1946
BO-180		340, Zelenodolsk	387	-					Listed 28.7.1945, cancelled 23.7.1946

Design based on the *Project 115* NKVD Border Guard patrol ship developed in 1939 by the bureau of Yard No 194 (A. Marti) in Leningrad. When the *Tamir-1* sonar was expected to become available in 1940, the naval authorities joined the project with a view to producing a dual-purpose Border Guard patrol boat and naval subchaser. The design (code *Project 122*) was modified to house the sonar, initial first work being done by the bureau of Yard No 189 (Baltic) and finally the job was trfd to the TsKB-51 bureau at Gorki.

The three-shaft power plant consisted of three diesel engines with the centre shaft powered by one unit placed in the forward engine room together with a donkey boiler and the outer shafts powered by engines placed in the aft machinery room. Because of wartime shortages of diesels, the *Series II* boats were fitted with Lend-Lease General Motors units. The first boats had a light tripod mast fitted.

Mass production was planned in Yard No 300 at Kiev, Yard No 340 at Zelenodolsk, Yd No 402 at Molotovsk, Yd No 199 at Komsomolsk-on-Amur and the fishing yard at Diamid bight at Vladivostok (subordinated to the Fishing Industry, so had no number assigned). As welding technology was not developed at most of the yards, a riveted version was prepared (*Series II*).

The first four were ordered by the NKVD and following sea trials of *OKhT-1* and *OKhT-2* the design was modified to *Project 122a* and the remaining boats (launched in 1939) were to be completed to the modified version. The next NKVD pair were requisitioned by the Navy in June 1941 and, transferred *via* the inland waterways, ran trials in the Caspian Sea. The naval trials proved to be disappointing as the three-shaft power plant generated so much noise at speeds above 6kts that the *Tamir-1* sonar was jammed, while the ship could not operate effectively at less than about 9kts. Therefore because of shortages of sonar supply it was decided to complete subchasers without any hydroacoustic equipment.

The improved design coded *Project-122-bis* was developed by the TSKB-51 in 1943, with the technical design approved on 20.7.1944. Body lines were modified to improve seakeeping to sea state 9, range was increased and *Tamir-9* sonar fitted. The production of the *Series I* was cancelled in 1946 after the US diesels became unavailable, but the project continued with the *Series II* produced on a mass scale from 1950 onwards using Soviet diesels and the improved *Tamir-10* sonar capable at speeds up to 8kts.

BO-185 of the *Project 122bis Series I* with her mast lowered for passing under a bridge. Note the twin Colt MGs.
Przemysław Budzbon Collection

12.2. Lend-Lease

US SC (110ft) class (BO-2 class)

Displacement:	86.8t standard, 110t normal, 126.4t full load
Dimensions:	34.2 x 5.47 x 1.87m
Machinery:	2-shaft General-Motors EMD Pancake 16-184-A diesels, 1960hp =17kts. Oil fuel 15.7t, range 1450nm at 12kts
Armament:	1-40 mm/56 Bofors, 3-20 mm Oerlikon, 2 Mousetrap Mk-20 (40 charges), 2 Mk-6 DCTs, 10 DC rack, 18 B-1 DCs, 20 M-1 DCs
Sensors:	SF-1 radar, QBE-3A sonar
Complement:	32

Data according to Russian sources.

BO-202 (ex-US *SC-1284*) flying Soviet colours in 1943 following the transfer.
Naval History and Heritage Command NH 85453

No	Builder	Comp	Delivered to Comm	Fleet	Remarks
BO-201 ex-*SC-1283* (1943)	Elizabeth	1943	Polarnoye 30.10.1943	N BS	Trfd 10.7.1944 to the Black Sea Fleet. Returned to the US 4.8.1945 at Maltepe, Turkey
BO-202 ex-*SC-1284* (1943)	Elizabeth	1943	Polarnoye 30.10.1943	N BS	Trfd 15.7.1944 to the Black Sea Fleet. Returned to the US 4.8.1945 at Maltepe, Turkey
BO-203 ex-*SC-1285* (1943)	Elizabeth	1943	Polarnoye 30.10.1943	N	Training boat from 15.1.1945 to 12.3.1945. Deleted 25.6.1956, scuttled off Kildin Island
BO-204 ex-*SC-1286* (1943)	Elizabeth	1943	Polarnoye 30.10.1943	N BS	Trfd 10.7.1944 to the Black Sea Fleet. Returned to the US 4.8.1945 at Maltepe, Turkey
BO-205 ex-*SC-1287* (1943)	Elizabeth	1943	Polarnoye 30.10.1943	N BS	Trfd 10.7.1944 to the Black Sea Fleet. Returned to the US 4.8.1945 at Maltepe, Turkey
BO-206 ex-*SC-1073* (1943)	Mathis	1943	Polarnoye 30.10.1943	N	Deleted 25.6.1956, scuttled off Kildin Island
BO-207 ex-*SC-1074* (1943)	Mathis	1943	Polarnoye 24.11.1943	N	Deleted 25.6.1956, scuttled off Kildin Island
BO-208 ex-*SC-1075* (1943)	Mathis	1943	Polarnoye 29.2.1944	N BS	Trfd 15.7.1944 to the Black Sea Fleet. Returned to the US 4.8.1945 at Maltepe, Turkey
BO-209 ex-*SC-1076* (1943)	Mathis	1943	Polarnoye 29.2.1944	N	Deleted 25.6.1956, scuttled off Kildin Island
BO-210 ex-*SC-719* (1943)	Fisher	1943	Polarnoye 30.10.1943	N	Deleted 25.6.1956, scuttled off Kildin Island
BO-211 ex-*SC-720* (1943)	Fisher	1943	Polarnoye 29.2.1944	N BS	Trfd 15.7.1944 to the Black Sea Fleet. Returned to the US 4.8.1945 at Maltepe, Turkey
BO-212 ex-*SC-721* (1943)	Fisher	1943	Polarnoye 24.11.1943	N	Deleted 25.6.1956, scuttled off Kildin Island
BO-213 ex-*SC-1484* (1944)	Elizabeth	1944	Polarnoye 25.8.1944	N	Laid up 17.10.1955. Deleted 25.6.1956, scuttled off Kildin Island
BO-214 ex-*SC-1480* (1944)	Rice Bros	1944	Polarnoye 25.8.1944	N	Laid up 15.3.1954. Deleted 25.6.1956, scuttled off Kildin Island
BO-215 ex-*SC-1496* (1944)	Vinyard	1944	Polarnoye 25.8.1944	N	Deleted 25.6.1956, scuttled off Kildin Island
BO-216 ex-*SC-1488* (1944)	Elizabeth	1944	Polarnoye 25.8.1944	N	Laid up 15.3.1954. Deleted 25.6.1956, scuttled off Kildin Island
BO-217 ex-*SC-1489* (1944)	Elizabeth	1944	Polarnoye 23.9.1944	N	Deleted 25.6.1956, scuttled off Kildin Island
BO-218 ex-*SC-1492* (1944)	Simms	1944	Polarnoye 25.8.1944	N	Deleted 25.6.1956, scuttled off Kildin Island
BO-219 ex-*SC-1475* (1944)	Quincy	1944	Polarnoye 25.8.1944	N B	Trfd 23.11.1945 to the Baltic Fleet. Returned 29.6.1955 to the US at Kiel (Germany)
BO-220 ex-*SC-1490* (1944)	Elizabeth	1944	Polarnoye 26.8.1944	N	Trfd 23.11.1945 to the Baltic Fleet. Returned 29.6.1955 to the US at Kiel (Germany)

BO-220 (ex-US *SC-1490*) during exercises.
Przemysław Budzbon Collection

No	Builder	Comp	Delivered to Comm	Fleet	Remarks
BO-221 ex-*SC-1481* (1944)	Rice Bros	1944	Polarnoye 27.8.1944	N	Trfd 23.11.1945 to the Baltic Fleet. Returned 29.6.1955 to the US at Kiel (Germany)
BO-222 ex-*SC-1498* (1944)	Knutson	1944	Polarnoye 25.8.1944	N	Training boat from 15.1.1945 to 12.3.1945. Conv 17.10.1955 to guard ship *BRN-4*. Deleted 25.6.1956, scuttled off Kildin Island
BO-223 ex-*SC-1476* (1944)	Quincy Adams	1944	Polarnoye 25.8.1944	N	Training boat from 15.1.1945 to 12.3.1945. Laid up 26.2.1948. Deleted 25.6.1956, scuttled off Kildin Island
BO-224 ex-*SC-1507* (1944)	Harris & Parsons	1944	Polarnoye 25.8.1944	N	Training boat from 15.1.1945. Sunk 2.3.1945 by *U-995* off Kildin Island
BO-225 ex-*SC-1517* (1944)	Petersen	1944	Polarnoye 28.10.1944	N	Laid up 25.11.1946. Conv 17.10.1955 to guard ship *BRN-5*. Deleted 25.6.1956, scuttled off Kildin Island
BO-226 ex-*SC-1510* (1944)	Perkins & Vaughn	1944	Polarnoye 28.10.1944	N	Laid up 25.11.1946. Deleted 1.5.1955, BU
BO-227 ex-*SC-1502* (1944)	Calderwood	1944	Polarnoye 28.10.1944	N	Trfd 23.11.1945 to the Baltic Fleet. Laid up 2.4.1952, conv to accommodation hulk. Conv 17.10.1955 to guard ship *BRN-3*. Returned 29.6.1955 to the US at Kiel (Germany)
BO-228 ex-*SC-1504* (1944)	Donovan	1944	Polarnoye 28.10.1944	N	Laid up 25.11.1946. Deleted 25.6.1956, scuttled off Kildin Island
BO-229 ex-*SC-1485* (1944)	Daytona Beach	1944	Polarnoye 28.10.1944	N	Sunk 7.12.1944 by *U-997* off Kildin Island
BO-230 ex-*SC-1477* (1944)	Quincy Adams	1944	Polarnoye 28.10.1944	N	Sunk 5.12.1944 by *U-365* off Teriberka, Kola Peninsula
BO-231 ex-*SC-1493* (1944)	Simms	1944	Polarnoye 25.4.1945	N	Laid up 25.11.1946. Deleted 25.6.1956, scuttled off Kildin Island

BO-232 ex-*SC-1482* (1944)	Rice Bros	1944	Polarnoye 25.4.1945	N	Laid up 25.11.1946. Deleted 25.6.1956, scuttled off Kildin Island	
BO-233 ex-*SC-1511* (1945)	Perkins & Vaughn	1944	Polarnoye 25.4.1945	N	Laid up 25.11.1946. Deleted 25.6.1956, scuttled off Kildin Island	
BO-234 ex-*SC-1505* (1945)	Donovan	1944	Polarnoye 25.4.1945	N	Laid up 25.11.1946. Deleted 25.6.1956, scuttled off Kildin Island	
BO-235 ex-*SC-1486* (1945)	Daytona Beach	1944	Polarnoye 25.4.1945	N	Laid up 16.7.1947. Deleted 25.6.1956, scuttled off Kildin Island	
BO-236 ex-*SC-1497* (1945)	Vinyard	1944	Polarnoye 25.4.1945	N	Trfd 23.11.1945 to the Baltic Fleet. Laid up 25.11.1946, conv to accommodation hulk. Conv 17.10.1955 to guard ship *BRN-6*. Deleted 25.6.1956, scuttled off Kildin Island	
BO-237 ex-*SC-1491* (1945)	Elisabeth	1944	Polarnoye 25.4.1945	N	Deleted 25.6.1956, scuttled off Kildin Island	
BO-238 ex-*SC-1478* (1945)	Quincy Adams	1944	Polarnoye 25.4.1945	N	Deleted 25.6.1956, scuttled off Kildin Island.	
BO-239 ex-*SC-1483* (1945)	Rice Bros	1944	Polarnoye 25.4.1945	N	Laid up 26.2.1948. Deleted 25.6.1956, scuttled off Kildin Island	
BO-240 ex-*SC-1508* (1945)	Harris & Parsons	1944	Polarnoye 25.4.1945	N	Deleted 25.6.1956, scuttled off Kildin Island	
BO-241 ex-*SC-1506* (1945)	Donovan	1944	Polarnoye 25.4.1945	N	Laid up 15.3.1954. Deleted 25.6.1956, scuttled off Kildin Island	
BO-242 ex-*SC-1499* (1945)	Knutson	1944	Polarnoye 26.4.1945	N	Deleted 25.6.1956, scuttled off Kildin Island	
BO-243 ex-*SC-1503* (1945)	Calderwood	1944	Polarnoye 27.4.1945	N	Deleted 25.6.1956, scuttled off Kildin Island	
BO-244 ex-*SC-1479* (1945)	Quincy Adams	1944	Polarnoye 25.4.1945	N	Laid up 26.2.1948. Deleted 25.6.1956, scuttled off Kildin Island	
BO-245 ex-*SC-1487* (1945)	Daytona Beach	1944	Polarnoye 25.4.1945	N	Laid up 17.10.1955. Deleted 25.6.1956, scuttled off Kildin Island	
BO-246 ex-*SC-1512* (1945)	Perkins & Vaughn	1944	Polarnoye 25.4.1945	N	Conv 22.4.1947 to salvage vessel. Deleted 25.6.1956, scuttled off Kildin Island	
BO-301 ex-*SC-687* (1945)	American Cruiser	1943	Petropavlovsk 8.6.1945	P	Laid up 1.2.1954, BU	
BO-302 ex-*SC-685* (1945)	American Cruiser	1943	Petropavlovsk 30.7.1945	P	Stranded 18.12.1947 at Cape Crillion. Raised 24.12.1947, sank under to	
BO-303 ex-*SC-661* (1945)	Burger	1942	Petropavlovsk 8.6.1945	P	Laid up 1.2.1954, BU	
BO-304 ex-*SC-539* (1945)	Petersen	1942	Petropavlovsk 8.6.1945	P	Laid up 1.2.1954, BU	
BO-305 ex-*SC-986* (1945)	Matton	1943	Petropavlovsk 17.6.1945	P	Laid up 1.2.1954, BU	
BO-306 ex-*SC-674* (1945)	Hiltebrant	1942	Petropavlovsk 8.6.1945	P	Conv 30.5.1949 to salvage boat *SPK-11*. Deleted 7.7.1956, BU	
BO-307 ex-*SC-657* (1945)	Snow	1942	Petropavlovsk 17.6.1945	P	Laid up 1.2.1954, BU	
BO-308 ex-*SC-647* (1945)	Robinson	1942	Petropavlovsk 17.6.1945	P	Conv 12.11.1953 to training boat. Deleted 11.7.1956, BU	
BO-309 ex-*SC-634* (1945)	Mathis	1942	Petropavlovsk 22.6.1945	P	Laid up 18.12.1954. Conv 31.7.1955 to training boat. Deleted 7.10.1955, BU	
BO-310 ex-*SC-654* (1945)	Westergard	1943	Petropavlovsk 30.7.1945	P	Conv 8.7.1950 to communication craft *RK-1483*, conv 23.6.1951 to dispatch vessel *Irtek*. Deleted 25.6.1956, scuttled in the Strait of Tartary	
BO-311 ex-*SC-660* (1945)	Burger	1942	Petropavlovsk 22.6.1945	P	Deleted 11.7.1956, BU	
BO-312 ex-*SC-1021* (1945)	Luders	1943	Petropavlovsk 17.6.1945	P	Laid up 15.4.1955. Deleted 7.10.1955, BU	
BO-313 ex-*SC-713* (1945)	Fisher	1942	Petropavlovsk 17.6.1945	P	Laid up 15.4.1955. Deleted 7.10.1955, BU	
BO-314 ex-*SC-675* (1945)	Hiltebrant	1942	Petropavlovsk 22.6.1945	P	Laid up 15.4.1955. Deleted 11.7.1956, BU	
BO-315 ex-*SC-1324* (1945)	Harris & Parsons	1943	Petropavlovsk 22.6.1945	P	Deleted 11.7.1956, BU	
BO-316 ex-*SC-673* (1945)	Knutson	1942	Petropavlovsk 17.6.1945	P	Laid up 15.4.1955. Deleted 11.7.1956, BU	

No	Builder	Comp	Delivered to Comm	Fleet	Remarks
BO-317 ex-SC-1060 (1945)	Burger	1943	Petropavlovsk 17.6.1945	P	Laid up 15.4.1955. Deleted 7.10.1955, BU
BO-318 ex-SC-663 (1945)	Fisher	1942	Petropavlovsk 17.6.1945	P	Laid up 15.4.1955. Deleted 7.10.1955, BU
BO-319 ex-SC-500 (1945)	Fisher	1942	Petropavlovsk 22.6.1945	P	Deleted 25.6.1956, scuttled in the Strait of Tartary
BO-320 ex-SC-1295 (1945)	W.A. Robinson	1943	Petropavlovsk 22.6.1945	P	Trfd 27.10.1945 to the NKVD Border Guard. Discarded 28.7.1960. Scuttled off Nakhodka
BO-321 ex-SC-538 (1945)	Peterson	1942	Petropavlovsk 26.8.1945	P	Deleted 25.6.1956, BU
BO-322 ex-SC-643 (1945)	Peterson	1942	Petropavlovsk 26.8.1945	P	Deleted 11.7.1956, BU
BO-323 ex-SC-774 (1945)	Peyton	1943	Petropavlovsk 26.8.1945	P	Laid up 15.4.1955. Deleted 11.7.1956, BU
BO-324 ex-SC-754 (45)	Robinson	1943	Petropavlovsk 31.8.1945	P	Deleted 7.10.1956, BU
BO-325 ex-SC-752 (1945)	Robinson	1942	Petropavlovsk 31.8.1945	P	Deleted 7.10.1956, BU
BO-326 ex-SC-997 (1945)	Island	1942	Petropavlovsk 31.8.1945	P	Conv 10.3.1953 to training boat *UBO-326*. Laid up 3.6.1955. Deleted 28.8.1956, BU
BO-327 ex-SC-1011 (1945)	Fellows	1943	Petropavlovsk 3.9.1945	P	Deleted 7.10.1955, BU
BO-328 ex-SC-1031 (1945)	Peterson	1943	Petropavlovsk 3.9.1945	P	Trfd 21.8.1950 to the NKVD Border Guard. Discarded 28.7.1960. Scuttled off Nakhodka
BO-329 ex-SC-1365 (1945)	Peyton	1944	Petropavlovsk 3.9.1945	P	Deleted 7.10.1955, BU.
BO-331 ex-SC-1364 (1945)	Peyton	1943	Petropavlovsk 3.9.1945	P	Conv 3.6.1953 to training boat. Laid up 15.4.1955. Deleted 28.8.1956, BU
BO-332 ex-SC-1007 (1945)	Fellows	1943	Petropavlovsk 3.9.1945	P	Trfd 21.8.1950 to the NKVD Border Guard. Discarded 28.7.1960. Scuttled off Nakhodka
BO-335 ex-SC-756 (1945)	Robinson	1943	Petropavlovsk 11.9.1945	P	Laid up 1.2.1954. Deleted 25.6.1956, scuttled in the Strait of Tartary

A total of 78 were transferred to the Soviet Union, 46 boats under the Lend-Lease programme while 32 went to the Pacific Fleet under Project Hula in anticipation of the Soviets eventually joining the war against Japan, specifically in preparation for planned Soviet invasions of southern Sakhalin and the Kurils.

Some were deleted after the war and BU in the Soviet Union; the surviving boats were returned to the US in 1955, those declared unfit having been scuttled under US supervision.

12.3. War prizes – Southeast Europe, 1944

German **Minen-Räumboote 1940**

Displacement: 110t standard, 128t (*BO-54* 120t) full load
Dimensions: 36.2 (*BO-54* 35.4) x 5.55 x 1.5m
Machinery: 2-shaft diesels, 1800hp = 23.5kts. Oil fuel 10t, range 1100nm at 15kts
Armament: 2-45mm/68.6 21-KM, 2-37mm/67.5 70-K, 1-0.5in DShK MG
Complement: 37

No	Comp	Comm	Fleet	Remarks
BO-51 ex-R-204 (Ger, 1944)	27.6.1943	30.11.1944	BS	Sunk 11.4.1944 by Soviet aircraft at Theodosia. Captured, raised and recomm
BO-52 ex-R-205 (Ger, 1944)	17.7.1943	30.11.1944	BS	Sunk 25.8.1944 by Soviet aircraft at Constanța. Captured, raised and recomm
BO-53 ex-R-206 (Ger, 1944)	28.5.1943	30.11.1944	BS	Sunk 30.08.1944 by Soviet aircraft at Constanța. Captured, raised and recomm
BO-54 ex-SK-751 (1945) ex-R-163 (Ger, 1944)	5.3.1941	19.9.1945	BS	Captured 8.9.1944 at Varna, comm as patrol boat. Conv 19.9.1945 to large submarine hunter. BU 1958

13. Small submarines hunters

Малые охотники за подводными лодками

13.1. The 'unitary' MO types

The high priority accorded to closing the sea border against potential penetration from outside, and against those wishing to leave the Soviet paradise, drove a massive demand for patrol boats of a small size. By the mid-1920s the Border Guard flotillas were worn out and obsolete while the requirement was estimated at more than 400 boats. The long-time experience of the Lodejnopl'ska Yard and the private NEP Zolotov boatyard was utilised during design and construction of the wooden-hulled *PK* (15t), *GK* (20–30t) and *ZK* (19t) types of patrol boats. The yards were unable to produce them in sufficient number and with Lodejnopl'ska Yard closed (converted to the base for the Onega Flotilla) by the end of 1920s the capacity had been reduced to less than a dozen per year. The Zolotov boatyard was nationalised in 1930 (A. Zolotov who lost his business twice – in 1918 and 1930 – was employed as designer and constructor) and incorporated as detachment (Workshop No 6) into the new OGPU Border Guard Yard devoted to mass-production of the *KM* type patrol boats.

In 1931 the massive OGPU Border Guard construction programme was launched with two basic types of wooden patrol-boats: *dimensional* of 30t (transportable by rail) and *unitary* of 80–100t; the latter was to be shared with the Red Navy. The common characteristics of the *unitary* boat were approved on 11.9.1931 by the Namorsi (Director of the Naval Forces) Orlov and the planning included construction of 270 boats.

This specification called for a dual-purpose peacetime patrol boat and wartime anti-submarine boat. In 1932 the bureau of the OGPU Yard prepared sketch designs for 80–100t, 30–36m wooden-hulled boats powered by AM-34K petrol engines, armed with either 3in or 45mm guns, two 0.5in MGs, 16 DCs and towed hydrophone. As the design proved to be too costly in terms of material and workmanship, the modified requirements were issued in June 1933 with displacement reduced to 50t and the possibility of rail transportation added. The reduced size allowed the doubling of shipyard output in terms of the number of units completed. The characteristics of the reduced design were as following: 47t full load; 26.2 x 3.8 x 1.1m; 3-shaft GAM-34 petrol engines, 2025hp = 27kts; radius 500nm; 1-3in/55 34-K, 1-45mm/46 21-K, 3-0.5in MGs, 8DCs. The prototype designated *MO-1* was laid down in Dec 1933 but the project was modified to reflect the lack of the GAM type engines. The MO designation stands for Malyj Okhotnik (Small Hunter) which applied just as well to hunting for fugitives or submarines.

Following the mobilisation plan, on 22 June 1941 the NKVD patrol boats were operationally detached to the naval command, while official commissioning for most of the boats followed within a few weeks.

MO-1

Displacement:	51.1t full load
Dimensions:	26.0 x 3.8 x 1.2m
Machinery:	2-shaft Sterling Viking petrol engines, 1130hp = 14kts. Radius 400nm
Armament:	2-0.5in DShK MGs (initially 2-0.3in Maxim MGs), 2 DC chutes, 20 BM-1 DCs, 1 KAT sweep
Complement:	21

Data for 1941.

NKVD No	SKA № 1941	SKA № 26.11.1943	No 21.5.1944	YN	Laid down	Launched	Comp	Comm	Fleet	Remarks
Builder: OGPU Border Guard Yard, Leningrad										
PK-139 ex-*PK-202* (9.1.1941)	№ 0132	№ 02[2]	SK-132	1	Dec 1933	1935	1935	19.7.1941	BS	Decomm 31.8.1943 for repairs, recomm 7.5.1944. Returned 21.6.1945 to the NKVD Border Guard, renumbered *PK-119*. Trfd 18.5.1947 to Leningrad, discarded 1.4.1953

MO-2 type

Displacement:	51t full load
Dimensions:	26.2 x 3.95 x 1.15m
Machinery:	3-shaft AM-34K (GAM-34BS on some) petrol engines, 2025hp (2550hp) = 26.5kts. Range 530nm at 15kts
Armament:	2-45mm/46 21-K, 2-0.5in DShK (initially 0.3in Maxim) MGs, 2 DC chutes, 8 BB-1 DCs, 12 BM-1 DCs
Sensors:	Posejdon towed hydrophone
Complement:	21

NKVD No	MO №* SKA №** on Comm	MO №*S KA №** 1941	SKA № 1943	No 1944	YN	Laid	Comp down	Comm	Fleet	Remarks
Builder: NKVD Border Guard Yard, Leningrad										
PK-115 ex-PK-258 (9.1.1941)		№ 0112				1935	1936	19.7.1941	BS	Numbered as patrol craft. Sunk 2.7.1942 by German MTBs S-27, S-28, S-40 and S-102 off Ai-Todor
PK-117 ex-PK-259 (9.1.1941)		№ 064[4] № 015[5]		MO-15	1	1935		19.7.1941	BS	Numbered as patrol craft until 7.5.1944. Sunk 19.4.1943 by artillery fire off Novorossijsk, raised and recomm. Returned 21.6.1945 to the NKVD Border Guard
PK-124 ex-PK-260 (9.1.1941)		№ 082		MO-82	7	1935		19.7.1941	BS	Numbered as patrol craft until 7.5.1944. Returned 21.6.1945 to the NKVD Border Guard
PK-126 ex-PK-265 (9.1.1941)		№ 0122			8	1935		19.7.1941	BS	Numbered as patrol craft. Sunk 8.11.1943 by a German MFP off Kerch
PK-127		№ 0142	№ 056[7]	MO-56	15	1935		19.7.1941	BS	Numbered as patrol craft until 7.5.1944. Returned 21.6.1945 to the NKVD Border Guard
PK-128		№ 054[4] № 075[5]		MO-75		1935		19.7.1941	BS	Numbered as patrol craft until 7.5.1944. Returned 21.6.1945 to the NKVD Border Guard, renumbered PK-143 on 21.9.1945. Discarded 1.11.1950
PK-140 ex-PK-264 (9.1.1941)		№ 066[3]		MO-66	14	1935		19.7.1941	BS	Numbered as patrol craft until 7.5.1944. Returned 21.6.1945 to the NKVD Border Guard
PK-171 ex-PK-200 (9.1.1941)	№ 934	№ 171[1]	№ 062	MO-171 MO-161[8]	13	1935	1936	25.7.1941	B BS	Trfd 29.9.1943 to the Black Sea Fleet, numbered as patrol craft. Returned 21.6.1945 to the NKVD Border Guard
PK-172 ex-PK-201 (9.1.1941)	№ 935	№ 111			11	1935	1936	25.7.1941	B	Returned 4.7.1945 to the NKVD Border Guard
PK-173 ex-PK-203 (9.1.1941)	№ 936	№ 173			12	1935	1936	25.7.1941	B La	Trdf 9.8.1941 to the Ladoga Flotilla. Sunk 30.8.1941 by artillery fire on the Neva River
PK-174 ex-PK-204 (9.1.1941)	№ 701	№ 174			16	1935	1936	25.7.1941	B La	Trdf 9.8.1941 to the Ladoga Flotilla. Scuttled 30.8.1941 after damage by artillery fire on the Neva River.
PK-175 ex-PK-205 (9.1.1941)	№ 702	№ 175			17	1935	1936	25.7.1941	B La	Trdf 9.8.1941 to the Ladoga Flotilla. Sank 20.11.1941 crushed by ice, raised and recomm. Sunk 9.10.1942 by German warships off Konevitsa Island
PK-176 ex-PK-206 (9.1.1941)	№ 703	№ 110			18	1935	1936	25.7.1941	B	Mined 6.9.1943 on the Vigrung shoal
PK-177 ex-PK-207 (9.1.1941)	№ 704	№ 702[2] № 177[6]			19		1936	25.7.1941	B	From 8.9.1941 to 3.1.1942 detached to the Red Army command of the Leningrad Front and carried the number MO-L-177. Sunk 22.6.1943 by German aircraft off Laavansaari Island
PK-216 ex-PK-210 (9.1.1941)	№ 405					1935	1936	25.7.1941	B	Sunk 16.9.1941 by German aircraft off Saaremaa Island

13.0 Small submarines hunters

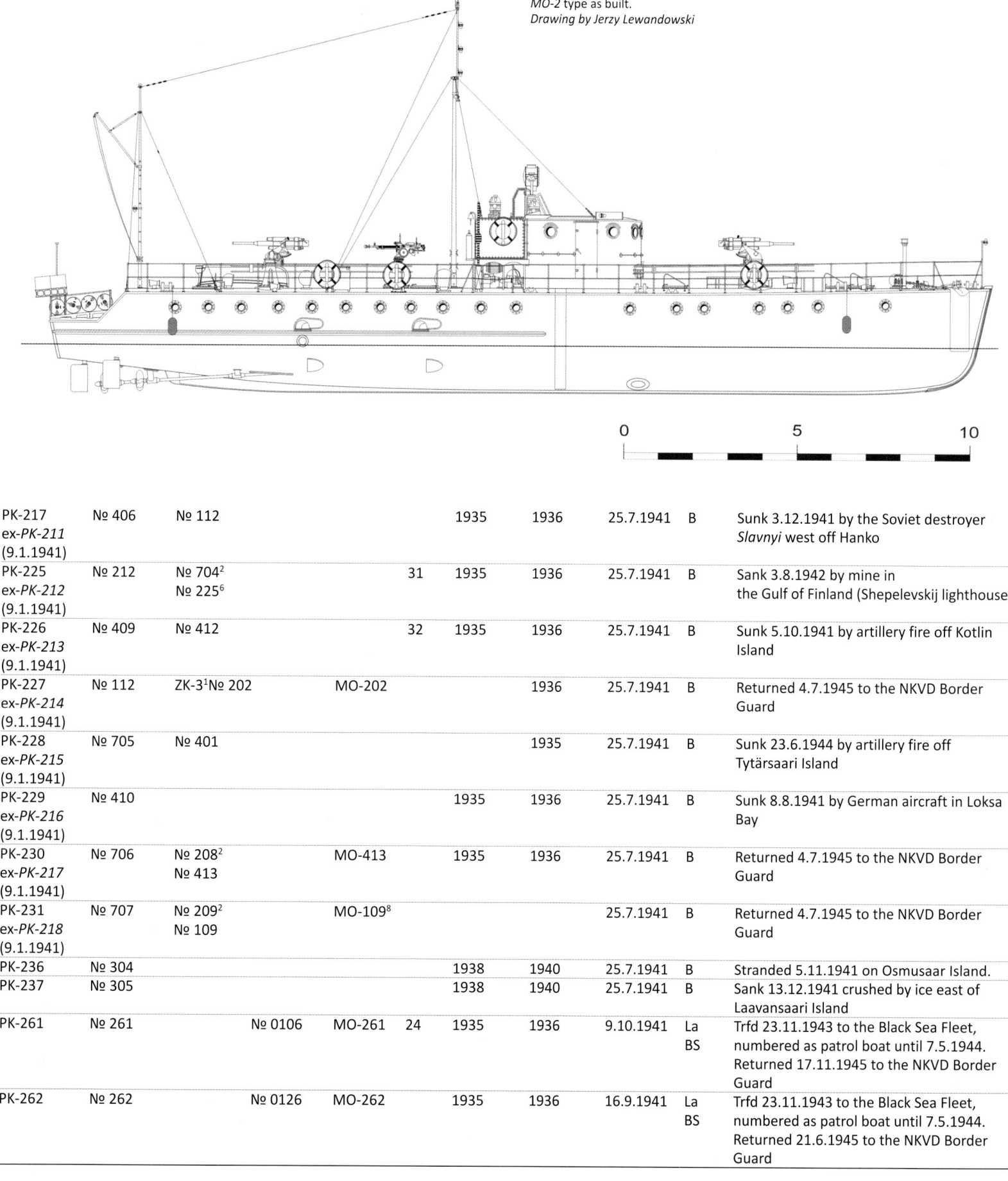

MO-2 type as built.
Drawing by Jerzy Lewandowski

PK-217 ex-*PK-211* (9.1.1941)	№ 406	№ 112			1935	1936	25.7.1941	B	Sunk 3.12.1941 by the Soviet destroyer *Slavnyi* west off Hanko
PK-225 ex-*PK-212* (9.1.1941)	№ 212	№ 704² № 225⁶		31	1935	1936	25.7.1941	B	Sank 3.8.1942 by mine in the Gulf of Finland (Shepelevskij lighthouse)
PK-226 ex-*PK-213* (9.1.1941)	№ 409	№ 412		32	1935	1936	25.7.1941	B	Sunk 5.10.1941 by artillery fire off Kotlin Island
PK-227 ex-*PK-214* (9.1.1941)	№ 112	ZK-3¹№ 202	MO-202			1936	25.7.1941	B	Returned 4.7.1945 to the NKVD Border Guard
PK-228 ex-*PK-215* (9.1.1941)	№ 705	№ 401			1935		25.7.1941	B	Sunk 23.6.1944 by artillery fire off Tytärsaari Island
PK-229 ex-*PK-216* (9.1.1941)	№ 410				1935	1936	25.7.1941	B	Sunk 8.8.1941 by German aircraft in Loksa Bay
PK-230 ex-*PK-217* (9.1.1941)	№ 706	№ 208² № 413	MO-413		1935	1936	25.7.1941	B	Returned 4.7.1945 to the NKVD Border Guard
PK-231 ex-*PK-218* (9.1.1941)	№ 707	№ 209² № 109	MO-109⁸				25.7.1941	B	Returned 4.7.1945 to the NKVD Border Guard
PK-236	№ 304				1938	1940	25.7.1941	B	Stranded 5.11.1941 on Osmusaar Island.
PK-237	№ 305				1938	1940	25.7.1941	B	Sank 13.12.1941 crushed by ice east of Laavansaari Island
PK-261	№ 261		№ 0106	MO-261	24	1935	1936	9.10.1941	La BS	Trfd 23.11.1943 to the Black Sea Fleet, numbered as patrol boat until 7.5.1944. Returned 17.11.1945 to the NKVD Border Guard
PK-262	№ 262		№ 0126	MO-262		1935	1936	16.9.1941	La BS	Trfd 23.11.1943 to the Black Sea Fleet, numbered as patrol boat until 7.5.1944. Returned 21.6.1945 to the NKVD Border Guard

* The Baltic Fleet designation.   ** The Black Sea Fleet designation.

Warships of the Soviet Fleets, 1939–1945

MO-2 type boat of the Black Sea Fleet passing by the cruiser Voroshilov *in 1943.*
Vitalij Kostrichenko Collection

MO-2 type boat at right accompanied by one of the MO-4 type at left. Note the camouflage schemes. Boris Lemachko Collection

The effective dates of Pennant Numbers change orders.

Year	Fleet	Date
1941	La	9.8.1941
	B	7.9.1941
1943	BS	25.11.1943
1944	BS	7.5.1944
	B	13.12.1944

Exceptions noted in the main table.

No	Year	Date	Fleet
1	1941	9.8.1941	B
2		22.8.1941	B
3		3.9.1941	BS
4		10.12.1941	BS
5		17.12.1941	BS
6		8.9.1941	B
7	1942	30.4.1942	BS
8	1945	6.1.1945	B

* The Baltic Fleet designation. ** The Black Sea Fleet designation.

The *unitary* design was modified following trials of the prototype *MO-1*. During the sea trials of YN 10 the boat was destroyed by the explosion of gasoline fumes, killing six of the crew and blowing away the CT. This was caused by negligence and poor ventilation. Construction changes resulting from that experience were introduced in nine boats already completed and the remainder of the series. The design was generally reviewed and modified and production was resumed under the designation *MO-4*.

MO-2 type boat during the war.
Boris Lemachko Collection

MO-3 type

Displacement:	51t full load
Dimensions:	26.2 x 3.95 x 1.28m
Machinery:	3-shaft Sterling Viking petrol engines, 1695hp = 27kts. Range 430nm
Armament:	2-45mm/46 21-K, 2-0.5in DShK (initially 0.3in Maxim) MGs, 2 DC chutes, 8 BB-1 DCs, 12 BM-1 DCs
Sensors:	Posejdon towed hydrophone
Complement:	21

The *MO-2* design modified by installation of the Sterling Viking engines because of delays with the AM-34K supply.

NKVD Border Guard patrol boat *PK-75* in the Caspian Sea. Following transfer to the Black Sea in Nov 1943 she received the naval number *Storozhevoj kater № 068* which was changed to *MO-305* five months later. Boris Lemachko Collection

NKVD No	SKA № 25.11.1943	No 7.5.1944	YN	Comp	Comm	Fleet	Remarks
Builder: NKVD Border Guard Yard, Leningrad							
PK-73 ex-*PK-269* (9.1.1941)	№ 048	MO-73	14	1935	22.6.1941	Cs BS	Trfd 26.11.1943 to the Black Sea Fleet, renumbered with the patrol boat number. Returned 21.6.1945 to the NKVD Border Guard
PK-74 ex-*PK-266* (9.1.1941)	№ 058	MO-301	11	1935	22.6.1941	Cs BS	Trfd 26.11.1943 to the Black Sea Fleet, renumbered with the patrol boat number. Returned 21.6.1945 to the NKVD Border Guard
PK-75 ex-*PK-268* (9.1.1941)	№ 068	MO-305	13	1935	22.6.1941	Cs BS	Trfd 26.11.1943 to the Black Sea Fleet, renumbered with the patrol boat number. Returned 21.6.1945 to the NKVD Border Guard
PK-76 ex-*PK-267* (9.1.1941)	№ 088		12	1935	22.6.1941	Cs BS	Trfd 26.11.1943 to the Black Sea Fleet, renumbered with the patrol boat number. Sunk 31.10.1943 by *U-13* off Suchumi

MO-4 type (*Project P-10, Project 174*)

Displacement:	54.0t normal, 56.5t full load
Dimensions:	26.9 x 3.9 x 1.25m
Machinery:	3-shaft GAM-34BS petrol engines, 2550hp = 26kts (*Project 174*: 2-shaft Packard 4M-2000 petrol engines, 2400hp). Petrol 5.2t, radius 495nm at 10kts
Armament:	2-45mm/46 21-K, 2-0.5in DShK MGs, 2 DC chutes, 8 BB-1 DCs, 24 BM-1 DCs, could carry 4 M1908 mines (see note)
Sensors:	Posejdon hydrophone (see note)
Complement:	24

PK-237 and PK-239 in NKVD livery in 1941. Boris Lemachko Collection

Builders

Builder	Period	Number completed	Remarks
NKVD Border Guard Yard, Leningrad 5 NKVD Yard, Leningrad from 1939	1936–1945	225	
640, Sosnovka	1943–1945	12	Completed to the *Project 174* design. Including fitting of 3 hulls built by Yard No 345, Yaroslav
345, Yaroslav		1	Three additional hulls evacuated to Yd No 640
Kirov Yd, Astrakhan	1943	5	Part of the MSV was evacuated to the Kirov Yd
MSV, Moscow	1943–1945		

Submarine chasers

MO № No on Comm	MO № 1940	MO № Feb-Mar 1941	MO № 25.7.1941	MO № 9.8.1941	MO № 7.9.1941	MO № 19.12.1941	MO № 1942	MO № 3.2.1943	MO № 25.11.1943	No 1944	No 1945
№ 1											
№ 11[2]										MO-11	
№ 12										MO-12	
№ 13										MO-13	
№ 14										MO-14	
№ 15										MO-7	
№ 16										MO-16	
№ 17										MO-17	
№ 18										MO-8	
№ 19										MO-19	
№ 20										MO-20	
№ 21										MO-21	
№ 22										MO-9	
№ 23										MO-23	
№ 24										MO-24	
№ 25										MO-25	
№ 26										MO-1	
№ 27										MO-27	
№ 28										MO-30	
№ 29										MO-29	
№ 106										MO-106	
№ 107										MO-107	
№ 108										MO-118	
№ 113				№ 205[5]			№ 124			MO-144	
№ 114			ZK-1		№ 207					MO-217	
ex-PK-• (1941)											
№ 115				ZK-4							
№ 131							№ 123				
№ 131			№ 501		№ 301						
№ 131		№ 311	№ 103		№ 701[5]	№ 101					
№ 132							№ 122			MO-423	
№ 132			№ 502		№ 302						MO-302
№ 132		№ 312	№ 104		№ 102						
№ 133		№ 313	№ 105		№ 103						MO-103
№ 133							№ 121				
№ 133			№ 503		№ 303						MO-303
№ 141		№ 311	№ 301			№ 313					MO-313
№ 141							№ 124				
№ 141			№ 106		№ 104						MO-104
№ 142		№ 312	№ 302			№ 314					MO-314
№ 142							№ 125			MO-426	
№ 142			№ 107		№ 105						
№ 143		№ 313	№ 303								
№ 143											
№ 143							№ 126			MO-424	
№ 153							№ 133			MO-431	
№ 161 ex-PK-• (1941)							№ 135			MO-430	
№ 162 ex-PK-223 (1941)							№ 132			MO-429	

13.0 Small submarines hunters

YN	Laid down	Launched	Comp	Comm	Fleet	Remarks
37	1937	Sum 1938	6.12.1938	1938	P	Trfd 25.4.1944 to the NKVD Border Guard, renumbered *PK-3*. Discarded 3.1.1957
81	1938	Sum 1939	16.9.1939	1939	P	Trfd 25.4.1944 to the NKVD Border Guard, renumbered *PK-5*. Discarded 10.1.1956
82	1938	Sum 1939	16.9.1939	1939	P	Trfd 25.4.1944 to the NKVD Border Guard, renumbered *PK-25*, renumbered *PSKR-15* on 19.9.1957. Discarded 23.5.1959
83	1938	Sum 1939	16.9.1939	1939	P	Trfd 25.4.1944 to the NKVD Border Guard, renumbered *PK-26*, renumbered *PSKR-16* on 19.9.1957. Discarded 3.1.1957
84	1938	Sum 1939	16.9.1939	1939	P	Trfd 25.4.1944 to the NKVD Border Guard, renumbered *PK-37*, renumbered *PSKR-8* on 19.9.1957. Discarded 11.11.1957
85	1938	1939	16.9.1939	1939	P	Survived the war
86	1938	Sum 1939	16.9.1939	1939	P	Trfd 25.4.1944 to the NKVD Border Guard. Discarded 23.5.1959
141	1939	Sum 1940	28.12.1940	3.3.1941	P	Survived the war
142	1939	Sum 1940	28.12.1940	3.3.1941	P	Survived the war
143	1939	Sum 1940	28.12.1940	3.3.1941	P	Survived the war
144	1939	Sum 1940	28.12.1940	3.3.1941	P	Survived the war
145	1939	Sum 1940	28.12.1940	3.3.1941	P	Survived the war
146	1939	Sum 1940	28.12.1940	3.3.1941	P	Survived the war
147	1939	Sum 1940	28.12.1940	3.3.1941	P	Survived the war
148	1939	Sum 1940	28.12.1940	3.3.1941	P	Survived the war
149	1939	Sum 1940	28.12.1940	3.3.1941	P	Survived the war
150	1939	Sum 1940	28.12.1940	3.3.1941	P	Survived the war
151	1939	Sum 1940	28.12.1940	3.3.1941	P	Survived the war
152	1939	Sum 1940	28.12.1940	3.3.1941	P	Survived the war
	Aut 1940	Sum 1941	2.9.1941	7.9.1941	B	Survived the war
225	Aut 1940	Sum 1941	2.9.1941	7.9.1941	B	Lost bow 28.7.1944 torpedoed by *U-475* south of Koivisto Island, repaired and recomm
	Aut 1940	Sum 1941	9.9.1941	7.9.1941	B	Decomm 2.6.1942 for repairs, recomm 21.11.1942
	Aut 1940	Spr 1941	26.6.1941	25.7.1941	B	Survived the war
195	Aut 1940	Spr 1941	26.6.1941 25.7.1941		B	Laid down as NKVD patrol boat, taken over by the Navy on completion. Returned renum 4.7.1945 to the NKVD Border Guard, renumbered *PK-212* on 10.10.1945, renumbered *PSKR-37* on 19.9.1957. Discarded 5.10.1959
197	Aut 1940	Spr 1941	26.6.1941	25.7.1941	B	Sank or abandoned 30.8.1941 after hitting a mine
167	29.5.1940	Aut 1940	20.12.1940	29.12.1940	N	Sunk 21.7.1943 by German aircraft in the Motovsky Gulf
131	4.5.1940	23.8.1940	11.11.1940	4.2.1941	B	Sank 14.11.1941 by mine east of Hanko
111	1939	Sum 1939	6.11.1939	16.1.1940	B	Sunk 31.7.1944 by *U-370* south of Laavansaari
168	29.5.1940	Aut 1940	15.12.1940	29.12.1940	N	Survived the war
	2.5.1940	23.8.1940	11.11.1940	4.2.1941	B	Survived the war
112	1939	Sum 1939	14.11.1939	16.1.1940	B	Sunk 19.4.1942 by artillery fire at Kronshtadt
113	1939	Sum 1939	12.11.1939	16.1.1940	B	Sunk 11.6.1943 by aircraft at Bukhta Batareynaya in the Gulf of Finland. Raised 27.6.1943 and recomm
169	Spr 1940	Aut 1940	18.12.1940	29.12.1940	N	Sunk 21.7.1943 by German aircraft in the Motovsky Gulf
	10.5.1940	28.8.1940	27.10.1940	4.2.1941	B	Survived the war
114	1939	Sum 1939	12.11.1939	16.1.1940	B	Survived the war
172	Spr 1940	Aut 1940	20.12.1940	29.12.1940	N	Sunk 6.10.1943 by German aircraft off Kuvshinskaya Salma, Kola Peninsula
161	10.5.1940	28.8.1940	27.10.1940	4.2.1941	B	Survived the war
115	1939	Sum 1939	6.11.1939	16.1.1940	B	Survived the war
171	Spr 1940	Aut 1940	20.10.1940	29.12.1940	N	Survived the war
165	20.5.1940	4.9.1940	27.10.1940	4.2.1941	B	Sunk 30.7.1944 by *U-250* in Vyborg Bay
116	1939	Sum 1939	16.11.1939	16.1.1940	B	Sank 11.12.1941 crushed by ice off Laavansaari Island
166	20.5.1940	4.9.1940	27.10.1940	4.2.1941	B	Sank 30.6.1941 by mine
	Spr 1940	Aut 1940	16.12.1940	29.12.1940	N	Survived the war
211	1940	Spr 1941	22.7.1941	22.7.1941	B N	Trfd 8.8.1941 to the Northern Fleet
212	1940	Spr 1941	22.7.1941	22.7.1941	B N	Laid down as NKVD patrol boat, taken over by the Navy on completion. Trfd 8.8.1941 to the Northern Fleet. Returned 16.1.1946 to the NKVD Border Guard, renumbered *PK-258* on 1.2.1946. Deleted 16.3.1955
223	1940	Spr 1941	22.7.1941	22.7.1941	B N	Laid down as NKVD patrol boat, taken over by the Navy on completion. Trfd 8.8.1941 to the Northern Fleet. Deleted 21.6.1948 to civilian service

MO № No on Comm	MO № 1940	MO № Feb-Mar 1941	MO № 25.7.1941	MO № 9.8.1941	MO № 7.9.1941	MO № 19.12.1941	MO № 1942	MO № 3.2.1943	MO № 25.11.1943	No 1944	No 1945
№ 163 ex-*PK-222*(1941)							№ 131			MO-434	
№ 204				ZK-5	№ 209						
№ 208									№ 042	MO-208	
№ 209									№ 025	MO-209	
№ 210							№ 125				
№ 213				№ 199						MO-199	
№ 213 ex-*PK-*• (1941)										MO-213	MO-223
№ 214				ZK-2	№ 208						
№ 214									№ 045	MO-214	
№ 215 ex-*PK-*• (1941)										MO-215	
№ 216											
№ 227										MO-227	
№ 228										MO-228	
№ 307											
№ 308											
№ 309 ex-*PK-*• (1941)										MO-309	
№ 310											
№ 311 VR-21[1] № 111[3]											
№ 312 VR-22[1] № 112[3]			№ 101		MO-L-112[8]						MO-131
№ 313 VR-23[1] № 113[3]			№ 102								
№ 321 VR-24[1] № 121[3]			№ 931	№ 121							MO-121
№ 322 VR-25[1] № 122[3]			№ 932	№ 122	MO-L-122[8]						MO-122
№ 323 VR-26[1] № 123[3]			№ 933	№ 123							
		№ 311									
№ 411				№ 196							

13.0 Small submarines hunters

YN	Laid down	Launched	Comp	Comm	Fleet	Remarks
222	1940	Spr 1941	22.7.1941	22.7.1941	B N	Laid down as NKVD patrol boat, taken over by the Navy on completion. Trfd 8.8.1941 to the Northern Fleet. Deleted 2.2.1950
204	1940	Spr 1941	5.7.1941	25.7.1941	B	Sank 7.5.1943 by mine off Suursaari Island
208	1940	Spr 1941	Aug 1941	9.8.1941	B BS	Trfd 11.6 1942 to the Ladoga Flotilla. Trfd 29.9.1943 to the Black Sea Fleet, *rated as patrol boat*
209	1940	Spr 1941	Aug 1941	9.8.1941	B La BS	Trfd 11.6 1942 to the Ladoga Flotilla. Trfd 29.9.1943 to the Black Sea Fleet, *rated as patrol boat*
210	1940	Spr 1941	15.7.1941	9.8.1941	B	Sank 27.7.1943 by mine in the Gulf of Finland
199	1940	Spr 1941	1.7.1941	25.7.1941	B La	Trfd 13.4.1942 to the Ladoga Flotilla, returned 13.10.1944
213	1940	Spr 1941	Aug 1941	16.9.1941	B La B	Laid down as NKVD patrol boat, taken over by the Navy on completion. Trfd 9.10.1941 to the Ladoga Flotilla, returned 13.10.1944. Returned 4.7.1945 to the NKVD Border Guard, renumbered *PK-207* on 10.10.1945, renumbered *PSKR-48* on 19.9.1957. Discarded 3.2.1959
	1940	Spr 1941	1.7.1941	25.7.1941	B	Sank 19.9.1942 by mine off Laavansaari Island
	1940	Spr 1941	Aug 1941	16.9.1941	B BS	Trfd 11.6.1942 to the Ladoga Flotilla, trfd 29.9.1943 to the Black Sea Fleet, *rated as patrol boat*
215	1940	Spr 1941	Aug 1941	16.9.1941	B La B	Laid down as NKVD patrol boat, taken over by the Navy on completion. Trfd 9.10.1941 to the Ladoga Flotilla, returned 13.10.1944. Returned 4.7.1945 to the NKVD Border Guard, renumbered *PK-220* on 10.10.1945, renumbered *PSKR-41* on 19.9.1957. Discarded 21.2.1959
216	1940	Spr 1941	Aug 1941	4.10.1941	La	Sank 27.11.1941 crushed by ice in the Murjajoki River estuary
227	1941	Sum 1941	9.9.1941	Sept 1941	B La B	Trfd 11.6.1942 to the Ladoga Flotilla, returned 13.10.1944
228	1941	Sum 1941	9.9.1941	Sept 1941	B La B	Trfd 11.6.1942 to the Ladoga Flotilla, returned 13.10.1944
221	1941	Spr 1941	27.8.1941	7.9.1941	B	Sank 11.12.1941 crushed by ice off Laavansaari Island
217	1941	Spr 1941	25.8.1941	7.9.1941	B	Sank 13.8.1942 by mine off Laavansaari Island
218	1941	Spr 1941	25.8.1941	7.9.1941	B	Laid down as NKVD patrol boat, taken over by the Navy on completion. Returned 12.9.1945 to the NKVD Border Guard, renumbered *PK-221* on 10.10.1945. Discarded 3.1.1957
221	1941	Spr 1941	25.8.1941	7.9.1941	B	Damaged 11.10.1941 in collision with the submarine *Shch-322*, immobilised, blown up 8.12.1941 at Suurkylä, Laavansaari Island
	1937	Sum 1937	29.11.1937	9.5.1938	B	Crushed by ice 9.1.1940 off Tallinn
	1937	Sum 1937	29.11.1937	9.5.1938	B	From 16.9.1941 to 14.10.1941 detached to the Red Army command of the Leningrad Front. Survived the war
	1937	Sum 1937	29.11.1937	9.5.1938	B	Sank 7.6.1943 by mine off Laavansaari Island
	1937	Spr 1938	4.8.1938	13.8.1941	B	Survived the war
	1937	Spr 1938	27.8.1938	21.9.1938	B	Survived the war
	1937	Spr 1938	19.9.1938	21.9.1938	B	Damaged 7.6.1943 by mine off Laavansaari Island, constructive total loss
220	1941	Spr 1941	25.8.1941	7.9.1941	B	Scuttled 13.10.1941 following mine damage off Ekholm Island, Saaristomeri (Turku Sea).
196	1940	Spr 1941	27.6.1941	25.7.1941	B La	Trfd 9.8.1941 to the Ladoga Flotilla. Sunk 27.9.1941 by artillery fire off Shlisselburg

Warships of the Soviet Fleets, 1939–1945

MO № No on Comm	MO № 1940	MO № Feb-Mar 1941	MO № 25.7.1941	MO № 9.8.1941	MO № 7.9.1941	MO № 19.12.1941	MO № 1942	MO № 3.2.1943	MO № 25.11.1943	No 1944	No 1945
№ 504 ex-*PK*-• (1941)				№ 198						MO-198	
№ 505				№ 201						MO-201	
№ 506				№ 202							
№ 507					№ 304						MO-304
№ 508					№ 305						
№ 509				№ 206						MO-206	
№ 510					№ 306						
M-11								№ 0412		MO-412	
M-12							№ 045				
M-12								№ 0112		MO-112	
M-13							№ 0155				
M-13								№ 0212			
M-14								№ 0312			
M-15								№ 0712		MO-712	
MO-1								№ 0612 № 0410[7]	№ 064[8] № 094	MO-307	
MO-2									№ 0104[8]	MO-210	
MO-3									№ 0114[8]	MO-320	
MO-4								№ 0812 № 0110[7]	№ 04[8] № 064		
MO-5									№ 054[8]		
MO-6								№ 0912 № 0210[7]	№ 084		
MO-11	№ 122						№ 114			MO-422[9]	
MO-12	№ 123						№ 116			MO-433	
MO-13 № 113[4]							№ 115			MO-425	
MO-14	№ 152						№ 134			MO-459[10]	
MO-15	№ 121						№ 113			MO-421[9]	
MO-16	№ 111									MO-427	
MO-17	№ 151						№ 136			MO-428	

13.0 Small submarines hunters

YN	Laid down	Launched	Comp	Comm	Fleet	Remarks
198	1940	Spr 1941	27.6.1941	25.7.1941	B La	Laid down as NKVD patrol boat, taken over by the Navy on completion. Trfd 7.8.1941 to the Ladoga Flotilla, returned 13.10.1944. Returned 12.9.1945 to the NKVD Border Guard, renumbered *PK-218* on 10.10.1945, renumbered *PSKR-40* on 19.9.1957. Discarded 21.2.1959
201	1940	Spr 1941	10.7.1941	25.7.1941	B La	Trfd 7.8.1941 to the Ladoga Flotilla, returned 13.10.1944
202	1940	Spr 1941	9.7.1941	25.7.1941	B	Sunk 30.8.1941 by artillery fire on the Neva River
203	1940	Spr 1941	10.7.1941	25.7.1941	B	Survived the war
205	1940	Spr 1941	9.7.1941	25.7.1941	B	Sunk 28.9.1941 by aircraft off Sommers Island
206	1940	Spr 1941	7.7.1941	25.7.1941	B La B	Trfd 9.8.1941 to the Ladoga Flotilla, returned 13.10.1944
207	1940	Spr 1941	7.7.1941	25.7.1941	B	Sunk 9.7.1942 by artillery fire off Someri Island
106	1939	Sum 1939	2.12.1939	1939/40	Cs Az	Trfd 4.4.1943 to the Azov Flotilla, *rated as patrol boat*
1304	1941	9.1.1942	19.3.1942	1.4.1942	Cs BS	Trfd 18.4.1942 to the Black Sea Flotilla, *rated as patrol boat*. Sunk 8.4.1943 by German MTBs off Myschako
38001	Aut 1941	Spr 1942	24.8.1942	17.9.1942	Cs Az	Trfd 4.4.1943 to the Azov Flotilla, *rated as patrol boat*
1305	1941	9.1.1942	29.3.1942	1.4.1942	Cs BS	Trfd 22.5.1942 to the Black Sea Fleet, *rated as patrol boat*. Sunk 21.6.1942 by German aircraft at Sevastopol
38002	Aut 1941	Spr 1942	5.9.1942	17.9.1942	Cs Az	Trfd 4.4.1943 to the Azov Flotilla, *rated as patrol boat*. Sunk 25.4.1943 German aircraft in the Azov Sea off Primorsko-Achtarsk
38003	Aut 1941	Spr 1942	18.9.1942	29.9.1942	Cs Az	Trfd 4.4.1943 to the Azov Flotilla, *rated as patrol boat*. Sunk 25.4.1943 German aircraft in the Azov Sea off Primorsko-Achtarsk
38004	1942	Sum 1942	Oct 1942	18.11.1942	Cs Az	Trfd 4.4.1943 to the Azov Flotilla, *rated as patrol boat*
1731	1941	Sum 1942	Aut 1942	31.10.1942	Vo BS	Trfd 24.10.1943 to the Black Sea Fleet, *rated as patrol boat*
1732	1941	Sum 1942	Aut 1942	16.11.1942	Vo On Vo BS	Trfd 19.1.1943 to Onega Flotilla, returned 15.5.1943. Trfd 26.10.1943 to the Black Sea Fleet, *rated as patrol boat*
1733	Aut 1941	Spr 1942	20.5.1942	28.7.1942	Cs Vo On Vo BS	Trfd 18.8.1942 to the Volga Flotilla, trfd 19.1.1943 to the Onega Flotilla, returned 15.5.1943. Trfd 26.10.1943 to the Black Sea Fleet, *rated as patrol boat*
6	Aut 1941	Spr 1942	18.6.1942	16.11.1942	Vo On Az Vo BS	Trfd 19.1.1943 to the Onega Flotilla, trfd 13.2.1943 to the Azov Flotilla, *rated as patrol boat*. Returned 15.5.1943 to the Volga Flotilla, trfd 24.10.1943 to the Black Sea Fleet. Sank 2.11.1943 on mines in the Kerch Strait
5	Aut 1941	Spr 1942	30.6.1942	16.11.1942	Vo On Vo BS	Trfd 19.1.1943 to the Onega Flotilla, returned 15.5.1943. Trfd 26.10.1943 to the Black Sea Fleet, *rated as patrol boat*. Sunk 3.11.1943 by artillery fire in the Kerch Strait
7	Aut 1941	Spr 1942	31.5.1942	28.7.1942	Vo On Vo BS	Trfd 19.1.1943 to the Onega Flotilla, returned 15.5.1943. Trfd 24.10.1943 to the Black Sea Fleet, *rated as patrol boat*. Sank 2.11.1943 by mine in the Kerch Strait
54	1938	1.6.1938	1.12.1938	1938/9	N BS	Trfd 21.5.1944 to the Black Sea Fleet
59	1938	1.6.1938	1.12.1938	1938/9	N	Survived the war
60	1938	1.6.1938	1.12.1938	1939	N	Survived the war
63	1938	1.6.1938	1.12.1938	1938/9	N	Conv 26.6.1943 to service craft, reverted 11.5.1944
102	1939	Sum 1939	Nov 1939	1939	N BS	Trfd 21.5.1944 to the Black Sea Fleet
103	1939	Sum 1939	Nov 1939	1939	N	Survived the war
105	1939	Sum 1939	Nov 1939	1939/40	N	Survived the war

Warships of the Soviet Fleets, 1939–1945

MO № No on Comm	MO № 1940	MO № Feb-Mar 1941	MO № 25.7.1941	MO № 9.8.1941	MO № 7.9.1941	MO № 19.12.1941	MO № 1942	MO № 3.2.1943	MO № 25.11.1943	No 1944	No 1945
MO-18	№ 112[4]								MO-432		
MO-32											
MO-33											
MO-34											
MO-114											

The effective dates of Pennant Numbers change orders.

Year	Fleet	Date
1940	P	11.2.1940
	B	29.12.1940
1941	B	4.2.1941
	N	26.3.1941
	B	25.7.1941
	B	9.8.1941
	B	7.9.1941
1942	A	5.4.1942
	B	25.8.1942
1943	Cs	3.2.1943
	Vo	
	BS	25.11.1943
1944	P	11.2.1944
	N	1.4.1944
	BS	7.5.1944
	B	13.12.1944
1945	B	2.1.1945
	La	20.3.1945

Exceptions noted in the main table.

No	Year	Date	Fleet
1	1939	11.5.1939	B
2		16.9.1939	P
3		10.10.1939	B
4	1940	29.12.1940	A
5	1941	22.8.1941	B
6		14.10.1941	B
7	1943	13.4.1943	Vo On
8		26.10.1943	BS
9	1944	14.2.1944	N
10		11.5.1944	N

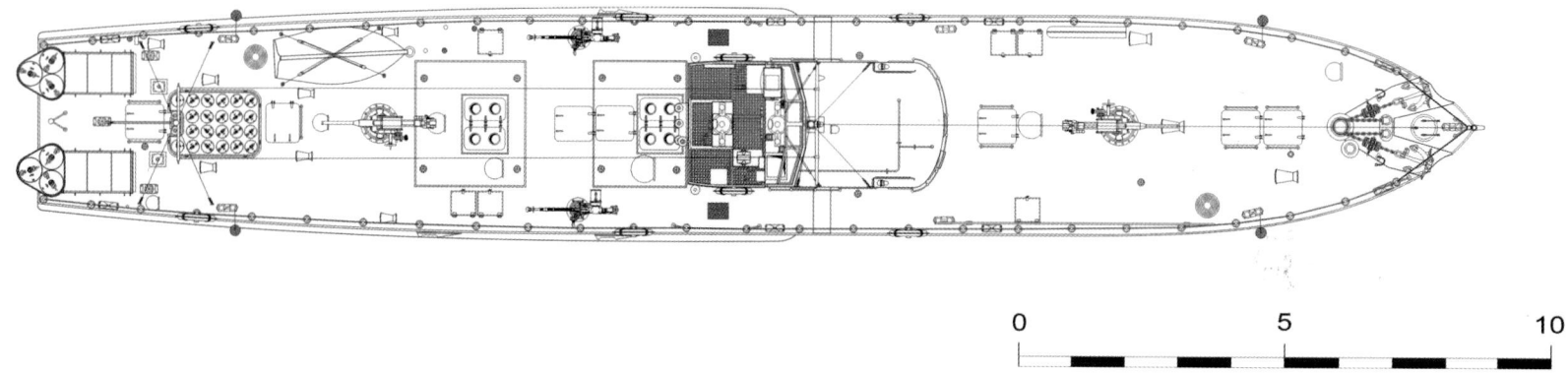

MO-4 type in 1939.
Drawing by Jerzy Lewandowski

YN	Laid down	Launched	Comp	Comm	Fleet	Remarks
106	1939	Sum 1939	Nov 1939	1939	N	Survived the war
	Spr 1943	Sum 1944	11.11.1944	1944	Cs	Survived the war
	Spr 1943	Sum 1945	Aug 45	19.9.1945	Cs	Survived the war
	Spr 1943	Sum 1945	1.9.1945	19.9.1945	Cs	Survived the war
	Spr 1943	Sum 1944	15.9.1944	30.9.1944	Cs B	Trfd 21.11.1944 to the Baltic Fleet

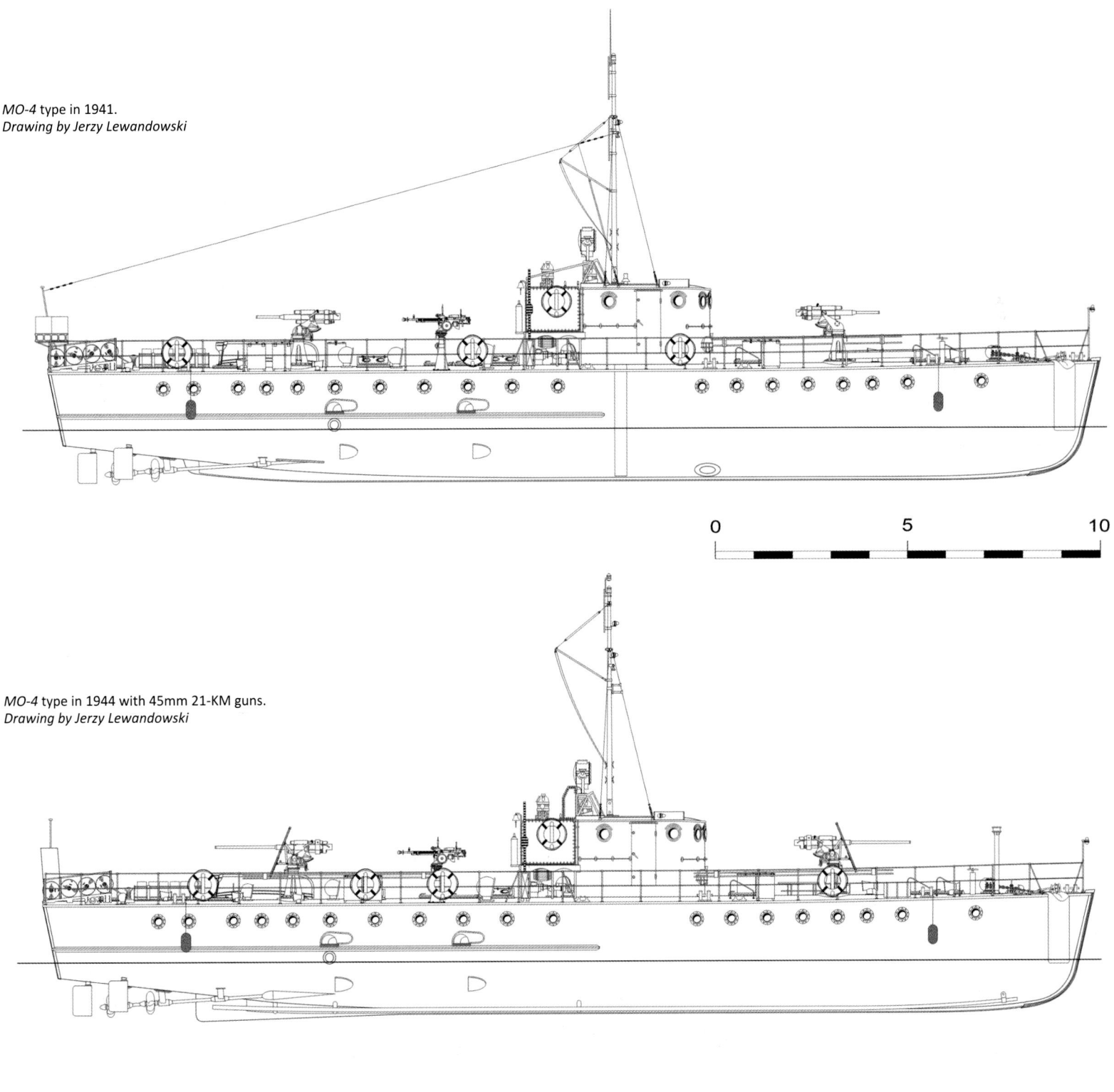

MO-4 type in 1941.
Drawing by Jerzy Lewandowski

MO-4 type in 1944 with 45mm 21-KM guns.
Drawing by Jerzy Lewandowski

WARSHIPS OF THE SOVIET FLEETS, 1939–1945

The Black Sea submarine hunters (rated as patrol boats)

SKA № on Comm	SKA № 2.7.1941	SKA № 4.9.1941	SKA № 10.12.1941	SKA № 17.12.1941	SKA № 3.7.1942	SKA № 13.4.1943	SKA № 25.11.1943	SKA № No 7.5.1944	YN
№ 013		№ 046[1]						MO-46	179
№ 014				№ 0118	№ 079[2]				185
№ 017	№ 042		№ 044	№ 0105				MO-105	117
№ 018	№ 012		№ 014	№ 085				MO-85	118
№ 019	№ 022								119
№ 020	№ 032		№ 034	№ 095					120
№ 021	№ 011								121
№ 022	№ 021								131
№ 023	№ 015		№ 0131						132
№ 023				№ 094					184
№ 024	№ 051								133
№ 024		№ 036[6]						MO-36	186
№ 025	№ 041								134
№ 026	№ 025		№ 0141					MO-141	135
№ 027	№ 061								136
№ 028	№ 081							MO-81	137
№ 031								MO-31	177
№ 033				№ 0104					181
№ 043				№ 0114					182
№ 052			№ 024	№ 0115				MO-115	187
№ 053				№ 0124					183
№ 058									1730
№ 062				№ 0125					188
№ 063		№ 056[6]							184
№ 071					№ 011		№ 03	SK-11[10] MO-11[11]	171
№ 091								MO-91	175
№ 095								MO-95	
№ 099							№ 055[8]	№ 099[9] MO-99	38008
№ 0100								MO-100	38009
№ 0101								MO-101	176
№ 0111								MO-111	174
№ 0121									178
№ 0122							№ 098[7]	MO-98	23
№ 0132							№ 0129[7]	MO-129	
№ 0165					№ 049			MO-49	
№ 0175					№ 059				
№ 1012						№ 0812	№ 014[6]	MO-812	8
№ 1112						№ 0912			9
№ 1212						№ 1012			10
№ 1312						№ 0512		MO-512	11
№ 1412						№ 0612			12
№ 1512						№ 0810[5] № 0162	№ 012	MO-162	13
№ 1612						№ 0710[5] № 0152	№ 032	MO-152	20
№ 1712						№ 0510 № 051[4]	№ 0124	MO-124	38006
№ 1812						№ 0610 № 038[4]		MO-38	38007

13.0 Small submarines hunters

Laid down	Launched	Comp	Comm	Fleet	Remarks
1940	1941	25.6.1941	2.7.1941	BS	Survived the war
1940	1941	25.6.1941	2.7.1941	BS	Sunk 6.6.1943 by aircraft in Tsemes Bay. Raised and recomm. Sunk 3.11.1943 by artillery fire off Kerch
1939	1940	27.6.1940	1940	BS	Survived the war
1939	1940	27.6.1940	1940	BS	Survived the war
1939	1940	27.6.1940	1940	BS	Sunk 22.9.1941 by German aircraft off the Tendra Spit
1939	1940	27.6.1940	1940	BS	Sank 5.4.1943 by mine off Myschako
1939	Spr 1940	11.7.1940	1940	BS	Sunk 15.11.1941 by German aircraft off Sevastopol
1939	Spr 1940	11.7.1940	1940	BS	Sunk 2.7.1942 off Yalta
1939	Spr 1940	11.7.1940	1940	BS	Used as experimental vessel from 19.3.1941 to 4.9.1941. Damaged 30.12.1941 by artillery fire at Theodosia and sunk 6.1.1943 by aircraft there
1940	1941	20.6.1941	2.7.1941	BS	Sunk 31.12.1941 by aircraft at the Kerch Strait
1939	1940	11.7.1940	1940	BS	Sank 4.2.1943 by mine off Novorossiysk
1940	1941	20.6.1941	2.7.1941	BS	Survived the war
1939	Spr 1940	11.7.1940	1940	BS	Sunk 22.5.1943 by aircraft off Gelendzhik
1939	Spr 1940	11.7.1940	1940	BS	Used as experimental vessel from 19.3.1941 to 4.9.1941. Sank 4.2.1943 by mine off Novorossiysk. Raised and recomm
1939	Spr 1940	23.7.1940	1940	BS	Sunk 27.6.1941 by aircraft at Sevastopol
1939	Spr 1940	23.7.1940	1940	BS	Survived the war
31.7.1940	25.10.1940	21.1.1941	28.4.1941	BS	Survived the war
1940	Spr 1941	20.6.1941	2.7.1941	BS	Deleted Oct 1943, presumably lost
1940	Spr 1941	20.6.1941	2.7.1941	BS	Deleted 20.7.1941(?), presumably lost
1940	Spr 1941	28.6.1941	2.7.1941	BS	Sank 24.2.1943 at Gelendzhik because of overload, raised and recomm
1940	Spr 1941	28.6.1941	2.7.1941	BS	Sunk 2.7.1943 by German MTBs off Sevastopol
Aut 1941	Spr 1942	Jul 1942	1942	Cs BS	Trfd 23.9.1942 to the Black Sa Fleet. Sank 24.4.1943 by mine off Myschako
1940	Spr 1941	28.6.1941	2.7.1941	BS	Sunk 21.6.1942 by aircraft at Sevastopol
1940	Spr 1941	20.6.1941	2.7.1941	BS	Sunk 29.12.1941 by artillery fire at Theodosia
12.7.1940	22.10.1940	21.1.1941	28.4.1941	BS	Conv 31.5.1943 to service craft, reverted 15.7.1944
18.7.1940	24.10.1940	28.1.1941	28.4.1941	BS	Survived the war
Jun 1942	Sum 1943	4.10.1943	1943	Cs BS	Trfd 3.11.1943 to the Black Sea Fleet
1942	Sum 1943	17.11.1943	4.12.1943	Cs BS	Trfd 12.2.1944 to the Black Sea Fleet
1942	Aut 1943	Feb 1944	8.3.1944	BS	
18.7.1940	24.10.1940	23.1.1941	28.4.1941	BS	Stranded 9.7.1941 off Cape Lukull near Sevastopol. Raised and recomm
12.7.1940	22.10.1940	23.1.1941	28.4.1941	BS	Survived the war
31.7.1940	26.10.1940	23.1.1941	28.4.1941	BS	Sunk 25.3.1942 by artillery fire at Sevastopol.
cze.42	Sum 1943	25.10.1943	1943	Cs BS	Trfd 14.4.1944 to the Black Sea Fleet
cze.42	Sum 1943	Aut 1943	14.12.1943	BS	Survived the war
1941	9.1.1942	26.4.1942	1942	Cs BS	Trfd 24.5.1942 to the Black Sea Fleet
1941	9.1.1942	Apr 1942	1942	Cs	Trfd 24.5.1942 to the Black Sea Fleet
1942	Spr 1943	13.8.1943	1943	BS	Name: *Morskaia dusha*. Trfd 25.8.1943 to the Black Sea Fleet
1942	Jul 1943	30.9.1943	1943	BS	Stranded 1.11.1943 off Eltigen and sunk by artillery fire
1942	Jul 1943	12.9.1943	1943	BS	Sank 31.10.1943 by mine in the Kerch Strait
1942	Jul 1943	29.9.1943	1943	BS	
1942	Spr 1943	24.7.1943	25.8.1943	BS	Sunk 10.1.1944 by aircraft off Cape Tarkhan
1942	Sum 1943	30.9.1943	25.11.1943	BS	Survived the war
May 1942	Sum 1943	30.9.1943	25.11.1943	BS	Survived the war
1942	Sum 1943	14.10.1943	25.11.1943	BS	Survived the war
1942	Sum 1943	16.10.1943	25.11.1943	BS	Survived the war

Exceptions noted in the main table.

No	Year	Date	Fleet
1	1941	3.9.1941	BS
2	1942	26.5.1942	BS
3		19.7.1942	BS
4	1943	25.5.1943	BS
5		20.6.1943	BS
6		22.9.1943	BS
7		22.12.1943	BS
8		30.12.1943	BS
9	1944	22.3.1944	Cs
10		21.4.1944	BS
11		15.7.1944	Bs

The NKVD Border Guard patrol boats

NKVD No	MO №* SKA №** 25.7.1941	MO № 9.8.1941	MO №* SKA №*** Sep 1941	SKA № 10.12.1941	SKA № 17.12.1941	SKA № 25.11.1943	No 1944	YN
PK-3 *ex-PK-227 (9.1.1941)*							MO-337[8]	33
PK-5 *ex-PK-229 (9.1.1941)*							MO-338[8]	36
PK-25							MO-339[8]	40
PK-26							MO-347[8]	41
PK-27							MO-348[8]	42
PK-37							MO-349[8]	69
PK-77						№ 028	MO-77	48
PK-78						№ 098	MO-306	49
PK-91 *ex-PK-250 (9.1.1941)*				№ 018	№ 05		MO-18	32
PK-92 *ex-PK-282 (9.1.1941)*				№ 028	№ 06		MO-28	52
PK-93 *ex-PK-283 (9.1.1941)*				№ 069[5]	№ 038[7]		MO-69	55
PK-94 *ex-PK-284 (9.1.1941)*				№ 048				56
PK-95 *ex-PK-285 (9.1.1941)*			№ 016[3]					57
PK-96 *ex-PK-286 (9.1.1941)*			№ 026[3]				MO-26	62
PK-97 *ex-PK-293 (9.1.1941)*				№ 058				11
PK-98 *ex-PK-294 (9.1.1941)*				№ 068				13
PK-99 *ex-PK-295 (9.1.1941)*				№ 078			MO-78	87
PK-100 *ex-PK-296 (9.1.1941)*				№ 088				92
PK-101 *ex-PK-297 (9.1.1941)*				№ 098				90
PK-102 *ex-PK-298 (9.1.1941)*				№ 0108			MO-108	91
PK-116 *ex-PK-261 (9.1.1941)*				№ 0154	№ 019			58
PK-118				№ 074	№ 025			65
PK-119					№ 035	№ 084[6]	MO-35	66
PK-120				№ 084	№ 045			
PK-121								
PK-122				№ 0104	№ 055			
PK-123 *ex-PK-263 (9.1.1941)*				№ 0114	№ 029	№ 07	SK-29	58
PK-125				№ 0124	№ 065		MO-65	51
PK-129 *ex-PK-274 (9.1.1941)*				№ 0164	№ 039			64
PK-130 *ex-PK-287 (9.1.1941)*			№ 022				MO-22	61

13.0 Small submarines hunters

Laid down	Launched	Comp	Comm	Fleet	Remarks
1937		1938	25.4.1944	P BS	Trfd 12.5.1944 to the Black Sea Fleet. Deleted 10.7.1954
1937		1938	25.4.1944	P BS	Trfd 12.5.1944 to the Black Sea Fleet. Conv 10.5.1945 to service craft. Renumbered *SK-338* on 27.12.1956, *SPK-22* on 19.2.1959. Deleted 24.9.1960
1937		1938	25.4.1944	P BS	Trfd 12.5.1944 to the Black Sea Fleet. Deleted 10.7.1954
1937		1938	25.4.1944	P BS	Trfd 12.5.1944 to the Black Sea Fleet. Deleted 10.7.1954
1937		1938	25.4.1944	P BS	Trfd 12.5.1944 to the Black Sea Fleet. Conv 9.5.1953 to service craft, deleted 3.9.1953
1937		1938	25.4.1944	P BS	Trfd 12.5.1944 to the Black Sea Fleet. Deleted 10.7.1954
		1938	22.6.1941	Cs BS	Trfd 18.9.1943 to the Black Sea Fleet, *rated as patrol boat*. Returned 21.6.1945 to the NKVD Border Guard, renumbered *PK-144* on 21.9.1945. Discarded 10.1.1956
		1938	22.6.1941	Cs BS	Trfd 18.9.1943 to the Black Sea Fleet, *rated as patrol boat*. Returned 21.6.1945 to the NKVD Border Guard, renumbered *PK-94* on 21.9.1945. Discarded 7.3.1951
1936		1937	19.7.1941	BS	*Rated as patrol boat*. Returned 21.6.1945 to the NKVD Border Guard, renumbered *PK-140* on 21.9.1945. Discarded 1.11.1950
		1938	19.7.1941	BS	*Rated as patrol boat*. Returned 21.6.1945 to the NKVD Border Guard. Recomm 14.8.1954 to the Baltic Fleet as communication boat *POK-69*. Deleted 27.7.1956
		1938	19.7.1941	BS	*Rated as patrol boat*. Returned 21.6.1945 to the NKVD Border Guard, renumbered *PK-133* on 21.9.1945. Discarded late 1940s
		1938	19.7.1941	BS	*Rated as patrol boat*. Sunk 26.9.1943 by mine off Anapa. Raised 18.11.1943, BU?
		1938	19.7.1941	BS	Sunk 25.5.1943 by artillery fire off Myschako
		1938	19.7.1941	BS	*Rated as patrol boat*. Returned 21.6.1945 to the NKVD Border Guard, renumbered *PK-116* on 21.9.1945. Discarded 16.3.1955
1936		1937	19.7.1941	BS	*Rated as patrol boat*. Sunk 4.1.1942 by German aircraft off Theodosia
1936		1937	19.7.1941	BS	*Rated as patrol boat*. Sunk 29.11.1941 by artillery fire off Theodosia
		1938	19.7.1941	BS	*Rated as patrol boat*. Returned 21.6.1945 to the NKVD Border Guard, renumbered *PK-93* on 21.9.1945, renumbered *PSKR-28* on 19.9.1957. Discarded 27.9.1957
		1938	19.7.1941	BS	*Rated as patrol boat*. Sank 17.3.1943 by mine in Tsemes Bay
		1938	19.7.1941	BS	*Rated as patrol boat*. Sank 10.5.1943 by mine off Myschako
		1939	19.7.1941	BS	*Rated as patrol boat*. Returned 21.6.1945 to the NKVD Border Guard, renumbered *PK-101* on 21.9.1945. Discarded 10.1.1956
		1938	19.7.1941	BS Az BS	*Rated as patrol boat*. Trfd 17.12.1941 to the Azov Flotilla, returned 1.10.1942. Sank 1.11.1943 by mine off Eltigen
		1938	19.7.1941	BS	*Rated as patrol boat*. Sunk 10.9.1943 by artillery fire off Novorossiysk
		1938	19.7.1941	BS	*Rated as patrol boat*. Returned 21.6.1945 to the NKVD Border Guard, renumbered *PK-141* on 21.9.1945, renumbered *PSKR-29* on 19.9.1957. Discarded 11.11.1957
1937		1938	19.7.1941	BS	*Rated as patrol boat*. Sunk 31.10.1941 by German aircraft off Evpatoria
1937		1938	19.7.1941	BS	Sunk 20.9.1941 by aircraft off the Tendra Spit
1937		1938	19.7.1941	BS	*Rated as patrol boat*. Sank 2.11.1943 by mine off Eltigen
		1938	19.7.1941	BS Az BS	*Rated as patrol boat*. Trfd 17.12.1941 to the Azov Flotilla, returned 1.10.1942. Damaged 19.4.1943 by artillery fire at Myschako, relegated conv 3.7.1943 to service craft. Returned 21.6.1945 to the NKVD Border Guard, renumbered *PK-117* on 21.9.1945, renumbered *PSKR-32* on 19.9.1957. Discarded 21.2.1959
		1938	19.7.1941	BS	*Rated as patrol boat*. Returned 21.6.1945 to the NKVD Border Guard, renumbered *PK-65* on 21.9.1945, renumbered *PSKR-31* on 19.9.1957. Discarded 11.11.1957
		1938	19.7.1941	BS Az	*Rated as patrol boat*. Trfd 17.12.1941 to the Azov Flotilla, returned 1.10.1942. Sunk 6.6.1943 by aircraft off Myschako
		1938	19.7.1941	BS	*Rated as patrol boat*. Returned 21.6.1945 to the NKVD Border Guard, renumbered *PK-130* on 21.9.1945. Discarded late 1940s

Warships of the Soviet Fleets, 1939–1945

NKVD No	MO №* SKA №** 25.7.1941	MO № 9.8.1941	MO №* SKA №*** Sep 1941	SKA № 10.12.1941	SKA № 17.12.1941	SKA № 25.11.1943	No 1944	YN
PK-131 ex-PK-288 (9.1.1941)			№ 012					93
PK-132 ex-PK-289 (9.1.1941)			№ 032					94
PK-133 ex-PK-290 (9.1.1941)			№ 042					95
PK-134 ex-PK-291 (9.1.1941)			№ 052				MO-52	96
PK-135 ex-PK-292 (9.1.1941)			№ 062			№ 04	SK-62 MO-62[10]	97
PK-136 ex-PK-313 (9.1.1941)			№ 092					98
PK-137 ex-PK-314 (9.1.1941)			№ 072				MO-72	99
PK-138 ex-PK-315 (9.1.1941)			№ 0102				MO-102	100
PK-141 ex-PK-270 (9.1.1941)					№ 014			5
PK-142 ex-PK-271 (9.1.1941)					№ 024			
PK-143 ex-PK-273 (9.1.1941)					№ 034			
PK-144 ex-PK-272 (9.1.1941)					№ 044		MO-44	3 or 4
PK-145 ex-PK-278 (9.1.1941)					№ 054			125
PK-146					№ 064			126
PK-147					№ 074		MO-74	127
PK-148					№ 084			128
PK-200			№ 403				MO-403[11]	
PK-201	№ 201	№ 108[2]	№ 201					
PK-202	№ 202		№ 402				MO-402[11]	
PK-203	№ 203	№ 109[2]						
PK-204 ex-PK-300 (9.1.1941)			№ 204				MO-204	
PK-205	№ 207	№ 201[2]	№ 205[4]				MO-205	
PK-206	№ 109	ZK-7	№ 206					
PK-207	№ 207		№ 407					
PK-208	№ 208	№ 203[2]	№ 408				MO-408[11]	
PK-209	№ 209	№ 204[2]	№ 409				MO-409[11]	
PK-210	№ 110	ZK-8	№ 210					
PK-211	№ 111	ZK-9	№ 211					
PK-212	№ 401		№ 405					
PK-213	№ 402		№ 406					
PK-214	№ 403		№ 410					
PK-215	№ 404							
PK-218	№ 407							
PK-219			№ 213				MO-213	138

13.0 Small submarines hunters

Laid down	Launched	Comp	Comm	Fleet	Remarks
1937		1938	19.7.1941	BS	*Rated as patrol boat.* Stranded 21.1.1942 off Gelendzhik, abandoned
		1939	19.7.1941	BS	*Rated as patrol boat.* Sunk 10.9.1943 by artillery fire off Novorossiysk
		1939	19.7.1941	BS	*Rated as patrol boat.* Sank 14.4.1942 by mine in the Kerch Strait
		1939	19.7.1941	BS	*Rated as patrol boat.* Returned 21.6.1945 to the NKVD Border Guard, renumbered *PK-131* on 21.9.1945. Discarded 5.2.1952
		1939	19.7.1941	BS	*Rated as patrol boat.* Conv 8.4.1942 to service craft, reverted 15.7.1944. Returned 21.6.1945 to the NKVD Border Guard, renumbered *PK-118* on 21.9.1945. Discarded 10.1.1956
		1939	19.7.1941	BS	*Rated as patrol boat.* Sunk 13.6.1942 by German aircraft off Cape Fiolent
		1939	19.7.1941	BS	*Rated as patrol boat.* Returned 21.6.1945 to the NKVD Border Guard, renumbered *PK-134* on 21.9.1945. Discarded 12.11.1952
		1939	19.7.1941	BS	*Rated as patrol boat.* Returned 21.6.1945 to the NKVD Border Guard, renumbered *PK-100* on 21.9.1945. Discarded 1.10.1947
		1937	19.7.1941	BS	*Rated as patrol boat.* Sank 27.7.1943 by mine off Myschako
1937		1938	19.7.1941	BS	*Rated as patrol boat.* Sank 15.4.1942 by mine at the Kerch Strait south east of Kamysh-Burun
1937		1938	19.7.1941	BS	*Rated as patrol boat.* Sunk 26.12.1941 by artillery fire off Kamysh-Burun
		1937	19.7.1941	BS	*Rated as patrol boat.* Sunk 1.11.1943 by aircraft off Eltigen, raised and recomm. Returned 21.6.1945 to the NKVD Border Guard, renumbered *PK-142* on 21.9.1945, renumbered *PSKR-34* on 19.9.1957. Discarded 20.9.1957
		1939	19.7.1941	BS	*Rated as patrol boat.* Sank 8.4.1943 by mine off Gelendzhik
		1939	19.7.1941	BS	*Rated as patrol boat.* Sunk 10.9.1943 by artillery fire off Novorossiysk
		1939	19.7.1941	BS	*Rated as patrol boat.* Stranded 5.2.1943 of Novorossiysk and damaged by artillery fire. Deleted 20.6.1943, raised 1.8.1943, considered constructive total loss on 12.7.1944
		1939	19.7.1941	BS	*Rated as patrol boat.* Sunk 11.9.1943 by artillery fire off Novorossiysk. Raised 1944, apparently considered constructive total loss
		1940	7.9.1941	B	Returned 4.7.1945 to the NKVD Border Guard, renumbered *PK-202* on 21.9.1945, renumbered *PSKR-47* on 19.9.1957. Discarded early 1960s
1940	1941	25.4.1941	25.7.1941	B	Sunk 27.6.1942 by aircraft off Seiskari Island
		1940	25.7.1941	B	Returned 4.7.1945 to the NKVD Border Guard, renumbered *PK-201* on 21.9.1945. Discarded 3.1.1957
		1940	25.7.1941	B	Sank 29.8.1941 by mine northwest of Cape Juminda
		1939	25.7.1941	B	Returned 4.7.1945 to the NKVD Border Guard, renumbered *PK-206* on 21.9.1945. Discarded 11.1.1954
1939		1940	25.7.1941	B / La / B	Trfd 7.8.1941 to the Ladoga Flotilla, returned 13.10.1944. Returned 4.7.1945 to the NKVD Border Guard, renumbered *PK-209* on 21.9.1945. Discarded 7.8.1953
1940	Spr 1941	1.7.1941	25.7.1941	B	Stranded 30.9.1941 off Kronshtadt, raised and recomm Oct 1941. Sunk 29.10.1941 by aircraft in the Gulf of Finland off the Shepelevskiy lighthouse
		1940	25.7.1941	B	Sank 10.12.1941 crushed by ice west of Laavansaari Island
		1940	25.7.1941	B	Returned 4.7.1945 to the NKVD Border Guard, renumbered *PK-214* on 21.9.1945, renumbered *PSKR-38* on 19.9.1957. Discarded early 1960s
		1940	25.7.1941	B	Returned 4.7.1945 to the NKVD Border Guard, renumbered *PK-203* on 21.9.1945. Conv 11.1.1954 to service craft *PS-100*. Discarded late 1950s
1940		1941	25.7.1941	B	Sunk 15.8.1942 by German aircraft off Seiskari Island
1940	1941	15.6.1941	25.7.1941	B	Sunk 15.8.142 by mine off Seiskari Island
		1938	25.7.1941	B	Sunk 13.12.1941 crushed by ice west of Laavansaari Island
		1939	25.7.1941	B	Sank 14.12.1941 crushed by ice off Penisari Island
		1940	25.7.1941	B	Conv 27.6.1943 to service craft because of damage. Sunk 22.11.1944 by mine off Tallinn
1938		1940	25.7.1941	B	Sunk 5/6.9.1941 by artillery fire off Koivisto
1938		1940	25.7.1941	B	Sunk 6.9.1941 by artillery fire off Koivisto
		1939	25.7.1941	B	Returned 4.7.1945 to the NKVD Border Guard, renumbered *PK-219* on 21.9.1945, renumbered *PSKR-35* on 19.9.1957. Discarded 3.2.1958

NKVD No	MO №* SKA №** 25.7.1941	MO № 9.8.1941	MO №* SKA №*** Sep 1941	SKA № 10.12.1941	SKA № 17.12.1941	SKA № 25.11.1943	No 1944	YN
PK-220	№ 210	№ 206[2]	№ 404					
PK-221	№ 211	№ 207[2]	№ 212					
PK-232	№ 108	ZK-6	№ 203				MO-203[12]	
PK-238	№ 306							
PK-239	№ 307							221
PK-251	№ 251[1]						MO-251[9]	
PK-252	№ 252[1]						MO-252[9]	

** The Northern Fleet designation. *** The Black Sea Fleet designation.

The effective dates of Pennant Numbers change orders.

Year	Fleet	Date
1941	B	25.7.1941
	BS	4.9.1941
	B	7.9.1941
	BS	10.12.1941
1943	BS	25.11.1943
1944	BS	7.5.1944
	B	13.12.1944

Exceptions noted in the main table.

No	Year	Date	Fleet
1	1941	23.6.1941	N
2		22.8.1941	B
3		3.9.1941	BS
4		4.10.1941	La
5	1942	26.7.1942	BS
6	1943	10.12.1943	BS
7		17.12.1943	BS
8	1944	24.5.1944	BS
9		11.6.1944	N
10		17.7.1944	BS
11		21.10.1944	B
12	1945	2.1.1945	B

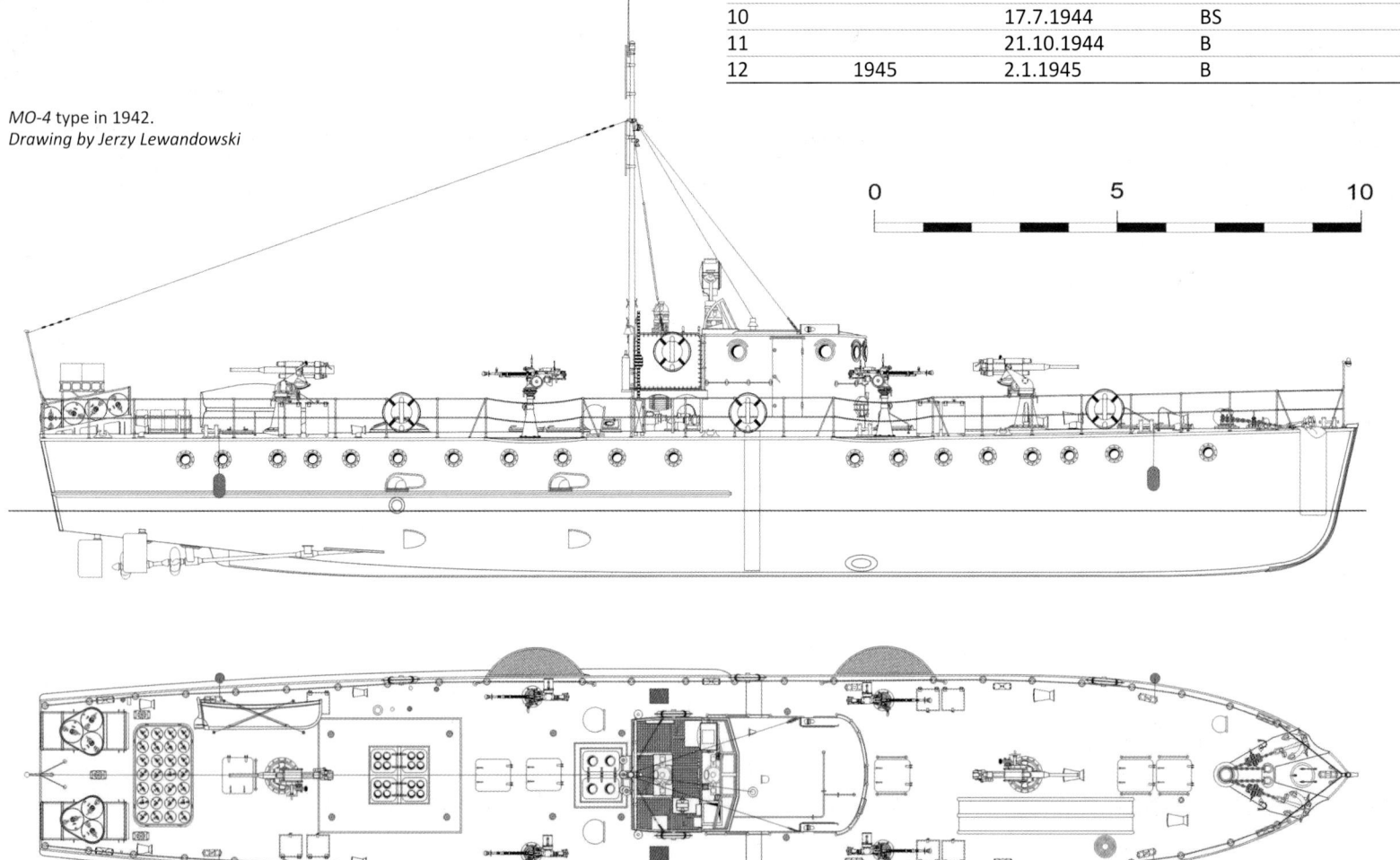

MO-4 type in 1942.
Drawing by Jerzy Lewandowski

13.0 SMALL SUBMARINES HUNTERS

Laid down	Launched	Comp	Comm	Fleet	Remarks
1940	1941	15.6.1941	25.7.1941	B	Sunk 13.5.1944 by aircraft off Laavansaari Island
1940	1941	15.6.1941	25.7.1941	B	Sunk 3.8.1942 by mine in the Gulf of Finland south east of Seiskari Island
1940		1941	25.7.1941	B	Returned 4.7.1945 to the NKVD Border Guard, renumbered *PK-200* on 21.9.1945, renumbered *PSKR-45* on 19.9.1957. Discarded early 1960s
1938		1940	25.7.1941	B	Sunk 26.7.1941 by the Finnish gunboat *Uusimaa* off Bengtskär Island near Hanko
1938		1940	25.7.1941	B	Sank 13.12 1941 crushed by ice off Laavansaari Island
1938		1940	23.6.1941	N Wh N	Trfd to the White Sea Flotilla, returned 16.2.1945. Returned 15.1.1946 to the NKVD Border Guard
1938		1940	23.6.1941	N Wh N	Trfd to the White Sea Flotilla, returned 16.2.1945. Returned 15.1.1946 to the NKVD Border Guard, renumbered *PK-252* on 21.9.1945, renumbered *PSKR-36* on 19.9.1957. Discarded early 1960s* The Baltic Fleet designation.

Aerial view of *MO-812*, named *Morskaia dusha* (Sea Soul) after the book of stories by regime writer Leonid Sobolev who handed over his 1943 Stalin Prize to the Defence Fund with request to build a boat. *Przemysław Budzbon Collection*

Storozhevoj kater № 023 in spring 1941 during the May Day parade passing the cruiser *Krasnyj Kavkaz* in the background. At that time she was detached to the experimental ships division, so a hyphen precedes her number 23 with O pennant standing for Opytovyj = Experimental. On 2.7.1941 her number was changed to *Storozhevoj kater № 015* while from 4.9.1941 it was altered again to *Storozhevoj kater № 0131*. *Boris Lemachko Collection*

Malyj okhotnik № 135 of the Northern Fleet presenting her camouflage painting. Former NKVD Border Guard patrol boat taken over by the Soviet Navy on completion and numbered *Malyj okhotnik № 161* to be renumbered on 5.4.1942. Two years later she was renamed *MO-430*. *Boris Lemachko Collection*

13.0 SMALL SUBMARINES HUNTERS

Storozhevoj kater № 0111 of the Black Sea Fleet.
Boris Lemachko Collection

MO-201 in May 1945 at Bornholm. Note 45mm 21-KM gun forward and 37mm 70-K gun aft.
Boris Lemachko Collection

Storozhevoj kater № 061 (formerly *№ 027*) in the choppy waters of the Black Sea, photographed between 2.7.1941 (when her number was changed) and her loss on 27.6.1941.
Przemysław Budzbon Collection

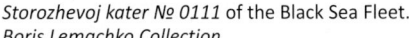

Above: Storozhevoj kater № 038 of the Black Sea Fleet, photographed in the first half of 1944 before her number was changed to *MO-69*. She was the former NKVD Border Guard patrol boat *PK-93* (until 9.1.1941 she carried the number *PK-282*), renumbered by the Navy *Storozhevoj kater № 069* on 26.7.1942, later changed to *№ 038* on 17.12.1943.
Jerzy Miciński Collection

Left: MO-108 of the Black Sea Fleet photographed after May 1944. Note her main armament of 45mm 21-KM guns.
Przemysław Budzbon Collection

13.0 Small submarines hunters

MO-4 type boats of the Black Sea Fleet. An *Artillerist* class *Project 122a Series I* boat scan be seen in the background left.
Przemysław Budzbon Collection

MO-432 and MO-434 of the Northern Fleet embarking troops. Photo taken after May 1944.
Boris Lemachko Collection

Storozhevoj kater № 031 of the Black Sea Fleet damaged off Kerch in Nov 1943. She was repaired, recommissioned, and renumbered *MO-31* on 7.5.1944. *Boris Lemachko Collection*

Storozhevoj kater № 0141 of the Black Sea Fleet damaged off Novorossiysk in Sept 1943. *Vitalij Kostrichenko Collection*

13.0 SMALL SUBMARINES HUNTERS

Above: The forward 45mm 21-K gun of an *MO-4* type boat during pre-war exercises.
Przemysław Budzbon Collection

Right: Close up of the after part of an *MO-4* type boat. Photo taken in 1942.
Vitalij Kostrichenko Collection

The NKVD Border Guard patrol boats detached to naval service but not commissioned.

NKVD No	YN	Built	Station	Remarks
PK-7 ex-*PK-239* (9.1.1941)		1937	Far East	Discarded 15.8.1956
PK-8 ex-*PK-240* (9.1.1941)		1937	Far East	Sunk 18.8.1945 by artillery fire off Shumshu Island
PK-9 ex-*PK-256* (9.1.1941)		1937	Far East	Discarded 15.8.1956
PK-10 ex-*PK-257* (9.1.1941)		1937	Far East	Discarded 15.8.1956
PK-11 ex-*PK-241* (9.1.1941)		1937	Far East	Discarded 7.3.1955
PK-12 ex-*PK-242* (9.1.1941)		1937	Far East	Discarded 7.3.1955
PK-13 ex-*PK-245* (9.1.1941)		1937	Far East	Discarded 16.3.1955
PK-16 ex-*PK-253* (9.1.1941)		1937	Far East	Discarded 16.3.1955
PK-17 ex-*PK-254* (9.1.1941)		1937	Far East	Stranded 15.1.1950
PK-18 ex-*PK-255* (9.1.1941)		1937	Far East	Discarded 17.9.1951
PK-19 ex-*PK-235* (9.1.1941)		1937	Far East	Discarded 16.3.1955
PK-23 ex-*PK-248* (9.1.1941)			Far East	Renumbered *PSKR-12* on 19.9.1957. Discarded 25.9.1959
PK-24 ex-*PK-249* (9.1.1941)			Far East	Renumbered *PSKR-14* on 19.9.1957. Discarded 25.9.1959
PK-28	43	1938	Far East	Renumbered *PSKR-18* on 19.9.1957. Discarded 1.11.1958
PK-29	44	1938	Far East	Discarded 10.1.1956
PK-30	43	1938	Far East	Discarded 7.3.1955
PK-33 ex-*PK-233* (9.1.1941)		1938	Far East	Renumbered *PSKR-20* on 19.9.1957. Discarded 17.6.1958
PK-34 ex-*PK-234* (9.1.1941)		1938	Far East	Discarded 16.3.1955
PK-35 ex-*PK-246* (9.1.1941)			Far East	Renumbered *PSKR-21* on 19.9.1957. Discarded 3.2.1958
PK-36 ex-*PK-247* (9.1.1941)			Far East	Discarded 7.3.1955
PK-38	70	1938	Far East	Renumbered *PSKR-22* on 19.9.1957. Discarded 10.8.1958
PK-39	71	1938	Far East	Renumbered *PSKR-23* on 19.9.1957. Discarded 10.8.1958
PK-40	72	1938	Far East	Renumbered *PSKR-24* on 19.9.1957. Discarded 27.9.1957
PK-41	73	1938	Far East	Discarded 7.3.1955
PK-42	74	1938	Far East	Renumbered *PSKR-25* on 19.9.1957. Discarded early 1960s
PK-61			Far East	Discarded 16.3.1955
PK-62			Far East	Discarded 16.3.1955
PK-63			Far East	Renumbered *PSKR-26* on 19.9.1957. Discarded 27.9.1957
PK-64			Far East	Discarded 16.3.1955
PK-65			Far East	Discarded 16.3.1955
PK-66			Far East	Renumbered *PSKR-27* on 19.9.1957. Discarded 3.2.1958
PK-233		1940	Baltic	Sunk before commissioning on 10.9.1941 by German aircraft in the Gulf of Vyborg
PK-234		1940	Baltic	Sunk before commissioning on 10.9.1941 by German aircraft in the Gulf of Vyborg
PK-235		1940	Baltic	Sunk before commissioning on 25.6.1941 by mine in the Gulf of Finland off the Shepelevskiy lighthouse

The design based on the *MO-2* type with numerous improvements relating to stability and seakeeping: flare was increased at bow and stern, depth of the hull was reduced by 100mm with engine foundations lowered by 200mm; aft recess was removed while construction of the weather deck fittings and gun reinforces was lightened.

The wooden hull comprised three layers of pine planking of 30mm total thickness, with longitudinal oak framing and steel foundations for engines and petrol tanks. The whole construction was exceptionally sturdy, which stood up well in real operating conditions carrying heavy loads close to well-defended enemy shores. The 3-shaft machinery plant was placed in two compartments, the forward one for the engines powering the outer shafts, the aft one housing the engine powering the centre shaft and auxiliary generator. The engine safe-life of 400 hours was extended in wartime conditions to 900 hours. A low speed could be attained within 30 seconds, the full speed within 5 minutes. The petrol tanks employed butt-joined and supply was improved by use of siphoned fuel feed with high pressure valves. From 1942 fuel tanks were fitted with an inert gas installation. Because of wartime shortages of GAM-34BS diesels, the wartime production boats were completed to the *Project 174* design, with two-shaft Packard diesel propulsion.

The pre-production series included four boats which were completed with twin rudder steering gear. However, following trials in the Gulf of Finland the steering gear was changed to a three-rudder arrangement. The boats ran final acceptance trials in the Black Sea and were accepted for mass production. In 1937 one boat was completed with a 3in gun and the trials lasted until 1940 when the plan to augment the main armament was rejected because of stability issues. During the war the MG outfit was increased up to 4, while later in the war the 45mm/46 21-K mountings were replaced by 45mm/68.5 21-KM long-barrelled guns with shields. In the closing stages of hostilities in the Black Sea the menace of German and Italian submarines diminished so 42 boats were fitted with additional AA weapons instead. The additional 20mm Oerlikon gun was mounted abaft the after 45mm mounting in place of M-1 DCs rack, but because of stability issues the pedestal was shortened by 400mm. Later they were replaced by 1in/83 72-K guns on 84-KM mounts. Some boats were fitted with four 8-M-8 82mm rocket launchers installed in pairs on each side of the bow forward of the 45mm gun.

The first boats were fitted with *Posejdon* or *Tsefej-2* hydrophones which could be used only with the boat hove-to. From 1940 they were fitted with the Tamir-1 type sonar and later with the British asdic Type 134A.

The boats numbered PK-1 (ex-*PK-225*), PK-2 (ex-*PK-226*), PK-4 (ex-*PK-228*), PK-6 (ex-*PK-230*), PK-21 (ex-*PK-237*), PK-22 (ex-*PK-238*), PK-31 (ex-*PK-231*), PK-32 (ex-*PK-232*) were operated by NKVD during the war.

MO-5

Displacement: 58t standard, 60t full load
Dimensions: 29.0 x 4.0 x 1.05m
Machinery: 3-shaft GAM-34BS petrol engines, 2550hp = 26kts. Range 495nm at 15kts
Armament: 2-45mm/46 21-K, 2-0.5in DShK MGs, 2 DC chutes, 8 BB-1 DCs, 24 BM-1 DCs
Complement: 21

MO № on Comm	MO №* 1941	No 1943-45	YN	Laid down	Launched	Comp	Comm	Fleet	Remarks
Builder: 5, Leningrad									
№ 113 ex-*MO-5* (1941)	№ 113	MO-113	1	1939	1940	lip.41	9.9.1941	B	YN 1, built for the NKVD Border Guard, taken over by the Navy on completion. Returned 4.7.1945 to the NKVD, renumbered *PK-213*. Discarded 11.1.1954

Enlarged MO-4 type, only the prototype was built.

MO-6 type (*Project 164*)

Displacement: 66t full load
Dimensions: 26.8 x 4.0 x 1.4m
Machinery: 3-shaft GAM-34FN petrol engines, 3600hp = 23kts. Range 700nm at 8kts
Armament: 2-45mm/68.5 21-KM, 2-0.5in DShK MGs, 2 DC chutes
Complement: 23

SKA № on Comm	SKA № 31.12.1943	SKA № 14.4.1944	No 7.5.1944	Laid down	Launched	Comp	Comm	Fleet	Remarks
Builder: 661, Balakhov									
№ 034	№ 024		MO-308	May 1942	Sum 1943	09.11.1943	25.11.1943	BS	Survived the war
№ 054	№ 0151		MO-151	Jun 1942	Sum 1943	14.10.1943	25.11.1943	BS	Survived the war
№ 061	№ 84	№ 061	MO-61	Jun 1942	Sum 1943	31.10.1943	27.11.1943	Cs BS	Trfd 30.12.1944 to the Black Sea Fleet
№ 0512	№ 0310[1] № 0172[2] № 024[3]	№ 0172	MO-172	May 1942	Sum 1943	Oct 1943	1943	Cs BS	Trfd 25.11.1943 to the Black Sea Fleet

Exceptions noted in the main table.

No	Year	Date	Fleet
1	1943	13.4.1943	
2		20.6.1943	
3		25.11.1943	

Steel-hulled version of the MO-4 type designed 1939/40 by the bureau of the NKVD Yard No 5. Series construction abandoned because of wartime shortage of steel.

13.2. The war-built standard types

OD-200 type (*Project P-26*)

Displacement: 47.2t full load
Dimensions: 23.4 x 4.0 x 1.35m
Machinery: 2-shaft Packard 4M-2500 petrol engines, 2400hp = 24.8kts (max 29.7kts for duration of 15 minutes), 2 Kermath cruising engines, 170hp = 9kts cruising speed. Petrol 6t, range 1500nm at 9kts
Armament: 1-37mm/67.5 70-K, 2-0.5in DShK MTU-2 MGs, 2 DC chutes, 12 BB-1 DCs, 24 BM-1 DCs
Sensors: Tamir-7 sonar (see note)
Complement: 22

No	No	YN	Laid down	Launched	Compl	Comm	Fleet	Remarks
SKA № on Comm	7.5.1944							
Builder: 640, Sosnovka								
№ 0361 ex-№ 011 (22.12.1943)	MO-361	103	Spr 1943	Nov 1943	22.12.1943	31.12.1943	BS	Delivered 5.11.1943 to Batum for completion. Conv 7.5.1944 to submarine hunter. Laid up 30.4.1948. Deleted 29.8.1949, trfd to the DOSFLOT as training boat
№ 0389 ex-№ 021 (22.12.1943)	MO-389	104	Spr 1944	Nov 1943	22.12.1943	29.2.1944	BS	Delivered 5.11.1943 to Batum for completion. Conv 7.5.1944 to submarine hunter. Deleted 29.9.1950, trfd to civilian service as service craft
№ 0375 ex-№ 041 (22.12.1943)	MO-375	106	Spr 1943	Nov 1943	22.12.1943	31.12.1943	BS	Delivered 5.11.1943 to Batum for completion. Conv 7.5.1944 to submarine hunter. Laid up 31.1.1947. Deleted 29.8.1949, trfd to the DOSFLOT as training boat
№ 0398 ex-№ 051 (22.12.1943)	MO-398	105	Spr 1944	Nov 1943	10.2.1944	29.2.1944	BS	Delivered 10.12.1943 to Batum for completion. Conv 7.5.1944 to submarine hunter. Conv 27.1.1947 to patrol boat *SK-398*? Deleted 25.11.1942

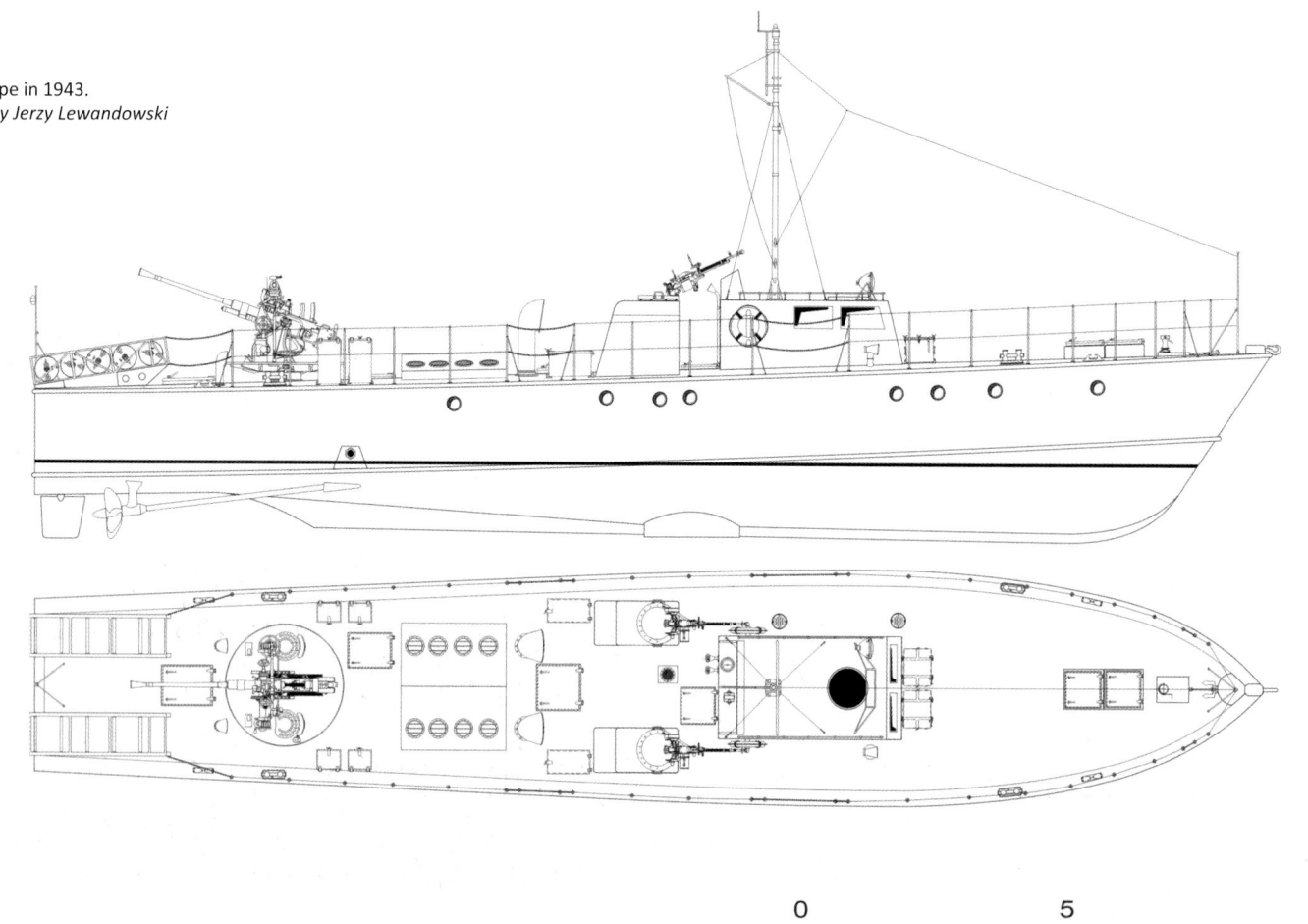

OD-200 type in 1943.
Drawing by Jerzy Lewandowski

13.0 SMALL SUBMARINES HUNTERS

№ 0340 ex-№ 061 (22.12.1943)	MO-340	107	Spr 1944	Nov 1943	10.2.1944	29.2.1944	BS	Delivered 10.12.1943 to Batum for completion. Conv 7.5.1944 to submarine hunter
№ 0354 ex-№ 071 (22.12.1943)	MO-354	108	Spr 1943	Dec 1943	10.2.1944	29.2.1944	BS	Delivered 10.12.1943 to Batum for completion. Conv 7.5.1944 to submarine hunter
№ 0317 ex-№ 092 (22.12.1943)	MO-317	101	Spr 1943	Nov 1943	22.12.1943	29.2.1944	BS	Delivered 10.12.1943 to Batum for completion. Conv 7.5.1944 to submarine hunter
№ 0336 ex-№ 0112 (22.12.1943)	MO-336	102	Spr 1943	Nov 1943	22.12.1943	29.2.1944	BS	Delivered 10.12.1943 to Batum for completion. Conv 7.5.1944 to submarine hunter
№ 0367 ex-№ 0121 (22.12.1943)	MO-367	109	Spr 1943	Dec 1943	10.2.1944	29.2.1944	BS	Delivered 5.11.1943 to Batum for completion. Conv 7.5.1944 to submarine hunter. Laid up 31.1.1947. Deleted 29.8.1949, trfd to the DOSFLOT as training boat
№ 0380 ex-№ 0131 (22.12.1943)	MO-380	110	Spr 1943	Dec 1943	10.2.1944	29.2.1944	BS	Delivered 10.12.1943 to Batum for completion. Conv 7.5.1944 to submarine hunter. Laid up 31.1.1947. Deleted 29.8.1949, trfd to the DOSFLOT as training boat
№ 0355	MO-355	100	Spr 1943	Aut 1943	1.1.1944	4.10.1943	Cs BS	Delivered 1.10.1943 to Baku for completion, trfd 29.2.1944 to the Black Sea Fleet. Laid up 31.1.1947, deleted 7.4.1950
№ 0356	MO-356	117	Sum 1943	Mar 1944	7.6.1944	14.6.1944	BS	Delivered 22.3.1944 to Batum for completion. Deleted 10.6.1955
№ 0385	MO-385	111	Sum 1943	Feb 1944	08.6.1944	14.6.1944	BS	Delivered 8.2.1944 to Batum for completion. Conv 7.5.1944 to submarine hunter. Laid up 31.1.1947, deleted 7.4.1950, trfd to the DOSFLOT as training boat
№ 0393	MO-393	112	Sum 1943	Feb 1944	30.3.1944	14.6.1944	BS	Delivered 8.2.1944 to Batum for completion. Conv 7.5.1944 to submarine hunter. Laid up 31.1.1947, deleted 7.4.1950, trfd to the DOSFLOT as training boat
MO Zav № 150		150	1943	Spr 1944	Sum 1944	30.9.1944	B	Conv 7.10.1948 to experimental boat *ISK-35*, renumbered *OK-18* on 24.5.1950. Deleted 10.7.1956
MO-211		175	1944	Jul 1945	Aug 1945	15.8.1945	P	Delivered 1.7.1945 to Vladivostok. Converted 1.11.1949 to smoke-screen layer boat *DZ-10*. Deleted 28.2.1961
MO-216		176	1944	Sum 1944	Aut 1945	3.11.1945	P	Conv 27.12.1956 to patrol boat *SK-216*. Deleted 12.3.1958
MO-217		177	1944	Sum 1944	Aut 1945	3.11.1945	P	Conv 27.12.1956 to patrol boat *SK-217*. Deleted 12.3.1958
MO-218		178	1944	Sum 1944	Aut 1945	3.11.1945	P	Conv 27.12.1956 to patrol boat *SK-218*. Deleted 12.3.1958
MO-219		179	1944	Sum 1945	Aut 1945	3.11.1945	P	Conv 27.12.1956 to patrol boat *SK-219*. Deleted 12.3.1958
MO-220		180	1944	Spr 1944	Sum 1945	11.8.1945	P	Conv 23.1.1956 to experimental boat *OK-41*. Deleted 25.8.1956
MO-221		181	1944	Spr 1944	Sum 1945	11.8.1945	P	Conv 23.1.1956 to experimental boat *OK-42*. Deleted 25.8.1956
MO-224		182	1944	Sum 1945	Aut 1945	3.11.1945	P	Conv 27.12.1956 to patrol boat *SK-224*. Deleted 12.3.1958
MO-225		183	1944	Sum 1945	Aut 1945	3.11.1945	P	Conv 27.12.1956 to patrol boat *SK-225*. Deleted 12.3.1958
MO-226		184	1944	Sum 1945	Aut 1945	3.11.1945	P	Deleted 31.7.1956

Launching of an *OD-200* type boat in 1943 at the No 640 Yard at Sosnovets. *Przemysław Budzbon Collection*

MO-328 in April 1946. *Jerzy Miciński Collection*

No SKA № on Comm	No 7.5.1944	YN	Laid down	Launched	Compl	Comm	Fleet	Remarks
MO-229		185	1944	Sum 1945	Aut 1945	3.11.1945	P	Deleted 31.7.1956
MO-230		156	Spr 1944	Aut 1944	1.2.1945	15.3.1945	Cs	Trfd 31.8.1951 to Bulgaria
MO-231		157	Spr 1944	Aut 1944	1.2.1945	15.3.1945	Cs	Trfd 29.9.1951 to the Pacific Fleet. Conv 27.12.1956 to patrol boat *SK-227*. Deleted 13.3.1958
MO-232		158	Spr 1944	Aut 1944	1.2.1945	15.3.1945	Cs	Trfd 31.8.1951 to Bulgaria
MO-233		159	Spr 1944	Aut 1944	1.2.1945	15.3.1945	Cs	Trfd 29.9.1951 to the Pacific Fleet. Trfd 16.7.1954 to North Korea
MO-234		160	Spr 1944	Aut 1944	1.2.1945	15.3.1945	Cs	Trfd 29.9.1951 to the Pacific Fleet. Trfd 16.7.1954 to North Korea
MO-235		161	Spr 1944	Aut 1944	1.2.1945	15.3.1945	Cs	Trfd 29.9.1951 to the Pacific Fleet. Conv 27.12.1956 to patrol boat *SK-238*. Deleted 13.3.1958
MO-236		162	Sum 1944	Jun 1945	Jul 1945	4.8.1945	P	Delivered 30.5.1945 to Vladivostok. Conv 27.12.1956 to patrol boat *SK-229*. Deleted 12.3.1958
MO-237		163	Sum 1944	Jun 1945	Jul 1945	4.8.1945	P	Delivered 30.5.1945 to Vladivostok. Deleted 10.6.1955
MO-238		164	Sum 1944	Jun 1945	Jul 1945	4.8.1945	P	Delivered 30.5.1945 to Vladivostok. Deleted 18.10.1956
MO-239		165	Sum 1944	Jun 1945	Jul 1945	4.8.1945	P	Delivered 30.5.1945 to Vladivostok. Deleted 18.10.1956
MO-240		166	Sum 1944	Jun 1945	Jul 1945	4.8.1945	P	Delivered 30.5.1945 to Vladivostok. Deleted 7.4.1956
MO-241		167	Sum 1944	Jun 1945	Jul 1945	4.8.1945	P	Delivered 30.5.1945 to Vladivostok. Conv 27.12.1956 to patrol boat *SK-220*. Deleted 12.3.1958
MO-242		168	Sum 1944	Jun 1945	Jul 1945	4.8.1945	P	Delivered 30.5.1945 to Vladivostok. Deleted 6.2.1950
MO-243		169	Sum 1944	Jun 1945	Jul 1945	4.8.1945	P	Delivered 30.5.1945 to Vladivostok. Deleted 7.4.1956
MO-244		170	Sum 1944	Jul 1945	Aug 1945	4.8.1945	P	Delivered 1.7.1945 to Vladivostok. Deleted 6.2.1950
MO-245		171	Sum 1944	Jul 1945	Aug 1945	4.8.1945	P	Delivered 1.7.1945 to Vladivostok. Deleted 7.4.1956
MO-246		172	Sum 1944	Jul 1945	Aug 1945	4.8.1945	P	Delivered 1.7.1945 to Vladivostok. Conv 27.12.1956 to patrol boat *SK-246*. Deleted 12.3.1958
MO-247		173	Sum 1944	Jul 1945	Aug 1945	4.8.1945	P	Delivered 1.7.1945 to Vladivostok. Deleted 6.2.1950
MO-248		174	Sum 1944	Jul 1945	Aug 1945	4.8.1945	P	Delivered 1.7.1945 to Vladivostok. Converted 1.11.1949 to smoke-screen layer boat *DZ-11*. Deleted 30.12.1955

MO-354 in 1944 following cessation of hostilities in the Black Sea. *Vitalij Kostrichenko Collection*

13.0 SMALL SUBMARINES HUNTERS

MO-249	186	1944	Sum 1945	Aut 1945	3.11.1945	P	Delivered 1945 to Vladivostok. Conv 27.12.1956 to patrol boat *SK-226*. Deleted 12.3.1958
MO-250	187	1944	Sum 1945	Aut 1945	3.11.1945	P	Delivered 1945 to Vladivostok. Deleted 31.7.1954
MO-321	122	1943	Apr 1944	7.6.1944	14.6.1944	BS	Delivered 30.3.1944 to Batum for completion. Deleted 10.7.1954
MO-322	123	1943	Apr 1944	7.6.1944	14.6.1944	BS	Delivered 30.3.1944 to Batum for completion. Deleted 30.12.1955
MO-323	124	1943	Apr 1944	12.6.1944	14.6.1944	BS	Delivered 30.3.1944 to Batum for completion. Conv 27.1.1947 to patrol boat *SK-631*. Deleted 21.5.1956
MO-324	125	1943	Apr 1944	7.6.1944	14.6.1944	BS B	Delivered 30.3.1944 to Batum for completion. Trfd 10.11.1944 to the Baltic Fleet, conv to 19.2.1958 to training boat *USK-324*. Deleted 19.1.1959
MO-325	126	1943	Apr 1944	20.7.1944	25.7.1944	BS B	Delivered 20.4.1944 to Batum for completion. Trfd 13.11.1944 to the Baltic Fleet. Trfd 5.4.1946 to Poland, renamed *Bezwzględny*. Deleted 25.1.1959
MO-326	127	1943	Apr 1944	06.8.1944	7.8.1944	BS B	Delivered 20.4.1944 to Batum for completion. Trfd 13.11.1944 to the Baltic Fleet. Trfd 5.4.1946 to Poland, renamed *Bystry*. Deleted 25.1.1959
MO-327	128	1943	Apr 1944	06.8.1944	7.8.1944	BS B	Delivered 20.4.1944 to Batum for completion. Trfd 13.11.1944 to the Baltic Fleet. Trfd 5.4.1946 to Poland, renamed *Dziarski*. Deleted 1959
MO-328	129	1943	Apr 1944	17.7.1944	25.7.1944	BS B	Delivered 20.4.1944 to Batum for completion. Trfd 13.11.1944 to the Baltic Fleet. Trfd 5.4.1946 to Poland, renamed *Dzielny*. Deleted 1959.
MO-329	130	1943	Apr 1944	7.9.1944	8.9.1944	BS B	Delivered 20.4.1944 to Batum for completion. Trfd 13.11.1944 to the Baltic Fleet. Trfd 5.4.1946 to Poland, renamed *Karny*. Deleted 25.1.1959
MO-357	118	1943	Mar 1944	24.5.1944	17.6.1944	BS	Delivered 22.3.1944 to Batum for completion. Conv 24.4.1955 to damage control training station *KBP-45*
MO-358	119	1943	Mar 1944	7.6.1944	14.6.1944	BS	Delivered 22.3.1944 to Batum for completion. Conv 12.3.1955 to patrol boat *SK-358*. Deleted 10.6.1958
MO-359	120	1943	Mar 1944	2.6.1944	14.6.1944	BS	Delivered 22.3.1944 to Batum for completion. Conv 24.4.1955 to damage control training station *KBP-46*

MO-231 in the Caspian Sea after the war. *Vitalij Kostrichenko Collection*

No SKA № on Comm	No 7.5.1944	YN	Laid down	Launched	Compl	Comm	Fleet	Remarks
MO-360		145	1943	Aug 1944	27.10.1944	31.12.1944	BS	Delivered 2.8.1944 to Batum for completion. Laid up 30.1.1947, deleted 21.7.1949, trfd to the DOSFLOT as training boat
MO-362		121	1943	Mar 1944	7.6.1944	14.6.1944	BS	Delivered 22.3.1944 to Batum for completion. Deleted 7.4.1950, trfd to the DOSFLOT as training boat
MO-368		131	1943	May 1944	25.7.1944	8.9.1944	BS B	Delivered 22.3.1944 to Batum for completion. Trfd 13.12.1944 to the Baltic Fleet. Trfd 5.4.1946 to Poland, renamed *Niedościgły*. Deleted 15.4.1960
MO-369		132	1943	May 1944	19.8.1944	23.9.1944	BS B	Delivered 15.5.1944 to Batum for completion. Trfd 13.12.1944 to the Baltic Fleet. Trfd 5.4.1946 to Poland, renamed *Nieuchwytny*. Deleted 25.1.1959
MO-370		133	1943	May 1944	12.8.1944	8.9.1944	BS B	Delivered 15.5.1944 to Batum for completion. Trfd 13.12.1944 to the Baltic Fleet. Trfd 5.4.1946 to Poland, renamed *Odważny*. Deleted 15.4.1960
MO-371		134	1943	May 1944	12.8.1944	8.9.1944	BS B	Delivered 15.5.1944 to Batum for completion. Trfd 13.12.1944 to the Baltic Fleet. Trfd 5.4.1946 to Poland, renamed *Śmiały*. Deleted 15.4.1960
MO-376		113	1943	Feb 1944	7.4.1944	7.5.1944	BS	Name: *Buzulukskij Komsomolets*. Torpedoed 13.5.1944 by submarine off Poti, the stern part sank, the bow towed to Poti. Deleted 5.6.1944
MO-377		114	1943	Feb 1944	18.5.1944	17.6.1944	BS	Delivered 8.2.1944 to Batum for completion. Laid up 30.4.1948, deleted 21.8.1949, trfd to the DOSFLOT as training boat
MO-378		115	1943	Feb 1944	18.5.1944	17.6.1944	BS	Delivered 8.2.1944 to Batum for completion. Laid up 31.7.1947, deleted 7.4.1950, trfd to the DOSFLOT as training boat
MO-379		116	1943	Feb 1944	11.5.1944	17.6.1944	BS	Delivered 8.2.1944 to Batum for completion. Deleted 29.9.1950, trfd to civilian service as craft
MO-461		148	1944	Sum 1944	Aut 1944	9.10.1944	N	Training boat until 16.2.1945. Laid up 26.2.1948. Deleted 14.3.1953
MO-462		149	1944	Sum 1944	Aut 1944	9.10.1944	N	Training boat until 16.2.1945. Laid up 26.2.1948. Deleted 14.3.1953
MO-547		135	1943	Jul 1944	12.8.1944	1.9.1944	BS	Delivered 1.7.1944 to Batum for completion. Laid up 31.1.1947, deleted 4.8.1949, trfd to the DOSFLOT as training boat
MO-548		136	1943	Jul 1944	17.8.1944	1.9.1944	BS	Delivered 1.7.1944 to Batum for completion. Deleted 4.8.1949, trfd to the DOSFLOT as training boat

MO-328 in Apr 1946 during transfer to Poland. *Jerzy Miciński Collection*

13.0 SMALL SUBMARINES HUNTERS

MO-549	137	1943	Jul 1944	18.8.1944	1.9.1944	BS	Delivered 1.7.1944 to Batum for completion. Deleted 21.7.1949, trfd to the DOSFLOT as training boat
MO-550	138	1943	Jul 1944	31.8.1944	30.9.1944	BS	Delivered 1.7.1944 to Batum for completion. Conv 27.1.1947 to patrol boat *SK-635*. Deleted 10.7.1956
MO-551	139	1943	Jul 1944	31.8.1944	30.9.1944	BS	Delivered 1.7.1944 to Batum for completion. Conv 27.1.1947 to patrol boat *SK-636*. Deleted 6.8.1958
MO-552	140	1943	Jul 1944	18.8.1944	23.9.1944	BS B	Delivered 1.7.1944 to Batum for completion. Trfd 13.12.1944 to the Baltic Fleet. Trfd 5.4.1946 to Poland, renamed *Sprawny*. Deleted 15.4.1960
MO-553	141	1943	Jul 1944	23.8.1944	23.9.1944	BS B	Delivered 1.7.1944 to Batum for completion. Trfd 13.12.1944 to the Baltic Fleet. Trfd 5.4.1946 to Poland, renamed *Szybki*. Deleted 15.4.1960
MO-554	142	1943	Jul 1944	31.8.1944	30.9.1944	BS	Delivered 1.7.1944 to Batum for completion. Laid up 31.1.1947, deleted 7.4.1950, trfd to the DOSFLOT as training boat
MO-555	143	1943	Aug 1944	07.10.1944	27.10.1944	BS	Delivered 2.8.1944 to Batum for completion. Conv 27.1.1947 to patrol boat *SK-637*. Deleted 10.5.1955
MO-556	144	1943	Aug 1944	21.10.1944	27.10.1944	BS	Delivered 2.8.1944 to Batum for completion. Conv 27.1.1947 to patrol boat *SK-638*. Deleted 10.6.1955
MO-558	146	1944	Aug 1944	07.10.1944	28.10.1944	BS	Delivered 2.8.1944 to Batum for completion. Conv 27.1.1947 to patrol boat *SK-639*. Deleted 6.3.1958
MO-559	147	1944	Aug 1944	03.10.1944	28.10.1944	BS	Delivered 2.8.1944 to Batum for completion. Conv 27.1.1947 to patrol boat *SK-640*. Deleted 21.5.1956
MO-563	151	1944	Oct 1944	27.11.1944	28.10.1944	BS	Delivered 2.8.1944 to Batum for completion. Laid up 31.1.1947, deleted 21.7.1949, trfd to the DOSFLOT as training boat
MO-564	152	1944	Oct 1944	27.11.1944	11.12.1944	BS	Delivered 18.10.1944 to Batum for completion. Trfd 30.12.1947 to Bulgaria
MO-565	153	1944	Oct 1944	01.12.1944	11.12.1944	BS	Delivered 18.10.1944 to Batum for completion. Sank 27.11.1947 in a gale off Nikolaev, raised and recomm. Laid up 30.4.1948. Deleted 19.4.1950
MO-566	154	1944	Oct 1944	30.11.1944	11.12.1944	BS	Delivered 18.10.1944 to Batum for completion. Trfd 30.12.1947 to Bulgaria
MO-567	155	1944	Oct 1944	30.11.1944	11.12.1944	BS	Delivered 18.10.1944 to Batum for completion. Sank 27.11.1947 in a gale off Nikolaev, raised and recomm. Deleted 30.12.1955

The wooden-hulled version of the *Project 200* design of the unitary MTB/subchaser (see chapter on MTBs). The design was produced by the construction bureau at Yd No 640 at Sosnovka (900km east of Moscow) where part of the NKVD Yd No 5 was evacuated. OD-200 stands for Okhotnik Dereviannyj 200 = Subchaser Wooden 200).

The prototype boat run trials on the Caspian Sea, and the series production began in 1943. The whole series was built under conditions of shortages – of skilled workers, quality materials and fittings. The use of unseasoned timber for their construction adversely affected the strength and life of the hulls. The late-war production boats received the newer types of sonar: *Tamir-8* and *Tamir-9*.

The design was considered poor by the Navy so numerous changes were introduced in the follow-on *Project 201*. It was planned to start production in 1944, but this did not happen. Instead, after the war the design was modified by adopting Soviet M-50 type diesels and increasing the armament by adding a 1in/83 72-K gun on 84-KM mounting forward and replacing single DShK turrets with the twin MSTU type. In total, 63-boats of the *OD-200-bis* were built during 1946-1948.

Details of *OD-200* type boats at Gdynia, April 1946.
Jerzy Miciński Collection

BMO type (*Project 194*) — *Armoured submarine hunters*

Displacement: 55.2t full load
Dimensions: 24.8 x 4.2 x 1.6m
Machinery: 2-shaft Packard 4M-2500 petrol engines, 2400hp = 21kts, 1-shaft ZIS-5 50hp cruising engine. Petrol 7.2t, range 1330nm at 8.4kts
Armament: 1-37mm/67.5 70-K, 1-0.5in DShK MG, 4-0.5in Colt (2x2) MGs, 2 DC chutes, 16 BB-1 DCs, could carry 10 KB-3 mines (see note)
Armour: side 10mm, deck 8mm, CT sides 12mm, roof 10mm
Sensors: Tamir-7 or Tamir-8 asdic
Complement: 24

No	No	YN	Laid down	Launched	Comp	Fleet	Remarks
on Comm	23.01.1945						
Builder: 196, Leningrad							
SK-318 ex-№ 318 (19.4.1943)	166		Sum 1942	1942	21.6.1943	B	Mined 30.10.1943 off Tytärsaari Island
SK-418 ex-№ 418 (19.4.1943)	MO-418	161	Sum 1942	5.11.1942	21.6.1943	B	Deleted 6.10.1949
SK-501	MO-501	167	Sum 1942	1942	13.6.1943	B	Deleted 6.10.1949
SK-502	MO-502	168	Sum 1942	Spr 1943	21.6.1943	B	Deleted 6.10.1949
SK-503		169	Aut 1942	Spr 1943	30.6.1943	B	Mined 4.7.1944 off Teikarsaari Island
SK-504	MO-504	170	Aut 1942	Spr 1943	20.7.1943	B	Deleted 6.10.1949
SK-505	MO-505	171	1942	Spr 1943	19.8.1943	B	Deleted 6.10.1949
SK-506		172	1942	Spr 1943	30.7.1943	B	Sunk 1.7.1944 by mine off Teikarsaari Island.
SK-507	MO-507	173	1942	Spr 1943	30.7.1943	B	Deleted 6.10.1949
SK-508	MO-508	174	1942	Spr 1943	31.8.1943	B	Deleted 9.8.1955
SK-509	MO-509	175	1942	Spr 1943	31.8.1943	B	Deleted 9.8.1955
SK-510		176	1943	Spr 1943	18.9.1943	B	Sunk 14.2.1944 by artillery fire off Meriküla
SK-511		177	1943	Spr 1943	28.9.1943	B	Sunk 14.2.1944 by artillery fire off Meriküla
SK-512		178	1943	Spr 1943	18.9.1943	B	Sunk 17.10.1944 by *U-1165* NW off Cape Suurupi
SK-513	MO-513	179	1943	Sum 1943	19.10.1943	B	Deleted 7.4.1956
SK-514	MO-514	180	1943	Sum 1943	30.10.1943	B	Deleted 9.8.1955
SK-515	MO-515	181	1943	Sum 1943	31.10.1943	B	Deleted 9.8.1955
SK-516	MO-516	182	1943	Sum 1943	28.11.1943	B	Deleted 28.11.1957
SK-517		183	1943	Sum 1943	30.11.1943	B	Sunk 9.6.1944 by mine off the Vigrund Bight
SK-518	MO-518	184	1943	Sum 1943	30.11.1943	B	Deleted 28.11.1957
SK-519	MO-519	185	1943	Aut 1943	15.12.1943	B	Deleted 28.11.1957
SK-520	MO-520	186	Oct 1943	Spr 1944	28.5.1944	B	Name: *Chkalovets*. Deleted 28.11.1957
SK-521	MO-521	187	Nov 1943	Spr 1944	26.6.1944	B	Name: *Iunyj chkalovets*, renamed *Chkalovskij komsomolets* on 22.5.1944. Deleted 28.11.1957
SK-522		188	Nov 1943	Spr 1944	14.6.1944	B	Name: *Chkalovskij pionier*. Mined 6.8.1944 in Narva Bay
SK-523	MO-523	189	Dec 1943	Spr 1944	26.7.1944	B	Name: *Khabarovskij komsomol*. Deleted 25.9.1950
SK-524		190	Nov 1943	Spr 1944	14.6.1944	B	Name: *Baltiets*. Sunk 4.8.1944 by German aircraft in Narva Bay
SK-525	MO-525	191	Dec 1943	Spr 1944	30.6.1944	B	Name: *Geroj Sovetskogo Soiuza Kotov*. Sunk in Jun 1945 by mine off Danzig. Apparently raised and recomm. Deleted 28.11.1957
SK-526	MO-526	192	Jan 1944	Spr 1944	30.6.1944	B	Deleted 9.8.1955
SK-527	MO-527	193	Jan 1944	Spr 1944	31.7.1944.	B	Name: *Tambovskij osoaviakhimovets*. Sunk 17.10.1944 by *U-1165* off Naissaar Island
SK-528	MO-528	194	Feb 1944	June 1944	31.7.1944	B	Deleted 11.6.1957
SK-529	MO-529	195	1944	July 1944	20.8.1944	B	Training boat from 12.9.1945. Deleted 28.11.1953
SK-530	MO-530	196	1944	Spr 1944	26.6.1944	B	Name: *Konstruktor-sudostroitiel'*. Deleted 11.6.1957
SK-531	MO-531	197	1944	Spr 1944	30.6.1944	B	Deleted 7.4.1956
SK-532	MO-532	198	1944	Spr 1944	29.6.1944	B	Deleted 9.8.1955
MO-533		199	1944	Spr 1944	21.7.1944	B	Deleted 9.8.1955
MO-534		200	1944	Spr 1944	31.7.1944	B	Deleted 9.8.1955
MO-535		201	1944	Spr 1944	26.8.1944	B	Deleted 28.11.1953
MO-536		202	1944	June 1944	31.8.1944	B	Deleted 28.11.1953
MO-537		203	1944	June 1944	31.8.1944	B	Deleted 28.11.1953
MO-538		204	Spr 1944	Sum 1944	25.9.1944	B	Name: *Sovetskij staratiel'*. Deleted 28.11.1953
MO-539		205	Spr 1944	Sum 1944	30.9.1944	B	Deleted 28.11.1953
MO-540		206	Spr 1944	Sum 1944	30.9.1944	B	Deleted 9.8.1955
MO-541		207	Spr 1944	Sum 1944	21.10.1944	B	Deleted 7.4.1956
MO-542		208	Spr 1944	Sum 1944	29.10.1944	B	Deleted 9.8.1955

13.0 SMALL SUBMARINES HUNTERS

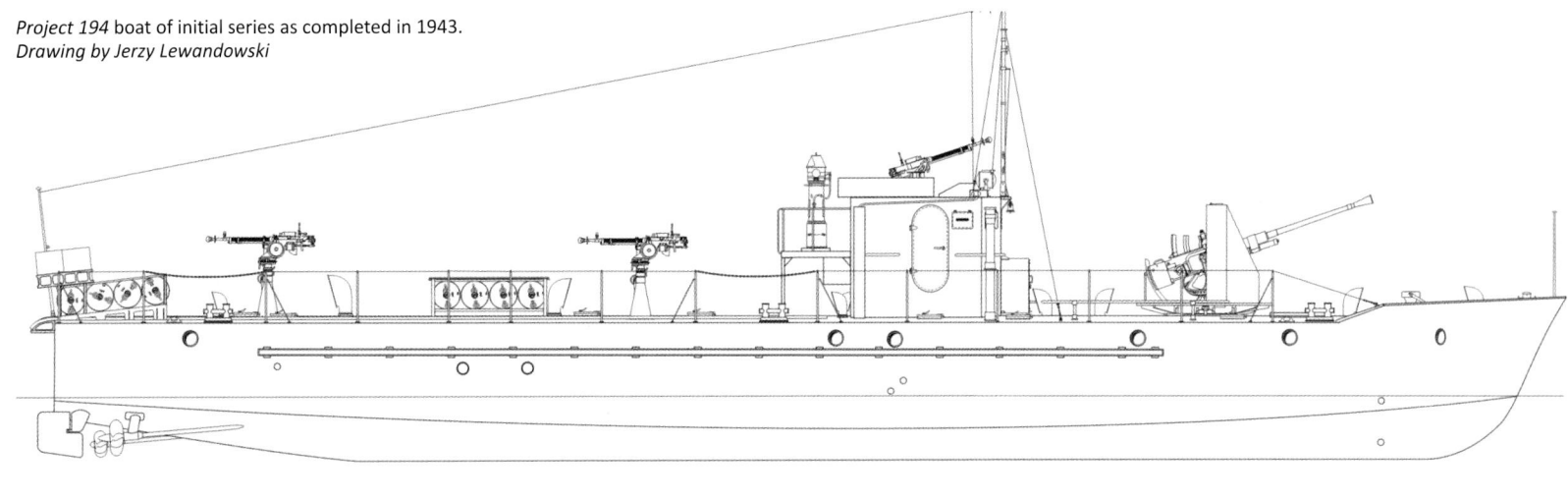

Project 194 boat of initial series as completed in 1943.
Drawing by Jerzy Lewandowski

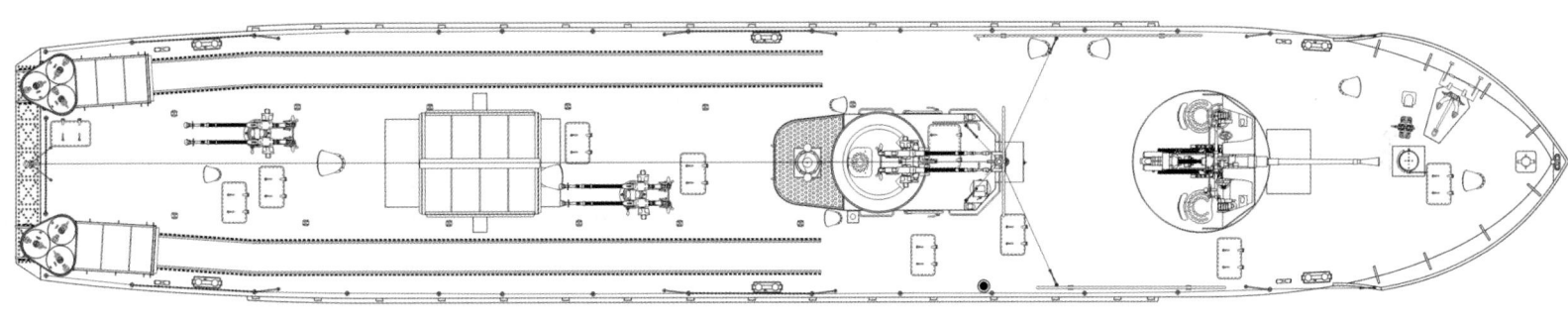

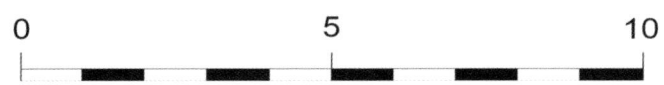

MO-543	209	Spr 1944	Sum 1944	31.10.1944	B	Deleted 9.8.1955
MO-544	210	Spr 1944	Sum 1944	31.10.1944	B	Deleted 9.8.1955
MO-545	211	Spr 1944	Sum 1944	29.11.1944	B	Sunk 2.7.1945 by mine off Pillau
MO-546	212	Spr 1944	Sum 1944	30.11.1944	B	Trfd 18.4.1946 to Poland, comm as *Błyskawiczny*. Deleted Apr 1960
MO-621	213	1944	Spr 1945	Jun 1945	B	Comm 3.7.1945. Deleted 24.7.1954
MO-622	214	1944	Sum 1945	Jun 1945	B	Comm 6.10.1945. Deleted 29.12.1954
MO-623	215	1944	Sum 1945	Sept 1945	B	Comm 6.10.1945. Deleted 24.7.1954
MO-624	216	1944	Sum 1945	Jun 1945	B	Comm 6.10.1945. Deleted 29.12.1954
MO-625	217	1944	Spr 1945	Jun 1945	B	Comm 3.7.1945. Deleted 24.7.1954
MO-626	218	1944	Spr 1945	Jun 1945	B	Comm 3.7.1945. Deleted 24.7.1954
MO-627	219	1945	Spr 1945	Sum 1945	B	Comm 5.9.1945. Deleted 24.7.1954
MO-628	220	1945	Spr 1945	Aug 1945	B	Comm 5.9.1945. Deleted 24.7.1954
MO-629	221	1945	Spr 1945	Aug 1945	B	Comm 5.9.1945. Renumbered *KBP-376* on 28.1.1955. Deleted 25.8.1956
MO-630	222	1945	Spr 1945	Jul 1945	B	Comm 4.8.1945. Deleted 24.7.1954
MO-631	223	1945	Spr 1945	Aug 1945	B	Comm 5.9.1945. Deleted 24.7.1954
MO-632	224	1945	Spr 1945	Aug 1945	B	Comm 5.9.1945. Renumbered *KBP-377* on 28.1.1955. Deleted 25.8.1956
MO-633	225	Spr 1945	Sum 1945	Sep 1945	B	Comm 6.10.1945. Deleted 29.12.1954
MO-634	226	Spr 1945	Sum 1945	Oct 1945	B	Comm 3.11.1945. Renumbered *KTs-20* on 15.10.1952. Deleted 16.9.1957
MO-635	227	Spr 1945	Sum 1945	Oct 1945	B	Comm 3.11.1945. Renumbered *KTs-30* on 15.10.1952. Deleted 16.9.1957
MO-636	230	Spr 1945	Sum 1945	Oct 1945	B	Comm 3.11.1945. Deleted 28.11.1953
MO-637	231	Spr 1945	Sum 1945	Oct 1945	B	Comm 30.11.1945. Deleted 24.7.1954
MO-638	232	Spr 1945	Sum 1945	Oct 1945	B	Comm 30.11.1945. Deleted 29.7.1954

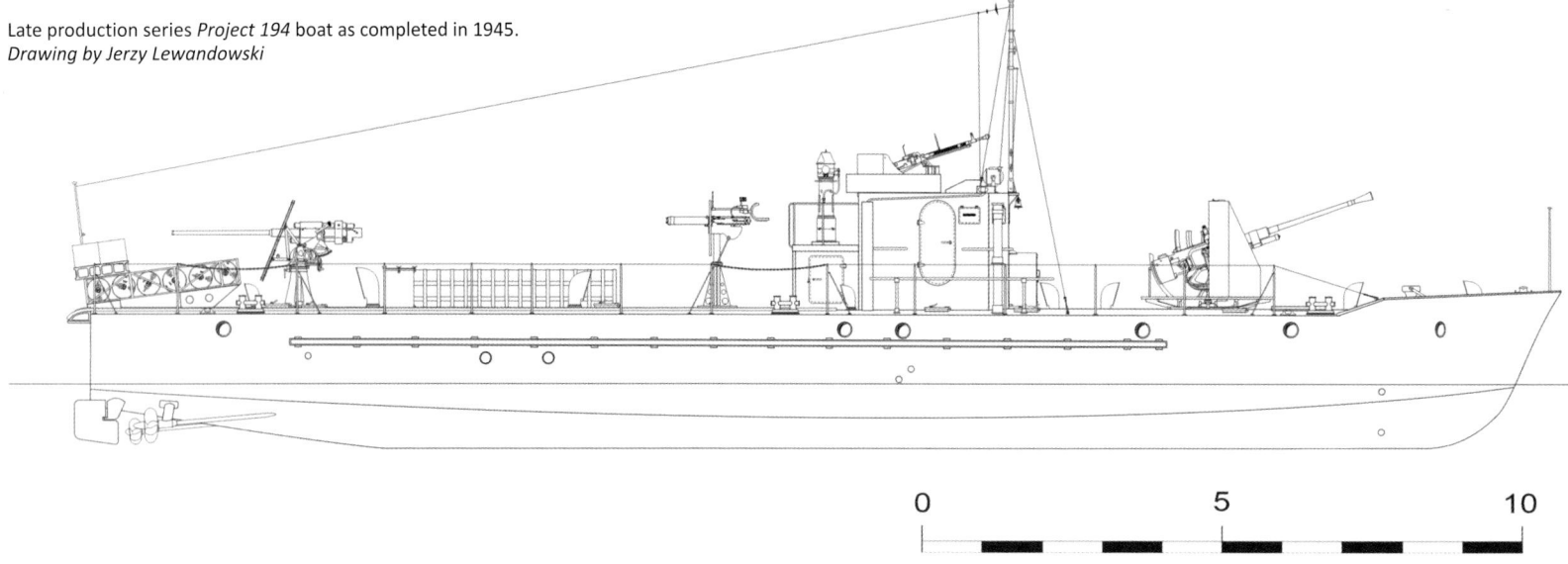

Late production series *Project 194* boat as completed in 1945. *Drawing by Jerzy Lewandowski*

The experience gained from 1941 operations of *MO-2* and *MO-4* type subchasers in the Baltic Fleet led to the conclusion that it was necessary to increase armament and above all to introduce protection against automatic and light infantry weapons. This was not possible to achieve on existing boats while the *P-10* design had no margin for such modifications. Therefore, in June 1942 the War Soviet of the Leningrad Front issued characteristics for a new type of armoured subchaser, called BMO (Bronirovannyj Malyj Okhotnik = Armoured Small Subchaser). The design coded *Project 194* was produced by the bureau of Yard No 196 (Sudomekh) at Leningrad and the technical project was approved on 24.8.1942. The steel-hulled boat had an armoured citadel around the machinery and the fuel tank spaces and the CT was protected as well, offering a much better defence than was the case for the *Project 1124* and *Project 1125* AMGBs. Unused armour plates designated for light tanks was used, as production this type of tank had been discontinued. The power plant included a 50hp ZIS-5 type cruising engine, which was replaced in 1944 it by a Lend-Lease Continental Motors Kermath 93hp engine.

In contrast to the *D-3* type its derivatives, the main 37mm gun was mounted forward of the CT thus offering a good firing position in close combat. However, that was at the cost of the boat trimming by the head and shipping water forward, while the gun crews had practically no protection against even light fire. In some boats the aft MG was replaced by a 45mm/68.6 21-KM type gun or two additional DShK MGs in twin MSTU turrets added atop the CT. To carry mines, the mine rails required the DC chutes to be rearranged, with one landed and the second moved to the centreline.

The prototype was launched on 5.11.1942, five weeks after the first steel was cut, while the first sea trials began in Kronshtadt at the end of the month. The series production was ordered on 16.12.1942 in batches of six, with the lead time from three to six months per boat. The whole project was an impressive production achievement, considering conditions in the besieged city of Leningrad. Because of their armour protection the boats were nicknamed 'irons' and were tactically designated to provide protection against enemy S-boats or R-boats. In practice they were often forced to withdraw under cover of a smokescreen as their armour was inadequate against automatic 20mm and 40mm guns.

Production was cancelled after the cessation of hostilities and the whole concept was discontinued in favour of seagoing AMGBs.

SK-508 during the war. *Boris Lemachko Collection*

BMO type in a choppy sea. *Przemysław Budzbon Collection*

13.0 Small submarines hunters

Cross reference: rated as small submarine hunters

MO № No	Details	Type	From	To	Fate
MO-588 – MO-593	D-3 Project P-19-OK	MTB	21.10.1944		Survived the war
MO-594	D-3 Project P-19-OK	MTB	28.11.1944	24.12.1944	Lost
MO-595	D-3 Project P-19-OK	MTB	28.11.1944	6.5.1945	Lost
MO-596	D-3 Project P-19-OK	MTB	28.11.1944		Survived the war
MO-600	D-3 Project P-19-OK	MTB	1944		Survived the war
MO-601	D-3 Project P-19-OK	MTB	1944		Survived the war
MO-603 – MO-611	D-3 Project P-19-OK	MTB	31.12.1945		Survived the war
MO-613 – MO-617	D-3 Project P-19-OK	MTB	31.12.1945		Survived the war
№ 12	D-3 Project P-19	MTB	17.11.1942	6.10.1944	Conv to patrol boat SK-181
№ 22	D-3 Project P-19	MTB	17.11.1942	6.10.1944	Conv to patrol boat SK-185
№ 32	D-3 Project P-19	MTB	17.11.1942	6.10.1944	Conv to patrol boat SK-183
№ 42	D-3 Project P-19-O	MTB	20.8.1943		Survived the war
№ 52	D-3 Project P-19-O	MTB	30.7.1943		Survived the war
№ 62	D-3 Project P-19-O	MTB	30.7.1943	18.11.1944	Lost
№ 72	D-3 Project P-19-O	MTB	30.7.1943		Survived the war
№ 82	D-3 Project P-19-O	MTB	30.7.1943		Survived the war
№ 92	D-3 Project P-19-O	MTB	30.7.1943		Survived the war
№ 102	D-3 Project P-19	MTB	17.11.1942	6.10.1944	Conv to patrol boat SK-102
№ 112	D-3 Project P-19	MTB	17.11.1942	6.10.1944	Conv to patrol boat SK-112
№ 122	D-3 Project P-19-O	MTB	20.8.1943	14.5.1944	Lost
№ 132	D-3 Project P-19-O	MTB	30.7.1943		Survived the war
№ 142	D-3 Project P-19-O	MTB	20.8.1943		Survived the war
№ 152	D-3 Project P-19-O	MTB	20.8.1943		Survived the war
№ 162	D-3 Project P-19-O	MTB	20.8.1943		Survived the war
№ 164	SM-4	MTB	26.6.1942	11.8.1943	Reverted to MTB
SK-171	D-3 Project P-19-O	MTB	14.7.1944		Survived the war
SK-172	D-3 Project P-19-O	MTB	14.7.1944		Survived the war
SK-173	D-3 Project P-19-O	MTB	14.7.1944		Survived the war
SK-174	D-3 Project P-19-O	MTB	14.7.1944		Survived the war
SK-175	D-3 Project P-19-O	MTB	20.1.1944		Survived the war
SK-176	D-3 Project P-19-O	MTB	20.1.1944		Survived the war
SK-177	D-3 Project P-19-O	MTB	20.1.1944		Survived the war
SK-272	D-3 Project P-19-O	MTB	12.12.1943		Survived the war
SK-282	D-3 Project P-19-O	MTB	12.12.1943		Survived the war
SK-292	D-3 Project P-19-O	MTB	12.12.1943		Survived the war

BMO type in Nov 1943. Note the camouflage painting. *Boris Lemachko Collection*

Aerial view of the BMO type in original configuration with twin Colt MGs. *Boris Lemachko Collection*

SK-506 with camouflage painting.
Vitalij Kostrichenko Collection

MO-622 after the war.
Przemysław Budzbon Collection

BMO type in 1944. Note DShK MG abaft the bridge and 45mm 21-KM gun aft. *Przemysław Budzbon Collection Naval History and Heritage Command NH 79319*

13.3. Miscellaneous

Russian Nikson type — *Combatants*

Displacement: 75t full load
Dimensions: 27.5 x 3.6 x 1.4m
Machinery: 2-shaft, 6 cyl petrol engines, 750hp = 16.5kts. Range 600nm at 11kts
Armament: 2-45mm/46 21-K, 2-0.5in DShK MGs, 2 DC chutes
Complement: 21

MO № No / Name Istrebitel' №	SKA № 10.10.1939	MO № 2.7.1941	MO № 7.9.1941	No 2.1.1945	Comp	Comm	Fleet	Remarks
Builder: Lewis Nixon Yd, Perth, NY								
№ 351 ex-*VR-11* (10.5.1939) ex-*Istrebitel № 1* (20.9.1937) ex-*Gregory* (US, 1904)	№ 211	№ 511	№ 312	MO-312	1904	20.9.1937	B	Conv 31.1.1940 to service craft, reverted 2.7.1941 to submarine hunter. Conv 28.1.1950 to service craft *RK-1442*
Builder: Flint, Bath, ME*								
№ 352 ex-*VR-12* (10.5.1939) ex-*Istrebitel № 2* (20.9.1937)	№ 212				1906	20.9.1937	B	Conv 31.1.1940 to training boat. Deleted 1.12.1940
№ 353 ex-*VR-13* (10.5.1939) ex-*IS-1* (20.9.1937) ex-*Inzhener* (16.4.1937) ex-*Istrebitel № 4* (1.1.1932)	№ 213				1906	10.5.1929	B	Conv 31.1.1940 to training boat. Deleted 1.12.1940
№ 354 ex-*VR-14* (11.5.1939) ex-*VS-4* (20.9.1937) ex-*V-3* (16.4.1937) ex-*Pilot* (1.1.1932) ex-*Istrebitel № 5* (1929)	№ 214				1906	1929	B	Conv 31.1.1940 to training boat. Deleted 1.12.1940
№ 355 ex-*VR-15* (11.5.1939) ex-*V-2* (20.9.1937) ex-*Morlet* (1.1.1932) ex-*Istrebitel № 6* (1929)	№ 215				1906	1929	B	Conv 31.1.1940 to training boat. Deleted 1.12.1940
№ 356 ex-*VR-16* (11.5.1939) ex-*Istrebitel № 7* (20.9.1937)	№ 216				1906	20.9.1937	B	Conv 31.1.1940 to training boat. Deleted 1.12.1940
№ 357 ex-*VR-17* (11.5.1939) ex-*Istrebitel № 9* (20.9.1937)	№ 217				1906	20.9.1937	B	Conv 31.1.1940 to training boat. Deleted 1.12.1940

* Delivered in parts, assembled by Admiralty Yd, Sevastopol

Ten motor yachts purchased 1904 by the Imperial Russian Navy and comm with the Black Sea Fleet as patrol boats, later small torpedo boats and then combatants with pennant Isterbitel' = Fighter. The № 1 was delivered fully completed under the name *Gregory*, the rest delivered in parts for assembly. Trfd 1907 to the Baltic Fleet, conv to torpedo boats and armed with 450mm TT. Laid up 1921, reactivated by mid-1930s. Conv 1937 to submarine hunters.

Nikson type boat in the late 1930s. *Przemysław Budzbon Collection*

BK-02 type
NKVD patrol boat

Displacement: 58t
Dimensions: 26.8 x 3.8 x 1.9m
Machinery: 3-shaft GAM-34 petrol engines (?), 2250hp = 24kts. Range 285nm
Armament: 2-45mm/46 21-K, 2-0.5in DShK MGs, 2 DC chutes, 8 BB-1 DCs, 24 BM-1 DCs, 4 mines
Complement: 20

NKVD No	MO № 25.7.1941	MO № 7.9.1941	No 2.1.1945	Comp	Comm	Fleet	Remarks
Builder: 5, Leningrad							
PK-224 ex-*PK-199* (9.1.1941)	№ 408	№ 411	MO-411	1940	25.7.1941	B	NKVD Border Guard. Returned 4.7.1945 to the NKVD, renumbered *PK-208*. Discarded 27.3.1952

NKVD experimental boat.

Cross reference: rated as small submarine hunters

Name	Details	Type	From	To	Fate
PAPANIN	*Papanin*	Minesweeping boat	30.10.1941	6.5.1942	Conv to minesweeping boat *KT-809*

MO-1 class (US AVT-63-foot type) temporarily rated as submarine hunters for duration of a few months: MO-230 – MO-249 and MO-435 – MO-458. See page 115

Malyj okhotnik № 411 off Laavansaari in 1944.
Boris Lemachko Collection

13.4. War prizes – Southeast Europe

Cross reference: Rated as submarine hunters.

MO №	Details	Type	From	To	Fate
MO-851	*German KFK*	Minesweeper	20.10.1944	27.1.1945	Conv to minesweeper *T-668*
MO-852	*German KFK*	Minesweeper	20.10.1944	27.1.1945	Conv to minesweeper *T-666*
MO-853	*German KFK*	Minesweeper	20.10.1944	27.1.1945	Conv to minesweeper *T-667*

14. Patrol boats

Сторожевые катера (СКР)

14.1. Standard types

ZK type *NKVD patrol boats*

Displacement: 19t full load
Dimensions: 19.8 x 3.3 x 1.2m
Machinery: 2-shaft Sterling Dolphin petrol engines, 600hp = 16kts. Range 350nm at 13kts
Armament: 1-45mm/46 21-K, 1 to 3-0.3in Maxim MG (replaced by up to 2-0.5in DShK MGs), 8 BM-1 DCs
Complement: 12

NKVD No	SKA № 1941	SKA № 25.11.1943	No 1944	Laid down	Comp	Comm	Fleet	Remarks
Builder: Zolotov boatyard / Workshop No 6 of OGPU Border Guard Yard, Leningrad								
K-193 ex-*PK-55* (9.1.1941)	№ 013			1930	1931	19.7.1941	Da BS	Trfd 4.9.1941 to the Black Sea Fleet. Deleted 20.6.1942 following damage off Kerch in Jan 1942
K-194 ex-*PK-56* (9.1.1941)	№ 023	SK-23		1930	1931	19.7.1941	Da BS	Trfd 4.9.1941 to the Black Sea Fleet. Returned 21.6.1945 to the NKVD Border Guard
K-195 ex-*PK-57* (9.1.1941)	№ 033	SK-33		1930	1931	19.7.1941	Da BS	Trfd 4.9.1941 to the Black Sea Fleet. Returned 21.6.1945 to the NKVD Border Guard.
K-196 ex-*PK-58* (9.1.1941)	№ 0128[1]			1930	1931	19.7.1941	BS	Sunk 1.11.1943 by artillery fire off Eltigen
K-206	№ 043	№ 08	SK-43	1930	1931	19.07.1941	Da BS	Trfd 4.9.1941 to the Black Sea Fleet. Conv to service craft 20.8.1942, reverted 5.8.1944. Returned 21.6.1945 to the NKVD Border Guard
K-207	№ 063			1930	1931	19.07.1941	Da BS	Trfd 4.9.1941 to the Black Sea Fleet. Sunk 29.12.1941 by artillery fire off Theodosia
K-208 ex-*PK-62* (9.1.1941)	№ 073	SK-73		1930	1931	19.07.1941	Da BS	Trfd 4.9.1941 to the Black Sea Fleet. Sunk 7.11.1943 by artillery fire off Eltigen. Raised and recomm
K-220 ex-*PK-54* (9.1.1941)	№ 053			1930	1931	19.07.1941	Da BS	Trfd 4.9.1941 to the Black Sea Fleet. Damaged 11.12.1943 by artillery fire off Eltigen, deleted 3.1.1944
K-229	№ 093	SK-93			1931	19.7.1941	BS	Returned 21.6.1945 to the NKVD Border Guard
K-325 ex-*PK-63* (9.1.1941)	I-34	SK-34			1932	11.09.1941	B	Returned 30.8.1945 to the NKVD Border Guard
K-326 ex-*PK-64* (9.1.1941)	I-35	SK-35			1932	11.09.1941	B	Returned 30.8.1945 to the NKVD Border Guard

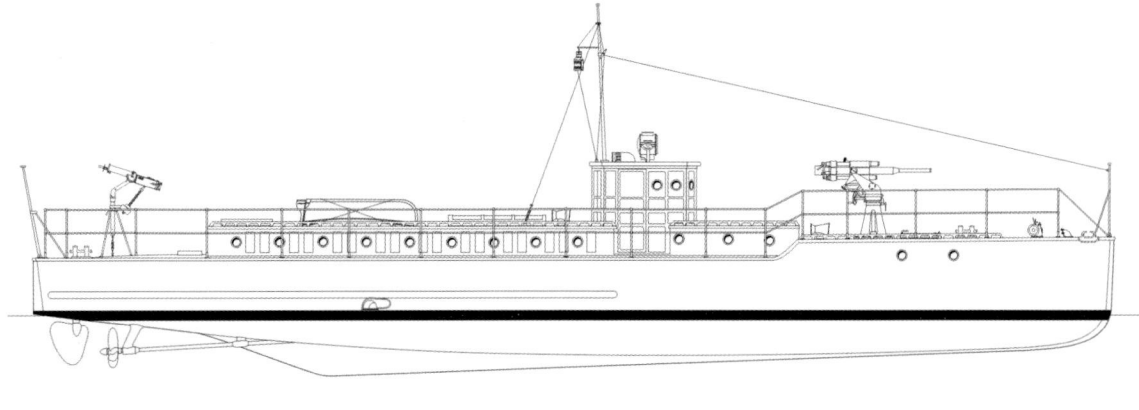

ZK type in the mid-1930s.
Drawing by Jerzy Lewandowski

NKVD No	SKA № 1941	SKA № 25.11.1943	No 1944	Laid down	Comp	Comm	Fleet	Remarks
K-327 ex-*PK-65* (9.1.1941)	I-36		SK-36		1932	11.09.1941	B	Returned 30.8.1945 to the NKVD Border Guard
K-328 ex-*PK-66* (9.1.1941)	I-37				1932	11.09.1941	B	Sunk 30.10.1941 in collision off Björk Island
K-329 ex-*PK-67* (9.1.1941)	I-38		SK-38		1932	11.09.1941	B	Returned 30.8.1945 to the NKVD Border Guard
K-330 ex-*PK-68* (9.1.1941)	I-39		SK-39		1932	11.09.1941	B	Returned 30.8.1945 to the NKVD Border Guard
K-331 ex-*PK-69* (9.1.1941)	I-40		SK-40		1932	11.09.1941	B	Returned 30.8.1945 to the NKVD Border Guard

The effective dates of Pennant Numbers change orders.

Year	Fleet	Date
1941	BS	4.9.1941
	B	11.9.1941
1944	BS	21.5.1944
		6.10.1944

Exceptions noted in the main table.

No	Year	Date	Fleet
1.	1941	17.12.1941	BS

Wooden-hulled 65ft patrol boats designed at the private NEP boatyard of A. Zolotov who was experienced in the construction of similar boats for the Imperial Russian Navy. The ZK designation meant Zolotovskij kater (Zolotov's boat) but the boatyard was nationalised in 1930 (Zolotov who lost his business twice – in 1918 and 1930 – was employed as designer and constructor) and incorporated into the new OGPU Yard. The boats were sturdy and capable of handling very rough sea.

Above and below: The patrol boat *I-36* seen during the war. Note the camouflage. *Boris Lemachko Collection*

NKVD Border Guard patrol boat *PK-57* in the Black Sea in the early 1930s. The cruisers *Profintern* and *Chervona Ukraina* can be seen in the background. *Boris Lemachko Collection*

14.0 Patrol boats

R type
Patrol boats / Minesweeping boats

Displacement:	26t normal, 30t full load
Dimensions:	20.8 x 3.3 x 1.1m
Machinery:	2-shaft ZiS-5 petrol engines, 126hp = 9.3kts. Range 890nm at 7kts
Armament:	1 or 2-0.3in Maxim MG, minesweeping boats fitted with 1 OTSh-2 or OZT sweep and 1 KT-1 sweep
Complement:	11–12

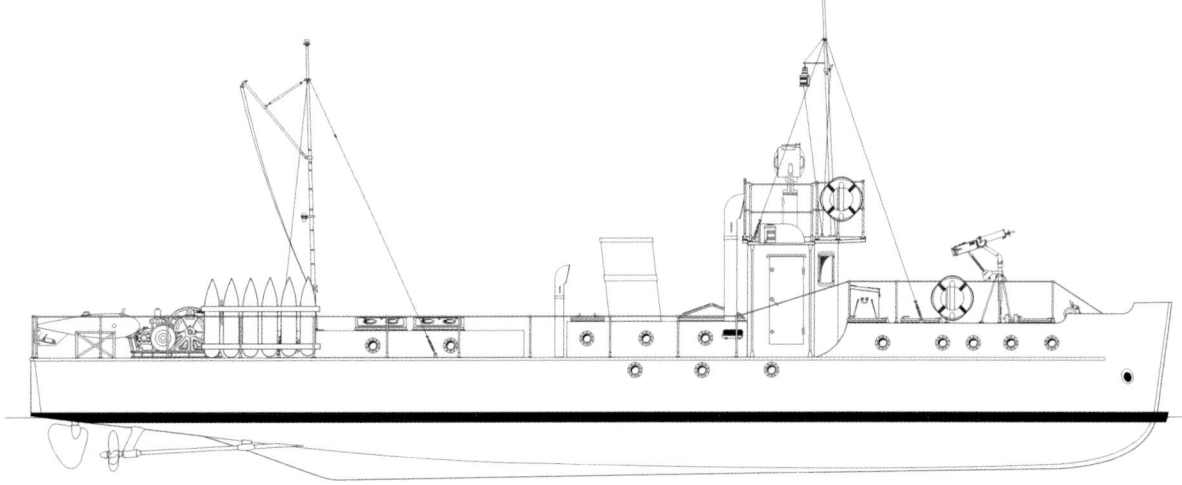

R type minesweeping boat.
Drawing by Jerzy Lewandowski

An *R type* training boat of the Frunze Naval Academy at the late 1930s. The pennant number has been censored.
Przemysław Budzbon Collection

SKA № 11.5.1939	SKA № 10.10.1939	SKA № 28.04.1940	SKA № 1.12.1940	KATShch № 25.7.1941	KATShch № 7.9.1941	KATShch № 11.9.1941	KATShch № 26.5.1942	No 12.11.1944
Builder: 341, Rybinsk								
Patrol boats				**Minesweeping boats**				
	№ 311 ex-*MU-32* (1939)			№ 1102[4]	№ 802			KT-802
	№ 312 ex-*MU-33* (1939)		№ 311	№ 1203	№ 703			KT-703
	№ 313 ex-*MU-34* (1939)							
	№ 314 ex-*MU-35* (1939)			№ 1104[4]	№ 804			
	№ 315 ex-*MU-46* (1939)	№ 323		№ 906[4]		№ 15		
	№ 316 ex-*MU-48* (1939)	№ 315						
	№ 317 ex-*MU-52* (1939)	№ 321						
	№ 321 ex-*MU-54* (1939)	№ 322						
	№ 322 ex-*MU-56* (1939)	№ 324						
	№ 323 ex-*MU-57* (1939)	№ 325						
			№ 323 ex-• (1940)	№ 1208	№ 707			KT-707
			№ 324 ex-• (1940)	№ 1209	№ 708			
	№ 324 ex-*NS-5* (1939)							
	№ 325 ex-*TK-12* (1939)							
	№ 326 ex-*VS-55* (1939)		№ 312	№ 1204	№ 704			KT-704
	№ 327 ex-*VS-56* (1939)		№ 313	№ 1205	№ 705			
№ 361 ex-*VR-3* (1939)	№ 221			№ 914[3]		№ 13		
№ 362 ex-*VR-4* (1939)	№ 222			№ 1509[3]	№ 709			
№ 363 ex-*VR-5* (1939)	№ 223			№ 1510[3]	№ 710			KT-710
№ 364 ex-*VR-6* (1939)	№ 224			№ 1511[3]	№ 711			KT-711
№ 365 ex-*VR-8* (1939)	№ 225			№ 1512[3]	№ 712			KT-712
№ 366 ex-*VR-9* (1939)	№ 226			№ 1513[3]				
№ 367 ex-*VR-10* (1939)	№ 227			№ 1514[3]	№ 810			KT-810
	№ 411 ex-*MU-31* (1939)			№ 1101[4]	№ 801			KT-801
	№ 412 ex-*MU-36* (1939)		№ 212	№ 1201	№ 701			KT-701
	№ 413 ex-*MU-37* (1939)		№ 213	№ 911		№ 10		KT-811
	№ 414 ex-*MU-45* (1939)							
	№ 415 ex-*MU-47* (1939)			№ 1109[4]	№ 809			KT-809
	№ 416 ex-*MU-51* (1939)							

Laid down	Comp	Comm	Fleet	Remarks
1936	1937	10.10.1939 1941	B	Training boat of UVMUZ, mobilised 16.9.1939, conv to patrol boat. Returned 10.12.1940, name reverted. Mobilised 25.7.1941, conv to minesweeping boat
1936	1937	10.10.1939	B	Training boat of UVMUZ, mobilised 22.9.1939, conv to patrol boat. Conv 25.7.1941 to minesweeping boat
1936	1937	10.10.1939	B	Training boat of UVZMU, mobilised 16.9.1939, conv to patrol boat. Returned 10.12.1940, name reverted
1936	1937	10.10.1939 1941	B	Training boat of UVMUZ, mobilised 16.9.1939, conv to patrol boat. Returned 10.12.1940, name reverted. Mobilised 25.7.1941, conv to minesweeping boat. Sunk 30.7.1944 by U-481 at the Narva Bay
1936	1937	10.10.1939 1941	B	Training boat of UVZMU, mobilised 16.9.1939, conv to patrol boat. Returned 10.12.1940, name reverted. Mobilised 25.7.1941, conv to minesweeping boat. Sunk 4.8.1944 by mine off the Vigrung shoal
1936	1937	10.10.1939	B	Training boat of UVMUZ, mobilised 16.9.1939, conv to patrol boat. Returned 24.6.1940, name reverted
1936	1937	10.10.1939	B	Training boat of UVMUZ, mobilised 16.9.1939, conv to patrol boat. Returned 24.6.1940, name reverted
1936	1937	10.10.1939	B	Training boat of UVMUZ, mobilised 16.9.1939, conv to patrol boat. Returned 10.12.1940, name reverted
1936	1937	10.10.1939	B	Training boat of UVMUZ, mobilised 16.9.1939, conv to patrol boat. Returned 10.12.1940, name reverted
1936	1937	10.10.1939	B	Training boat of UVMUZ, mobilised 16.9.1939, conv to patrol boat. Returned 28.6.1940, name reverted
1936	1937	1.12.1940	B	Naval launch, conv 1940 to patrol craft. Conv 25.7.1941 to minesweeping boat
1936	1937	1.12.1940	B	Naval launch, conv 1940 to patrol craft. Conv 25.7.1941 to minesweeping boat. Sunk 5.8.1944 by aircraft off Laavansaari Island
1936	1937	10.10.1939	B	Naval launch, mobilised 16.9.1939, conv to patrol craft. Reverted 9.1.1940 to service craft
1935	1936	10.10.1939	B	Naval launch, mobilised 16.9.1939, conv to patrol craft. Reverted 9.1.1940 to service craft
1936	1937	10.10.1939	B	Naval aviation launch, mobilised 16.9.1939, conv to patrol craft. Conv 25.7.1941 to minesweeping boat
1936	1937	10.10.1939	B	Naval aviation launch, mobilised 16.9.1939, conv to patrol craft. Conv 25.7.1941 to minesweeping boat. Sunk 26.6.1944 by mine off Tytärsaari
	1937	1937	B	Naval launch, diving tender, conv 11.5.1939 to patrol boat, conv 19.8.1941 to minesweeping boat. Mined 5.9.1943 off the Vigrung shoal
	1937	1937	B	Naval launch, diving tender, conv 11.5.1939 to patrol boat, conv 19.8.1941 to minesweeping boat. Sunk 22.9.1944 by mine in the Narva Bay
	1937	1937	B	Naval launch, diving tender, conv 11.5.1939 to patrol boat, conv 19.8.1941 to minesweeping boat
	1937	1937	B	Naval launch, diving tender, conv 11.5.1939 to patrol boat, conv 19.8.1941 to minesweeping boat
	1937	1937	B	Naval launch, diving tender, conv 11.5.1939 to patrol boat, conv 19.8.1941 to minesweeping boat
	1937	1937	B	Naval launch, diving tender, conv 11.5.1939 to patrol boat, conv 19.8.1941 to minesweeping boat. Sunk Aug 1941 by aircraft at Tallinn
	1937	1937	B	Naval launch, diving tender, conv 11.5.1939 to patrol boat, conv 19.8.1941 to minesweeping boat
1936	1937	10.10.1939 1941	B	Training boat of UVMUZ, mobilised 29.9.1939, conv to patrol boat. Returned late 1940, name reverted. Mobilised 25.7.1941, conv to minesweeping boat
1936	1937	10.10.1939	B	Training boat of UVMUZ, mobilised 29.9.1939, conv to patrol boat. Conv 25.7.1941 to minesweeping boat
1936	1937	10.10.1939	B	Training boat of UVMUZ, mobilised 29.9.1939, conv to patrol boat. Stranded 1.12.1939 at Nizhnye Nikulasy on Lake Ladoga. Raised and recomm, conv 25.7.1941 to minesweeping boat
1936	1937	10.10.1939	B	Training boat of UVZMU, mobilised 29.9.1939, conv to patrol boat. Returned 6.01.1940, name reverted
1936	1937	10.10.1939 1941	B	Training boat of UVMUZ, mobilised 29.9.1939, conv to patrol boat. Returned 6.1.1940, name reverted. Mobilised 25.7.1941, conv to minesweeping boat
1936	1937	10.10.1939	B	Training boat of UVZMU, mobilised 29.9.1939, conv to patrol boat. Sunk 8.12.1939 in collision with the minesweeper № 30 at Saunsaari. Raised, repaired and returned 6.1.1940, name reverted

SKA № 11.5.1939	SKA № 10.10.1939	SKA № 28.04.1940	SKA № 1.12.1940	KATShch № 25.7.1941	KATShch № 7.9.1941	KATShch № 11.9.1941	KATShch № 26.5.1942	No 12.11.1944
	№ 417 ex-*MU-53* (1939)							
	№ 421 ex-*MU-55* (1939)							
	№ 422 ex-*MU-58* (1939)	№ 214	№ 912			№ 11		KT-817
	№ 423 ex-*MU-59* (1939)							
	№ 424 ex-*US-1* (1939)	№ 215	№ 1202			№ 702		KT-702
	№ 425 ex-*US-2* (1939)	№ 216	№ 913			№ 12 № 812[6A]		KT-812
	№ 426 ex-*US-3* (1939)	№ 314	№ 1209					
	№ 427 ex-*US-4* (1939)							
						№ 44[6] ex-*MU-44* (1941)		KT-377[9]
				№ 81[2] ex-•			KATShch-553	
				№ 82[2] ex-•			KATShch-554	
				№ 83[2] ex-•			KATShch-555	
				№ 84[2] ex-•			KATShch-556	
				№ 85[2] ex-•			KATShch-557	
				№ 86[2] ex-•			KATShch-558	KT-558[10]
				№ 87[2] ex-•			KATShch-559	
							№ 120[7] ex-*Sh-2* (1942) KATShch-570	KT-570[9]
					№ 127[5]		KATShch-567	KT-567[9]
					№ 128[5]		KATShch-568	KT-568[9]
							№ 129[7] ex-*Sh-1* (1942)	
				№ 1103 ex-*MU-33* 1941)	№ 803			KT-803
				№ 1105 ex-*MU-36* (1941)	№ 805			KT-805
				№ 1106 ex-*MU-41* (1941)	№ 806		№ 41[8]	KT-376[11]
				№ 1107 ex-*MU-42* (1941)	№ 807			
				№ 1108 ex-*MU-43* (1941)	№ 808			KT-808
								KT-717[10] ex-*IS-3* (1944)
							OVR-13	KT-844[12]
							№ 5385	KEMTShch-661[9]
							№ 6684	KEMTShch-660[9]
							№ 6685	

							No 20.8.1942	No 15.1.1943
Air warning & AA defence boats								
							PVO-41 ex-*№ 27*	PVO-11

14.0 Patrol boats

Laid down	Comp	Comm	Fleet	Remarks
1936	1937	10.10.1939	B	Training boat of UVMUZ, mobilised 29.9.1939, conv to patrol boat. Returned 6.1.1940, name reverted
1936	1937	10.10.1939	B	Training boat of UVMUZ, mobilised 29.9.1939, conv to patrol boat. Returned 6.1.1940, name reverted
1936	1937	10.10.1939	B	Training boat of UVMUZ, mobilised 22.9.1939, conv to patrol boat. Conv 25.7.1941 to minesweeping boat
1936	1937	10.10.1939	B	Training boat of UVMUZ, mobilised 29.9.1939, conv to patrol boat. Returned 6.1.1940, name reverted
1936	1937	10.10.1939	B	Training boat of UVMUZ, mobilised 22.9.1939, conv to patrol boat. Conv 25.7.1941 to minesweeping boat
1936	1937	10.10.1939	B	Training boat of UVMUZ, mobilised 22.9.1939, conv to patrol boat. Conv 25.7.1941 to minesweeping boat. Sunk 16.9.1941 by aircraft at Leningrad, raised and recomm
1936	1937	10.10.1939	B	Training boat of UVMUZ, mobilised 22.9.1939, conv to patrol boat. Conv 25.7.1941 to minesweeping boat. Fate unknown, probably stranded off Leningrad late 1942
1936	1937	10.10.1939	B	Training boat of UVMUZ, mobilised 29.9.1939, conv to patrol boat. Returned 6.1.1940, name reverted
1936	1937	Oct 1941	B La Ba	Mobilised 4.10.1941, conv to minesweeping boat. Trfd to the Ladoga Flotilla, returned 6.10.1944
1936	1937	July 1941	BS	Training boat of UVMUZ, mobilised 5.7.1941, conv to minesweeping boat
1936	1937	July 1941	BS	Training boat of UVMUZ, mobilised 5.7.1941, conv to minesweeping boat
1936	1937	July 1941	BS	Training boat of UVMUZ, mobilised 5.7.1941, conv to minesweeping boat
1936	1937	July 1941	BS	Training boat of UVMUZ, mobilised 5.7.1941, conv to minesweeping boat
1936	1937	July 1941	BS	Training boat of UVMUZ, mobilised 5.7.1941, conv to minesweeping boat. Sank 1.11.1943 in a gale north of Kerch
1936	1937	July 1941	BS	Training boat of UVMUZ, mobilised 5.7.1941, conv to minesweeping boat
1936	1937	July 1941	BS	Training boat of UVMUZ, mobilised 5.7.1941, conv to minesweeping boat. Damaged 5.11.1943 by artillery fire off Eltigen
1936	1937	1937	BS	Launch of the staff of the Black Sea Fleet, conv 12.3.1942 to minesweeping boat. Decomm 15.7.1942 for repairs, recomm 2.2.1943
1936	1937	1937	BS	Name: *Rybinskij № 1*. Launch of the staff of the Black Sea Fleet, conv 4.9.1941 to minesweeping boat
1936	1937	1937	BS	Name: *Rybinskij № 2*. Launch of the staff of the Black Sea Fleet, conv 4.9.1941 to minesweeping boat
1936	1937	1937	B	Launch of the staff of the Black Sea Fleet, conv 12.3.1942 to minesweeping boat
1936	1937	1941	B	Training boat of UVMUZ, mobilised 25.7.1941, conv to minesweeping boat
1936	1937	1941	B	Training boat of UVMUZ, mobilised 25.7.1941, conv to minesweeping boat
1936	1937	1941	B La B	Training boat of UVMUZ, mobilised 25.7.1941, conv to minesweeping boat. Trfd 16.2.1942 to the Ladoga Flotilla. Damaged 30.7.1944 by *U-481* in Narva Bay, repaired and recomm. Returned 6.10.1944 to the Baltic Fleet
1936	1937	25.7.1941	B	Training boat of UVZMU, mobilised 24.6.1941, conv to minesweeping boat. Sunk 30.7.1944 by *U-481* at the Narva Bay
1936	1937	25.7.1941	B	Training boat of UVMUZ, mobilised 24.6.1941, conv to minesweeping boat
1936	1937	19.8.1944	B	Launch of the naval research institute, mobilised Aug 1944, conv to minesweeping boat
1936	1937	1937	B	Naval launch, conv 16.3.1943 to minesweeping boat
1936	1937	1937	BS	Naval launch, conv 18.9.1943 to minesweeping boat
1936	1937	1937	BS	Naval launch, conv 12.3.1942 to minesweeping boat
1936	1937	1937	BS	Naval launch, conv 12.3.1942 to minesweeping boat. Sank 2.11.1943 in a gale off Eltigen

Laid down	Comp	Comm	Fleet	Remarks
	1936	20.8.1942	Cs	Conv 18.2.1943 to service craft *AK-37*, renumbered *OShK-37* on 4.1.1944

Exceptions noted in the main table.

No	Year	Date	Remarks
1.	1940	6.1.1940	
2.	1941	5.7.1941	
3.		19.8.1941	
4.		25.7.1941	Recommissioned
5.		4.9.1941	
6.		11.9.1941	
6A.		29.12.1941	
7.	1942	12.3.1942	
8.		16.2.1942	
9.	1944	21.6.1944	
10.		19.8.1944	
11.		6.10.1944	
12.		21.10.1944	

Steel-hulled boats built as communication, naval training and various service craft, nicknamed *Rybinets*. Converted to patrol boats or minesweeping boats.

Kater-tral'shchik № 704 in 1943. Boris Lemachko Collection

Close up of minesweeping gear of the *R type* boats in 1945. *KT-810* is in the background. *Przemysław Budzbon Collection*

An *R type* minesweeping boat at sea during the war. *Przemysław Budzbon Collection*

Several *R type* minesweeping boats laid up at Pillau in 1945. *KT-716* is in the foreground. *Vitalij Kostrichenko Collection*

Training boats of the Frunze Naval Academy at sea in 1937. *MU-43* at left was mobilised on 24.6.1946 and converted to the minesweeping boat *Kater-tral'shchik № 1108*, to be renumbered to *Kater-tral'shchik № 808* on 7.9.1941. From 12.11.1944 she received a permanent number, probably *KT-716*. *Boris Lemachko Collection*

KM-2 type

Patrol boats / Minesweeping boats

Displacement: 7.5t full load
Dimensions: 13.8 x 3.1 x 0.8m
Machinery: 1-shaft ZiS-5 petrol engine, 63hp = 9kts. Range 200nm
Armament: 1-0.3in Maxim MG (replaced on some by 1-0.5in DShK during the war), 1 KT-1 sweep on minesweeping boats
Complement: 10

Launching *K-223* from a slip at Laavensaari using *Stalinets S-65* tracked artillery tractors.
Boris Lemachko Collection

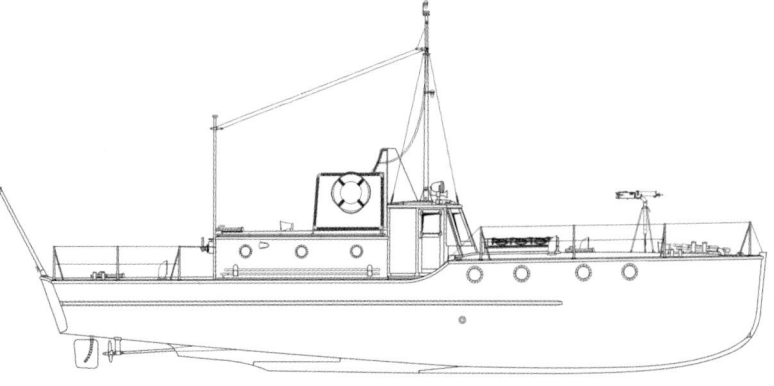

KM-2 type as built.
Drawing by Jerzy Lewandowski

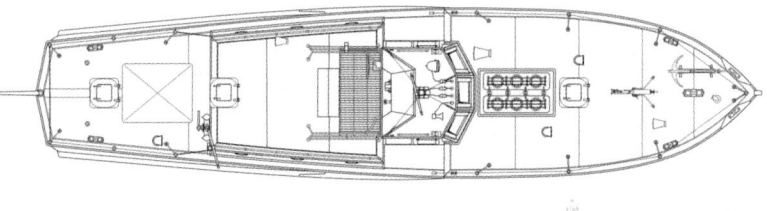

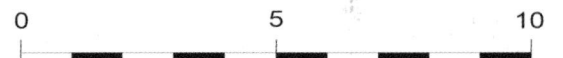

Former NKVD Border Guard patrol boats

NKVD No	SKA № KATShch №* on Comm	No 1944	Laid down	Comp	Comm	Fleet	Remarks
Builder: 5, Leningrad							
K-•	№ 1304*				25.7.1941	B	Conv 25.7.1941 to minesweeping boat. Sunk 16.9.1941 by German aircraft off Saaremaa Island. Identified by photograph of the wreck
K-•	№ 1308*				25.7.1941	B	Conv 25.7.1941 to minesweeping boat. Sunk 14.9.1941 by German aircraft off Hiiumaa Island
K-•	№ 1312*				25.7.1941	B	Conv 25.7.1941 to minesweeping boat. Sunk 16.9.1941 by German aircraft off Saaremaa Island
K-161 ex-*K-48* (9.1.1941)				1937	9.4.1942	Cs	Trfd 22.6.1941 to the Caspian Flotilla, comm as service craft. Conv 9.4.1942 to patrol boat. Returned 1.8.1944 to the NKVD Border Guard
K-162 ex-*K-49* (9.1.1941)				1937	9.4.1942	Cs	Trfd 22.6.1941 to the Caspian Flotilla, comm as service craft. Conv 9.4.1942 to patrol boat. Returned 1.8.1944 to the NKVD Border Guard
K-163 ex-*K-51* (9.1.1941)				1937	9.4.1942	Cs	Trfd 22.6.1941 to the Caspian Flotilla, comm as service craft. Conv 9.4.1942 to patrol boat. Returned 1.8.1944 to the NKVD Border Guard
K-166 ex-*K-133* (9.1.1941)				1937	9.4.1942	Cs	Trfd 22.6.1941 to the Caspian Flotilla, comm as service craft. Conv 9.4.1942 to patrol boat. Returned 1.8.1944 to the NKVD Border Guard
K-167 ex-*K-134* (9.1.1941)				1937	9.4.1942	Cs	Trfd 22.6.1941 to the Caspian Flotilla, comm as service craft. Conv 9.4.1942 to patrol boat. Returned 1.8.1944 to the NKVD Border Guard
K-168 ex-*K-135* (9.1.1941)				1937	9.4.1942	Cs	Trfd 22.6.1941 to the Caspian Flotilla, comm as service craft. Conv 9.4.1942 to patrol boat. Returned 1.8.1944 to the NKVD Border Guard
K-188	№ 0168		1934	1935	17.12.1941	BS	Sunk 1.11.1943 by artillery fire at Eltigen
K-189	№ 0178		1934	1935	17.12.1941	BS	Sunk 1.11.1943 by artillery fire at Eltigen
K-190	№ 0188		1934	1935	17.12.1941	BS	Sunk 1.11.1943 by artillery fire at Eltigen
K-212	№ 0117	SK-117	1935	1936	17.12.1941	BS	Returned 21.6.1945 to the NKVD Border Guard

NKVD No	SKA № on Comm	No 1944	Laid down	Comp	Comm	Fleet	Remarks
K-213	№ 0174 № 0087[2]	SK-87	1935	1936	17.12.1941	BS	Returned 21.6.1945 to the NKVD Border Guard
K-214 ex-*K-46* (9.1.1941)	№ 0127	SK-127	1935	1936	17.12.1941	BS	Returned 21.6.1945 to the NKVD Border Guard
K-215 ex-*K-47* (9.1.1941)	№ 096	SK-96	1935	1936	17.12.1941	BS	Returned 21.6.1945 to the NKVD Border Guard
K-216 ex-*K-45* (9.1.1941)	№ 0106		1935	1936	17.12.1941	BS	Deleted 13.11.1942, presumably lost
K-217 ex-*K-63* (9.1.1941)	№ 0137		1935	1936	17.12.1941	BS	Sunk 17.5.1942 by artillery fire at Yeni-Kale
K-218 ex-*K-64* (9.1.1941)	№ 0135	SK-135	1935	1936	17.12.1941	BS	Conv 21.5.1944 to service craft. Returned 21.6.1945 to the NKVD Border Guard
K-221	№ 0173		1935	1936	4.9.1941	BS	Deleted 8.3.1942, presumably lost
K-222	№ 0113		1935	1936	4.9.1941	BS	Sunk 16.11.1941 by aircraft at Sevastopol
K-223 ex-*K-62* (9.1.1941)	№ 0183		1935	1936	4.9.1941	BS	Deleted 19.7.1942, presumably lost
K-224	№ 076		1935	1936	4.9.1941	BS	Sunk 2.11.1943 by aircraft at Taman. Raised and conv 13.12.1944 to service craft
K-225	№ 086		1935	1936	4.9.1941	BS	Deleted 13.11.1942. Presumably lost
K-226	№ 0123		1935	1936	4.9.1941	BS	Sunk 2.11.1943 by mine off Eltigen
K-228	№ 0134 № 0145[2]	SK-145	1935	1936	10.12.1941	BS	Returned 21.6.1945 to the NKVD Border Guard
K-236	№ 0116	SK-116	1935	1936	17.12.1941	BS	Returned 21.6.1945 to the NKVD Border Guard
K-237					-	BS	Scuttled 16.10.1941 at Odessa
K-238	№ 0174		1935	1936	17.12.1941	BS	Deleted 22.11.1942. Presumably lost
K-241	№ 0153		1935	1936	4.9.1941	BS	Sunk 16.11.1941 by aircraft at Sevastopol
K-242	№ 0163	SK-163	1935	1936	4.9.1941	BS	Returned 21.6.1945 to the NKVD Border Guard
K-243 ex-*K-56* (9.1.1941)					-	BS	Presumably lost June–July 1941
K-277	№ 1306*				25.7.1941	B	Conv 25.7.1941 to minesweeping boat. Sunk 16.9.1941 by German aircraft off Saaremaa Island
K-278	№ 1307*				25.7.1941	B	Conv 25.7.1941 to minesweeping boat. Sunk 16.9.1941 by German aircraft off Saaremaa Island
K-279	№ 614* I-21[1]	KT-845[3]	1936	1937	25.7.1941	B BS	Conv 29.12.1941 to minesweeping boat. Trfd 7.2.1945 to the Black Sea Fleet, conv 16.2.1945 to service craft
K-280	№ 615* I-22[1]	KT-846[3]	1936	1937	25.7.1941	B	Conv 29.12.1941 to minesweeping boat. Survived the war
K-281	№ 1309*				25.7.1941	B	Conv 25.7.1941 to minesweeping boat. Sunk 16.9.1941 by German aircraft off Saaremaa Island
K-282	№ 1310*				25.7.1941	B	Conv 25.7.1941 to minesweeping boat. Sunk 16.9.1941 by German aircraft off Saaremaa Island
K-283	№ 1318*				25.7.1941	B	Conv 25.7.1941 to minesweeping boat. Sunk 16.9.1941 by German aircraft off Saaremaa Island
K-284	№ 616* I-23[1]	KT-455[5]			25.7.1941	B	Conv 29.12.1941 to minesweeping boat, reverted 25.7.1944 to patrol boat, back to minesweeping boat 14.11.1944. Survived the war
K-285	№ 617*				25.7.1941	B	Conv 25.7.1941 to minesweeping boat. Sunk 28-29.8.1941 by mine
K-286	№ 618*				25.7.1941	B	Conv 25.7.1941 to minesweeping boat. Sunk 28-29.8.1941 by mine
K-287					-	B	Presumably lost June–July 1941
K-288	I-24	SK-24	1935		7.9.1941	B La B	Trfd 3.1.1942 to the Ladoga Flotilla, returned 13.12.1944. Returned 30.8.1945 to the NKVD Border Guard
K-289	I-27		1935		7.9.1941	B	Conv 29.12.1941 to minesweeping boat, reverted 25.7.1944 to patrol boat. Sunk 16/17.8.1944, by aircraft on Lake Lämmijärv
K-291					-	B	Lost early Sept 1941
K-292	I-25		1935		7.9.1941	B	Conv 29.12.1941 to minesweeping boat, reverted 25.7.1944 to patrol boat. Conv 14.11.1944 to service craft
K-293					-	B	Lost June–Aug 1941
K-294	I-26		1935		7.9.1941	B	Conv 29.12.1941 to minesweeping boat, reverted 25.7.1944 to patrol boat. Conv 14.11.1944 to service craft
K-295	I-29		1935		7.9.1941	B	Sunk 1.11.1941 by German aircraft west of Hiiuuma
K-296	№ 619*				25.7.1941	B	Conv 25.7.1941 to minesweeping boat. Sunk 28-29.8.1941 by mine

K-297					25.7.1941	B	Sunk 28-29.8.1941 by mine
K-298	I-28			1935	7.9.1941	B	Conv 29.12.1941 to minesweeping boat, reverted 25.7.1944 to patrol boat. Conv 14.11.1944 to service craft
K-316	I-30	SK-30		1935	7.9.1941	B La B	Trfd 3.1.1942 to the Ladoga Flotilla, returned 13.12.1944. Returned 30.8.1945 to the NKVD Border Guard
K-317	I-41			1935	7.9.1941	B	Lost 1941?
K-318	I-42			1935	11.9.1941	B	Sank 25.6.1944 in a gale off Tuloksa on Lake Onega, raised
K-336	I-48		1935	1937	11.9.1941	B	Conv 29.12.1941 to minesweeping boat. Sunk 13.5.1944 by aircraft off Laavansaari Island
K-337	I-32	KT-32[4]	1935	1937	11.9.1941	B	Conv 29.12.1941 to minesweeping boat. Survived the war
K-338	I-49	SK-49	1935	1937	11.9.1941	B La B	Trfd 3.1.1942 to the Ladoga Flotilla, returned 13.12.1944. Survived the war
K-340	I-33		1935	1937	11.9.1941	B	Conv 29.12.1941 to minesweeping boat, conv 6.10.1944 to service craft
K-356					-	N	Fate unknown, presumably lost June–July 1941
K-357					-	N	Fate unknown, presumably lost June–July 1941
K-360					-	La	Fate unknown, presumably lost June–July 1941
K-371 ex-*K-89* (9.1.1941)					-	N	Lost, presumably June–July 1941
K-372 ex-*K-90* (9.1.1941)					-	N	Fate unknown, presumably lost June–July 1941
K-374 ex-*K-92* (9.1.1941)					-	N	Fate unknown, presumably lost June–July 1941
K-387	№ 606	SK-606		1936	9.7.1941	Wh	Returned 19.10.1945 to the NKVD Border Guard
K-407	№ 407*				June 1941	B	Service boat, conv 1.10.1943 to minesweeping boat. Sunk 27.9.1944 by mine off Juminda Cape

* KATShch № pennant.

The effective dates of Pennant Numbers change orders.

Year	Fleet	Date
1944	BS	21.5.1944
	B	13.12.1944

Exceptions noted in the main table.

No	Year	Date	Fleet
1.	1941	7.9.1944	B
2.		17.12.1941	BS
3.	1944	21.10.1944	B
4.		12.11.1944	B
5.		14.11.1944	B

NKVD Border Guard patrol boats detached to the naval service.

NKVD No	Built	Station	Remarks
K-1	1935	Far East	Extant 1946
K-2	1935	Far East	Extant 1946
K-3	1935	Far East	Extant 1946
K-4	1935	Far East	Extant 1946
K-12		Far East	Extant 1945
K-14		Far East	Extant 1945
K-15		Far East	Extant 1945
K-16		Far East	Extant 1945
K-18		Far East	Extant 1945
K-25		Far East	Extant 1945
K-26		Far East	Extant 1945
K-27		Far East	Extant 1946
K-28		Far East	Extant 1946
K-35	1934	Far East	Extant 1946
K-37	1934	Far East	Extant 1946
K-38	1934	Far East	Extant 1946
K-43		Far East	
K-47	1937	Far East	Extant 1946
K-67	1936	Amur	
K-68	1936	Amur	
K-69	1936	Amur	
K-70	1936	Amur	
K-71	1936	Amur	
K-72	1932	Amur	
K-73		Amur	
K-83		Amur	
K-84		Amur	
K-92		Amur	
K-99		Amur	
K-107		Amur	
K-112	1936	Amur	
K-113	1936	Amur	
K-114	1936	Amur	
K-373 ex-*K-91* (9.1.1941)		Arctic	Renumbered *ShK-15* on 23.6.1941. Fate unknown

KM-2 type boat at left with the D-2, D-4 type boat (see page 241) at right. Boris Lemachko Collection

Naval boats (patrol, minesweeping and service boats)

No SKA № on Comm	No 1944 KATSHch №*	No 2.1.1945	Laid down	Comp	Comm	Fleet	Remarks
Builder: 5, Leningrad							
OV-161	SK-161		1941	1942	19.6.1942	P	Patrol boat. Survived the war
OV-162	SK-162		1941	1942	19.6.1942	P	Patrol boat. Survived the war
OV-163	SK-163		1941	1942	19.6.1942	P	Patrol boat. Survived the war
OV-164	SK-164		1941	1942	19.6.1942	P	Patrol boat. Survived the war
OV-165	SK-165		1941	1942	19.6.1942	P	Patrol boat. Survived the war
№ 12	SK-12[5]		1940	1941	4.10.1941	B	Patrol boat. Trfd to the Ladoga Flotilla, returned 28.11.1944
№ 14	SK-14[5]		1940	1941	4.10.1941	B / La / B	Patrol boat. Trfd to the Ladoga Flotilla, returned 28.11.1944. Survived the war
№ 15	SK-15[4]		1940	1941	4.10.1941	B / La / B	Patrol boat. Trfd to the Ladoga Flotilla. Decomm 12.7.1944 for repairs, recomm 28.11.1944 and returned to the Baltic Fleet
№ 18		SK-18	1941	1942	18.12.1942	B	Patrol boat. Trfd 30.8.1945 to the NKVD Border Guard
№ 21	SK-21[5]		1940	1941	4.10.1941	B / La	Patrol boat. Trfd to the Ladoga Flotilla, returned 13.12.1944. Survived the war
№ 22			1940	1941	21.11.1941	La	Patrol boat. Lost 1941?
№ 23	SK-23[5]		1940	1941	21.11.1941	B / La / B	Patrol boat. Trfd to the Ladoga Flotilla, returned 13.12.1944. Survived the war
№ 25	SK-25[5]		1940	1941	4.10.1941	B / La / B	Patrol boat. Trfd to the Ladoga Flotilla, returned 13.12.1944. Survived the war
№ 26 / № 26*			1940	1941	7.10.1941	B	Patrol boat. Conv 3.1.1942 to minesweeping boat. Decomm 5.6.1944, BU
№ 27 / № 27*			1940	1941	7.10.1941	B	Patrol boat. Conv 3.1.1942 to minesweeping boat. Sunk 1.9.1942 by mine off Seiskari Island
№ 28		SK-28	1941	1942	18.12.1942	B	Patrol boat. Trfd 30.8.1945 to the NKVD Border Guard
№ 38		SK-38	1941	1942	18.12.1942	B	Patrol boat. Trfd 30.8.1945 to the NKVD Border Guard
№ 48		SK-48	1941	1942	18.12.1942	B	Patrol boat. Trfd 30.8.1945 to the NKVD Border Guard

KM-2 type boat after the war.
Vitalij Kostrichenko Collection

KATSchch № SKA №* No on Comm	SKA № 15.3.1943	No 1944	Laid down	Comp	Comm	Fleet	Remarks
Builder: 5, Leningrad							
№ 620			1941	1942	21.10.1942	B	Conv 6.10.1944 to service craft.
№ 920 ex-AO-1 (1942)	№ 920	DZ-920[1]			21.10.1942	B	Service boat of artillery service conv to minesweeping boat. Conv 15.3.1943 to patrol boat, conv 14.8.1944 to smoke screen layer boat. Reverted 12.6.1945 to service boat
№ 921 ex-BPL-1 (1942)	№ 921	DZ-921[1]			21.10.1942	B	Service boat of the Submarine Brigade conv to minesweeping boat. Conv 15.3.1943 to patrol boat, conv 14.8.1944 to smoke screen layer boat. Conv 12.6.1945 to service boat
№ 922 ex-BPL-2 (1942)	№ 922	DZ-922[1]			21.10.1942	B	Service boat of the Submarine Brigade conv to minesweeping boat. Conv 15.3.1943 to patrol boat, conv 14.8.1944 to smoke screen layer boat. Conv 12.6.1945 to service boat
№ 923 ex-PVO-4 (1942)	№ 923	DZ-923[1]			21.10.1942	B	Service boat of AA defence conv to minesweeping boat. Conv 15.3.1943 to patrol boat, conv 14.8.1944 to smoke screen layer boat. Reverted 12.6.1945 to service boat
№ 924 ex-T-1 (1942)	№ 924	DZ-924[1]			21.10.1942	B	Service boat of military court conv to minesweeping boat. Conv 15.3.1943 to patrol boat, conv 14.8.1944 to smoke screen layer boat. Reverted 12.6.1945 to service boat
№ 602* ex-MA-2 (1941) № 602		KT-454[3]	1935	1936	25.7.1941	B	Service boat of Naval Academy, comm as patrol boat but remained attached to the academy. Conv 1.6.1942 to minesweeping boat. Survived the war
PP-1		KT-810	1938	1939	7.10.1941	B	Service boat of submarine service, conv to minesweeping boat. Survived the war

SKA № on Comm	KATSchch № on Conv	No 12.11.1944	Laid down	Comp	Comm	Fleet	Remarks
Builder: 5, Leningrad							
№ 603 ex-MA-3 (1941)	№ 603			1935	25.7.1941	B	Training boat of the Naval Academy. Mobilised 1941, conv to patrol boat. Conv 29.12.1941 to minesweeping boat. Returned 6.10.1944 6.10.1944 to Naval Academy
№ 604 ex-MA-4 (1941)	№ 604	KT-604[2]		1935	25.7.1941	B	Training boat of the Naval Academy. Mobilised 1941, conv to patrol boat. Conv 18.10.1941 to minesweeping boat. Survived the war
№ 605 ex-PU-1 (1941)	№ 605			1935	25.7.1941	B	Naval service boat, conv to patrol boat. Conv 3.1.1942 to minesweeping boat. Sunk 30.8.1943 by German R-boats in the Gulf of Finland off Strelna
№ 606 ex-PU-2 (1941)	№ 606			1935	25.7.1941	B	Naval service boat, conv to patrol boat. Conv 3.1.1942 to minesweeping boat. Sunk 28.6.1943 by artillery fire in Neva Bay
№ 607 ex-PU-3 (1941)	№ 607	KT-407[2]		1935	25.7.1941	B	Naval service boat, conv to patrol boat. Conv 3.1.1942 to minesweeping boat. Survived the war
	№ 17	KT-117	1941	1942	18.12.1942	B	Minesweeping boat. Survived the war
	№ 25	KT-821	1940	1941	7.10.1941	B	Minesweeping boat. Survived the war
	№ 27	KT-127	1941	1942	18.12.1942	B	Minesweeping boat. Survived the war
	№ 28	KT-822	1940	1941	7.10.1941	B	Minesweeping boat. Survived the war
	№ 29	KT-29	1940	1941	7.10.1941	B	Minesweeping boat. Survived the war
	№ 30	KT-30	1940	1941	7.10.1941	B	Minesweeping boat. Survived the war
	№ 37	KT-37	1941	1944	18.12.1942	B	Minesweeping boat. Survived the war
	№ 47	KT-137	1941	1942	18.12.1942	B	Minesweeping boat. Survived the war
	№ 57	KT-237	1941	1942	18.12.1942	B	Minesweeping boat. Survived the war
	№ 606 ex-Sh-6 (1943)	KT-608			30.7.1943	B	Naval staff communication boat, conv to minesweeping boat. Survived the war

The effective dates of Pennant Numbers change orders.

Year	Fleet	Date
1944	P	13.9.1944
	B	12.11.1944

Exceptions noted in the main table.

No	Year	Date	Fleet
1.	1944	14.8.1944	B
2.		21.10.1944	B
3.		14.11.1944	B
4.		28.11.1944	B
5.		13.12.1944	B

Built under the 1931 NKVD Programme as coastal patrol boats. Construction based on the German steel-hulled *Polizeiboot* (11.5m, 70hp = 14.3kts), from design drawings purchased in Germany in 1930. The design was adapted to local conditions by change of hull material from steel to wood which resulted in an increase in dimensions; combined with the adoption of the less powerful 63hp ZiS-5 truck engine, this resulted in a speed reduced to 9kts.

KM-2 type boat in a moderate sea.
Przemysław Budzbon Collection

KM-4 type   *Patrol boats / Minesweeping boats*

Displacement: 12t full load
Dimensions: 19.3 x 3.4 x 0.8m
Machinery: 2-shaft ZiS-5 petrol engines, 126hp = 10kts. Range 220nm
Armament: 1-0.3in Maxim MG (replaced on some by 1-0.5in DShK during the war), 1 KT-1 sweep on minesweeping boats
Complement: 10

NKVD Border Guard patrol boats

Patrol boat Storozhevoj kater № 911.
Przemysław Budzbon Collection

NKVD No	SKA № on Comm	No 1944	Laid down	Comp	Comm	Fleet	Remarks
Builder: 5, Leningrad							
K-186	№ 0208	SK-208	1938	1939	17.12.1941	BS	Returned 21.6.1945 to the NKVD Border Guard
K-187	№ 0218		1938	1939	17.12.1941	BS	Deleted 2.4.1942. Presumably lost
K-191	№ 0198	SK-198	1938	1939	17.12.1941	BS	Returned 21.6.1945 to the NKVD Border Guard
K-211	№ 0107	SK-107	1938	1939	17.12.1941	BS	Returned 21.6.1945 to the NKVD Border Guard
K-227	№ 0184[2] № 097	SK-97	1938	1939	17.12.1941	BS	Returned 21.6.1945 to the NKVD Border Guard
K-235	№ 0164		1938	1939	17.12.1941	BS	Deleted 20.6.1943. Presumably lost
K-285	№ 617				25.7.1941	B	Sunk 28-29.8.1941 by mine
K-319	I-31	KT-847	1938	1940	7.9.1941	B	Conv 29.12.1941 to minesweeping boat. Survived the war
K-320	I-43	KT-43[3]	1939	1940	11.9.1941	B	Conv 3.1.1942 to minesweeping boat. Survived the war
K-321	I-44	KT-44[3]	1938	1940	11.9.1941	B	Conv 3.1.1942 to minesweeping boat. Survived the war
K-322	I-45	KT-848	1938	1940	11.9.1941	B	Conv 29.12.1941 to minesweeping boat. Survived the war
K-323	I-46		1938	1940	11.9.1941	B	Conv 18.7.1944 to service craft
K-324	I-47	KT-849	1938	1940	11.9.1941	B	Conv 29.12.1941 to minesweeping boat. Survived the war
K-358				-		N	Fate unknown
K-359				-		N	Fate unknown
K-388	№ 607[1]	SK-607		1938	09.7.1941	Wh	Returned 15.7.1945 to the NKVD Border Guard
K-389	№ 608[1]	SK-608		1938	09.7.1941	Wh	Returned 15.7.1945 to the NKVD Border Guard
K-406						B	Fate unknown
K-411						BS	Fate unknown
K-412	•				•	BS	Stranded 10.10.1942 off Novorossisk
K-413	•				•	BS	Lost. Deleted 10.10.1942
K-421						Cs	Fate unknown
K-422						Cs	Fate unknown
K-423						Cs	Fate unknown
K-424						Cs	Fate unknown

The effective dates of Pennant Numbers change orders.

Year	Fleet	Date
1944	BS	21.5.1944
	Wh	31.5.1944
	B	21.10.1944

Exceptions noted in the main table.

No	Year	Date	Fleet
1.	1941	29.9.1941	Wh
2.		10.12.1941	BS
3.	1944	12.11.1944	B

NKVD Border Guard patrol boats left in NKVD service

NKVD No	Built	Station	Remarks
K-13	1939	Far East	
K-39	1938	Far East	
K-40	1940	Far East	
K-41	1940	Far East	
K-42	1938	Far East	
K-44	1938	Far East	
K-45	1938	Far East	
K-46	1939	Far East	
K-48	1938	Far East	
K-61		Far East	
K-62		Far East	Extant 1945
K-90		Far East	
K-91		Far East	
K-100		Amur	
K-101		Amur	
K-102		Amur	
K-108		Far East	
K-109		Far East	
K-110		Far East	
K-111		Far East	
K-200		Moskva	Communication boat

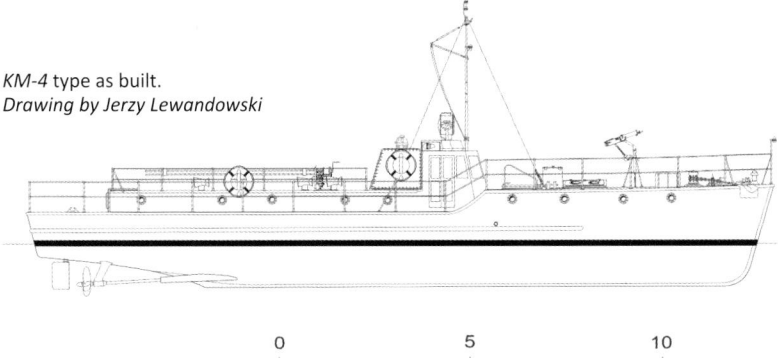

KM-4 type as built.
Drawing by Jerzy Lewandowski

Kater-tral'shchik № 203 in the background. Note rudimentary sweeping gear.
Vitalij Kostrichenko Collection

KT-609 at sea. Boris Lemachko Collection

Naval boats

No SKA № on Comm	KATShch No on Conv	No 1944	No 1945	Laid down	Lauched	Comm	Fleet	Remarks
Builder: 5, Leningrad								
Patrol boats								
OV-211		SK-211		1941	1942	08.9.1942	P	Survived the war
OV-212		SK-212		1941	1942	08.9.1942	P	Survived the war
OV-213		SK-213		1941	1942	08.9.1942	P	Survived the war
OV-214		SK-214		1941	1942	08.9.1942	P	Survived the war
OV-311		SK-311		1942	1943	30.12.1943	P	Survived the war
OV-312		SK-312		1942	1943	30.12.1943	P	Survived the war
OV-313		SK-313		1942	1943	30.12.1943	P	Survived the war
OV-314		SK-314		1942	1943	30.12.1943	P	Survived the war
OV-315		SK-315		1942	1943	30.12.1943	P	Survived the war
OV-316		SK-316		1942	1943	30.12.1943	P	Survived the war
№ 16		SK-16[6]		1940	1941	4.10.1941	B La B	Trfd to the Ladoga Flotilla, returned 13.12.1944
№ 26		SK-26[6]		1941	1942	13.4.1942	B La B	Trfd to the Ladoga Flotilla, returned 13.12.1944. Trfd 4.7.1945 to the NKVD Border Guard
№ 31	№ 31	KT-609[5]		1940	1941	7.10.1941	B	Conv 3.10.1942 to minesweeping boat
№ 32		SK-32[6]		1940	1941	21.11.1941	B La B	Trfd to the Ladoga Flotilla, returned 13.12.1944
№ 58			SK-58[7]	1941	1942	18.12.1942	B	Trfd 30.8.1945 to the NKVD Border Guard
№ 68			SK-68[7] KT-406[9]		1942	18.12.1942	B	Conv 21.6.1945 to minesweeping boat
№ 78			SK-78[7] KT-407[9]		1942	18.12.1942	B	Conv 21.6.1945 to minesweeping boat
№ 88			SK-88[7] KT-408[9]		1942	18.12.1942	B	Conv 21.6.1945 to minesweeping boat
№ 93	№ 93	KT-93		1941	1942	13.4.1942	B La B	Trfd to the Ladoga Flotilla, conv 11.9.1942 to minesweeping boat. Returned to the Baltic Fleet 21.10.1944.
№ 94		SK-94[6]		1940	1941	4.10.1941	B La B	Trfd to the Ladoga Flotilla, returned 13.12.1944
№ 95	№ 95	KT-95			1941	4.10.1941	B La B	Trfd to the Ladoga Flotilla, conv 11.9.1942 to minesweeping boat. Returned to the Baltic Fleet 21.10.1944
№ 98		KT-98		1941	1942	13.4.1942	B La B	Trfd to the Ladoga Flotilla, conv 11.9.1942 to minesweeping boat. Returned to the Baltic Fleet 21.10.1944
№ 98			SK-98[7] KT-409[9]		1942	18.12.1942	B	Conv 21.6.1945 to minesweeping boat
№ 99	№ 99	KT-99		1941	1942	13.4.1942	B La B	Trfd to the Ladoga Flotilla, conv 11.9.1942 to minesweeping boat. Returned to the Baltic Fleet 21.10.1944
№ 102	№ 102	KT-102[5]			1941	14.10.1941	B	Conv 16.3.1942 to minesweeping boat
№ 107	№ 107	KT-119			1941	4.10.1941	B La B	Trfd to the Ladoga Flotilla, conv 11.9.1942 to minesweeping boat. Returned to the Baltic Fleet 21.10.1944
№ 108			SK-108[7] KT-410[9]		1942	18.12.1942	B	Conv 21.6.1945 to minesweeping boat
№ 110	№ 110	KT-110[5]			1941	14.10.1941	B	Conv 16.3.1942 to minesweeping boat
№ 112	№ 112	KT-112			1941	4.10.1941	B La B	Trfd to the Ladoga Flotilla, conv 11.9.1942 to minesweeping boat. Returned to the Baltic Fleet 21.10.1944

14.0 Patrol boats

Training boat *OShK-26* as smokescreen-laying boat *DZ-7*. Boris Lemachko Collection

Kater-tral'shchik № 113 at the foreground with others of the *KM-4* type astern. Vitalij Kostrichenko Collection

KATShch № on Comm	KATShch № 30.1.1944	No 1944	No 1945	Laid down	Lauched	Comm	Fleet	Remarks
Builder: 5, Leningrad								
Minesweeping boats								
№ 13	№ 301	KT-301			1943	30.7.1943	B	Survived the war
№ 23	№ 302	KT-302			1943	21.9.1943	B	Survived the war
№ 33	№ 303	KT-303			1943	21.9.1943	B	Survived the war
№ 43	№ 304	KT-304			1943	21.9.1943	B	Survived the war
№ 53	№ 305	KT-305			1943	30.7.1943	B	Survived the war
№ 63	№ 306	KT-306			1943	21.9.1943	B	Survived the war
№ 67					1942	18.12.1942	B	Mined 28.9.1944 in Narva Bay
№ 73	№ 307	KT-307			1943	21.9.1943	B	Survived the war
№ 77		KT-77			1942	18.12.1942	B	Survived the war
№ 83	№ 308	KT-308			1943	21.9.1943	B	Survived the war
№ 87			KT-87[8]		1942	18.12.1942	B	Mined 4.7.1944 off Teikarsaari. Raised and recomm 12.4.1945
№ 93	№ 309	KT-309			1943	30.7.1943	B	Survived the war
№ 97		KT-97[5]			1942	18.12.1942	B	Survived the war
№ 103	№ 310	KT-310			1943	30.7.1943	B	Survived the war
№ 104 RK № 104 SKA № 104 SKA № 102 SKA № 112[1]	№ 112 № 104[2]	KT-263			1941	28.11.1941	Vo On La B	Conv 15.3.1942 to service boat *Raz"ezdnoj kater № 104*, trfd 11.5.1942 to the Onega Flotilla, conv 29.6.1942 to patrol boat *Storozhevoj kater № 104*, renumbered № 102 on 29.6.1942, № 112 on 2.8.1942. Reverted 29.1.1944 to minesweeping boat, trfd 21.7.1944 to the Ladoga Flotilla, trfd 23.1.1945 to the Baltic Fleet
№ 105		KT-105			1941	3.1.1942	B La B	Trfd to the Ladoga Flotilla, returned 21.10.1944
№ 107					1942	18.12.1942	B	Mined 20.8.1944 in Narva Bay
№ 111 RK № 111 SKA № 111		KT-264			1941	28.11.1941	Vo On La	Conv 15.3.1942 to service boat *Raz"ezdnoj kater № 111* trfd 11.5.1942 to the Onega Flotilla, conv 29.6.1942 to patrol boat *Storozevoj kater № 111*. Reverted 29.1.1944 to minesweeping boat, trfd 21.7.1944 to the Ladoga Flotilla, trfd 23.1.1945 to the Baltic Fleet
№ 113	№ 311	KT-311			1943	21.9.1943	B	Survived the war
№ 115		KT-115			1941	3.1.1942	B	Survived the war
№ 118		KT-118			1941	3.1.1942	B	Survived the war
№ 121		KT-121			1941	3.1.1942	B La	Trfd 20.8.1942 to the Ladoga Flotilla, returned 21.10.1944
№ 123	№ 312	KT-312			1943	30.7.1943	B	Survived the war
№ 133	№ 313	KT-313			1943	30.7.1943	B	Survived the war
№ 143	№ 314	KT-314			1943	30.7.1943	B	Survived the war
№ 153	№ 315	KT-315			1943	30.7.1943	B	Survived the war
№ 163	№ 316				1943	30.7.1943	B	Sunk 9.7.1944 by artillery fire in Vyborg Bay
№ 173	№ 317				1943	30.7.1943	B	Sunk 30.5.1944 by mine off Seiskaari Island
№ 183	№ 318	KT-318			1943	30.7.1943	B	Survived the war
№ 193	№ 319	KT-319			1943	21.9.1941	B	Survived the war

KATShch № on Comm	KATShch № 30.1.1944	No 1944	No 1945	Laid down	Lauched	Comm	Fleet	Remarks
№ 203	№ 320	KT-320			1943	21.9.1941	B	Survived the war
№ 213	№ 335	KT-335[5]			1943	21.9.1941	B	Survived the war
№ 223	№ 336	KT-336[4]			1943	10.11.1943	B	Survived the war
№ 233	№ 337	KT-337[4]			1943	10.11.1943	B	Mined 9.9.1944 in Vyborg Bay. Raised and recomm
№ 243	№ 338	KT-338[4]			1943	10.11.1943	B	Survived the war
№ 253	№ 339	KT-339[4]			1943	10.11.1943	B	Survived the war
№ 263	№ 340	KT-340[4]			1943	10.11.1943	B	Sunk 20.10.1944 by mine in the Gulf of Riga
№ 273	№ 341	KT-341[5]			1943	10.11.1943	B	Survived the war
№ 283	№ 342	KT-342[5]			1943	10.11.1943	B	Survived the war
№ 293	№ 343	KT-343[5]			1943	10.11.1943	B	Survived the war
№ 303	№ 344	KT-344			1943	10.11.1943	B	Survived the war
№ 313	№ 345	KT-345			1943	10.11.1943	B	Sunk 24.10.1944 by mine in the Gulf of Riga
№ 346		KT-346		1943	1944	30.1.1944	B BS	Trfd 7.2.1945 to the Black Sea Fleet
№ 347		KT-347		1943	1944	30.1.1944	B	Survived the war
№ 348		KT-348		1943	1944	30.1.1944	B	Survived the war
№ 373	№ 321				1943	10.11.1943	B	Sunk 10.10.1944 by mine in the Gulf of Riga
№ 383	№ 322	KT-322[5]			1943	10.11.1943	B	Survived the war
№ 393	№ 323				1943	10.11.1943	B	Sunk 30.7.1944 by mine in Narva Bay
№ 403	№ 324	KT-324[5]			1943	10.11.1943	B	Survived the war
№ 413	№ 325	KT-325[5]			1943	10.11.1943	B	Survived the war
№ 423	№ 326	KT-326[5]			1943	10.11.1943	B	Survived the war
№ 433	№ 327	KT-327[5]			1843	10.11.1943	B	Survived the war
№ 443	№ 328	KT-328[5]			1943	21.9.1943	B	Survived the war
№ 453	№ 329	KT-329[5]			1943	10.11.1943	B	Survived the war
№ 463	№ 330	KT-330[5]			1943	10.11.1943	B	Survived the war
№ 473	№ 331	KT-331[5]			1943	10.11.1943	B	Survived the war
№ 483	№ 322	KT-322[5]			1943	21.9.1943	B	Survived the war
№ 493	№ 333	KT-333[5]			1943	10.11.1943	B	Survived the war
№ 503	№ 334	KT-334[5]			1943	10.11.1943	B	Survived the war

KATShch № on Comm	KATShch № 7.9.1941	SKA № 15.3.1943	No 1945	Laid down	Lauched	Comm	Fleet	Remarks
Builder: 5, Leningrad								
№ 901			KT-621		1941	7.9.1941	B	Sunk 7.11.1942 in collision with the patrol boat *OVR-10* off Kronshtadt, raised and recomm 30.7.1943 as the patrol boat with the smoke screen generator. Reverted 20.4.1945 to minesweeping boat
№ 1401	№ 902			1938	1941	25.7.1941	D	Sunk 5.10.1941 by artillery fire off Peterhof
№ 1402	№ 903	№ 903		1938	1941	25.7.1941	B	Conv 15.3.1943 to patrol boat with a smoke screen generator. Renamed *Leningrad* on 30.1.1944. Conv 7.6.1944 to service craft
№ 1403	№ 904	№ 904	KT-622		1941	25.7.1941	B	Conv 15.3.1943 to patrol boat with a smoke screen generator. Reverted 20.4.1945 to minesweeping boat
№ 1404	№ 905	№ 905		1938	1941	25.7.1941	B	Sunk 7.10.1941 by aircraft at Leningrad, raised and recomm. Conv 15.3.1943 to patrol boat with a smoke screen generator. Sunk 21.6.1944 by German warships off Björk Island
№ 1405	№ 906	№ 906	KT-623	1938	1941	25.7.1941	B	Conv 15.3.1943 to patrol boat with a smoke screen generator. Reverted 20.4.1945 to minesweeping boat
№ 1406	№ 907	№ 907			1938	25.7.1941	B	Former naval service boat *№ 406*, conv 25.7.1941 to minesweeping boat. Conv 15.3.1943 to patrol boat with a smoke screen generator. Deleted 5.8.1944, presumably lost
№ 1407	№ 908	№ 908	KT-624	1938	1941	25.7.1941	B	Conv 15.3.1943 to patrol boat with a smoke screen generator. Reverted 20.4.1945 to minesweeping boat
№ 1408	№ 909	№ 909		1938	1941	25.7.1941	B	Conv 15.3.1943 to patrol boat with a smoke screen generator. Deleted 9.7.1944, presumably lost
№ 1409	№ 910	№ 910	KT-625	1938	1941	25.7.1941	B	Conv 15.3.1943 to patrol boat with a smoke screen generator. Reverted 20.4.1945 to minesweeping boat
№ 1410	№ 911	№ 911	KT-626	1938	1941	25.7.1941	B	Conv 15.3.1943 to patrol boat with a smoke screen generator. Reverted 20.4.1945 to minesweeping boat

№ 1411	№ 912	№ 912	KT-627	1938	1941	25.7.1941	B	Conv 15.3.1943 to patrol boat with a smoke screen generator. Reverted 20.4.1945 to minesweeping boat
№ 1412	№ 913	№ 913		1938	1941	25.7.1941	B	Conv 15.3.1943 to patrol boat with a smoke screen generator. Deleted 9.7.1944, presumably lost
№ 1413	№ 914	№ 914	KT-628	1938	1941	25.7.1941	B	Conv 15.3.1943 to patrol boat with a smoke screen generator. Reverted 20.4.1945 to minesweeping boat
№ 1414	№ 915	№ 915		1938	1941	25.7.1941	B	Conv 15.3.1943 to patrol boat with a smoke screen generator. Reverted 20.4.1945 to minesweeping boat. Deleted 24.10.1944, presumably lost
№ 1415	№ 916	№ 916			1941	25.7.1941	B	Sunk 26.5.1942 by artillery fire off Kronshtad
№ 1416	№ 917	№ 917	KT-629	1938	1941	25.7.1941	B	Conv 15.3.1943 to patrol boat with a smoke screen generator. Reverted 20.4.1945 to minesweeping boat
MI-8						7.10.1941	B	Naval engineering service craft, conv to minesweeping boat. Was active in July 1944. Fate unknown

No on Comm	No 23.2.1943	No 27.11.1943	No 21.6.1944	Laid down	Lauched	Comm	Fleet	Remarks
Training boats								
OSHK-26	KEMTShch-7	RTShch-101	KEMTShch-101	1938	1940	8.8.1942	Cs BS	Naval training boat, conv 8.8.1942 to patrol boat. Conv 23.2.1943 to magnetic minesweeping boat, trfd 27.11.1943 to the Black Sea Fleet, comm as river minesweeper. Conv 31.12.1945 to service craft *Raze"zdnyj kater № 238*
OSHK-28	KEMTShch-8	RTShch-109	KEMTShch-109	1938	1940	8.8.1942	Cs BS	Naval training boat, conv 8.8.1942 to patrol boat. Conv 23.2.1943 to magnetic minesweeping boat, trfd 27.11.1943 to the Black Sea Fleet, comm as river minesweeper. Conv 31.12.1945 to service craft

The effective dates of Pennant Numbers change orders.

Year	Fleet	Date
1944	BS	21.6.1944
	La	21.7.1944
	P	13.9.1944
	B	21.10.1944
1945	B	20.4.1945

Exceptions noted in the main table.

No	Year	Date	Fleet
1.	1942	2.8.1942	Vo
2.	30.1.1944	22.5.1944	On
4.	1944	21.9.1944	B
5.		12.11.1944	B
6.		13.12.1944	B
7.	1945	2.1.1945	B
8.		12.4.1945	B
9.		21.6.1945	B

Left and above: *KM-4* type minesweeping boats.
Vitalij Kostrichenko Collection

Late war production minesweeping boats

No	Laid down	Comp	Comm	Fleet	Remarks
Builder: 5, Leningrad					
KT-210	1944	1945	16.2.1945	BS	Survived the war
KT-231	1944	1945	28.6.1945	BS	Conv 31.12.1945 to service craft Raz"ezdnoj kater № 248
KT-239	1944	1945	28.6.1945	BS	Conv 31.12.1945 to service craft Raz"ezdnoj kater № 245
KT-265		1944	19.8.1944	B	Survived the war
KT-266	1944	1945	25.11.1945	B	Survived the war
KT-283		1944	19.12.1944	B	Survived the war
KT-284	1944	1945	1.9.1945	B	Survived the war
KT-285	1944	1945	1.9.1945	B	Survived the war
KT-291	1943	1944	19.8.1944	B	Survived the war
KT-292	1943	1944	19.8.1944	B	Survived the war
KT-294	1944	1945	25.11.1945	B	Survived the war
KT-295	1943	1944	19.8.1944	B	Survived the war
KT-298		1944	19.12.1944	B	Survived the war
KT-349	1943	1944	23.6.1944	B	Survived the war
KT-350	1943	1944	23.6.1944	B	Survived the war
KT-351	1943	1944	23.6.1944	B / BS	Trfd 7.2.1945 to the Black Sea Fleet
KT-352	1943	1944	23.6.1944	B	Survived the war
KT-353	1943	1944	23.6.1944	B	Survived the war
KT-354	1943	1944	23.6.1944	B	Survived the war
KT-355	1943	1944	28.6.1944	B	Mined 30.7.1944 in Narva Bay
KT-356		1944	23.6.1944	B	Survived the war
KT-358		1944	23.6.1944	B	Survived the war
KT-359		1944	23.6.1944	B	Survived the war
KT-360		1944	23.6.1944	B	Survived the war
KT-363	1944	1945	2.2.1945	B	Survived the war
KT-381		1944	21.9.1944	B	Survived the war
KT-382		1944	21.9.1944	B	Survived the war
KT-383		1944	21.9.1944	B	Survived the war
KT-384		1944	21.9.1944	B	Survived the war
KT-385		1944	21.9.1944	B	Survived the war
KT-386		1944	21.9.1944	B	Survived the war
KT-387		1944	21.9.1944	B	Survived the war
KT-388		1944	21.9.1944	B	Survived the war
KT-389		1944	21.9.1944	B	Survived the war
KT-390		1944	21.9.1944	B	Survived the war
KT-664		1944	21.10.1944	B	Survived the war
KT-665		1944	21.10.1944	B	Survived the war
KT-666		1944	21.10.1944	B	Survived the war
KT-667		1944	21.10.1944	B	Sank 6.11.1944 in a gale off Nerva Island, raised and recomm 12.4.1945
KT-668		1944	21.10.1944	B	Survived the war
KT-669		1944	21.10.1944	B	Survived the war
KT-670		1944	21.10.1944	B	Survived the war
KT-671		1944	21.10.1944	B	Survived the war
KT-672		1944	21.10.1944	B	Survived the war
KT-673		1944	21.10.1944	B	Survived the war
KT-674		1944	21.10.1944	B	Survived the war
KT-675		1944	21.10.1944	B	Survived the war
KT-676		1944	21.10.1944	B	Survived the war
KT-677		1944	21.10.1944	B	Survived the war
KT-678		1944	21.10.1944	B	Survived the war
KT-679		1944	21.10.1944	B	Survived the war
KT-680		1944	21.10.1944	B	Sank 16.11.1944 in collision at Tallinn
KT-681		1944	21.10.1944	B	Survived the war
KT-682		1944	21.10.1944	B	Survived the war
KT-851	1944	1945	16.2.1945	BS	Survived the war
KT-852	1944	1945	16.2.1945	BS	Survived the war
KT-853	1944	1945	16.2.1945	BS	Survived the war
KT-854	1944	1945	16.2.1945	BS	Survived the war
KT-855	1944	1945	16.2.1945	BS	Survived the war

KT-856	1944	1945	16.2.1945	BS	Survived the war	
KT-857	1944	1945	16.2.1945	BS	Survived the war	
KT-952		1945	19.12.1945	B	Survived the war	
KT-954		1945	19.12.1945	B	Survived the war	
KT-955		1945	19.12.1945	B	Survived the war	
KT-958		1945	1.9.1945	B	Survived the war	
KT-960		1945	25.11.1945	B	Survived the war	
KT-962		1945	1.9.1945	B	Survived the war	
KT-965		1945	25.11.1945	B	Survived the war	
KT-966		1945	25.11.1945	B	Survived the war	
KT-967		1945	25.11.1945	B	Survived the war	
KT-968		1945	1.9.1945	B	Survived the war	
KT-972		1945	1.9.1945	B	Survived the war	
KT-973		1945	25.11.1945	B	Survived the war	
KT-974		1945	1.9.1945	B	Survived the war	
KT-975		1945	19.12.1945	B	Survived the war	
KT-976		1945	19.12.1945	B	Survived the war	
KT-977		1945	19.12.1945	B	Survived the war	
KT-978		1945	19.12.1945	B	Survived the war	
KT-979		1945	19.12.1945	B	Survived the war	
KEMTShch-280	1943	1944	4.8.1944	BS	Conv 31.12.1945 to service craft *Raz"ezdnoj kater № 239*	
KEMTShch-281	1943	1944	4.8.1944	BS	Survived the war	
KEMTShch-282	1943	1944	4.8.1944	BS	Conv 31.12.1945 to service craft *Raz"ezdnoj kater № 240*	
KEMTShch-287	1943	1944	4.8.1944	BS	Conv 31.12.1945 to service craft *Raz"ezdnoj kater № 249*	
KEMTShch-288	1943	1944	4.8.1944	BS	Conv 31.12.1945 to service craft *Raz"ezdnoj kater № 247*	
KEMTShch-289	1943	1944	4.8.1944	BS	Conv 31.12.1945 to service craft *Raz"ezdnoj kater № 243*	
KEMTShch-290	1943	1944	4.8.1944	BS	Conv 31.12.1945 to service craft *Raz"ezdnoj kater № 246*	

Two-shaft version of the *KM-2* type; production started as successor to the *ZK* type.

A class (*Project 78*) *Patrol boats / Minesweeping boats*

Displacement: 8t full load
Dimensions: 15.6 x 3.0 x 0.6m
Machinery: 1-shaft GAZ-11 petrol engine, 63hp = 8kts
Armament: 1-0.5in DShK MG, 1-0.3in Maxim MG
Complement: 6

No SKA № co Comm	SKA № 24.3.1943	No 13.6.1944	No 21.7.1944	Laid down	Comp	Comm	Fleet	Remarks
Builder: 341, Rybinsk								
DZ-221*	№ 11	SK-11		1941	1942	16.11.1942	Vo Dn	Conv 10.2.1943 to patrol boat. Trfd 31.5.1944 to the Dnieper Flotilla
DZ-215*	№ 12	SK-12		1941	1942	16.11.1942	Vo Dn	Conv 10.2.1943 to patrol boat. Trfd 31.5.1944 to the Dnieper Flotilla
DZ-222*	№ 13	SK-13		1941	1942	16.11.1942	Vo	Conv 10.2.1943 to patrol boat. Trfd 31.5.1944 to the Dnieper Flotilla
№ 14	№ 14	SK-14		1941	1942	10.2.1943	Vo Dn	Trfd 31.5.1944 to the Dnieper Flotilla
DZ-216 *	№ 15	SK-15		1941	1942	16.11.1942	Vo Dn	Conv 10.2.1943 to patrol boat. Trfd 31.5.1944 to the Dnieper Flotilla
DZ-217*	№ 16	SK-16		1941	1942	16.11.1942	Vo Dn	Conv 10.2.1943 to patrol boat. Trfd 31.5.1944 to the Dnieper Flotilla.
DZ-218*	№ 17	SK-17		1941	1942	16.11.1942	Vo Dn	Conv 10.2.1943 to patrol boat. Trfd 31.5.1944 to the Dnieper Flotilla
DZ-211*	№ 21	SK-21[4]		1941	1942	16.11.1942	Vo Dn	Conv 10.2.1943 to patrol boat. Trfd 18.3.1944 to the Dnieper Flotilla. Handed over 1950s to the DOSAAF as training boat, renamed *DOSAAF-322*. Discarded 1972
DZ-212*	№ 22	SK-22[4]		1941	1942	16.11.1942	Vo Dn	Conv 10.2.1943 to patrol boat. Trfd 18.3.1944 to the Dnieper Flotilla.
DZ-219*	№ 23	SK-23[4]		1941	1942	16.11.1942	Vo Dn	Conv 10.2.1943 to patrol boat. Trfd 18.3.1944 to the Dnieper Flotilla

Warships of the Soviet Fleets, 1939–1945

No SKA № co Comm	SKA № 24.3.1943	No 13.6.1944	No 21.7.1944	Laid down	Comp	Comm	Fleet	Remarks
DZ-213*	№ 24	SK-24[4]		1941	1942	16.11.1942	Vo Dn	Conv 10.2.1943 to patrol boat. Trfd 18.3.1944 to the Dnieper Flotilla
DZ-220*	№ 25	SK-25[4]		1941	1942	16.11.1942	Vo Dn	Conv 10.2.1943 to patrol boat. Trfd 18.3.1944 to the Dnieper Flotilla
DZ-214*	№ 26	SK-26[4]		1941	1942	16.11.1942	Vo Dn	Conv 10.2.1943 to patrol boat. Trfd 18.3.1944 to the Dnieper Flotilla
№ 47[1]	№ 121[3]	SK-47[1]	SK-668[1]	1939	1940	Sept 1941	Wh On La B	Former service boat Kater № 47 of the NKVD. Mobilised 30.8.1941, conv to minesweeping boat. Trfd 31.10.1941 to the Onega Flotilla, conv 29.6.1942 to patrol boat. Trfd 21.7.1944 to the Ladoga Flotilla, trfd 23.1.1945 to the Baltic Fleet
№ 49[2]	№ 122[3]	SK-49[2]	SK-669[2]	1939	1940	Sept 1941	Wh On La B	Former service boat Kater № 49 of the NKVD. Mobilised 30.8.1941, conv to minesweeping boat. Trfd 31.10.1941 to the Onega Flotilla, conv 29.6.1942 to patrol boat. Trfd 21.7.1944 to the Ladoga Flotilla, trfd 23.1.1945 to the Baltic Fleet
№ 661 ex-KATShch № 135** (1942/3)			SK-661	1942	1943	29.1.1944	On La B	Trfd 21.7.1944 to the Ladoga Flotilla. Trfd 23.1.1945 to the Baltic Fleet
№ 662 ex-№ 1 (1942/3)			SK-662	1942	1943	29.1.1944	On La B	Trfd 21.7.1944 to the Ladoga Flotilla. Trfd 23.1.1945 to the Baltic Fleet
№ 663 ex-№ 2 (1942/3)			SK-663	1942	1943	29.1.1944	On La B	Trfd 21.7.1944 to the Ladoga Flotilla. Trfd 23.1.1945 to the Baltic Fleet
№ 664 ex-№ 3 (1942/3)			SK-664	1942	1943	29.1.1944	On La B	Trfd 21.7.1944 to the Ladoga Flotilla. Trfd 23.1.1945 to the Baltic Fleet
№ 665 ex-№ 4 (1942/3)			SK-665	1942	1943	29.1.1944	On La B	Trfd 21.7.1944 to the Ladoga Flotilla. Trfd 23.1.1945 to the Baltic Fleet
№ 666 ex-KATShch № 133** (1942/3)			SK-666	1942	1943	29.1.1944	On	Trfd 21.7.1944 to the Ladoga Flotilla. Trfd 23.1.1945 to the Baltic Fleet
№ 667 ex-KATShch № 134** (1942/3)			SK-667	1942	1943	29.1.1944	On	Trfd 21.7.1944 to the Ladoga Flotilla. Trfd 23.1.1945 to the Baltic Fleet

Notes on construction:
* Completed as smoke screen layer boats, later converted to patrol boats.
** Laid down as minesweeping boats, converted during construction to patrol boats with Pt Nos changed accordingly.

Notes on Pt Nos:
1. Commissioned as the minesweeping boat № 47 (Kater-tral'shchik № 47), number changed to № 423 on 15.10.1941, then reverted to № 47 on 28.11.1941. Following conversion to patrol boat retained the № 47 (Storozhevoi Kater № 47), changed to № 121 on 2.8.1942, given the permanent number SK-47 on 8.3.1944, which was changed again to SK-668 on 21.7.1944.
2. Commissioned as the minesweeping boat № 49 (Kater-tral'shchik № 49), Pt No changed to № 443 on 15.10.1941, then reverted to № 49 on 28.11.1941. Following conversion to patrol boat retained the № 49 (Storozhevoi Kater № 49), changed to № 122 on 2.8.1942, given the permanent number SK-49 on 8.3.1944, which was changed again to SK-669 on 21.7.1944.
3. Pt Nos changed 2.8.1942.
4. Pt Nos changed 7.3.1944.

Communication and service boats, conv during construction.

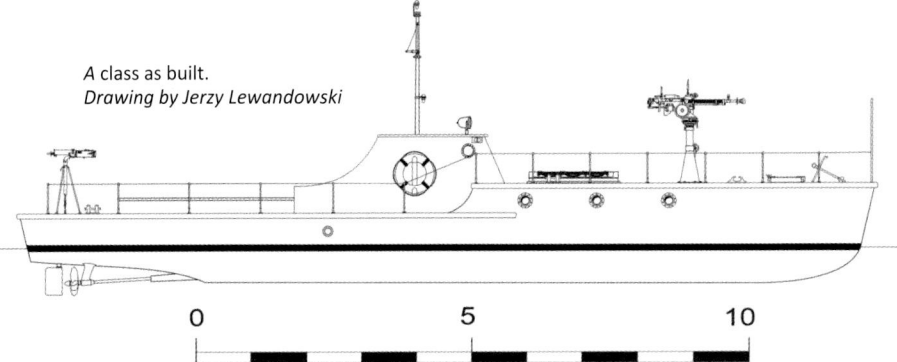

A class as built.
Drawing by Jerzy Lewandowski

SK-22 boat of the *A* class. Przemysław Budzbon Collection

Cross reference: rated as patrol boats

SKA № No Name	Details	Type	From	To	Fate
ChU-1 – ChU-2	Ia-5 type	Rocket boat	29.9.1941	27.4.1945	Conv to service craft
№ 2	KLT type	Minesweeping boat	1940	25.7.1941	Conv to minesweeping boat
№ 3	KLT type	Minesweeping boat	1940	25.7.1941	Conv to minesweeping boat
№ 41	BKM-2 type	Rocket boat	17.7.1944		Survived the war
№ 42	BKM-2 type	Rocket boat	17.7.1944		Survived the war
№ 42	D-3 Project P-19-O	MTB	20.8.1943		Survived the war
№ 43	BKM-2 type	Rocket boat	17.7.1944		Survived the war
№ 44	BKM-2 type	Rocket boat	17.7.1944		Survived the war
№ 52	D-3 Project P-19-O	MTB	30.7.1943		Survived the war
№ 62	D-3 Project P-19-O	MTB	30.7.1943	18.11.1944	Lost
№ 72	D-3 Project P-19-O	MTB	30.7.1943		Survived the war
№ 82	D-3 Project P-19-O	MTB	30.7.1943		Survived the war
№ 92	D-3 Project P-19-O	MTB	30.7.1943		Survived the war
SK-37	D-3 Project P-19	MTB	7.2.1945		
SK-102	D-3 Project P-19	MTB	6.10.1944		Survived the war
SK-112	D-3 Project P-19	MTB	6.10.1944		Survived the war
№ 122	D-3 Project P-19-O	MTB	20.8.1943	14.5.1944	Lost
№ 132	D-3 Project P-19-O	MTB	30.7.1943		Survived the war
№ 142	D-3 Project P-19-O	MTB	20.8.1943		Survived the war
№ 152	D-3 Project P-19-O	MTB	20.8.1943		Survived the war
№ 162	D-3 Project P-19-O	MTB	20.8.1943		Survived the war
SK-171	D-3 Project P-19-O	MTB	14.7.1944		Survived the war
SK-172	D-3 Project P-19-O	MTB	14.7.1944		Survived the war
SK-173	D-3 Project P-19-O	MTB	14.7.1944		Survived the war
SK-174	D-3 Project P-19-O	MTB	14.7.1944		Survived the war
SK-175	D-3 Project P-19-O	MTB	20.1.1944		Survived the war
SK-176	D-3 Project P-19-O	MTB	20.1.1944		Survived the war
SK-177	D-3 Project P-19-O	MTB	20.1.1944		Survived the war
SK-181	D-3 Project P-19	MTB	6.10.1944		Survived the war
SK-182	D-3 Project P-19	MTB	15.3.1943		Survived the war
SK-183	D-3 Project P-19	MTB	6.10.1944		Survived the war
SK-184	D-3 Project P-19	MTB	15.3.1943		Survived the war
SK-185	D-3 Project P-19	MTB	6.10.1944		Survived the war
SK-192	D-3 Project P-19	MTB	15.3.1943		Survived the war
SK-202	D-3 Project P-19	MTB	15.3.1943		Survived the war
SK-272	D-3 Project P-19-O	MTB	12.12.1943		Survived the war
SK-282	D-3 Project P-19-O	MTB	12.12.1943		Survived the war
SK-292	D-3 Project P-19-O	MTB	12.12.1943		Survived the war
SK-320 – SK-327	G-5 type	MTB	26.11.1943	16.10.1944	Revetred to MTBs
SK-655	BKM-2 type	Rocket boat	20.3.1945		Survived the war
SOL'TSY	MSV-30 type	Depot ship	28.7.1941	2.10.1944	Conv to depot ship
UG-1	Ia-5 type	Rocket boat	3.1.1942	27.4.1945	Conv to minesweeping boat
UG-2	Ia-5 type	Rocket boat	3.1.1942	27.4.1945	Conv to minesweeping boat

14.2. Lend-Lease boats

MO-1 class (US AVR 63-foot) — *Patrol craft*

Displacement: 27.2t full load
Dimensions: 19.2 x 4.6 x 1.2m
Machinery: 2-shaft Hall-Scott Defender petrol engines, 1260hp =25kts. Range 490nm at 9kts
Armament: 1-20mm Oerlikon, 4-0.5in (2x2) MGs, 4 DC chutes, 32 DCs
Complement: 12

Data according to Russian sources.

No on Comm	No 3.7.1944	No 4.9.1944	Delivered To	Comm	Fleet	Remarks
Builder: John Trumpy & Sons, Miami, FL						
MO-230 ex-*PTC-31* (US, 1944)		SK-230	31.3.1944 Petropavlovsk	6.4.1944	P	Conv 28.11.1953 to communication boats. Deleted 4.12.1956, handed over to BU
MO-231 ex-*PTC-32* (US, 1944)		SK-231	31.3.1944 Petropavlovsk	6.4.1944	P	Conv 28.11.1953 to communication boats. Deleted 4.12.1956, handed over to BU
MO-232 ex-*PTC-34* (US, 1944)		SK-232	31.3.1944 Petropavlovsk	6.4.1944	P	Conv 28.11.1953 to communication boats. Deleted 4.12.1956, handed over to BU
MO-233 ex-*PTC-36* (US, 1944)		SK-233	31.3.1944 Petropavlovsk	6.4.1944	P	Conv 28.11.1953 to communication boats. Deleted 4.12.1956, handed over to BU
MO-234 ex-*PTC-30* (US, 1944)		SK-234	31.3.1944 Petropavlovsk	6.4.1944	P	Conv 7.10.1953 to communication boats. Deleted 4.12.1956, handed over to BU
MO-235 ex-*PTC-53* (US, 1944)		SK-235	31.3.1944 Petropavlovsk	6.4.1944	P	Conv 7.10.1953 to communication boats. Deleted 21.12.1954, handed over to BU
MO-236 ex-*PTC-39* (US, 1944)		SK-236	31.3.1944 Petropavlovsk	6.4.1944	P	Laid up 13.3.1954, deleted 21.5.1955, handed over to BU
MO-237 ex-*PTC-40* (US, 1944)		SK-237	31.3.1944 Petropavlovsk	6.4.1944	P	Conv 26.7.1953 to training boat, deleted 24.10.1955, handed over to BU
MO-238 ex-*PTC-37* (US, 1944)		SK-238	31.3.1944 Petropavlovsk	6.4.1944	P	Deleted 11.2.1955, trfd to PRC?
MO-239 ex-*PTC-38* (US, 1944)		SK-239	31.3.1944k Petropavlovs	6.4.1944	P	Conv 9.12.1955 to communication boat of naval aviation. Deleted 1956, handed over to BU
MO-240 ex-*PTC-48* (US, 1944)		SK-240	31.3.1944 Petropavlovsk	6.4.1944	P	Deleted 10.6.1955, handed over to BU
MO-241 ex-*PTC-49* (US, 1944)		SK-241	31.3.1944 Petropavlovsk	6.4.1944	P	Deleted 9.8.1955, handed over to BU
MO-242 ex-*PTC-35* (US, 1944)		SK-242	31.3.1944 Petropavlovsk	6.4.1944	P	Deleted 23.4.1955, returned to the US at Maizuru, Japan
MO-243 ex-*PTC-44* (US, 1944)		SK-243	31.3.1944 Petropavlovsk	6.4.1944	P	Deleted 23.4.1955, returned to the US at Maizuru, Japan
MO-244 ex-*PTC-46* (US, 1944)		SK-244	31.3.1944 Petropavlovsk	6.4.1944	P	Deleted 23.4.1955, returned to the US at Maizuru, Japan
MO-245 ex-*PTC-47* (US, 1944)		SK-245	31.3.1944 Petropavlovsk	6.4.1944	P	Laid up 3.7.1954, deleted 4.12.1956, handed over to BU
MO-246 ex-*PTC-41* (US, 1944)		SK-246	31.3.1944 Petropavlovsk	6.4.1944	P	Conv 26.7.1953 to training boat, deleted 24.10.1955, handed over to BU
MO-247 ex-*PTC-43* (US, 1944)		SK-247	31.3.1944 Petropavlovsk	6.4.1944	P	Laid up 13.3.1954, deleted 7.10.1955, handed over to BU.
MO-248 ex-*PTC-42* (US, 1944)		SK-248	31.3.1944 Petropavlovsk	6.4.1944	P	Conv 9.12.1955 to communication boat of naval aviation. Deleted 1956, handed over to BU
MO-249 ex-*PTC-45* (US, 1944)		SK-249	31.3.1944 Petropavlovsk	6.4.1944	P	Deleted 7.10.1955, handed over to BU
MO 435 ex-*PTC-37* (US, 1944)			1.2.1944 Murmansk	20.2.1944	N	Sunk 9.5.1944 by German aircraft in the Barents Sea, north of Kuvshinskaya Salma
MO-436 ex-*PTC-42* (US, 1944)	SK-436		1.2.1944 Murmansk	20.2.1944	N BS	Trfd 29.6.1944 to the Black Sea Fleet. Laid up 30.4.1948, deleted 4.8.1954, returned to the US at Maltepe, Turkey
MO-437 ex-*PTC-40* (US, 1944)			27.2.1944 Murmansk	1.4.1944	N	Sunk 9.5.1944 by German aircraft in the Barents Sea, north of Kuvshinskaya Salma
MO-438 ex-*PTC-41* (US, 1944)	SK-438		27.2.1944 Murmansk	1.4.1944	N BS	Trfd 29.6.1944 to the Black Sea Fleet. Laid up 30.4.1948, deleted 4.8.1954, returned to the US at Maltepe, Turkey
MO-439 ex-*PTC-43* (US, 1944)			27.2.1944 Murmansk	1.4.1944	N	Sunk 9.5.1944 by German aircraft in the Barents Sea, north of Kuvshinskaya Salma
MO-440 ex-*PTC-44* (US, 1944)	SK-440		27.2.1944 Murmansk	1.4.1944	N BS	Trfd 29.6.1944 to the Black Sea Fleet. Laid up 30.4.1948, deleted 4.8.1954, returned to the US at Maltepe, Turkey
MO-441 ex-*PTC-45* (US, 1944)	SK-441		27.2.1944 Murmansk	1.4.1944	N BS	Trfd 29.6.1944 to the Black Sea Fleet. Laid up 30.4.1948, deleted 4.8.1954, returned to the US at Maltepe, Turkey
MO-442 ex-*PTC-46* (US, 1944)	SK-442		27.2.1944 Murmansk	1.4.1944	N BS	Trfd 29.6.1944 to the Black Sea Fleet. Laid up 30.4.1948, deleted 4.8.1954, returned to the US at Maltepe, Turkey
MO-443 ex-*PTC-47* (US, 1944)			27.2.1944 Murmansk	1.4.1944	N	Sunk 9.5.1944 by German aircraft in the Barents Sea, north of Kuvshinskaya Salma
MO-444 ex-*PTC-48* (US, 1944)	SK-444		Apr 1944 Murmansk	27.4.1944	N BS	Trfd 2.7.1944 to the Black Sea Fleet. Laid up 30.4.1948, deleted 4.8.1954, returned to the US at Maltepe, Turkey

Name	Former	Laid down / Builder	Commissioned	Fleet	Fate
MO-445 ex-*PTC-49* (US, 1944)	SK-445	Apr 1944 Murmansk	27.4.1944	N BS	Trfd 2.7.1944 to the Black Sea Fleet. Laid up 2.11.1948, deleted 4.8.1954, returned to the US at Maltepe, Turkey
MO-446 ex-*RPC-1* (US, 1944)	SK-446	Apr 1944 Murmansk	27.4.1944	N BS	Trfd 2.7.1944 to the Black Sea Fleet. Laid up 2.11.1948, deleted 4.8.1954, returned to the US at Maltepe, Turkey
MO-447 ex-*RPC-2* (US, 1944)	SK-447	Apr 1944 Murmansk	27.4.1944	N BS	Trfd 2.7.1944 to the Black Sea Fleet. Laid up 31.7.1947, deleted 4.8.1954, returned to the US at Maltepe, Turkey
MO-448 ex-*RPC-3* (US, 1944)	SK-448	Apr 1944 Murmansk	27.4.1944	N BS	Trfd 2.7.1944 to the Black Sea Fleet. Laid up 2.11.1953, deleted 4.8.1954, returned to the US at Maltepe, Turkey
MO-449 ex-*RPC-4* (US, 1944)	SK-449	Apr 1944 Murmansk	27.4.1944	N BS	Trfd 2.7.1944 to the Black Sea Fleet. Laid up 2.11.1953, deleted 4.8.1954, returned to the US at Maltepe, Turkey
MO-450 ex-*RPC-5* (US, 1944)	SK-450	Apr 1944 Murmansk	27.4.1944	N BS	Trfd 2.7.1944 to the Black Sea Fleet. Laid up 2.11.1953, deleted 4.8.1954, returned to the US at Maltepe, Turkey
MO-451 ex-*RPC-6* (US, 1944)	SK-451	Apr 1944 Murmansk	27.4.1944	N BS	Trfd 2.7.1944 to the Black Sea Fleet. Laid up 30.4.1948, deleted deleted 4.8.1954, returned to the US at Maltepe, Turkey
MO-452 ex-*RPC-7* (US, 1944)	SK-452	Apr 1944 Murmansk	27.4.1944	N BS	Trfd 2.7.1944 to the Black Sea Fleet. Laid up 31.7.1947, deleted deleted 4.8.1954, returned to the US at Maltepe, Turkey
MO-453 ex-*RPC-10* (US, 1944)	SK-453	Apr 1944 Murmansk	27.4.1944	N BS	Trfd 2.7.1944 to the Black Sea Fleet. Laid up 31.7.1947, deleted 4.8.1954, returned to the US at Maltepe, Turkey
MO-454 ex-*RPC-12* (US, 1944)	SK-454	Apr 1944 Murmansk	27.4.1944	N BS	Trfd 2.7.1944 to the Black Sea Fleet. Laid up 2.7.1947, deleted 4.8.1954, returned to the US at Maltepe, Turkey
MO-455 ex-*RPC-13* (US, 1944)	SK-455	Apr 1944 Murmansk	27.4.1944	N BS	Trfd 2.7.1944 to the Black Sea Fleet. Laid up 2.7.1947, deleted 4.8.1954, returned to the US at Maltepe, Turkey
MO-456 ex-*RPC-14* (US, 1944)	SK-456	Apr 1944 Murmansk	27.4.1944	N BS	Trfd 2.7.1944 to the Black Sea Fleet. Laid up 31.1.1947, deleted 4.8.1954, returned to the US at Maltepe, Turkey
MO-457 ex-*RPC-15* (US, 1944)	SK-457	Apr 1944 Murmansk	27.4.1944	N BS	Trfd 2.7.1944 to the Black Sea Fleet. Laid up 31.1.1947, deleted 4.8.1954, returned to the US at Maltepe, Turkey
MO-458 ex-*RPC-16* (US, 1944)	SK-458	Apr 1944 Murmansk	27.4.1944	N BS	Trfd 2.7.1944 to the Black Sea Fleet. Laid up 2.11.1953, deleted 4.8.1954, returned to the US at Maltepe, Turkey
SK-250 ex-*RPC-8* (US, 1944)		9.8.1944 Nikolaevsk	30.8.1944	P	Deleted 23.4.1955, returned to the US at Maizuru, Japan
SK-251 ex-*PTC-60* (US, 1944)		9.8.1944 Nikolaevsk	30.8.1944	P	Deleted 10.6.1955, handed over to BU
SK-252 ex-*PTC-54* (US, 1944)		23.10.1944 Petropavlovsk	14.11.1944	P	Conv 7.10.1953 to communication boat. Deleted 4.12.1956, handed over to BU
SK-253 ex-*PTC-56* (US, 1944)		23.10.1944 Petropavlovsk	14.11.1944	P	Conv 28.11.1953 to communication boat. Deleted 1.2.1954, handed over to BU
SK-254 ex-*PTC-470* (US, 1944)		14.11.1944 Petropavlovsk	28.11.1944	P	Decomm 1.5.1945, trfd to civilian aviation as salvage boat. Recomm 24.12.1946, trfd to the Kamchatka Flotilla. Deleted 10.6.1955, handed over to BU
SK-255 ex-*PTC-55* (US, 1944)		3.1.1945 Petropavlovsk	29.1.1945	P	Conv 7.10.1953 to communication boat. Deleted 4.12.1956, handed over to BU
SK-256 ex-*PTC-57* (US, 1944)		3.1.1945 Petropavlovsk	29.1.1945	P	Deleted 10.6.1955, handed over to BU
SK-257 ex-*PTC-58* (US, 1944)		3.1.1945 Petropavlovsk	29.1.1945	P	Deleted 7.10.1955, handed over to BU
SK-258 ex-*PTC-59* (US, 1944)		3.1.1945 Petropavlovsk	29.1.1945	P	Deleted 10.6.1955, handed over to BU
SK-521 ex-*PTC-61* (US, 1944)		26.8.1944 Murmansk	18.9.1944	N	Conv 25.11.1945 to communication boat, recomm 2.11.1949. Scuttled 28–30.6.1955 off Kildin Island, deleted 8.7.1956
SK-522 ex-*PTC-62* (US, 1944)		26.8.1944 Murmansk	18.9.1944	N	Conv 2.4.1945 to service craft, recomm 2.11.1949. Conv 28.11.1957 to communication boat, deleted 8.8.1959, handed over to BU
SK-523 ex-*PTC-63* (US, 1944)		26.8.1944 Murmansk	18.9.1944	N	Communication boat from 2.4.1945 to 29.6.1945 and from 26.11.1945 to 19.1.1946. Laid up 15.6.1956, deleted 25.6.1956, scuttled 28–30.6.1955 off Kildin Island
SK-524 ex-*RPC-9* (US, 1944)		26.8.1944 Murmansk	18.9.1944	N BS	Trfd 31.7.1945 to the Baltic Fleet. Conv 16.9.1945 to training boat, deleted 9.8.1955, returned to the US at Kiel, Germany
SK-525 ex-*PTC-64* (US, 1944)		6.11.1944 Murmansk	1944	N BS	Trfd 31.7.1945 to the Baltic Fleet. Conv 16.9.1945 to training boat, deleted 9.8.1955, returned to the US at Kiel, Germany
SK-526 ex-*PTC-65* (US, 1944)		6.11.1944 Murmansk	1944	N	Conv 13.11.1944 to communication boat, laid up 15.6.1956, reactivated 18.6.1957. Deleted 18.5.1959, handed over to BU
SK-527 ex-*PTC-66* (US, 1944)		6.11.1944 Murmansk	1944	N	Conv 13.11.1944 to communication boat, laid up 11.4.1953, reactivated 3.11.1956. Deleted 1962, handed over to BU

Note: The ex-US numbers according to Russian sources.

US air-sea rescue boats designated as AVR (Aircraft Vessels, Rescue). Designed by the Miami Shipbuilding Corporation, the version delivered to the Soviet Union (*Model 293*) was a flush-decked subchaser version of the Model 314. Four DC racks were added to each side toward the stern. This model was not intended for air-sea rescue work, so the aft areas were reconfigured to accommodate more fuel, DCs and ammunition. The elimination of the aft cockpit (as fitted to the previous models) provided space for mounting the single 20mm Oerlikon Those delivered to the Soviet Union were referred to as RPC (Russian Patrol Craft). They were initially rated as submarine hunters, but as no sonar was fitted, they were re-rated as patrol boats in the Soviet Union.

The US *AVR 63-foot* type *RPC-6* before transfer to the Soviet Union. Following delivery to Murmansk in Apr 1944 she became *MO-451* of the Northern Fleet. *Naval History and Heritage Command NH 80-G-212747*

14.3. Miscellaneous NKVD patrol boats

Subtype	K-164	K-165	K-197	RPK	K-271	K-332	K-333
Displacement:	14t	15.5t	12t	32t	18t	15t	13t
Length:	12.9m	17.0m	15.2m	23.0m	•	12.9m	•
Beam:	2.7	3.4m	2.9m	3.8m	•	2.9m	•
Draught:	1.2	0.8m	1.0m	1.1m	•	1.4m	•
Total power:	100hp	720hp	300hp	1500hp + 72hp	450hp	100hp	100hp
Speed:	10kts	13kts	10kts	23kts	10kts	8kts	10kts
Range:	160nm	200nm at 10kts	180nm at 8kts	400nm	180nm	330nm	220nm
MGs:	1-0.3in Maxim	1-3in Maxim	2-0.3in Maxim	2-0.5in DShK	2-0.3in Maxim	2-0.3in Maxim	2-0.3in Maxim
Complement:	7	9	11	12	7 (*K-272* 11)	10	6

Subtype	K-334	PK-2	BKM-1	K-17	K-18	KP-11
Displacement:	15t	15t	38t	17t	14t	89t
Length:	12.9m	15.3m	21.7m	18.9m	13.6m	24.1m
Beam:	2.9m	2.9m	4.0m	3.6m	2.8m	6.1m
Draught:	1.4m	1.4m	1.1m	1.4m	1.7m	3.1m
Total power:	100hp	800hp	280hp	600hp	300hp	292hp
Speed:	8kts	12kts	12.5kts	11kts	7kts	•
Range:	330nm	255nm at 10kts	575nm at 11.5kts	100nm at 9kts	120nm at 6.5kts	•
MGs:	2-0.3in Maxim	1-7.92mm, 1-0.3in Maxim	6-0.3in Maxim (1x4, 2x1)	1-7.92mm, 1-0.3in Maxim	1-7.92mm, 1-0.3in Maxim	•
Complement:	10	10	12	9	•	•

NKVD No Kater №	SKA № 1941-43	No 1944	Comp	Subtype	Comm	Fleet	Remarks
K-164 ex-*PK-13* (9.1.1941) ex-*K-19* (1929) ex-*Pulemet* (1928)	№ 0103	SK-164	1917	K-164	8.8.1942	Cs BS	Trfd 25.11.1943 to the Black Sea Fleet. Returned 28.6.1945 to the NKVD Border Guard
K-165 ex-*PK-93* (9.1.1941)	№ 0113[2]	SK-165	1935	K-165	8.8.1942	Cs BS	Trfd 25.11.1943 to the Black Sea Fleet. Returned 28.6.1945 to the NKVD Border Guard
K-197 ex-*PK-70* (9.1.1941)	№ 0158[2]	SK-158	1917	K-197	19.7.1941	BS	Returned 21.6.1945 to the NKVD Border Guard
K-219	№ 083[1]		1936	RPK	19.7.1941	Da BS	Builder: 5, Leningrad. Trfd 4.9.1941 to the Black Sea Fleet. Sunk 12.5.1942 by aircraft off Kerch
K-271 ex-*PK-71* (9.1.1941)				K-271	-	B	Fate unknown. Presumably lost June–July 1941
K-272 ex-*PK-72* (9.1.1941)				K-271	-	B	Lost June–July 1941
K-332 ex-*K-1* (9.1.1941)				K-332	-	B	Lost June–July 1941
K-333 ex-*K-3* (9.1.1941) ex-*№ 3* (1928)			1915?	K-333	-	B	Lost June–July 1941
K-334 ex-*K-2* (9.1.1941) ex-*№ 2* (1928)			1915?	K-334	-	B	Lost June–July 1941
K-386 ex-*PK-50* (9.1.1941)	№ 605	SK-605	1936	PK-2	9.7.1941	Wh	Returned 15.7.1945 to the NKVD Border Guard
K-390	№ 609	SK-609	1940	BKM-1	9.7.1941	Wh	Returned 15.7.1945 to the NKVD Border Guard
		SK-210[5]	1942	BKM-1	6.10.1942	Vo BS	Comm as service craft *RK № 754*. Trfd 5.7.1944 to the Black Sea Fleet. Conv 27.9.1945 to patrol boat
K-396 ex-*K-17* (9.1.1941)	№ 615	SK-615	1931	K-17	9.7.1941	Wh	Returned 15.7.1945 to the NKVD Border Guard
K-397 ex-*K-18* (9.1.1941)	№ 616	SK-616	1930	K-18	9.7.1941	Wh	Returned 15.7.1945 to the NKVD Border Guard
KP-11				KP-11	-	B	Sunk June–July 1941 by aircraft off Saaremaa Island

The effective dates of Pennant Numbers change orders.

Year	Fleet	Date
1941	B	11.9.1941
	Wh	29.9.1941
	BS	17.12.1941
1944	BS	21.5.1944
	Wh	31.5.1944

Exceptions noted in the main table.

No	Year	Date	Fleet
1.	1941	4.9.1941	BS/Da
2.	1943	25.11.1943	BS
3.		27.9.1945	BS

RPK type NKVD Border Guard patrol boats left in NKVD service

NKVD No	Built	Station
K-11		Far East
K-103	1934	Far East
K-104	1934	Far East
K-105	1934	Far East
K-106	1934	Far East
K-131		Amur
K-132		Amur
K-133		Amur
K-134		Amur
K-135		Far East
K-136		Far East
K-137		Far East

Typical to the type, built in 1918 by Zolotov Yd, the Border Guard patrol boat *PK-51 Kommunist*. She was discarded by the 1930s.
Boris Lemachko Collection

PK type
NKVD patrol boats

Displacement: 35t full load
Dimensions: 22.6 x 3.8 x 1.5m
Machinery: 300hp = 15kts. Range 450nm
Armament: 1-45mm/46 21-K, 1-0.3in Maxim MG
Complement: 12

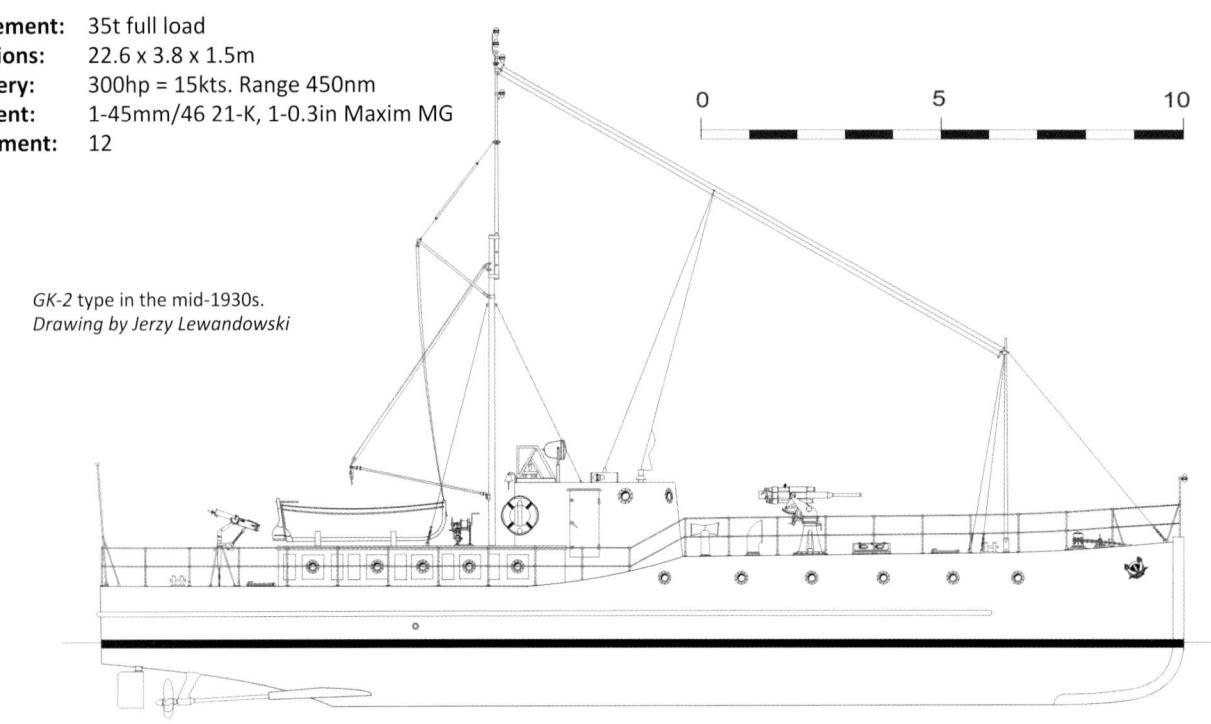

GK-2 type in the mid-1930s.
Drawing by Jerzy Lewandowski

Left: *PK-108 as completed. Przemysław Budzbon Collection*

NKVD No	SKA № 10.12.1941	No 21.5.1944	Comp	Comm	Fleet	Remarks
Builder: Lodejnopol'ska Yard						
K-230 ex-*PK-108* (9.1.1941)	№ 0134	SK-134	1930	19.7.1941	BS	Sunk 3.2.1943 by artillery fire off Myshako. Raised and recomm. Survived the war
K-426 ex-*PK-105* (9.1.1941)	№ 0143	SK-143	21.1.1928	4.9.1941	BS	Returned 21.6.1945 to the NKVD Border Guard
K-425 ex-*PK-103* (9.1.1941)	№ 0103		1.9.1927	19.7.1941	BS	Scuttled 14.11.1941 at Balaklava
K-240 ex-*PK-102* (9.1.1941)	№ 0133		20.5.1927	19.7.1941	BS	Sunk 12.5.1942 by aircraft off Kerch
K-244 ex-*PK-101* (9.1.1941)			20.5.1927	-	BS	Fate unknown, presumably lost 1941
K-427 ex-*PK-104* (9.1.1941)			20.5.1927	-	BS	Fate unknown, presumably lost 1941
K-428 ex-*PK-107* (9.1.1941)			21.1.1920	-	BS	Fate unknown, presumably lost 1941

Wooden-hulled boats; PK meant *Pogranichnyj kater* (Frontier boat).

K-1 type
NKVD patrol boats

Displacement: 13t full load
Dimensions: 12.9 x 2.9 x 1.4m
Machinery: 100hp = 10kts. Range 200nm
Armament: 1-7.92mm MG, 2-0.3in Maxim MGs
Complement: 8

NKVD No	SKA № 29.9.1941	No 31.5.1944	Comp	Comm	Fleet	Remarks
K-391 ex-*K-4* (9.1.1941)	№ 610	SK-610	1928	9.7.1941	Wh	Returned 15.7.1945 to the NKVD Border Guard
K-392 ex-*K-5* (9.1.1941)	№ 611	SK-611	1928	9.7.1941	Wh	Returned 15.7.1945 to the NKVD Border Guard
K-393 ex-*K-6* (9.1.1941)	№ 612	SK-612	1928	9.7.1941	Wh	Returned 15.7.1945 to the NKVD Border Guard
K-394 ex-*K-7* (9.1.1941)	№ 613	SK-613	1928	9.7.1941	Wh	Returned 15.7.1945 to the NKVD Border Guard
K-395 ex-*K-9* (9.1.1941)	№ 614	SK-614	1928	9.7.1941	Wh	Returned 15.7.1945 to the NKVD Border Guard

GK types
NKVD patrol boats

Type	GK-1	GK-2	GK-3	GK-4
Displacement (full):	35t	36t	30t	
Length:	22.6m	24.0m	24.0m	
Beam:	3.8m	3.9m	3.9m	
Draught:	1.5m	1.1m	1.0m	
Petrol engines (2-shaft):	•	Sterling Viking	AM-34	Fiat
Total power:	300hp	1130hp	1350hp	1650hp
Speed (max):	15kts	22kts	24kts	23kts
Range:	300nm at 8kts	300nm at 8kts	300nm	320nm at 17kts
Main armament:	1-20mm Oerlikon	1-45mm/46 21-K	1-45mm/46 21-K	1-45mm/46 21-K
MGs:	1-0.5in DShK MG	1-0.3in Maxim	1-0.3in Maxim	•
DCs:	8 BB-1	8 BB-1	8 BB-1, 18 BM-1	•
Complement:	12	13	16	10

Storozhevoj kater № 0144 during the war.
Przemysław Budzbon Collection

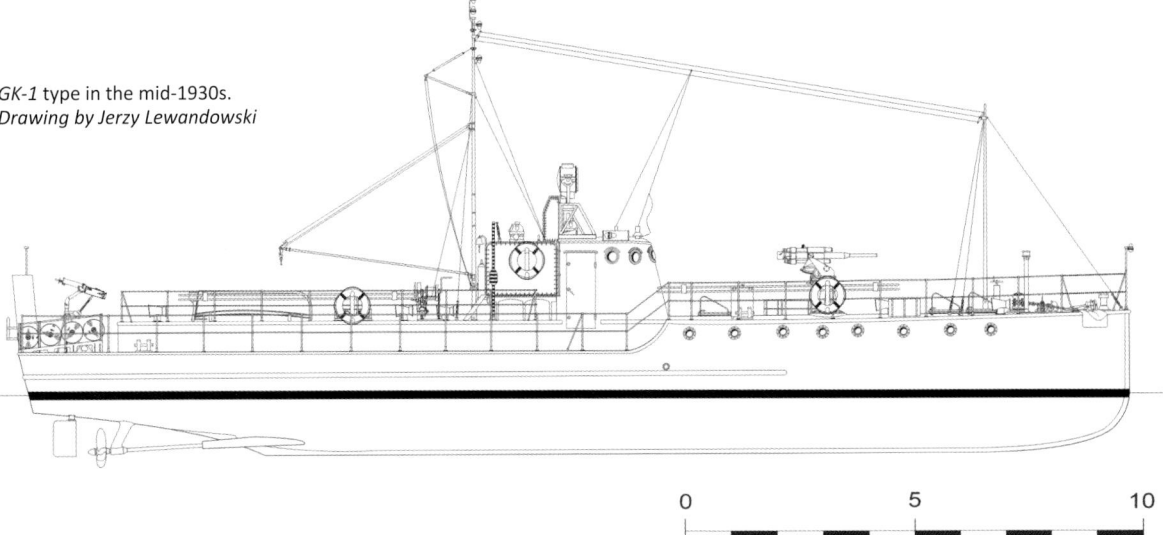

GK-1 type in the mid-1930s.
Drawing by Jerzy Lewandowski

NKVD No	SKA № 17.12.1941	No 21.5.1944	Laid down	Comp	Type	Comm	Fleet	Remarks
Builder: OGPU Border Guard Yard, Leningrad								
K-231	№ 0144	SK-144	1930	1930	GK-1	19.7.1941	BS	Returned 21.6.1945 to the NKVD Border Guard
K-232 ex-*PK-126* (9.1.1941)	№ 047	SK-47	1930	1931	GK-4	19.7.1941	BS	Returned 21.6.1945 to the NKVD Border Guard
K-233 ex-*PK-110* (9.1.1941)	№ 057 № 01		1930	1931	GK-3	19.7.1941	BS	Laid up June 1941, recomm Aug 1942. Conv 16.2.1943 to service craft, renumbered № 01 on 25.11.1943. Mined 7.11.1943 in the Kerch Strait

Wooden-hulled boats designed by the OKTB-2 bureau of the OGPU Border Guard Yard. *GK-4* type was completed as state yacht. GK meant *Granichnyj kater* (Border boat).

NKVD Border Guard patrol boats remaining in NKVD service

NKVD No	Type	Station
K-19 ex-*PK-116* (9.1.1941)	GK-2	Far East
K-20 ex-*PK-117* (9.1.1941)	GK-2	Far East
K-21 ex-*PK-118* (9.1.1941)	GK-2	Far East
K-22 ex-*PK-119* (9.1.1941)	GK-2	Far East
K-23 ex-*PK-120* (9.1.1941)	GK-2	Far East
K-24 ex-*PK-121* (9.1.1941)	GK-2	Far East
K-29 ex-*PK-109* (9.1.1941)	GK-3	Far East
K-30 ex-*PK-110* (9.1.1941)	GK-3	Far East
K-31 ex-*PK-112* (9.1.1941)	GK-3	Far East
K-32 ex-*PK-113* (9.1.1941)	GK-3	Far East
K-33 ex-*PK-114* (9.1.1941)	GK-3	Far East
K-34 ex-*PK-115* (9.1.1941)	GK-3	Far East
K-79 ex-*PK-122* (9.1.1941)	GK-2	Amur
K-80 ex-*PK-123* (9.1.1941)	GK-2	Amur
K-81 ex-*PK-124* (9.1.1941)	GK-3	Amur
K-82 ex-*PK-125* (9.1.1941)	GK-3	Amur

GK type boat under repair, 1940. *Przemysław Budzbon Collection*

MKM type

NKVD patrol boats

Displacement: 18.3t
Dimensions: 16.2 x 3.6 x 1.2m
Machinery: 1-shaft GAM-34BS petrol engine, 1 cruising engine of 72hp, 850hp = 21kts. Range 370nm at 8.5kts
Armament: 1-0.5in DShK MG and/or 1-0.3in Maxim MG (*№ 0138* from 1943 replaced by 1-20mm Oerlikon)
Complement: 12

NKVD No	No 11.9.1941	SKA № 17.12.1941	No 21.5.1945	No 2.1.1945	Laid down	Comp	Comm	Fleet	Remarks
Builder: Taganrog Works, Taganrog									
K-192		№ 0138	SK-138		1939	1940	17.12.1941	BS	YN 52. Stranded 4.11.1943 off Lake Tobechik on the Kerch Peninsula. Raised and recomm. Returned 21.6.1945 to the NKVD Border Guard
K-210		№ 967	SK-67		1939	1940	17.12.1941	BS	YN 63. Returned 21.6.1945 to the NKVD Border Guard
K-234		№ 0154			1939	1940	17.12.1941	BS	YN 7. Sunk 6.2.1943 by artillery fire off Stanichka
K-273	I-50			SK-50	1939	1940	11.9.1941	B	YN 54. Returned 30.8.1945 to the NKVD Border Guard
K-274	I-51			SK-51	1939	1940	11.9.1941	B	YN 56. Returned 30.8.1945 to the NKVD Border Guard
K-335				SK-335[1]	1939	1940	4.3.1942	B	Survived the warExceptions noted in the main table.

Exceptions noted in the main table.

No	Year	Date	Fleet
1.	1944	6.10.1944	B

14.0 Patrol boats

BK-4 type
NKVD patrol boats

Displacement: 20.3t full load
Dimensions: 17.6 x 3.85 x 1.3m
Machinery: 2-shaft GAM-34BS petrol engines, 1700hp = 32kts. Range 220nm at 18kts
Armament: 2-0.5in DShK MGs, 8 BM-1 DCs
Complement: 8

BK-4 type interceptor, from a shipyard drawing.
Przemysław Budzbon Collection

NKVD No	SKA № 17.12.1941	No 21.5.1944	YN	Laid down	Comp	Comm	Fleet	Remarks
Builder: 5, Leningrad								
K-209	№ 0144[1] № 017	SK-17	1	1939	1940	19.7.1941	BS Da	Returned 21.6.1945 to the NKVD Border Guard
K-198	№ 027	SK-27	2	1940	1941	17.12.1941	BS	Taken over from the NKVD during sea trials. Mined 18.4.1944 at the entrance to Odessa, raised and recomm 21.5.1944 as service craft. Returned 21.6.1945 to the NKVD Border Guard
K-239	№ 037			1940	1941	17.12.1941	BS	Taken over from the NKVD during sea trials. Deleted 19.10.1942. Returned 21.6.1945 to the NKVD Border Guard
BK-1	SK-1[2]				1941	6.2.1942	B	Returned 30.8.1945 to the NKVD Border Guard
BK-2	SK-2[2]				1941	6.2.1942	B	Returned 30.8.1945 to the NKVD Border Guard

Exceptions noted in the main table.

No	Year	Date	Fleet
1.	1941	10.12.1941	BS
2.	1945	2.1.1945	B

Wooden-hulled fast interception boats; only *K-209* was delivered to the NKVD before the German invasion, the others being taken over by the Navy during construction. BK meant *Bystrokhodnyj kater* (Fast boat).

14.4. Army conversions

BKM-70 type
Army tugboats

Displacement: 5t
Dimensions: 7.1 x 3.4 x 0.6m
Machinery: 1-shaft GAZ-11 petrol engine, 52hp = 6kts
Armament: 1-0.3in MG
Complement: 5

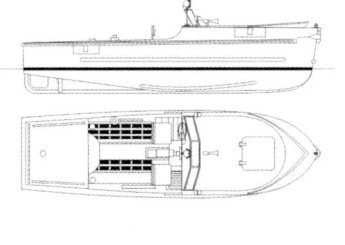

BKM type as built.
Drawing by Jerzy Lewandowski

A BKM-70 type boat.
Przemysław Budzbon Collection

SKA № on Comm 2.4.1944	No	Laid down	Comp	Fleet	Comm	Remarks
№ 1	SK-221	1942	1943	Im B	24.4.1943	Trfd 2.4.1944 to the Baltic Fleet. Survived the war
№ 2	SK-222	1942	1943	Im B	24.4.1943	Trfd 2.4.1944 to the Baltic Fleet. Survived the war
№ 3	SK-223	1942	1943	Im B	24.4.1943	Trfd 2.4.1944 to the Baltic Fleet. Survived the war
№ 4	SK-224	1942	1943	Im B	24.4.1943	Trfd 2.4.1944 to the Baltic Fleet. Survived the war
№ 5	SK-225	1942	1943	Im B	24.4.1943	Trfd 2.4.1944 to the Baltic Fleet. Survived the war

Tugboats of the engineering troops of the North-Western Front of the Red Army, trfd 1943 to the Ilmen Flotilla and conv to patrol boats. The BKM stands for Buksirnyj Kater Motornyj (Motor Tug Boat). Reportedly could carry 0.5in DShK MG.

14.5. Civilian conversions

14.5.1. Mobilised passenger vessels

Opyt type   *River ferries*

Displacement: 65t
Dimensions: 30.0 x 5.6 x 0.7m
Machinery: 2-shaft diesels, 150hp = 11kts.
Armament: 2 to 4-45mm/46 (see note), 1 or 2-0.3in Maxim MGs

No 1941	Name	Comm	Fleet	Remarks
	Builder: 300, Kiev			
S-1	PT-1 PAVLIK MOROZOV	26.7.1941	Pn	Mobilised 22.7.1941, comm with the Berezina Detachment. Sunk 31.8.1941 by artillery fire on the Dnieper off Domantovo. Raised 1944, rebuilt, to civilian service
S-2	PT-2	26.7.1941	Pn	Mobilised 22.7.1941, comm with the Berezina Detachment. Scuttled 18.9.1941 at Kiev
S-3	PT-3 TOVARISHCH	26.7.1941	Pn	Mobilised 22.7.1941, comm with the Berezina Detachment. Heavily damaged 18.8.1941 by German aircraft, scuttled 18.9.1941 at Kiev
S-4	PT-4	Aug 1941	Pn	Mobilised summer 1941 comm with the Chernigov Detachment. Scuttled 11.9.1941 on Desna River at Ladinski creek. Raised 1943, BU
S-5	PT-5	-	Pn	Mobilised summer 1941, conv abandoned because of poor condition
S-6	PT-6	-	Pn	Mobilised summer 1941, conv abandoned because of poor condition
S-7	PT-7	Aug 1941	Pn	Mobilised summer 1941, comm with the Dnepropetrovsk Detachment. Scuttled 25.8.1941 at Dnepropetrovsk
S-8	PT-8	-	Pn	Mobilised summer 1941, conv abandoned because of poor condition
S-9	PT-9	Aug 1941	Pn	Mobilised summer 1941, comm with the Chernigov Detachment. Sunk 9.9.1941 by artillery fire on Desna River off Shestovits
S-10	PT-10	Aug 1941	Pn	Mobilised summer 1941, comm with the Dnepropetrovsk Detachment. Scuttled at Dnepropetrovsk
S-12	PT-12	Aug 1941	Pn	Mobilised summer 1941, comm with the Dnepropetrovsk Detachment. Abandoned 25.8.1941 at Dnepropetrovsk, seized by the Germans

Converted small river passenger ferries ('river trams') built 1935-1940, six of them were armed with two 45mm turrets (either 41-K type twin or 40-K single) designed for river monitors or two 45mm in single 21-K type mountings.

14.5.2. NKVD Border Guard fishing vessel types

STOROZHEVOJ KATER № 601   *Drifter*

Displacement: 110t
Dimensions: 25.9 x 5.0 x 2.5m
Machinery: 1-shaft, 100hp diesel = 5.8kts. Range 1084тm at 6.5kts
Armament: 6-0.3in Maxim (1x4, 2x1) MGs
Complement: 16

Nikolai Knipovich back in civilian service after the war.
www.littorina.info

SKA № 29.9.1941	No 1.4.1944	NKVD No	Built	Comm	Fleet	Remarks
№ 601	SK-601	PS-1 ex-*PSh-9* (9.1.1941)	1937	9.7.1941	N Wh	Mobilised 22.6.1941, trfd 25.8.1941 to the White Sea Flotilla. Conv 31.3.1945 to service craft, returned 15.7.1945, numbered *PS-1*, discarded late 1940s

Storozhevoj kater № 602 class

Motorboats

Displacement: 53.5t
Dimensions: 17.0 x 4.9 x 2.4m
Machinery: 1-shaft diesel, 50hp = 5kts. Range 960nm
Armament: 2-0.3in MGs
Complement: 7

NKVD No	SKA № 29.9.1941	No 1.4.1944	Built	Comm	Fleet	Remarks
PS-2	№ 602	SK-602	1940	9.7.1941	N Wh	Mobilised 22.6.1941, trfd 25.8.1941 to the White Sea Flotilla. Returned 15.7.1945, number reverted. Discarded 1950s
PS-3	№ 603	SK-603	1940	9.7.1941	N Wh	Mobilised 22.6.1941, trfd 25.8.1941 to the White Sea Flotilla. Returned 15.7.1945, number reverted. Discarded 1950s
PS-4	№ 604	SK-604	1940	9.7.1941	N Wh	Mobilised 22.6.1941, trfd 25.8.1941 to the White Sea Flotilla. Returned 15.7.1945, number reverted. Discarded 1950s

Storozhevoj kater № 619 class

Drifters

Displacement: 58.7t
Dimensions: 16.6 x 4.9 x 2.4m
Machinery: 1-shaft ICE, 50hp = 7kts. Range 760nm at 6.5kts
Armament: 1-0.5in DShK MG, 1-0.3in MG
№ 621, № 622, № 624: 2-0.3in MGs
Complement: 17

*Storozhevoj kater № 619 during the war.
Przemysław Budzbon Collection*

SKA № 6.7.1942	No 31.5.1944	Built	Comm	Fleet	Remarks
№ 619	SK-619	1942	6.7.1942	Wh	
№ 620	SK-620	1942	6.7.1942	Wh	Service craft between 16.6.1944 and 16.2.1945
№ 621		1942	6.7.1942	Wh	Conv 18.5.1944 to diving tender *VM-20*. Survived the war
№ 622	SK-622	1942	6.7.1942	Wh	
№ 623	SK-623	1942	6.7.1942	Wh	Service craft between 22.7.1944 and 16.2.1945
№ 624	SK-624	1942	6.7.1942	Wh	
№ 625	SK-625	1942	6.7.1942	Wh	
№ 626	SK-625	1942	6.7.1942	Wh	

Ordered in 1940 by NKVD in local Arctic yards, design based on drifter type fishing vessel. Taken over by the Navy upon completion and fitted as patrol boats.

Motorboats

NKVD No	No 23.6.1941	Name	Comm	Fleet	Remarks
PS-2	IK-8	AKULA	23.6.1941	N	Mobilised 22.6.1941. Fate unknown
PS-3	IK-9	DEL'FIN	23.6.1941	N	Ship confiscated for violating sea border. Mobilised 22.6.1941. Fate unknown
PS-4	IK-10	OPS-1	23.6.1941	N	Mobilised 22.6.1941. Lost during the war
PS-5	•	•	23.6.1941	N	*Kasatka* type. Mobilised 22.6.1941. Lost during the war
PS-9	•	SHTIL'	23.6.1941	N	Ship confiscated for violating sea border. Mobilised 22.6.1941. Lost during the war

Steam tugboat

NKVD No	No 21.5.1944	Details	Comm	Fleet	Remarks
PS-6 ex-*K-10* (9.1.1941)	ShK-17	10 men	22.6.1941	N	Survived the war

Sail-motor schooners

NKVD No	SKA № 29.9.1941	No 21.5.1944	Details	Comm	Fleet	Remarks
PS-1	№ 077	SK-77	125t; 26.0 x 5.5 x 3.0m; 280hp = 9 w. 400mm, 1-45mm/46 21-K, 1-0.5in MG; 9 men.	19.7.1941	BS	Built 1936. Mobilised 22.6.1941 renumbered on 17.12.1941, renumbered on 21.5.1944. Returned 21.6.1945 to NKVD.
PS-1 ex-*PSh-13* (9.1.1941)			46t; 20.5 x 4.4 x 1.7m; 100hp = 9.2; 880nm at 7.7kts; 1-45mm/46 21-K, 2-0.3in; 12 men	9.4.1942	Cs	Built 1930. Mobilised 22.6.1941 as service craft, conv to patrol boat. Returned 1.8.1944 to NKVD
PS-2 ex-*PSh-14* (9.1.1941)				9.4.1942	Cs	Built 1930. Mobilised 22.6.1941 as service craft, conv to 9.4.1942 patrol boat. Returned 1.8.1944 to NKVD
PS-3 ex-*PSh-8* (9.1.1941)			22.6x5.1 x 1.4m; 50hp=4kts; 10men	June 1941	Cs	Mobilised 22.6.1941. Returned 1.8.1944 to NKVD
PS-4			•	23.6.1941	B	Built 1909. Tugboat, mobilised 22.6.1941. Returned 4.7.1945, renamed *PS-230*, discarded 18.5.1950
PS-4			•	23.6.1941	BS	Mobilised 22.6.1941. Fate unknown
PS-5 ex-*K-50* (9.1.1941)			8t; 150hp; 3 men	22.6.1941	N	Mobilised 22.6.1941. Fate unknown

An OGPU Border Guard motor-sail schooner slipped at Novorossiysk, 1930s. *Przemysław Budzbon Collection*

An OGPU Border Guard motor-sail schooner wintering at Odessa, 1930s. Note the sentry with long rifle and bayonet. *Przemysław Budzbon Collection*

14.5.3. Mobilised fishing vessels

Kungas-Kavasaki types *Motorboats*

Displacement: 26t
Dimensions: 16.2 x 3.65 x 1.1m
Machinery: 1-shaft, ICE, 30hp (see note*) = 6.5kts. Radius 300–500nm at 5kts
Armament: 1-0.3in MG, 1 KAT sweep, 4 mines
Complement: 6

Mobilised fishing boats

Patrol boats

No on Comm	No 19.9.1944	Comm	Fleet	Remarks
OV-45		Oct 1941	P	Mobilised 7.10.1941. Decomm 5.7.1943 to civilian service
OV-46		Oct 1941	P	Mobilised 7.10.1941. Decomm 5.7.1943 to civilian service
OV-51		Oct 1941	P	Mobilised 7.10.1941. Decomm 5.7.1943 to civilian service
OV-52		Oct 1941	P	Mobilised 7.10.1941. Decomm 5.7.1943 to civilian service
OV-53		Oct 1941	P	Mobilised 7.10.1941. Decomm 5.7.1943 to civilian service
OV-54		Oct 1941	P	Mobilised 7.10.1941. Decomm 5.7.1943 to civilian service
OV-55		Oct 1941	P	Mobilised 7.10.1941. Decomm 5.7.1943 to civilian service
OV-61	SK-61	Oct 1941	P	Mobilised 7.10.1941. Conv 30.10.1945 to service craft
OV-62	SK-62	Oct 1941	P	Mobilised 7.10.1941. Decomm 30.10.1945 to civilian service
OV-63	SK-63	Oct 1941	P	Mobilised 7.10.1941. Conv 20.10.1945 to service craft
OV-64	SK-64	Oct 1941	P	Mobilised 7.10.1941. Decomm 30.4.1945 to civilian service
OV-65		Oct 1941	P	Mobilised 7.10.1941. Decomm 5.7.1943 to civilian service
OV-71		Oct 1941	P	Mobilised 7.10.1941. Decomm 5.7.1943 to civilian service
OV-72		Oct 1941	P	Mobilised 7.10.1941. Decomm 5.7.1943 to civilian service
OV-73		Oct 1941	P	Mobilised 7.10.1941. Decomm 5.7.1943 to civilian service
OV-74		Oct 1941	P	Mobilised 7.10.1941. Decomm 5.7.1943 to civilian service
OV-75		Oct 1941	P	Mobilised 7.10.1941. Decomm 5.7.1943 to civilian service
OV-81		Oct 1941	P	Mobilised 7.10.1941. Decomm 5.7.1943 to civilian service
OV-82		Oct 1941	P	Mobilised 7.10.1941. Decomm 5.7.1943 to civilian service
OV-83		Oct 1941	P	Mobilised 7.10.1941. Decomm 5.7.1943 to civilian service
OV-84		Oct 1941	P	Mobilised 7.10.1941. Decomm 5.7.1943 to civilian service
OV-85		Oct 1941	P	Mobilised 7.10.1941. Decomm 5.7.1943 to civilian service
OV-91		Oct 1941	P	Mobilised 7.10.1941. Decomm 5.7.1943 to civilian service
OV-92		Oct 1941	P	Mobilised 7.10.1941. Decomm 5.7.1943 to civilian service
OV-93		Oct 1941	P	Mobilised 7.10.1941. Decomm 5.7.1943 to civilian service
OV-94		Oct 1941	P	Mobilised 7.10.1941. Decomm 5.7.1943 to civilian service
OV-95		Oct 1941	P	Mobilised 7.10.1941. Decomm 5.7.1943 to civilian service
OV-101 ex-*Razvedchik № 12* (1941)	SK-101	Oct 1941	P	Mobilised 7.10.1941. Conv 20.10.1945 to service craft
OV-102	SK-102	Oct 1941	P	Mobilised 7.10.1941. Conv 20.10.1945 to service craft
OV-103	SK-103	Oct 1941	P	Mobilised 7.10.1941. Conv 20.10.1945 to service craft
OV-104	SK-104	Oct 1941	P	Mobilised 7.10.1941. Conv 20.10.1945 to service craft
OV-105	SK-105	Oct 1941	P	Mobilised 7.10.1941. Conv 20.10.1945 to service craft
OV-106	SK-106	Oct 1941	P	Mobilised 7.10.1941. Conv 20.10.1945 to service craft
OV-107		Oct 1941	P	Mobilised 7.10.1941. Decomm 5.7.1943 to civilian service
OV-121	SK-121	Oct 1941	P	Mobilised 7.10.1941. Decomm before Aug 1945 to civilian service
OV-122	SK-122	Oct 1941	P	Mobilised 7.10.1941. Survived the war
OV-123	SK-123	Oct 1941	P	Mobilised 7.10.1941. Survived the war
OV-124	SK-124	Oct 1941	P	Mobilised 7.10.1941. Survived the war
OV-125	SK-125	Oct 1941	P	Mobilised 7.10.1941. Survived the war
OV-126	SK-126	Oct 1941	P	Mobilised 7.10.1941. Survived the war
OV-131 ex-*MK-19* (1941)		Oct 1941	P	Mobilised 7.10.1941. Decomm 5.7.1943 to civilian service
OV-132 ex-*MK-20* (1941)		Oct 1941	P	Mobilised 7.10.1941. Decomm 5.7.1943 to civilian service
OV-133 ex-*MK-21* (1941)		Oct 1941	P	Mobilised 7.10.1941. Decomm 5.7.1943 to civilian service
OV-134 ex-*MK-22* (1941)		Oct 1941	P	Mobilised 7.10.1941. Decomm 5.7.1943 to civilian service
OV-135 ex-*MK-23* (1941)		Oct 1941	P	Mobilised 7.10.1941. Decomm 5.7.1943 to civilian service
OV-136 ex-*MK-24* (1941)		Oct 1941	P	Mobilised 7.10.1941. Decomm 5.7.1943 to civilian service
OV-141		Oct 1941	P	Mobilised 7.10.1941. Decomm 5.7.1943 to civilian service
OV-142		Oct 1941	P	Mobilised 7.10.1941. Decomm 5.7.1943 to civilian service

No on Comm	No 19.9.1944	Comm	Fleet	Remarks
OV-143		Oct 1941	P	Mobilised 7.10.1941. Decomm 5.7.1943 to civilian service
OV-144		Oct 1941	P	Mobilised 7.10.1941. Decomm 5.7.1943 to civilian service
OV-145		Oct 1941	P	Mobilised 7.10.1941. Conv 5.8.1943 to coastal diving tender *VRD-53*
OV-146		Oct 1941	P	Mobilised 7.10.1941. Decomm 5.7.1943 to civilian service
OV-147	SK-147[1]	Aut 1941	P	Mobilised autumn 1941 as service craft. Conv 5.7.1943 to patrol boat. Reverted 20.10.1945 to service craft
OV-148	SK-148[1]	Aut 1941	P	Mobilised autumn 1941 as service craft. Conv 5.7.1943 to patrol boat. Reverted 20.10.1945 to service craft
OV-149	SK-149[1]	Aut 1941	P	Mobilised autumn 1941 as service craft. Conv 5.7.1943 to patrol boat. Reverted 20.10.1945 to service craft
OV-152		Aut 1941	P	Mobilised autumn 1941. Decomm 5.2.1943 to civilian service
OV-153		Aut 1941	P	Mobilised autumn 1941. Decomm 5.2.1943 to civilian service
OV-154		Aut 1941	P	Mobilised autumn 1941. Decomm 5.2.1943 to civilian service
OV-155		Aut 1941	P	Mobilised autumn 1941. Decomm 5.2.1943 to civilian service
OV-156		Aut 1941	P	Mobilised autumn 1941. Decomm 5.2.1943 to civilian service
SK-117		7.10.1941	P	Mobilised 7.10.1941 as service craft. Conv 13.9.1944 to patrol boat. Reverted 20.10.1945 to service craft
SK-118		7.10.1941	P	Mobilised 7.10.1941 as service craft. Conv 13.9.1944 to patrol boat. Reverted 20.10.1945 to service craft
SK-127		7.10.1941	P	Mobilised 7.10.1941 as service craft. Conv 13.9.1944 to patrol boat. Survived the war
SK-128 ex-*Oktiabr'* (1944)		7.10.1941	P	Mobilised 7.10.1941 as service craft. Conv 13.9.1944 to patrol boat. Survived the war
SK-237 ex-*Cheliuskinets* (1944)		7.10.1941	P	Mobilised 7.10.1941 as service craft. Conv 13.9.1944 to patrol boat. Survived the war
SK-238 ex-*Udarnik* (1944)		7.10.1941	P	Mobilised 7.10.1941 as service craft. Conv 13.9.1944 to patrol boat. Survived the war
SK-239 ex-*Chkalov* (1944)		7.10.1941	P	Mobilised 7.10.1941 as service craft. Conv 13.9.1944 to patrol boat. Survived the war
SK-761		Aug 1945	P	Mobilised 10.8.1945. Conv 20.9.1945 to service craft
SK-762		Aug 1945	P	Mobilised 10.8.1945. Conv 20.9.1945 to service craft
SK-763		Aug 1945	P	Mobilised 10.8.1945. Conv 20.9.1945 to service craft
SK-764		Aug 1945	P	Mobilised 10.8.1945. Conv 20.9.1945 to service craft
SK-765		Aug 1945	P	Mobilised 10.8.1945. Conv 20.9.1945 to service craft
SK-766		Aug 1945	P	Mobilised 10.8.1945. Conv 20.9.1945 to service craft
SK-767		Aug 1945	P	Mobilised 10.8.1945. Conv 20.9.1945 to service craft
SK-768		Aug 1945	P	Mobilised 10.8.1945. Conv 20.9.1945 to service craft
SK-769		Aug 1945	P	Mobilised 10.8.1945. Conv 20.9.1945 to service craft
SK-770		Aug 1945	P	Mobilised 10.8.1945. Conv 20.9.1945 to service craft
SK-771		Aug 1945	P	Mobilised 10.8.1945. Conv 20.9.1945 to service craft
SK-772		Aug 1945	P	Mobilised 10.8.1945. Conv 20.9.1945 to service craft
SK-773		Aug 1945	P	Mobilised 10.8.1945. Conv 20.9.1945 to service craft
SK-774		Aug 1945	P	Mobilised 10.8.1945. Conv 20.9.1945 to service craft
SK-775		Aug 1945	P	Mobilised 10.8.1945. Conv 20.9.1945 to service craft
SK-776		Aug 1945	P	Mobilised 10.8.1945. Conv 20.9.1945 to service craft
SK-777		Aug 1945	P	Mobilised 10.8.1945. Conv 20.9.1945 to service craft
SK-778		Aug 1945	P	Mobilised 10.8.1945. Conv 20.9.1945 to service craft
SK-779		Aug 1945	P	Mobilised 10.8.1945. Conv 20.9.1945 to service craft
SK-780		Aug 1945	P	Mobilised 10.8.1945. Conv 20.9.1945 to service craft
SK-781		Aug 1945	P	Mobilised 10.8.1945. Conv 20.9.1945 to service craft
SK-782		Aug 1945	P	Mobilised 10.8.1945. Conv 20.9.1945 to service craft
SK-783		Aug 1945	P	Mobilised 10.8.1945. Conv 20.9.1945 to service craft
SK-784		Aug 1945	P	Mobilised 10.8.1945. Conv 20.9.1945 to service craft
SK-785		Aug 1945	P	Mobilised 10.8.1945. Conv 20.9.1945 to service craft
SK-786		Aug 1945	P	Mobilised 10.8.1945. Conv 20.9.1945 to service craft
SK-787		Aug 1945	P	Mobilised 10.8.1945. Conv 20.9.1945 to service craft
SK-788		Aug 1945	P	Mobilised 10.8.1945. Conv 20.9.1945 to service craft
SK-789		Aug 1945	P	Mobilised 10.8.1945. Conv 20.9.1945 to service craft
SK-790		Aug 1945	P	Mobilised 10.8.1945. Conv 20.9.1945 to service craft
SK-791		Aug 1945	P	Mobilised 10.8.1945. Conv 20.9.1945 to service craft
SK-792		Aug 1945	P	Mobilised 10.8.1945. Conv 20.9.1945 to service craft
SK-793		Aug 1945	P	Mobilised 10.8.1945. Conv 20.9.1945 to service craft

14.0 Patrol boats

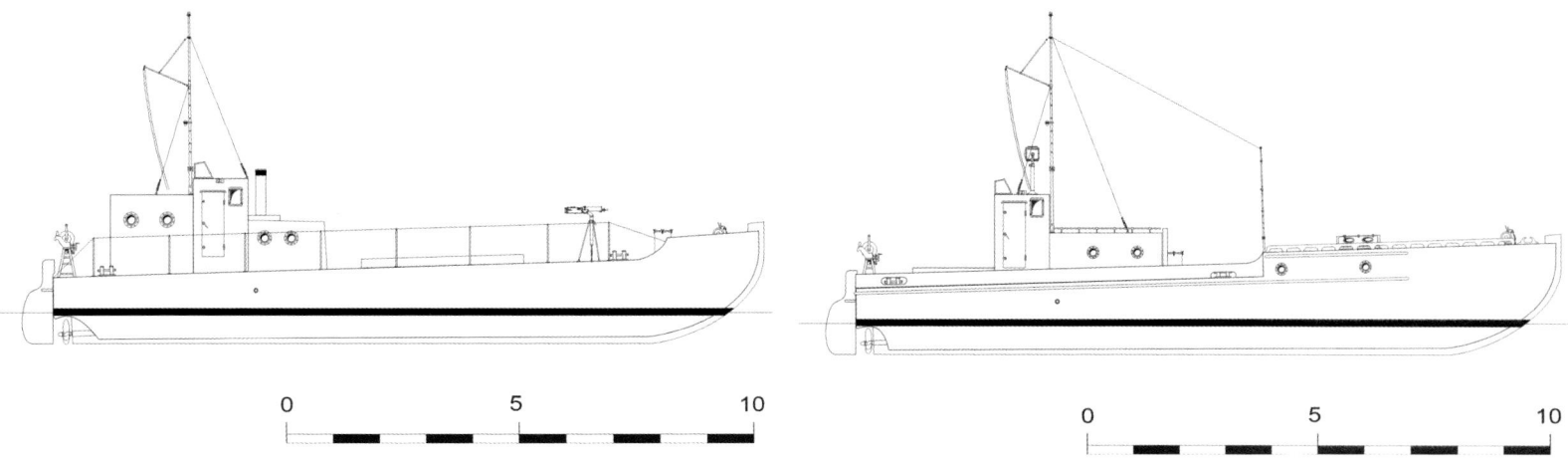

Kungas-Kavasaki type patrol boat.
Drawing by Jerzy Lewandowski

Kungas-Kavasaki type minesweeping boat with long forecastle.
Drawing by Jerzy Lewandowski

SK-794	Aug 1945	P	Mobilised 10.8.1945. Conv 20.9.1945 to service craft
SK-795	Aug 1945	P	Mobilised 10.8.1945. Conv 20.9.1945 to service craft
SK-796	Aug 1945	P	Mobilised 10.8.1945. Conv 20.9.1945 to service craft
SK-797	Aug 1945	P	Mobilised 10.8.1945. Conv 20.9.1945 to service craft
SK-798	Aug 1945	P	Mobilised 10.8.1945. Conv 20.9.1945 to service craft
SK-799	Aug 1945	P	Mobilised 10.8.1945. Conv 20.9.1945 to service craft
SK-800	Aug 1945	P	Mobilised 10.8.1945. Conv 20.9.1945 to service craft
SK-801	Aug 1945	P	Mobilised 10.8.1945. Conv 20.9.1945 to service craft
SK-802	Aug 1945	P	Mobilised 10.8.1945. Conv 20.9.1945 to service craft
SK-803	Aug 1945	P	Mobilised 10.8.1945. Conv 20.9.1945 to service craft
SK-804	Aug 1945	P	Mobilised 10.8.1945. Conv 20.9.1945 to service craft
SK-805	Aug 1945	P	Mobilised 10.8.1945. Conv 20.9.1945 to service craft
SK-806	Aug 1945	P	Mobilised 10.8.1945. Conv 20.9.1945 to service craft
SK-807	Aug 1945	P	Mobilised 10.8.1945. Conv 20.9.1945 to service craft
SK-808	Aug 1945	P	Mobilised 10.8.1945. Conv 20.9.1945 to service craft
SK-809	Aug 1945	P	Mobilised 10.8.1945. Conv 20.9.1945 to service craft
SK-812	Aug 1945	P	Mobilised 10.8.1945. Conv 20.9.1945 to service craft
SK-813	Aug 1945	P	Mobilised 10.8.1945. Conv 20.9.1945 to service craft
SK-814	Aug 1945	P	Mobilised 10.8.1945. Conv 20.9.1945 to service craft
SK-815	Aug 1945	P	Mobilised 10.8.1945. Conv 20.9.1945 to service craft
SK-816	Aug 1945	P	Mobilised 10.8.1945. Conv 20.9.1945 to service craft
SK-817	Aug 1945	P	Mobilised 10.8.1945. Conv 20.9.1945 to service craft
SK-818	Aug 1945	P	Mobilised 10.8.1945. Conv 20.9.1945 to service craft
SK-819	Aug 1945	P	Mobilised 10.8.1945. Conv 20.9.1945 to service craft
SK-820	Aug 1945	P	Mobilised 10.8.1945. Conv 20.9.1945 to service craft
SK-821	Aug 1945	P	Mobilised 10.8.1945. Conv 20.9.1945 to service craft
SK-822	Aug 1945	P	Mobilised 10.8.1945. Conv 20.9.1945 to service craft
SK-823	Aug 1945	P	Mobilised 10.8.1945. Conv 20.9.1945 to service craft
SK-824	Aug 1945	P	Mobilised 10.8.1945. Conv 20.9.1945 to service craft
SK-825	Aug 1945	P	Mobilised 10.8.1945. Conv 20.9.1945 to service craft
SK-826	Aug 1945	P	Mobilised 10.8.1945. Conv 20.9.1945 to service craft
SK-827	Aug 1945	P	Mobilised 10.8.1945. Conv 20.9.1945 to service craft
SK-828	Aug 1945	P	Mobilised 10.8.1945. Conv 20.9.1945 to service craft
SK-829	Aug 1945	P	Mobilised 10.8.1945. Conv 20.9.1945 to service craft
SK-830	Aug 1945	P	Mobilised 10.8.1945. Conv 20.9.1945 to service craft
SK-831	Aug 1945	P	Mobilised 10.8.1945. Conv 20.9.1945 to service craft
SK-832	Aug 1945	P	Mobilised 10.8.1945. Conv 20.9.1945 to service craft
SK-833	Aug 1945	P	Mobilised 10.8.1945. Conv 20.9.1945 to service craft
SK-834	Aug 1945	P	Mobilised 10.8.1945. Conv 20.9.1945 to service craft
SK-835	Aug 1945	P	Mobilised 10.8.1945. Conv 20.9.1945 to service craft
SK-836	Aug 1945	P	Mobilised 10.8.1945. Conv 20.9.1945 to service craft
SK-837	Aug 1945	P	Mobilised 10.8.1945. Conv 20.9.1945 to service craft
SK-838	Aug 1945	P	Mobilised 10.8.1945. Conv 20.9.1945 to service craft
SK-839	Aug 1945	P	Mobilised 10.8.1945. Conv 20.9.1945 to service craft
SK-840	Aug 1945	P	Mobilised 10.8.1945. Conv 20.9.1945 to service craft

No	No	Comm	Fleet	Remarks
on Comm	19.9.1944			
SK-841		Aug 1945	P	Mobilised 10.8.1945. Conv 20.9.1945 to service craft
SK-848		Aug 1945	P	Mobilised 10.8.1945. Conv 20.9.1945 to service craft
SK-849		Aug 1945	P	Mobilised 10.8.1945. Conv 20.9.1945 to service craft
SK-850		Aug 1945	P	Mobilised 10.8.1945. Conv 20.9.1945 to service craft
SK-851		Aug 1945	P	Mobilised 10.8.1945. Conv 20.9.1945 to service craft
SK-852		Aug 1945	P	Mobilised 10.8.1945. Conv 20.9.1945 to service craft
SK-853		Aug 1945	P	Mobilised 10.8.1945. Conv 20.9.1945 to service craft
SK-854		Aug 1945	P	Mobilised 10.8.1945. Conv 20.9.1945 to service craft
SK-855		Aug 1945	P	Mobilised 10.8.1945. Conv 20.9.1945 to service craft

Air warning service craft

No	Name	Comm	Fleet	Remarks
3.10.1942				
VNOS-16	ANAKRIIA	Aug 1942	Cs	Built 1937. Mobilised 20.8.1942. Renumbered VNOS-21 on 30.10.1942. Conv 25.11.1943 to service craft
VNOS-17	MARKSIST	Aug 1942	Cs	Built 1937. Mobilised 20.8.1942. Renumbered VNOS-22 on 30.10.1942. Conv 25.11.1943 to service craft
VNOS-18	ROT-FRONT	Aug 1942	Cs	Built 1937. Mobilised 20.8.1942. Renumbered VNOS-23 on 30.10.1942. Conv 25.11.1943 to service craft
VNOS-19	SUKHUMI	Aug 1942	Cs	Built 1937. Mobilised 20.8.1942. Renumbered VNOS-24 on 30.10.1942. Conv 25.11.1943 to service craft
VNOS-20	MORIANA	Aug 1942	Cs	Built 1937. Mobilised 20.8.1942. Renumbered VNOS-25 on 30.10.1942. Conv 25.11.1943 to service craft

Coastal minelayers

No	Comm	Fleet	Remarks
1942			
ZM-12	Aug 1942	P	Mobilised 24.8.1942, conv to coastal minelayer. Conv 5.2.1943 to service craft
ZM-13	Aug 1942	P	Mobilised 24.8.1942, conv to coastal minelayer. Conv 5.2.1943 to service craft
ZM-14	Aug 1942	P	Mobilised 24.8.1942, conv to coastal minelayer. Conv 5.2.1943 to service craft
ZM-15	Aug 1942	P	Mobilised 24.8.1942, conv to coastal minelayer. Conv 5.2.1943 to service craft
ZM-16	Aug 1942	P	Mobilised 24.8.1942, conv to coastal minelayer. Conv 5.2.1943 to service craft
ZM-17	Aug 1942	P	Mobilised 24.8.1942, conv to coastal minelayer. Conv 5.2.1943 to service craft
ZM-22	Aug 1942	P	Mobilised 24.8.1942, conv to coastal minelayer. Conv 5.2.1943 to service craft
ZM-23	Aug 1942	P	Mobilised 24.8.1942, conv to coastal minelayer. Conv 5.2.1943 to service craft
ZM-24	Aug 1942	P	Mobilised 24.8.1942, conv to coastal minelayer. Conv 5.2.1943 to service craft
ZM-25	Aug 1942	P	Mobilised 24.8.1942, conv to coastal minelayer. Conv 5.2.1943 to service craft
ZM-26	Aug 1942	P	Mobilised 24.8.1942, conv to coastal minelayer. Conv 5.2.1943 to service craft
ZM-27	Aug 1942	P	Mobilised 24.8.1942, conv to coastal minelayer. Conv 5.2.1943 to service craft
ZM-32	Aug 1942	P	Mobilised 24.8.1942, conv to coastal minelayer. Conv 5.2.1943 to service craft
ZM-33	Aug 1942	P	Mobilised 24.8.1942, conv to coastal minelayer. Conv 5.2.1943 to service craft
ZM-34	Aug 1942	P	Mobilised 24.8.1942, conv to coastal minelayer. Conv 5.2.1943 to service craft
ZM-35	Aug 1942	P	Mobilised 24.8.1942, conv to coastal minelayer. Conv 5.2.1943 to service craft
ZM-36	Aug 1942	P	Mobilised 24.8.1942, conv to coastal minelayer. Conv 5.2.1943 to service craft
ZM-37	Aug 1942	P	Mobilised 24.8.1942, conv to coastal minelayer. Conv 5.2.1943 to service craft
ZM-42	Aug 1942	P	Mobilised 24.8.1942, conv to coastal minelayer. Conv 5.2.1943 to service craft
ZM-43	Aug 1942	P	Mobilised 24.8.1942, conv to coastal minelayer. Conv 5.2.1943 to service craft
ZM-44	Aug 1942	P	Mobilised 24.8.1942, conv to coastal minelayer. Conv 5.2.1943 to service craft
ZM-45	Aug 1942	P	Mobilised 24.8.1942, conv to coastal minelayer. Conv 5.2.1943 to service craft
ZM-46	Aug 1942	P	Mobilised 24.8.1942, conv to coastal minelayer. Conv 5.2.1943 to service craft
ZM-47	Aug 1942	P	Mobilised 24.8.1942, conv to coastal minelayer. Conv 5.2.1943 to service craft

NKVD conversions

Patrol boats

NKVD No	Comm	Fleet	Remarks
PS-5	June 1941	Cs	Lost
PS-6	June 1941	Cs	Lost
•	June 1941	B	Fate unknown

14.0 Patrol boats

Tugboats

No	No	Comm	Fleet	Remarks
		12.5.1943		
NK-1 (1943) ex-№ 1 (1943) ex-PS-10 (1941)	SK-528	12.5.1943	Wh	Former NKVD Border Guard patrol boat PS-10 (?), taken over in 1941. Conv 1943 to tugboat of the naval base at Novaya Zemlya. Renumbered NMB-9 on 23.6.1943. Conv 12.5.1943 to patrol boat. Survived the war
NK-2 (1943) ex-№ 2 (1943) ex-PS-11 (1941)	SK-529	12.5.1943	Wh	Former NKVD Border Guard patrol boat PS-11 (?), taken over in 1941. Conv 1943 to tugboat of the naval base at Novaya Zemlya. Renumbered NMB-10 on 23.6.1943. Conv 12.5.1943 to patrol boat. Survived the war
	•	9.8.1945~	P	Survived the war

Naval conversions

Minesweeping boats (Naval conversions)

Name	No	Comm	Fleet	Remarks
KATshch № 1941		9.10.1942		
MEDUZA № 53	OV-56	22.10.1942	P	Mobilised 7.10.1941, conv to minesweeping boat. Conv 22.10.1942 to patrol boat. Decomm 5.7.1943 to civilian service
PELENGAS № 54	OV-66 SK-66²	22.10.1942	P	Mobilised 7.10.1941, conv to minesweeping boat. Conv 9.10.1942 to patrol boat. Survived the war

NKVD patrol boat *PS-5*. Przemysław Budzbon Collection

Small wooden-hull flat bottomed drifters powered by semi-Diesel engines. Their concept was based on Far East *kungas* launches and Japanese *kawasaki* crab boats. Mass-built from early 1930s at various local yards on the Soviet Pacific coast for the fishing industry. At least three basic types are known, designated *KK-1*, *KK-2* and *KK-3*. They may have differed in size, but the main distinguishing feature was output of the engine; mostly 30hp, 50hp and 75hp power units were fitted, with 18hp (*) units for those operating inland. Total number built not known, but the following figures may indicate the scale: in 1938 the Pacific Fleet mobilised 273 boats of this type as transports during the Khasan Lake battles, while the general mobilisation plans for the Far East estimated the possibility of sourcing up to 1500 boats from local operators. In total, 187 boats were mobilised during the war as patrol boats, netlayers, minelayers or air warning service craft. In practice, they were allowed to continue fishing operations on condition that could be combat-ready within 24 hours.

The boats remaining in NKVD Border Guard service

From 1935 this design was accepted as the standard NKVD Border Guard small patrol craft, fitted with a wireless set and 0.3in Maxim machine gun. Approximately 85 were built.

NKVD No	Area	NKVD No	Area
PS-1	Far East	PS-30	Far East
PS-1	Far East	PS-31	Far East
PS-2	Far East	PS-32	Far East
PS-3	Far East	PS-34	Far East
PS-4	Far East	PS-35	Far East
PS-4	Karelia	PS-59	Bashkiria
PS-5	Far East	PS-60	Bashkiria
PS-5	Karelia	PS-61	Bashkiria
PS-6	Far East	PS-62	Bashkiria
PS-6	Far East	PS-63	Bashkiria
PS-6	Karelia	PS-64	Bashkiria
PS-7	Far East	PS-65	Bashkiria
PS-7	Far East	PS-66	Bashkiria
PS-7	Arctic	PS-79	Amur
PS-8	Far East	PS-80	Far East
PS-8	Far East	PS-80	Amur
PS-9	Far East	PS-81	Far East
PS-10	Far East	PS-82	Far East
PS-11	Far East	PS-84	Far East
PS-12	Far East	PS-85	Far East
PS-12	Far East	PS-86	Far East
PS-13	Far East	PS-87	Far East
PS-13	Far East	PS-88	Far East
PS-14	Far East	PS-89	Far East
PS-17	Far East	PS-90	Far East
PS-18	Far East	PS-91	Far East
PS-19	Far East	PS-92	Far East
PS-21	Far East	PS-93	Far East
PS-22	Far East	PS-94	Far East
PS-22	Amur	PS-96	Far East
PS-23	Far East	PS-108	Far East
PS-23	Amur	PS-109	Far East
PS-24	Far East	PS-110	Far East
PS-24	Amur	PS-111	Far East
PS-25	Amur	PS-112	Far East
PS-26	Far East	PS-113	Far East
PS-26	Amur	PS-123	Far East
PS-27	Far East	PS-124	Far East
PS-28	Far East	PS-125	Far East
PS-29	Far East	PS-128 (ex-*KK-10*)	Far East

Motorboats

Pt-No 1941	SKA № on Comm	No 7.7.1944	Name	Details	Comm	Fleet	Remarks
225	№ 13	SK-13	SHIP	95t; 15.2 x 5.0 x 2.0m; 50hp = 6kts; 990nm at 5kts; 1-0.3in MG; 7 men	July 1941	N	Built 1938. Mobilised 29.7.1941, conv 3.3.1945 to service craft
214	№ 14		PUZANOK	•	July 1941	N	Mobilised 29.7.1941, conv to patrol boat, conv 25.11.1941 to service craft. Renumbered TO-5 on 21.3.1942, PMB-46 on 19.6.1943
215	№ 15		KIL'KA	85t; 16.0 x 4.9 x 1.8m; 50hp = 6kts; 260nm at 5kts; 1-0.3in MG; 7 men	July 1941	N	Built 1935. Mobilised 29.7.1941, decomm 15.5.1944 to civilian service
216	№ 16		RIF	•	July 1941	N	Mobilised 29.7.1941, damaged 18.9.1942 by aircraft at Litsa Bay, stranded, wreck burned
223	№ 17		VOZHAK	130t; 140hp	July 1941	N	Mobilised 29.7.1941, sunk 2.8.1941 by aircraft at Litsa Bay
217	№ 18		V'IUN	95t; 15.8 x 5.0 x 1.8m; 50hp = 5kts; 960nm at 4.5kts; 1-0.5in MG; 7 men	July 1941	N	Built 1938. Mobilised 29.7.1941, decomm 31.12.1943 to civilian service
226	№ 21		MOGILEVICH	87.5t; 16.5 x 4.4 x 2.0m; 50hp = 6; 343nm at 5kts; 1-0.5in MG; 7 men	July 1941	N	Built 1934. Mobilised 29.7.1941, decomm 31.12.1943 to civilian service
218	№ 22	SK-22[1]	FEDOROV	95t; 15.8 x 5.0 x 1.8m; 50hp = 5kts; 690nm at 4.5kts; 1-0.5in MG; 7 men	July 1941	N	Built 1938. Mobilised 29.7.1941, renumbered on. Conv 8.3.1945 to service craft
219	№ 23		KAGANOVICH	95t; 16.0 x 5.0 x 2.4m; 50hp = 6/5kts; 228nm; 1-0.3in MG; 7 men	July 1941	N	Built 1935. Mobilised 2.7.1941, decomm 31.12.1943 to civilian service
228	№ 31		GROMOV	95t; 15.8 x 5.0 x 1.8m; 50hp = 6.5/5kts; 900nm; 1-0.3in MG; 7 men	July 1941	N	Built 1938. Mobilised 29.7.1941, decomm 31.12.1943 to civilian service
227	№ 32		KRENKEL	50t; 50hp	July 1941	N	Mobilised 29.7.1941, sunk 18.11.1941 by artillery fire at Zapadnaia Litsa Bay
224	№ 40	SK-40	LINEK	92.8t; 15.8 x 4.6 x 2.6m; 50hp = 6/5kts; 257nm; 1-0.5in MG, 1 -0.3in MG; 7 men	July 1941	N	Built 1935. Mobilised 2.7.1941, decomm 3.3.1945 to civilian service
	№ 56	SK-56[2]	VELIKAN	35 – 40t; 13.5 x 3.7 x 1.9m; 35hp = 5kts; 1MG	26.6.1943	B	Mobilised 13.6.1942 as motorboat. Conv 26.6.1943 to patrol boat, conv 6.10.1945 to service craft
	№ 57	SK-57[2]	ORYOL		26.6.1943	B	Mobilised 22.6.1941 as motorboat. Conv 26.6.1943 to patrol boat, conv 6.10.1945 to service craft
	№ 58		SOKOL		26.6.1943	B	Mobilised 22.6.1941 as motorboat. Conv 26.6.1943 to patrol boat, conv 2.7.1943 to service craft
	№ 58		BOEVOJ		2.7.1943	B	Mobilised 22.6.1941 as motorboat. Conv 2.7.1943 to patrol boat conv 7.10.1944 to service craft
	№ 59		SHTURVAL		26.6.1943	B	Mobilised 22.6.1941 as motorboat. Conv 26.6.1943 to patrol boat, conv 2.7.1943 to service craft
	№ 59	SK-59[2]	KRASNYJ RYBAK		2.7.1943	B	Mobilised 22.6.1941 as motorboat. Conv 2.7.1943 to patrol boat, conv 6.10.1945 to service craft
	№ 75		VENERA		26.6.1943	B	Ex-Finnish? Mobilised 22.6.1941 as motorboat. Conv 26.6.1943 to patrol boat. Detached 18.7.1944 to the Red Army command of the Leningrad Front
	№ 83	SK-83[2]	POLIUS		26.6.1943	B	Mobilised 22.6.1941 as motorboat. Conv 26.6.1943 to patrol boat, conv 6.10.1945 to service craft
	№ 85		GORDYJ		26.6.1943	B	Mobilised 22.6.1941 as motorboat. Conv 26.6.1943 to patrol boat. Detached 18.7.1944 to the Red Army command of the Leningrad Front, lost the same day at Berksund for unknown reasons
	№ 92	SK-92[2]	LIUBIMETS		26.6.1943	B	Mobilised 22.6.1941 as motorboat. Conv 26.6.1943 to patrol boat, conv 6.10.1945 to service craft.
	№ 94	SK-94[2]	LASTOCHKA		26.6.1943	B	Mobilised 22.6.1941 as motorboat. Conv 26.6.1943 to patrol boat, conv 6.10.1945 to service craft
	№ 117	SK-117[2]	BODRYJ		26.6.1943	B	Mobilised 22.6.1941 as motorboat. Conv 26.6.1943 to patrol boat, conv 6.10.1945 to service craft

No		Name	Specs	Date		Notes
№ 511		LASTOLA	38.9t; 15.1 x 5.0 x 2.3m; 50hp = 5kts; 720nm; 2-0.3in MGs; 8 men	29.9.1941	Wh	Built 1939. Mobilised 12.8.1941, comm 20.8.1941 as naval pilot boat, conv 29.9.1941 to patrol boat. Conv 19.4.1943 to service craft
№ 512	SK-512	PRIMORETS	42.2t; 16.4 x 4.9 x 2.9m; 35hp = 5.5kts; 520nm; 1 x 2-0.3in MG; 8 men	29.9.1941	Wh	Built 1936. Mobilised 12.8.1941, comm 20.8.1941 as naval pilot boat, conv 29.9.1941 to patrol boat. Decomm 8.3.1945 to civilian service
№ 513		BELEK	40.5t; 14.4 x 5.2 x 2.7m; 50hp = 4.5kts; 360nm; 2 x 2-0.3in MG; 8 men	29.9.1941	Wh	Built 1933. Mobilised 12.8.1941, comm 20.8.1941 as naval pilot boat, conv 29.9.1941 to patrol boat. Decomm 30.12.1943 to civilian service
№ 514	SK-514	LEBEDIN	29.6t; 15.8 x 4.1 x 2.7m; 50hp = 5.5kts; 1000nm; 1 x 2-0.3in MG; 8 men	29.9.1941	Wh	Built 1938. Mobilised 12.8.1941, comm 20.8.1941 as naval pilot boat, conv 29.9.1941 to patrol boat. Decomm 24.3.1945 to civilian service
№ 515		RS-6	50.6t; 15.8 x 5.6 x 2.9m; 50hp = 5kts; 840nm; 1 x 2-0.3in MG; 8 men	29.9.1941	Wh	Built 1933. Mobilised 12.8.1941, comm 20.8.1941 as naval pilot boat, conv 29.9.1941 to patrol boat. Decomm 31.12.1943 to civilian service
№ 516		RASKOVA	40.2t; 15.1 x 5.0 x 2.4m; 65hp = 7kts; 800nm; 1-0.3in MG; 8 men	29.9.1941	Wh	Built 1939. Mobilised 12.8.1941, comm 20.8.1941 as naval pilot boat, conv 29.9.1941 to patrol boat. Decomm 31.12.1943 to civilian service
№ 517		MOTOBOT № 8	47.4t; 15.7 x 5.7 x 2.8m; 50hp = 5kts; 960nm; 1-0.3in MG; 8 men	29.9.1941	Wh	Built 1935. Mobilised 3.8.1941, comm 20.8.1941 as naval pilot boat, conv 29.9.1941 to patrol boat. Decomm 31.12.1943 to civilian service
№ 518	SK-518	RS-1	53.5t; 17.0 x 4.9 x 2.4m; 50hp = 5kts; 960nm; 2-0.3in MG; 7 men	29.9.1941	Wh	Built 1933. Mobilised Aug 1941 comm 20.8.1941 as naval pilot boat, conv 29.9.1941 to patrol boat. Renumbered on 7.7.1941. Decomm 3.3.1945 to civilian service

Exceptions noted in the main table.

No	Year	Date
1	1944	1.4.1944
2		7.10.1944

Storozhevoj kater № 13 Ship during press presentation.
Gangut

Seiners

SKA № on Comm	SKA № 3.6.1942	Name	Details	Comm	Fleet	Remarks
№ 111	№ 0111	SUVOROV	67t	Apr 1942	BS	Mobilised 27.4.1942. Deleted 5.2.1943, presumably lost
№ 112	№ 0211	BK-4	37t; 16.1 x 3.9 x 1.8m; 65hp = 7kts; 700nm at 6.2kts; 1-0.5in MG, 4-0.3in (1x4) MGs; 12 men	Apr 1942	BS	Mobilised 27.4.1942. Sunk 8.11.1943 by mines off Tuzla spit
№ 113	№ 0311	KRASNYJ KRYM	37t; 16.5 x 4.0 x 1.8m; 50hp = 7kts; 1100nm at 6kts; 1-0.5in MG, 1 KAT sweep; 12 men	Apr 1942	BS	Mobilised 27.4.1942. Conv 21.6.1944 to minesweeping boat *KT-816*. Survived the war
№ 114	№ 0411	OST	40t; 16.7 x 4.6 x 1.8m; 65hp = 7.0kts; 1150nm at 6.2kts; 1 MG, 12 men	Apr 1942	BS	Mobilised 27.4.1942. Sunk 8.11.1943 on mines off Tuzla spit
№ 115	№ 0511	BUREVESTNIK	55.4t	6.5.1942	BS	Mobilised 27.4.1942, conv to patrol boat, conv 18.3.1943 to salvage tender. Survived the war
№ 116	№ 0611	20 LET OKTIABRIA	47.4t	Apr 1942	BS	Mobilised 27.4.1942. Deleted 31.7.1942, presumably lost
№ 117	№ 0711	SEINER № 5	40t; 16.7 x 1.8m; 65hp = 7kts; 1150nm at 6.2kts; 1 MG, 12 men	Apr 1942	BS	Mobilised 27.4.1942. In repairs during 3.7.1942–11.11.1942. Deleted 21.6.1944
№ 118	№ 0811	SEINER № 6	51.7t; 23.0 x 4.1 x 1.6m; 50hp = 7kts; 850nm at 6kts; 1 MG, 12 men	Apr 1942	BS	Mobilised 27.4.1942. In repairs during 3.7.1942–11.11.1942. Deleted 21.6.1944
№ 120	№ 1110[1] № 1011	SEL'D'	96.4t	27.4.1942	BS	Mobilised 1.10.1941 as service craft, conv 27.4.1942 to patrol boat. Mined 15.4.1942 off Kamych-Burun. She was deleted from the navy list 31.7.1942, so had the № 1110, then № 1011 allocated
№ 121	№ 1111[1]	KOKKINAKI	52.3t	27.4.1942	BS	Mobilised 1.10.1941 as service craft, conv 27.4.1942 to patrol boat. Deleted 15.1.1943, presumably lost
№ 122	№ 1112[1] № 1211	KOMINTERN	48t		BS	Mobilised 1.10.1941. Deleted 15.1.1943, presumably lost

Exceptions noted in the main table.

No	Year	Date
1	1942	30.4.1942

OV-11 class
Inshore drifters

Displacement: 10t
Dimensions: 14.7 x 3.6 x 1.4m
Machinery: 1-shaft ICE, 20hp = 7kts. Range 500nm at 5kts
Armament: 1-0.3in MG, 4 mines, 1 KTA sweep, 1 magnetic tail sweep
Complement: 6

No 1941	No 13.9.1944	Comm	Fleet	Remarks
OV-111	SK-111	Oct 1941	P	Mobilised 7.10.1941. Survived the war
OV-112	SK-112	Oct 1941	P	Mobilised 7.10.1941. Survived the war
OV-113	SK-113	July 1941	P	Mobilised 7.10.1941. Survived the war
OV-114	SK-114	Oct 1941	P	Mobilised 7.10.1941. Survived the war
OV-115		Oct 1941	P	Mobilised 7.10.1941. Decomm 5.7.1943 to civilian service
OV-116		Oct 1941	P	Mobilised 7.10.1941. Decomm 5.7.1943 to civilian service

Drifters

Pt-No 1941	SKA № on Comm	No 1944	Name	Details	Comm	Fleet	Remarks
211	№ 9		NOKUEV	233t; 26.7 x 6.4 x 2.8m; 140hp = 8kts; 1020nm at 7kts; 1-45mm/46 21-K, 2-0.3in MGs : (1943: 1-20mm Oerlikon, 12-0.5in MGs (3x4),2-0.3in MGs (1x2)]; 15 men	July 1941	N	Built 1939. Mobilised 2.7.1941. Sunk 19.8.1943 by aircraft off Cape Sharapov
212	№ 10		KHARLOV	233t; 26.7 x 6.4 x 2.8m; 140hp = 8kts; 1020nm at 7kts; 2-45-mm. 2-0.5in MGs,; 2-0.3in MGs; 15 men	July 1941	N	Built 1939. Mobilised 2.7.1941. Decomm 15.5.1944 to civilian service
213	№ 11		RYNDA	233t; 26.7 x 6.5 x 2.5m; 140hp = 8kts; 1020nm at 7kts; 2-45mm/46 21-K, 2-0.5in MGs, 2-0.3in MG; 15 men	July 1941	N	Built 1940. Mobilised 2.7.1941. Decomm 15.5.1944 to civilian service
222	№ 42		TAJFUN	264t; 25.7 x 6.5 x 2.8m; 140hp = 7kts; 1300nm at 6kts; 1-45mm/46 21-K, 1-0.5in MGs, 2-0.3in MGs [MGs replaced 1943 by 18-0.5in MGs (4x4, 1x2)]; 15 men	July 1941	N	Built 1937. Mobilised 2.7.1941. Sunk 19.8.1943 by aircraft at Eina Gulf
221	№ 5[1] № 46[2]	SK-46[5]	EJNA	233t; 26.0 x 6.4 x 2.8m; 140hp = 8kts; 1020nm at 7kts; 2-45mm/46 21-K, 2-0.5in MGs, 2-0.3in MGs, KAT sweep; 15 men	Dec 1939 July 1941	N	Built 1938. Mobilised 2.12.1939, conv to patrol boat, conv 4.3.1940 to escort ship renamed *Raduga*, decomm 4.3.1941 to civilian service, name reverted. Mobilised 29.7.1941, conv to patrol boat. Decomm 23.4.1945 to civilian service
	№ 501	SK-501[6]	ARA	150t; 25 x 5.5 x 3.2m; 140hp = 6kts; 1200nm; 1-45mm/46 21-K, 1-0.5in MGs, 1-0.3in MGs; 15 men	10.8.1941	Wh	Built 1940. Mobilised 1.8.1941, decomm 2.3.1945 to civilian service
	№ 502		GOLETS	180t; 35.0 x 4.8 x 3.3m; 170hp = 7kts; 840nm; 1-45mm/46 21-K, 1-0.3in MGs; 15 men	10.8.1941	Wh	Built 1940. Mobilised 1.8.1941, decomm 5.6.1944 to civilian service
	№ 503[3]		KNIPOVICH	180t; 30.0 x 4.8 x 3.3m; 120hp = 4kts; 1200nm; 1-45mm/46 21-K, 1-0.3in MG; 15 men	29.7.1941	N Wh	Built 1940. Mobilised 29.7.1941 as service craft; conv 25.8.1941 to patrol craft, trfd to the White Sea Flotilla. Conv 29.3.1944 to surveying vessel, name reverted. Decomm 30.1.1945 to civilian service, renamed *Nikolai Knipovich*. Discarded 1959, abandoned and sank, raised 1986, BU 1991
	№ 504[3]	SK-504[6]	DRIFTER № 277	133t; 28.7 x 6.5 x 3.3m; 110hp = 5kts; 1200nm; 1-45mm/46 21-K, 1-0.3in MG; 15 men	25.8.1941	Wh	Built 1937. Mobilised 29.7.1941, decomm 2.3.1945 to civilian service
	№ 505[3]		ORDEN	213t; 30.0 x 6.7 x 3.4m; 100hp = 5kts; 1200nm; 1-45mm/46 21-K, 1-0.5in MG, 0.3in MG; 15 men	10.8.1941	Wh	Built 1935. Mobilised 1.8.1941, conv to patrol boat, conv 20.3.1944 to degaussing station *SBR-6*, trfd to the Northern Fleet; renamed *SBR-23* on 18.9.1945
	№ 506		SEVERNYJ	213t; 30.0 x 6.7 x 3.4m; 100hp = 5kts; 1200nm; 1-45mm/46 21-K, 1-0.5in MG, 1-0.3in MG; 15 men	25.8.1941	N Wh	Built 1935. Mobilised 29.7.1941, conv to patrol boat, trfd 7.9.1941 to the White Sea Flotilla. Conv 20.3.1944 to degaussing station *SBR-23*, trfd to the Northern Fleet. Deleted 28.2.1945
	№ 507		DRIFTER № 276 ZELENETS	133t; 28.7 x 6.5 x 3.3m; 110hp = 5kts; 1200nm; 1-45mm/46 21-K, 1-0.3in MGs; 15 men	19.9.1941	Wh	Built 1937. Mobilised 16.9.1941.Conv 5.4.1942 to service craft of the naval postal service, renumbered *AS-1*, renumbered *S-1* on 12.5.1943, renumbered *AMB-31* on 23.6.1943. Survived the war
	№ 508	SK-508[6]	RK-1 KOMBAJN-1	170t; 28.7 x 6.8 x 3.4m; 100hp = 5kts; 1200nm; 1-45mm/46 21-K, 1-0.3in MG; 15 men	29.9.1941	Wh	Built 1931.Mobilised 25.8.1941, decomm 24.3.1945 to civilian service
	№ 509	SK-509[6]	DRIFTER № 111	100t; 26.0 x 4.5 x 3.0m; 100hp = 6.5kts; 780nm; 2-45mm/46 21-K, 1-0.5in MG; 15 men	29.9.1941	Wh	Built 1941. Mobilised 1941. Survived the war

Pt-No 1941	SKA № on Comm	No 1944	Name	Details	Comm	Fleet	Remarks
	№ 510	SK-510[4]	DRIFTER № 112	100t; 26.0 x 4.5 x 3.0m; 100hp = 6.5kts; 780nm; 2-45mm/46 21-K, 2-0.3in MGs; 15 men	29.9.1941	Wh	Built 1941. Mobilised 1941, deleted 14.11.1944
	№ 519	SK-519[6]	DRIFTER № 113	100t; 26.0 x 4.5 x 3.0m; 100hp = 6.5kts; 780nm; 2-45mm/46 21-K, 1-0.5in MG, 0.3in MGs; 15 men	29.9.1941	Wh	Built 1941. Mobilised 1941, conv to patrol boat, renamed on 7.4.1944, conv 18.4.1945 to dispatch vessel *AMB-75*. Survived the war
		SK-520[7]	AVANGARD	•	29.9.1941	Wh	Mobilised 5.6.1944. Decomm 1.12.1944 to civilian service

Exceptions noted in the main table.

No	Year	Date
1	1939	2.12.1939
2	1941	29.7.1941
3		29.9.1941
4	1944	1.4.1944
5		10.6.1944
6		7.7.1944
7		29.9.1944

SK-510 in wartime camouflage.
Przemysław Budzbon Collection

Sail-motor schooners

SKA № on Comm	Name	Details	Comm	Fleet	Remarks
	BELUGA	61t; 16.0 x 5.75 x 1.65m; 25hp = 3.2kts; radius 320nm at 2kts; 1 MG; 6 men	27.6.1941	BS	Built 1930. Mobilised 23.6.1941, stranded 22.1.1942 off Kamysh-Burun, deleted 2.4.1942. Repaired, recomm 30.10.1942 as transport *ChFMSh-8*. Survived the war
№ 32	KOMSOMOLETS	160t	21.7.1941	BS	Mobilised 23.6.1941, deleted 2.4.1942. Presumably lost
	KOMSOMOLKA	140t	27.6.1941	BS	Mobilised 23.6.1941, conv 18.4.1944 to degaussing station, renamed *SBR-35*. Survived the war
	NORD-VEST	47t; 13.0 x 4.0 x 1.8m; 35hp = 5kts	Nov 1941	BS	Built 1933. Mobilised 30.10.1941, conv 6.5.1942 to minesweeping boat. Decomm 6.11.1943, after repairs recomm 30.3.1944 as service craft. Survived the war
	SKUMBRIA	22.8t	27.6.1941	BS	Mobilised 23.6.1941, deleted 28.12.1941. Presumably lost

14.5.4. Tugs

Seagoing tugs

No	Fleet	Remarks
SK-105	N	Mobilised, conv to patrol boat. Reverted to tug 19.6.1943, numbered *M-12*. Conv to salvage vessel 1.9.1944
SK-109	N	Mobilised, conv to patrol boat. Reverted to tug 19.6.1943, numbered *M-11*. Conv to salvage vessel 1.9.1944

Tugboats

SKA № 27.4.1942	SKA № 3.6.1942	Name	Details	Comm	Fleet	Remarks
№ 119	№ 0911	BK № 8	27.6t	27.4.1942	BS	Mobilised as service craft, conv 27.4.1942 to patrol boat. Sunk 27.4.1943 by German aircraft off the Achuevskaya Spit
		N. SHCHORS		26.7.1942	Az	Mobilised 26.7.1942. Scuttled 22.8.1942 in Temryuk Bay
		POLIANKA		26.7.1942	Az	Mobilised 26.7.1942. Scuttled 21.8.1942 on Kuban River

Cross reference: Rated as patrol boats

No	Name	Details	Type	From	To	Fate
SK-113		*VP-4*	Coastal tug	21.1.1945		Survived the war
	MIKULA	*Mikula*	Experimental ship	22.11.1939	1940	Reverted to auxiliary vessel

14.5.5. Naval auxiliaries

Cross reference: Rated as patrol boats

Name	Details	Type	From	To	Fate
SVIAZIST	*Sviazist*	Experimental vessel	Nov 1939	1940	Reverted to experimental vessel

14.6. War prizes

14.6.1. Poland, 1939

Cross reference: Rated as patrol boats

SKA №	Details	Type	From	To	Fate
№ 51	Polish *Linz* type	AMGB	Mar 1941	12.4.1941	Re-rated as AMGB
№ 52	Polish *Linz* type	AMGB	Mar 1941	12.4.1941	Re-rated as AMGB
№ 53	Polish *Linz* type	AMGB	Mar 1941	12.4.1941	Re-rated as AMGB
№ 54	Polish *KM* type	AMGB	24.10.1939	12.4.1941	Re-rated as AMGB
№ 55	Polish *KM* type	AMGB	24.10.1939	12.4.1941	Re-rated as AMGB

14.6.2. Finland, 1940

Storozhevoj kater № 617 class
Motorboats

Displacement: 32t
Dimensions: 18.2 x 3.5 x 1.8m
Machinery: 1-shaft ICE, 50hp = 6.5kts. Range 500nm
Armament: 2-0.303in MGs, 2-0.3in MGs
Complement: 11

SKA № 1941	No 31.5.1944	Comm	Fleet	Remarks
№ 617	SK-617	5.4.1942	Wh	Conv 24.9.1945 to service craft, *PMB-73*
№ 618	SK-618	5.4.1942	Wh	Conv 24.9.1945 to service craft, *PMB-74*

Finnish motorboats captured in 1940, rebuilt as patrol boats.

Sail-motor schooners

NKVD No	Comm	Fleet	Remarks
PS-2	23.6.1941	B	Finnish, captured 1940. Mobilised 22.6.1941. Lost 1941?
PS-3	23.6.1941	B	Finnish, captured 1940. Mobilised 22.6.1941. Lost 1941?

14.6.3. Lithuania, 1940

Lithuanian Partizanas
Patrol boat

Displacement: 60t full load
Dimensions: 21.5 x 4.5 x 1.3m
Machinery: 1-shaft Deutz-Humbolt diesel, 200hp = 12kts
Armament: 1-57mm, 1-20mm Oerlikon, 2-7.98 Maxim 08 MGs
Complement: 13 (in Lithuanian service)

Lithuanian Police Border Guard boat, trfd to the Lithuanian Navy in July 1940. Captured by the Soviets, trfd 24.7.1940 to the NKVD Border Guard, 22.6.1941 dispatched to the Baltic Fleet, lost before formal comm.

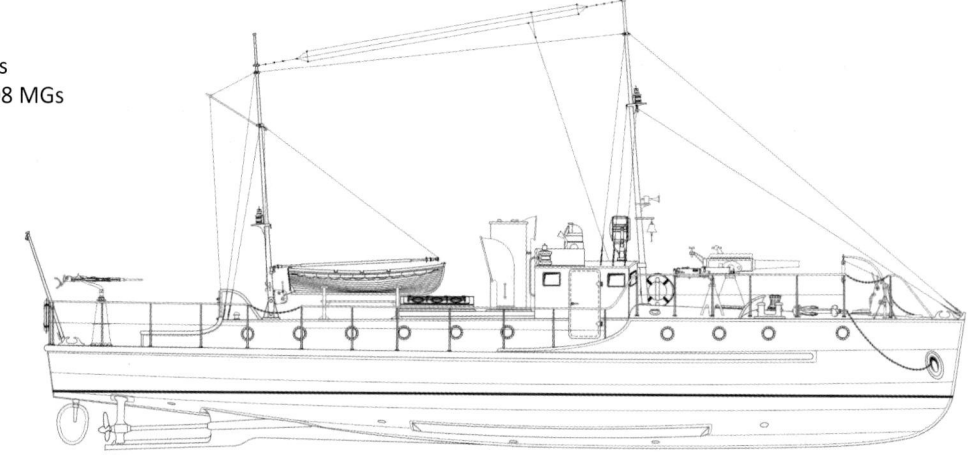

Partizan in 1940.
Drawing by Jerzy Lewandowski

NKVD No	Laid down	Comp	Comm	Fleet	Remarks
Builder: Schiffswerft Memel-Lindenau, Klaipėda					
K-276 ex-*Partizan* (9.1.1941) ex-*Partizanas* (Lit, 1940)	1932	1933	-	B	Stranded 13.10.1941 off Osmussaar Island

14.6.4. IRAN, 1941

Iranian **Azerbaijan** class
Patrol craft

Displacement: 32t full load
Dimensions: 20.9 x 3.8 x 1.1m
Machinery: diesel engine 240hp = 14kts. Range 680nm at 10kts
Armament: 1-45mm/46 21-K, 1-0.5in DShK MG
Complement: 15

SKA-1 in Soviet service.
Drawing by Jerzy Lewandowski

No on Comm	No 22.11.1941	Comp	Comm	Fleet	Remarks
SKA-1 ex-*Azerbaijan* (Irn, 1941)	SKA-200	1935	23.9.1941	Cs	Returned 1947 to Iran, renamed *Babolsar*, discarded 1972
SKA-2 ex-*Gehlani* (Irn, 1941)	SKA-201	1935	23.9.1941	Cs	Returned 1947 to Iran, renamed *Gorgan*, discarded 1972
SKA-3 ex-*Mazenderand* (Irn, 1941)	SKA-202	1935	23.9.1941	Cs	Returned 1947 to Iran, renamed *Sefidreude*, discarded 1972

Captured during Anglo-Soviet invasion of Iran, returned after Soviet withdrawal in May 1946.

14.6.5. SOUTHEAST EUROPE, 1944

No	Details	Comm	Fleet	Remarks
SK-752	51.3t; 23.0 x 4.5 x 1.3m; 220hp = 11kts; 1-37mm?	20.10.1944	BS	German SM-222 (ex-*G-3182*, ex-*RA-52*, ex-*R-202*, ex-*RH-2*) and SM-223 (ex-*G-3183*, ex-*RA-56*, ex-*R-206*) captured by the Germans in 1940 in the Netherlands. Captured 8.9.1944 at Varna, comm as patrol boats
SK-753		20.10.1944	BS	
SK-754	50t; 32.0 x 4.4 x 1.0m; 700hp = 20.3kts; 1-47mm, 1-20mm; 18 men	30.10.1944	Da	Romanian vintage riverine torpedo boats (vedetă torpiloare fluvială) of the *Căpitan Nicolae Lascăr Bogdan* class, captured 1944 on the Danube, conv to patrol boats. Names: *Vedeta No 3* (*Căpitan Romano*), *Vedeta No 5* (*Maior Grigore Ioan*), *Vedeta No 7* (*Locotenent Călinescu*). Presumably BU mid-1940s
SK-755		30.10.1944	Da	
SK-756		30.10.1944	Da	
SK-757	87t; 33.5 x 4.3 x 1.2m; 600hp = 12.5kts	20.11.1944	BS	Bulgarian *Belomorets* Elco-built SC boat *C-80* purchased by Bulgaria in 1922 in France. Captured 9.9.1944 at Varna, conv to patrol boats. Returned 19.4.1945
SK-758	87t; 33.5 x 4.3 x 1.2m; 600hp = 12.5kts	20.11.1944	BS	Bulgarian *Chernomorets* Elco-built SC boat *C-27* purchased by Bulgaria in 1922 in France. Captured 9.9.1944 at Varna, conv to patrol boats. Returned 19.4.1945

Cross reference: rated as patrol boat

No	Details	Type	From	To	Fate
SK-751	German *Minen-Räumboote 1940*	Large Submarine Hunter	20.10.1944	19.9.1945	Re-rated as large submarine hunter

14.6.6. Manchukuo, 1945

No	Details	Comm	Fleet	Remarks
SK-265 ex-*Ta Tung* (Man, 1945)	56t; 30.5 x 4.9 x 0.75m; 240hp = 10.5kts; 1-57mm/40, 3-0.303in MGs	24.8.1945	Am	Manchukuo, Kobe-built river gunboat *Ta Tung* captured 20.8.1945 at Habrin. Comm as patrol boat
SK-266 ex-*Li Min* (Man, 1945)		24.8.1945	Am	Manchukuo, Kobe-built river gunboat *Li Min* captured 20.8.1945 at Habrin. Comm as patrol boats
SK-267 ex-*Hai Tein* (Man, 1945) ex-*Kozakura* (Jap, 1939)	30t; 25.0 x 3.65 x 0.6m; 120hp = 13.2kts; 2-0.303in MGs	24.8.1945	Am	Japanese Harima-built river gunboat *Kozakura* trfd to Manchukuo in 1939, comm as *Hai Tien*. Captured 20.8.1945 at Habrin. Comm as patrol boat
SK-268 ex-*Hui Min* (Man, 1945)	15t; 17.1 x 3.4 x 0.8m; 80hp = 8.5kts; 3-0.303in MGs	24.8.1945	Am	Manchukuo, Kawasaki-built river gunboat *Hui Min* captured 20.8.1945 at Habrin. Comm as patrol boat
SK-269 ex-*Pu Min* (Man, 1945)	15t; 17.1 x 3.4 x 0.8m; 80hp = 8.5kts; 3-0.303in MGs	24.8.1945	Am	Manchukuo, Kawasaki-built river gunboat *Pu Min* captured 20.8.1945 at Habrin. Comm as patrol boat
SK-270 ex-*Nr 203*(?) (Man, 1945)	•	24.8.1945	Am	Manchukuo, river gunboat *Nr 203*(?) captured 20.8.1945 at Habrin. Comm as patrol boat

14.7. Motor launches

NKL-5 type *Aero-hydroplanes*

Displacement: 1.2t full load
Dimensions: 6.4 x 1.8 x 0.2m
Machinery: 1 aircraft propeller, M-11 petrol engine, 110hp = 32kts
Armament: 1-0.3in DT MG
Complement: 4

The prototype was built in 1935, to a design based on aviation industry components: aluminium alloy hull, engine and MG mounting. Used for communication and assault. The most noticeable use was noted during seizure of the Reichsbrücke (Imperial Bridge) in Vienna. They were referred to as Aeroglissery (aero-hydroplanes).

Total number of craft commissioned by the naval forces is not known, but the following information is available:

*NKL-5 type boat of the Dnieper Flotilla.
Vitalij Kostrichenko Collection*

Flotilla	Number of craft in service	In commission
Pinsk	7	1941
Danube	6	1941
	6	1944/5

NKL-27 type — *Hydroplanes*

Displacement: 1.45t full load
Dimensions: 7.0 x 1.6 x 0.55m
Machinery: 1-shaft, GAZ-MM petrol engine, 50hp = 19–20kts
Armament: 1-0.3in Maxim MG
Complement: 2

Basically a tourist launch designed around a petrol car engine in 1934. Wooden hull, in mass production as both service craft and leisure boats for Communist dignitaries. During the war large numbers were used by the engineering units of the Red Army. The Red Navy employed them as harbour communication launches, while the most common employment was by the riverine flotillas in multiple roles: communication, transport, reconnaissance, depth sounding, patrol service, troop landing and evacuation. Could carry up to 5 passengers. The PG prefix stands for *PoluGlisser* (half-hydroplane).

The following numbers have been identified, but it is certain that many more were in commission.

The Baltic Fleet

Number	In commission	
№ 688[1]	1940[1]	Slightly different type / series

The Black Sea Fleet

Number	Listed	Deleted
•[2]	25.9.1941	19.7.1942
PG-5	25.9.1941	22.4.1942
PG-20	25.9.1941	22.4.1942
PG-33	20.4.1943	2.8.1943
PG-34	20.4.1943	26.11.1943
PG-35	20.4.1943	27.3.1944
PG-36	20.4.1943	26.11.1943
PG-37	20.4.1943	5.7.1943
PG-38	20.4.1943	27.3.1944
PG-39	20.4.1943	26.11.1943
PG-40	20.4.1943	10.9.1943
PG-41	20.4.1943	26.11.1943
PG-42	20.4.1943	26.11.1943
PG-43	20.4.1943	27.3.1944
PG-44	20.4.1943	26.11.1943
PG-50	5.2.1944	13.4.1944
PG-51	5.2.1944	12.4.1944
PG-52	5.2.1944	12.4.1944
PG-53	5.2.1944	12.4.1944
PG-54	5.2.1944	12.4.1944
PG-55	5.2.1944	12.4.1944
PG-56	5.2.1944	12.4.1944
PG-57	5.2.1944	12.4.1944
PG-58	5.2.1944	12.4.1944
PG-59	5.2.1944	12.4.1944
PG-60	5.2.1944	12.4.1944
PG-61	5.2.1944	12.4.1944
PG-81	23.3.1943	26.11.1943
PG-82	23.3.1943	26.11.1943
PG-83	23.3.1943	31.3.1944
PG-84	23.3.1943	26.11.1943
PG-85	23.3.1943	26.11.1943
PG-86	23.3.1943	26.11.1943
PG-87	23.3.1943	31.3.1944
PG-88	23.3.1943	26.11.1943
PG-89	23.3.1943	31.3.1944
PG-90	23.3.1943	5.6.1941
PG-91	23.3.1943	26.11.1943
PG-92	23.3.1943	26.11.1943
PG-110	25.9.1941	22.4.1942
PG-200	25.9.1941	5.9.1942
PG-385	25.9.1941	22.4.1942
PG-427	25.9.1941	22.4.1942
PG-432	25.9.1941	22.4.1942
PG-437	25.9.1941	22.4.1942
PG-587/10	25.9.1941	22.4.1942
PG-1088	25.9.1941	22.4.1942

[2] Sevastopol Naval Base Defence Forces

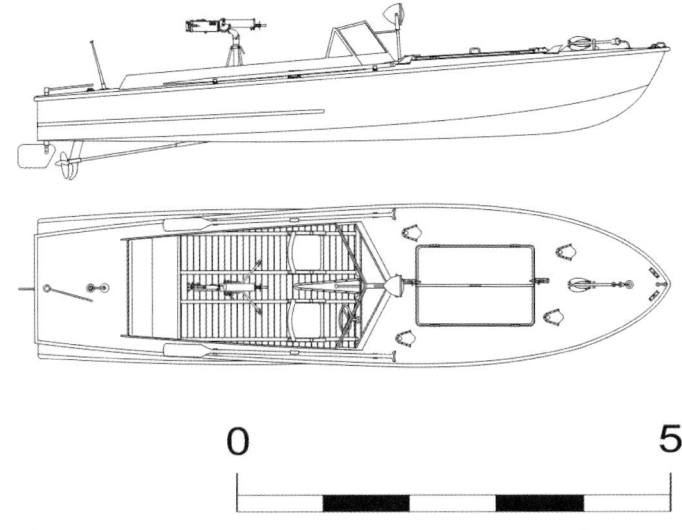

NKL-27 type. Drawing by Jerzy Lewandowski

The Pinsk Flotilla

Number Poluglisser №	Listed	Remarks
№ 1 (DM-1)	1941	Sunk 16.7.1941 by artillery fire on Berezina River
№ 2 (PG-7)	1941	Sunk 16.7.1941 by artillery fire on Berezina River
Sh-1	1941	Scuttled, some raised and recomm by the Germans (one name identified: *Möwe*)
Sh-2	1941	
•	1941	

The Volga Flotilla

Status on 25.11.1942~	16.8.1943	Jan 1944
PG-1 – PG-44	PG-11, PG-12	PG-8, PG-9
	PG-15, PG-17	PG-11 – PG-17
	T-11 – T-13	allocated for transfer
	T-21 – T-23	to the Dnieper Flotilla:
	T-31 – T-33	PG-1 – PG-7
	T-41 – T-43	PG-50 – PG-60
	T-51 – T-53	PG-62, PG-63
	T-61 – T-63	PG-65 – PG 67
	T-71 – T-73	
	T-83 – T-85	

The Dnieper Flotilla

Poluglisser №	Listed	Remarks
№ 18, № 19	7.3.1944	Deleted 23.11.1944
№ 20, № 22	6.4.1944	Deleted 1.10.1944
№ 21	6.4.1944	Deleted 24.12.1944
№ 23	7.3.1944	Lost. Deleted 13.8.1944
№ 62 – № 65	7.3.1944	Deleted 15.2.1945
№ 66	7.3.1944	Deleted 11.11.1944
№ 67, № 68	7.3.1944	Deleted 15.2.1945
№ 69	7.3.1944	Sunk 29.10.1944 by artillery fire on the Bug River. Deleted 11.11.1944
№ 70 – № 87	7.3.1944	Survived the war
№ 101	3.5.1944	Survived the war
№ 102	18.4.1944	Survived the war
№ 103	18.4.1944	Lost. Deleted 13.8.1944
№ 104 – № 106	18.4.1944	Survived the war
№ 107	18.4.1944	Sunk 23.4.1944 by artillery fire on the Spree
№ 108 – № 112	18.4.1944	Survived the war
№ 113 – № 114	3.5.1944	Lost. Deleted 1.9.1944
№ 115 – № 118	29.9.1944	Survived the war
№ 119 – № 121	29.9.1944	Deleted 15.2.1945
№ 122 – № 132	25.2.1945	Survived the war

The Danube Flotilla

Number	Listed	Remarks
5 craft[3]	22.6.1941~	Deleted 23.7.1941. Presumably lost
PG-8, PG-9	23.12.1944	Survived the war
PG-33, PG-34	1944	
PG-36, PG-37	1944	
PG-39	1944	
PG-41, PG-42	1944	
PG-44	1944	
PG-50, PG-51[3]	20.4.1944	Survived the war
PG-52[3]	20.4.1944	Deleted 4.10.1944
PG-53[3]	20.4.1944	Survived the war
PG-54[3]	20.4.1944	Deleted 10.3.1945
PG-55[3]	20.4.1944	Deleted 1.11.1944
PG-56 – PG-60[3]	20.4.1944	Survived the war
PG-61[3]	20.4.1944	Deleted 14.11.1944
PG-81 – PG-85	1944/5	
PG-91, PG-92	1944/5	

[3] Slightly different type/ series

The Amur Flotilla (1945)

Number
PG-1 – PG-5
PG-201 – PG-211

The Il'men Flotilla (1945)

Number	Listed
№ 1 – № 4	24.4.1943
№ 5 – № 9	10.9.1943

Left: Ammunition delivery by a *PG-82* boat of the Dnieper Flotilla. Note Maxim MG and camouflage painting. *Vitalij Kostrichenko Collection*

Below: *NKL-27* type boats of the Dnieper Flotilla. *Vitalij Kostrichenko Collection*

K-ZiS-5 type

Harbour launches

Displacement: 3.06t full load
Dimensions: 10.0 x 2.0 x 0.65m
Machinery: 1-shaft ZIS-5 petrol engine, 75hp = 12–15kts. Range 180nm
Complement: 2

Service and communication launches built at Leningrad, Yaroslavl and other inland and small yards. Several hundred built, and used on all coastal and inland areas by the naval forces, Red Army and NKVD. There was no official numbering system, and the data presented below are fragmentary; the numbers might be the yard production numbers.

K-ZiS-5 type boat. Przemysław Budzbon Collection

No Raz"ezdnoj kater №	Fleet	Listed	Remarks
KP-110	B	1938	1940 in Kronstadt
KP-111	B	1938	1940 in Kronstadt
№ 0115, № 0116, № 0215, № 0216, № 0315, № 0316, № 0415, № 0416, № 0516, № 0615, № 0715, № 0716, № 0815, № 0816, № 0915, № 0916, № 1015, № 1115, № 1116, № 1215, № 1216, № 1315, № 1316, № 1415, № 1416	Az	1941~	Scuttled 22.8.1942 on the Kuban River
№ 0515, № 0616, № 1016	Az	1941~	Sunk Aug 1942 by artillery fire on the Kuban River
№ 0306, № 0309	Il La	20.7.1941	Trfd 20.10.1941 to the Ladoga Flotilla
RSK-1	Az	1941~	Sunk 17.10.1941 by artillery fire off Taganrog
RSK-2, RSK-4, RSK-5, RSK-8–RSK-10	Az	1941~	Scuttled 26.7.1942 on the Don River
RSK-3	Az	1941~	Sunk 17.10.1941 by artillery fire off Rostov-on-Don
RSK-7	Az	1941~	Scuttled 27.7.1942 on the Manych River
SP-48 (№ 1176)	BS	1942	Extant 1944
SP-49	BS	1940	Extant 1944
SP-54	BS	1939	Extant 1944

Miscellaneous types

Hydroplanes

No	Fleet	Listed	Deleted	Remarks
•	C	25.9.1941	19.7.1942	Sevastopol Naval Base
№ 7	C	22.6.1941~	17.12.1942	Staff of the Sevastopol Naval Base
•	C	22.6.1941~	17.12.1942	Staff of the Black Sea Fleet
•	C	22.6.1941~	17.12.1942	Staff of the Black Sea Fleet
•	C	22.6.1941~	17.12.1942	Staff of the Black Sea Fleet
•	C	22.6.1941~	17.12.1942	Staff of the Black Sea Fleet

15. Floating artillery batteries

Плавучие артиллерийские батареи

PBAB № on Comm ex-Barzha №	No 1944	Details	Comm	Fleet	Remarks
№ 4	PAB-4	365t; 37.0 x 7.0 x 0.7m; 3-100mm/56 B-34, 1-37mm/67.5 70-K, added 1943: 2-20mm Oerlikon, 5-0.5in DShK MGs (1x4, 1x1), 2-0.3in MGs, 83 men	11.10.1941	Az BS Da	Mobilised summer 1941, conv to floating battery. Trfd 1.10.1942 to the Black Sea Fleet, trfd 13.4.1944 to the Danube Flotilla, renumbered *PAB-4* on 14.11.1944
№ 97		2-6in field guns, 2-120mm mortars, 4-0.5in MGs	30.6.1942	On Vo	Mobilised spring 1942, conv to floating battery. Trfd 17.7.1942 to the Volga Flotilla. Disarmed 9.2.1943, conv 20.2.1943 to service craft
№ 98		2-6in field guns, 2-120mm mortars, 4-0.5in MGs	30.6.1942	On Vo	Mobilised spring 1942, conv to floating battery. Trfd 17.7.1942 to the Volga Flotilla. Disarmed 9.2.1943, conv 20.2.1943 to service craft
№ 99		2-6in field guns, 2-120mm mortars, 4-0.5in MGs	18.8.1942	Vo	Mobilised autumn 1942, conv to floating battery. Disarmed 9.2.1943, conv 20.2.1943 to service craft
№ 100		2-6in field guns, 2-120mm mortars, 4-0.5in MGs	18.8.1942	Vo	Mobilised autumn 1942, conv to floating battery. Disarmed 9.2.1943, conv 20.2.1943 to service craft.

Cross reference: Rated as floating artillery batteries

PAB №	Details	Type	From	To	Fate
№ 1220	*DB* type	Landing craft	14.9.1944		Survived the war
№ 1225	*DB* type	Landing craft	1943		Survived the war
№ 1226	*DB* type	Landing craft	1943		Survived the war
№ 1227	*DB* type	Landing craft	1943		Survived the war
№ 1228	*DB* type	Landing craft	1943		Survived the war
№ 1229	*DB* type	Landing craft	1943		Survived the war
№ 1271	*DB* type	Landing craft	31.10.1944		Survived the war
№ 1272	*DB* type	Landing craft	31.10.1944		Survived the war
№ 1273	*DB* type	Landing craft	31.10.1944		Survived the war

Gadir Usejnov, later *Plavuchaia zenitnaia batereia № 1139 Zaria*, as completed in 1903. *Boris Lemachko Collection*

Polius, later *PZB-1*, as completed in 1897. *Boris Lemachko Collection*

Volodarskij, later *Plavuchaia zenitnaia batereia № 1140*, in 1930s. *Boris Lemachko Collection*

16. AA defence ships

Корабли ПВО

16.1. Floating AA batteries

Плавучие зенитные батареи

Cargo steamers

No 1941	Name	Details	Comm	Fleet	Remarks
PZB-1	POLIUS	2080t; 71.7 x 9.9 x 4.0m; 720hp = 7.5kts; 4-3in/55 34-K,	29.8.1941	Cs	Built 1897. Mobilised 23.8.1941, conv to AA battery. Decomm 5.11.1943 to civilian service
PZB-2	MERIDIAN	1-37mm/67.5 70-K, 1-23mm VIa aircraft gun, 2-0.5in MGs, 4-0.5in (4x1) MGs; 110 men	3.8.1941	Cs	Built 1897. Mobilised 1.8.1941, conv to AA battery. Decomm 2.11.1943 to civilian service
PZB-3	EKVATOR	2045t; 71.1 x 9.9 x 4.1m; 520hp = 9kts; 4-3in/55, 1-37mm/67.5 70-K, 1-23mm VIa aircraft gun, 2-0.5in MGs, 4-0.5in (4x1) MGs; 117 men	14.7.1941	Cs	Built 1899. Mobilised 13.7.1941, conv to AA battery. Decomm 31.10.1943 to civilian service

PZB-2 Meridian during the war. Note 3in 34-K type guns and camouflage painting. Przemysław Budzbon Collection

Oilers

PZB № on Comm	Name	Details	Comm	Fleet	Remarks
№ 1139	ZARIA ex-*Gadir* (1924) ex-*Gadir Usejnov* (1920)	1395grt; 70.2 x 9.9 x 5.7m; 850hp; 4-3in/55 34-K, 6-20mm Oerlikon	6.10.1943	Cs	Built 1903. Mobilised 14.7.1943, conv to AA battery. Decomm 7.12.1943 to civilian service
№ 1140	VOLODARSKIJ ex-*Aleksandra Zelenaia* (1924) ex-*Aleksandra Kolesnikova* (1920)	1350grt; 71.4 x 9.7 x 5.7m; 800hp; 4-3in/55 34-K, 6-20mm Oerlikon	7.10.1943	Cs	Built 1903. Mobilised 14.7.1943, conv to AA battery. Decomm 24.11.1943 to civilian service

Steam tug *P-9* following conversion to AA battery *Zenit* with 37mm 70-K guns forward and three 45mm 21-KM shielded guns aft. *Przemysław Budzbon Collection*

Paddle steam tugs

PZB № No on Comm	Name	Details	Comm	Fleet	Remarks
	ZENIT ex-*P-9*	400t standard, 480t full load; 61.0 x 16.5/• x 1.2m; 400hp = 11.5kts; 4-45mm/68.6 21-KM, 3-37mm/67.5 70-K, 4-0.5in DShK MGs; 71 men	15.4.1942	Am	Built 1935, Leninskaia kuznitsa. Mobilised 1942, refurbished and conv to AA defence ship, conv 24.8.1943 to AA battery, numbered № 1234. Survived the war
№ 1232		8-37mm/67.5 70-K, 8-0.5in MGs	29.9.1943	Am	Mobilised 1943, conv to AA battery. Survived the war

Barge

No on Comm	Name	Details	Comm	Fleet	Remarks
PVO-1270		30t; 19.5 x 4.2 x 0.8m; 144hp = 7kts; 2-37mm/67.5 70-K, 2-0.5in MGs; 13 men	15.5.1944	Dn	Mobilised 1944, conv to AA battery. Survived the war

Dumb barges

PZB № No on Comm	Name Barzha №	Details	Comm	Fleet	Remarks
№ 586	P-8 AVRORA	400t; 58.7 x 8.5 x 1.3m; 4-3in/55 34-K, 2-0.3in MGs, 60 men	27.10.1941	Am	Built 1894. Mobilised Oct 1941, conv to AA battery. Decomm 5.2.1943?
№ 587	P-11	2-4in	27.10.1941	Am	Built 1894. Mobilised Oct 1941, conv to AA battery. Decomm 5.2.1943
№ 588		2-3in	27.10.1941	Am	Built 1894. Mobilised Oct 1941, conv to AA battery. Decomm 5.2.1943?
№ 614	№ 614	•	16.11.1942	Vo	Mobilised Nov 1942, conv to AA batteries. Decomm 9.2.1943 to civilian service
№ 615	№ 615	•	16.11.1942	Vo	Mobilised Nov 1942, conv to AA batteries. Decomm 9.2.1943 to civilian service

Dumb barge *P-8 Avrora* following conversion to AA battery *PZB № 586*, armed with 3in 34-K guns.
Przemysław Budzbon Collection

№ 616	№ 616	•		16.11.1942	Vo	Mobilised Nov 1942, conv to AA batteries. Decomm 9.2.1943 to civilian service
№ 617	№ 617	•		16.11.1942	Vo	Mobilised Nov 1942, conv to AA batteries. Decomm 9.2.1943 to civilian service
№ 618	№ 618	•		16.11.1942	Vo	Mobilised Nov 1942, conv to AA batteries. Decomm 9.2.1943 to civilian service
PB-1	ex-K-• (Pol, 1939)	47.8t; 28.8 x 4.5 x 0.5m; 2-37mm/67.5 70-K	July 1941	Pn	Built late 1930s. Ex-Polish Pinsk Flotilla barge, scuttled 1939, raised and conv to AA battery. Scuttled ~26.9.1941 at Kiev
PB-2	ex-K-• (Pol, 1939)	47.8t; 28.8 x 4.5 x 0.5m; 2-37mm/67.5 70-K	July 1941	Pn	Built late 1930s. Ex-Polish Pinsk Flotilla barge, scuttled 1939, raised and conv to AA battery. Scuttled ~26.9.1941 at Kiev
PB-3	ex-K-• (Pol, 1939)	47.8t; 28.8 x 4.5 x 0.5m; 1-37mm/67.5 70-K	July 1941	Pn	Built late 1930s. Ex-Polish Pinsk Flotilla barge, scuttled 1939, raised and conv to AA battery. Scuttled ~26.9.1941 at Kiev

Test compartment

PZB № on Comm	Name	Details	Comm	Fleet	Remarks
№ 3	[NE TRON' MENIA]*	50.0 x 30.0 x 15(depth)m; non propelled; 2-130mm/50 B-13 (removed Oct 1941), 4-3in/55 34-K, 3-37mm/67.5 70-K, 3-0.5in DShK MGs, 4-0.3in (1x4) Maxim MGs	3.8.1941	BS	Test compartment for *Sovetskij Soiuz* class battleships. Conv to artillery battery moored at entrance to Sevastopol, conv Oct 1941 to AA battery, towed 11.11.1941 to Kazachaia Bay and beached to avoid sinking by enemy aircraft. Decomm 27.06.1942 and abandoned. Raised late 1940s and BU

* Nickname

Abandoned battery *PZB № 3*.
Boris Lemachko Collection

Cross reference: Rated as floating AA batteries

PZB № No Name	Details	Type	From	To	Fate
ASHKADAR	T-422	River minesweeper	5.8.1943	12.11.1943	Decomm
BAKEN	T-846	River minesweeper	5.8.1943	26.9.1944	Decomm
CHEBOKSARY	T-126	River minesweeper	5.8.1943	30.5.1944	Decomm
INZHENER BEGAM	T-845	River minesweeper	5.8.1943	24.4.1944	Decomm
KOKKINAKI	Project SB-47	Gunboat	-	Sept 1941	Scuttled
LOMONOSOV	Project SB-47	Gunboat	-	Sept 1941	Scuttled
MAIAKOVSKIJ	T-425	River minesweeper	5.8.1943	20.6.1944	Decomm
№ 1220	DB type	Landing craft	6.7.1943	14.9.1944	Re-rated as floating artillery battery
№ 1221	DB type	Landing craft	19.5.1943	24.6.1943	Renumbered PVO-28
№ 1222	DB type	Landing craft	19.5.1943	24.6.1943	Renumbered PVO-29
№ 1223	DB type	Landing craft	16.8.1943	July 1944	Conv to service craft
№ 1224	DB type	Landing craft	16.8.1943	July 1944	Conv to service craft
№ 1230	G type	Landing craft	29.8.1943		Survived the war
№ 1231	G type	Landing craft	29.8.1943		Survived the war
№ 1232	G type	Landing craft	29.8.1943		Survived the war
SERGEJ KOSTRIKOV	T-424	River minesweeper	5.8.1943	20.6.1944	Decomm
SHTURVAL'NYJ	T-322	River minesweeper	5.8.1943	20.6.1944	Decomm
VISLIANA	T-521	River minesweeper	5.8.1943	30.6.1944	Reverted to tug
ZUBR	T-121	River minesweeper	5.8.1943	30.5.1944	Decomm

16.2. Air warning service ships

Корабли ВНОС

The Soviet fleet of air warning ships and boats on the Caspian Sea is a perfect illustration of the truth that the military is always well prepared for every war except the one they have to fight. The mobilisation scheme was prepared in case of war with the British-French alliance who in 1940 had plans to bomb the Baku oilfields (Operation Pike). The huge fleet of mobilised ships was soon relegated to other duties. A new type of AA defence boat was comm in the areas where they were really needed.

Tel'man in civilian service before the war.
Boris Lemachko Collection

Cargo-passenger motorships

No 1941	Name	Details	Comm	Fleet	Remarks
VN-12	BOEVOJ ex-*Chernogoriia* (1921) ex-*Duel'* (1914)	1188t; 59.0 x 8.9 x 3.0m; 1200hp = 9.7kts; (from 1942/3: 1-20mm Oerlikon), 1-0.5in MG, 4-0.45in MGs	July 1941	Cs	Built 1898 Ganz Danubius. Mobilised 1920 as transport, decomm 1920 to civilian service. Mobilised July 1941, conv to air warning ship. Conv 10.10.1941 to transport, name reverted. Survived the war
VN-13	SPARTAK ex-*Mush* (1914)	1357t; 63.4 x 8.4 x 3.4m; 2 x 240hp = 8.2kts; 3-0.45in MGs	9.8.1941	Cs	Built 1891. Mobilised 30.7.1941, conv to air warning ship. Conv 28.8.1941 to transport, name reverted. Survived the war
VN-14	TEL'MAN ex-*Trud* (1935) ex-*Geok-Tepe* (1922	1352t; 73.0 x 11.0 x 4.0m; 720hp = 10kts; 4550nm at 8.5kts; 4-45mm/46 21-K, 2-0.5in MGs, 1-0.3in MG; 83 men	1.7.1941	Cs	Built 1883 for the Caspian Flotilla as steam paddle harbour vessel, conv 1911 to dispatch vessel. Seized 1918 by White Russians, recovered 1920, conv 1923 to minelayer, conv 1925 to surveying vessel. Deleted 1929, to civilian service, rebuilt as screw motorship. Mobilised 30.6.1941, conv to air warning ship. Conv 15.1.1942 to depot ship, name reverted. Decomm 30.10.1943 to civilian service. Sunk 21.4.1944, raised and repaired. Discarded 1.4.1958

16.0 AA Defence ships

Cargo-passenger steamers

No 1941	Name	Details	Comm	Fleet	Remarks
VN-1	CHICHERIN ex-*Mikhail Kolesnikov* (1920)	2227t; 66.3 x 9.6 x 4.6m; 2 x 400hp = 10kts; 2-45mm/46 21-K, 2-0.3in MGs (from Apr 1942: 1-45mm/46 21-K, 1-0.5in MG, 4-0.45in MGs)	22.7.1941	Cs	Built 1898. Mobilised 21.7.1941, conv to air warning ship. Conv 16.10.1941 to training ship, name reverted. Conv 13.4.1942 to transport. Survived the war
VN-2	SHAUMIAN ex-*Tov. Fomin* (1937) ex-*Skobelev* (1923)	1624t; 72.6 x 8.5 x 4.3m; 2 x 500hp = 11.8; 1780nm at 9kts; 2-45mm/46 21-K, 3-0.3in; 89 men	June 1941	Cs	Built 1902. Mobilised 25.6.1941, conv to air warning ship. Conv 16.10.1941 to training ship of the KVVMU, name reverted. Returned 9.5.1945
VN-3	KOMSOMOLETS ex-*Dem'ian Bednyj* (1939) ex-*Ali Usejnov* (1921)	1055t; 47.1 x 8.6 x 3.6m; 400hp = 9.5kts; 1-45mm/46 21-K, 4-0.45in MGs, 1-0.303in MG	Aug 1941	Cs	Built 1894 Bergsunds. Mobilised 23.8.1941, conv to air warning ship. Conv 13.10.1941 to transport, name reverted. Survived the war
VN-4	KARL MARKS ex-*Sedaget* (1923) ex-*Ivan Kolesnikov* (1918)	2191t; 66.8 x 9.7 x 4.6m; 2 x 400hp = 10kts; 1-45mm/46 21-K, 1-0.5in MG, 4-0.45in MGs	28.8.1941	Cs	Built 1898. Mobilised July 1941, conv to air warning ship. Conv 8.10.1941 to transport, name reverted. Survived the war
VN-5	ASTRAKHAN'	2180t; 65.0 x 9.0 x 4.2m; 900hp = 9.6kts; 1-45mm/46 21-K, (added 1942/3: 1-20mm Oerlikon), 4-0.45in MG	28.8.1941	Cs	Built 1897. Mobilised 7.1941, conv to air warning ship. Conv 2.10.1941 to transport, name reverted. Survived the war
VN-11	POLTORATSK ex-*Akperiia* (1924)	1060t; 47.1 x 8.4 x 3.7m; 400hp = 9.2kts; 1-45mm/46 21-K, 3-0.45in MGs, 1-0.303in MGs	July 1941	Cs	Built 1894 Bergsunds. Mobilised July 1941, conv to air warning ship. Conv 3.10.1941 to transport, name reverted. Survived the war
VN-13	MOSKVA ex-*Imperatritsa Aleksandra* (1917)	2050t; 76.2 x 10.4 x 4.1m; 1200hp = 11.6kts; 2-45mm/46 21-K, (added 1942/3: 1-20mm Oerlikon), 1-0.5in MG, 4-0.45in MGs	28.8.1941	Cs	Built 1896 Kavkaz i Merkuri. Mobilised 24.8.1941, conv to air warning ship. Conv 12.10.1941 to transport, name reverted. Conv 6.6.1942 to sanitary transport for 250 beds. Reverted to transport 2.2.1943. Survived the war, Rebuilt 1958, hulked at Baku 1960s, BU 1980

Ali Usejnov, future *VN-3 Komsomolets*, as built.
Sjöhistoriska museet Fo44600

Valerij Chkalov back in civilian service in the 1950s.
Boris Lemachko Collection

Cargo steamers

No 1941	Name	Details	Comm	Fleet	Remarks
VN-7	FIOLETOV ex-*Kokkum* (1924)	958t; 47.8 x 8.5 x 3.8m; 360hp = 8.4kts; 1-45mm/46 21-K, 3-11.43mm, 1-0.303in MG	July 1941	Cs	Built 1880. Mobilised July 1941, conv to air warning ship. Conv 13.10.1941 to transport, name reverted. Survived the war
VN-8	MOLOT ex-*Nedzhef* (1924)	955t; 6.5 x 8.4 x 3.3m; 300hp = 7.8kts; 2-45mm/46 21-K, 3-0.3in	1.7.1941	Cs	Built 1897. Mobilised 30.6.1941, conv to air warning ship. Conv 13.10.1941 to transport, name reverted. Survived the war
VN-9	MARY ex-*Merv* (1937)	1585t; 65.8 x 8.5 x 3.9m; 2 x 340hp = 8.1kts; 1-45mm/46 21-K, 4-0.45in MGs, 1-0.303in MG	July 1941	Cs	Built 1882. Tanker, conv 1920. Mobilised 16.7.1941, conv to air warning ship. Conv 17.10.1941 to transport, name reverted. Survived the war
VN-10	CHKALOV ex-*Grigorij Artsruni* (1937)	1106t; 47.3 x 8.5 x 3.6m; 400hp = 8.1kts; 1-45mm/46 21-K, 1-0.303in MG	July 1941	Cs	Built 1894. Mobilised July 1941, conv to air warning ship. Conv 6.10.1941 to transport, name reverted. Decomm 1944 to civilian service, renamed *V. Chkalov*

Water carrier

No 1941	Name	Details	Comm	Fleet	Remarks
VN-3	DIMITROV ex-*Trud* (1935) ex-*Mariia* (1924)	2330t; 69.8 x 8.5 x 4.8m; 2 x 450hp = 9kts; (added 1942/3: 1-20mm Oerlikon), 3-0.45in MGs, 1-0.303in MG	July 1941	Cs	Built 1901. Mobilised 17.7.1941, conv to air warning ship. Conv 28.8.1941 to transport, name reverted. Survived the war

Service craft

No 1941	Name	Details	Comm	Fleet	Remarks
VN-15	DAGESTANETS	•	7.7.1941	Cs	Mobilised 3.7.1941, conv to air warning ship. Conv 15.10.1941 to service craft

16.3. Air warning & AA defence boats

AA defence boats
Катера ПВО
Air warning boats
Катера ВНОС (Air surveillance and communication boats)

Motorboats

No 1942	Name	Details	Comm	Fleet	Remarks
PVO-21	CHTZ-17	•	Oct 1942	Cs	Mobilised 3.10.1942, conv to AA defence boat. Conv 18.2.1943 to service craft *RSK-36*
PVO-22	GEROJ CHKALOV	72t; 18.4 x 6.2 x 1.5m; 35hp = 5kts; 1400nm; 2-0.3in (1x2) MGs; 18 men	Oct 1942	Cs	Mobilised 3.10.1942 conv to AA defence boat. Conv 16.2.1943 to service craft, name reverted
PVO-23	DOLBAN		Oct 1942	Cs	Mobilised 3.10.1942 conv to AA defence boat. Conv 16.2.1943 to service craft, name reverted
PVO-25	TATARIN		Oct 1942	Cs	Mobilised 3.10.1942 conv to AA defence boat. Conv 16.2.1943 to service craft, name reverted
PVO-110	KAMYNIN	72t; 18.4 x 6.2 x 1.5m; 35hp = 5kts; 1400nm; 2-0.3in (1x2) MGs; 18 men	June 1943	Cs	Mobilised 18.6.1943, conv to AA defence boat. Conv 25.10.1943 to service craft. Sank 7.12.1943 in a gale off Krotkovo, raised and repaired
VN-19	10 LET SOVETSKOJ TURKMENII ex-*10 let Turkmenistana*	18.05 x 5.95 x 1.15m; 35hp = 6kts; 1-0.3in MG	7.7.1941	Cs	Built 1938. Mobilised 3.7.1941, conv to air warning boat. Conv 12.10.1941 to service craft
VN-20	KIZIL-SU	18.2 x 6.2 x 1.6m; 35hp = 6kts; 1-0.3in MG	7.7.1941	Cs	Built 1938. Mobilised 3.7.1941, conv to air warning boat. Deleted 4.9.1941
VN-22	DMITRIEV	87t; 22.0 x 6.0 x 1.4m; 35hp = 5kts; 1000nm; 16 men	7.7.1941	Cs	Built 1938. Mobilised 2.7.1941 conv to air warning boat. Conv 12.10.1941 to service craft
VN-24	BALAKHNA	75t; 17.6 x 6.3 x 1.8m; 35hp = 7kts; 2300nm; 4-0.3in (1x4) MGs; 18 men	7.7.1941	Cs	Built 1938. Mobilised 2.7.1941, conv to air warning boat. Deleted 4.9.1941
VN-26	TIMIRIAZEV		7.7.1941	Cs	Built 1938. Mobilised 2.7.1941 conv to air warning boat. Conv 12.10.1941 to service craft

Seiners

No 1942	Name	Details	Comm	Fleet	Remarks
PVO-12	VOSKHOD	17.5 x 5.0 x 1.6m; 65hp; 2-0.5in DShK	Oct 1942	Cs	Built 1940. Mobilised 3.10.1942, conv to AA defence boat. Conv 15.2.1943 to service craft. Sunk 21.11.1943 by artillery off Eltigen
PVO-13	IVA	17.5 x 5.0 x 1.6m; 65hp; 2-0.5in DShK	Aug 1942	Cs	Built 1940. Mobilised 20.8.1942, conv to AA defence boat. Conv 15.2.1943 to service craft
PVO-15	GROMOBOJ	17.5 x 5.0 x 1.6m; 65hp; 2-0.5in DShK	Oct 1942	Cs	Built 1940. Mobilised 3.10.1942, conv to AA defence boat. Conv 15.2.1943 to service craft
PVO-16	CHELIABINSK	17.5 x 5.0 x 1.6m; 65hp; 2-0.5in DShK	Oct 1942	Cs	Built 1940. Mobilised 3.10.1942, conv to AA defence boat. Conv 15.2.1943 to service craft
PVO-26	REKORD	17.5 x 5.0 x 1.6m; 65hp; 2-0.5in DShK	Aug 1942	Cs	Built 1940. Mobilised 20.8.1942, conv to AA defence boat. Conv 16.2.1943 to service craft. Sank 15.11.1943 in a gale off Tulza Spit
PVO-33	BURIAT	68t; 18.2 x 6.4 x 2.3m; 35hp = 7kts; 2200nm at 5.5kts; 2-0.5in MGs	Aug 1942	Cs	Built 1940. Mobilised 20.8.1942, conv to AA defence boat. Conv 16.2.1943 to service craft. Sank 15.11.1943 in a gale off Tulza Spit
PVO-35	KARELIIA	68t; 18.2 x 6.4 x 2.3m; 35hp = 7kts; 2200nm at 5.5kts; 2-0.5in MGs	Aug 1942	Cs	Built 1940. Mobilised 20.8.1942, conv to AA defence boat. Conv 15.2.1943 to service craft
PVO-36	KAGANOVICH	68t; 18.2 x 6.4 x 2.3m; 35hp = 7kts; 2200nm at 5.5kts; 2-0.5in MGs	Oct 1942	Cs	Built 1940. Mobilised 3.10.1942, conv to AA defence boat. Conv 15.2.1943 to service craft

No	Name	Details	Comm	Fleet	Remarks
1942					
PVO-42	STROITEL'	68t; 18.2 x 6.4 x 2.3m; 35hp = 7kts; 2200nm at 5.5kts; 2-0.5in MGs	Aug 1942	Cs	Built 1940. Mobilised 20.8.1942, conv to AA defence boat. Renamed *PVO-14* on 15.1.1943. Conv 15.2.1943 to service craft
PVO-43	KOSA	68t; 18.2 x 6.4 x 2.3m; 35hp = 7kts; 2200nm at 5.5kts; 2-0.5in MGs	Aug 1942	Cs	Built 1940. Mobilised 20.8.1942, conv to AA defence boat. Renamed *PVO-24* on 15.1.1943. Conv 16.2.1943 to service craft
PVO-45	AVIATOR	68t; 18.2 x 6.4 x 2.3m; 35hp = 7kts; 2200nm at 5.5kts; 2-0.5in MGs	Aug 1942	Cs	Built 1940. Mobilised 20.8.1942, conv to AA defence boat. Renamed *PVO-31* on 15.1.1943. Conv 16.2.1943 to service craft
PVO-101	UDARNIK	68t; 18.2 x 6.4 x 2.3m; 35hp = 7kts; 2200nm at 5.5kts; 2-0.5in MGs, 1 MKhT sweep; 10 men	29.5.1943	Cs	Built 1940. Mobilised 26.5.1943, conv to AA defence boat. Conv 14.11.1943 to service craft
PVO-103	KRASNOZNAMENETS		7.6.1943	Cs	Built 1940. Mobilised 6.6.1943, conv to AA defence boat. Conv 25.10.1943 to service craft
PVO-104	STRATOSTAT		2.6.1943	Cs	Built 1940. Mobilised 1.6.1943, conv to AA defence boat. Conv 25.10.1943 to service craft
PVO-105	GROMKIJ		9.6.1943	Cs	Built 1940. Mobilised 8.6.1943, conv to AA defence boat. Conv 25.10.1943 to service craft
PVO-106	STAKHANOV		7.6.1943	Cs	Built 1940. Mobilised 30.5.1943, conv to AA defence boat. Conv 25.10.1943 to service craft
PVO-107	TALOVETS		30.5.1943	Cs	Built 1940. Mobilised 26.5.1943, conv to AA defence boat. Conv 14.11.1943 to service craft
PVO-108	SEJNER № 83		June 1943	Cs	Built 1940. Mobilised 13.6.1943, conv to AA defence boat. Conv 25.10.1943 to service craft
PVO-109	LEJTENANT SHMIDT		May 1943	Cs	Built 1940. Mobilised 26.5.1943, conv to AA defence boat. Conv 25.10.1943 to service craft

Cross reference: Rated as air warning & AA defence ships and boats

No	Details	Type	From	To	Fate
B-10	*Zubr*	Minesweeper	5.8.1943	20.6.1944	Reverted to tug
B-15	*Cheboksary*	Minesweeper	5.8.1943	20.6.1944	Reverted to tug
B-18	*Shturval'nyj*	Minesweeper	5.8.1943	20.6.1944	Reverted to tug
B-24	*Ashkadar*	Minesweeper	5.8.1943	20.6.1944	Reverted to tug
B-26	*Maiakovskij*	Minesweeper	5.8.1943	20.6.1944	Reverted to tug
B-27	*Sergej Kostrikov*	Minesweeper	5.8.1943	20.6.1944	Reverted to tug
B-30	*Visliana*	Minesweeper	5.8.1943	20.6.1944	Reverted to tug
B-48	*Inzhener Begam*	Minesweeper	5.8.1943	20.6.1944	Reverted to tug
B-49	*Baken*	Minesweeper	5.8.1943	20.6.1944	Reverted to tug
PVO-9	*KLT* type	Minesweeping boat	1940	16.6.1944	Conv to minesweeping boat
PVO-10	*DB* type	Landing motorboat	24.6.1943	17.11.1943	Lost
PVO-11	*R* type	Patrol boat	15.1.1943	18.2.1943	Conv to service craft
PVO-11	*DB* type	Landing motorboat	24.6.1943	18.4.1944	Conv to minesweeping boat
PVO-11	*Temir*	Minesweeping boat	Aug 1942	15.1.1943	Conv to magnetic minesweeper
PVO-12	*Iranets*	Minesweeping boat	Aug 1942	3.9.1942	Conv to tug for minesweeping raft
PVO-12	*DB* type	Landing motorboat	24.6.1943	21.11.1943	Lost
PVO-13	*DB* type	Landing motorboat	24.6.1943	18.4.1944	Conv to minesweeping boat
PVO-14	*DB* type	Landing motorboat	24.6.1943	18.4.1944	Conv to minesweeping boat
PVO-14	*Drifter № 80*	Minesweeping boat	Aug 1942	15.1.1943	Conv to magnetic minesweeper
PVO-15	*DB* type	Landing motorboat	24.6.1943	18.4.1944	Conv to minesweeping boat
PVO-16	*DB* type	Landing motorboat	24.6.1943	18.4.1944	Conv to minesweeping boat
PVO-17	*DB* type	Landing motorboat	24.6.1943	18.4.1944	Conv to minesweeping boat
PVO-18	*DB* type	Landing motorboat	24.6.1943	18.4.1944	Conv to minesweeping boat
PVO-19	*DB* type	Landing motorboat	24.6.1943	18.4.1944	Conv to minesweeping boat
PVO-20	*DB* type	Landing motorboat	24.6.1943	21.11.1943	Lost
PVO-21	*Komarovets*	Minesweeping boat	20.8.1942	3.10.1942	Renumbered *PVO-31*
PVO-21	*DB* type	Landing motorboat	24.6.1943	10.1.1944	Lost
PVO-22	*Samosdelets*	Minesweeping boat	20.8.1942	3.10.1942	Renumbered *PVO-32*
PVO-22	*DB* type	Landing motorboat	24.6.1943	21.11.1943	Lost
PVO-23	*DB* type	Landing motorboat	24.6.1943		Survived the war
PVO-24	*DB* type	Landing motorboat	24.6.1943	26.11.1943	Lost
PVO-24	*Drifter № 79*	Minesweeping boat	Aug 1942	15.1.1943	Conv to magnetic minesweeper

PVO-25	*KM 16m* type	Training motorboat	20.8.1942	18.2.1943	Conv to communication boat
PVO-25	*DB* type	Landing motorboat	24.6.1943	18.4.1944	Conv to minesweeping boat
PVO-26	*DB* type	Landing motorboat	24.6.1943	15.11.1943	Lost
PVO-27	*DB* type	Landing motorboat	24.6.1943	23.11.1943	Lost
PVO-28	*DB* type	Landing motorboat	24.6.1943	18.4.1944	Conv to minesweeping boat *KATShch-236*
PVO-29	*DB* type	Landing motorboat	24.6.1943		Survived the war
PVO-31	*Komarovets*	Minesweeping boat	3.10.1942	15.1.1943	Conv to minesweeping boat
PVO-32	*Surkovets*	Minesweeping boat	20.8.1942	3.9.1942	Conv to minesweeping boat
PVO-32	*Samosdelets*	Minesweeping boat	3.10.1942	15.1.1943	Conv to minesweeping boat
PVO-32	*UK-1* type	Training ship	13.1.1943	18.2.1943	Conv to service craft
PVO-34	*Evdokiia Vinogradova*	Minesweeping boat	Aug 1942	15.1.1943	Conv to magnetic minesweeper
PVO-36	*KM 16m* type	Training motorboat	20.8.1942	18.2.1943	Conv to communication boat
PVO-41	*R* type	Patrol boat	20.8.1942	15.1.1943	Renumbered *PVO-11*
PVO-44	*KM 16m* type	Training motorboat	30.10.1942	18.2.1943	Conv to communication boat
PVO-46	*KM 16m* type	Training motorboat	3.9.1942	18.2.1943	Conv to communication boat
PVO-51	*UK-1* type	Training ship	3.10.1942	13.1.1943	Renumbered *PVO-32*
PVO-52	*Beketovets*	Minesweeping boat	Aug 1942	15.1.1943	Conv to magnetic minesweeper
PVO-53	*Maiachnyj*	Minesweeping boat	Aug 1942	15.1.1943	Conv to magnetic minesweeper
PVO-54	*Il'Inets*	Minesweeping boat	Aug 1942	15.1.1943	Conv to magnetic minesweeper
PVO-55	*KM 16m* type	Training motorboat	30.10.1942	18.2.1943	Conv to communication boat
PVO-56	*Bakhtemirovets*	Minesweeping boat	Aug 1942	15.1.1943	Conv to magnetic minesweeper
PVO-61	*DB* type	Landing motorboat	30.6.1944		Survived the war
PVO-62	*DB* type	Landing motorboat	30.6.1944		Survived the war
PVO-63	*DB* type	Landing motorboat	30.6.1944		Survived the war
PVO-64	*DB* type	Landing motorboat	30.6.1944		Survived the war
PVO-65	*DB* type	Landing motorboat	30.6.1944		Survived the war
PVO-66	*DB* type	Landing motorboat	30.6.1944		Survived the war
PVO-67	*DB* type	Landing motorboat	30.6.1944		Survived the war
PVO-68	*DB* type	Landing motorboat	30.6.1944		Survived the war
PVO-69	*DB* type	Landing motorboat	30.8.1944	17.9.1945	Conv to armed (rocket) boat
PVO-70	*DB* type	Landing motorboat	30.8.1944	17.9.1945	Conv to armed (rocket) boat
PVO-71	*DB* type	Landing motorboat	30.8.1944		Survived the war
PVO-72	*DB* type	Landing motorboat	30.8.1944		Survived the war
PVO-73	*DB* type	Landing motorboat	30.8.1944		Survived the war
PVO-74	*DB* type	Landing motorboat	30.8.1944		Survived the war
PVO-75	*DB* type	Landing motorboat	30.8.1944		Survived the war
PVO-76	*DB* type	Landing motorboat	30.8.1944		Survived the war
PVO-77	*DB* type	Landing motorboat	30.8.1944		Survived the war
PVO-78	*DB* type	Landing motorboat	30.8.1944		Survived the war
PVO-79	*DB* type	Landing motorboat	30.8.1944		Survived the war
PVO-80	*DB* type	Landing motorboat	30.8.1944		Survived the war
PVO-102	*Temir*	Minesweeping boat	26.5.1943	25.10.1945	Conv to service craft
PVO-110	*Dar'lal*	Minesweeping boat	14.6.1943	19.7.1943	Conv to magnetic minesweeper *EMTShch-93*
VN-6	*Pioner*	Transport (built 1935)	3.7.1941	15.10.1941	Reverted to transport
VN-16	*Izotermichka № 13*	Minesweeping boat	7.7.1941	12.10.1941	Decomm to civilian service
VN-17	*Izotermichka № 7*	Minesweeping boat	7.7.1941	15.11.1941	Conv to magnetic minesweeper *EMT-03*
VN-18	*Izotermichka № 9*	Minesweeping boat	7.7.1941	12.10.1941	Decomm to civilian service
VN-21	*Sverdlov*	Minesweeping boat	7.7.1941	15.11.1941	Conv to magnetic minesweeper *EMT-01*
VN-23	*Izotermichka № 10*	Minesweeping boat	7.7.1941	15.11.1941	Conv to magnetic minesweeper *EMT-02*
VN-25	*Tarta*	Minesweeping boat	7.7.1941	12.10.1941	Decomm to civilian service
VN-27	*Frunze*	Minesweeping boat	7.7.1941	12.10.1941	Decomm to civilian service
VN-28	*Serov*	Minesweeping boat	7.7.1941	12.10.1941	Decomm to civilian service
VNOS-10	*Kater № 22*	Minesweeping boat	Sept 1942	3.10.1942	Renumbered *VNOS-11*
VNOS-11	*Kater № 22*	Minesweeping boat	3.10.1942	18.2.1943	Conv to magnetic minesweeping boat *KEMTShch-1*
VNOS-12	*Kater № 28*	Minesweeping boat	Sept 1942	18.2.1943	Conv to magnetic minesweeping boat *KEMTShch-2*
VNOS-13	*Kater № 38*	Minesweeping boat	Sept 1942	18.2.1943	Conv to magnetic minesweeping boat *KEMTShch-3*
VNOS-14	*Kater № 44*	Minesweeping boat	Sept 1942	18.2.1943	Conv to magnetic minesweeping boat *KEMTShch-4*
VNOS-15	*Kater № 45*	Minesweeping boat	Sept 1942	18.2.1943	Conv to magnetic minesweeping boat *KEMTShch-5*
VNOS-16	*Kungas-Kavasaki* type	Patrol craft	Aug 1942	25.11.1943	Conv to service craft
VNOS-16	*Kater № 46*	Minesweeping boat	3.10.1942	18.2.1943	Conv to magnetic minesweeping boat *KEMTShch-6*
VNOS-17	*Kungas-Kavasaki* type	Patrol craft	Aug 1942	25.11.1943	Conv to service craft
VNOS-18	*Kungas-Kavasaki* type	Patrol craft	Aug 1942	25.11.1943	Conv to service craft
VNOS-19	*Kungas-Kavasaki* type	Patrol craft	Aug 1942	25.11.1943	Conv to service craft
VNOS-20	*Kungas-Kavasaki* type	Patrol craft	Aug 1942	25.11.1943	Conv to service craft
VNOS-26	*Kemtshch-6*	Minesweeping boat	24.6.1943	29.12.1943	Conv to service craft

17. Minelayers

Минные заградители

17.1. Naval construction

Russian **Bug** class

Displacement:	1380t
Dimensions:	62.2 x 10.4 x 4.6m
Machinery:	2-shaft VTE, 4 boilers, 1500hp = 10.5kts. Coal, range 1000nm at 5kts
Armament:	1-3in/30 Lender, 230 mines
Complement:	59

Minelayer *Dunaj*, laid up in Apr 1918. Changed hands several times during the Civil War, then captured 14.11.1920 by the Red Army at Sevastopol. Relegated 1922 to transport, then reverted to minelayer. Conv 29.10.1924 to surveying vessel, reverted 28.4.1928 to minelayer. Reverted 4.6.1940 to surveying vessel. Sank 19 miles east of Yalta following damage by German aircraft.

*1 Maia (ex-Dunaj), future Bug in 1924.
Boris Lemachko Collection*

Name	Builder	Laid down	Launched	Comp	Comm	Fleet	Fate
GIDROGRAF ex-*1 Maia* (1.1.1932) ex-*Dunaj* (31.12.1922)	Motala	Feb 1891	13.11.1891	20.4.1892	Dec 1920	BS	Lost 4.11.1941

Russian **Teplokhod** class

Coastal minelayer

Displacement:	50t full load
Dimensions:	23.2 (*Vajndlo* 21.2) x 5.0 x 1.0m
Machinery:	2-shaft, Orel (*Vajndlo* Bolinder) diesel motor, 86hp = 7.5kts. Oil fuel 1.25t, range 360nm at 7kts
Armament:	1 MG, 40 mines
Complement:	8

Name	Builder	Compl	Comm	Fleet	Fate
KERI ex-*Keri* (Est, 1940) ex-*Kalev* (Est, 1936) ex-*M-8* (Est, 1919) ex-*KM-1* (Ger, 1919) ex-*Teplokhod № 8* (Rus, 1918)	Björneborg	1915	13.8.1940	B	Deleted 28.8.1948
VAJNDLO ex-*Vajndlo* (Est, 1940) ex-*M-10* (Est, 1919) ex-*Olev* (Est, 1936) ex-*KM-3* (Ger, 1919) ex-*№ Teplokhod № 10* (Rus, 1918)	Crichton, Okhta	1914	13.8.1940	B	Deleted 28.8.1948

Belonged to the series of small coastal minelayers built in four groups at local yards for the Baltic Fleet. There is fundamental disagreement in various sources concerning the identity of these vessels while photographic documentation is scare and misidentified. After evaluating all available material, the authors decided to follow the recommendation of Sergej Berezhnoj (see 0.2.2 Sources). Teplokhod = Motor ship

Keri: built within the № 6 group (wheelhouse forward), abandoned 1918 at Reval and captured by the Germans, comm as *KM-1*, trfd 1919 to Estonia, renamed *M-8*, comm 1919 as minesweeper *Kalev*, later renamed *Keri*. Seized 1940, comm as minelayer. Conv to 15.7.1941 to minesweeping boat *Katertral'shchik № 2*, renamed *№ 1502* on 25.7.1941. Stranded 28.8.1941 at Tallinn. Raised by the Germans, comm May 1942 as staff vessel, conv August 1942 to guardship (KS-Boot) *156*, renumbered *O.Re 76* in September

1942. Conv late 1943 to dispatch boat *Keri*, sold 1.8.1944 to local civilian owners, conv to seiner *Koit*. Interned in Sweden autumn 1944, returned September 1945. Presumably BU late 1940s.

Vajndlo: built within the *№ 10* group (wheelhouse amidships), abandoned 1918 at Reval and captured by the Germans, comm as *KM-3*, trfd 1919 to Estonia, renamed *M-10*, comm 1919 as minesweeper *Olev*, later renamed *Vajndlo*. Seized 1940, comm as minelayer. Conv to 15.7.1941 to minesweeping boat *Kater-tral'shchik № 1*, renamed *№ 1501* on 25.7.1941, reverted 7.9.1941 to minelayer, name reverted. Laid up 1.10.1942. Conv 3.8.1944 to diving tender *VRD-84*, renamed *VRD-105* on 17.7.1946.

PINA *River minelayer*

Displacement:	60.8t
Dimensions:	35.0 x 5.25 x 0.5m
Machinery:	1-shaft, Glennifer diesel motor, 120hp = 7.1kts. Oil fuel 1.25t, range 360nm at 7kts
Armament:	2-45mm/46 21-K, 4-0.3in Maxim (1x4) MGs, 160 mines
Complement:	18 (1939)

Name	Comm	Fleet	Fate
PINA	24.10.1939	DnPn	Lost 26.8.1941
ex-*Mątwa* (Pol, 1939)			
ex-• (Pol, 1925)			
ex-*K-5* (Rus, 1920)			

Former Russian dumb barge captured March 1920 by the Poles, comm with the Polish Pinsk Flotilla as mine depot. Fitted with engine and rebuilt 1925 to minelayer-chemical warfare ship, renamed *Mątwa*. Scuttled 18.9.1939 at Prypiat, raised 30.9.1939 by the Soviets and comm. Trfd 17.6.1940 to the Pinsk Flotilla. Sunk by artillery fire off Domantovo at Dnieper. Wreck raised 25.5.1944 and BU.

Pina in 1941.
Drawing by Tomasz Grotnik

17.2. Conversions

17.2.2. NAVAL CONVERSIONS

MARTI *Imperial yacht*

Displacement:	5655t standard; 5980t normal; 6189t full load
Dimensions:	122.3 x15.4 x 7.0m
Machinery:	2-shaft VTS, 4 Yarrow boilers (16.5kG/cm², 202°C), 11,426hp = 18.7kts. Oil fuel 400t, range 2260nm at 12kts
Armament:	4-130mm/55, 7-3in/55 34-K, 3-45mm/46 21-K, (added 1943 2-0.5in DShK MGs, 4-0.5in Vickers (1x4) MGs), 320 KB mines
Armour:	CT 12mm roof, 12mm sides, guns shields 70mm face, 35mm sides
Complement:	390

Marti in 1940. Note that she still lacks her 3in 34-K guns. *Boris Lemachko Collection*

Marti in 1937.
Drawing by Jerzy Lewandowski

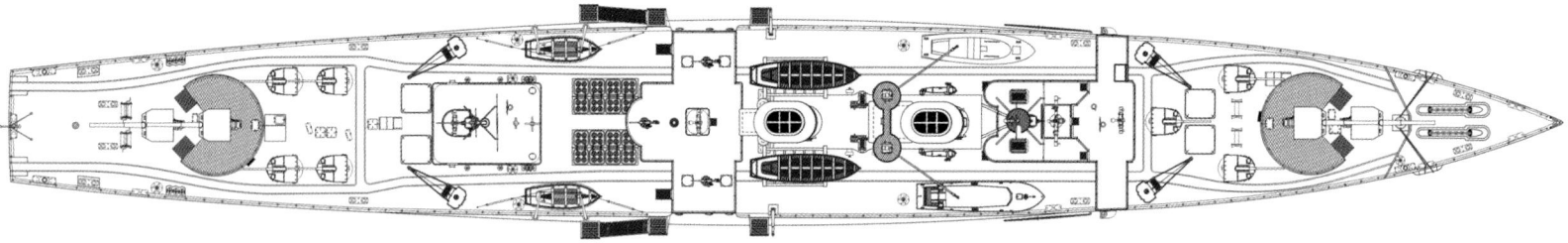

Camouflaged *Marti* at Leningrad in 1942.
Przemysław Budzbon Collection

Oka (ex-*Marti*) in 1948.
Vitalij Kostrichenko Collection

Built as the imperial yacht of Nicholas II. Laid up from May 1918 to 1932, during which time bore the name 18 marta, then taken in hand for minelayer conversion, which changed her appearance drastically. The conversion was not an outstanding success as only 320 mines were carried on 6000t displacement and she proved too slow for offensive minelaying (although she reached 14kts in normal operational conditions). During the war she played the key role in Soviet mining operations in the Gulf of Finland and evacuation of Hanko garrison. Following damage to machinery and boilers inflicted on 2.11.1941 by a mine exploding on a paravane, she did not go to a sea until end of the war and was used as a floating battery during the defence of Leningrad. Overhauled and re-engined at Rostock during the late 1940s she was conv to a training ship, renamed *Oka* in 1948. Conv 1950s to accommodation hulk, was used 1961 as target for missile practice.

Name	Builder	Laid down	Launched	Comp	Comm	Fleet	Fate
MARTI	B&W, Copenhagen	1.10.1893	4.8.1895	1896	25.12.1936	B	BU 1960s
ex-*Shtandart* (28.8.1934)							

17.0 MINELAYERS

SIL'NYJ
Armed paddle steamer

Displacement: 190t normal, 300t full load
Dimensions: 55.7 x 16.6/• x 1.5m
Machinery: 2 side wheels, reciprocating, 450hp = 11kts
Armament: 3-45mm/46 21-K, 11-0.3in (12x4, 3x1) Maxim MGs, 50 M1908 mines or 150 R-1 mines
Complement: 71

Ordered as armed steamer for the Amur Flotilla. Captured 1918 by the Japanese, returned 1.5.1925, conv to minelayer, comm with the Naval Forces of the Far East, trfd 27.6.1931 to the Amur Flotilla. Modernised 1928, rearmed 1930s.

Sil'nyj in the late 1920s armed with a vintage 47mm gun. *Przemysław Budzbon Collection*

Name	Builder	Built	Comm	Fleet	Fate
SIL'NYJ	Nizhny Novgorod	1910	12.1.1926	Am	BU after the war.

Cross reference: Rated as minelayers

Name	Details	Type	From	To	Fate
KOMINTERN	*Komintern*	Training cruiser	early 1941	10.10.1942	Scuttled
MURMAN	*Okean* class	Surveying ship	8.5.1939	8.12.1945	Reverted to surveying ship
OKEAN	*Okean* class	Surveying ship	24.6.1942	29.7.1945	Reverted to surveying ship
OKHOTSK	*Okean* class	Surveying ship	31.7.1941	29.7.1945	Reverted to surveying ship
ZIUJD	*Ost* class	Surveying ship	23.8.1941	12.11.1943	Reverted to surveying ship

17.2.3. CIVILIAN CONVERSIONS

VOROSHILOVSK
Cargo-passenger steamer

Displacement: 2300t full load
Dimensions: 63.5 x 10.0 x 4.6m
Machinery: 1-shaft VTE, 750hp = 10.5kts. Coal 600t, range 4000nm at 6kts
Armament: 4-3in/55 34-K, 8-0.3in (2x4) MGs, 268 mines
Complement: 155

Mobilised 1923 as secondary cruiser, decomm 1923 to civilian service. Comm 24.12.1931 as surveying vessel of the Ubeko DV, mobilised 3.5.1932, conv to minelayer, mine depot July–Dec 1934, renamed 8.6.1935 *Voroshilovsk*. Modernised 1938–1939. Sunk in explosion of mines at Novik bay, wreck raised 1951 and BU.

Stavropol, future *Voroshilovsk*, in civilian service in the mid-1920s. *Boris Lemachko Collection*

Name	Builder	YN	Built	Comm	Fleet	Fate
VOROSHYLOVSK ex-*Stavropol* (1935) ex-*Kotik* (1912)	Nüscke	142	1907	21.12.1931	P	Lost 30.10.1950

Russian **Tver'** type

Cargo-passenger steamers

Displacement:	*Astrakhan'* 2986t standard, 3618t normal, 3725t full load (*Teodor Nette* 3765t, *Sergej Kirov* 4690t, *Tomsk* 4466t)
Dimensions:	91.1 x 12.3 x 5.2m
Machinery:	1-shaft VTE, 2 Scotch cylindrical boilers (191°C, 12 kG/cm^2); 1150hp = 10.5kts (see note). Coal 300t. Range 4200nm at 6.6kts
Armament:	*Astrakhan'* (1944): 2-4in/60, 2-3in/30 Lender, 1-45mm/46 21-K, 12-0.3in Maxim MGs (3x4), 820 M1912 mines, 550 M1926 mines, 4 mine rails *Teodor Nette*: 1-4in/60, 2-3in/30 Lender, 1-45mm/46 21-K, 2-0.3in Maxim MGs, 200 mines *Tomsk*: 9-45mm/46 21-K, 2-0.3in MGs, 420 mines *Sergej Kirov*: 2-4in/60, 2-75mm, (added 1940/41) 1-37mm/67.5 70-K, 2-0.3in Maxim MGs, 500 mines
Complement:	*Astrakhan'* and *Tomsk* 164 *Teodor Nette* 143, *Sergej Kirov* 121

Tomsk in the early 1930s armed with 130mm guns.
Przemysław Budzbon Collection

Name	Builder	Built	Comm	Type	Fleet	Fate
ASTRAKHAN'	Nevskiy	1913	7.6.1934	Minelayer	P	Presumably scrapped 1990s
SERGEJ KIROV ex-*Erivan'* (1935)	Nevskiy	1913	15.8.1932	Mine hulk Depot ship	P	Deleted 20.5.1957
TEODOR NETTE ex-*Soria* (1926) ex-*Tver'* (1921)	Nevskiy	1912	25.6.1934	Depot ship Minelayer	P	Deleted 28.2.1953
TOBOL'SK	Nevskiy	1912	1940	Depot ship	P	BU 1953
TOMSK ex-*Glavkom Uborevich* (1923) ex-*Tomsk* (1922) ex-*Vladivostok* (1913)	Nevskiy	1913	Aug 1932	Minelayer Depot ship	P	Deleted 9.11.1956

The class of six 340-passenger vessels built for the Dobroflot for the Okhotsk–Kamchatka route. Were able to attain between 6 and 9 kts in 1940s.

Astrakhan': mobilised 20.12.1933 and conv to minelayer. Relegated 20.12.1950 to accommodation hulk *PKZ-33*. Deleted 20.04.1956 and used as mooring berth.

Sergej Kirov: seized 1921 by the White Russians, returned 1923. Mobilised 22.4.1932, conv to minelayer. Renamed 12.4.1935 *Sergej Kirov*, conv Feb 1937 to transport. Because of worn-out engine conv 20.4.1939 to mine hulk, conv 17.6.1940 to depot ship at Vladivostok, renamed *Aldan*. Conv 27.17.1956 to accommodation hulk *PKZ-118*.

Teodor Nette: captured 1918 by White Russians, sold December 1921 to the Italian owner, renamed *Soria*. Repurchased 1926. Mobilised 25.6.1934, conv to minelayer. Disarmed and conv 20.4.1939 to depot ship of the 4th Submarine Brigade, from February 1941 of the 2nd Submarine Brigade. Reverted 9.7.1941 to minelayer, conv 23.10.1945 to naval transport, reverted 6.3.1946 to depot ship. Laid up 1947 as heater, accommodation *PKZ-28* from 13.6.1950. Damaged by a gale in the winter 1953 and deleted. Used as mooring berth afterwards.

Tobol'sk: seized 1918 by the British, trfd 1919 to the White Russians. Repurchased 1924, stranded 15.11.1936, raised 10.1.1937, from 1940 accommodation hulk of the EPRON. Decomm 1946 to the civilian service, recomm 12.6.1947, deleted 28.7.1947 because of poor technical condition.

Tomsk: mobilised 1922 as transport, decomm 1923 to civilian service. Following general repair mobilised 14.7.1932, conv to minelayer, mine hulk 5.11.1940–2.7.1941. Conv 17.4.1945 to depot ship, conv 9.11.1952 to accommodation hulk.

Simferopol' of this type stranded off Sakhalin in a gale in October 1930. Raised and scrapped in 1950.

Tomsk in late 1920s.
Boris Lemachko Collection

S. ORDZHONIKIDZE

Cargo-passenger steamer

Displacement:	3638t standard, 4151t normal, 5400t full load
Dimensions:	97.0 x 13.7 x 5.5m
Machinery:	1-shaft VTE, 2 boilers (187°C, 12.7kG/cm^2), 1550hp = 11kts (minelaying speed 8kts). Coal 600t, range 4820nm at 8kts
Armament:	4-130mm/55, 3-3in/30 Lender (replaced by 2-3in/55 34-K in 1945), 4-37mm/67.5 70-K (from 1940/41), 9-0.3in (2x4, 1x1) Maxim MGs, 2 DC rails, 530 M1936 mines, or 370 KB mines or 703 M1908/30 mines; 4 mine rails
Complement:	196 (1943)

Purchased 1933 for the Far East. Mobilised 11.3.1936, conv to minelayer. Renamed *Argun'* 20.10.1940.

Minelayer *Argun'* in the late 1940s. *Boris Lemachko Collection*

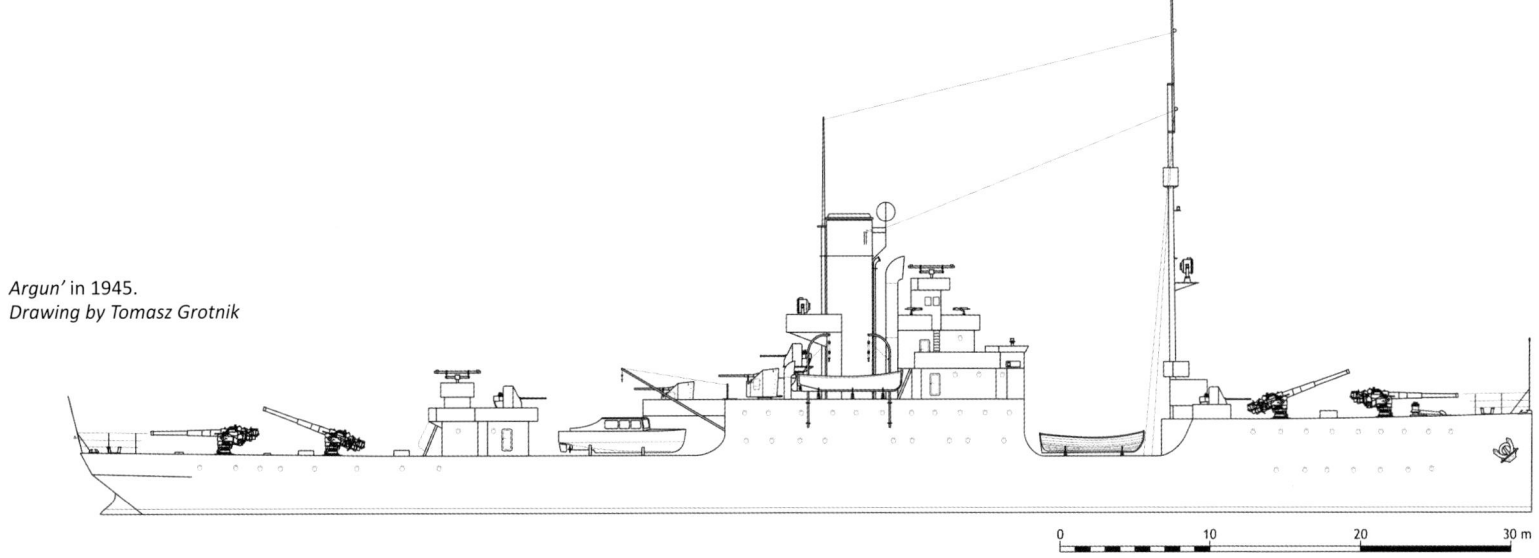

Argun' in 1945. *Drawing by Tomasz Grotnik*

Name	Builder	YN	Built	Comm	Fleet	Fate
S. ORDZHONIKIDZE ex-*Amur* (1936) ex-*Japix* (Br, 1933)	Great Britain		1923	22.2.1937	P	Deleted 1950s.

IUSHAR

Cargo-passenger steamer

Displacement:	1000t standard, 1354 normal, 2020t full load
Dimensions:	75.5 x 10.7 x 3.9m
Machinery:	1-shaft VTE, 2 Scotch boilers (190°C, 12 kG/cm^2), 848hp = 11kts. Coal 240t, range 2250nm at 9kts
Armament:	1 (added 1943: 3)-3in/55 34-K, 2 (from 1944: 4)-45mm/46 21-K, (added 1943: 1-20mm Oerlikon), 6-0.3in (1x4, 2x1) Maxim MGs, 125 KB mines, 2 mine rails, 20 DCs
Complement:	132

Mobilised 1916 to the Arctic Ocean Flotilla, conv to dispatch vessel. Seized 1918 by the British, recovered 1920. Mobilised 1920, decomm 1920 to civilian service. Mobilised 12.7.1941, conv to minelayer. Decomm 9.10.1945 to civilian service.

Iushar after 1943 displaying her 3in 34-K guns and camouflage. *Przemysław Budzbon Collection*

Pt-No 12.6.1941	Name	Builder	YN	Built	Comm	Fleet	Fate
93	IUSHAR ex-*Kolguev* (1921)	Swan Hunter	956	1915	13.8.1941	Wh	Discarded 1968

Cargo-passenger steamers

Pt-No 12.6.1941	Name	Details	Comm	Fleet	Remarks
91	KANIN ex-*Proletarij* (1921) ex-*Sergej Vitte* (1920)	1163t; 60 x 8.5 x 5.4m, 550hp = 10kts; 1-3in/55 34-K, (added 1942: 1-20mm Oerlikon), 4-0.3in (2x2) Maxim MGs, • mines	23.8.1941	Wh	Built 1898 Wigham. Mobilised 3.7.1941, conv to minelayer. Decomm 25.8.1942 to civilian service. Discarded 1959
92	SOSNOVETS ex-*Sever* (1921) ex-*Velikaia kniaginia Kseniia* (1917)	1335t; 62.8 x 8.5 x 5.8m; 850hp = 10kts; 2-4in, 1-3in/55 34-K, 2-0.3in Maxim MG, • mines	23.8.1941	Wh	Built 1895. Mobilised 1920 White Sea Flotilla, conv to minelayer. Decomm 11.8.1942 to civilian service. Discarded May 1953

Zaria type

Coastal passenger motorships

Displacement: 353.7t full load
Dimensions: 32.3 x 5.6 x 2.6m
Machinery: 1-shaft Benz diesel, 220hp = 9kts; Range 3315nm
Armament: 2-45mm/46 21-K, 2-0.5in DShK MGs, 10 mines
Complement: 33

Pt-No 12.6.1941	Name	Builder	Built	Comm	Fleet	Fate
•	LUKOMSKIJ ex-*Pyotr Lukomskij* ex-*Zarnitsa* (1935)	A. Marti, Odessa	1929	6.7.1941	BS	Fate unknown
61	ZARIA	A. Marti, Odessa	1929	15.7.1941	BS	Lost 5.3.1943

Built for service between Yalta.

Lukomskij: mobilised 23.6.1941, conv to coastal minelayer. Multipurpose use as staff vessel, depot and transport. Decomm 3.1.1945 to civilian service.

Zaria: mobilised 22.6.1941, conv to coastal minelayer. Sunk by mines near the Doob Cape off Kabardinka.

Coastal passenger motorship

Pt-No 12.6.1941	Name	Details	Comm	Fleet	Remarks
61	DOOB	150t; 24.4 x 5.3 x 2.9m; 120hp = 9kts; 300nm; -45mm/46 21-K, 2-0.3in MG, • mines	15.7.1941	BS	Built 1929. Mobilised 22.6.1941, conv to minelayer. Sunk 11.2.1942 by mines off Sevastopol.

KOLKHOZNIK

Inland cargo motorship

Displacement: 210t normal
Dimensions: 50.4 x 10.6 x 0.7m
Machinery: 2-shaft Scripps kerosene motors, 200hp = 5.3kts. Oil 5t, range 400km
Armament: 2-3in/30 Lender, 6-0.3in Maxim (1x4, 2x1) MGs, 104 M1908 or 500 R-1 mines, 2 mine rails
Complement: 32

Project SB-11. Mobilised following completion, conv to minelayer armed with 1-3in/30 and 7 MGs. In 1939 one Maxim MG was replaced by additional 3in/30 gun. Trfd 8.7.1940 to the Danube Flotilla, conv to mine depot. Sunk by German aircraft off Kinburn Spit in the Black Sea.

Name	Builder	YN	Built	Comm	Fleet	Fate
KOLKHOZNIK	Leninskaia kuznitsa, Kiev		15.6.1930	June 1932	Dn Da	Lost 21.9.1941

Russian **Apostol Pyotr** type

Paddle cargo-passenger steamers

Displacement: 500t normal, 600t full load
Dimensions: 60.0 x 15.5/7.9 x 2.2m
Machinery: 2 side wheels VDE, 1 cylindrical boiler, 220hp = 9kts. Coal 54t, range 800nm at 8.5kts
Armament: 175 M1908 mines, *Ristna* from 1943: 2-37mm
Complement: 51

Ristna in the 1950s. *Boris Lemachko Collection*

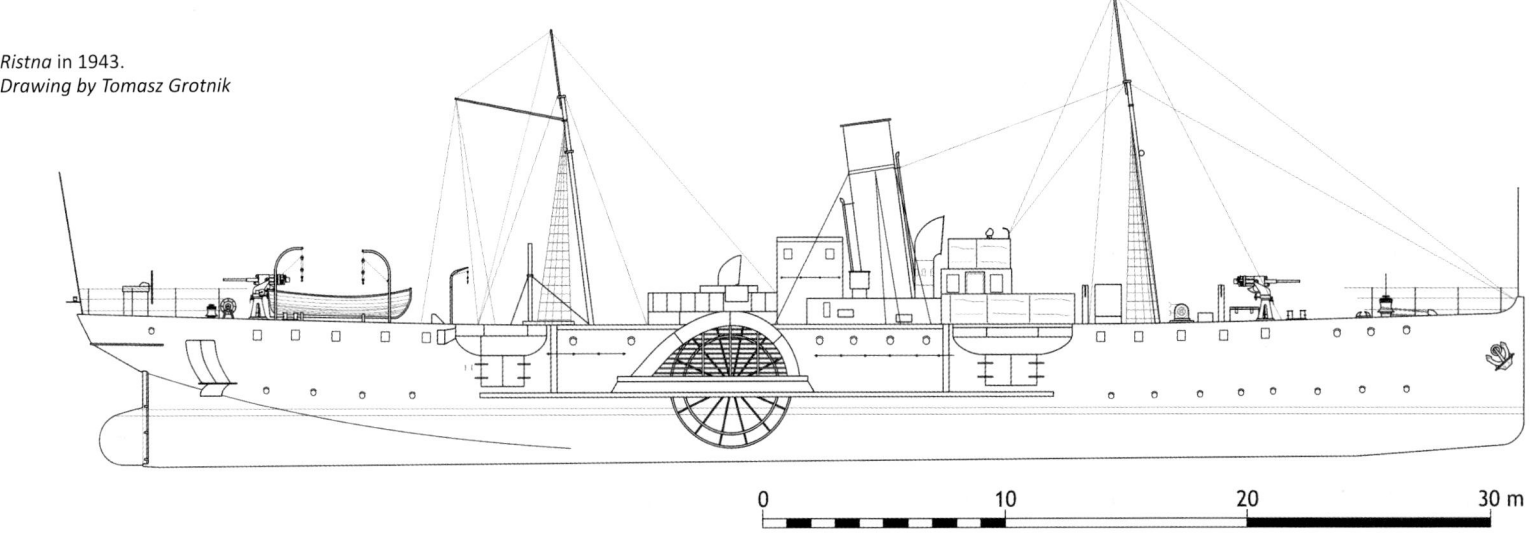

Ristna in 1943. *Drawing by Tomasz Grotnik*

Name	Builder	YN	Built	Comm	Fleet	Fate
RISTNA	Grangemouth	282	1906	13.8.1940	B	Deleted 7.4.1956
ex-*Ristna* (Est, 1940)						
ex-*TShch № 18* (1922)						
ex-*Apostol Pyotr* (1915)						
SUROP	Grangemouth	283	1906	13.8.1940	B	Lost 11.8.1941
ex-*Suurop* (Est, 1940						
ex-*TShch № 19* (1915)						
ex-*Apostol Pavel* (1915)						

Both mobilised 1915 in the Baltic Fleet, conv to minesweepers. Captured 1918 by Estonians, to civilian service. Purchased 1927 and conv to minelayers of the Estonian Navy. Seized 1940 by the Soviets.

***Ristna*:** conv November 1941 to depot ship, after 1945 to training ship. BU 1958.

***Surop*:** mined near Virstu in the Gulf of Riga.

Seiners

No	Details	Comm	Fleet	Remarks
ZM-11	56t; 19.3 x 5.1 x 2.3m; 65hp = 8kts; 1350nm at 6kts; 2-0.3in MGs; • mines; 13 men	Aug 1942	P	Mobilised 24.8.1942, conv to coastal minelayer. Conv 5.2.1943 to service craft
ZM-21		Aug 1942	P	Mobilised 24.8.1942, conv to coastal minelayer. Conv 5.2.1943 to service craft
ZM-31		Aug 1942	P	Mobilised 24.8.1942, conv to coastal minelayer. Conv 5.2.1943 to service craft
ZM-41		Aug 1942	P	Mobilised 24.8.1942, conv to coastal minelayer. Conv 5.2.1943 to service craft

Paddle steam tugs

Name	Comm	Fleet	Remarks
BIDZHAN ex-*N-23* (1943)	9.1.1944	P	Mobilised 8.12.1943, conv to minelayer
BIRA ex-*K-19* (1943)	9.1.1944	P	Mobilised 8.12.1943, conv to minelayer

Cross reference: Rated as minelayers

Name	Details	Type	From	To	Fate
AIAN	*Pioner* type	Transport	14.8.1939		Survived the war
FELIKS DZERZHINSKIJ	*Aleksej Rykov* type	Transport	Nov 1939	25.10.1940	Renamed *Ural*
GIZHIGA	*Pioner* type	Transport	3.11.1939		Survived the war
MINNALAJD	*Minnalajd*	Transport	-	28.8.1941	Lost
OSTROVSKIJ	*Del'fin* type	Sanitary transport	8.7.1940	23.3.1942	Lost
PUSHKIN	*Tovarishch Stalin* type	Transport	7.12.1939	10.11.1940	Decomm
RAA	*Raa*	Transport	-	28.8.1941	Lost
SYZRAN'	*Sikhali* type	Transport	8.7.1940	Aut 1940	Decomm
SYZRAN'	*Sikhali* type	Transport	22.7.1941		Fate unknown
URAL	*Aleksej Rykov* type	Transport	25.10.1940	1942	Conv to depot ship
ZM-12	*Kungas-Kavasaki* type	Patrol motorboats	Aug 1942	5.2.1943	Conv to service craft
ZM-13	*Kungas-Kavasaki* type	Patrol motorboats	Aug 1942	5.2.1943	Conv to service craft
ZM-14	*Kungas-Kavasaki* type	Patrol motorboats	Aug 1942	5.2.1943	Conv to service craft
ZM-15	*Kungas-Kavasaki* type	Patrol motorboats	Aug 1942	5.2.1943	Conv to service craft
ZM-16	*Kungas-Kavasaki* type	Patrol motorboats	Aug 1942	5.2.1943	Conv to service craft
ZM-17	*Kungas-Kavasaki* type	Patrol motorboats	Aug 1942	5.2.1943	Conv to service craft
ZM-22	*Kungas-Kavasaki* type	Patrol motorboats	Aug 1942	5.2.1943	Conv to service craft
ZM-23	*Kungas-Kavasaki* type	Patrol motorboats	Aug 1942	5.2.1943	Conv to service craft
ZM-24	*Kungas-Kavasaki* type	Patrol motorboats	Aug 1942	5.2.1943	Conv to service craft
ZM-25	*Kungas-Kavasaki* type	Patrol motorboats	Aug 1942	5.2.1943	Conv to service craft
ZM-26	*Kungas-Kavasaki* type	Patrol motorboats	Aug 1942	5.2.1943	Conv to service craft
ZM-27	*Kungas-Kavasaki* type	Patrol motorboats	Aug 1942	5.2.1943	Conv to service craft
ZM-32	*Kungas-Kavasaki* type	Patrol motorboats	Aug 1942	5.2.1943	Conv to service craft
ZM-33	*Kungas-Kavasaki* type	Patrol motorboats	Aug 1942	5.2.1943	Conv to service craft
ZM-34	*Kungas-Kavasaki* type	Patrol motorboats	Aug 1942	5.2.1943	Conv to service craft
ZM-35	*Kungas-Kavasaki* type	Patrol motorboats	Aug 1942	5.2.1943	Conv to service craft
ZM-36	*Kungas-Kavasaki* type	Patrol motorboats	Aug 1942	5.2.1943	Conv to service craft
ZM-37	*Kungas-Kavasaki* type	Patrol motorboats	Aug 1942	5.2.1943	Conv to service craft
ZM-42	*Kungas-Kavasaki* type	Patrol motorboats	Aug 1942	5.2.1943	Conv to service craft
ZM-43	*Kungas-Kavasaki* type	Patrol motorboats	Aug 1942	5.2.1943	Conv to service craft
ZM-44	*Kungas-Kavasaki* type	Patrol motorboats	Aug 1942	5.2.1943	Conv to service craft
ZM-45	*Kungas-Kavasaki* type	Patrol motorboats	Aug 1942	5.2.1943	Conv to service craft
ZM-46	*Kungas-Kavasaki* type	Patrol motorboats	Aug 1942	5.2.1943	Conv to service craft
ZM-47	*Kungas-Kavasaki* type	Patrol motorboats	Aug 1942	5.2.1943	Conv to service craft

18. Netlayers

Сетевые заградители

Onega class (*Project 149*)

Displacement: 420t standard; 527t full load
Dimensions: 56.8 x 9.8 x 1.7m
Machinery: 3-shaft two 4SD-19/32, one 2SD-20/30 diesels, 330hp = 8kts. Oil fuel 14t, range 1280nm at 4.5kts
Armament: 3-45mm/46 21-K, 4-0.5in Vickers (1x4) MGs (*Iset'* 2-0.5in DShK MGs), 96 M1908 mines, 2 MTSh sweeps, 2 MZT sweeps, antisubmarine net of 6nm
Complement: 54 – 55

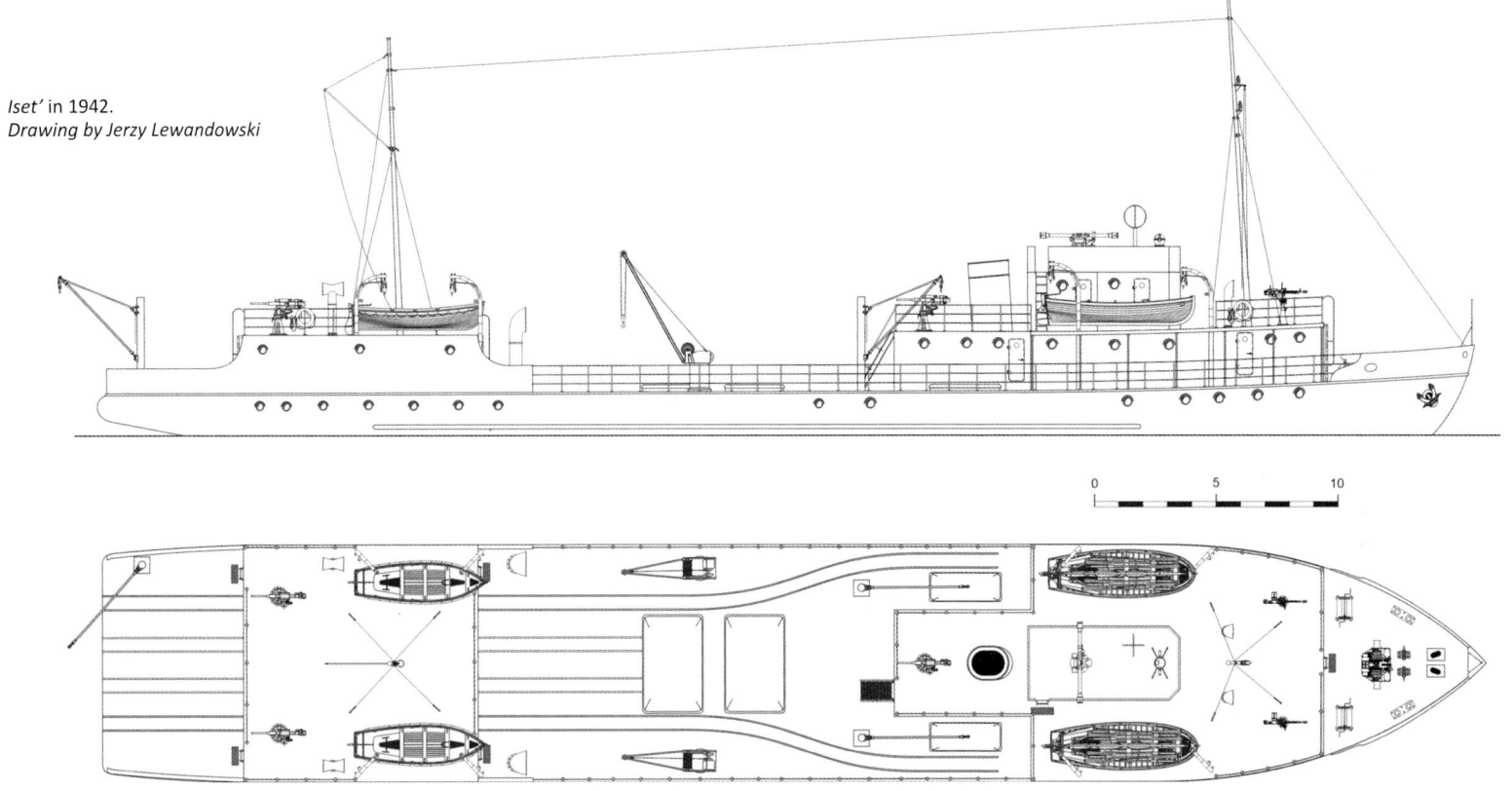

Iset' in 1942.
Drawing by Jerzy Lewandowski

Name	Builder	YN	Laid down	Launched	Comp	Comm	Fleet	Remarks
ISET'	264, Krasnoarmeisk	91	1939	•	1941	1941	Vo Cs	Deleted 17.8.1967
MEZEN'	264, Krasnoarmeisk 368, Khabarovsk-on-Amur	107	1940	1944	1946	1946	P	Deleted 28.2.1961
MOLOGA	264, Krasnoarmeisk 368, Khabarovsk-on-Amur	106	3.7.1941	1.8.1944	11.9.1944	30.12.1944	P	Deleted 28.2.1961
ONEGA	264, Krasnoarmeisk		1938	1940	22.7.1941	31.7.1941	B	Deleted 7.6.1961
SUKHONA	264, Krasnoarmeisk, 368, Khabarovsk-on-Amur	105	31.8.1941	1944	31.12.1944	19.2.1945	P	Deleted 19.1.1972
TURA	264, Krasnoarmeisk	92	8.1939	26.6.1940	8.9.1941	1941	Vo Cs	Deleted 10.2.1977
VIATKA	264, Krasnoarmeisk		5.1939	20.5.1940	19.7.1941	31.7.1041	B	Deleted 20.12.1969
VYCHEGDA	264, Krasnoarmeisk 368, Khabarovsk-on-Amur	108	1940	1944	1946	1946	P	Deleted 22.10.1967

Viatka on 8.10.1944 in the Gulf of Finland. Note camouflage. *Naval History and Heritage Command NH 79334*

This series of 12 combined netlayers/minelayers was authorised under the 3rd Five-Year Programme. Construction of four each designated for the Baltic and Pacific Fleets was begun at Stalingrad before the German invasion.

Iset': comm with the Volga Flotilla on completion, conv 25.7.1942 to communication vessel. Trfd in second half of to the Caspian Flotilla. Conv 2.6.1952 to depot ship *PB-40*, conv 3.8.1966 to accommodation hulk *PKZ-72*.

Mezen': delivered 1941/2 in parts to Khabarovsk for assembly, comp after the war.

Mologa: delivered 1941/2 in parts to Khabarovsk for assembly.

Onega: following completion delivered to Leningrad *via* inland waterways.

Sukhona: delivered 1941/2 in parts to Khabarovsk for assembly. Conv 28.10.1963 to non-propelled depot ship *PBN-1*, conv 8.6.1966 to heater *OT-2*.

Tura: comm with the Volga Flotilla on completion, conv 25.7.1942 to staff vessel and depot ship. Trfd 1944 to the Caspian Flotilla, conv to torpedo experimental vessel with the bank of three 450mm TTs installed. Conv 4.12.1945 to training ship, conv 28.2.1961 to floating workshop *PM-137*.

Viatka: following completion delivered to Leningrad *via* inland waterways.

Vychegda: delivered 1941/2 in parts to Khabarovsk for assembly, comp after the war. Conv 31.7.1967 to accommodation hulk *PKZ-64*.

Viatka on 14.10.1944 at the Gulf of Finland. Compare the port camouflage from the previous photo with the scheme on the starboard. Two *D-3 type* patrol boats *SK-182* and *SK-192* are moored alongside. *Naval History and Heritage Command NH 79334*

SB-58 following conversion to netlayer. *Przemysław Budzbon Collection*

18.1. Conversions

PROFSOIUZ
Cargo steamer

Displacement: 1535t full load
Dimensions: 67 x 11.5 x 2.8m
Machinery: 1-shaft, reciprocating, 520hp = 8kts. Coal 100t, range 1600nm at 7kts
Armament: 1-45mm/46 21-K, 2-0.3in MGs
Complement: 70

Camouflaged *Profsoiuz* during the war.
Przemysław Budzbon Collection

Pt-No 1941	Name	Builder	YN	Built	Comm	Fleet	Fate
94	PROFSOIUZ ex-*Lovat'* (1922) ex-*№ 3* (1915) ex-*Runo* (1914)	Scotts	238	1912	Nov 1939	N	Discarded 1973

Mobilised 1914 in the Baltic Fleet, conv to transport, conv 21.5.1915 to minesweeper, conv 18.10.1915 to minelayer *Lovat'*. Laid up 1918, 1922 to civilian service. Mobilised 9.11.1939, conv to netlayer. Decomm 17.10.1940 to civilian service. Mobilised 3.7.1941, conv to minelayer. Decomm 26.9.1945 to civilian service.

Sail-motor schooner

Name	Details	Comm	Fleet	Remarks
SUKHUMI	•	Sept 1941	BS	Mobilised 4.9.1941, conv to service craft. Conv 19.9.1944 to netlayer, conv 3.2.1945 to minesweeping boat, numbered *KT-394*.

Miscellaneous

SZ № 18.9.1941	Name	Details	Comm	Fleet	Remarks
№ 1	BUJREP ex-*Zeia* (1941)	56t; 19.3 x 5.1 x 2.3m; 65hp = 8kts; 1350nm at 6kts; 2-0.3in MGs, 13 men	18.9.1941	P	Built 1941, seiner. Mobilised 5.9.1941, conv to netlayer. Name reverted 13.10.1941 to *Zeia*. Survived the war
№ 2	PATRON ex-*Bureia* (1941)		18.9.1941	P	Built 1941, seiner. Mobilised 5.9.1941, conv to netlayer. Tame reverted 13.10.1941 to *Bureia*. Survived the war
-	GARIBAL'DI ex-*PS № 2* (1919) ex-*Shkval* (1918)	200t; 42.8 x 10.2 /• x 2.2m; 400hp = 7.5kts; 205nm at 5kts; 1-45mm/46 21-K, 2-0.3in MGs, 28 men	2.7.1941	B	Built 1903, paddle steamer. Mobilised 1919 in the Onega Flotilla, conv to dispatch vessel, decomm 1919 to civilian service. Mobilised 29.10.1939, convto netlayer. Decomm 30.11.1944, returned 26.2.1945 to civilian service
*	SB-58 ex-*P-15* (1941)	459t; 61.2 x 17.0/• x 1.2m; 400hp = 9.5kts; 23in/55 34-K, 60 mines; 47 men	1941	P	Built 1939, paddle steam tug. Mobilised 1941, conv to netlayer. Renamed *ZBS-1* in 1945. Survived the war

Cross reference: Rated as netlayers

Name	Details	Type	From	To	Fate
ASTRONOM	*Astronom*	Surveying vessel	6.7.1940	28.8.1941	Lost
AZIMUT	*Azimut*	Surveying vessel	31.7.1941	18.10.1941	Reverted to surveying vessel

19. Minesweepers

Тральщики

19.1. Russian-built

The Russians were among the pioneers of mine warfare in both laying and sweeping techniques. This knowledge and World War 1 experience did not disappear in the Red Navy but expertise faded and lagged behind technical development in the 1930s.

Russian **Minrep** / **Udarnik** class

Inshore minesweepers

Displacement:	190t normal, 210t full load (*Zapal* 205t)
Dimensions:	43.7 (*Zapal* 45.0) x 6.1 x 2.5m
Machinery:	2-shaft VDE, 2 boilers, 375hp (*Zapal* 300hp) = 11kts. Oil fuel 18t, range 500nm at 8kts
Armament:	1-3in/30 Lender, 1-45mm/46 21-K, 2-0.3in MGs, 1 MTSh sweep, 2 MZT sweeps, 2 KAT sweeps, 36 (*Zapal*) 32 M1926 mines
Complement:	37

Data for 1941

Kliuz as built.
Boris Lemachko Collection

TShch № 25.7.1941	TShch № 7.9.1941	Name	Builder	Laid down	Launched	Comp	Comm	Fleet	Fate
№ 54	№ 56	KLIUZ	Russo-Baltic Wks, Reval	Jan 1916	1916	19.11.1917	Apr 1918	B	Sank 25.11.1941.
№ 53	№ 57	UDARNIK	Putilov Yd, Helsingfors	Feb 1916	23.7.1916	14.7.1917	Apr 1918	B	Sank 2.10.1942.
		ZAPAL	Izhora, St.Petersburg	Dec 1910	Dec 1911	Jul 1912	Apr 1918	B	BU 1964.

The three survived Imperial Navy minesweepers were of two similar classes: *Zapal* of *Minrep* class, the two others of the *Udarnik* class. These ships were quite successful and oil-fired which was uncommon in the 1910s.

Kliuz: mined east of Hanko.

Udarnik: mined off Seskar.

Zapal: detached to the surveying service from 29.7.1936 to autumn 1939. Decomm 1940-1945 for repairs. Conv 7.2.1948 to surveying ship *Tuman*, renamed 21.10.1949 *Indikator*. Laid up 1962.

19.2. Standard Soviet-built types

Vladimir Polukhin class (*Project 59*)

Fleet minesweepers

Displacement:	690t standard, 784t normal, 879t full load
Dimensions:	79.1 x 8.1 x 2.5m
Machinery:	2-shaft DK-1 turbines, 2 water tube boilers (28kG/cm^2, 370°C), 8000hp = 22.4kts (15.5kts with a sweep). Oil fuel 173t normal, 191t max, range 2000nm at 11kts
Armament:	2-100mm/56 B-24-BM, 1-45mm/46 21-K, 3-37mm/67.5 70-K (3x1), 2-20mm Oerlikon, 4-0.5in Colt MG's, 2 DC chutes, 20 B-1 DCs, 20 M-1 DCs, 2 MTSh sweeps, 2 MZT sweeps, 20 KB mines
Complement:	125

Data for 1944

Valdimir Polukhin as completed in 1942. Note that her topmast was removed to make detection difficult by German reconnaissance planes and artillery.
Boris Lemachko Collection

19.0 Minesweepers

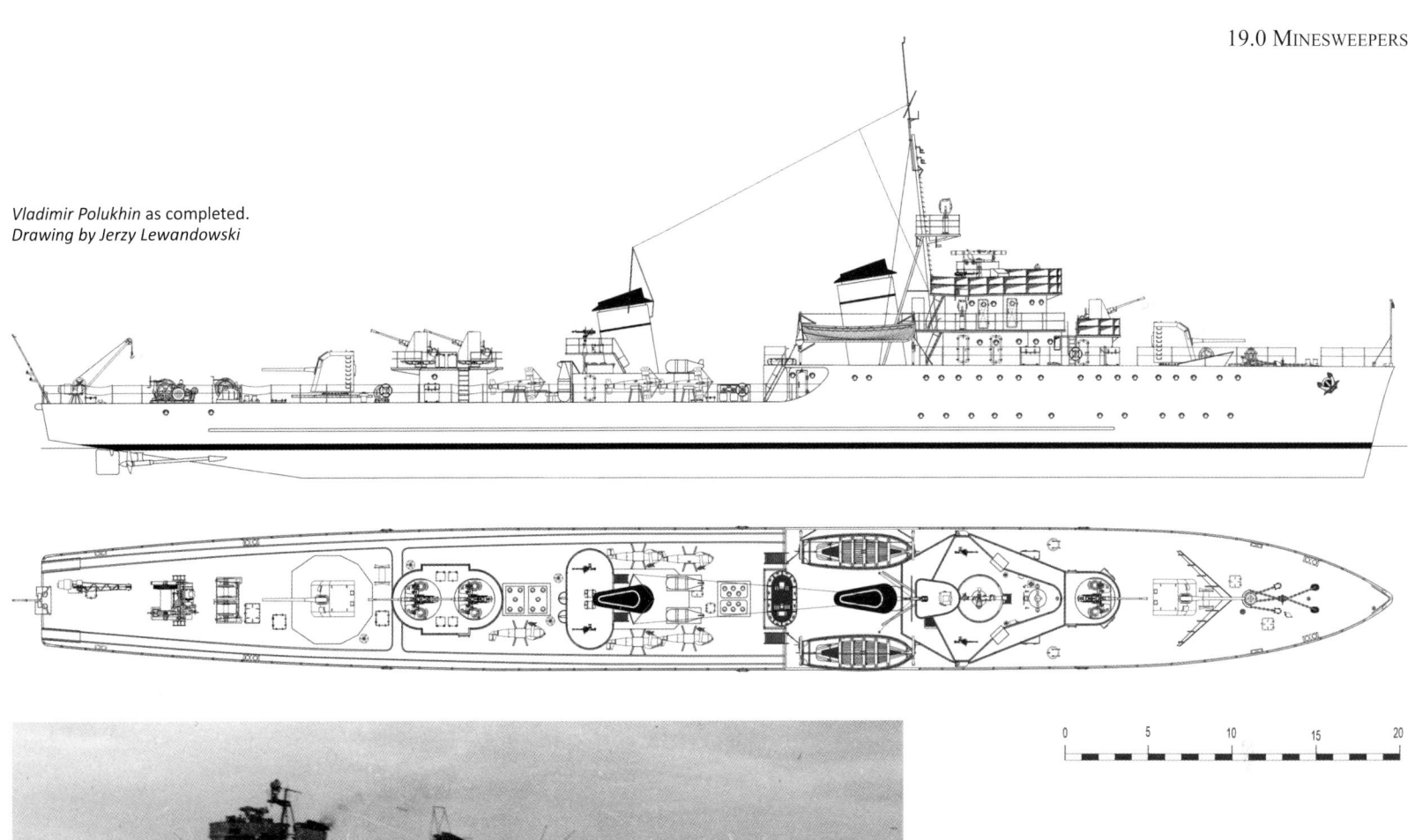

Vladimir Polukhin as completed.
Drawing by Jerzy Lewandowski

Valdimir Polukhin as completed in 1942.
Przemysław Budzbon Collection

No	Name	Builder	YN	Laid down	Launched	Comp	Comm	Fleet	Remarks
	25.9.1940								
T-250	VLADIMIR POLUKHIN	370, Leningrad	108	28.5.1939	30.03.1940	19.10.1942	7.11.1942	B	Hulked 1957
T-251	PAVEL KHOKHRIAKOV	370, Leningrad	109	28.5.1939	31.03.1940	25.11.1949*	1949	B	BU 1972
T-252	ALEKSANDR PETROV	370, Leningrad	110	20.4.1940	20.11.1940	25.11.1949*	8.12.1949	B	BU 1959
T-253	KARL ZEDIN	370, Leningrad	111	29.4.1940	30.11.1940	18.9.1948*	10.9.1948	B	
T-254	VASILIJ GROMOV	363, Leningrad	23	29.5.1939	8.10 1940	23.9.1943	9.12.1943	B	Deleted 26.5.1958
T-255	ANDRIAN ZASIMOV	363[1], Leningrad	25	10.8.1939	15.9.1940	29.12.1949*	15.2.1950	B	
T-256	VLADIMIR TREFOLEV	363, Leningrad	26	10.2.1940	9.12.1940	17.11.1947*	27.12.1947	B	BU 1988
T-257	TIMOFEJ ULIANTSEV	370, Leningrad	124	30.11.1940	30.5.1941	10.12.1948*	4.1.1949	B	BU 1964
T-258	MIKHAIL MARTYNOV	370, Leningrad	125	10.12.1940	30.5.1941	12.8.1948*	1948	B	BU 1959
T-259	FYODOR MITROFANOV	363[1], Leningrad	29	20.8.1940	17.5.1941	7.11.1947*	1947	B	BU 1960
T-260	LUKA PANKOV	363[1], Leningrad	30	21.9.1940	June 1941	31.12.1947*	23.2.1948	B	
T-261	PAVEL VINOGRADOV	363[1], Leningrad	31	17.10.1940	July 1941	2.9.1949*	Sept 1949	B	BU 1972
T-262	STEPAN GRADUSHKO	363[1], Leningrad	32	20.12.1941	July 1941	24.8.1949*	Sept 1949	B	BU 1958
T-263	SEMYON PELIKHOV	363[1], Leningrad	33	19.12.1940	July 1941	26.8.1949*	Sept 1949	B	BU 1977
T-450	PAVEL GOLOVIN	201, Sevastopol	250	6.8.1939	8.2.1940	-	-	C	Stranded 22.1.1942
T-451	IVAN BORISOV	201[2], Sevastopol	249	4.4.1939	31.12.1939	13.12.1943**	13.12.1943	C	Deleted 1958.
						31.8.1949*	Sept 1949	C	
T-452	SERGEJ SHUVALOV	201[2], Sevastopol	251	20.11.1939	24.2.1941	13.12.1943**	13.12.1943	C	Deleted 1958.
						0.8.1948*	Apr 1948	C	
T-453	SEMYON ROSHAL'	201, Sevastopol	252	31.12.1939	16.1.1941	-	-	C	Stranded 19.12.1944
T-454	IVAN SLADKOV	201[2], Sevastopol	253	14.2.1940	20.3.1941	18.3.1948*	1948	C	BU 1964
T-455	NIKOLAJ MARKIN	201, Sevastopol	258	Oct 1941	-	-	-	C	BU by the Germans on slipway
T-456	BORIS ZHEMCHUZHIN	201, Sevastopol	259	-	-	-	-	C	Cancelled 19.10.1940
T-457	NIKOŁAJ POZHAROV	201, Sevastopol	260	-	-	-	-	C	Cancelled 19.10.1940

Notes:

* Completed to the *Project 73K*. ** Completed as a non-propelled landing craft. 1) Completed at Yard No 370, Leningrad. 2) Completed at Yard No 445, Leningrad.

The type of fast fleet minesweepers, designed in 1938 and intended for mine surveillance in distant areas and protection of large surface ships. To ensure a squadron speed of 20kts they were powered by turbines, which was unique for minesweepers. To ensure survival during surveillance missions they were given a strong gun armament like the *Project 29* escort ships.

It was planned to lay down 46 ships by the end of 1942, and the construction of 22 hulls began during 1939/40 with comm of first pair planned for early 1940. Delays in the delivery of turbines and boilers extended the schedules, so none was ready before the German invasion, which found 5 hulls already launched at Sevastopol and 12 at Leningrad with two sets of turbines and boilers available. Eventually, the fitting-out of *T-250* and *T-254* was continued but in the conditions of besieged Leningrad it took one year to complete the first and two years for the second.

With no prospect of obtaining turbines during wartime it was decided to complete the ships with diesel engines. The design coded *Project 73* was completed in January 1942 with the power plant changed to two General Motors GM-16-278A. In total, 24 engines were delivered under Lend-Lease to the Soviet Union by 1945, which made it possible to complete twelve ships after the war. In spring 1945 the design was modified to the *Project 73K*, with the main armament changed to 85mm/52 90-K and sensors added (in reality, only sonars were fitted in the majority) and the dozen GM-engined hulls were fitted like that. The other three *Project 73K* hulls received Soviet-made 6D diesels.

A *Project 73* minesweeper as completed. *Boris Lemachko Collection*

Project 73K characteristics (as completed)

Displacement:	720t standard, 800t normal, 880t full load
Dimensions:	79.6 x 8.1 x 2.5m
Machinery:	2-shaft General-Motors GM-16-278A diesels, 3200hp = 16kts (12.5kts with a sweep). Oil fuel 132.5t, range 3700nm at 16kts
	T-251, T-252, T-255: 2-shaft 6D diesels, 3400hp = 17kts (13kts with a sweep). Oil fuel 132.5t, range 3500nm at 17kts
Armament:	2-85mm/52 90-K, 3-37mm/67.5 70-K, 4-0.5in DShKM MGs, 2 BMB-1 DCs, 20 B-1 DCs, 24 M-1 DCs, MT-2 sweep, US TEM-VI Mk IV magnetic sweep, BAT-2 acoustic sweep, 20 M1926 mines
Sensors:	Tamir-5N sonar (except *T-259, T-260*)
Complement:	119

T-250 *Vladimir Polukhin*: completed to the original design with turbine machinery; during gunnery acceptance trials in September 1942 she fired at German troops. Seriously damaged 4.6.1943 following collision with a sunken barge, but repaired and recomm. Conv December 1954 to experimental ship *Forel'*, conv December 1956 to floating workshop *PM-73*, from Jan 1957 to accommodation hulk *PKZ-129*.

T-251 *Pavel Khokhriakov*: towed in 1941 to the Volga, returned after the war and completed to the *Project 73K* with Soviet-made 6D diesels.

T-252 *Aleksandr Petrov*: towed in 1941 to the Volga, returned after the war and completed to the *Project 73K* with Soviet-made 6D diesels.

T-253 *Karl Zedin*: towed in 1941 to the Volga, returned after the war and completed to the *Project 73K*.

T-254 *Vasilij Gromov*: completed to the original design with the turbine machinery. Conv January 1956 to floating workshop *PM-69*.

T-255 *Andrian Zasimov*: towed in 1941 to the Volga, returned after the war and completed to the *Project 73K* with Soviet-made 6D diesels.

T-256 *Vladimir Trefolev*: remained at Leningrad during the siege, slightly damaged, completed after the war to the *Project 73K*.

T-257 *Timofej Uliantsev*: remained at Leningrad during the siege, slightly damaged, completed after the war to the *Project 73K*.

T-258 *Mikhail Martynov*: remained at Leningrad during the siege, slightly damaged, completed after the war to the *Project 73K*.

T-259 *Fyodor Mitrofanov*: remained at Leningrad during the siege, slightly damaged, completed after the war to the *Project 73K*.

T-260 *Luka Pankov*: remained at Leningrad during the siege, slightly damaged, completed after the war to the *Project 73K*.

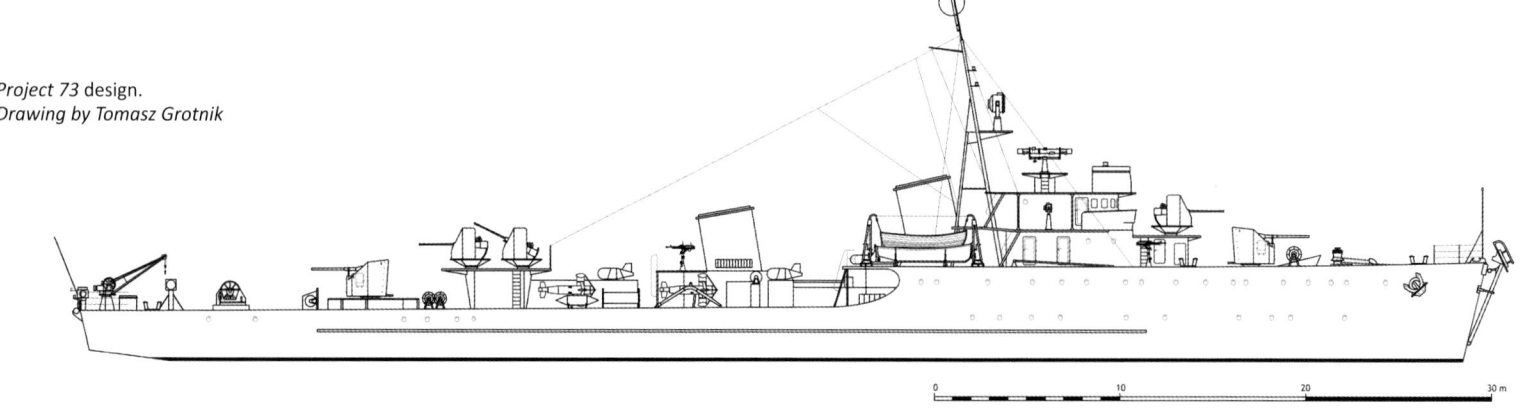

Project 73 design.
Drawing by Tomasz Grotnik

T-261 *Pavel Vinogradov:* remained at Leningrad during the siege, slightly damaged, completed after the war to the *Project 73K*.

T-262 *Stepan Gradushko:* remained at Leningrad during the siege, slightly damaged, completed after the war to the *Project 73K*.

T-263 *Semyon Pelikhov:* remained at Leningrad during the siege, slightly damaged, completed after the war to the *Project 73K*.

T-450 *Pavel Golovin:* foundered during gale off Tuapse when towed to Caucasian port.

T-451 *Ivan Borisov:* towed 1942 to Caucasian port, provisionally completed in 1943 as non-propelled troop transport. Completed after the war to the *Project 73K*.

T-452 *Sergej Shuvalov:* towed 1942 to Caucasian port, provisionally completed in 1943 as non-propelled troop transport. Completed after the war to the *Project 73K*.

T-453 *Semyon Roshal':* towed 1942 to Caucasian port. Foundered during a gale.

T-454 *Ivan Sladkov:* towed 1942 to Caucasian port. Completed after the war K.

Final configuration of *Project 73* in the late 1960s. Note radar outfit and funnel bands. *Boris Lemachko Collection*

T-455 *Nikolaj Markin:* destroyed on a slipway, the remains BU by the Germans.

T-456 *Boris Zhemchuzhin:* construction cancelled before being laid down.

T-457 *Nikolaj Pozharov:* construction cancelled before being laid down.

Fugas class (*Project 3, Project 53, Project 53U, Project 58*) — *Coastal minesweepers*

Project	Project 3	Project 53		Project 53U	Project 58
Number:	T-204	T-1	T-406	T-217	T-5
Data for year:	1941	1943	1943	1943	1938
Displacement (standard):	428t	431t	400t	430t	406t
Displacement (normal):	•	490t	418t	447t	•
Displacement (full):	445t	535t	494t	490t	459t
Length:	62.0m				
Beam:	7.2m			7.4m	7.2m
Draught:	2.0m	2.5m	2.2m	2.4m	2.3m
Diesel engines (2-shaft):	42-BMRN-6			6D	42-BMRN-6
Total power:	2800hp	3200hp	2800hp		
Speed (max):	18.5kts	17.5kts	18.5kts	18kts	18.5kts
Speed (with sweep):	14.9kts	12.7kts	13kts	14.5kts	14.7kts
Oil fuel (max):	•	97.6t	94t	100t	90t
Range:	2900nm at 12kts	7200nm at 12kts	3300nm at 16kts	2360nm at 14kts	3300nm at 14.7kts
Main armament:	1-100mm/51 B-24-IIs	1-100mm/56 B-24-BM	1-100mm/51 B-24-IIs		
AA armament:	1-45mm/46 21-K	1-37mm/67.5 70-K	1-45mm/46 21-K, 3-37mm/67.5 70-K	1-45mm/46 21-K, 2-20mm Oerlikon	1-45mm
MGs:	2	2-0.5in DShK	2-0.5in DShK, 1-0.5in Browning	4-0.5in DShK	4-0.5in (2x2) MGs
Sweeps:	1 MTSh, 1 MZT, 1 electromagnetic experimental*	1 MTSh, 1MZT 1 MShchT-2*	1 MTSh, 1 MZT*	2 MTSh, 2 MZT*	1 MTSh, 1 MZT*
Paravanes:	2	2	1	3	•
Spar buoys KS-39:	•	20	5	•	
DCTs / DC chutes:	- / 2	2 BMB-1 / 2	- / 2	- / 2	•
DCs:	20 B-1, 20 M-1	20 M-1	10 B1, 30 M-1	•	
Mines:	31 M1926			20 M1926	28 M1926
Complement:	42	61	66	60	47

* From 1944 they carried additionally British electromagnetic and acoustic sweeps

Project 3 as completed.
Drawing by Jerzy Lewandowski

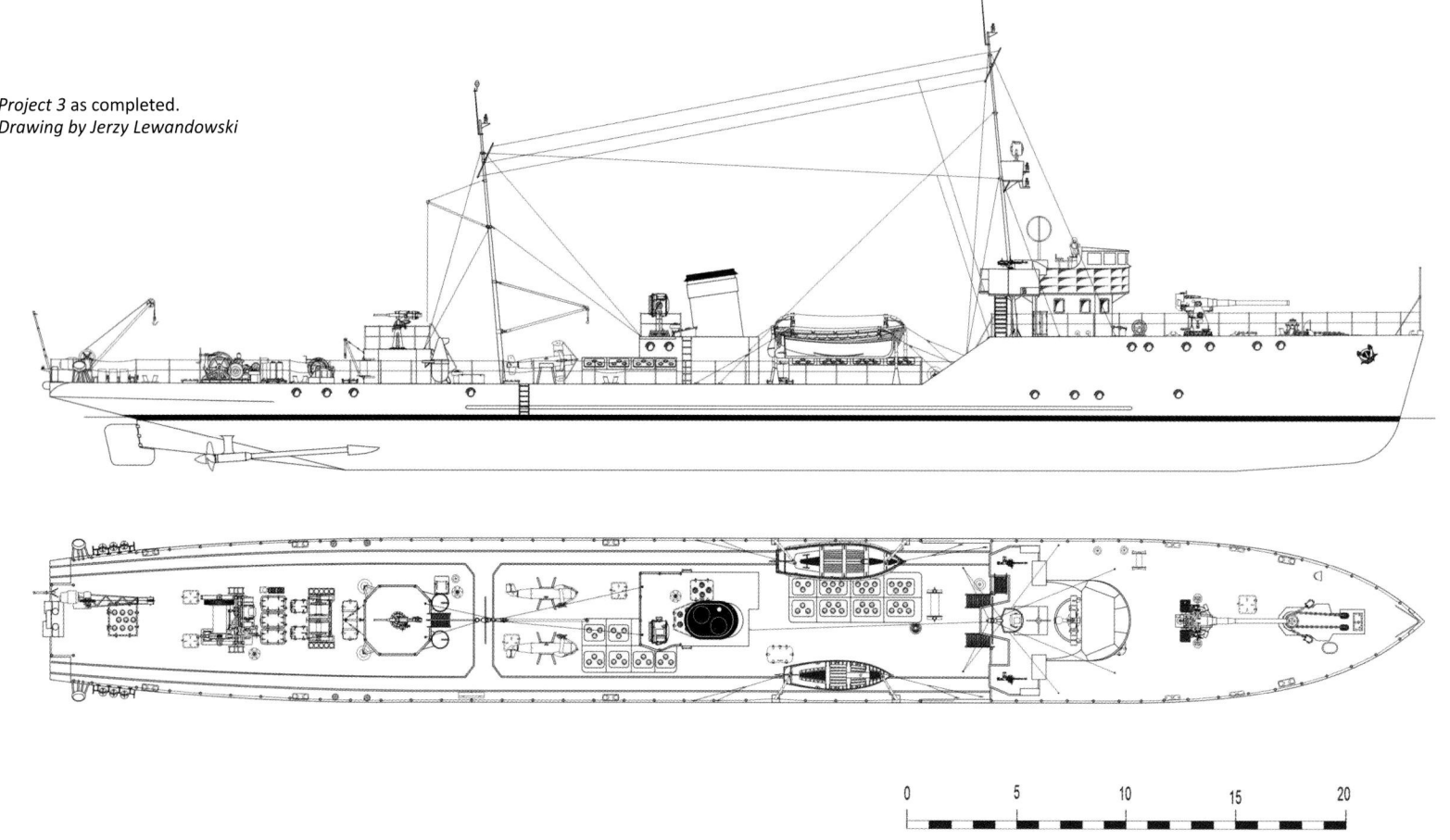

Pt-No 12.6.1941	Pt-No 17.7.1942	Pt-No Apr 1944	No 25.7.1939	Name	Builder	YN	Laid down	Launched	Comp	Comm	Fleet	Fate
Project 3												
			T-201	ZARIAD	190, Leningrad	459	12.10.1933	10.10.1934	26.12.1936	28.7.1937	B	Sunk 30.7.1941
			T-202	BUJ	190, Leningrad	460	12.12.1933	5.11.1934	11.8.1938	13.8.1938	B	Sunk 14.8.1941
			T-203	PATRON	190, Leningrad	461	28.12.1933	25.10.1934	4.7.1938	1938	B	Sunk 25.10.1941
			T-204	FUGAS	190, Leningrad	462	5.1.1934	25.10.1934	10.12.1936	28.2.1937	B	Sunk 24.8.1942
11	11	401	T-401 EMTShch-401[1]	TRAL	201, Sevastopol	67	5.11.1933	23.08.1934	22.5.1937	24.8.1937	BS	Expended as target 1955
12			T-402	MINREP	201, Sevastopol	68	5.11.1933	14.1.1935	28.1.1937	22.05.1937	BS	Sunk 12.9.1941
13	12	403	T-403	GRUZ	201, Sevastopol	69	20.3.1934	21.9.1935	25.7.1937	24.8.1937	BS	Sunk 27.2.1943
14	13	404	T-404	SHCHIT	201, Sevastopol	70	17.1.1934	10.12.1935	30.10.1937	9.12.1937	BS	Experimental vessel 7.4.1956
Project 53												
			T-1	STRELA	190, Leningrad, 196 Leningrad	491 111	10.05.1935	17.05.1936	13.8.1938	24.9.1938	P	Surveying vessel 1.9.1955
			T-2	TROS	190, Leningrad 196, Leningrad	492 112	22.05.1935	24.6.1936	24.9.1938	1938	P	Trfd Dec 1953 to North Korea
			T-3	PROVODNIK	190, Leningrad 196, Leningrad	493 113	30.6.1035	30.6.1936	4.12.1938	23.2.1939	P	Deleted 30.6.1950
			T-4	PODSEKATEL'	190, Leningrad 196, Leningrad	494 114	16.11.1935	10.12.1936	15.12.1938	23.2.1939	P	Trfd 11.10.1950 to the Border Guard
			T-7	VEKHA	201, Sevastopol	179	30.12.1936	14.3.1938	16.9.1938	24.9.1938	P	Trfd 11.10.1950 to the Border Guard
			T-8	CHEKA	201, Sevastopol	180	27.12.1936	14.3.1938	2.11.1938	7.11.1938	P	Trfd Dec 1953 to North Korea
			T-405	VZRYVATEL'	201, Sevastopol	175	21.7.1936	27.4.1937	27.4.1938	9.5.1938	BS	Lost 5.1.1942
21	21	406	T-406	ISKATEL'	201, Sevastopol	176	30.7.1936	29.8.1937	29.4.1938	9.5.1938	BS	Extant 1990
22	22	407	T-407 EMTShch-407[1]	MINA	201, Sevastopol	178	25.2.1937	20.8.1937	19.8.1938	26.8.1938	BS	Sunk Sept 1992
26	14		T-411	ZASHCHITNIK	201, Sevastopol	177	25.12.1936	31.7.1937	31.7.1938	20.8.1938	BS	Sunk 15.6.1943

19.0 Minesweepers

Project 53U

		T-205	GAFEL'	363, Leningrad	14	12.10.1937	29.7.1938	21.7.1939	23.7.1939	B	Conv to service craft 17.10.1955
		T-206	VERP	363, Leningrad	15	12.10.1937	17.6.1938	17.6.1939	1939	B	Sunk 14.11.1941
		T-207	SHPIL'	363, Leningrad	16	17.11.1937	18.8.1938	23.9.1939	24.10.1939	B	Conv to service craft 17.10.1955
		T-208	SHKIV	363, Leningrad / 196, Leningrad	17 / 129	18.11.1937	31.10.1938	12.10.1939	1939	B	Sunk 25.6.1941
		T-209	KNEKHT	363, Leningrad	18	16.6.1938	17.8.1939	3.6.1940	30.6.1940	B	Sunk 24.8.1941
		T-210	GAK	363, Leningrad	19	8.8.1938	15.4.1939	14.11.1939	30.11.1939	B	Deleted 13.1.1961
		T-211	RYM	363, Leningrad	20	21.9.1938	5.5.1939	25.6.1940	6.7.1940	B	Deleted 12.2.1960
		T-212	SHTAG	363, Leningrad	21	6.11.1938	2.12.1939	26.7.1940	1940	B	Sunk 3.8.1941
		T-213	KRAMBOL	370, Leningrad	92	26.8.1938	31.1.1939	30.11.1939	25.4.1940	B	Sunk 11.8.1941
		T-214	BUGEL'	370, Leningrad	93	26.8.1938	31.1.1939	29.6.1940	6.7.1940	B	Sunk 24.8.1941
		T-215		363, Leningrad	24	23.4.1939	17.12.1939	30.9.1940	23.10.1940	B	Deleted 9.2.1962
		T-216		363, Leningrad	27	17.9.1939	30.4.1940	24.12.1940		B	Sunk 6.7.1941
		T-217	KONTR-ADMIRAL IURKOWSKIJ	363, Leningrad	28	21.9.1939	31.7.1940	26.8.1941	30.8.1941	B	Deleted 7.6.1961
		T-218		363, Leningrad	22	20.3.1939	24.11.1939	30.11.1940	23.12.1940	B	Deleted 7.3.1958
		T-219	KONTR-ADMIRAL KHOROSHKHIN	363, Leningrad / 370, Leningrad	34	27.4.1941	24.06.1943	25.9.1944	7.10.1944	B	Deleted 7.3.1958
		T-220		363, Leningrad / 370, Leningrad	35	10.4.1941	16.11.1943	16.10.1946	1946	B	Deleted 13.1.1960
		T-221	DMITRIJ LYSOV	363, Leningrad	36	27.6.1941	6.6.1946	5.11.1946	1946	B	Deleted 1960s
		T-222	-	370, Leningrad	134	-	-	-	-	B	Cancelled 1941
		T-223	-	370, Leningrad	135	-	-	-	-	B	Cancelled 1941
Project 58											
		T-5	PARAVAN	201, Sevastopol	187	15.3.1937	28.1.1938	28.1.1939	4.2.1939	P	Trfd 11.10.1950 to the Border Guard
		T-6	KAPSIUL'	201, Sevastopol	188	21.3.1937	28.1.1938	28.1.1939	4.2.1939	P	Trfd Jan 1946 to the Border Guard
23	23	408	T-408	IAKOR'	201, Sevastopol	189	28.3.1937	4.1.1938	15.2.1939	19.3.1939	BS	Conv to experimental vessel 7.4.1956
24	24	409	T-409	GARPUN	201, Sevastopol	190	27.4.1937	28.3.1938	20.2.1939	19.3.1939	BS	BU 1960
25	25	410	T-410	VZRYV	201, Sevastopol	191	29.4.1937	29.4.1938	9.3.1939	1.4.1939	BS	Sunk 2.9.1944
16	15	412	T-412	A. RASSKIN	201, Sevastopol	255	13.4.1939	5.11.1939	3.3.1941	23.4.1941	BS	BU 1958
27			T-413	-	201, Sevastopol	256	29.10.1939	12.10.1940	21.4.1941	1.5.1941	BS	Sunk 13.6.1942
			T-414	-	201, Sevastopol	267	3.1.1941	29.4.1941	-	-	BS	BU late 1940s
			T-415	-	201, Sevastopol	268	20.3.1941	5.11.1947	-	-	BS	Destroyed 1942

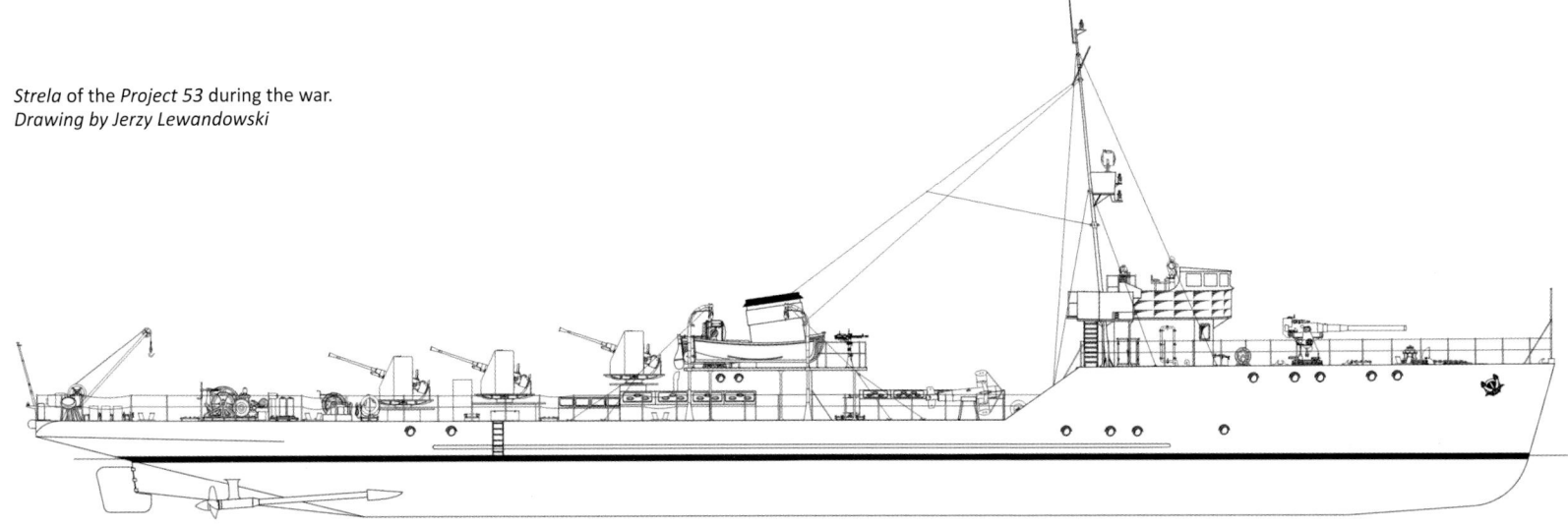

Strela of the *Project 53* during the war.
Drawing by Jerzy Lewandowski

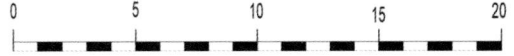

Provodnik (*T-3*) during transfer from Baltic to Vladivostok, approaching Panama Canal on 17.7.1939. *Naval History and Heritage Command NH 58834*

The first ten 330t Fast Minesweepers (Bystrokhodnye Tral'shchiki) of 19kts were authorised under the supplementary 1930 Programme, five each for the Baltic and the Black Sea. The design concept was based on the French diesel *Friponne* class avisos, tasked with sweeping fairways and anchorages, and escorting submarines and bigger ships. Too much was demanded from a ship of this size which, in addition to minesweeping gear, received a 100mm gun as main armament and a full outfit of AS weapons. The design, coded *Project 3* with a displacement of 383t standard, was approved on 27.3.1933. In contrast to the standard Soviet practice of that time, the first series of eight ships (the programme was reduced by 20%) were not laid down until several months later due to shortages of steel. After launching, the construction schedule was further extended, this time due to delays in the delivery of diesels.

On trials the prototype *Fugas* proved to be top heavy with a metacentric height of 42cm, instead of the designed 72cm. With the planned load of mines onboard, the height of the metacentre was reduced to 23cm. This was a combination of design flaws and the centre of gravity of the diesels which was substantially higher than assumed during their design. This was remedied by plating of double bottom stringers and girders in tanks to reduce free surfaces and by shipping 15t of pig iron ballast. As a result, the standard displacement rose to 428t and the designed speed was missed by 0.5kts. By the time this was revealed, construction of the second batch (built to the slightly modified design coded *Project 53*) was well advanced, so the only solution was to ship an additional 10t of pig iron, the whole load reaching 6.5% of displacement. Therefore, it was decided to increase the beam by

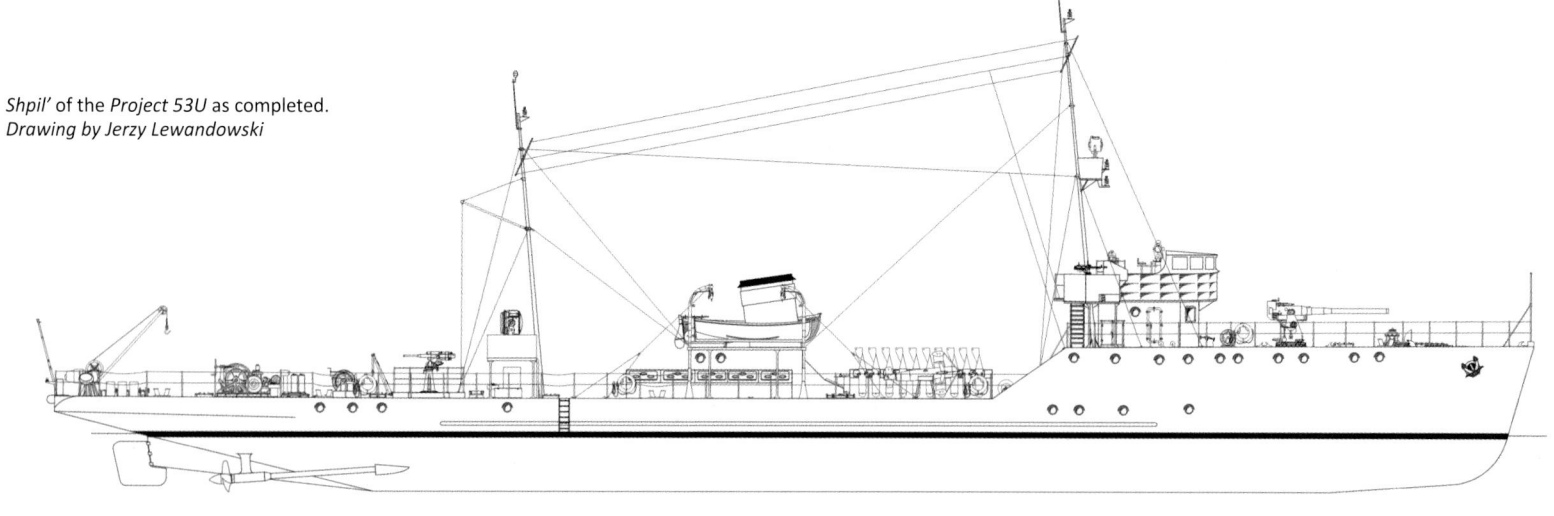

Shpil' of the *Project 53U* as completed.
Drawing by Jerzy Lewandowski

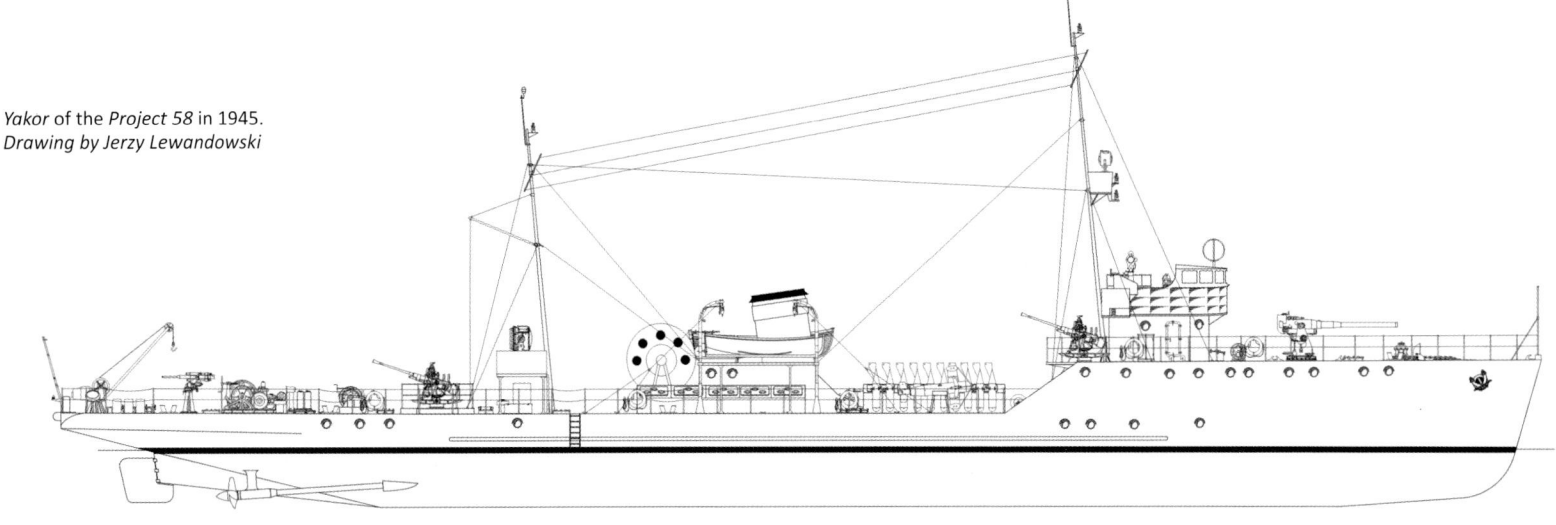

Yakor of the *Project 58* in 1945.
Drawing by Jerzy Lewandowski

20cm and the modified design coded *Project 53U* (U for Ushirennyi = Widened) was applied at the third batch which entered production in 1937 at Yard No 363 in Leningrad. On the other hand, Yard No 201 at Sevastopol modified the design coded *Project 58* by lowering the fittings, so they continued construction based on the earlier hull. At that time, they became rated as coastal minesweepers – Base Minesweepers in Russian nomenclature (Bazovye Tral'shchiki) – as the fast minesweeper concept was to materialise as *Project 59*.

During the war their AA armament and minesweeping outfit was augmented, further adding to the stability problems. One of most curious modifications took place in January 1943 when *Garpun* and *Iskatel'* received two torpedo drop-collars each on their already crowded main deck. In May 1943 they were moved to the forecastle deck close to the bridge but following some attempts at their employment, the drop-collars were finally removed. The idea came about because of experience fighting German cargo transports when the 100mm guns proved to be ineffective.

Regardless of their faults, the ships turned out to be sturdy and were successfully employed in a variety of tasks far from minesweeping, like escort work, attacks on enemy shipping, landing operations and fire support.

Bugel' (*T-214*) and *Shkiv* (*T-208*) in 1940 with their pennant numbers in the 1939 scheme.
Boris Lemachko Collection

Fugas class minesweeper early in the war. *IWM RUS 469*

Wreck of *Vzryvatel'* off Eupatoria in Jan 1942. *Jerzy Miciński Collection*

T-201 *Zariad*: experimental ship from 1.9.1939 until 4.2.1941 with a break between December 1939 and March 1940 because of employment in the Winter War. Mined off Ristna lighthouse, west of Hiuumaa.

T-202 *Buj*: mined off Cape Juminda.

T-203 *Patron*: mined off Keri.

T-204 *Fugas*: mined off Laavansaari.

T-401 *Tral*: damaged 27.6.1942 by bombs, repaired. Conv 24.8.1944 to the electromagnetic minesweeper, renumbered *EMTShch-401*. Conv 1.9.1955 to target ship.

T-402 *Minrep*: under repair until end of August 1941. Sunk by mine when sailing from Feodosia.

T-403 *Gruz*: damaged 16.2.1942 by aircraft off Kyz-Aul Cape, under repair until end of 1942. Sunk by German MTBs off Myshako.

T-404 *Shchit*: conv 7.4.1956 to experimental vessel.

T-1 *Strela*: trfd 15.6.–24.8.1939 from Kronshtadt to Far East *via* the Panama Canal. Took part in sweeping south of Askold Island during the Soviet-Japanese War. Conv 1.9.1955 to surveying ship *Reduktor*.

T-2 *Tros*: trfd 15.6.–24.8.1939 from Kronshtadt to Far East *via* the Panama Canal. Trfd to North Korea, conv to patrol ship.

T-3 *Provodnik*: trfd 15.6.–24.8.1939 from Kronshtadt to Far East *via* the Panama Canal.

T-4 *Podsekatel'*: trfd 15.6.–24.8.1939 from Kronshtadt to Far East *via* the Panama Canal.

T-7 *Vekha*: trfd 14.6.–17.5.1939 from Sevastopol to Far East *via* the Suez Canal. Took part in landing on Shumshu during the Soviet-Japanese War.

T-8 *Cheka*: trfd 14.6.–17.5.1939 from Sevastopol to Far East *via* the Suez Canal. Took part in sweeping south of Askold Island during the Soviet-Japanese War. Trfd to North Korea, conv to patrol ship.

T-405 *Vzryvatel'*: damaged by artillery fire during landing at Eupatoria and beached. Wreck destroyed by artillery fire by end of the day.

T-406 *Iskatel'*: took part 9.9.1944 in landing at Burgas. Conv 18.12.1954 to experimental vessel.

T-407 *Mina*: damaged 27.6.1942 by German aircraft, repaired. Took part in December 1942 in attacks on German communication lines. Damaged 22.5.1943 by aircraft, under repair in Poti for several months. Conv 24.8.1944 to the electromagnetic minesweeper, renumbered *EMTShch-407*. Conv 7.4.1956 to training station *UTS-255*. Sank at Sevastopol during BU.

T-411 *Zashchitnik*: sunk by *U-24* west of Sukhumi.

T-205 *Gafel'*: took part in July 1942 in landing on Sommers. Stranded 5.8.1942 off Lavensaari but salvaged. Conv to dumb ammunition depot *BAMT-31250*.

T-206 *Verp*: Sunk by mine off Keri.

T-207 *Shpil'*: conv to dumb floating workshop *PM-93*.

T-208 *Shkiv*: mined north-east of Hiumaa when escorting damaged cruiser *Maksim Gorkij*.

T-209 *Knekht*: mined off Keri.

T-210 Gak: damaged 13.11.1941 by artillery fire at Leningrad, repaired. Damaged 9.5.1943 by mine off Laavansaari but survived and repaired. Sunk 2.7.1944 by mine in the Bay of Vyborg, raised and recomm.

T-211 Rym: conv 19.2.1959 to guard ship.

T-212 Shtag: mined north of Saaremaa when escorting the submarine *Shch-322*.

T-213 Krambol: mined off Cape Juminda.

T-214 Bugel': mined off Keri.

T-215: damaged 10.6.1943 by aircraft, repaired. Conv 7.6.1961 to accommodation hulk *PKZ-33*.

T-216: training ship between 71.1.1941 and 22.6.1941.

T-217 Kontr-admiral Iurkowskij: damaged 6.6.1943 by artillery fire when escorting submarines from Kronshadt, repaired.

T-218: damaged 9.11.1941 in collision with the minesweeper *T-204*, repaired. Damaged 4.12.1941 by mine when assisting damaged transport *Iosif Stalin*, repaired. Heavily damaged 10.6.1943 by aircraft escorting submarines from Kronshadt, repaired. Conv 3.4.1954 to experimental vessel, numbered *OS-9* on 27.12.1957.

T-219 Kontr-admiral Khoroshkhin: conv 30.12.1955 to experimental vessel, trfd 17.11.1956 to the Northern Fleet, numbered *OS-10* on 27.12.1957.

T-220: completed after the war with armament of 1-100mm/56 B-24-BM, 2-1in O4-K, 4-0.5in DShK.

T-221 Dmitrij Lysov: completed after the war with armament of 1-100mm/56 B-24-BM, 2-1in O4-K, 4-0.5in DShK.

T-5 Paravan: trfd 14.6.–17.5.1939 from Sevastopol to Far East *via* the Suez Canal. Took part in sweeping south of Askold Island during the Soviet-Japanese War.

T-6 Kapsiul': trfd 14.6.–17.5.1939 from Sevastopol to Far East *via* the Suez Canal.

T-408 Iakor': conv 17.10.1953 to service craft of Naval Mine Department, conv to experimental vessel *Leshch*.

T-409 Garpun: conv 7.4.1956 to training station.

T-410 Vzryv: damaged 30.9.1941 by aircraft at Sevastopol, repaired. Took part in the Kerch landing in December 1941/January 1942. Damaged 14.8.1942 by aircraft off Anapa, stranded and helped by the tug *Simeiz* to put out fires. Refloated, towed to Novorossisk, repaired. Sunk by *U-19* off Constanța.

T-412 A. Rasskin: took part in landings at Kerch in December 1941/January 1942 and Novorossisk in September 1943. Renamed 24.8.1944 *Arsenij Rasskin*.

T-413: sunk by aircraft of Cape Fiolent. Wreck raised 1947 and BU.

T-414: hull towed January 1942 to Tuapse, then April 1942 to Poti, returned to Nikolaev April 1944 for completion but cancelled.

T-415: hull destroyed on the slipway in 1942 to avoid capture by the Germans.

Left and below: Details of *A. Rasskin* in 1943.
Vitalij Kostrichenko Collection

Warships of the Soviet Fleets, 1939–1945

Camouflaged *Fugas* class minesweeper in the Baltic during the war.
Boris Lemachko Collection

Tral in 1943.
Jerzy Miciński Collection

Left and right: *Tral* with electromagnetic minesweeper suite as *EMTShch-401* in Sept 1944.
Przemysław Budzbon Collection

Left: *Gafel'* at the Finnish port of Abo in Feb 1945. Note the short mast and camouflage scheme.
Boris Lemachko Collection

Iakor' (Pt No 408) and three others of the class at a Black Sea port in 1945.
Vitalij Kostrichenko Collection

MT types (*Project 253-L*) — *Inshore minesweepers*

Type	MT-1	MT-2
Data for year:	1944	1945
Displacement (standard):	113.2t	128t
Displacement (normal):	118.6t	135t
Displacement (full):	126.7t	141.3t
Length:	38.0m	
Beam:	5.7m	5.72m
Draught:	1.37m	1.44m
Diesel engines (3-shaft):	Superior	Superior
Total power:	690hp	480hp
Speed (max):	14kts	12.6kts
Oil fuel (max):	10t	11.7t
Range:	2500nm at 8.6kts	3100nm at 6.2kts
Main armament:	2-45mm/68.6 21-KM	
MGs:	2-0.5in DShK	4-0.5in Colt (2x2)
Sweeps:	1-OTSh, 1 KAT, 1 BAT-2, 1 PEMT	
DCTs / DC chutes:	-/2	
DCs:	12 (18max) M-1	
Mines:	12 M1931	
Complement:	21	•

T-239 after the war.
Boris Lemachko Collection

Project 253L MT-2 type as built.
Drawing by Jerzy Lewandowski

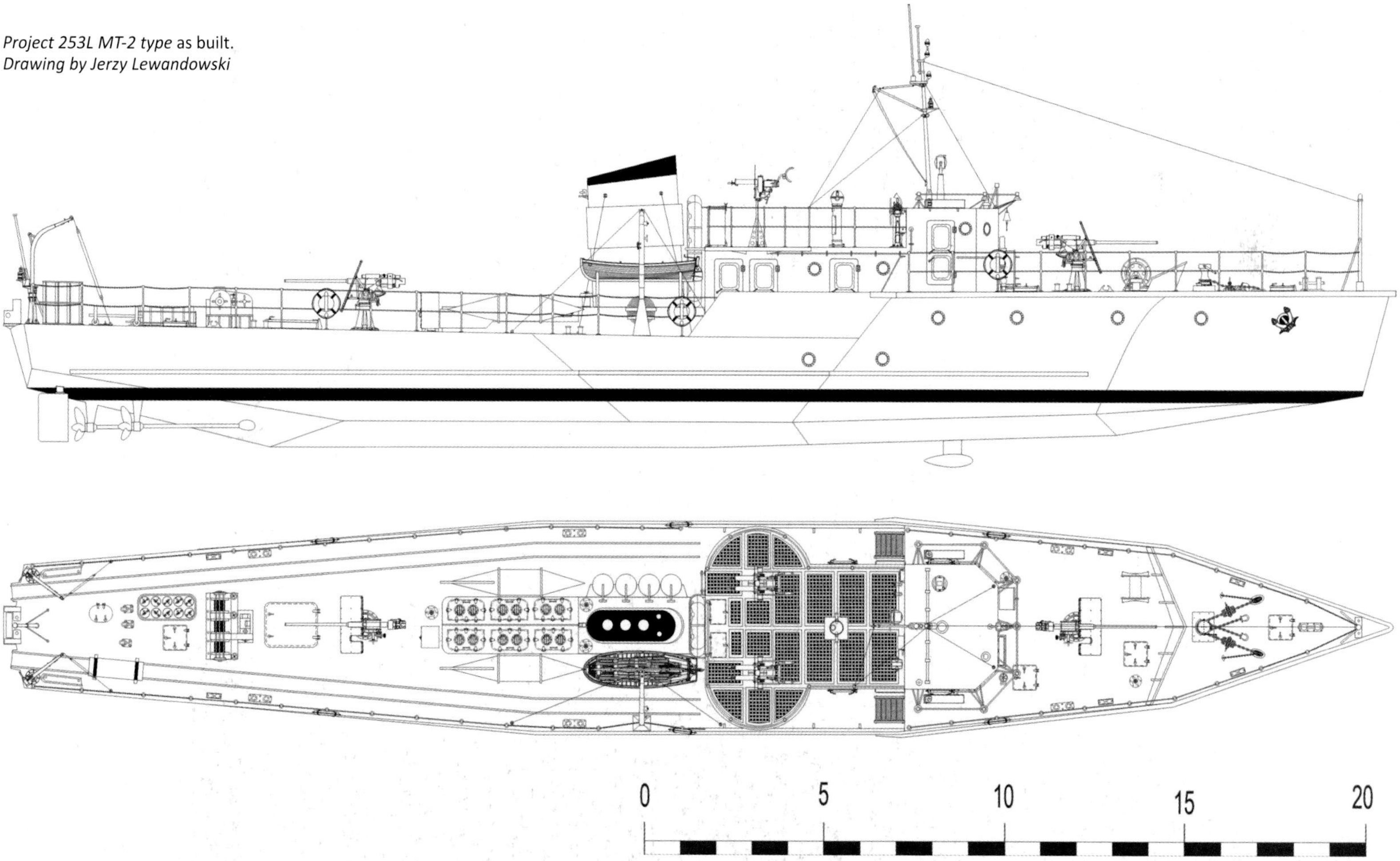

No	YN	Laid down	Launched	Comp	Comm	Fleet	Fate
MT-1 type							
Builder: 189, Leningrad							
T-351	314	12.6.1943	Sum 1943	1943	20.1.1944	B	Survived the war
T-352	315	12.6.1943	1944	31.5.1944	8.7.1944	B	Survived the war
T-353	316	24.8.1943	1944	31.5.1944	8.7.1944	B	Sunk 8.9.1944
T-354	317	24.8.1943	1944	31.5.1944	8.7.1944	B	Survived the war
T-355	320	12.10.1943	Spr 1944	29.6.1944	8.7.1944	B	Sunk 20.8.1945
T-356	321	12.10.1943	Spr 1944	29.6.1944	8.7.1944	B	Survived the war
T-357	322	30.11.1943	Sum 1944	18.10.1944	1944	B	Survived the war
T-358	323	30.11.1943	Sum 1944	18.10.1944	1944	B	Survived the war
T-359	324	30.11.1943	Sum 1944	18.10.1944	1944	B	Survived the war
T-360	325	30.11.1943	Sum 1944	18.10.1944	1944	B	Survived the war
T-361	326	29.12.1943	Spr 1944	3.7.1944	31.8.1944	B	Survived the war
T-362	327	29.12.1943	Spr 1944	3.7.1944	31.8.1944	B	Survived the war
T-363	328	29.12.1943	Spr 1944	17.8.1944	31.8.1944	B	Survived the war
T-364	329	29.12.1943	Spr 1944	17.8.1944	31.8.1944	B	Survived the war
T-386	330	29.2.1944	Sum 1944	20.10.1944	1944	B	Survived the war
T-387	331	29.2.1944	Sum 1944	20.10.1944	1944	B	Sunk 28.11.1944
T-388	332	31.3.1944	Aut 1944	27.12.1944	1944/5	B	Survived the war
T-389	333	31.3.1944	Aut 1944	27.12.1944	1944/5	B	Survived the war
Builder: 190, Leningrad							
T-370	568	Sum 1943	Spr 1944	9.7.1944	1944	B	Survived the war
T-371	569	Sum 1943	Spr 1944	9.7.1944	1944	B	Survived the war
T-372	570	Sum 1943	Spr 1944	17.8.1944	1944	B	Survived the war
T-373	571	Sum 1943	Spr 1944	12.8.1944	1944	B	Survived the war
T-374	573	end 1943	Sum 1944	30.9.1944	1944	B	Survived the war
T-375	574	end 1943	Sum 1944	30.9.1944	1944	B	Survived the war
T-376	575	end 1943	Sum 1944	20.10.1944	1944	B	Survived the war
T-377	576	end 1943	Spr 1944	20.10.1944	1944	B	Sunk 5.12.1944

MT type boats slipped out. Note angular body lines.
Przemysław Budzbon Collection

Builder: 370, Leningrad

T-378	151	8.8.1943	Spr 1944	9.7.1944	1944	B	Survived the war
T-379	152	8.8.1943	Spr 1944	17.8.1944	1944	B	Lost 23.10.1944
T-380	153	beg 1944	Sum 1944	20.10.1944	1944	B	Survived the war
T-381	154	27.10.1943	Sum 1944	27.12.1944	1944/5	B	Survived the war
T-382	155	31.12.1943	Aut 1944	14.2.1945	1945	B	Survived the war
T-383	156	27.2.1944	Spr 1945	4.8.1945	1.9.1945	B	
T-384	157	27.2.1944	Spr 1945	4.8.1945	1.9.1945	B	
T-385	158	29.3.1944	Sum 1945	Aut 1945	3.11.1945	B	

MT-2 type

Builder: 189, Leningrad

T-222	345	30.11.1944	Spr 1945	4.8.1945	1.9.1945	B	
T-223	346	30.11.1944	Spr 1945	4.8.1945	1.9.1945	B	
T-224	347	30.11.1944	Spr 1945	4.8.1945	1.9.1945	B	
T-225	348	30.11.1944	Spr 1945	31.8.1945	19.11.1945	B	Trfd 5.4.1946 to Poland
T-226	349	30.11.1944	Spr 1945	31.8.1945	19.11.1945	B	
T-227	350	30.11.1944	Spr 1945	31.8.1945	19.11.1945	B	
T-228	351	30.11.1944	Spr 1945	31.8.1945	19.11.1945	B	Trfd 5.4.1946 to Poland
T-229	352	30.11.1944	Spr 1945	1946	1946	B	
T-230	353	30.11.1944	Spr 1945	1946	1946	B	
T-231	354	30.11.1944	Spr 1945	31.8.1945	19.11.1945	B	Trfd 5.4.1946 to Poland
T-232	355	30.11.1944	Spr 1945	19.9.1945	16.11.1945	B	
T-233	356	1944	Spr 1945	29.9.1945	19.11.1945	B	
T-234	357	1944	Spr 1945	29.9.1945	19.11.1945	B	Conv 1956 to diving tender
T-235	358	1944	Spr 1945	29.9.1945	19.11.1945	B	
T-236	359	1944	Spr 1945	29.9.1945	19.11.1945	B	Conv 1956 to diving tender
T-237	360	1945	Sum 1945	25.10.1945	19.11.1945	B	
T-238	361	1945	Sum 1945	25.10.1945	19.11.1945	B	
T-239	362	1945	Sum 1945	25.10.1945	19.11.1945	B	
T-240	363	1945	Sum 1945	25.10.1945	19.11.1945	B	
T-241	364	1945	Sum 1945	25.10.1945	19.11.1945	B	Trfd 5.4.1946 to Poland
T-242	365	1945	Sum 1945	05.12.1945	1945/6	B	Conv 1957 to training station
T-243	366	1945	Sum 1945	05.12.1945	1945/6	B	Trfd 5.4.1946 to Poland
T-244	367	1945	Sum 1945	05.12.1945	1945/6	B	Trfd 5.4.1946 to Poland
T-245	368	1945	Sum 1945	05.12.1945	1945/6	B	
T-246	369	1945	Sum 1945	05.12.1945	1945/6	B	
T-247	370	1945	Aut 1945	Dec 1945	1945/6	B	Conv 1956 to diving tender
T-248	371	1945	Aut 1945	Dec 1945	1945/6	B	
T-249	372	1945	Aut 1945	Dec 1945	1945/6	B	
T-365	340	Spr 1944	Spr 1945	Jun 1945	3.7.1945	B	
T-366	341	Spr 1944	Spr 1945	Jul 1945	4.8.1945	B	
T-367	342	Sum 1944	Spr 1945	Jul 1945	15.8.1945	B	
T-368	343	Spr 1944	Spr 1945	Jun 1945	3.7.1945	B	
T-369	344	Sum 1944	Spr 1945	Jul 1945	15.8.1945	B	

From the left, *T-369*, *T-223* and unidentified boat of the *MT* type during fitting out. *Boris Lemachko Collection*

T-375 packed with minesweeping equipment. Photo apparently taken after the war, *Przemysław Budzbon Collection*

No	YN	Laid down	Launched	Comp	Comm	Fleet	Fate
T-390	336	30.6.1944	Aut 1944	Dec 1944	6.1.1945	B	Survived the war
T-391	337	30.6.1944	Aut 1944	Dec 1944	17.1.1945	B	Survived the war
T-440	338	31.7.1944	Spr 1945	Jun 1945	3.7.1945	B	
T-441	339	25.8.1944	Spr 1945	Jun 1945	3.7.1945	B	
T-459	334	30.4.1944	Aut 1944	8.11.1944	9.12.1944	B	Survived the war
T-460	335	30.4.1944	Aut 1944	8.11.1944	9.12.1944	B	Survived the war
Builder: 370, Leningrad							
T-434	162	beg 1945	Aut 1945	Nov 1945	20.12.1945	B	
T-435	163	beg 1945	Aut 1945	1945	1945	B	Conv 1955 to diving tender
T-439	164	beg 1945	Aut 1945	1945	1945	B	
Builder: 190, Leningrad							
T-461	579	1945	Spr 1945	Jun 1945	3.7.1945	B	
T-462	580	1945	Spr 1945	Jun 1945	3.7.1945	B	
T-463	581	1945	Spr 1945	Jul 1945	4.8.1945	B	
T-464	582	1945	Spr 1945	Jul 1945	4.8.1945	B	
T-465	583	25.12.1944	Aut 1945	1945	1945	B	Trfd 5.4.1946 to Poland
T-466	584	29.3.1945	Spr 1945	Sum 1945	5.9.1945	B	
T-467	585	30.3.1945	Aut 1945	1945	1945	B	Trfd 5.4.1946 to Poland
T-468	586	1945	Spr 1945	Sum 1945	29.9.1945	B	
T-469	587	1945	Spr 1945	Sum 1945	29.9.1945	B	
T-470	588	1945	Spr 1945	Sum 1945	29.9.1945	B	
T-472	590	1945	Sum 1945	1945	20.12.1945	B	
T-473	591	1945	Sum 1945	1945	20.12.1945	B	Conv 1956 to diving tender
T-474	592	1945	Sum 1945	1945	20.12.1945	B	
T-475	593	1945	Sum 1945	1945	20.12.1945	B	Conv 1956 to diving tender
T-476	594	1945	Sum 1945	1945	20.12.1945	B	
T-477	595	1945	Sum 1945	Aut 1945	25.10.1945	B	
T-478	596	1945	Sum 1945	1945	20.12.1945	B	
T-479	597	1945	Spr 1945	Sum 1945	29.9.1945	B	

MT type boats of the post-war series in line ahead.
Jerzy Miciński Collection

A *Project 255-K* minesweeper as completed.
Vitalij Kostrichenko Collection

The specification for a 60t, 16kt inshore minesweeper for the Baltic Fleet was issued in April 1942 and the design coded *Project 253* was delivered by the TsKB-51 in November 1942 in two variants, with either wooden or steel hull. It was rejected by the Narkomat of Shipbuilding because of design flaws and a general lack of confidence in a bureau specialised in riverine vessels. Therefore, the design was reviewed and modified at Leningrad's Yd No 189 with displacement increased almost two-fold. The design was accepted for steel-hulled ships, but to facilitate production under siege conditions at Leningrad the workshop drawings were simplified with angular lines to eliminate bending and the use of a low-quality steel (design code *Project 253-L*). Following acceptance of the prototype, series production was implemented with 30 ships delivered by the end of 1944. The type was designated MT, which stands for Malyj Tral'shchik (Small Minesweeper), and they were nicknamed '100-tonners'.

The design was modified in 1944 by dividing the machinery room into two compartments and adding a third generator. The modified type was given the designation MT-2, while retrospectively the former type became MT-1.

When the stock of Lend-Lease Superior diesels was exhausted the design was modified (*Project 255-K*) to apply Soviet-made ZD-12 diesels. Around eighty-eight ships were completed by 1952 at Yd No 341 at Rybinsk.

The type was phased out in the late 1950s, but some served much longer in satellite navies.

19.3. Lend-Lease ships

US **Admirable** class *Minesweepers*

Displacement:	625t standard, 806t normal, 877t full load
Dimensions:	56.7 x 10.2 x 4.3m
Machinery:	2-shaft ALCO-539 diesels, 1800hp =15.3kts. Oil fuel 123 t; range 6200nm at 12.7kts
Armament:	2-3in/50 M-22, 8-20mm Oerlikon, 1 Hedgehog Mk-10, 2 Mk-6 DCTs, 2 DC chutes, 148 Mk-10 DCs, 84 B-1 DCs, 3 Oropesa sweeps, 2 acoustic sweeps, 1 Mk-5 electromagnetic sweep
Sensors:	SL-1 radar, QCS-1 sonar
Complement:	95

Data for 1944 according to Russian sources.

T-115 (ex-US *Apex*, AM-142) with Soviet Navy pennant number.
Przemysław Budzbon Collection

T-285 (ex-US *Bond*, AM-152) after the war. *Przemysław Budzbon Collection*

Warships of the Soviet Fleets, 1939–1945

No	Builder	YN	Laid down	Launched	Comp	Trfd Location	Comm	Fleet	Fate
T-111 ex-AM-138 *Advocate* (US, 1943)	Tampa	48	8.4.1942	1.11.1942	Jun 1943	25.6.1943 St Petersburg	30.10.1943	N	Name: *Starshij lejtenant Lekarev*. Deleted 4.6.1969
T-112 ex-AM-139 *Agent* (US, 1943)	Tampa	49	8.4.1942	1.11.1942	Jul 1943	7.7.1943 St Petersburg	30.10.1943	N	Name: *Starshij lejtenant Vladimirov*. Extant 2010s
T-113 ex-AM-140 *Alarm* (US, 1943)	Tampa	50	8.6.1942	7.12.1942	Aug 1943	5.8.1943 St Petersburg	30.10.1943	N	Deleted 14.3.1960
T-114 ex-AM-141 *Alchemy* (US, 1943)	Tampa	51	8.6.1942	7.12.1942	Aug 1943	11.8.1943 St Petersburg	30.10.1943	N	Sunk 13.8.1944
T-115 ex-AM-142 *Apex* (US, 1943)	Tampa	52	8.6.1942	7.12.1942	Aug 1943	17.8.1943 St Petersburg	30.10.1943	N	Deleted 28.2.1961
T-116 ex-AM-143 *Arcade* (US, 1943)	Tampa	53	8.6.1942	7.12.1942	Aug 1943	26.8.1943 St Petersburg	24.11.1943	N	Deleted 4.5.1963
T-117 ex-AM-144 *Arch* (US, 1943)	Tampa	54	18.10.1942	7.12.1942	6.9.1943	9.9.1943 St Petersburg	24.11.1943	N	Deleted 19.9.1967
T-118 ex-AM-145 *Armada* (US, 1943)	Tampa	55	18.10.1942	7.12.1942	Sep 1943	16.9.1943 Key West	29.2.1944	N	Sunk 12.8.1944
T-119 ex-AM-146 *Aspire* (US, 1943)	Tampa	56	1.11.1942	27.12.1942	Sep 1943	29.9.1943 Key West	29.2.1944	N	Deleted 4.11.1966
T-120 ex-AM-147 *Assail* (US, 1943)	Tampa	57	1.11.1942	27.12.1942	Oct 1943	5.10.1943 Key West	29.2.1944	N	Sunk 24.9.1944
T-271 ex-AM-222 *Disdain* (US, 1945)	Tampa		23.10.1943	25.3.1944	26.12.1944	21.5.1945 Cold Bay	5.6.1945	P	Discarded early 1960s
T-272 ex-AM-234 *Fancy* (US, 1945)	Puget Sound Bridge	41	12.5.1944	4.9.1944	13.12.1944	20.5.1945 Cold Bay	17.6.1945	P	Discarded early 1960s
T-273 ex-AM-250 *Indicative* (US, 1945)	Savannah		29.9.1943	12.12.1943	26.5.1944	20.5.1945 Cold Bay	8.6.1945	P	Discarded early 1960s
T-274 ex-AM-262 *Marvel* (US, 1945)	ASBC Lorain		12.4.1943	31.7.1943	6.9.1944	20.5.1945 Cold Bay	8.6.1945	P	Discarded early 1960s
T-275 ex-AM-263 *Measure* (US, 1945)	ASBC Lorain		5.6.1943	29.10.1943	3.5.1944	21.5.1945 Cold Bay	8.6.1945	P	Discarded early 1960s
T-276 ex-AM-264 *Method* (US, 1945)	ASBC Lorain		7.6.1943	23.10.1943	10.7.1944	20.5.1945 Cold Bay	7.6.1945	P	Discarded early 1960s
T-277 ex-AM-265 *Mirth* (US, 1945)	ASBC Lorain		31.7.1943	24.12.1943	12.8.1944	21.5.1945 Cold Bay	22.6.1946	P	Discarded early 1960s
T-278 ex-AM-268 *Nucleus* (US, 1945)	Gulf	11	7.9.1942	25.6.1943	19.1.1944	21.5.1945 Cold Bay	17.6.1945	P	Discarded early 1960s
T-279 ex-AM-270 *Palisade* (US, 1945)	Gulf	14	21.9.1942	26.6.1943	9.3.1944	21.5.1945 Cold Bay	22.6.1945	P	Deleted 31.7.1957
T-280 ex-AM-271 *Penetrate* (US, 1945)	Gulf		5.1.1943	11.9.1943	31.3.1944	21.5.1945 Cold Bay	27.6.1945	P	Discarded early 1960s
T-281 ex-AM-272 *Peril* (US, 1945)	Gulf	16	1.2.1943	25.7.1943	20.4.1944	21.5.1945 Cold Bay	27.6.1945	P	Deleted 18.1.1960
T-282 ex-AM-282 *Rampart* (US, 1945)	Gulf	26	24.11.1943	30.3.1944	18.11.1944	20.5.1945 Cold Bay	5.6.1945	P	Discarded early 1960s
T-283 ex-AM-154 *Candid* (US, 1945)	WISCO		27.4.1942	14.10.1942	31.10.1943	16.8.1945 Cold Bay	3.9.1945	P	Deleted 11.3.1958
T-284 ex-AM-158 *Caution* (US, 1945)	WISCO		29.5.1942	7.12.1942	10.2.1944	16.8.1945 Cold Bay	31.8.1945	P	Deleted 18.1.1960
T-285 ex-AM-152 *Bond* (US, 1945)	WISCO		11.4.1942	21.10.1942	30.8.1943	16.8.1945 Cold Bay	31.8.1945	P	Deleted 18.1.1960
T-331 ex-AM-136 *Admirable* (US, 1945)	Tampa	46	8.4.1942	18.10.1942	20.4.1943	17.5.1945 Cold Bay	1.8.1945	P	Deleted 11.3.1958
T-332 ex-AM-137 *Adopt* (US, 1945)	Tampa	47	8.4.1942	18.10.1942	31.5.1943	17.5.1945 Cold Bay	1.8.1945	P	Deleted 28.3.1960
T-333 ex-AM-148 *Astute* (US, 1945)	Tampa	58	7.12.1942	23.2.1943	17.1.1944	17.5.1945 Cold Bay	1.8.1945	P	Deleted 18.1.1960
T-334 ex-AM-149 *Augury* (US, 1945)	Tampa	59	7.12.1942	23.2.1943	17.3.1944	17.5.1945 Cold Bay	30.7.1945	P	Deleted early 1960s
T-335 ex-AM-150 *Barrier* (US, 1945)	Tampa	60	7.12.1942	23.2.1943	10.5.1944	17.5.1945 Cold Bay	7.8.1945	P	Deleted 11.7.1956
T-336 ex-AM-151 *Bombard* (US, 1945)	Tampa	61	7.12.1942	23.2.1943	31.5.1944	17.5.1945 Cold Bay	11.8.1945	P	Deleted 12.2.1963

T-337 ex-AM-157 *Caravan* (US, 1945)	WISCO	16.5.1942	27.10.1942	21.1.1944	17.8.1945 Cold Bay	3.9.1945	P	Deleted 17.1.1960
T-338 ex-AM-156 *Captivate* (US, 1945)	WISCO	12.5.1942	1.12.1942	30.12.1943	16.8.1945 Cold Bay	31.8.1945	P	Deleted 18.1.1960
T-339 ex-AM-155 *Capable* (US, 1945)	WISCO	28.4.1942	16.11.1942	5.12.1943	16.8.1945 Cold Bay	31.8.1945	P	Deleted 18.1.1960

Ten ships were delivered to the Soviet Union in 1943 under Lend-Lease and after manning by the Soviet crews sailed to Murmansk to be comm with the Northern Fleet. Another two dozen units were delivered to the Pacific Fleet under Project Hula in anticipation of the Soviets eventually joining the war against Japan, specifically in preparation for planned Soviet invasions of southern Sakhalin and the Kurils. They were the most modern minesweepers in the Soviet Navy, equipped with a full outfit of advanced sweeping gear and – most importantly – sonar and radar. Especially because of the latter, command positions on these ships were so highly regarded by some Soviet officers that they were even the envy of destroyer commanders.

T-111: training ship from 15.1.1945 to 12.3.1945. Conv 11.7.1956 to torpedo recovery vessel, renamed *TV-25* on 3.11.1956, conv 4.5.1963 to accommodation hulk *PKZ-35*.

T-112: training ship from 15.1.1945 to 12.3.1945. Conv 15.10.1955 to torpedo recovery vessel *TV-21*, rated 8.3.1966 as military transport *VTR-21*, conv 20.4.1972 to training station *UTS-288*. Decomm 31.1.1991, the hull remained extant in to 2010s.

T-113: training ship from 15.1.1945 to 12.3.1945. Conv 3.11.1956 to hulk *BSh-34*.

T-114: sunk by *U-365* off Bely Island in the Kara Sea.

T-115: training ship from 15.1.1945 to 12.3.1945. conv 17.10.1955 to dispatch vessel *Ajdar*.

T-116: conv 3.11.1956 to torpedo recovery vessel *TV-23*, conv 23.10.1962 to target ship *SM-7*.

T-117: conv 15.10.1955 to torpedo recovery vessel *TV-22*, rated 8.3.1966 as military transport *VTR-22*.

T-118: sunk by *U-365* off Bely Island in the Kara Sea.

T-119: conv 3.11.1956 to torpedo recovery vessel *TV-24*, rated 8.3.1966 as military transport *VTR-140*.

T-120: sunk by *U-739* in the Kara Sea.

T-271: 12.8.1945 landing at Unngi (Korea), decomm 14.7.1947 to civilian service, conv 7.8.1948 to whaler *Shtorm*.

T-272: decomm 23.10.1947 to civilian service, conv 7.8.1948 to whaler *V'iuga*.

T-273: decomm 24.6.1947 to civilian service, conv 7.8.1948 to whaler *Tsiklon*.

T-274: decomm 3.7.1947 to civilian service, conv 7.8.1948 to whaler *Passat*.

T-275: 15.8.1945 landing at Seishin (Korea), decomm 23.10.1947 to civilian service, conv 7.8.1948 to whaler *Buran*.

T-276: decomm 23.10.1947 to civilian service, conv 7.8.1948 to whaler *Purga*.

T-277: 21.8.1945 landing at Wŏnsan (Korea), decomm 24.6.1947 to civilian service, conv 7.8.1948 to whaler *Musson*.

T-278: 14.8.1945 landing at Seishin (Korea), 20.8.1945 landing at Maoka (Sakhalin), decomm 23.10.1947 to civilian service, conv 7.8.1948 to whaler *Uragan*.

T-279: 12.8.1945 landing at Rajin-Sŏnbong (Korea), conv 21.9.1951 to accommodation hulk *PKZ-38*.

T-280: 15.8.1945 landing at Seishin (Korea), decomm 24.6.1947 to civilian service, conv 7.8.1948 to whaler *Tajfun*.

T-281: 12.8.1945 landing at Rajin-Sŏnbong (Korea), conv to guard ship *VRN-32*.

T-282: 21.8.1945 landing at Wŏnsan (Korea), decomm 23.10.1947 to civilian service, conv 7.8.1948 to whaler *Shkval*.

T-283: conv 28.6.1947 to surveying ship *Gorizont*.

T-284: conv 5.11.1945 to training ship, conv 3.12.1956 to guard ship *VRN-36*.

T-285: conv 5.11.1945 to training ship, conv 3.12.1956 to guard ship *VRN-37*.

T-331: conv 28.6.1947 to surveying ship *Giroskop*.

T-332: conv 17.10.1955 to dispatch vessel *Kinel'*, conv 27.2.1956 to guard ship *VRN-10*.

T-333: conv 17.10.1955 to dispatch vessel *Kurchum*, conv 27.2.1956 to guard ship *VRN-9*.

T-334: Aug 1945 landing at Kuriles, conv 12.1.1955 to dispatch vessel *Gazimur*, conv 27.2.1956 to guard ship *VRN-12*, conv to floating workshop *PM-97*.

T-335: conv 17.10.1955 to dispatch vessel *Istok*.

T-336: conv 16.6.1954 to dispatch vessel *Gydan*.

T-337: conv 3.12.1956 to guard ship *VRN-33*.

T-338: conv 3.12.1956 to guard ship *VRN-34*.

T-339: conv 3.12.1956 to guard ship *VRN-35*.

Admirable class minesweepers following their arrival in the Arctic: ex-*AM-146*, ex-*AM-147* and ex-*AM-148*. Boris Lemachko Collection

US YMS class — *Inshore minesweepers*

Displacement: 345t full load
Dimensions: 41.45 x 7.46 x 3.87 m
Machinery: 2-shaft General Motors 8-268A diesels, 1000hp =14.8kts. Range 2030nm at 9.2kts
Armament: 1-3in/50, 2-20mm Oerlikon, 2-0.5in MGs, 2 Mk-6 DCTs, 1 MK-5 electromagnetic sweep, 3 acoustic sweeps
Sensors: SL-1 radar, QCS-1 sonar
Complement: 48

Data for 1945 from Russian sources.

No	Builder	Laid down	Launched	Comp	Trfd	Comm	Fleet	Fate
T-521 ex-*YMS-59* (US, 1945)	Gibbs	14.2.1941	30.12.1941	24.4.1942	5.6.1945	27.6.1945	P	Deleted 11.7.1956
T-590 ex-*YMS-75* (US, 1945)	Weaver	22.7.1941	26.5.1942	22.2.1943	17.7.1945	30.7.1945	P	Scuttled 30.6.1956
T-592 ex-*YMS-42* (US, 1945)	Wheeler	6.6.1941	17.3.1942	25.4.1942	17.7.1945	30.7.1945	P	Deleted 7.10.1955
T-593 ex-*YMS-38* (US, 1945)	Hiltebrant	2.5.1941	24.1.1942	3.4.1942	17.7.1945	30.7.1945	P	Deleted 1.9.1955
T-602 ex-*YMS-100* (US, 1945)	Astoria	15.7.1941	12.4.1942	20.6.1942	17.8.1945	31.8.1945	P	Scuttled 30.6.1956
T-603 ex-*YMS-33* (US, 1945)	Hiltebrant	8.5.1941	8.10.1941	10.6.1942	17.8.1945	31.8.1945	P	Scuttled 30.6.1956
T-604 ex-*YMS-85* (US, 1945)	Grebe	2.6.1941	19.3.1942	30.6.1942	17.8.1945	31.8.1945	P	Scuttled 30.6.1956
T-608 ex-*YMS-88* (US, 1945)	South Coast	20.6.1941	18.10.1941	5.5.1942	26.8.1945	5.9.1945	P	Trfd 11.2.1955 to Communist China
YMS-135 subclass								
T-522 ex-*YMS-143* (US, 1945)	San Diego	20.4.1942	30.6.1942	16.2.1943	16.5.1945	5.6.1945	P	Deleted 11.7.1956
T-523 ex-*YMS-144* (US, 1945)	San Diego	20.4.1942	30.7.1942	17.3.1943	16.5.1945	5.6.1945	P	Constructive total loss 15.10.1945
T-524 ex-*YMS-145* (US, 1945)	San Diego	8.5.1942	7.9.1942	21.4.1943	21.5.1945	5.6.1945	P	Scuttled 30.6.1956
T-525 ex-*YMS-428* (US, 1945)	Mojean	10.2.1944	5.6.1944	24.1.1945	16.5.1945	5.6.1945	P	Deleted 11.7.1956
T-526 ex-*YMS-435* (US, 1945)	Martinac	11.5.1944	30.9.1944	5.3.1945	16.5.1945	5.6.1945	P	Deleted 11.7.1956
T-527 ex-*YMS-260* (US, 1945)	South Coast	20.5.1942	6.9.1942	9.4.1943	20.8.1945	11.9.1945	P	Deleted 11.7.1956
T-588 ex-*YMS-178* (US, 1945)	Grebe	9.7.1942	24.4.1943	31.7.1943	17.7.1945	30.7.1945	P	Scuttled 30.6.1956
T-589 ex-*YMS-237* (US, 1945)	Stadium	6.6.1942	7.9.1942	18.2.1943	17.7.1945	30.7.1945	P	Deleted 11.7.1956
T-591 ex-*YMS-241* (US, 1945)	Tacoma	20.5.1942	7.9.1942	18.2.1943	17.7.1945	30.7.1945	P	Scuttled 30.6.1956
T-594 ex-*YMS-139* (US, 1945)	Astoria	4.1.1943	19.5.1943	24.6.1943	17.7.1945	1.8.1945	P	Deleted 1.9.1955
T-595 ex-*YMS-184* (US, 1945)	Greenport	15.4.1942	18.7.1942	25.1.1943	17.7.1945	1.8.1945	P	Deleted 7.10.1955
T-596 ex-*YMS-216* (US, 1945)	Martinac	16.6.1942	17.10.1942	26.2.1943	17.7.1945	1.8.1945	P	Deleted 7.10.1955
T-597 ex-*YMS-272* (US, 1945)	Bellingham	20.7.1942	14.11.1942	28.5.1943	17.7.1945	1.8.1945	P	Scuttled 30.6.1956
T-598 ex-*YMS-273* (US, 1945)	Bellingham	7.9.1942	26.12.1942	7.7.1943	17.7.1945	1.8.1945	P	Deleted 11.7.1956
T-599 ex-*YMS-295* (US, 1945)	Associated	10.7.1943	11.8.1943	9.11.1943	17.7.1945	1.8.1945	P	Scuttled 30.6.1956
T-600 ex-*YMS-288* (US, 1945)	Associated	12.8.1942	20.11.1942	19.4.1943	17.8.1945	31.8.1945	P	Scuttled 30.6.1956
T-601 ex-*YMS-266* (US, 1945)	Kruse & Banks	16.5.1942	24.12.1942	8.4.1943	17.8.1945	31.8.1945	P	Deleted 11.9.1956

T-605 ex-*YMS-301* (US, 1945)	Stone	14.11.1942	1.5.1943	11.9.1943	17.8.1945	31.8.1945	P	Trfd 11.2.1955 to Communist China
T-606 ex-*YMS-135* (US, 1945)	Astoria	20.5.1942	26.12.1942	26.2.1943	26.8.1945	5.9.1945	P	Trfd 11.2.1955 to Communist China
T-607 ex-*YMS-332* (US, 1945)	Ballard	3.3.1943	5.6.1943	12.10.1943	26.8.1945	5.9.1945	P	Trfd 11.2.1955 to Communist China
T-609 ex-*YMS-180* (US, 1945)	Grebe	27.10.1942	28.8.1943	10.9.1943	26.8.1945	5.9.1945	P	Trfd 11.2.1955 to Communist China
T-610 ex-*YMS-285* (US, 1945)	Northwestern	16.6.1942	20.3.1943	26.6.1943	2.9.1945	11.9.1945	P	Sunk 15.10.1945
T-611 ex-*YMS-287* (US, 1945)	Associated	16.7.1942	27.10.1942	15.3.1943	2.9.1945	11.9.1945	P	Trfd 11.2.1955 to Communist China
YMS-446 subclass								
T-181 ex-*YMS-447* (US, 1944)	Jakob	17.6.1943	15.9.1943	28.6.1944	27.3.1945	28.6.1945	B	Deleted 16.10.1957
T-182 ex-*YMS-457* (US, 1944)	Greenport	17.11.1943	8.1.1944	14.9.1944	31.3.1945	28.6.1945	B	Deleted 11.7.1956
T-183 ex-*YMS-460* (US, 1944)	Stadium	8.6.1943	4.12.1943	27.5.1944	5.4.1945	28.6.1945	B	Deleted 16.10.1957
T-184 ex-*YMS-462* (US, 1944)	Hiltebrant	5.4.1943	11.10.1943	10.6.1944	12.4.1945	28.6.1945	B	Deleted 9.6.1956
T-185 ex-*YMS-448* (US, 1944)	Jakob	22.6.1943	22.3.1944	25.7.1944	24.4.1945	28.6.1945	B	Deleted 19.4.1958
T-186 ex-*YMS-469* (US, 1944)	Gibbs	30.7.1943	17.3.1944	22.9.1944	30.4.1945	28.6.1945	B	Deleted 11.7.1956
T-187 ex-*YMS-465* (US, 1944)	Gibbs	21.6.1943	4.1.1944	17.6.1944	8.5.1945	4.8.1945	BS	Deleted 28.1.1958
T-188 ex-*YMS-464* (US, 1944)	Gibbs	14.5.1943	9.12.1943	13.6.1944	15.5.1945	4.8.1945	BS	Deleted 28.1.1958
T-189 ex-*YMS-453* (US, 1944)	Greenport	20.7.1943	2.10.1943	27.6.1944	24.5.1945	4.8.1945	BS	Deleted 2.6.1959
T-190 ex-*YMS-455* (US, 1944)	Greenport	21.8.1943	13.11.1943	21.7.1944	30.5.1945	4.8.1945	BS	Deleted 28.1.1958
T-191 ex-*YMS-456* (US, 1944)	Greenport	4.10.1943	11.12.1943	21.8.1944	16.5.1945	4.8.1945	BS	Deleted 28.1.1958
T-192 ex-*YMS-466* (US, 1944)	Gibbs	24.6.1943	22.1.1944	4.7.1944	31.5.1945	4.8.1945	BS	Deleted 17.11.1959

YMS-456 (future *T-191*) before transfer to the Soviets. *Boris Lemachko Collection*

US mass-built inshore minesweepers, 12 delivered under Lend-Lease to the Baltic and Black Sea Fleets, while 31 went to the Pacific Fleet under Project Hula in anticipation of the Soviets eventually joining the war against Japan, specifically in preparation for planned Soviet invasions of southern Sakhalin and the Kurils. The subclasses differ from the two-funnelled *YMS-1* class in number of stacks: *YMS-135* subclass had one, while *YMS-466* subclass had none. These small ships were packed with advanced sweeping technology, radars and sonars thus contributing with this technology much more to the Cold War Soviet Navy than to the World War 2 effort. Those delivered to the Baltic Fleet sailed in June 1945 directly to Bornholm (then occupied by the Soviets) and those to the Black Sea in August to Sevastopol.

T-181: conv 30.12.1955 to experimental vessel *OS-7*.

T-182: conv 12.1.1955 to diving tender *VM-77*, laid up 12.3.1955.

T-183: conv 30.12.1955 to experimental vessel *OS-8*.

T-184: conv 12.1.1955 to diving tender *VM-78*, laid up 12.3.1955.

T-185: conv 15.4.1955 to diving tender *VM-77*.

T-187: laid up 7.4.1956.

T-189: conv 12.1.1955 to degaussing station *SBR-123*.

T-190: conv 12.1.1955 to degaussing station *SBR-124*.

T-191: laid up 7.4.1956.

T-192: conv 28.1.1958 to degaussing station *SBR-124*.

T-521: laid up 15.4.1955.

T-522: August 1945 landing on Sakhalin, laid up 15.4.1955.

T-523: damaged 15.10.1945 by mine in a Soviet minefield; broke in half but both parts remained afloat and were towed to Petropavlovsk-Kamchatski for BU.

T-524: August 1945 landing on Sakhalin, deleted 25.6.1956 and scuttled at Tartar Bay under US supervision.

T-525: August 1945 landing on Kuriles, laid up 15.4.1955.

T-526: August 1945 landing on Sakhalin, laid up 17.10.1955.

T-527: August 1945 landing on Sakhalin, laid up 14.4.1955.

T-588: August 1945 landing on Sakhalin, laid up 1.9.1955, conv 27.2.1956 to guard ship *BRN-11*, scuttled at Tartar Bay under US supervision.

T-589: August 1945 landing on Sakhalin, laid up 17.10.1955.

T-590: August 1945 landing on Sakhalin, laid up 1.9.1955, scuttled at Tartar Bay under US supervision.

T-591: August 1945 landing on Sakhalin, conv 28.6.1947 to surveying vessel *Gidrofon*, scuttled at Tartar Bay under US supervision.

T-597: conv 28.6.1947 to surveying ship *Gigrometr*, scuttled at Tartar Bay under US supervision.

T-599: 25.08.1945 landing at Otomari (Sakhalin), scuttled under US supervision in the Sea of Japan.

T-600: scuttled under US supervision in the Sea of Japan.

T-601: conv 2.2.1956 to guard ship *BRN-13*.

T-602: laid up 17.10.1955, scuttled under US supervision in the Sea of Japan.

T-603: conv 27.2.1956 to guard ship *BRN-14*, scuttled under US supervision in the Sea of Japan.

T-604: scuttled under US supervision in the Sea of Japan.

T-605 – T-609: trfd to Communist China.

T-610: mined off Petropavlovsk-Kamchatski.

T-611: trfd to Communist China.

Ex-US *YMS* class minesweepers in the Black Sea after the war. *Przemysław Budzbon Collection*

British TAM class
Inshore minesweepers

Displacement: 480t normal, 540t full load
Dimensions: 36.3 x 6.5 x 4.16m
Machinery: 1-shaft VTE, 1 Scotch boiler (14.5 kG/cm^2), 850hp = 12.5kts (6kts with a sweep). Oli fuel 100t, range 1800nm at 11kts
Armament: 1-20mm Oerlikon, 1-0.5in Vickers MG, 18 M-1 DCs, 1 electromagnetic sweep, 1 acoustic sweep
Complement: 42

Data of *T-102* in 1943 from Russian sources.

No	Builder	YN	Build	Trfd Convoy	Comm	Fleet	Fate
T-101 ex-FY.1664 (Br, 1.3.1942) ex-*Shika* (Nor, Mar 1943)	Smith's Dock, Middlesbrough	893	1929	17.2.1942 PQ-9/10	14.3.1942	N	Returned 20.8.1948. Sank 1983
T-102 ex-FY.1759 (Br, 1.3.1942) ex-*Hav* (Nor, Mar 1943)	Akers, Oslo		1931	17.2.1942 PQ-9/10	14.3.1942	N	Returned 20.8.1948
T-103 ex-FY.1887 (Br, 22.4.1942) ex-*Stefa* (Nor, Mar 1943)	Smith's Dock, Middlesbrough	873	1929	21.3.1942 PQ-12	9.5.1942	N	Returned 20.8.1948. BU 1985
T-104 ex-FY.294 (Br, 22.4.1942) ex-*Vega* (Nor, Mar 1943)	Smith's Dock, Middlesbrough	877	1929	16.3.1942 PQ-12	9.5.1942	N	Returned 20.8.1948. BU 1983
T-105 ex-FY.1702 (Br, 22.4.1942) ex-*Shusa* (Nor, Mar 1943)	Smith's Dock, Middlesbrough	884	1931	17.4.1942 PQ-12	9.5.1942	N	Deleted 4.7.1964
T-106 ex-FY.297 (Br, 22.4.1942) ex-*Sunba* (Nor, Mar 1943)	Smith's Dock, Middlesbrough	887	1929	4.4.1942 PQ-13	9.5.1942	N	Returned 20.8.1948. BU 1957
T-107 ex-FY.301 (Br, 21.5.1942) ex-*Silja* (Nor, Mar 1943)	Smith's Dock, Middlesbrough	901	1929	15.5.1942 PQ-13	5.6.1942	N	Returned 20.8.1948. Sank 5.11.1948
FY.1724 ex-*Shera* (Nor, Mar 1943)	Smith's Dock, Middlesbrough		1929	-	-	N	Foundered 9.3.1942

Former Norwegian whalers, built in Britain. Following occupation of Norway in April 1940, they fled to British ports where they were mobilised and conv into acoustic-magnetic minesweepers. Trfd to the Soviet Union under Lend-Lease, arrived February/March 1942 with PQ convoys to Kola Bay manned by British crews and were handed over to the Northern Fleet. They became the first Soviet minesweepers capable of countering non-contact mines.

T-105: stranded 24.11.1942 at Danilov Island, raised summer 1943 and towed to Molotovsk, laid up and decomm 16.8.1943. Conv to training ship *Vaga*, recomm 19.10.1952, conv 27.12.1956 to training station *UTS-21*.

FY.1824, FY.1874: foundered on passage to Kola Bay.

British **MMS** class *Inshore minesweepers*

Type	105ft	126ft
Data for year:	1942	1944*
Displacement (full):	254t	450t
Length:	36.0m	44.3
Beam:	7.0m	7.3
Draught:	2.9m	4.0
Diesel engine (1-shaft):	•	Crossley
Total power:	375hp	500hp
Speed (max):	12kts	10.5kts
Oil fuel (max):	26t	55t
Range:	2400nm at 9.5kts	4800nm at 8.5kts
AA armament:	2-20mm Oerlikon	2-20mm Oerlikon
MGs:	2-0.5in	2-0.303in Lewis MGs
Sweeps:	electromagneticacoustic	LL electromagneticKango acoustic
DCs:	•	18 M-1
Complement:	25	31

*Data of T-121 in 1944 from Russian sources.

British motor minesweepers trfd to the Soviet Union under Lend-Lease, manned by the British crews arrived with PQ-18 and JW-55-A convoys to Kola Bay and were handed over to the Northern Fleet.

T-108: conv 2.5.1951 to diving tender *VM-30*.

T-109: foundered during a gale off Sangeiski Island in the Barents Sea.

T-110: conv 6.3.1951 to diving tender *VM-29*.

T-121: conv 6.3.1951 to pilot boat *LOTs-26*.

T-122: conv 6.3.1951 to pilot boat *LOTs-27*.

No	Builder	Laid down	Launched	Comp	Trfd Convoy	Comm	Fleeet	Fate
105ft MMS								
T-108 ex-*MMS-90* (Br, 1942)	Morris	1941	25.11.1941	17.6.1942	6.10.1942 PQ-18	10.10.1942	Wh	Deleted 9.6.1958. BU 1962?
T-109 ex-*MMS-203* (Br, 1942)	Curtis	1942	13.4.1942	21.7.1942	6.10.1942 PQ-18	10.10.1942	Wh	Foundered 22.11.1944
T-110 ex-*MMS-212* (Br, 1942)	Humphrey	1942	23.4.1942	17.6.1942	6.10.1942 PQ-18	10.10.1942	Wh	Deleted 20.4.1956
126ft MMS								
T-121 ex-*MMS-1005* (Br, 1943)	East Anglian	1942	30.7.1942	5.1.1943	5.1.1944 JW-55-A	24.1.1944	N	Deleted 21.12.1954
T-122 ex-*MMS-1023* (Br, 1943)	Humphrey	1942	22.10.1942	29.12.1942	29.12.1943 JW-55-A	24.1.1944	N	Deleted mid-1950s

19.4. War prizes

19.4.1. POLAND, 1939

Polish **T-4** class *River motor minesweepers*

Displacement:	4.8t full load
Dimensions:	9.0 x 3.8/2.2 x 0.25m
Machinery:	2 side wheels, Praha L petrol engine, 20hp = 6.4kts. Range 150nm
Armament:	1-0.3in Maxim MG, 1 MTSh (light) sweep, • R-1 mines
Complement:	5–6

TShch № 1939	TShch № 22.6.1941	Built	Comm	Fleet	Remarks
	Builder: WPMW				
№ 3	№ 33	1928	24.10.1939	Dn Pn	Scuttled 18.9.1941 at Kiev
№ 4	№ 34	1929	24.10.1939	Dn Pn	Sunk 19.8.1941
№ 5	№ 35	1929	24.10.1939	Dn Pn	Sunk 17/18.9.1941

Polish river minesweepers scuttled 21.9.1939 in the Prypiat' basin near Kużliczyn, raised 8.10.1939 and repaired at the former Polish Pinsk workshop, named by the Soviets as Harbour Workshops of the Pinsk Base of the Dnieper Flotilla.

They were ceremonially presented as war prizes and formally comm with the Dnieper Flotilla.

Tral'shchik № 3: former Polish *T-4*, trfd 17.7.1940 to the Pinsk Flotilla, renumbered *№ 33* on 22.6.1941, scuttled at Kiev.

Tral'shchik № 4: former Polish *T-6 (ex-T-2)*, trfd 17.7.1940 to the Pinsk Flotilla, renumbered *№ 34* on 22.6.1941. Sank off Cherkasy on the Dnieper following damage by artillery fire.

Tral'shchik № 5: former Polish *T-7 (ex-T-3)*, trfd 17.7.1940 to the Pinsk Flotilla, renumbered *№ 35* on 22.6.1941. Sunk by German tanks off Svarom on the Dnieper.

Note: Two ex-Polish riverine craft were commissioned in 1939 in the Dnieper Flotilla as minesweepers *TShch № 1* and *TShch № 2*. Following transfer to the Pinsk Flotilla in 1940 they were renumbered as *TShch № 31* and *TShch № 32*. Apparently both were lost in 1941.

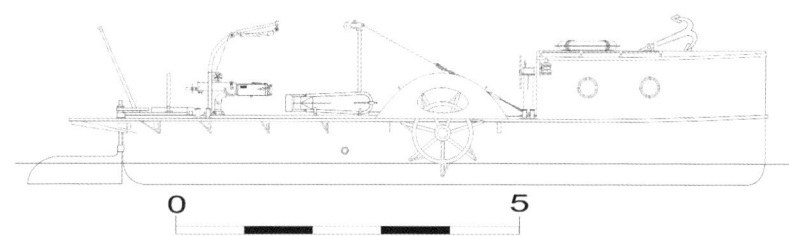
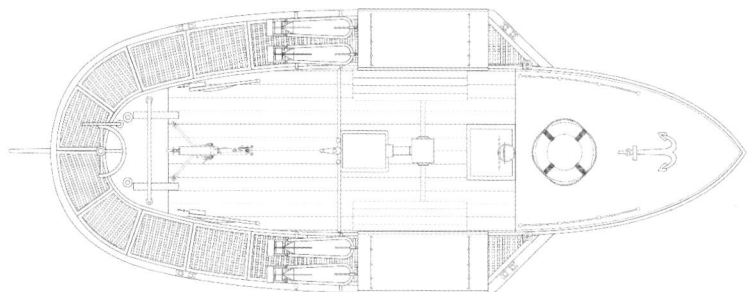

T-4 class in Soviet service. *Drawing by Jerzy Lewandowski*

19.4.2. BALTIC STATES, 1940

German **M1916** type — *Minesweepers*

Former Imperial German Navy minesweepers purchased by Lithuania and Latvia.

Korall: purchased by Lithuania in July 1927 as the first and only warship of the Lithuanian Navy which was only formed in 1935. Seized 15.6.1940, renamed *Primunas,* trfd to the NKVD Border Guard 19.8.1940, renamed *Korall*. Dispatched to the naval command on 22.6.1941, rated as escort ship and comm 19.8.1941 with the Baltic Fleet. Rated as minesweeper 25.11.1943. Sunk by mine off Aegna.

Virsajtis: seized 19.8.1940, rated 25.7.1941 as escort ship. Sunk by mine off Hanko.

Name	Virsajtis	Korall
Data for year:	1941	1943
Displacement (normal):	525t	600t
Displacement (full):	•	650t
Length:	56.1m	
Beam:	7.3m	
Draught:	2.4m	2.7m
2-shaft:	VTE	
Boiler:	2 •	2 Kraft-Schultz (15kG/cm^2)
Total power:	800hp	
Speed (max):	15kts	16kts
Coal (max):	120t	
Range:	1000nm at 10kts	1200nm at 10kts
Main armament:	4-83.5mm/55 Škoda vz.22/24	2-3in/55 34-K
AA armament:	2-57mm	-
MGs:	4-0.303in Vickers	4-0.5in DShK
Sweeps:	1 MTSh, 1 MZT	
DCTs / DC chutes:	-	•
DCs:	-	•
Mines:	40 M1908	•
Complement:	57	70

No 17.10.1940	TShch № 7.9.1941	No 29.8.1944	No/Name	Builder	YN	Laid down	Launched	Comp	Comm	Fleet	Fate
	№ 76	T-33	KORALL ex-*Primunas* (19.8.1940) ex-*Anastasas Smetona* (Lit, 22.6.1940) ex-*Prezidentas Smetona* (Lit, 1934) ex-*M-59* (Ger, 2.8.1922)	Deschimag, Seebeck	402	Sum 1917	31.10.1917	30.11.1917	19.8.1941	B	Sunk 11.1.1945
T-297			VIRSAJTIS ex-*Virsajtis* (Lat, 17.10.1940) ex-*Sarkana Latvija* (Lat, Jun 1919) ex-*M-68* (Ger, Jan 1919)	Neptun, Rostock	382	1917	25.7.1917	6.10.1917	19.8.1940	B	Sunk 3.12.1941

Latvian **Viesturs** class — *Minesweepers*

Name	Imanta	Viesturs
Data for year:	1941	1943
Displacement (normal):	255t	280t
Displacement (full):	•	310t
Length:	46.0m	
Beam:	6.45m	6.4m
Draught:	1.7m	1.8m
2-shaft:	VTE	
Boiler:	2 Normand (15kG/cm^2)	
Total power:	730hp	
Speed (max):	14kts	
Coal (max):	28t	
Range:	700nm at 7kts	672nm at 7kts
Main armament:	1-75mm/36 Schneider	1-3in/55 34-K
AA armament:	-	1-45mm/46 21-K
MGs:	4-0.303in Vickers	3-0.5in DShK
Sweeps:	1 MTSh, 1 MZT	
DCTs / DC chutes:	-	•
DCs:	-	• M-1
Mines:	30 M1908	30 M1908
Complement:	29	49

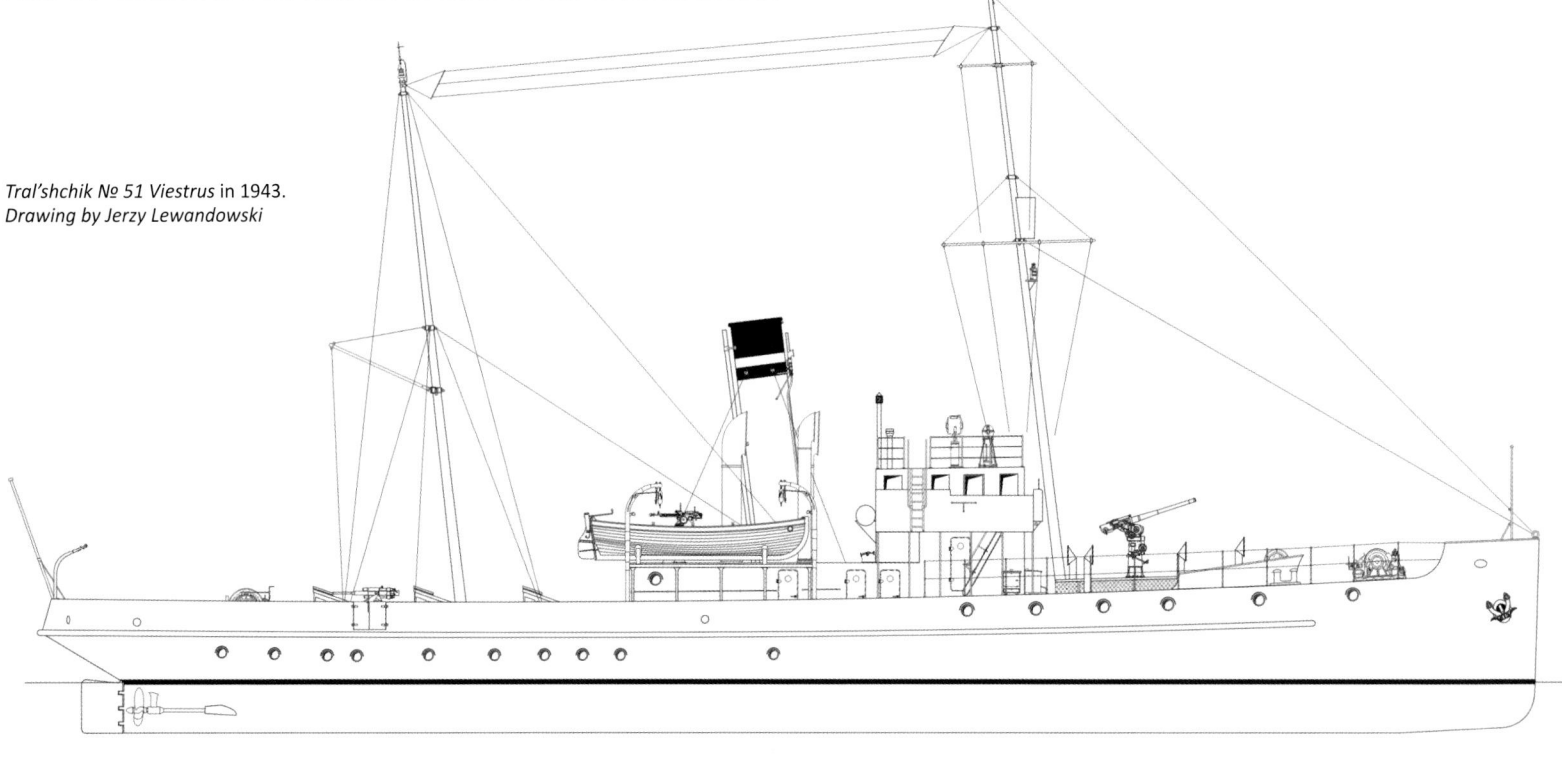

Tral'shchik № 51 Viestrus in 1943. Drawing by Jerzy Lewandowski

Latvian minesweepers, design based on a tug, seized on annexation of Latvia and comm with the Baltic Fleet.

Imanta: seized 13.8.1940, mined north of Saaremaa.

Viesturs: seized 13.8.1940, conv 7.2.1948 to surveying vessel.

No 17.10.1940	TShch № 25.7.1941	TShch № 7.9.1941	No 29.8.1944	Name	Builder	Laid down	Launched	Comp	Comm	Fleet	Fate
T-299				IMANTA ex-*Imanta* (Lat, 1940)	Dubigeon, Nantes	Spr 1926	11.08.1926	1926	13.8.1940	B	Sank 1.7.1941
T-298	№ 57	№ 51	T-298	VIESTURS ex-*Viestrus* (Lat, 1940)	Dubigeon, Nantes	1926	27.05.1926	Aut 1926	13.8.1940	B	Deleted 28.1.1959

19.4.3. SOUTHEAST EUROPE, 1944-1945

German **KFK** types
Inshore minesweepers

Displacement: 103t standard, 110t full load
Dimensions: 23.0 x 6.0 x 1.2m
Machinery: 1-shaft diesel 120hp = 12kts. Oil fuel 6–7t, range 1200nm at 7kts
Armament: 1-37mm, 4-20mm
Complement: 15

No	Builder	YN	Comp	Comm	Fleet	Fate
T-651 ex-*KFK-1* (Ger, 1944) ex-*KFK-38* (Ger, Aug 1944)	Cherson Werft		1943	6.11.1944	BS	Deleted 17.6.1947
T-652 ex-*KFK-2* (Ger, 1944) ex-*KFK-39* (Ger, Aug 1944)	Cherson Werft		1943	6.11.1944	BS	Deleted 17.6.1947
T-653 ex-*KFK-3* (Ger, 1944) ex-*KFK-40* (Ger, Aug 1944)	Cherson Werft		1943	6.11.1944	BS	Deleted 17.6.1947
T-654 ex-*KFK-4* (Ger, 1944) ex-*KFK-41* (Ger, Aug 1944)	Cherson Werft		1943	6.11.1944	BS	Deleted 23.3.1951
T-655 ex-*KFK-5* (Ger, 1944 ex-*KFK-42* (Ger, Aug 1944)	Cherson Werft		1944	6.11.1944	BS	Deleted 10.1.1956
T-666 ex-*MO-851* (1945) ex-*VS-1* (Rom, 1944) ex-*UJ-311* (Ger, Aug 1944) ex-*KFK-198* (Ger, May 1943)	Swinemünde		1943	20.10.1944	BS	Deleted 13.11.1947
T-667 ex-*MO-852* (1945) ex-*VS-2* (Rom, 1944) ex-*UJ-319* (Ger, Aug 1944) ex-*KFK-199* (Ger, May 1943)	Swinemünde		1943	20.10.1944	BS	Deleted 13.11.1947
T-668 ex-*MO-853* (1945) ex-*VS-3* (Rom, 1944) ex-*KFK-201* (Ger, Aug 1944)	Swinemünde		1943	20.10.1944	BS	Conv 12.2.1948 to degaussing station
T-669 ex-*KFK-•* (Ger, 1945)	Varnenska Yd		1944	28.2.1945	BS	Deleted 12.5.1948
T-671 ex-*KFK-574* (Ger, 1945)	Varnenska Yd	19	1945	5.1.1945	BS	Deleted 10.1.1956
T-672 ex-*KFK-575* (Ger, 1945)	Varnenska Yd	20	1945	5.1.1945	BS	Deleted 17.6.1947
T-673 ex-*KFK-576* (Ger, 1945)	Varnenska Yd	21	1945	5.1.1945	BS	Deleted 13.1.1947
T-674 ex-*KFK-577* (Ger, 1945)	Koralovag, Burgas	19	1945	5.1.1945	BS	Deleted 10.1.1956
T-675 ex-*KFK-578* (Ger, 1945)	Koralovag, Burgas	20	1945	5.1.1945	BS	Deleted 17.6.1947
T-676 ex-*KFK-579* (Ger, 1945)	Koralovag, Burgas	21	1945	5.1.1945	BS	Deleted 17.6.1947
T-677 ex-*KFK-580* (Ger, 1945)	Koralovag, Burgas	22	1945	5.1.1945	BS	Deleted 17.6.1947
T-678 ex-*KFK-•* (Ger, 1945)	Varnenska Yd	40	1944	25.6.1945	BS	Deleted 1950s
T-679 ex-*KFK-581* (Ger, 1945)	Varnenska Yd	41	1944	25.6.1945	BS	Deleted 1950s
T-680 ex-*KFK-582* (Ger, 1945)	Varnenska Yd	42	1945	25.6.1945	BS	Deleted 1950s

No	Builder	YN	Comp	Comm	Fleet	Fate
T-685 ex-*KFK-583* (Ger, 1945)	Varnenska Yd	22	1945	24.4.1945	BS	Deleted 20.3.1948
T-686 ex-*KFK-584* (Ger, 1945)	Varnenska Yd	23	1945	20.4.1945	BS	Deleted 20.3.1948
T-687 ex-*KFK-585* (Ger, 1945)	Varnenska Yd	24	1945	20.4.1945	BS	Deleted 28.10.1947
T-688 ex-*KFK-586* (Ger, 1945)	Varnenska Yd	23	1945	20.4.1945	BS	Deleted 17.6.1947
T-689 ex-*KFK-587* (Ger, 1945)	Koralovag, Burgas	24	1945	20.4.1945	BS	Deleted 17.6.1947
T-690 ex-*KFK-?* (Ger, 1945)	Varnenska Yd	25	1944	20.4.1945	BS	Deleted 10.1.1956
T-691 ex-*KFK-588* (Ger, 1945)	Varnenska Yd	26	1944	25.6.1945	BS	Deleted 1950s
T-692 ex-*KFK-589* (Ger, 1945)	Varnenska Yd	27	1945	25.6.1945	BS	Deleted 13.11.1947
T-693 ex-*KFK-590* (Ger, 1945)	Varnenska Yd	28	1945	25.6.1945	BS	Deleted 1950s
T-694 ex-*KFK-591* (Ger, 1945)	Varnenska Yd	29	1945	25.6.1945	BS	Deleted 1950s

German standard armed trawler – *Kriegsfischkutter* – built during the war in various local yards. Wooden hull with steel framing. Apart from the 29 units captured by the Soviets, the Red Navy received 147 boats after the war as its share in the German Navy.

T-651: captured 29.8.1944 at Constanța, comm as minesweeper, rated 5.2.1947 as minesweeping boat *KT-1261*. Decomm and trfd to civilian service as fishing trawler *MRT-1261*.

T-652: captured 29.8.1944 at Constanța, comm as minesweeper, rated 5.2.1947 as minesweeping boat *KT-1262*. Decomm and trfd to civilian service as fishing trawler *MRT-1262*.

T-653: captured 29.8.1944 at Constanța, comm as minesweeper, rated 5.2.1947 as minesweeping boat *KT-1263*. Decomm and trfd to civilian service as fishing trawler *MRT-1232*.

T-654: captured 29.8.1944 at Constanța, comm as minesweeper, rated 5.2.1947 as minesweeping boat *KT-1264*. Decomm detached to civilian service as fishing trawler *MRT-1264*. Deleted from the navy list 23.3.1951, BU.

T-655: captured 29.8.1944 at Constanța, comm as minesweeper rated 5.2.1947 as minesweeping boat *KT-1265*.

T-666: captured 29.8.1944 at Constanța, comm as small submarine hunter *MO-851*, conv 27.1.1945 to minesweeper, rated 5.2.1947 as minesweeping boat *KT-1266*. Decomm and trfd to civilian service as fishing trawler *MRT-1266*, renamed 6.12.1948 *Vladimir Vorob'ev*.

T-667: captured 29.8.1944 at Constanța, comm as small submarine hunter *MO-852*, conv 27.1.1945 to minesweeper, rated 5.2.1947 as minesweeping boat *KT-1267*. Decomm and trfd to civilian service as fishing trawler *MRT-1267*.

T-668: captured 29.8.1944 at Constanța, comm as small submarine hunter *MO-853*, conv 27.1.1945 to minesweeper, rated 5.2.1947 as minesweeping boat *KT-1268*. Conv 12.2.1948 to degaussing station.

T-669: sunk Aug 1944 by Soviet aircraft at Varna, raised by the Soviets 1944, comm as minesweeper, rated 5.2.1947 as minesweeping boat *KT-1269*. Decomm and trfd to civilian service as fishing trawler *MRT-1269*, renumbered *ChMT-236* on 3.12.1948, named *Otvazhnyj*.

T-671: captured 9.9.1944 on slipway at Varna, comm as minesweeper, rated 5.2.1947 as minesweeping boat *KT-1270*.

T-672: captured on slipway at Varna, comm as minesweeper, rated 5.2.1947 as minesweeping boat *KT-1271*. Decomm and trfd to civilian service as fishing trawler *MRT-1271*.

T-673: captured 9.9.1944 on slipway at Varna, comm as minesweeper, rated 5.2.1947 as minesweeping boat *KT-1272*. Decomm and trfd to civilian service as fishing trawler *MRT-1272*.

T-674: captured 9.9.1944 on slipway at Burgas, comm as minesweeper, rated 5.2.1947 as minesweeping boat *KT-1273*. Conv 20.3.1948 to salvage service craft.

T-675: captured 9.9.1944 on slipway at Burgas, comm as minesweeper, rated 5.2.1947 as minesweeping boat *KT-1274*. Decomm and trfd to civilian service as fishing trawler *MRT-1274*.

T-676: captured 9.9.1944 on slipway at Burgas, comm as minesweeper, rated 5.2.1947 as minesweeping boat *KT-1275*. Decomm and trfd to civilian service as fishing trawler *MRT-1275*.

T-677: captured 9.9.1944 on slipway at Varna, comm as minesweeper, rated 5.2.1947 as minesweeping boat *KT-1276*. Decomm and trfd to civilian service as fishing trawler *MRT-1276*.

T-678: sunk August 1944 by Soviet aircraft at Varna, raised by the Soviets 1944, comm as minesweeper. Conv 26.9.1945 to service craft *RK № 232*.

T-679: sunk August 1944 by Soviet aircraft at Varna, raised by the Soviets 1944, comm as minesweeper. Conv 26.9.1945 to surveying boat *GK-32*, rated 16.5.1949 as inshore craft *RBZ-119*.

T-680: sunk August 1944 by Soviet aircraft at Varna, raised by the Soviets 1944, comm as minesweeper. Conv 26.9.1945 to surveying boat *GK-33*, rated 16.5.1949 as inshore craft *RBZ-120*.

T-685: captured 9.9.1944 on slipway at Varna, comm as minesweeper, rated 5.2.1947 as minesweeping boat *KT-1277*. Decomm and trfd to civilian service as fishing trawler *MRT-1277*, renamed 3.12.1948 *Dnestrovodets*.

T-686: captured 9.9.1944 on slipway at Varna, comm as minesweeper, rated 5.2.1947 as minesweeping boat *KT-1278*. Decomm and trfd to civilian service as fishing trawler *MRT-1278*, renamed 3.12.1948 *Dunaets*.

T-687: captured 9.9.1944 on slipway at Varna, comm as minesweeper, rated 5.2.1947 as minesweeping boat *KT-1279*. Decomm and trfd to civilian service as fishing trawler *MRT-1279*.

T-688: captured 9.9.1944 on slipway at Burgas, comm as minesweeper, rated 5.2.1947 as minesweeping boat *KT-1280*. Decomm and trfd to civilian service as fishing trawler *MRT-1280*.

T-689: captured 9.9.1944 on slipway at Burgas, comm as minesweeper, rated 5.2.1947 as minesweeping boat *KT-1281*. Decomm and trfd to civilian service as fishing trawler *MRT-1281*.

T-690: sunk August 1944 by Soviet aircraft at Varna, raised by the Soviets 1944, comm as minesweeper detached to the salvage service. Rated 5.2.1947 as minesweeping boat *KT-1282* but remained in salvage service.

T-691: sunk August 1944 by Soviet aircraft at Varna, raised by the Soviets 1944, comm as minesweeper, rated 5.2.1947 as minesweeping boat *KT-1283*. Conv 14.6.1947 to degaussing station *SBR-30*, renumbered *SBR-22* on 16.5.1949.

T-692: captured 9.9.1944 on slipway at Varna, comm as minesweeper, rated 5.2.1947 as minesweeping boat *KT-1284*. Decomm and trfd to civilian service as fishing trawler *MRT-1284*.

T-693: captured 9.9.1944 on slipway at Varna, comm as minesweeper, rated 5.2.1947 as minesweeping boat *KT-1285*. Conv 12.2.1948 to degaussing station.

T-694: captured 9.9.1944 on slipway at Varna, comm as minesweeper, rated 5.2.1947 as minesweeping boat *KT-1286*. Conv 12.2.1948 to degaussing station.

19.5. Conversions

19.5.1. Mobilised trawlers

Initially, the World War 1 vintage mobilisation trawlers were converted, as well as one newly built (*Rolik*), to gain some experience. They were armed with the available 4in/60 and 0.3in Maxim MGs, but after 45mm/46 21-K and 3in/55 34-K guns entered production, the mobilisation conversion project was adapted to mount the new weaponry. The minesweeper conversion project - designated *Project 33* - provided for the installation of two 45mm guns (one each on forecastle deck and poop), and two single 0.3in MGs on M-1 type mountings on the wheelhouse deck. To clear the firing arcs of the aft 45mm gun, the boat davits were moved to amidships. Trawlers were already fitted with a trawl hoist, so the only thing required was to equip them with MTSh and MZT sweeps.

During the war, the armament was increased by replacing 45mm/46 guns with 3in/55 ones, installing 20mm Oerlikons and replacing Maxim MGs with 0.5in DShK ones. Some were given acoustic trawls and DC rails.

Nalim class	*Steam trawlers*
Displacement:	500t normal, 613t full load
Dimensions:	46.0 x 7.4 x 4.1m
Machinery:	1-shaft VTE, Scotch boiler (10kG/cm²), 600hp = 11kts. Coal 105t, range 3000nm at 8kts
Armament:	2-45mm/46 21-K (1 replaced 1943/5 by 37mm/67.5 70-K), 8-0.3in Maxim MGs (2x4) (replaced 1943/5 by 2-0.5in DShL MGs), 18 M-1 DCs, 1 MTSh sweep, 2 MZT sweeps, 10–15 KS-39 spar buoys
Complement:	44

T-890 with the 1939 style pennant number. Przemysław Budzbon Collection

Pt-No 12.6.1941	No on Comm	No 23.11.1939	Name	Built	Comm	Type	Fleet	Remarks
			Builder: Smith's Dock					
17	T-33	T-891	FOREL' ex-*Plamia* (1924) ex-*Altair* (Fin, 1922 ex-*Plamia* (Rus, 1918)	1913	1933	Minesweeper	N	Decomm 17.4.1947
18	T-31	T-890	NALIM ex-*Patron* (1923)	1913	1933	Minesweeper	N	Sunk 9.7.1941

Purchased 1913 for the Siberian Flotilla as harbour vessels but remained in the Baltic. Conv 1914 to minesweepers, comm 1915 with the Baltic Fleet, 1918 rated as escort ships.

Forel': interned 1918 in Finland, comm with the Finnish Navy. Returned 1922, trfd to the OGPU Border Guard, decomm 1924 to civilian service, trfd to the Arctic. Mobilised 9.8.1933, conv to minesweeper. Decomm to the civilian service.

Nalim: decomm 1921 to civilian service, trfd to the Arctic. Mobilised 9.8.1933, conv to minesweeper.
Sunk by aircraft in Zapadnaia Litsa bay, north of Murmansk.

Feliks Dzerzhinskij type

Steam trawlers

Displacement: 1306t
Dimensions: *Series 1:* 48.3 x 7.65 x 4.95m
Series 2: 51.1 x 9.0 x 4.8m
Machinery: 1-shaft VTE, 1 boiler, *Series 1:* 550hp, *Series 2:* 700hp = 9kts. Coal fuel, range 3800nm at 7kts
Armament: *Series 1:* not armed
Series 2: № 11: 1-4in/60, 3-0.3in MGs, 1 MTSh sweep, 1 MZT sweep, 1 KAT sweep, 70 mines;
№ 17: 1-3in/30 Lender, 1 MTSh sweep, 1 MZT sweep, 40 mines
Complement: about 50

Plastun in surveying service in the 1950s.
Boris Lemachko Collection

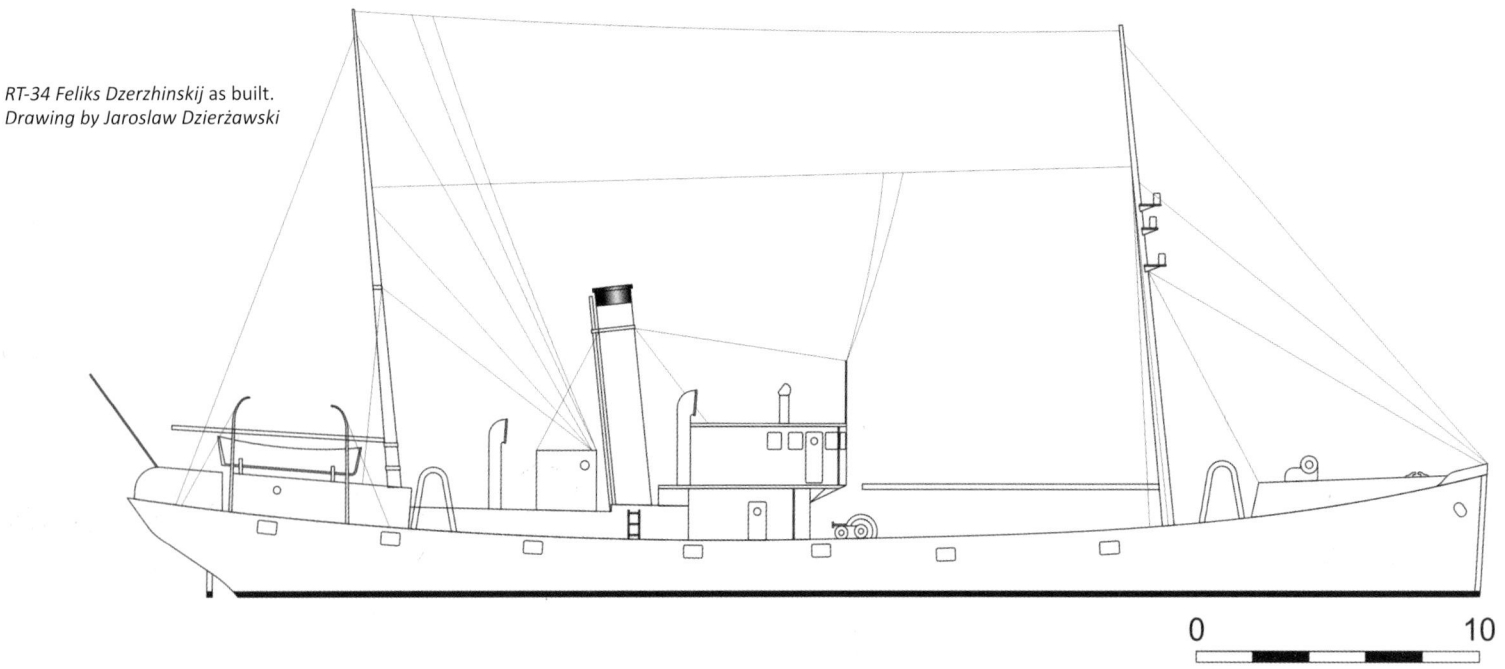

RT-34 Feliks Dzerzhinskij as built.
Drawing by Jaroslaw Dzierżawski

TShch № on Comm	No 13.9.1944	FN	Name	YN	Built	Comm	Type	Fleet	Remarks
			Series 1						
			Builder: Seebeckwerft						
		RT-34	FELIKS DZERZHINSKIJ	463	1927	10.11.1941	Heater	N	Mobilised 1941. Decomm 17.3.1942 to civilian service. Discarded 1960s
			Series 2						
			Builder: Weser Seebeck						
№ 11	T-11		PLASTUN	508	1931	1.5.1934	Minesweeper Cable layer	P	Mobilised 2.12.1933, conv to minesweeper. Conv 18.4.1945 to cable layer. Deleted 1960s
№ 17	T-17		TEREK		1931	1938	Minesweeper	P	Mobilised 3.9.1938, conv to minesweeper. Employed as transport May 1939–Aug 1940 during Khalkhin-Gol battles. Deleted 1960s

RT-406 Lebed' (P) and *Toporok* (P) of this type in civilian service during the war.

19.0 Minesweepers

Arkhangel'sk type
Steam trawlers

Displacement: 1100t
Dimensions: 48.2 x 8.5 x 4.4m
Machinery: 1-shaft VTE, 1 boiler, 650hp = 9.5kts. Coal fuel, range 4100nm
Armament: 2-45mm/46 21-K (1943 replaced by 2-3in/55 34-K), (1943 added 2-20mm Oerlikon), 2-0.3in MGs, 2 DC racks, 18DCs, 1 MTSh sweep, 2 MZT
Complement: 43

Pt-No	No on Comm 1941	FN	Name	YN	Built	Comm	Type	Fleet	Remarks
			Builder: Wollheim						
55	T-901	RT-20	ARKHANGEL'SK	725	1928	29.11.1941	Minesweeper	Wh	Mobilised 13.8.1941. Decomm 18.3.1945 to civilian service. Discarded 29.5.1959

RT-22 Murmansk (N) of this type in civilian service during the war.

Maksim Gor'kij type
Steam trawlers

Displacement: 1107t
Dimensions: 49.3 x 8.5 x 4.8m
Machinery: 1-shaft VTE, 1 boiler, 675hp = 9kts. Coal fuel, range 8500nm at 7kts
Armament: *№ 14*: 1-4in/60, 2-45mm/46 21-K, 5-0.3in MGs, 1 MTSh sweep, 1 MZT sweep, 1 KAT sweep, 40 mines
T-908: 2-45mm/46 21-K, (1943 added 2-20mm Oerlikon), 2-0.3in MGs, 1 MTSh sweep, 2 MZT sweeps, 1 AT sweep
T-909: 2-45mm/46 21-K (1943 replaced by 2-3in/55 34-K, 2-20mm Oerlikon), 1-0.3in MG, 1 MTSh sweep, 2 MZT sweeps, 1 AT sweep
Complement: 58

Dal'nevostochnik during the handing-over ceremony. Note the crowd ashore. At that time the Soviet Union enjoyed a positive image in much of Western European society.
Boris Lemachko Collection

Pt-No	TShch № on Comm	No on Comm	No 13.9.1944	FN	Name	YN	Built	Comm	Type	Fleet	Remarks
					Builder: Union Giesserei						
	№ 14		T-14		BAKLAN		1930	7.6.1934	Minesweeper	P	Mobilised 14.12.1934. Employed Aug 1939 as transport during the Khasan Lake battles. Deleted 1960s
62		T-908		RT-41	M. GOR'KIJ ex-*Maksim Gor'kij* (1941)	245	1928	5.10.1941	Minesweeper	Wh	Mobilised 26.8.1941. Decomm 18.3.1945 to civilian service. Discarded by 1965
63		T-909		RT-36	BOL'SHEVIK	249	1929	20.5.1942	Minesweeper	Wh	Mobilised 20.9.1941. Decomm 28.2.1945 to civilian service, stranded 18.2.1961, total loss

Dal'nevostochnik (P) of this type in civilian service during the war.

Gagara type
Steam trawlers

Displacement:	1250t
Dimensions:	54.8 x 9.0 x 4.4m
Machinery:	1-shaft VTE, 1 boiler, 770hp = 10kts. Coal fuel, range 8500 nm
Armament:	№ 13: 1-4in/60, 5-0.3in MGs, 1 MTSh sweep, 1 MZT sweep, 1 KAT sweep, 50 mines
	№ 16: 1-3in/30 Lender, 1 MTSh sweep, 1 MZT sweep, 1 KAT sweep, 40 mines
Complement:	№ 13: 58

Gagra during launching. Przemysław Budzbon Collection

TShch № on Comm	No 13.9.1944	FN	Name	YN	Built	Comm	Type	Fleet	Remarks
			Builder: Tirreno						
№ 13	T-13	RT-4	GAGARA	112	1931	6.8.1934	Minesweeper	P	Mobilised 14.2.1934. Employed Aug 1939 as transport during Khasan Lake battles. Deleted 1960s
№ 16	T-16		SOKOL		1931	1938	Minesweeper	P	Mobilised 3.9.1938. Employed May 1939-Aug battles. Discarded 1960s

Paltus (P) of this type in civilian service during the war.

Rolik type
Steam trawlers

Displacement:	1150t (*T-879:* 1036t, *RT-12:* 1218t)
Dimensions:	51.1 x 9.05 x 4.5m
Machinery:	1-shaft VTE, 1 water tube boiler, 675hp = 10kts. Coal 270t, range 4300 nm
Armament:	*DK-10:* 2-45mm/46 21-K, 2-0.3in MGs, 2 DC racks, 18 DCs
	RT-12: not armed.
	T-879: 2-45mm/46 21-K, 2-0.3in MGs (1943 added 2-20mm Oerlikon, 2-0.3in MGs,) 1 MTSh sweep, 2 MZT sweeps, 1 KAT sweep, (added 1943 1 BAT-2 sweep)
	T-880: 2-45mm/46 21-K, 2-0.303in MGs, 1 MTSh sweep, 2 MZT sweeps
Complement:	43; *T-880:* 45

Rolik on delivery. Boris Lemachko Collection

19.0 Minesweepers

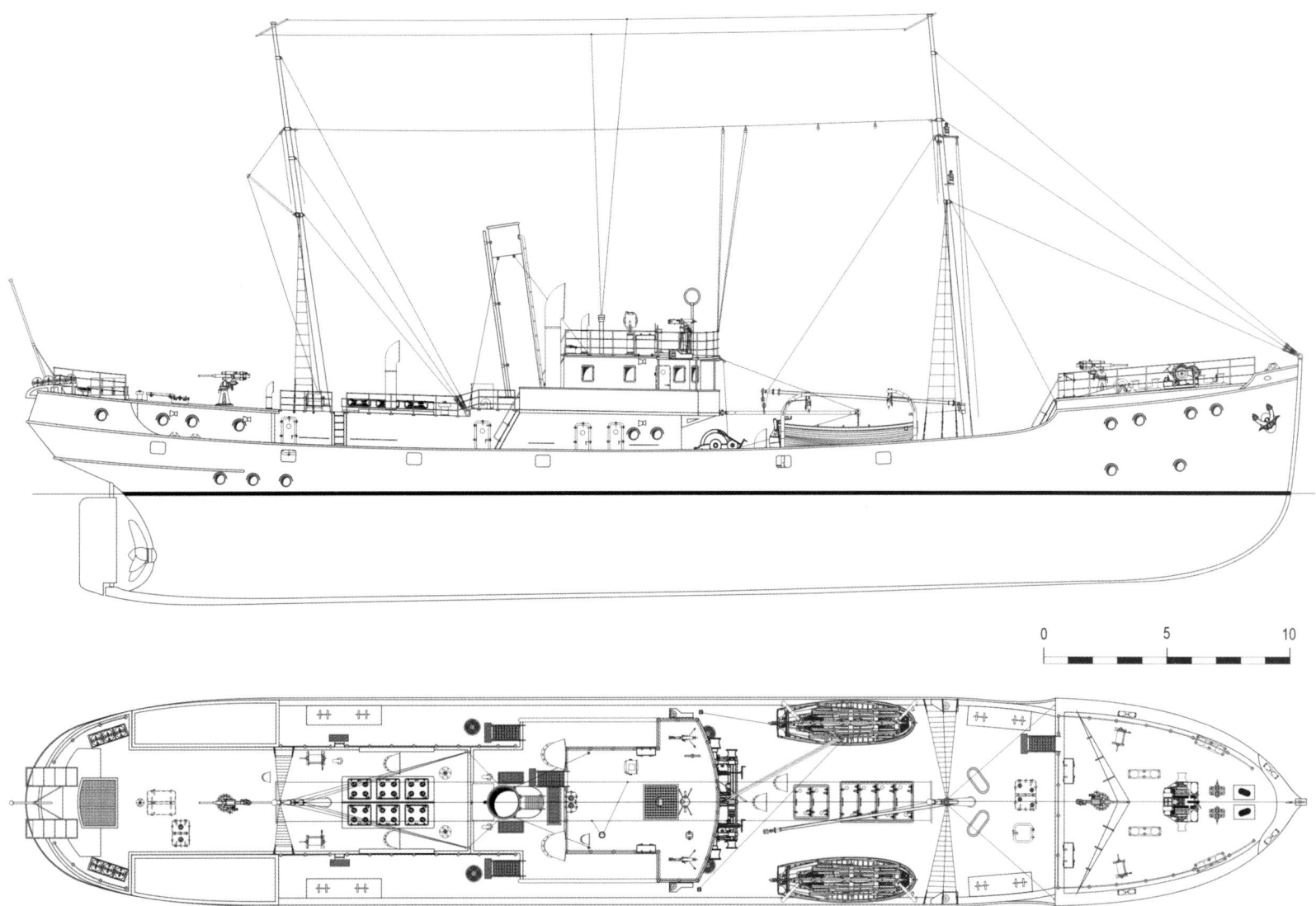

Tuman in the patrol ship configuration.
Drawing by Jerzy Lewandowski

Pt-No 1941	No on Comm	FN	Name	YN	Built	Comm	Type	Fleet	Remarks
			Builder: Klawitter						
12	DK-10	RT-10	LEBEDKA	449	1930	1939	Escort ship	N	Mobilised 19.12.1939, conv to escort ship. Renamed *Tuman* 4.3.1940, sunk by gunfire from German destroyers off Kildin Island 10.8.1941
		RT-12	TRAL	451	1930	10.11.1941	Heater Degaussing station	N	Mobilised 1941, conv 6.6.1943 to degaussing station *SBR-5*, decom 1945 to civilian service. Discarded 1960
54	T-879	RT-9	ROLIK	448	1930	1933	Minesweeper	N	Mobilised 1933, conv to minesweeper. Decomm 1934/5? to civilian service. Mobilised 14.7.1941, conv to minesweeper. Decomm 18.3.1945 to civilian service. Discarded mid-1960s
53	T-880	RT-11	VAER	450	1931	26.8.1941	Minesweeper	N	Mobilised 14.7.1941. Decomm 9.5.1945 to civilian service. Discarded 1967

Rolik was converted to a minesweeper as the prototype and test of mobilisation plans for the newly built trawlers. The conversion project designated *Project 33* was to be applied for all minesweeper conversions. A similar scheme, based on the same principles, was apparently prepared for the escort ship conversions.

Krasnoarmeets type
Steam trawlers

Displacement: 1150t
Dimensions: 51.15 x 9.05 x 4.3m
Machinery: 1-shaft VTE, 1 water tube boiler, 700hp = 10.5kts. Coal 286t, range 4100nm at 9kts
Armament: *BS-1:* 1- or 2-45mm/46 21-K
T-886: 2-3in/55 34-K, (1943 added 2-20mm Oerlikon), 2-0.3in MGs, 1 MTSh sweep, 1 MZT sweep
T-889: 2-3in/55 34-K, 2-0.3in MGs, 1 MTSh sweep, 1 MZT sweep
T-907: 2-45mm/46 21-K (replaced 1943 by 2-3in/55 34-K), 2-20mm Oerlikon, 2-0.3in MGs, 1 MTSh sweep, 2 MZT sweep
Complement: 43 (*T-886:* 52)

Pt-No 1941	No on Comm	FN	Name	YN	Built	Comm	Type	Fleet	Remarks
			Builder: Nordseewerke						
	BS-1	RT-13	MIKOIAN	166	1930	1941	Guardship Heater	N	Mobilised 29.7.1941, conv to guardship. Conv 20.9.1942 to heater, name reverted, decomm 1945 to civilian service. Renamed 1950s *Olenegorsk*. Discarded early 1960s
31	T-886	RT-15	ZASOL'SHCHIK	163	1930	29.7.1941	Minesweeper	N Wh	Mobilised 25.6.1941. Trfd 13.8.1941 to the White Sea Flotilla, sunk by German aircraft off Toros Island 9.5.1944
34	T-889	RT-3	KRASNOARMEETS	162	1930	29.7.1941	Minesweeper	N Wh	Mobilised 25.6.1941. Trfd 13.8.1941 to the White Sea Flotilla. Sunk 15.11.1941 by *U-752* near Ludki Island, Barents Sea
61	T-907	RT-21	TRALMEJSTER	164	1930	29.9.1941	Minesweeper	Wh	Mobilised 15.8.1941. Decomm after the war to civilian service

RT-14 Stalin (N) and *RT-23 Chajka* (N) of this type in civilian service during the war.

Lenin type
Steam trawlers

Displacement: *Series 1:* 1100t; *Series 2:* 1450t (*T-888:* 1416t)
Dimensions: *Series 1:* 51.2 x 9.05 x 4.4m; *Series 2:* 51.25 x 9.05 x 4.5m
Machinery: 1-shaft Lentz compound, 1 boiler 600hp (*Series 2:* 675hp) = 11kts. Coal 250t (*Series 2:* 260t). Range 3500–5000nm at 8kts
Armament: *T-885:* 2-3in/55 34-K, 3-0.3in MGs, 1 MTSh sweep, 1 MZT sweep
T-902: 2-45mm/46 21-K (1943 replaced by 2-3in/55 34-K, 2-20mm Oerlikon), 2-0.3in MGs, 1 MTSh sweep, 2 MZT sweeps
DK-5: 2-45mm/46 21-K, 2-0.3in Maxim MGs
Syomga: not armed
T-888: 2-3in/55 34-K, (1943 added 1-37mm/67.5 70-K, 1-20mm Oerlikon), 2-0.5in DShK MGs, 1 MTSh sweep, 1 MZT sweep
Complement: 54 (*T-888:* 52, *T-902:* 43)

Pt-No 1941	No on Comm	FN	Name	YN	Built	Comm	Type	Fleet	Remarks
			Builder: Schichau						
	MIP-2		**Series 1** FINVAL ex-*Bliukher* (1938) ex-*Stalin* (1930)	1217	1930	9.8.1945~	Experimental vessel	P	Decomm after the war. Discarded 1960
39	T-885	RT-16	LENIN	1213	1930	29.7.1941	Minesweeper	N	Mobilised 25.6.1941. Decomm after the war to civilian service. Discarded 1964
56	T-902	RT-18	PROFINTERN	1214	1930	20.9.1941	Minesweeper	N	Mobilised 13.8.1941. Decomm. 1.2.1943 to civilian service, renamed *I. Sivkov* after the war. Discarded 1960
14	DK-5	RT-5	**Series 2** KRAB	1249	1932	1939	Escort ship	N	Mobilised 2.12.1939, renamed 4.2.1940 *Priliv*, sunk by German aircraft in Kildin Strait 3.8.1943
		RT-7	SYOMGA	1251	1931	31.12.1942	Heater	N	Mobilised 1942, conv to heater. Damaged by German aircraft at Murmansk 5.04.1942, repaired. Decomm after the war to civilian service. Discarded 1967
33	T-888	RT-6	KIT	1250	1931	29.7.1941	Minesweeper	N	Decomm 1945. Discarded early 1960s

Series 1: RT-17 KIM, RT-19 Komintern), Burevestnik and *Series 2: RT-1 Akula, RT-2 Ersh, RT-3 Kasatka, RT-4 Navaga, RT-8 Sel'd'* (sunk 27.8.1941 by *U-752*) in civilian service during the war.

Dnepr type
Steam trawlers

Displacement: 1150t
Dimensions: 57.1 x 9.0 x 4.5m
Machinery: 1-shaft VTE,1 boiler, 650hp = 11kts. Coal 220t, range 5190nm.
Armament: *BS-2:* 2-45mm/46 21-K, 2-0.3in Maxim MGs, 2 DC rails
T-884: 2-3in/55 34-K, (added 1944: 1-37mm/67.5 70-K, 1-20mm Oerlikon, 2-0.5in DShK MGs), 2-0.3in Maxim MGs, 1 MTSh sweep, 1 MZT sweep, (added 1944: 2 DCTs)
Complement: *BS-2*: 34, *T-884*: 52

Pt-No 1941	No on Comm	FN	Name	YN	Built	Comm	Type	Fleet	Remarks
			Builder: Frerix						
	BS-2	RT-43	RYBETS	557	1931	July 1941	Guardship Escort ship	N	Mobilised 29.7.1941, conv to guardship. Conv 1.9.1942 to escort ship *SKR-31*, sunk 12.5.1943 by German aircraft in Barents Sea north of Murmansk
38	T-884	RT-29	KIROV ex-*Dnepr* (1932)	556	1932	29.7.1941	Minesweeper	N	Mobilised 1941. Decomm after the war to civilian service, name reverted. Discarded 1960

Neva type
Steam trawlers

Displacement: 1140t
Dimensions: 51.1 x 9.0 x 4.5m
Machinery: 1-shaft VTE, 1 boiler, 690hp = 10kts. Coal fuel, range 4000nm
Armament: *SKR-61:* 2-45mm/46 21-K, (added 1943: 3-20mm Oerlikon), 2-0.3in Maxim MGs, 1 MTSh sweep, 2 MZT sweeps, (added 1943: 1-AT sweep)
T-883: 2-3in/55 34-K, (added 1943: 2-20mm Oerlikon), 2-0.3in MGs, 1 MTSh sweep, 2 MZT sweeps, 1 KAT sweep, (added 1943: 1 AT sweep)
T-887: 2-3in/55 34-K, (added 1943: 1-37mm/67.5 70-K, 1-20mm Oerlikon, 2-0.5in DShK MGs), 2-0.3in Maxim MGs, 1 MTSh sweep, 1 MZT sweep, 1 KAT sweep, (added 1943: 1 AT sweep)
Complement: 43; *T-883*: 49; *T-887*: 52

Dvina during launching.
Boris Lemachko Collection

Pt-No 1941	No on Comm	FN	Name	YN	Built	Comm	Type	Fleet	Remarks
			Builder: Neptun						
5359[1]	SKR-61 T-905[1]	RT-44	NEVA	428	1931	July 1941	Escort ship Minesweeper	N Wh	Mobilised 4.7.1941, conv to escort ship. Trfd 13.8.1941 to the White Sea Flotilla. Decomm 18.3.1945 to civilian service. Discarded early 1960s
37	T-883	RT-45	DVINA	429	1931	29.7.1941	Minesweeper	N Wh	Mobilised 25.6.1941, conv to minesweeper, trfd 13.8.1941 to the White Sea Flotilla. Sunk 29.12.1944 by *U-995* SW off Cape Svyatoy Nos
32	T-887	RT-46	LOSOS'	430	1931	19.7.1941	Minesweeper	N Wh	Mobilised 25.6.1941, conv to minesweeper, trfd 13.8.1941 to the White Sea Flotilla. Decomm after the war to civilian service. Discarded 1966

Exceptions noted in the main table.

No	Year	Date
1	1941	20.9.1941

Gaga type *Steam trawlers*

Displacement: 1250t
Dimensions: 54.8 x 9.4 x 5.0m
Machinery: 1-shaft VTE, 1 boiler, 650hp = 8.5kts. Coal fuel, range 2850nm
Armament: № 12: 1-4in/60, 2-45mm/46 21-K, 5-0.3in Maxim MGs (1x4, 1x1), 1 MTSh sweep, 1 MZT sweep, 50 mines
T-906: 2-45mm/46 21-K, 2-0.3in Maxim MGs, 1 MTSh sweep, 1 MZT sweep
Complement: № 12: 59; T-906: 43

Tral'shchik № 12 Ara in the mid-1930s.
Przemysław Budzbon Collection

Pt-No 1941	No on Comm	No 13.9.1944	FN	Name	YN	Built	Comm	Type	Fleet	Remarks
				Builder: Breda						
	№ 12	T-12		ARA		1933	18.8.1934	Minesweeper	P	Mobilised 1.12.1933. Deleted 1960s
60	T-906		RT-410	PELIKAN	33	1932	1.9.1941	Minesweeper	Wh	Mobilised 13.8.1941. Decomm after the war to civilian service

R-407 Gaga and *RT-409 Nyrok* of this type in civilian service during the war.

19.5.2. MOBILISED TUGS

19.5.2.1. SEAGOING AND COASTAL TUGS

Severoles type (*Project 129*) *Steam tugs*

Displacement: 104t light, 145t full load
Tonnage: 77grt
Dimensions: 24.5 oa, 22.9 pp x 5.5 x 1.6m moulded, 1.8m max
Machinery: 1-shaft, VTE 180–240hp = 9.4kts. Coal 20t. Bollard pull 1.57T for 180hp boats, 1.94T for 200hp boats.
Armament: minesweepers: 1-45mm/46 21-K, 2-0.3in Maxim MGs (replaced by 0.5in DShK later during the war), 1 MTSh sweep, 1 MZT sweep
escort ships: 1-45mm/46 21-K, 2-0.3in Maxim MGs
gunboats: *Izhorets № 9*: 1-45mm M1937 field gun, 1-85mm mortar, 6-0.3in Maxim MGs (1x4, 2x1); *KL-13*: 1-45mm/46 21-K, 1-37mm/67.5 70-K
Complement: 12 men (peacetime tug), 22 (gunboat), 31 (minesweeper)

Severoles type tug mobilised as minesweeper in 1939.
Boris Lemachko Collection

19.0 Minesweepers

TShch № 1939	TShch № 22.6.1941	TShch № 25.7.1941	TShch № 7.9.1941	No 11.10.1944	No/Name	YN	Built	Comm	Type	Fleet	Remarks
					Builder: 370, Leningrad (Petrozavod)						
					Series 1 BP-1 ex-*Iakov Vorob'yov* (1941) ex-*BP № 1* (1940)	1	1933	15.9.1941	Tug	N On	Built for civilian service, mobilised 1941. Numbered *A-32* from 30.6.1943. Decomm after the war to civilian service, renamed *BO-19-S* in 1956. Discarded 1961
			T-621[7] B-36[8]		BP № 2 (1943)	2	1933	24.6.1943	Mine-sweeping tug Tug	Vo	Built for civilian service, mobilised 12.5.1943, conv to tug for minesweeping rafts, reverted 22.6.1944 to tug. Decomm 1.7.1945, to civilian service, renamed *Kingisepp*. Discarded 1960
					IZHORETS-3 ex-*BP № 3* (1942)	3	1933	25.6.1941 31.6.1942	Tug	B	Built for civilian service, mobilised 25.6.1941, reverted 30.10.1941 to civilian service. Mobilised 1942, decomm 9.8.1946 to civilian service. Discarded 1960
					BP № 5	5	1934	-	Tug	B	Built for civilian service, included in the 1941 Mobilisation Plan but not actually comm. Renamed *Osinovets* after the war. Discarded 1960
					Series 2 KP-42 ex-*BP № 6* (1941)	6	1934	25.6.1941	Tug	B	Built for civilian service, mobilised 1941. Probably sunk, raised and recomm 13.6.1942. Decomm 15.5.1944 to civilian service, renamed *Chudovo*. Discarded 1960
					IZHORETS № 8 (?) ex-*BP № 8* (1941)	8	1934	25.6.1941	Tug	B La	Built for civilian service, mobilised 1941, trfd to the Ladoga Flotilla. Decomm 1.7.1945 to civilian service, renamed *Karedzhi* in 1962, preserved 1976 as *Izhorets-8*. Not listed in the *Register No 19*
					IZHORETS № 9 ex-*BP № 9* (1941)	9	1934	28.8.1941	Gunboat Tug	Im La	Built for civilian service, mobilised 25.6.1941, conv to gunboat. Disarmed 19.10.1941 reverted to tug, trfd to the Ladoga Flotilla. Sank 20.11.1941 crushed by ice
					Series 3 LF-150 ex-*BP № 11* (1941)	11	1934	5.8.1941	Tug	B	Built for civilian service, mobilised 1941 as replacement for *BP № 19*. Decomm 3.5.1945 to civilian service, name reverted. Fate after 1947 unknown. Not listed in the *Register No 19*
№ 101	№ 93	№ 41			LENVODPUT' № 12	12	1934	29.10.1939 28.6.1941	Minesweeper	B	Built for civilian service, mobilised 1939, conv to minesweeper. Decomm 12.12.1940 to civilian service. Mobilised June 1941, conv to minesweeper. Sunk 13.8.1941 by a German MTB north of Cape Juminda
№ 102	№ 94	№ 42			LENVODPUT' № 13	13	1934	29.10.1939 28.6.1941	Minesweeper	B	Built for civilian service, mobilised 1939, conv to minesweeper. Decomm 12.12.1940 to civilian service. Mobilised June 1941, conv to minesweeper. Sunk 28.8.1941 by mine off Cape Juminda
					BPL-1	14	1933	1934	Tug	B	Built for naval service. Deleted 6.8.1942. Presumably lost
№ 103					LENVODPUT' № 15	15	1934	29.10.1939	Minesweeper	B	Built for civilian service, mobilised 1939 conv to minesweeper. Deleted 28.12.1939, lost?
№ 104					*Series 4* LENVODPUT' № 16	16	1934	29.10.1939	Minesweeper	B	Built for civilian service, mobilised 1939 conv to minesweeper. Deleted 28.12.1939, lost?

TShch № 1939	TShch № 22.6.1941	TShch № 25.7.1941	TShch № 7.9.1941	No 11.10.1944	No/Name	YN	Built	Comm	Type	Fleet	Remarks
	№ 95	№ 43	№ 52	T-52	LENVODPUT' № 17	17	1934	25.7.1941	Minesweeper	B	Built for civilian service, mobilised 30.6.1941. Detached to the Ladoga Flotilla during 24.4.1944 to 3.7.1944. Decomm after the war, to civilian service, renamed *BP № 17*
					KL-13 ex-*BP № 18* (1941)	18	1935	9.9.1941	Gunboat	On Vo	Built for civilian service, mobilised 7.8.1941, conv to gunboat. Trfd 28.11.1941 to the Volga Flotilla, returned 25.5.1942. Lost 31.7.1942 in a gale
	№ 76	№ 94	№ 59[5]	T-59[9]	BP № 20	20	1935	16.6.1941 19.12.1941	Minesweeper	B	Built for civilian service, mobilised 13.5.1941. Decomm 10.9.1941 to civilian service, renamed *Izhorets-20*. Mobilised Dec 1941, reverted to minesweeper. Decomm late in 1945 to civilian service. Discarded 1970
					BPL-36	36	1936	1936	Tug	B	Built for naval service
					Series 6 CHAPAEV	49	1936	30.6.1941	Escort ship	B	Built for civilian service, mobilised 25.6.1941, conv to escort ship. Laid up 8.8.1942, decomm 1946 to civilian service. Fate after 1965 unknown.
					SHCHORS	51	1936	30.6.1941	Escort ship	B	Built for civilian service, mobilised 25.6.1941, conv to escort ship. Mined 29.8.1941 off Lavansaari Island
					KP-52 (?)	52	1936	1936	Tug	B	Built for naval service. Lost during the war in the eastern part of the Gulf of Finland
	№ 128		№ 67		BP № 53	53	1936	13.7.1941	Minesweeper	B	Built for civilian service, mobilised 7.7.1941. Reverted 25.7.1941 to tug, renamed *Izhorets-53*. Reverted 7.9.1941 to minesweeper. Sunk 30.11.1941 by German aircraft in the Gulf of Finland
	№ 81			T-81[12]	*Series 7* BP № 81	81	1936*	7.7.1941	Minesweeper	B La B	Built for civilian service, mobilised 23.6.1941. Trfd 13.7.1941 to the Ladoga Flotilla, reverted 30.10.1941 to tug. Trfd 18.10.1944 to the Baltic Fleet, reverted to minesweeper. Decomm after Sept 1945 to civilian service. Fate after 1958 unknown
	№ 79		№ 82[2]	T-82[12]	BP № 82	82	1937*	22.6.1941	Minesweeper	La B	Built for civilian service, mobilised 9.6.1941. Reverted 30.10.1941 to tug. Trfd 18.10.1944 to the Baltic Fleet, reverted to minesweeper. Sunk 15.9.1944 by German aircraft off Ust-Dvinsk
	№ 77	№ 89			BP № 83	83	1937*	22.6.1941	Minesweeper	B	Built for civilian service, mobilised 9.6.1941. Fled to Sweden in Sept 1941, interned. Returned 1945 to civilian service. Fate after 1960 unknown
	№ 176		№ 176[6]	T-176[12]	BP № 85	85	1936*	19.8.1941	Minesweeper	B La B	Built for Baltekhflot of NKVD. Mobilised 6.8.1941, conv to minesweeper. Reverted 13.12.1941 to tug renamed *KP-19*. Trfd 3.4.1942 to the Ladoga Flotilla, conv to minesweeper. Returned to the Baltic Fleet 18.10.1944. Decomm 8.4.1945 to civilian service, renamed *Bager*. Further fate unknown
					Series 8 IZHORETS-87 ex-*BP № 87* (1941)	87	1936	22.6.1941	Tug	B	Built for civilian service, mobilised 22.6.1941. Survived the war

19.0 Minesweepers

					IZHORETS-88 ex-*BP № 88* (1941)	88	1938	22.6.1941	Tug	B	Built for civilian service, mobilised 22.6.1941. Survived the war
					Series 10 IZHORETS-92	92	1939	13.6.1942	Tug	B	Survived the war
	№ 85	№ 59	№ 59[5]	T-43[10]	FURMANOV	93	1939	30.6.1941 19.12.1941	Minesweeper	B	Built for civilian service, mobilised 26.6.1941, conv to minesweeper, decomm 7.9.1941 to civilian service, name reverted. Mobilised 10.12.1941, conv to minesweeper
	№ 73	№ 48	№ 45	T-45[9]	ANTIKAJNEN	94	1940	30.6.1941	Minesweeper	B	Built for civilian service, mobilised 26.6.1941. Sunk 26.8.1944 by *U-745* off Narvi Island
					Builder: 363, Izhora (Izhora Yd)						
					Series 5						
№ 21	№ 48	№ 80			BP № 21 ex-*BP № 1* (1934)	21	1934	13.7.1939 30.6.1941	Minesweeper	B	Built for civilian service, mobilised 15.5.1939, conv to minesweeper. Decomm 12.12.1940 to civilian service, name reverted. Mobilised June 1941, conv to minesweeper. Sunk 19.8.1941 by the German MTB *S-58* off Moonsound Island
№ 22[1]	№ 78	№ 81			BP № 22 ex-*BP № 2* (1934)	22	1934	22.6.1941	Minesweeper	B	Built for civilian service, mobilised. Sunk 16.9.1941 by German aircraft north-west of Paldiski
№ 23	№ 108	№ 82			BP № 23 ex-*BP № 3* (1934)	23	1934	13.7.1939 3.7.1941	Minesweeper	B	Built for civilianservice, mobilised 13.5.1939, conv to minesweeper. Decomm 28.12.1939 to civilian service. Mobilised June 1941, conv to minesweeper. Fled to Sweden Sept 1941, interned, returned 1945. Further fate unknown
					BP № 5 ex-*BP № 24* (1941) ex-*BP № 4* (1936)	24	1936	30.6.1941	Tug	Wh	Built for civilian service, mobilised 1941. Numbered *A-35* from 30.6.1943. Decomm 1946 to civilian service, name reverted to *№ 24*. Fate after 1956 unknown

Severoles type tug as built.
Drawing by Jerzy Lewandowski

TShch № 1939	TShch № 22.6.1941	TShch № 25.7.1941	TShch № 7.9.1941	No 11.10.1944	No/Name	YN	Built	Comm	Type	Fleet	Remarks
	№ 96	№ 83	№ 46	T-46[13]	BP № 25	25	1935	8.7.1941	Minesweeper	B	Built for civilian service, mobilised 27.6.1941. Capsized when coaling and sank 31.7.1941 at Tallinn, raised next day. Detached to the Ladoga Flotilla during 24.4.1944 to 18.10.1944. Decomm after Sept 1945 to civilian service. Fate after 1960 unknown
№ 26	№ 44	№ 84	№ 47		BP № 26	26	1936	Nov 1939 30.6.1941	Minesweeper	B	Built for civilian service, mobilised 9.10.1939, conv to minesweeper. Decomm 12.12.1940 to civilian service. Mobilised June 1941, conv to minesweeper. Sunk 21.6.1944 by mine off the Bjerkesund Strait
	№ 175	№ 175[3]	T-175[12]		BP № 27	27	1936	19.8.1941	Minesweeper	B La B	Built for civilian service, mobilised 2.8.1941. Reverted to tug 13.12.1941, conv 3.4.1942 to minesweeper, trfd to Ladoga Flotilla. Sank in a gale 31.7.1942, raised, trfd 18.10.1944 to the Baltic Fleet. Decomm after Sept 1945, to civilian service, name reverted. Fate after 1962 unknown
№ 29	№ 106	№ 85			BP № 29	29	1936	Sept 1939 1.7.1941	Minesweeper	B	Built for civilian service, mobilised 20.9.1939, conv to minesweeper. Temporarily detached to the Ladoga Flotilla in Oct 1939. Decomm 12.12.1940 to civilian service. Mobilised June 1941, conv to minesweeper. Sunk in Sept 1941 by German aircraft while fleeing to Sweden
№ 30	№ 129		№ 68	T-68	BP № 30	30	1936	29.9.1939 21.7.1941	Minesweeper	B	Built for civilian service, mobilised 28.9.1939, conv to minesweeper. Temporarily detached to the Ladoga Flotilla in Nov 1939. Stranded 8.12.1939 at Saunasaari Bay. Raised, decomm 5.6.1940 to civilian service renamed *Izhorets-30*. Mobilised June 1941, conv to minesweeper. Decomm after Sept 1945 to civilian service. Renamed Feb 1959 *Entuziast*, fate after 2013 unknown

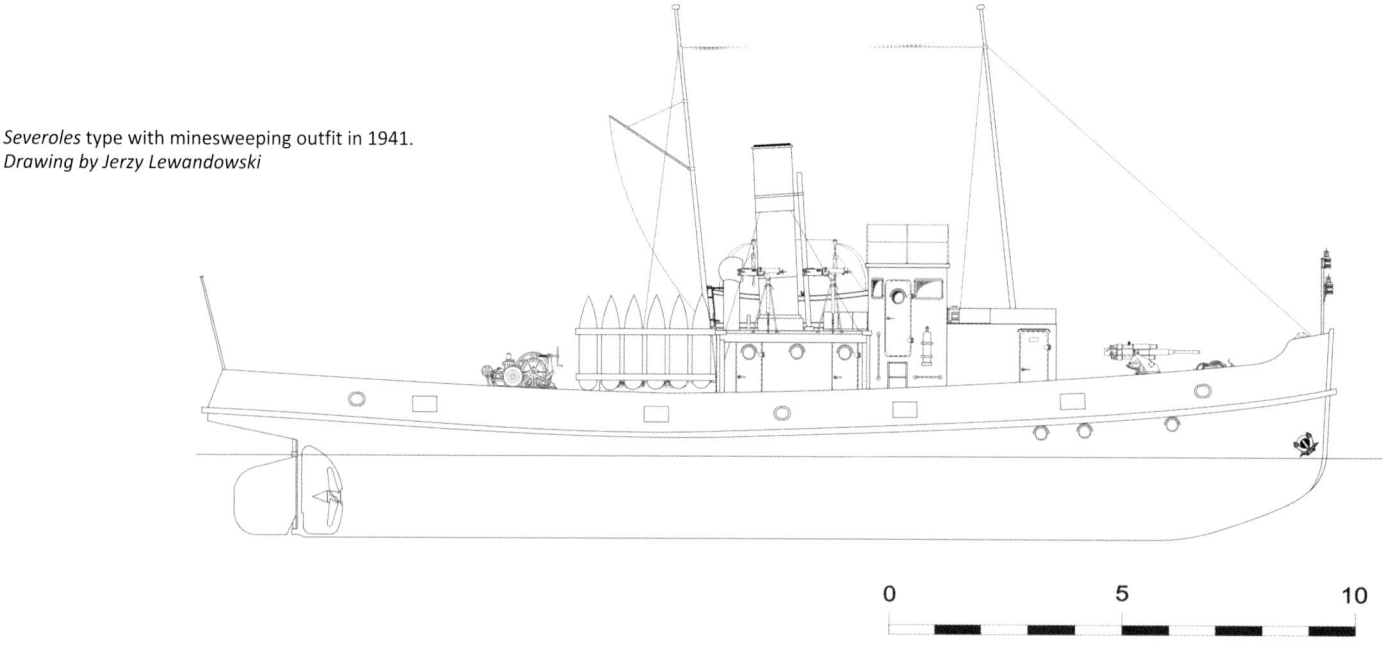

Severoles type with minesweeping outfit in 1941. Drawing by Jerzy Lewandowski

№ 31	№ 75	№ 88	№ 49		BP № 31	31	1936	Sept 1939 5.7.1941	Minesweeper	La B	Built for civilian service, mobilised 21.9.1939, conv to minesweeper. Damaged by Finnish artillery fire 3.12.1939. Decomm 5.6.1940 to civilian service. Mobilised June 1941 to the Baltic Fleet, conv to minesweeper. Sunk 19.9.1944 by mine off Vingrund shoals
№ 32	№ 127				BP № 32	32	1936	29.11.1939 8.7.1941	Minesweeper	B La	Built for civilian service, mobilised 21.9.1939. Sunk 29.1.1940 by Finnish aircraft in Saunasaari Bay, raised 1940, returned to civilian service. Mobilised 1941 to the Baltic Fleet, conv to minesweeper, trfd 4.10.1941 to the Ladoga Flotilla. Mined 3.8.1944 off Mantenisaar
№ 33	№ 107	№ 86	№ 48	T-48	BP № 33	33	1936	Dec 1939 2.7.1941	Minesweeper	B	Built for civilian service, mobilised 29.11.1939 for the Ladoga Flotilla. Conversion to minesweeper completed late in Dec 1939 so she was not able to reach Ladoga because of heavy ice. Decomm to civilian service 2.11.1940. Mobilised June 1941 for Baltic Fleet, conv to minesweeper. Sunk 20.11.1942 in collision with the minesweeper *TShch № 34 (Dzerzhinskij)* at the roadstead of Kronshtadt. Raised and recomm 15.11.1943. Decomm after Sept 1945 to civilian operator. Fate after 1965 unknown
№ 34	№ 105	№ 87			BP № 34	34	1936	29.11.1939 2.7.1941	Minesweeper	La	Built for civilian service, mobilised 21.9.1939, conv to minesweeper. Damaged 29.1.1940 by Finnish aircraft, decomm 5.6.1940 to civilian service. Mobilised June 1941 to the Baltic Fleet, conv to minesweeper. Fled to Sweden Sept 1941, interned, returned 1945. Further fate unknown
№ 35	№ 35		№ 69	T-69	BP № 35	35	1936	Oct 1939 30.6.1941	Minesweeper	B	Built for civilian service, mobilised 28.9.1939, conv to minesweeper. Decomm at the end Dec 1940 to civilian service. Mobilised June 1941 to the Baltic Fleet, conv to minesweeper. Decomm after Sept 1945 to civilian service. Fate after 1960 unknown
№ 37					BP № 37	37	1936	30.11.1939	Minesweeper	La	Built for civilian service, mobilised 20.9.1939. Stranded 4.12.1939 off the Taipaleenluoto light. Raised, deleted 5.6.1940 to civilian service. Mobilised Sept 1941 as tug, not recomm and laid up in Nov 1941. Returned after Sept 1945 to civilian service
№ 38	№ 45	№ 44	№ 38	T-38[11]	BP № 38	38	1936	13.10.1939 1.7.1941	Minesweeper	B La	Built for civilian service, mobilised 20.9.1939, conv to minesweeper. Trfd end Oct 1939 to the Baltic Fleet. Decomm 12.12.1940 to civilian service. Mobilised June 1941 to the Baltic Fleet, conv to minesweeper. Detached to the Ladoga Flotilla during 24.4.1943 to 18.10.1944. Decomm after Sept 1945 to civilian service. Further fate after 1946 unknown

Shch № 1939	TShch № 22.6.1941	TShch № 25.7.1941	TShch № 7.9.1941	No 11.10.1944	No/Name	YN	Built	Comm	Type	Fleet	Remarks
№ 39	№ 46	№ 45	№ 53		BP № 39	39	1936	Sept 1939 30.6.1941	Minesweeper	B	Built for civilian service, mobilised 20.9.1939, conv to minesweeper. Decomm 12.12.1940 to civilian service. Mobilised June 1941 to the Baltic Fleet, conv to minesweeper. Sunk 19.9.1941 in collision, raised and recomm 28.11.1942. Mined 21.6.1944 in Bjerkesund Strait
					Series 9						
					BURUN	61	1937	22.6.1941	Tug	B	Built for the NKVD Dal'stroi. Mobilised 1941. Survived the war
					SHKVAL	62	1937	13.6.1942	Tug	B	Built for the NKVD Dal'stroi. Mobilised 1941. Survived the war
№ 63	№ 63			T-63[12]	BP № 63	63	1937	Sept 1939 June 1941	Minesweeper	B La	Built for civilian service, mobilised 20.9.1939, conv to minesweeper. Decomm 20.7.1940 to civilian service name reverted. Mobilised 22.6.1941 to the Baltic Fleet, conv to minesweeper. Trfd 7.6.1942 to the Ladoga Flotilla. Decomm 15.9.1945 to civilian service. Conv 1958 to motor tug, fate after 1960 unknown
	№ 124		№ 65	T-65	BP № 64	64	1937	11.7.1941	Minesweeper	B	Built for civilian service, mobilised 30.6.1941, conv to minesweeper. Reverted 25.7.1941 to tug, renamed *Izhorets-64*. Reverted to minesweeper 7.9.1941
№ 65	№ 47	№ 46	№ 43		BP № 65	65	1937	Sept 1939 2.7.1941	Minesweeper	B	Built for civilian service, mobilised 20.9.1939, conv to minesweeper. Decomm 12.12.1940, to civilian service. Mobilised June 1941, conv to minesweeper. Stranded 1.11.1941 off the Lavansaari Island and abandoned

Severoles type tug mobilised as minesweeper in 1941.
Przemysław Budzbon Collection

19.0 Minesweepers

№ 126			T-126[12]	BP № 66	66	1938	12.7.1941	Minesweeper	B La B	Built for civilian service, mobilised 5.7.1941. Sunk 21.9.1941 by artillery fire off Shlisselburg, raised, trfd 20.20.1942 to the Ladoga Flotilla. Sunk 10.4.1943 by mine in Volkhovskaya Bay, raised 15.5.1943, trfd to the Baltic Fleet. Decomm after Sept 1946 to civilian service. Fate after 1959 unknown
№ 74	№ 47	№ 44	T-44	BP № 69	69	1937	30.6.1941	Minesweeper	B	Built for civilian service, mobilised 26.6.1941. During 24.4.1944 to 3.7.1944 detached to the Ladoga Flotilla. Decomm after Sept 1945, further fate unknown
	№ 179	№ 179[5]	T-179	MZ-1 ex-*BP № 70* (1938)	70	1938	6.8.1941 19.12.1941	Minesweeper	B	Built for civilian service, mobilised 4.8.1941. Decomm 8.9.1941 to civilian service, name reverted. Mobilised 19.12.1941, reverted to minesweeper. Sank 7.7.1943 in collision on the Neva. Raised and recomm in 1944
	№ 121	№ 64		BP № 71	71	1938	5.7.1941	Minesweeper	B	Built for civilian service, mobilised 30.6.1941. Reverted 25.7.1941 to tug, renamed *Izhorets-71*. Reverted 7.9.1941 to minesweeper. Sank 1.10.1941 in Luga Bay after ramming the wreck of Soviet survey vessel *Astronom* mistaken for an enemy submarine
				LK-2	72	1938	1938	Dispatch vessel Escort ship	B	Built for naval service, conv 2.7.1941 to escort ship. Sunk 15.7.1942 by mine east of Lavansaari.
			T-40[12]	LK-13	73	1938	1938	Tug Training vessel Minesweeper	B La B	Built for naval service, conv 1939 to the training vessel *UK-4*, trfd to the Ladoga Flotilla. Conv 3.8.1941 to minesweeper, trfd 18.10.1944 to the Baltic Fleet. Survived the war
		№ 65[6]		VVS-65	74	1938	1938	Tug Minesweeper	La	Built for the Baltic Fleet Air Forces. Conv 1941 to minesweeper. Reverted 5.7.1944 to tug
	№ 125	№ 66	T-66	BP № 75	75	1938	11.7.1941	Minesweeper	B	Built for the Svir'stroi of the NKVD. Mobilised 30.6.1941, conv to minesweeper. Reverted 25.7.1941 to tug, renamed *Izhorets-75*. Reverted 7.9.1941 to minesweeper
	№ 93	№ 63	T-63 T-83[14]	SOM	76	1939	23.3.1939	Experimental vessel	B	Built for the Ostekhbiuro, mobilised 1939. Conv 20.3.1940 to minesweeper
				KP-19	77	1939	1939	Tug	B	Built for Kronshtadt Naval Harbour. Survived the war
				KP-20	78	1939	1939	Tug	B	Built for Kronshtadt Naval Harbour. Heavily damaged by artillery fire in 1941, relegated to a heater. Deleted 6.8.1942
				KP-21	79	1939	1939	Tug	B	Built for Kronshtadt Naval Harbour. Destroyed 27.6.1941 by artillery fire, total loss. Deleted 26.9.1941
				KP-22	80	1939	1939	Tug	B	Built for Kronshtadt Naval Harbour. Not listed in the *Register No 19*

Builder: 340, Zelenodolsk

	BTShCh-14[3] TShCh-310[4]		B-30 ex-*BP-3* (1941)		1941	10.10.1941	Tug	Cs	Built for naval service, conv 4.1.1942 to minesweeper. Reverted to tug *RB-310* on 11.9.1944
	BTShCh-15[3] TShCh-311[4]		B-31 ex-*BP-4* (1941)		1941	10.10.1941	Tug	Cs	Built for naval service, conv 4.1.1942 to minesweeper. Reverted to tug *RB-311* on 11.9.1944

* Completed at Yard No 363, Ust-Izhora.

Exceptions noted in the main table.

No	Year	Date
1	1941	9.6.1941
2		3.8.1941
3		29.11.1941
4		12.12.1941
5		19.12.1941
6	1942	3.4.1942
7	1943	24.6.1943
8		9.7.1943
9	1944	5.6.1944
10		29.8.1944
11		6.10.1944
12		21.10.1944
13		12.11.1944
14	1945	28.3.1945

One of the largest series of civilian ships built in the Soviet Union before World War 2, in total 88 were completed (*YN 1–39, YN 43–53, YN 61–94*, plus four Zelenodolsk Works boats (YN not known). Design by the Rechsudproekt (TsKB-51), design based on the *Martiets* type tug built by the A. Marti Yd in 1930. Multipurpose workhorses of the northern regions, they could carry up to 15t of cargo and 12 passengers. Were strengthened for navigation in ice while those designated to assist floating timber on Siberian rivers were fitted to fire their boilers with wood instead of coal (inter alia *YN 24, 45, 47, 48, 50*).

Series production began at Petrozavod, with various improvements introduced in the subsequent series. From *Series 2* all-welded hull construction was introduced, while the companionway forward of the deckhouse was fitted following the first operational experience, to prevent flooding at large angles of heel. The boats of the first three series were fitted with 180hp machinery sets while from *Series 4* the power was increased to 200–215hp, culminating in the introduction of the 240hp sets in *Series 6*. The increasing volume of orders from various Soviet economic organisations produced a bottleneck at Petrozavod, so starting from the *Series 5* in 1934, orders were placed at Ust-Izhorskii Zavod at Kolpino. The first four hulls were named *BP № 1 to № 4* which was a source of confusion with the Petrozavod ships, so the YN and ship numeration was continued, and the boats renumbered *BP № 21 to № 24*. It was from Izhora that the tugs took their nickname, which was not the formal name of the type, although the ships built in Izhora carried the name *Izhorets* painted on the sides together with the yard number. The nickname *Izhorets* has become synonymous with the *Project 129* tugs, even those built at Petrozavod. It became the official name of the units mobilised by the Navy, and after the war it was carried over into official registers. However, used retrospectively, it is incorrect.

Most of them were conv to minesweepers by adding stiffeners for a gun and two MGs mountings, installation of a radio transmitter and a main mast for an aerial, 45cm searchlight, a sweeping winch and cable drums, and racking for trawl buoys. Furthermore, they received cast iron fairleads and a boom for operating otter boards. A two-and-a-half times increase in the complement made the boats extremely cramped. Preparing for war in 1939, the Baltic Fleet had already mobilised 10 ships for conversion to minesweepers during May-July, followed by an additional 11 in September. After the conclusion of the Winter War, most of them were disarmed between February and June 1940 and returned to their civilian operators to be mobilised again a year later, as well as others of the type, in the face of the German invasion. During the war they operated in the Baltic, as well as on Lakes Ladoga, Onega and Ilmen. Those at Ladoga were often employed in their tug role when supplying the besieged city of Leningrad. Sturdy and of simple construction, when lost in shallow water many were raised and following unsophisticated repairs returned to service – some of them more than once. Back in civilian service after the conclusion of hostilities, some were refitted with diesel motors. They remained in operation well until 1960s, and one reached the 21st century. *YN 8* was preserved in the *Road of Life Museum* at Kokkorevo on the shore of Lake Ladoga.

Tral'shchik № 53 (ex-Buksirnyj parokhod № 39) in 1941.
Przemysław Budzbon Collection

Izhorets № 24 (formerly naval tug A-35, ex-№ 5) after the war in civilian service.
Przemysław Budzbon Collection

Eksportles № 18 type
Steam tugs

Displacement: 450t full load
Dimensions: 31.6 x 6.7 x 3.3m
Machinery: 2-shaft, VTE, 1 boiler, 450hp = 11kts
Armament: 1-45mm/46 21-K, 2-0.3in MGs, 1 MTSh sweep, 1 MZT sweep
Complement: 48

Exportles № 18 carried numbers T-18, T-893 and T-892 when mobilized. Seen in 1995 carrying the name Skoryj. Boris Lemachko Collection

Pt-No 1941	No Oct 1939	No 23.11.1939	No 9.7.1941	Name	Built	Comm	Fleet	Remarks
				Builder: Crichton-Vulcan				
46	T-18	T-893	T-892	EKSPORTLES № 18	1933	Oct 1939 9.7.1941	N Wh	Mobilised 19.10.1939, conv to minesweeper. Decomm 1.5.1940 to civilian service. Mobilised 26.6.1941, conv to minesweeper. Trfd 13.8.1941 to the White Sea Flotilla. Decomm 2.12.1941 to civilian service, renamed *Skoryj*
47	T-19	T-892	T-893	EKSPORTLES № 19	1933	Oct 1939 9.7.1941	N Wh	Mobilised 19.10.1939, conv to minesweeper. Decomm 4.11.1940 to civilian service. Mobilised 26.6.1941, conv to minesweeper. Trfd 13.8.1941 to the White Sea Flotilla. Decomm 2.12.1941 to civilian service. Mobilised 28.8.1944 as tug *M-38*

Dzerzhinskij type
Steam tugs

Displacement: 470t full load
Dimensions: 38.1 x 7.6 x 3.0m
Machinery: 2-shaft, VTE, 1 boiler, 450hp = 9kts (*Menzhinskij* 400hp = 7.8kts). Coal 75t, range 1285nm at 6kts (*Menzhinskij* 600nm)
Armament: 1-45mm/46 21-K, 1-0.5in DShK MG, 1 MTSh sweep, 1 MZT sweep, (*Menzhinskij* 10 DCs)
Complement: 48

TShch № 29.6.1941	TShch № 2.7.1941	TShch № 25.7.1941	TShch № 7.9.1941	No 5.6.1944	Name	Built	Comm	Fleet	Remarks
					Builder: •				
№ 40	№ 43	№ 72	№ 34	T-34	DZERZHINSKIJ	1934	27.11.1939 2.7.1941	B	Mobilised 15.7.1939, conv to minesweeper, decomm 24.7.1940 to civilian service. Mobilised 27.6.1941, conv to minesweeper
№ 41	№ 42	№ 73	№ 35		MENZHINSKIJ	1934	27.11.1939 2.7.1941	B	Mobilised 25.7.1939, conv to minesweeper, decomm 29.9.1940 to civilian service. Mobilised 27.6.1941, conv to minesweeper. Mined 21.11.1941 east of Hanko
№ 43	№ 92	№ 75	№ 42	T-42	ORDZHONIKIDZE	1934	Aut 1938 2.7.1941	La B	Mobilised 1938, conv to gunboat, decomm 20.3.1940 to civilian service. Mobilised 27.6.1941, conv to minesweeper
№ 42	№ 91	№ 74	№ 41		SERGEJ KIROV	1934	2.7.1941	B	Mobilised 27.6.1941. Sunk 22.9.1941 by Finnish MTBs at the entrance to Suursaari harbour

GP-4 type
Steam naval tugs

Displacement: 369.5t full load
Dimensions: 31.6 x 7.2 x 3.0m
Machinery: 2-shaft, VTE, 400hp = 8/7kts. Range 420nm at 7kts
Armament: 2-45mm/46 21-K, 4-0.3in MGs, 1 MTSh sweep, 1 MZT sweep
Complement: 50

TShch № 7.10.1941	No 13.9.1944	Name	Built	Comm	Fleet	Remarks
№ 22	T-22	GP-4 ex-BP № 583	1938	7.10.1941	P	Tug of Naval Harbour of Vladivostok, conv 1941 to minesweeper
№ 23	T-23	BP № 584	1938	7.10.1941	P	Tug of Naval Harbour of Vladivostok, conv 1941 to minesweeper
№ 24	T-24	BP № 582	1938	7.10.1941	P	Tug of Naval Harbour of Vladivostok, conv 1941 to minesweeper

Beliakov type
Steam tugs

Displacement: 510t full load
Dimensions: 40.8 x 7.6 x 2.6m
Machinery: 2-shaft, VTE, 400hp = 9kts. Range 2000nm at 7kts
Armament: 2-45mm/46 21-K, 2-0.3in MGs, 1 MTSh sweep, 1 MZT sweep
Complement: 37

TShch № 7.10.1941	No 13.9.1944	Name	Built	Comm	Fleet	Remarks
131		BELIAKOV	1938	2.8.1941	P	Mobilised 23.7.1941. Decomm 5.2.1943 to civilian service. Recomm as tug for duration of the Soviet-Japanese War
132		CHKALOV	1938	2.8.1941	P	Mobilised 23.7.1941. Decomm 5.2.1943 to civilian service. Recomm as tug for duration of the Soviet-Japanese War
133		TUCHA	1938	2.8.1941	P	Mobilised 23.7.1941. Decomm 5.2.1943 to civilian service. Recomm as tug for duration of the Soviet-Japanese War
134		GROZA	1938	2.8.1941	P	Mobilised 25.7.1941. Decomm 5.2.1943 to civilian service
135	T-135	POLARNIK	1938	2.8.1941	P	Mobilised 25.7.1941
136	T-136	UDARNIK	1938	2.8.1941	P	Mobilised 25.7.1941

Sever type
Steam tugs

Displacement: 149.5t
Dimensions: 28.2 x 6.5 x 1.2m
Machinery: 1-shaft, reciprocating, 1 boiler; 200hp = 7kts. Range 190nm
Armament: 1-45mm/46 21-K, 2-0.5in MGs, 1 OTSh-2 sweep, 1 MKhT sweep
Complement: 32

RTShch-51 Sever during the war. Przemysław Budzbon Collection

No 7.9.1941	Name	Built	Comm	Fleet	Remarks
RTShch-48	KOSTROMA	1930	7.9.1941	Wh	Mobilised 25.6.1941. Decomm 24.2.1945 to civilian service
RTShch-49	SAKKO	1930	7.9.1941	Wh	Mobilised 25.6.1941. Decomm 24.2.1945 to civilian service. Discarded Sept 1960
RTShch-50	VANTSETTI	1930	7.9.1941	Wh	Mobilised 25.6.1941. Decomm 24.2.1945 to civilian service. Discarded Sept 1960
RTShch-51	SEVER	1930	7.9.1941	Wh	Mobilised 25.6.1941. Decomm 24.2.1945 to civilian service. Discarded March 1965
RTShch-52	BARBIUS	1930	7.9.1941	Wh	Mobilised 25.6.1941. Decomm 24.2.1945 to civilian service

Shchors type
Steam tugs

Displacement: 430t full load
Dimensions: 38.2 x 7.6 x 2.8m
Machinery: 2-shaft, VTE, 400hp = 7.5kts. Range 1166nm at 6.5kts
Armament: 1-45mm/46 21-K, 2-0.3in MGs, 1 MTSh sweep, 1 MZT sweep
Complement: 37

TShch № 7.10.1941	No 13.9.1944	Name	Built	Comm	Fleet	Remarks
№ 141	T-141	SHCHORS	1934	7.10.1941	P	Mobilised 16.7.1941
№ 142	T-142	CHAPAIEV	1934	7.10.1941	P	Mobilised 16.7.1941

Finnish Viipuri class
Steam tugs

Displacement: 335t full load
Dimensions: 31.6 x 7.5 x 4.0m
Machinery: 1-shaft, VTE, 368hp = 10kts
Armament: 2-45mm/46 21-K, 2-0.5in MGs

Tug *MB-57*, former minesweeper *EMTShch-71* in the early 1950s.
Naval History and Heritage Command NH 92270

No/Name	YN	Built	Comm	Fleet	Remarks
Builder: Crichton-Vulcan					
EMTSHCH-70 ex-*Viipuri* (Fin, 1944) ex-• (Rus, 1941)	761	June 1941	30.12.1944	B	Seized July 1941 by the Finnish Navy on completion, comm as minesweeper. Returned 3.11.1944, conv to magnetic minesweeper. Reverted 28.11.1950 to tug, numbered *MB-54* from 22.12.1950, *RB-169* from 7.7.1956. Decomm 8.8.1960 to civilian service, renamed *Shtorm*. Discarded after mid-1960s
EMTSHCH-71 ex-• (Fin, 1944) ex-• (Rus, 1941)	762	June 1941	30.12.1944	B	Seized July 1941 by the Finnish Navy on completion, comm as minesweeper. Returned 3.11.1944, conv to magnetic minesweeper. Reverted 20.11.1946 to tug, numbered *F-63*, *MB-57* from 15.5.1947, *RB-168* from 7.7.1956. Deleted 5.7.1973
EMTSHCH-72 ex-• (Fin, 1944) ex-• (Rus, 1941)	763	June 1941	30.12.1944	B	Seized July 1941 by the Finnish Navy on completion, comm as minesweeper. Returned 3.11.1944, conv to magnetic minesweeper. Reverted 28.11.1950 to tug, numbered *MB-55* from 22.12.1950, *RB-170* from 7.7.1956. Decomm 8.8.1960 to civilian service, renamed *Tugev*. Discarded 1978
EMTSHCH-73 ex-*Vilpula* (Fin, 1944) ex-• (Rus, 1941)	764	June 1941	30.12.1944	B	Seized July 1941 by the Finnish Navy on completion, comm as minesweeper. Returned 3.11.1944, conv to magnetic minesweeper. Reverted 20.11.1946 to tug, numbered *F-69*, *MB-19* from 15.5.1947, *RB-3* from 27.8.1964. Conv 25.8.1969 to heater *OT-12*. Deleted 22.4.1982

Tugs ordered by the Soviet Union in Finland and seized by the Finnish Navy in July 1941. Returned to the Soviet Union in 1944.

Steam tugs

Pt-No 1941	TShch № on Comm	No	Name TShch №	Details	Comm	Fleet	Remarks
	№ 14 ex-№ 15[1]	T-15[4]	PATROKL	480t; 31.2 x 6.8 x 4.6m; 750hp = 9kts; 760nm at 7kts; 1-75mm, 4-0.3in MGs, 1 MTSh sweep, 1 MZT sweep; 44 men	1.1.1933	P	Built 1921. Mobilised 26.11.1932. Survived the war
	№ 18	T-18[4]	№ 18	447t; 31.6 x 7.2 x 3.2m; 400hp = 9kts; 1120nm at 8kts; 2-45mm/46 21-K, 2-0.3in MGs, 6 mines, 1 MTSh sweep, 1 MZT sweep; 45 men	1935	P	Built 1935 for naval service. Conv 28.12.1935 to minesweeper. Survived the war
	№ 19	T-19[4]	№ 19		1935	P	Built 1935 for naval service. Conv 16.12.1935 to minesweeper. Survived the war
41		T-484[2]	KHENKIN	200t; 1-45mm/46 21-K, 2-0.3in MGs	29.1.1940 2.7.1941	BS	Built 1935. Mobilised 29.10.1939, conv to minesweeper. Decomm 5.10.1940 to civilian service. Mobilised 22.6.1941, conv to minesweeper. Stranded 7.11.1941 in a gale off Cape Sarych
42		T-485[2]	KAKHOVKA ex-*Kalugar'* (1938)	200t; 1-45mm/46 21-K, 2-0.3in MGs	29.1.1940 3.7.1941	BS	Built 1935. Mobilised 29.10.1939, conv to minesweeper. Decomm 29.1.1940 to civilian service. Mobilised 22.6.1941, conv to minesweeper. Sunk 28.12.1941 by German aircraft in the Kerch Strait., raised and recomm. Sunk 25.2.1942 by aircraft off Kamysch-Burun
44		T-487[2]	OCHAKOVSKIJ KANAL	248t; 30.6 x 6.7 x 3.5m; 350hp = 9kts; 1500nm at 8.5kts; 1-45mm/46 21-K, 2-0.3in MGs	29.1.1940 28.6.1941	BS	Built 1927. Mobilised 29.10.1939, conv to minesweeper. Decomm 5.10.1940 to civilian service. Mobilised 22.6.1941, conv to minesweeper. Sunk 19.8.1941 by artillery fire off Kherson. Wreck raised by the Germans
57		T-503[3]	BAJKAL	358t; 2-45mm/46 21-K, 2-0.3in MGs	2.7.1941	BS	Icebreaking tug. Mobilised 22.6.1941. Sunk 18.8.1941 by artillery fire off Ochakov. Wreck raised by the Germans, comm 20.10.1942 as minehunter *Bajkal*. Sunk 26.10.1942 off Yalta following damage by Allied bombers
67		T-515[3]	GELENDZHIK ex-*Gerkules* (1922)	325t; 35.6 x 6.2 x 3.7m; 450hp = 12kts; 1000nm at 10kts; 1-45mm/46 21-K, 2-0.3in MGs	30.6.1941	BS	Built 1890. Icebreaking tug. Mobilised in World War 1 for Black Sea Fleet, captured 1918 by the Germans, trfd to the White Russians, recovered 1920, decomm to civilian service 1921. Mobilised 22.6.1941, conv to minesweeper. Sunk 4.2.1943 by artillery fire off Yuzhnaya Ozereika, raised 19.10.1943, recomm 25.1.1944. Reverted 21.6.1944 to tug *ChF-8*. Survived the war
	71		KRAB	463.5t; 41.0 x 7.6 x 2.3m; 400hp = 8kts; 500nm at 6kts; 1-45mm, 2-0.3in MGs, 1 MTSh sweep, 1 MZT sweep; 31 men.	20.3.1940	B	Built 1938. Experimental vessel of the Ostekhburo, seized 23.3.1939. Conv 20.3.1940 to minesweeper, numbered № 71 from 25.7.1941. Mined 28.8.1941 off Cape Juminda

Exceptions noted in the main table.

No	Year	Date
1	1934	1.5.1934
2	1940	29.1.1940
3	1941	on Comm
4	1944	13.9.1944

T-487 Ochakovskij kanal stranded after shelling by German artillery. *Przemysław Budzbon Collection*

19.5.2.2. River tugs

300hp types
Paddle steam tugs

- **Displacement:** 293t
- **Dimensions:** 48.5 x 13.4/• x 1.5m
- **Machinery:** 2 side wheels, compound, 1 locomotive boiler; 150–200hp = 6kts
- **Armament:** 1-45mm/46 21-K, 8-0.5in (2 x 4) MGs, 1-0.3in MG, 1 OTSh-1 sweep, 1 KT sweep, 50 mines
- **Complement:** 47

No 1935	Name	Built	Comm	Fleet	Remarks
RTShch-1	LENINGRAD	1934	1935	Am	Mobilised 5.3.1935. Modernised 1940. Conv 7.5.1943 to decontamination depot ship *DPB-1*
RTShch-2	STALINGRAD	1934	1935	Am	Mobilised 5.3.1935. Modernised 1940
RTShch-3	KHAR'KOV	1934	1935	Am	Mobilised 5.3.1935. Decomm 6.11.1943 to civilian service
RTShch-4	KUZNETSK	1934	1935	Am	Mobilised 5.3.1935. Decomm 13.10.1943 to civilian service. Discarded Sept 1969

200hp types
Paddle steam tugs

Group	1	2	3
Displacement (full):	227t	250t	195–232t
Length:	49.0m	44.0	47.3m
Beam:	13.4/6.1m	14.2/• m	14.2/• m
Draught:	1.0m	0.9m	1.0m
Compound machinery (2 sidewheels):	1		
Boiler:	1		
Total power:	200hp		
Speed (max):	6.5–7.5kts		
Main armament:	1-45mm/46 21-K		
MGs:	8-0.3in (2x4)	3-0.5in	2-0.3in
Sweeps:	1 OTSh, 1 KT		
Mines:	40	50	
Complement:	48	48	

RTShch-64 Frunze in civilian service in the 1960s. Boris Lemachko Collection

No June 1941	Name	YN	Built	Comm	Fleet	Remarks
	Group 1 Builder: Cockerill					
RTShCh-56	ZHURAVLYOV ex-*Pavel Zhuravlyov* (1932) ex-*TZ-1* (1929) ex-*Pavel Zhuravlyov* (1929) ex-*A. Bubnov* (1923) ex-*Pavel Zhuravlyov* (1922) ex-*Al. Bubnov* (1920) ex-*Nikolaj* (1905)	214	1902	July 1941	Am	Mobilised 1920 for Amur Flotilla, conv to armed steamer, decomm 1922 to civilian service. Mobilised 25.7.1929, conv to minesweeper-layer *TZ-1*, decomm to civilian service Dec 1929, name reverted. Recomm 5.5.1932 renamed *Zhuravlyov*, decomm 24.5.1934 to civilian service. Mobilised 13.7.1941, conv to minesweeper. Decomm 24.10.1945 to civilian service. Discarded Aug 1963
RTShch-57	G. CHERNENKO ex-*TZ-2* (1929) ex-*G. CHERNENKO* (1929) ex-*V. Kovalevskij* (1923)	213	1907	July 1929	Am	Mobilised 1920 the Amur Flotilla, conv to armed steamer, decomm 1922 to civilian service. Mobilised 25.7.1929, conv to minesweeper-layer *TZ-2*, decomm to civilian service Dec 1929, name reverted. Recomm 5.5.1932 renamed *G. Chernenko*, decomm 24.5.1934 to civilian service. Mobilised 13.7.1941, conv to minesweeper. Decomm 24.10.1945 to civilian service
	Group 2 Builder: 344, Perm					
RTShch-64	FRUNZE	19	1932	Aug 1942	Am	Mobilised 21.8.1942. Decomm 22.10.1945 to civilian service
	Group 3 Builder: •					
RTShch-50	IUMASHEV		1938	June 1941	Am	Mobilised 13.7.1941. Decomm 22.10.1045 to civilian service
RTShch-51	BELIAKOV		1937	June 1941	Am	Mobilised 13.7.1941. Decomm 18.10.1045 to civilian service
RTShch-52	CHKALOV		1937	June 1941	Am	Mobilised 13.7.1941. Decomm 22.10.1045 to civilian service
RTShch-53	BAJDUKOV		1937	June 1941	Am	Mobilised 13.7.1941. Decomm 16.10.1045 to civilian service
RTShch-54	BABUSHKIN		1937	June 1941	Am	Mobilised 13.7.1941. Decomm 16.10.1045 to civilian service. Discarded Apr 1960
RTShch-55	PAPANIN		1938	June 1941	Am	Mobilised 13.7.1941. Decomm 16.10.1045 to civilian service
RTShch-58	MAZURUK		1937	June 1941	Am	Mobilised 13.7.1941. Decomm 19.10.1045 to civilian service
RTShch-59	DANILIN		1937	June 1941	Am	Mobilised 13.7.1941. Decomm 24.10.1045 to civilian service

150hp types — *Paddle steam tugs*

Displacement: 200t
Dimensions: 38.4 x •/6.0 x 0.8m
Machinery: 2 side wheels, compound, 1 boiler (8.7kG/cm^2); 150–200hp = 6kts. Range 190nm
Armament: 1-45mm/46 21-K, 2-0.5in MGs, 1 OTSh-2 sweep, 1 MKhT sweep
Complement: 26

RTShch № 1942	Name	Built	Comm	Fleet	Remarks
№ 429	OBORONA	1931	Aug 1942	Wh	Mobilised 18.8.1942. Reverted 29.10.1944 to tug, decomm 10.11.1944 to civilian service
№ 430	PLEKHANOV	1931	Aug 1942	Wh	Mobilised 18.8.1942. Reverted 23.10.1944 to tug, decomm 10.11.1944 to civilian service. Discarded Oct 1969
№ 431	LIMENDA	1931	Aug 1942	Wh	Mobilised 18.8.1942. Decomm 10.11.1944 to civilian service. Discarded July 1964
№ 432	NATSFLOT	1931	Aug 1942	Wh	Mobilised 18.8.1942. Reverted 23.10.1944 to tug, decomm 10.11.1944 to civilian service. Renamed *Solikamsk* in Feb 1960. Discarded Dec 1966.
№ 433	MOGUCHIJ	1931	Aug 1942	Wh	Mobilised 18.8.1942. Reverted 4.11.1944 to tug, decomm 10.11.1944 to civilian service. Discarded Oct 1973

Screw steam tugs

TShch № No on Comm 1941	TShch № 25.7.1941	TShch № 7.9.1941	No 1944	Name	Details	Comm	Fleet	Remarks
№ 102	№ 31	№ 36	T-36^3	MOSKVA	220t; 31.8 x 6.9 x 2.1m; 330hp = 10kts; 860nm at 8kts; 1-45mm/46 21-K, 2-0.3in MGs, 1 MTSh sweep, 1 MZT sweep; 37 men	Sept 1939 28.6.1941	B	Built 1891. Mobilised 18.9.1939, conv to minesweeper. Decomm 20.3.1940 to civilian service. Mobilised 23.6.1941, conv to minesweeper. Stranded 29.10.1941 in a gale, salvaged 1941. Decomm after the war to civilian service. Discarded Dec 1963
№ 87	№ 32	№ 31		OZERNOJ	200t; 1-45mm/46 21-K, 2-0.3in MGs, 1 MTSh sweep, 1 MZT sweep; 37 men	Aut 1939 29.6.1941	B	Mobilised autumn 1939, conv to minesweeper. Decomm 9.5.1940 to civilian service. Mobilised 23.6.1941, conv to minesweeper. Sunk 23.9.1941 by German aircraft at Kronstadt
№ 104	№ 33		T-51^5	OLONKA	160t; 29.6 x 6.0 x 1.6m; 400hp = 1-45mm/46 21-K, 2-0.3in MGs, 1 MTSh sweep, 1 MZT sweep; 31 men	2.7.1941	B	Built 1927. Mobilised 28.6.1941. Detached 10.9.1941 to civilian service, returned 3.1.1942, number reverted. Decomm after the war to civilian service. Discarded 1970
№ 103	№ 34			VIDLITSA	199t normal, 234t full load; 30.3 x 6.2 x 1.6m, 450hp = 8kts; 1000nm; (1939: 1-75mm, 2-0.3in MGs; 1942: 3-45mm/46 21-K, 1-0.5in MG; 1943: 1-85mm 52K, 1-37mm/67.5 70-K, 6-0.5in (3x2) Colt MGs, 1-82mm mortar), 1 MTSh sweep, 1 MZT sweep; 42–48 men	Oct 1939 28.6.1941	B On Vo On	Built 1928. Mobilised 29.10.1939, conv to minesweeper. Decomm 20.3.1940 to civilian service. Mobilised 23.6.1941, conv to minesweeper, Detached 10.9.1941 to civilian service. Mobilised and conv 26.10.1941 to gunboat *KL-16*, trfd to the Onega Flotilla. Temporarily with the Volga Flotilla during 28.11.1941 to 25.5.1942. *KL-41* from 30.4.1942. Decomm 21.7.1944 to civilian service, discarded 5.11.1958
№ 86	№ 35	№ 32	T-32^3	SHUIA	230t; 30.0 x 6.1 x 2.2m; 440hp = 8kts; 200nm at 7.5kts; 1-45mm/46 21-K, 1 MTSh sweep, 1 MZT sweep; 37 men	28.6.1941	B	Built 1927. Mobilised 24.6.1941. Decomm 11.10.1944 to civilian service. Renamed May 1950 *Strazha*, name reverted May 1953. Discarded Jan 1961
№ 83	№ 36	№ 33	T-61^5	MOLOTOV	200t; 28.3 x 6.0 x 1.6m; 375hp = 1-45mm/46 21-K, 1 MTSh sweep, 1 MZT sweep; 37 men	28.6.1941	B	Built 1927. Mobilised 23.6.1941. Sunk 20.9.1941 by German aircraft at Leningrad, raised and recomm 20.2.1942 without number allocation. Reverted 11.10.1944 to tug

19.0 Minesweepers

№ 72	№ 37		T-37[16]	BOEVOJ	196t; 29.0 x 5.3 x 2.3m; 300hp = 9kts; 1400nm at 7kts; 1-45mm/46 21-K, 2-0.5in MGs, 1-0.3in MGs, 1 MTSh sweep, 1 MZT sweep, 1 AT sweep; 38 men	Nov 1939 27.6.1941	B La B	Built 1927. Mobilised Nov 1939 as tug, decomm 1940 to civilian service. Mobilised 22.6.1941 conv to minesweeper. Detached 10.9.1941 to civilian service, recomm 21.11.1941, number reverted, trfd to the Ladoga Flotilla, returned to the Baltic Fleet 18.10.1944
№ 84	№ 38	№ 37	T-37[3]	TIULEN'	300t; 34.6 x 6.3 x 2.0m; 400hp = 8/6kts; 1200nm; 1-45mm/46 21-K, 2-0.3in MGs, 1 MTSh sweep, 1 MZT sweep; 37 men	Nov 1939 28.6.1941	B	Built 1912. Mobilised Nov 1939 as tug, decomm 1940 to civilian service. Mobilised 23.6.1941. Detached 8.9.1941 to civilian service, recomm 19.12.1941. Sunk 2.8.1944 by German aircraft in Narva Bay
	№ 52	№ 55	T-55[4]	BUEK ex-*Buj* (1937) ex-*Kingisepp* (1932) ex-*Tosmar* (1925)	325t; 32.7 x 6.3 x 3.4m; 500hp = 10kts; 600nm at 8kts; 1-45mm/46 21-K, 1 MTSh sweep; 38 men	21.4.1921	B	Built 1900 Ahlström. Mobilised 1921, detached during 1922 to the OGPU Border Guard, hulked 1922–1924, conv 27.8.1924 to dispatch vessel. Surveying vessel from 1932. Conv 28.9.1939 to minesweeper. Reverted 11.10.1944 to tug
№ 81	№ 58		T-60[5]	OSYOTR	29.3 x 5.3 x 1.7m; 415hp	30.6.1941	B	Built 1914. Mobilised 25.6.1941. Detached 6.9.1941 to civilian service, recomm 3.1.1942, number reverted. Reverted 8.10.1944 to tug. Discarded Apr 1960
№ 82	№ 91	№ 61		LIAPIDEVSKIJ	32.6 x 5.5 x 1.7m; 240hp	1.7.1941	B	Built 1912. Mobilised 25.6.1941. Hulked 1.10.1942, reverted to tug 30.4.1944. Fate unknown
№ 100			T-100[6]	UK-100 ex-*Aunus* (Fin, 1940)	150t; 26.0 x 5.6 x 2.3m; 280hp = 10.5/7kts; 750nm; 2-45mm/46 21-K, 2-0.5in DShK MGs, 1-0.3in MGs, 8 M1908 mines, 5 M1926 mines; 38 men	3.8.1941	La	Built 1900 Crichton, Abo. Captured 1940, conv 24.8.1940 to training ship. Conv 3.8.1941 to minesweeper. Trfd 18.10.1944 to the Baltic Fleet. Renamed *F-198* on 9.4.1947. Decomm 16.5.1949 to civilian service, renamed *RB-30*. Preserved 1982

T-100, former Finnish tug *Aunus*, in 1943.
Boris Lemachko Collection

№ 122				SOM	163t; 29.2 x 5.5 x 1.6m; 280hp = 10kts; 1-45mm/46 21-K, 2-0.3in MGs; 31 men	10.7.1941	La	Built 1913. Mobilised 2.7.1941. Sunk 17.9.1941 by German aircraft
№ 171				NOREK	23.2 x 5.5 x 2.5m; 232hp	19.8.1941	B	Built 1910. Mobilised 2.8.1941. Lost 30.11.1941
№ 173				MORIAK № 1	22.0 x 5.0 x 3.5m; 260hp = 10kts; 800nm at 8kts; 1-45mm/46 21-K, 1 MTSh sweep, 1 OTSh sweep; 32 men	10.9.1941	B	Built 1895. Mobilised 2.8.1941 as tug, conv 10.9.1941 to minesweeper. Detached 10.9.1941 to civilian service, recomm 19.12.1941, number reverted. Laid up 3.9.1943, decomm 30.4.1944 to civilian service
№ 174				EMEL'IAN PUGACHYOV ex-*Mikhail*	21.6 x 4.8 x 2.4m; 205hp	Aug 1941	B	Built 1870. Mobilised 4.8.1941. Reverted 13.12.1941 to tug, decomm 15.2.1943 to civilian service. Discarded Dec 1962
№ 177				BELUGA	185t; 26.8 x 4.7 x 2.0m; 240hp = 12kts; 740nm at 11kts; 1-45mm/46 21-K, 1 MTSh sweep, 1 OTSh sweep; 32 men	3.9.1941	B	Built 1897. Mobilised 5.8.1941. Sunk 3.11.1941 in collision with dispatch vessel *Piarnu* in Neva estuary. Raised 11.11.1941 and recomm. Reverted 10.11.1944 to tug. Survived the war

TShch № No on Comm	TShch № 25.7.1941	TShch № 7.9.1941	No 1944	Name	Details	Comm	Fleet	Remarks
№ 178				UL'IANOV ex-KL № 2 (1919) ex-Sever (1918) ex-VP № 2 (1918) ex-A. Ulianov (1918) ex-Sever (1918)	27.5 x 5.0 x 2.1m; 300hp	2.9.1941	B	Built 1912 Il'sa. Mobilised 1918 for Onega Flotilla, conv to armed (Vooruzhyonnyj parokhod), conv 1919 to gunboat. Decomm 1919 to civilian service. Mobilised 1.8.1941, conv to minesweeper. Sunk 7.11.1941 by German artillery when ice-bound on the Neva
			T-64[5]	STEPAN RAZIN ex-KL № 8 (1920) ex-Buksir-ledokol № 1 (1919) ex-Sten'ka Razin (1919)	180t; 30.2 x 5.7 x 2.1m; 430hp = 9kts; 400nm; 1-45mm/46 21-K, 1 MTSh sweep, 1 MZT sweep	25.7.1941 7.3.1943	B	Icebreaking tug. Mobilised 1919 for Onega Flotilla, conv 1919 to gunboat. Decomm 1920 to civilian service. Mobilised 22.6.1941, comm 26.6.1941 as tug. Conv 25.7.1941 to minesweeper, conv 7.9.1941 to escort ship. Reverted 24.2.1942 to tug, decomm 8.8.1942 to civilian service. Mobilised 7.3.1943, conv to minesweeper. Survived the war
BTShch-11				SERGEJ KIROV	48.9 x 7.9 x 2.0m; 600hp = 9kts; 2-45mm/46 21-K, 2-0.5in MGs	4.9.1941	Cs	Mobilised 25.8.1941. Decomm 23.2.1942 to civilian service
BTShch-12				CHERNYSHEVSKIJ	48.9 x 7.9 x 2.0m; 600hp = 9kts; 2-45mm/46 21-K, 2-0.5in MGs	4.9.1941	Cs	Mobilised 25.8.1941. Decomm 10.3.1942 to civilian service
№ 101		№ 39[2]		PETROZAVODSK ex-PS № 1 (1920) ex-VP № 1 (1920) ex-Petrozavodsk (1918)	275t; 47.0 x 2.1m; 280hp = 12kts; 1296nm at 9kts; 1-45mm/46 21-K, 1-0.3in MGs, 1 MTSh sweep, 1 MZT sweep; 37 men	29.6.1941	B	Built 1913 Lange. Mobilised 1918 for Onega Flotilla, conv to armed steamer, conv March 1919 to gunboat, conv June 1919 to dispatch vessel, conv 1920 to surveying vessel. Decomm 1921 to civilian service. Mobilised 25.6.1941 conv to minesweeper, mined 7.7.1941 in Kronstadt roadstead. Raised autumn 1941, recomm 21.11.1941 as. Sunk 3.8.1942 by mines off Seskar

Exceptions noted in the main table.

No	Year	Date
1	1941	25.7.1941
2		22.11.1941
3	1944	5.6.1944
4		8.7.1944
5		29.8.1944
6		21.10.1944

Tral'shchik № 101 Petrozavodsk as built. Boris Lemachko Collection

Paddle steam tugs

TShch № No on Comm	TShch № 25.7.1941	TShch № 3.1.1942	TShch № 13.8.1943	No 29.8.1944	Name	Details	Comm	Fleet	Remarks
№ 71		№ 71		T-50	BALMASHEV	295t; 36.1 x 11.0 x 2.4m; 250hp = 6kts; 365nm at 5kts; 1-45mm/46 21-K, 1-0.3in MG, 1 MTSh sweep, 1 OTSh sweep; 32 men	28.6.1941	B	Built 1903. Mobilised 1919 for Onega Flotilla, decomm 1919 to civilian service. Mobilised 23.6.1941, conv to minesweeper. Detached 6.9.1941 to civilian operator, returned 3.1.1942. Reverted to tug 11.10.1944
№ 88		№ 39	№ 39	T-35	SIGOVETS	240t; 460hp = 1-45mm /46 21-K, 2-0.3in MGs, 1 MTSh sweep, 1 MZT; 37 men	3.7.1941	B	Built 1897. Mobilised 25.6.1941, conv to minesweeper Detached 6.9.1941 to civilian operator, returned 3.1.1942. Reverted to tug 11.10.1944

19.0 Minesweepers

№ 172		T-172	ZHELIABOV ex-*PS № 3* (1920) ex-*Zheliabov* (1919)	185t; 29.0 x 5.5 x 1.4m; 320hp = 10kts; 1-45mm/46 21-K, 2-0.3in MGs	19.8.1941	B	Built 1897. Mobilised 1919 for Onega Flotilla, conv to dispatch vessel. Decomm 1920 to civilian service. Mobilised 1.8.1941 conv to minesweeper. Detached 6.9.1941 to civilian operator, returned 19.12.1941, number reverted. Discarded Sept 1965
MBTShch-115	EMTShch-58		REVOLUTSIIA	100hp	21.6.1943	Cs	Mobilised 20.6.1943, conv to magnetic minesweeper. Decomm 13.6.1944 to civilian service
MBTShch-118	EMTShch-61		PIONER	60hp	21.7.1943	Cs	Mobilised 19.7.1943, conv to magnetic minesweeper. Decomm 27.4.1944 to civilian service
MBTShch-211	EMTShch-62		LENINETS	120hp	21.6.1943	Cs	Mobilised 20.6.1943, conv to magnetic minesweeper. Decomm 14.6.1944 to civilian service
MBTShch-212	EMTShch-63		CHKALOV	107hp	12.6.1943	Cs	Mobilised 11.6.1943, conv to magnetic minesweeper. Decomm 11.6.1944 to civilian service
MBTShch-213	EMTShch-64		18-J PARTS"EZD VKP(b) •		14.6.1943	Cs	Mobilised 13.6.1943, conv to magnetic minesweeper. Decomm 12.6.1944 to civilian service
MBTShch-214	EMTShch-65		GORNIAK	100hp	12.6.1943	Cs	Mobilised 10.6.1943, conv to magnetic minesweeper. Decomm 11.5.1944 to civilian service
MBTShch-215	EMTShch-66		1-e MAIA	•	June 1943	Cs	Mobilised 14.6.1943, conv to magnetic minesweeper. Decomm 16.4.1944 to civilian service
MBTShch-217	EMTShch-68		KRASNOFLOTETS	110hp	16.6.1943	Cs	Mobilised 15.6.1943, conv to magnetic minesweeper. Decomm 18.11.1944 to civilian service
MBTShch-216	EMTShch-67		FEODOSIIA	100hp	14.6.1943	Cs	Mobilised 12.6.1943, conv to magnetic minesweeper. Decomm 17.11.1943 to civilian service
MBTShch-218	EMTShch-69		DZERZHINSKIJ	70hp	June 1943	Cs	Mobilised 16.6.1943, conv to magnetic minesweeper. Decomm 12.5.1944 to civilian service
MBTShch-322	EMTShch-83		ANASTAS MIKOIAN	•	3.6.1943	Cs	Mobilised 2.6.1943, conv to magnetic minesweeper. Decomm 14.3.1944 to civilian service
MBTShch-323	EMTSHCH-84		KRENKEL'	80hp	5.6.1943	Cs	Mobilised 3.6.1943, conv to magnetic minesweeper. Decomm 28.4.1944 to civilian service.
MBTShch-327	EMTShch-88		PROFINTERN	110hp	16.6.1943	Cs	Mobilised 15.6.1943, conv to magnetic minesweeper. Decomm 13.5.1944 to civilian service
MBTShch-328	EMTShch-89		TOWARISHCH CHAPAEV	72hp	16.6.1943	Cs	Mobilised 15.6.1943, conv to magnetic minesweeper. Decomm 15.6.1944 to civilian service
RTShch-3		MS-38		•	6.11.1943 17.8.1945	Am	NKVD Border Guard tug. Mobilised 13.10.1943, returned 1.1.1945. Mobilised Aug 1945, returned to the NKVD 3.9.1945
RTShch-4		MS-39		•	6.11.1943 17.8.1945	Am	NKVD Border Guard tug. Mobilised 13.10.1943, returned 1.1.1945. Mobilised Aug 1945, returned to the NKVD 3.9.1945

19.5.2.2.3. Volga tugs for minesweeping rafts

Буксиры тралбарж

Minesweeping rafts were introduced for the purpose of sweeping magnetic mines; these were loaded with iron and scrap steel to induce a strong magnetic field. The following barges were listed with the Volga Flotilla, identified by their Yard Numbers with the *Tralbarzha №* pennant:

№ 201 – № 203   № 344 – № 345   № 398 – № 405   № 408 – № 411

To operate magnetic mine barges, small river tugs were mobilised and formally commissioned on 24.6.1943 (although some were already in use), allocated numbers with a 'T' pennant and three digits (with two exceptions, which were soon changed). To separate them from regular minesweepers (which had been fitted with some minesweeping gear on top of towing hooks), they were renumbered on 9.7.1943 with a 'B' pennant and two-digit numbers.

The numbers are displayed in the 'No' column of the tables below; all exceptions are explained in the 'Remarks' column.

All ships reverted to regular tugs in 1944 and after few months decommissioned and returned to civilian operators.

River steam tugs

No on Comm	No 9.7.1943	Name	Details	Comm	Fleet	Remarks
T-122	B-13	ENERGICHNYJ ex-*Mars* (1928)	25.7 x 4.3 x 1.8m; 110hp = 1-37mm/67.5 70-K, 2-0.5in MGs; 7 men	24.6.1943	Vo	Built 1900 Sormovo. Mobilised 13.5.1943. Reverted 12.8.1943 to service craft, from 2.6.1944 to tug. Discarded Dec 1966
T-125	B-14	KURSK ex-*Brat'ia* (1928)	29.0 x 4.3 x 1.8m; 100hp = 1-37mm/67.5 70-K, 2-0.5in MGs; 8 men	24.6.1943	Vo	Built 1906. Mobilised 14.5.1943. Reverted 2.6.1944 to tug. Discarded Dec 1966
T-242	B-17	VTOROJ	19.8 x 3.7 x 2.0m; 116hp = 5kts; 1-0.5in MGs; 4 men	24.6.1943	Vo	Built 1906. Mobilised 16.5.1943. Reverted 2.6.1944 to tug
T-321	B-23	LOMONOSOV	17.5 x 4.2 x 1.8m; 150hp = 1-0.3in MGs; 7 men	24.6.1943	Vo	Built 1913. Mobilised 29.5.1943. Reverted 25.4.1944 to tug
T-421	B-28	NOVATOR	19.5 x 4.5 x 1.8m; 100hp = 7kts	24.6.1943	Vo	Built 1913. Mobilised 15.6.1943. Reverted 2.6.1944 to tug
T-423	B-29	MEZEN'	23.0 x 4.0 x 1.6m; 170hp = 6.3kts; 13 men	24.6.1943	Vo Cs	Built 1910. Mobilised 15.6.1943. Reverted 30.6.1944 to tug, trfd to the Caspian Flotilla. Decomm 22.11.1944 to civilian service. Discarded Apr 1970
T-522	B-31	DON	85t; 17.7 x 4.3 x 2.1m; 230hp = 8.6kts; 1-0.5in MG	24.6.1943	Vo	Built 1928. Mobilised 7.5.1943. Detached 13.8.1943 to civilian operator, reverted 12.11.1943 to tug
T-523	B-32	IOKOGANSHCHIK ex-*Iokan'shchik* (1939) ex-*Pioner* (1922) ex-*BP № 1* (1919) ex-*Pioner* (1919)	65t; 26.0 x 5.2 x 0.8m; 100hp = 11kts; 1-0.5in MG	24.6.1943	Vo Cs	Built 1912 Sandvikens. Mobilised 15.6.1943. Reverted 30.6.1944 to tug, trfd to the Caspian Flotilla. Decomm 22.11.1944 to civilian service
T-524	B-33	STARITSA	70t; 18.3 x 4.4 x 1.4m; 100hp = 7kts; 1-0.5in MG	24.6.1943	Vo	Built 1914 Tristan. Mobilised 17.5.1943. Reverted 2.6.1944 to tug. Discarded Dec 1964
T-622	B-37	MINSK ex-*Vperyod* (1936)	70t; 18.5 x 4.5 x 1.7m; 140hp = 7.5kts; 1-20mm Oerlikon	24.6.1943	Vo	Built 1910 St Petersburg. Mobilised 17.5.1943. Reverted 20.6.1944 to tug. Discarded March 1979
T-623	B-40	BRIGADIR	65t; 19.1 x 4.4 x 1.4m; 140hp = 6.7kts; 1-20mm Oerlikon	24.6.1943	Vo	Built 1912 St Petersburg. Mobilised 17.5.1943. Reverted 20.06.1944 to tug. Discarded July 1980
T-624	B-39	KOMMUNA	75t; 18.0 x 4.0 x 2.2m; 100hp = 8.5kts; 1-0.5in MG	24.6.1943	Vo	Built 1913. Mobilised 17.5.1943. Reverted 20.06.1944 to tug
T-625	B-41	OBDORSK	70t; 19.4 x 4.5 x 1.5m; 150hp = 9.1kts; 1-20mm Oerlikon	24.6.1943	Vo	Built 1911. Mobilised 13.5.1943. Detached 11.10.1943 to civilian operator. Reverted 20.06.1944 to tug
T-626	B-38	BELOMORSK	70t; 18.4 x 4.0 x 1.7m; 155hp = 7kts; 1-20mm Oerlikon	24.6.1943	Vo	Built 1914. Mobilised 12.5.1943. Reverted 20.06.1944 to tug
T-841	B-44	PAMIATI KUZNETSOVA	80t; 22.6 x 4.6 x 1.5m; 108hp = 8.5kts; 1-20mm Oerlikon	24.6.1943	Vo	Built 1914. Mobilised 14.5.1943. Reverted 2.06.1944 to tug
T-842	B-45	BORETS ZA KOMMUNU ex-*SS № 102* (1918) ex-*Peresvet* (1918)	75t; 17.4 x 4.3 x 1.8m; 110hp; = 1-0.5in MGs	24.6.1943	Vo	Built 1914. Mobilised 1918 for Volga Flotilla, conv to escort vessel (Storozhevoe sudno), decomm 1920 to civilian service. Mobilised 17.5.1943. Reverted 2.06.1944 to tug
T-843	B-46	BALTVOD	65t; 19.8 x 3.4 x 2.0m; 80hp = 8kts; 1-0.5in MGs	24.6.1943	Vo	Built 1913. Mobilised 18.5.1943. Reverted 20.06.1944 to tug. Discarded Sept 1960
T-844	B-47	STEREGUSHCHIJ ex-*SS № 107* (1919) ex-*Steregushchij* (1919)	75t; 25.3 x 4.1 x 1.4m; 120hp = 8.6kts; 1-20mm Oerlikon	24.6.1943	Vo	Built 1906. Mobilised 1918 for Volga Flotilla, conv to escort vessel (Storozhevoe sudno), decomm 1920 to civilian service. Mobilised 17.5.1943. Reverted 2.06.1944 to tug.

19.0 Minesweepers

T-125 Kursk in civilian service after the war. Boris Lemachko Collection

Paddle steam tugs

No on Comm	No 9.7.1943	Name	Details	Comm	Fleet	Remarks
T-121	B-10	ZUBR ex-*Osnovatel'* (1918)	38.4 x 13.0 x 0.7m; 100hp; 2-45mm/46 21-K, 2-20mm Oerlikn, 2-0.5in MGs	24.6.1943	Vo	Built 1911 Volosov. Mobilised 11.5.1943. Conv 5.8.1943 to AA defence ship. Reverted 30.5.1944 to tug. Renamed 1945 *Furmanov*. Discarded May 1959
T-123	B-11	POSTAVSHCHIK	160t; 37.8 x 10.5 x 0.7m; 100hp = 7kts; 1-0.5in MGs; 15 men	24.6.1943	Vo	Built 1913. Mobilised 14.5.1943. Reverted 30.5.1944 to tug
T-124	B-12	SOVKOMBAJN ex-*Fialka* (1918)	39.6 x 5.9 x 1.2m; 280hp; 1-37mm; 2-0.5in MGs	26.4.1943	Vo	Built 1913. Mobilised 15.5.1943. Reverted 12.11.1943 to tug
T-126	B-15	CHEBOKSARY	160t; 38.4 x 14.5 x 0.8m; 160hp = 7kts; 2-45mm/46 21-K, 2-20mm Oerlikon, 2-0.5in MGs; 15 men	24.6.1943	Vo	Built 1935. Mobilised 21.5.1943. Conv 5.8.1943 to AA defence ship. Reverted 30.5.1944 to tug. Discarded Feb 1961
T-241	B-16	PODTYOLKOV	43.1 x 11.6 x 1.5m; 150hp = 6kts; 2-0.5in MGs	24.6.1943	Vo	Built 1909. Mobilised 21.5.1943. Reverted 30.5.1944 to tug. Discarded Apr 1957
T-322	B-18	SHTURVAL'NYJ	160t; 42.0 x 14.0 x 0.7m; =190hp = 9.5kts; 2-45mm/46 21-K, 2-20mm Oerlikon 1-0.5in MGs; 16 men	24.6.1943	Vo	Built 1931 Gorokhovets. Mobilised 26.5.1943. Conv 5.8.1943 to AA defence ship. Reverted 20.6.1944 to tug. Refurbished 1955
T-323	B-19	VECHERKOVICH ex-*Rabotnik* ex-*Aleksandr* (1918)	150t; 31.4 x 12.9 x 1.1m; 130hp = 6.2kts; 2-0.3in MGs	24.6.1943	Vo	Built 1887. Mobilised 4.6.1943. Reverted 25.4.1944 to tug
T-324	B-20	PINSK	160t; 49.9 x 14.6 x 0.7m; 220hp = 10.2kts; 2-0.3in MGs; 17 men	24.6.1943	Vo	Built 1937 Kujbyshev. Mobilised 24.5.1943. Reverted 16.10.1943 to tug. Discarded Dec 1964

T-322 Shturval'nyj at the foreground in civilian service in the 1960s. Boris Lemachko Collection

No on Comm	No 9.7.1943	Name	Details	Comm	Fleet	Remarks
T-422	B-24	ASHKADAR	160t; 45.9 x 12.6 x 0.7m; 210hp = 9.1kts; 2-45mm/46 21-K, 2-20mm Oerlikon, 2-0.5in MGs; 16 men	24.6.1943	Vo	Built 1899 Yelabuga. Mobilised 23.5.1943. Conv 5.8.1943 to AA defence ship. Reverted 12.11.1943 to tug. Discarded Dec 1963
T-424	B-27	SERGEJ KOSTRIKOV	150t; 47.9 x 14.0 x 9.8m; 200hp = 9.1kts; 2-37mm/67.5 70-K, 2-20mm Oerlikon, 2-0.5in MGs; 17 men	24.6.1943	Vo	Built 1931. Mobilised 19.5.1943. Conv 5.8.1943 to AA defence ship. Reverted 20.6.1944 to tug
T-425	B-26	MAIAKOVSKIJ	150t; 42.5 x 12.1 x 0.8m; 140hp = 7kts; 2-45mm/46 21-K, 2-20mm Oerlikon, 2-0.5in MGs;17 men	24.6.1943	Vo	Built 1886. Mobilised 2.6.1943. Conv 5.8.1943 to AA defence ship. Reverted 20.6.1944 to tug
T-426	B-25	TRANSPORT	150t; 40.6 x 11.9 x 1.1m; 140hp = 7.5kts; 1-37mm/67.5 70-K, 2-0.5in MGs; 17 men	24.6.1943	Vo	Built 1905 Nozhnyi Novgorod. Mobilised 29.5.1943. Detached 13.8.1943 to civilian operator, reverted 12.11.1943 to tug. Discarded Dec 1961
T-521	B-30	VISLIANA	160t; 42.5 x 14.6 x 0.9m; 200hp = 10kts; 2-37mm/67.5 70-K, 2-20mm Oerlikon, 2-0.5inMGs; 17 men	24.6.1943	Vo Cs	Built 1934. Mobilised 8.5.1943. Conv 5.8.1943 to AA defence ship. Reverted 30.6.1944 to tug, trfd to the Caspian Flotilla. Decomm 22.11.1944 to civilian service
T-525	B-34	VYKSA ex-*Rabotnik* (1925) ex-*Pobeda* (1917) ex-*Vladelets* (1908)	170t; 46.7 x 12.2 x 0.9m; 130hp = 7kts; 1-20mm Oerlikon, 1-0.5in MGs	24.6.1943	Vo	Built 1887 Gaks-Kuznetsov. Mobilised 2.7.1943. Reverted 12.11.1943 to tug. Discarded Feb 1949
T-845	B-48	INZHENER BEGAM	160t; 48.6 x 14.6 x 0.8m; 210hp = 10.5kts; 2-45mm/46 21-K, 2-20mm, 2-0.5in MGs	24.6.1943	Vo	Built 1935. Mobilised 19.5.1943. Reverted 24.4.1944 to tug. Discarded July 1971
T-92 T-846[1]	B-49[2] T-847[3]	BAKEN	170t; 39.1 x 12.6 x 1.4m; 145hp = 9.1kts; 2-45mm/46 21-K, 2-20. 2-0.5in MGs	24.6.1943	Vo	Built 1895. Mobilised 19.5.1943. Rated from 5.8.1943 as AA defence ship, reverted 29.6.1944 to tug *B-49*. Discarded June 1960
T-91 T-845[1]	B-50[2] T-846[3]	NEVA	170t; 39.7 x 12.3 x 1.3m; 220hp = 9.1kts. 1-0.5in MGs	24.6.1943	Vo	Built 1900. Mobilised 27.5.1943. Reverted 12.11.1943 to tug *B-50*

Exceptions noted in the main table.

No	Year	Date
1	1943	7.7.1943
2		31.7.1943
3		16.8.1943

T-422 Ashkadar in civilian service in the 1950s.
Boris Lemachko Collection

19.0 Minesweepers

19.5.3. Naval & Army conversions

Tral'shchik № 01 class
Service steamers

Displacement: 17t
Dimensions: 19.0 x 5.7/3.0 x 0.6m
Machinery: 2 side wheels, compound, 1 boiler, 30hp = 9.7/5.4kts. Range 540nm at 8.1kts
Armament: 1-0.3in Maxim MG, 1 MTSh (light) sweep, 10 R-1 mines
Complement: 8

TShch № 1927	TShch № 22.6.1941	Built	Comm	Fleet	Remarks
	Builder: Iuzhnorski*				
№ 01		1926	1927	Dn	Sunk 26.8.1941 by artillery fire off Domantovo on Dnieper, raised by the Germans, comm as *Klaus*. Scuttled 1943 by the Germans off Rozhny on Desna River. Wreck raised Nov 1943
№ 02		1926	1927	Dn	Sunk 26.8.1941 by artillery fire off Domantovo on Dnieper, raised by the Germans, comm as *Morizt*. Scuttled 1944 by the Germans off Chernobyl on Pripyat River. Wreck raised Feb 1944
№ 03	№ 30	1926	1927	Dn	Lost Aug 1941 off Cherkasy at Dnieper
№ 04	№ 31	1926	1927	Dn	Scuttled Sept 1941 at Kiev
№ 05	№ 32	1926	1927	Dn	Scuttled Sept 1941 at Kiev

* launched 1916–1917, completed 1926.

River service craft ordered 1915 by the Russian Army, completed by the Soviets as river minesweepers. Designated in June 1940 for transfer to the Danube Flotilla, but actually remained on the Dnieper until German invasion.

Tral'shchik № 1 class river minesweeper in 1935.
Vitalij Kostrichenko Collection

Zmej in 1920s. Przemysław Budzbon Collection

Army yachts

TShch № 25.7.1941	TShch № 7.9.1941	TShch № 2.8.1944	Name	Details	Comm	Fleet	Remarks
№ 51			ZMEJ ex-*Zarnitsa* (1921)	245t; 40.2 x 6.0 x 2.8m; 375hp = 10/8kts; 700nm; 1-45mm/46 21-K, 2-0.3in MGs, 1 MTSH. 1 MZT; 37 men	11.2.1918	B	Built 1914, Helsingfors, yacht of CO of Kronshtadt Fortress. Mobilised 15.1.1918, conv 9.4.1921 to minesweeper, dispatch vessel 1923-1924. Rebuilt 1927, 1933, 1936 and 1939. Mined 30.7.1941 in the Solea Strait off Saarema Island
№ 92	№ 62	T-62	INZHENER	140t; 31.2 x 5.9 x 2.7m; 240hp = 8kts; 560nm at 4.5kts; 1-45mm/46 21-K, 2-0.5in MGs, 2-0.3in MGs, 1 MTSh sweep, 1 MZT sweep; 31 men	23.3.1939 25.6.1941	B	Built 1890. Icebreaking yacht of the Sveaborg Fortress. Conv 1921 to dispatch vessel, decomm 1926 to civilian service. Experimental vessel of Ostekhburo from 10.3.1927, seized 23.3.1939. Escort vessel 22.11.1939 to 12.12.1939, conv 25.6.1941 to minesweeper, numbered *№ 92* from 25.7.1941, *№ 62* from 7.9.1941, *T-62* from 2.8.1944. Conv *5.11.1945* to surveying vessel. Deleted 13.11.1953

Dispatch vessel

Name	Details	Comm	Fleet	Remarks
DZHALITA	400t; 40.5 x 6.2 x 2.9m; 300hp = 7/5 w. 277nm at 5kts; 1-45mm/46 21-K, 1 MTSh sweep, 1 MZT sweep, 6 mines; 41 men	1.8.1926 29.6.1941	BS	Built 1926, Nikolaev. Dispatch vessel, laid down 1914 at Petrograd for assembly at Nikolaev. Laid down 1916 at Nikolaev, captured 1918 by the Germans, recovered 1920. Comm 1.8.1926 as dispatch vessel, conv 4.2.1927 to minesweeper, numbered *Tral'shchik № 11* from Jan 1928, *№ 14* from Nov 1928. Conv 1.1.1939 to experimental vessel, reverted to minesweeper 29.6.1941. Sunk 29.8.1943 by *U-18* off Ochamchire

Cross reference: Rated as minesweepers

TShch № No	Name	Details	Type	From	To	Fate
BTShch-13	KUBAN'	*Demosfen* type	Gunboat	29.10.1941	23.2.1943	Decomm to civilian service
№ 49	LAJNE	*Lajne*	Escort ship	25.7.1941	19.12.1941	Conv to escort ship
T-301	ODESSA	*Piarnu*	Dispatch vessel	16.2.1942	12.7.1943	Reverted to tug *K-4*
T-31	RAZVEDCHIK	*Dozornyj* class	Escort ship	8.7.1942		Survived the war
№ 76	VAL	*Val*	Surveying ship	June 1941	8.8.1941	Lost
T-512	VALERIJ CHKALOV	*El'pidifor* class	Gunboat	8.7.1941	7.3.1942	Conv to cable vessel
№ 79	VOLNOREZ	*Volnorez*	Surveying ship	June 1941		Survived the war

Tral'shchik № 14 Dzhalita in the early 1930s. *Boris Lemachko Collection*

T-513 Nord in civilian service. *Boris Lemachko Collection*

19.5.4. CIVILIAN CONVERSIONS

Nord type
Passenger ships

Displacement: 285t full load
Dimensions: 37.6 x 6.6 x 2.9m
Machinery: 1-shaft, Benz diesel motors, 375hp = 12kts
Armament: 1-45mm/46 21-K, 2-0.5in MGs, 1 MTSh sweep, 1 MZT sweep
Complement: 35

Pt-No	No	Name	Built	Comm	Fleet	Remarks
1941	22.6.1941					
	Builder: A.Marti, Odessa					
65	T-513	NORD	1932	2.7.1941	BS	Mobilised 22.6.1941. Decomm 10.6.1946 to civilian service, renamed *Iug* from Feb 1950. Discarded 1968
66	T-514	OST	1932	2.7.1941	BS	Mobilised 22.6.1941. Sunk 4.3.1943 by mines off the Doob Cape

Kurortnik type
Passenger ships

Displacement: 148t (*Turist* 145.5t) full load
Dimensions: 26.7 x 6.0 x 2.4m
Machinery: 1-shaft, Benz diesel motors, 220hp = 9.5kts
Armament: 1-45mm/46 21-K, 2-0.3in MGs
Complement: 16

No 29.1.1940	No 25.6.1941	Name	Built	Comm	Fleet	Remarks
		Builder: A.Marti, Odessa				
T-488	AS-24	KURORTNIK	1931	29.1.1940 25.6.1941	BS	Mobilised autumn 1939, conv to minesweeper *T-488*. Decomm 19.3.1940 to civilian service. Mobilised 25.6.1941, conv to salvage vessel. Decomm 1946 to civilian service
T-489	AS-25	TURIST	1931	29.1.1940 25.6.1941	BS	Mobilised autumn 1939, conv to minesweeper *T-489*. Decomm 19.3.1940 to civilian service. Mobilised 25.6.1941, conv to salvage vessel. Decomm 1946 to civilian service

T-489 Turist in 1946.
Boris Lemachko Collection

Tramvaj type
River passenger ferries

Displacement: 120t full load
Dimensions: 29.9 x 5.6 x 1.2m
Machinery: 100hp = 6.2kts
Armament: 1-0.5in MGs

No 16.8.1943	No 26.10.1943	Name	Built	Comm	Fleet	Remarks
T-511	B-51	D-11	1935	16.8.1943	Vo	Mobilised 27.7.1943, conv to tug for minesweeping raft. Conv 28.4.1944 to service craft
T-512	B-52	D-15	1935	16.8.1943	Vo	Mobilised 27.7.1943, conv to tug for minesweeping raft. Conv 28.4.1944 to service craft

Cargo steamers

Pt-No 1941	No on Comm	No 21.6.1944	Name	Details	Comm	Fleet	Remarks
43	T-486	EMTShch-486	SOVETSKAIA ROSSIIA ex-*Sofiia* (1920) ex-*T-395* (1920) ex-*T-295* (1918) ex-*Sofiia* (1916) ex-*Omsk*	1005t; 58.4 x 8.6 x 2.9m; 360hp = 8kts; 420nm at 5kts; 3-45mm/46 21-K, (added 1943: 1-20mm), 2-0.5in MGs, 50 mines, 1 MTSh sweep, 1 MZT; 43 men	29.1.1940	BS Az BS	Built 1880 Mitchell. Mobilised 1916 for Black Sea Fleet, conv to minesweeper. Captured 1918 by the Germans, trfd to the White Russians, recovered 1920, conv to repair ship, decomm 1922 to civilian service. Mobilised 29.10.1939, conv to minesweeper. Temporarily trfd to the Azov Flotilla 10.04.1942 10.04.1942 to 7.9.1942. Torpedoed 15.10.1943 by *U-23*, survived. Conv 21.6.1944 to magnetic minesweeper. Decomm 22.1.1945 to civilian service. Discarded 5.3.1955
62	T-489	EMTShch-489	KHOSTA ex-*Georgij* (122) ex-*T-15* (1921) ex-*Georgij* (1921) ex-*T-261* (1918) ex-*Georgij* (1916)	1441t; 64.0 x 9.6 x 3.2m; 400hp = 7.5kts; 780nm; 1 (added 1943:2, added 1944:1)-45mm/46 21-K, 2-0.3in MGs, 1 MTSh sweep, 1 MZT; 40 men	5.7.1941	BS	Built 1910 Schlick. Mobilised 1916 for Black Sea Fleet, conv to minesweeper. Captured 1918 by the Germans, trfd to the White Russians, recovered 1920, recomm. Decomm 1921 to civilian service. Mobilised 22.6.1941, conv to minesweeper. Conv 21.6.1944 to magnetic minesweeper. Decomm 21.8.1946 to civilian service, discarded 1955
63	T-511		CHERVONYJ KAZAK ex-*KL № 11* (1921) ex-*Prorok Iona* (1920) ex-*T-335* (1918) ex-*T-235* (1918) ex-*Prorok Iona* (1916)	1050t; 56.7 x 9.4 x 2.7m; 300hp = 8.5kts; 1700nm at 6kts; 4-45mm/46 21-K, 2-0.3in MGs, 1 MTSh sweep, 1 ShChT sweep; 27 men	3.7.1941	BS	Built 1896 STT. Mobilised 1916 for Black Sea Fleet, conv to minesweeper. Captured 1918 by the Germans, Seized 1920, recomm the Azov Flotilla. Conv 1920 to gunboat № 1, decomm 1921 to civilian service. Mobilised 22.6.1941, conv to minesweeper. Sunk 26.3.1943 by German MTBs in Tsemes Bay
68	T-516	EMTShch-516	MAJKOP ex-*Novyj mir* (1922) ex-*Chervonyj kazak* (1921) ex-*Zelenyj partizan* (1920) ex-*Elena Kuppa* (1920) ex-*T-365* (1920) ex-*T-265* (1920) ex-*Elena Kuppa* (1916)	842t; 57.8 x 8.2 x 2.2m; 360hp = 8kts; 490nm at 5kta; 4-45mm/46 21-K, 1-20mm Oerlikon, 2-0.5in MGs, 1 MTSh sweep; 40 men	1.7.1941	BS	Built 1893 STT. Mobilised 1915 for Black Sea Fleet, conv to minesweeper. Captured 1918 by the Germans, trfd 1918 to the White Russians, recovered 1920, comm as transport, conv to gunboat. Scuttled 1920, raised 1921 to civilian service. Mobilised 22.6.1941, conv to minesweeper. Sunk 19.11.1941 by German aircraft off Anapa, raised and recomm. Conv 21.6.1944 to magnetic minesweeper
39			DOROTEIA	500t; 46.2 x 6.5 x 4.0m; 400hp = 8/5.5kts; 550nm; 2-45mm, 1 MTSh sweep, 1 MZT, 6 mines; 41 men	13.9.1924 5.7.1941	BS	Built 1898. Coastal steamer. Mobilised 9.8.1924, conv to minesweeper № 21, № 12 from 15.1.1938. Conv 1.1.1939 to experimental vessel, reverted to minesweeper 5.7.1941. Conv 9.10.1944 to depot ship, conv 6.1.1945 to experimental vessel

T-516 Majkop in civilian service.
Przemysław Budzbon Collection

T-501 Sivash in 1959 in civilian service.
Sergej Berezhnoj Collection

19.0 Minesweepers

Icebreaking tug

TShch № 25.7.1941	TShch № 7.9.1941	Name	Details	Comm	Fleet	Remarks
55	54	MOROZ ex-*Soldat* (?)	350t; 32.2 x 6.6 x 4.2m; 750hp = 11kts; 1060nm at 8kts; 1-45mm, 2-0.5in MGs, 1 MTSh sweep, 1 MZT sweep; 37 men	21.11.1939	B	Built 1914 Finland. Experimental vessel of the Ostekhburo, seized 23.3.1939. Reverted to tug 25.5.1944. Survived the war

Drifter type

Drifters

Displacement: 370t
Dimensions: 34.6 x 6.4 x 4.3m
Machinery: 1-shaft compound, 1 boiler, 350hp = 7.9kts. Range 672nm
Armament: 1-45/46 21-K, 2-0.3in MGs, 1 MTSh sweep, 1 MZT sweep
Complement: 45

TShch № on Comm	No 13.9.1944	Drifter №	Built	Comm	Fleet	Remarks
№ 20	T-20	№ 1	1930	June 1941	P	Mobilised 9.6.1941. Survived the war
№ 21	T-21	№ 2	1930	June 1941	P	Mobilised 9.6.1941. Survived the war

Sivash type

Steam hopper barges

Displacement: 500t full load
Dimensions: 49.1 x 9.3 x 2.4m
Machinery: reciprocating, 350hp = 5kts. Range 600nm at 4.5kts
Armament: 2(from 1944 1)-3in/55 34-K, (added 1944: 3-45mm/46 21-K), 2-0.5in MGs, 2-0.3in MGs, 1 MTSh sweep
Complement: 44

Pt-No 1941	No 1.7.1941	No 21.6.1944	Name	Built	Comm	Fleet	Remarks
		Builder: Taganrog Works					
45	T-501	EMTShch-501	SIVASH	1932	1.7.1941	BS	Built 1932 Taganrog. Mobilised 22.6.1941. Conv 21.6.1944 to magnetic minesweeper *EMTShch-501*. Decomm to civilian service after the war
46	T-502		MANYCH	1932	1.7.1941	BS	Built 1932 Taganrog. Mobilised 22.6.1941. Conv 1.10.1942 to naval tanker

Steam hopper barges

Pt-No 1941	No 1941	No 21.6.1944	Name	Details	Comm	Fleet	Remarks
51	T-491		KIZILTASH	444grt; 48.0 x 9.8 x 3.0m; 435hp = 6kts; 1030nm at 5kts; 2-45mm/46 21-K, 2-0.3in MGs	7.7.1941	BS	Built 1925. Mobilised 22.6.1941. Damaged 27.12.1941 by German aircraft in the Kerch Strait, sank 2.3.1942 under tow off Kuchugur
52	T-492	EMTShch-492	BIELOBIEREZH'E	700t; 46.2 x 8.0 x 3.8m; 230hp = 6.5kts; 575nm; 3-45mm/46 21-K, (added 1943: 1-20mm), 2-0.5in MGs, 1 MTSh sweep; 40 men	6.8.1941	BS	Built 1898. Mobilised 22.6.1941. Conv 21.6.1944 to magnetic minesweeper *EMTShch-492*. Decomm 26.9.1944.
53	T-493		KHADZHIBEJ	329.8grt; 42.5 x 8.0 x 3.8m; 230hp = 7kts; 1050nm; 2-45mm/46 21-K, 2-0.3in MGs	30.6.1941	BS	Built 1898 Lyon. Mobilised 1922, conv to surveying vessel, decomm 1924 to civilian service. Mobilised 22.6.1941, conv to minesweeper. Sunk 6.9.1941 by German aircraft at Odessa. Raised by the Germans, repaired. Recovered 28.9.1944 at Constanța

Pt-No 1941	No 1941	No 21.6.1944	Name	Details	Comm	Fleet	Remarks
54	T-494		SARY-KAMYSHI ex-*Olesh'e* (1922)	950t; 45.6 x 8.3 x 3.2m; 230hp = 7kts; 1000nm; 2-45mm/46 21-K, 2-0.3in MGs	30.6.1941	BS Az	Built 1889. Mobilised 22.6.1941. Trfd 10.04.1942 to the Azov Flotilla 7.9.1942. Sunk 25.4.1942 by German aircraft in Jasenskaja Bay
55	T-495	EMTShch-495	KONKA	520t; 43.0 x 9.2 x 4.8m; 375hp = 8kts; 1708nm at 6kts; 4-45mm/46 21-K, (added 1943: 1-20mm Oerlikon), 2-0.5in MGs	26.7.1941	BS	Mobilised 22.6.1941. Conv 21.6.1944 to magnetic minesweeper EMTShch-495. Decomm 4.3.1945
56	T-497		EGURCHA ex-*KL № 9* (1921) ex-*Krasnaia Zvezda* (1922) ex-*Egurcha* (1920)	1080t; 59.2 x 10.0 x 1.8m; 400hp = 6kts; 650nm; 2-45mm/46 21-K, 2-0.3in MGs	7.7.1941	BS	Mobilised 1920 for Azov Flotilla, conv to armed steamer, decomm 1921 to civilian service. Mobilised 22.6.1941 conv to minesweeper. Mined 2.11.1941 off Novorossiysk

Cross reference: Rated as minesweeper

TShch № No	Name	Details	Type	From	To	Fate
T-911	ASTRAKHAN'	*Smena* type	Escort ship	26.11.1941	30.7.1943	Lost
№ 155	AVACHA	*KATShch № 155*	Minesweeping boat	8.6.1943	1945	Survived the war
№ 56	BAROMETR	*Udalets*	Tug	4.11.1932	28.8.1941	Lost
T-903	BELOMORETS	*Smena* type	Escort ship	20.9.1941	2.2.1944	Conv to dispatch vessel
T-507	DELEGAT	*Pioner* type	Transport	17.7.1941	27.10.1941	Lost
T-712	GAZOKHOD № 72	*MSV-34* type	Minesweeping boat	24.6.1943	12.11.1943	Reverted to tug
T-2	GOL'FSTRIM	*Smena* type	Escort ship	19.10.1939	29.3.1940	Decomm to civilian service
T-895	GOL'FSTRIM	*Smena* type	Escort ship	29.7.1941	1.2.1943	Decomm to civilian service
T-881	I. PAPANIN	*Smena* type	Escort ship	29.7.1941	1945	Decomm to civilian service
T-6	KOLGUEVETS	*Smena* type	Escort ship	Oct 1939	29.3.1940	Decomm to civilian service
T-899	KOLGUEVETS	*Smena* type	Escort ship	29.7.1941	8.3.1945	Decomm to civilian service
T-910	KOLOMNA	*Smena* type	Escort ship	23.10.1941	1945	Decomm to civilian service
№ 10	KOMMUNAR	*MSV* type	Minesweeping boat	29.7.1941	Sum 1941	Lost
№ 08	KOMSOMOLETS	*MSV* type	Minesweeping boat	29.7.1941	Sum 1941	Lost
T-3	KRASNYJ ONEZHANIN	*Smena* type	Escort ship	Nov 1939	29.3.1940	Decomm to civilian service
T-896	KRASNYJ ONEZHANIN	*Smena* type	Escort ship	29.7.1941	1.10.1943	Lost
T-882	LENINGRAD	*Smena* type	Escort ship	29.7.1941	30.1.1943	Decomm to civilian service
T-506	MESTKOM	*Pioner* type	Transport	29.1.1940	24.6.1942	Reverted to transport
T-711	MRG-54	*MSV-34* type	Minesweeping boat	24.6.1943	5.10.1943	Reverted to tug
T-4	MUD'IUZHANIN	*Smena* type	Escort ship	Oct 1939	29.3.1940	Decomm to civilian service
T-897	MUD'IUZHANIN	*Smena* type	Escort ship	29.7.1941	30.1.1943	Decomm to civilian service
T-5	NENETS	*Smena* type	Escort ship	Oct 1939	29.3.1940	Decomm to civilian service
T-898	NENETS	*Smena* type	Escort ship	29.7.1941	25.8.1941	Lost
	NEPEREMOZHNYJ	*MSV* type	Minesweeping boat	29.7.1941	Sum 1941	Lost
T-481	PIONER	*Pioner* type	Transport	29.1.1940	23.9.1944	Reverted to transport
№ 06	PRIPIAT'	*MSV* type	Minesweeping boat	29.7.1941	Sum 1941	Lost
№ 07	PROGRESS	*MSV* type	Minesweeping boat	29.7.1941	Sum 1941	Lost
T-504	RABOTNIK	*Pioner* type	Transport	17.7.1941	2.11.1941	Lost
	RADUGA	*Raduga*	Tug	5.5.1943	23.12.1943	Lost
T-517	RAJKOMVOD	*Pioner* type	Transport	25.6.1941		Decomm after the war to civilian service
№ 91	SEJNER № 11	*KATShch № 91*	Minesweeping boat	8.6.1943	1945	Survived the war
№ 92	SEJNER № 12	*KATShch № 92*	Minesweeping boat	8.6.1943	1945	Survived the war
№ 93	SEJNER № 13	*KATShch № 93*	Minesweeping boat	8.6.1943	1945	Survived the war
№ 94	SEJNER № 14	*KATShch № 94*	Minesweeping boat	8.6.1943	1945	Survived the war
T-1	SEVERNYJ	*Smena* type	Escort ship	19.10.1939	29.3.1940	Decomm to civilian service
T-894	SEVERNYJ	*Smena* type	Escort ship	29.7.1941	15.5.1944	Decomm to civilian service
T-505	SUDKOM	*Pioner* type	Transport	24.6.1941		Decomm after the war to civilian service
T-483	TRAKTORIST	*Pioner* type	Transport	29.1.1940	24.6.1942	Reverted to transport
T-326	V-66	*MSV-34* type	Minesweeping boat	24.6.1943	23.9.1943	Reverted to tug
T-325	V-68	*MSV-34* type	Minesweeping boat	24.6.1943	23.9.1943	Reverted to tug
№ 156	VILIUJ	*KATShch № 156*	Minesweeping boat	8.6.1943	1945	Survived the war
T-87	ZARIAD	*Zariad*	Firefighting vessel	9.11.1944		Survived the war
T-30	ZARNITSA	*Zarnitsa*	Tug	12.4.1943		Survived the war
T-482	ZEMLIAK	*Pioner* type	Transport	29.1.1940	23.9.1944	Reverted to transport
T-904	ZHDANOV	*Smena* type	Escort ship	20.9.1941	25.7.1943	Lost

19.5.5. War prizes – Southeast Europe, 1944-1945

Miscellaneous

No	Details	Comm	Fleet	Remarks
EMTShch-631	•	24.5.1945	Da	Yugoslavian river steam tug *Chernogoriia* captured Oct 1944, conv to magnetic minesweeper. Returned to Yugoslavia after the war
EMTShch-648	•	31.8.1945	Da	German magnetic motor minesweeper *Mina* captured spring 1945. Conv 16.6.1949 to minesweeper *T-648*, decomm 24.7.1954, conv to mooring berth *PPR-57*
EMTShch-656	320t; 40 x 10.5 x 1.1m; 180hp = 9kts; 1-20mm Oerlikon, 1 magnetic sweep; 22 men	10.11.1944	Da	Romanian magnetic minesweeper, steamer *General Majkan*. Captured Aug 1944, conv 28.3.1947 to surveying vessel *Dolgota*, decomm 7.7.1956
EMTShch-657	1-37mm	10.11.1944	Da	Romanian magnetic minesweeper, steamer *Bessarab*. Captured Aug 1944. Deleted 13.11.1945, BU
EMTShch-659	•	10.11.1944	Da	Bulgarian magnetic minesweeper, steamer *Kiryl Popov*. Captured Sept 1944. Returned 10.8.1945 to Bulgaria
EMTShch-660	205t; 34.8 x 6.0 x 2.1m; 360hp	10.11.1944	Da	Built 1907 DDSG. French steam tug *Jacques Vuccino* (ex-*Sulina*, A-H, 1908), seized by the Germans, conv 1944 to magnetic minesweeper. Captured Aug 1944. Returned 23.5.1945 to France
EMTShch-660	•	24.5.1945	Da	Romanian river motor tug *Constanța*, captured Aug 1944, conv to magnetic minesweeper. Conv 12.1.1949 to minesweeper *T-660*, conv 30.12.1955 to dispatch vessel, renamed *POK-72* on 23.1.1956, conv 21.1.1957 to motor launch *PMB-48*, trfd 27.3.1960 to the Black Sea Fleet. Deleted 1960s
EMTShch-661	244t; 40.4 x 6.5 x 1.6m; 500hp = 10kts	10.11.1944	Da	Built 1912 ST. French steam tug *Pasteur* (ex-*Turn Severin*, A-H, 1918), seized by the Germans, conv 1944 to magnetic minesweeper. Captured Aug 1944, conv to magnetic minesweeper. Returned 24.9.1945 to France
EMTShch-662	241t; 35.0 x 7.0 x 1.85m; 320hp = 9kts	10.11.1944	Da	Built 1925 CRDA. Bulgarian magnetic minesweeper *Isk"r*, conv from steam tug. Captured Sept 1944. Returned 10.8.1945 to Bulgaria
EMTShch-663	103t; 28.8 x 6.5 x 2.75m; 345hp = 7kts; 1 magnetic sweep	10.11.1944	Da	Bulgarian magnetic minesweeper *Vasil Levski* conv from steam tug. Captured Sept 1944. Returned 31.8.1945 to Bulgaria
EMTShch-664	244t; 29.95 x 5.8 x 1.9m; 350hp = 8.5kts	10.11.1944	Da	Built 1921 Ganz Danubius. Romanian magnetic minesweeper *Motru* (ex-*Levendis*, Gre, 1940) conv from steam tug. Captured Aug 1944. Deleted 24.5.1945, BU
T-670	285t full load; 37.6 x 6.6 x 2.9m; 375hp = 12kts; 1-45mm/46 21-K, 2-0.5in MGs, 1 MTSh sweep, 1 MZT sweep; 35 men	10.11.1944	Da	Built 1942 Schiffswerft Linz. German tug *Grafenau* captured Aug 1944 on the Danube, conv to minesweeper. Trfd 25.4.1949 to the Black Sea Fleet, conv 23.01.1956 to dispatch vessel *POK-74*, 19.1.1959 to staff vessel *Desna*, 22.7.1961 to dispatch vessel *PS-10*, 28.6.1977 to communication vessel *SSV-10*. Trfd 1.5.1995 to Ukraine, conv 1997 to border guard boat *Dunaj*. Laid up 2011, trfd to naval school
T-680	180 t	27.12.1945	Da	Built 1930. German river motor tug. Captured spring 1945 on the Danube, conv to minesweeper. Conv 30.12.1955 to dispatch boat, renamed *POK-76* on 23.1.1956, *PMB-50* on 21.1.1957. Trfd 27.3.1960 to the Black Sea Fleet, conv 16.2.1964 to tug *RB-27*. Deleted 10.12.1969

EMTShch-648 (in the centre), 1945.
Przemysław Budzbon Collection

20. Minesweeping boats

Катера-тральщики

20.1. Standard types

K-15 (M-17) type

Displacement: 21.0 full load
Dimensions: 15.5 x 3.3 x 0.7m
Machinery: 1-shaft M-17 diesel, 75–100hp = 6.5–8kts. Range 850nm
Armament: 1-0.5in DShK or 1-0.3in Maxim MG; 1 sweep; KEMT-2 sweep or OTSH-2 or KT type
Complement: 8

KATShch № No on Comm	KATShch № No 1942	No 1943	No 1944	Laid down	Comp	Comm	Fleet	Remarks
Builder: KSMZ, Kostroma								
№ 155		RTShch-155	KT-155	1942	1943	15.6.1943	Vo Dn	Trfd 31.5.1944 to the Dnieper Flotilla. Survived the war
№ 156		RTShch-156	KT-156	1942	1943	15.6.1943	Vo Dn	Trfd 31.5.1944 to the Dnieper Flotilla. Survived the war
№ 157		RTShch-157	KT-157	1942	1943	15.6.1943	Vo Dn	Trfd 4.2.1944 to the Dnieper Flotilla. Survived the war
№ 158		RTShch-158	KT-158	1942	1943	15.6.1943	Vn Dn	Trfd 31.5.1944 to the Dnieper Flotilla. Survived the war
№ 159		RTShch-159	KT-159	1942	1943	15.6.1943	Vo Dn	Trfd 4.2.1944 to the Dnieper Flotilla. Survived the war
№ 160		RTShch-160	KT-160	1942	1943	15.6.1943	Vo Dn	Trfd 31.5.1944 to the Dnieper Flotilla. Survived the war
№ 161		RTShch-161	KT-161	1942	1943	15.6.1943	Vo Dn	Trfd 4.2.1944 to the Dnieper Flotilla. Survived the war
№ 162		RTShch-162	KT-162	1942	1943	15.6.1943	Vo Dn	Trfd 15.6.1943 to the Dnieper Flotilla. Survived the war
№ 163		RTShch-163	KT-163	1942	1943	15.6.1943	Vo Dn	Trfd 15.6.1943 to the Dnieper Flotilla. Survived the war
№ 314	RTShch-121 № 26[2]			1941	1942	25.2.1942	Vo	Mined 22.9.1942 at Staritskii Perekat
№ 315	RTShch-122 № 28[2]		KT-122	1941	1942	25.2.1942	Vo Cs Da	Trfd 3.6.1944 to the Caspian Flotilla, trfd 21.11.1944 to the Danube Flotilla. Survived the war

K-15 (M-17) type boat on the Danube during the war.
Vitalij Kostrichenko Collection

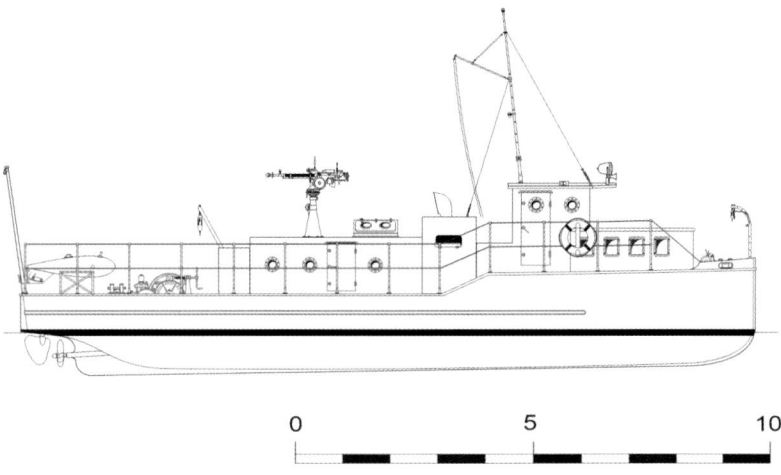

K-15 (M-17) type as built.
Drawing by Jerzy Lewandowski

№ 316	RTShch-123 № 24[2]		KT-123	1941	1942	25.2.1942	Vo Cs Da	Trfd 3.6.1944 to the Caspian Flotilla, trfd 21.11.1944 to the Danube Flotilla. Survived the war
№ 321	RTShch-124 № 25[2]			1941	1942	25.2.1942	Vo	Sunk 2.9.1942 by aircraft on the Volga off Zamor Island
№ 322	RTShch-125 № 23[2]		KT-125	1941	1942	25.2.1942	Vo Dn	Trfd 4.2.1944 to the Dnieper Flotilla. Sank 29.3.1945 in collision on the Vistula River off Warsaw. Raised and recomm
№ 323	RTShch-126 № 22[2]		KT-126	1941	1942	25.2.1942	Vo Cs Da	Trfd 30.6.1944 to the Caspian Flotilla, trfd 21.11.1944 to the Danube Flotilla. Survived the war
№ 324	RTShch-127 № 21[2]		KT-127	1941	1942	25.2.1942	Vo Cs Da	Trfd 30.6.1944 to the Caspian Flotilla, trfd 21.11.1944 to the Danube Flotilla. Survived the war
№ 325	RTShch-128 № 29[2]		KT-128	1941	1942	25.2.1942	Vo Cs Da	Trfd 30.6.1944 to the Caspian Flotilla, trfd 21.11.1944 to the Danube Flotilla. Survived the war
№ 326	RTShch-129 № 27[2]		KT-129	1941	1942	15.3.1942	Vo Dn	Trfd 4.2.1944 to the Dnieper Flotilla. Survived the war
№ 311	№ 570	RTShch-130[6]	KT-130	1940	1941	10.12.1941	Vo On La B	Trfd 13.4.1942 to the Onega Flotilla, trfd 28.7.1944 to the Ladoga Flotilla. Trfd 23.1.1945 to the Baltic Fleet. Survived the war
№ 312	№ 574	RTShch-131[6]	KT-131	1940	1941	10.12.1941	Vo On La B	Trfd 13.4.1942 to the Onega Flotilla, trfd 28.7.1944 to the Ladoga Flotilla. Trfd 23.1.1945 to the Baltic Fleet. Survived the war
№ 313	№ 575	RTShch-132[6]	KT-132	1940	1941	10.12.1941	Vo On La B	Trfd 13.4.1942 to the Onega Flotilla, trfd 28.7.1944 to the Ladoga Flotilla. Trfd 23.1.1945 to the Baltic Fleet. Survived the war
RTShch-7				1940	1941	17.4.1941	Am	Survived the war
RTShch-8				1940	1941	17.4.1941	Am	Survived the war

RTShch-126 on the Volga.
Vitalij Kostrichenko Collection

KATShch № No on Comm	KATShch № No 1942	No 1943	No 1944	Laid down	Comp	Comm	Fleet	Remarks
RTShch-9				1940	1941	17.4.1941	Am	Survived the war
RTShch-10				1940	1941	17.4.1941	Am	Survived the war
RTShch-11				1940	1941	17.4.1941	Am	Survived the war
RTShch-12				1940	1941	17.4.1941	Am	Survived the war
RTShch-18				1940	1941	8.8.1941	Am	Survived the war
RTShch-19				1940	1941	8.8.1941	Am	Survived the war
RTShch-20				1940	1941	8.8.1941	Am	Survived the war
RTShch-21				1940	1941	8.8.1941	Am	Survived the war
RTShch-22				1940	1941	14.10.1941	Am	Survived the war
RTShch-23				1940	1941	29.8.1941	Am	Survived the war
RTShch-24				1940	1941	12.4.1942	Am	Survived the war
RTShch-25				1940	1941	12.4.1942	Am	Survived the war
RTShch-26				1940	1941	12.4.1942	Am	Survived the war
RTShch-27				1940	1941	12.4.1942	Am	Survived the war
RTShch-28				1941	1942	12.4.1942	Am	Survived the war
RTShch-29			KEMTShch-29	1942		20.8.1942	Am BS	Trfd 20.11.1943 to the Black Sea Fleet. Survived the war
RTShch-30				1942		20.8.1942	Am	Survived the war
RTShch-31				1942		20.8.1942	Am	Survived the war
RTShch-32				1942		20.8.1942	Am	Survived the war
RTShch-33			KEMTShch-33	1942		20.8.1942	Am BS	Trfd 20.11.1943 to the Black Sea Fleet. Survived the war
RTShch-34			KEMTShch-34	1942		20.8.1942	Am BS	Trfd 20.11.1943 to the Black Sea Fleet. Survived the war
RTShch-35			KEMTShch-35	1942		20.8.1942	Am BS	Trfd 20.11.1943 to the Black Sea Fleet. Survived the war
RTShch-36			KEMTShch-36	1942		20.8.1942	Am BS	Trfd 20.11.1943 to the Black Sea Fleet. Survived the war
RTShch-37				1942		20.8.1942	Am BS	Trfd 20.11.1943 to the Black Sea Fleet. Sunk 19.4.1944 by mine off Feodosia
RTShch-38			KEMTShch-38	1942		20.8.1942	Am BS	Trfd 20.11.1943 to the Black Sea Fleet. Survived the war
RTShch-39			KEMTShch-39	1942		20.8.1942	Am BS	Trfd 20.11.1943 to the Black Sea Fleet. Survived the war
RTShch-40				1942		20.8.1942	Am	Survived the war
RTShch-41				1942		20.8.1942	Am	Survived the war
RTShch-42				1942		20.8.1942	Am	Survived the war
RTShch-43				1942		20.8.1942	Am	Survived the war
RTShch-103				1940	1941	7.3.1941	Da	Scuttled 8.7.1941 on Lake Kagul
RTShch-104				1940	1941	7.3.1941	Da BS	Trfd 21.11.1941 to the Black Sea Fleet. Sunk 10.9.1943 by artillery fire off Novorossiysk
RTShch-105				1940	1941	7.3.1941	Da BS	Trfd 21.11.1941 to the Black Sea Fleet. Sunk 7.12.1943 by German warships off Eltigen
RTShch-106				1940	1941	7.3.1941	Da	Scuttled 8.7.1941 on Lake Kagul
RTShch-107			KEMTShch-107	1940	1941	7.3.1941	Da BS	Trfd 21.11.1941 to the Black Sea Fleet. Survived the war
RTShch-108				1940	1941	14.7.1941	Pn	Lost 1941
RTShch-109	RTShch-108		KEMTShch-108	1940	1941	14.7.1941	Pn BS	Trfd 26.11.1942 to the Black Sea Fleet. Survived the war
RTShch-110 KATShch-21[1]	KATShch-110	KEMTShch-126[7] KATShch-110[8] KATShch-117[9]	KEMTShch-117	1940	1941	8.9.1941	Cs BS	Trfd 27.11.1943 to the Black Sea Fleet. Survived the war
RTShch-111 KATShch-22[1]	KATShch-111	KEMTShch-127[7] KATShch-111[8]		1940	1941	8.9.1941	Cs BS	Trfd 27.11.1943 to the Black Sea Fleet. Sunk 3.11.1943 by aircraft off Chushka Spit
RTShch-133	RTShch-112		KT-112	1941	1942	21.5.1942	Vo Da	Trfd 30.6.1944 to the Casipan Flotilla, trdf 21.11.1944 to the Danube Flotilla. Survived the war
RTShch-120	RTShch-113[4]		KT-113	1941	1942	28.5.1942	Vo Dn	Trfd 3.5.1944 to the Dnieper Flotilla. Survived the war
RTShch-112	RTShch-118[3]		KT-118	1941	1942	28.5.1942	Vo Dn	Trfd 4.2.1944 to the Dnieper Flotilla. Survived the war
RTShch-119				1941	1942	21.5.1942	Vo	Mined 12.5.1943 off Ekaterinovka

20.0 Minesweeping boats

RTShch-113	RTShch-120³	KT-120	1941	1942	28.5.1942	Vo Dn	Trfd 14.9.1943 to the Dnieper Flotilla. Survived the war
RTShch-118	RTShch-133³	KT-133	1941	1942	28.5.1942	Vo Dn	Trfd 4.2.1944 to the Dnieper Flotilla. Survived the war
RTShch-134		KT-134	1941	1942	21.5.1942	Vo Cs Da	Trfd 30.6.1944 to the Caspian Flotilla, trfd 21.11.1944 to the Danube Flotilla. Survived the war
RTShch-135		KT-135	1941	1942	21.5.1942	Vo Cs Da	Trfd 30.6.1944 to the Caspian Flotilla, trfd 21.11.1944 to the Danube Flotilla. Survived the war
RTShch-136		KT-136	1941	1942	21.5.1942	Vo Dn	Trfd 4.2.1944 to the Dnieper Flotilla. Survived the war
RTShch-137		KT-137	1941	1942	21.5.1942	Vo Dn	Trfd 4.2.1944 to the Dnieper Flotilla. Survived the war
RTShch-138		KT-138	1941	1942	21.5.1942	Vo Dn	Trfd 4.2.1944 to the Dnieper Flotilla. Survived the war
RTShch-139		KT-139	1941	1942	16.11.1942	Vo Cs Da	Trfd 30.6.1944 to the Caspian Flotilla, trfd 21.11.1944 to the Danube Flotilla. Survived the war
RTShch-140		KT-140		1942	16.11.1942	Dn	Trfd 16.11.1942 to the Dnieper Flotilla. Mined 4.5.1945 on the Oder at Stettin
RTShch-141		KT-141		1942	16.11.1942	Vo Dn	Trfd 31.5.1944 to the Dnieper Flotilla. Survived the war
RTShch-142		KT-142		1942	16.11.1942	Vo Dn	Trfd 31.5.1944 to the Dnieper Flotilla. Survived the war
RTShch-143		KT-143		1942	16.11.1942	Vo Dn	Trfd 14.9.1943 to the Dnieper Flotilla. Survived the war
RTShch-144		KT-144		1942	16.11.1942	Vo Dn	Trfd 4.2.1944 to the Dnieper Flotilla. Survived the war
RTShch-145		KT-145		1942	29.9.1942	Vo Cs Da	Trfd 30.6.1944 to the Caspian Flotilla, trfd 21.11.1944 to the Danube Flotilla. Survived the war

KT-146 in the foreground on the Volga. *Vitalij Kostrichenko Collection*

KATShch № No on Comm	KATShch № No 1942	No 1943	No 1944	Laid down	Comp	Comm	Fleet	Remarks
RTShch-146			KT-146		1942	29.9.1942	Vo Cs Da	Trfd 30.6.1944 to the Caspian Flotilla, trfd 21.11.1944 to the Danube Flotilla. Survived the war
RTShch-147			KT-147		1942	29.9.1942	Vo Cs Da	Trfd 30.6.1944 to the Caspian Flotilla, trfd 21.11.1944 to the Danube Flotilla. Survived the war
RTShch-148			KT-148		1942	29.9.1942	Vo Cs Da	Trfd 30.6.1944 to the Caspian Flotilla, trfd 21.11.1944 to the Danube Flotilla. Survived the war
RTShch-151		RTShch-149[6]	KT-149		1942	16.11.1942	Vo Dn	Trfd 31.5.1944 to the Dnieper Flotilla. Survived the war
RTShch-152		RTShch-150[6]	KT-150		1942	16.11.1942	Vo Dn	Trfd 31.5.1944 to the Dnieper Flotilla. Survived the war
RTShch-153		RTShch-151[6]	KT-151		1942	16.11.1942	Vo Dn	Trfd 4.2.1944 to the Dnieper Flotilla. Survived the war
RTShch-149		RTShch-152[6]	KT-152		1942	16.11.1942	Vo Dn	Trfd 4.2.1944 to the Dnieper Flotilla. Survived the war
RTShch-153		RTShch-150[6]	KT-153		1942	16.11.1942	Vo Dn	Trfd 31.5.1944 to the Dnieper Flotilla. Survived the war
RTShch-154			KT-154		1942	16.11.1942	Vo Dn	Trfd 14.9.1943 to the Dnieper Flotilla. Survived the war
RTShch-187			KT-187	1942	1943	27.9.1943	Vo Cs Da	Trfd 30.6.1944 to the Caspian Flotilla, trfd 21.11.1944 to the Danube Flotilla. Survived the war
RTShch-188			KT-188	1942	1943	27.9.1943	Vo C Da	Trfd 30.6.1944 to the Caspian Flotilla, trfd 21.11.1944 to the Danube Flotilla. Survived the war
RTShch-189			KT-189	1942	1943	27.9.1943	Vo Cs Da	Trfd 30.6.1944 to the Caspian Flotilla, trfd 21.11.1944 to the Danube Flotilla. Survived the war
RTShch-190			KT-190	1942	1943	27.9.1943	Vo Cs Da	Trfd 30.6.1944 to the Caspian Flotilla, trfd 21.11.1944 to the Danube Flotilla. Survived the war
RTShch-191			KT-191	1942	1943	27.9.1943	Vo Cs Da	Trfd 30.6.1944 to the Caspian Flotilla, trfd 21.11.1944 to the Danube Flotilla. Survived the war

The effective dates of Pennant Numbers change orders.

Year	Fleet	Date
1942	Vo	28.5.1942
	On	29.6.1942
	Cs	24.9.1942
	BS	26.11.1942
1943	On	13.1.1943
	Vo	16.8.1943
1944	BS	21.6.1944
	Cs	30.6.1944
	On	21.7.1944
	Dn	14.9.1944

Exceptions noted in the main table.

No	Year	Date	Fleet
1	1941	9.9.1941	Cs
2	1942	Number carried from 3 until 12 June 1942	Vo
3		12.6.1942	Vo
4		31.10.1942	Vo
5		16.11.1942	Vo
6	1943	18.1.1943	Vo
7		26.5.1943	Cs
8		13.8.1943	Cs
9		27.11.1943	BS

Wooden-hulled boats engined with the M-17 type tractor diesel designed as the power unit of the *Stalinets* type tractor. From 1943 production was shifted to the K-18 type fuelled by a wood gas generator.

K-18 type

Displacement: 17.5t full load
Dimensions: 15.9 x 3.3 x 0.7m
Machinery: 1-shaft MG-17 diesel with G-25 gas generator, 85–115hp = 4.75kts (with a sweep). Range 800nm
Armament: 1-0.5in DShK or 1-0.3in Maxim MG; 1 sweep; KEMT-2 sweep or OTSH-2 or KT type
Complement: 7

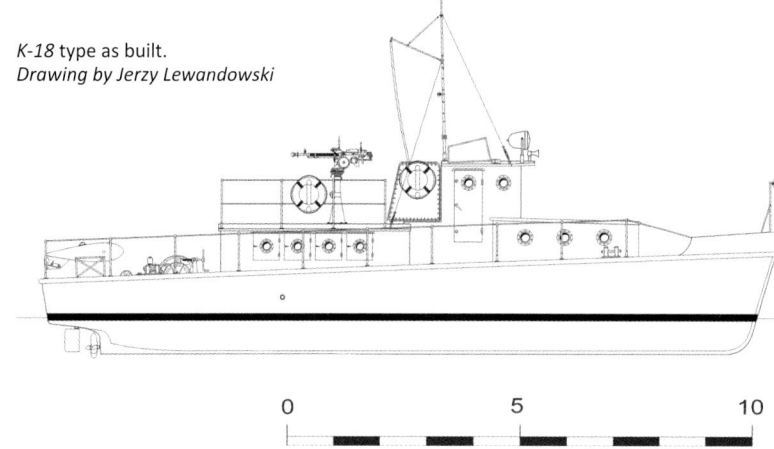

K-18 type as built. Drawing by Jerzy Lewandowski

No on Comm	KATShch № No 1944	Laid down	Comp	Comm	Fleet	Remarks
Builder: KSMZ, Kostroma						
KT-693				30.6.1944	Dn	Survived the war
KT-694				30.6.1944	Dn	Survived the war
KT-695				27.6.1944	Dn	Survived the war
KT-696		1943	1944	27.6.1944	Dn	Mined 8.5.1945 in the Pommersche Bucht. Survived the war
KT-697		1943	1944	27.6.1944	Dn Da	Trfd 13.11.1944 to the Danube Flotilla. Survived the war
KT-698		1943	1944	27.6.1944	Dn Da	Trfd 13.11.1944 to the Danube Flotilla. Survived the war
KT-699	93		1944	27.6.1944	Dn Da	Trfd 13.11.1944 to the Danube Flotilla. Survived the war
KT-700		1943	1944	27.6.1944	Dn Da	Trfd 13.11.1944 to the Danube Flotilla. Survived the war
KT-729		1943	1944	29.1.1945	Da	Sunk in error 28.3.1945 by Soviet artillery fire
KT-730		1943	1944	29.1.1945	Da	Survived the war
KT-731		1943	1944	27.6.1944	Dn Da	Trfd 13.11.1944 to the Danube Flotilla. Survived the war
KT-732		1943	1944	27.6.1944	Dn Da	Trfd 13.11.1944 to the Danube Flotilla. Survived the war
KT-733			1944	14.9.1944	Dn Da	Trfd 13.11.1944 to the Danube Flotilla. Survived the war

KT-221. Przemysław Budzbon Collection

K-18 type boats on the Danube. KT-732 and KT-733 nearest to camera. Vitalij Kostrichenko Collection

Pennant	Former	Laid down	Launched	Commissioned	Fleet	Fate
KT-734			1944	29.1.1945	Da	Survived the war
KT-735			1944	29.1.1945	Da	Survived the war
KT-736			1944	29.1.1945	Da	Survived the war
KT-737			1944	29.1.1945	Da	Survived the war
KT-738			1944	29.1.1945	Da	Survived the war
KT-739			1944	29.1.1945	Da	Survived the war
KT-742		1944	1945	4.5.1945	Da	Survived the war
KT-743		1944	1945	4.5.1945	Da	Survived the war
KT-744		1944	1945	4.5.1945	Da	Survived the war
KT-745		1944	1945	4.5.1945	Da	Survived the war
RTShch-205	№ 205[1], KT-205		1943	27.11.1943	Vo, Dn	Trfd 7.3.1944 to the Dnieper Flotilla. Sunk 13.7.1944 by artillery fire off Pinsk, raised and recomm 18.1.1945
RTShch-206	№ 206[1], KT-206		1943	27.11.1943	Vo, Dn	Trfd 7.3.1944 to the Dnieper Flotilla. Survived the war
RTShch-220	KT-220[2]	1943	1944	7.3.1944	Dn, BS, Da	Trfd 9.4.1944 to the Black Sea Fleet, trfd 13.4.1944 to the Danube Flotilla. Sunk 21.3.1945 by artillery fire on the Danube off Estergom
RTShch-221	KT-221[2]	1943	1944	7.3.1944	Dn, BS, Da	Trfd 9.4.1944 to the Black Sea Fleet, trfd 13.4.1944 to the Danube Flotilla. Survived the war
RTShch-222	KT-222[2]	1943	1944	7.3.1944	Dn, BS, Da	Trfd 9.4.1944 to the Black Sea Fleet, trfd 13.4.1944 to the Danube Flotilla. Sunk in error 28.3.1945 by Soviet artillery fire
RTShch-223	KT-223[2]	1943	1944	7.3.1944	Dn, BS, Da	Trfd 9.4.1944 to the Black Sea Fleet, trfd 13.4.1944 to the Danube Flotilla. Survived the war
RTShch-491	KEMTShch-491	1943	1944	12.5.1944	Da, BS	Trfd 21.6.1944 to the Black Sea Fleet. Survived the war
RTShch-492	KEMTShch-492	1943	1944	12.5.1944	Da, BS	Trfd 21.6.1944 to the Black Sea Fleet. Survived the war
RTShch-493	KEMTShch-493	1943	1944	12.5.1944	Da, BS	Trfd 21.6.1944 to the Black Sea Fleet. Survived the war
RTShch-494	KEMTShch-494	1943	1944	4.4.1944	BS, Da, BS	Trfd 13.4.1944 to the Danube Flotilla, returned 21.6.1944. Survived the war
RTShch-495	KEMTShch-495	1943	1944	4.4.1944	BS, Da, BS	Trfd 13.4.1944 to the Danube Flotilla, returned 21.6.1944. Survived the war
RTShch-496			1943	27.11.1943	Vo, BS, Da	Trfd 5.2.1944 to the Black Sea Fleet, trfd 13.4.1944 to the Danube Flotilla. Survived the war
RTShch-497	KT-497		1943	27.11.1943	Vo, BS, Da	Trfd 5.2.1944 to the Black Sea Fleet, trfd 13.4.1944 to the Danube Flotilla. Returned 21.6.1944 to the Black Sea Fleet. Survived the war
RTShch-498	KT-498		1943	27.11.1943	Vo, BS, Da	Trfd 5.2.1944 to the Black Sea Fleet, trfd 13.4.1944 to the Danube Flotilla. Returned 21.6.1944 to the Black Sea Fleet. Survived the war
RTShch-499	KEMTShch-499	1943	1944	4.4.1944	BS, Da, BS	Trfd 13.4.1944 to the Danube Flotilla, returned 21.6.1944. Survived the war
RTShch-500	KEMTShch-500	1943	1944	4.4.1944	BS, Da, BS	Trfd 13.4.1944 to the Danube Flotilla, returned 21.6.1944. Survived the war

The effective dates of Pennant Numbers change orders.

Year	Fleet	Date
1944	Da	21.6.1944
	BS	29.7.1944
	Dn	14.9.1944

Exceptions noted in the main table.

No	Year	Date	Fleet
1	1944	27.6.1944	Dn
2		15.11.1944	Da

The follow-on to the K-15 (M-17) type, designed to save material and use wood gas propulsion with modified version of the M-17 diesel designated MG-17 (G stands for Gaz = gas) fuelled by G-25 gas generator unit.

MSV-38 type

Displacement: 16.5t full load
Dimensions: 14.0 x 2.9 x 0.85m
Machinery: 1-shaft, petrol engine, 68–95hp = 8.5–9kts. Range 300nm
Armament: 1-0.3in Maxim MG, 1 KEMT-2 or 1 MKhT type sweep
Complement: 8

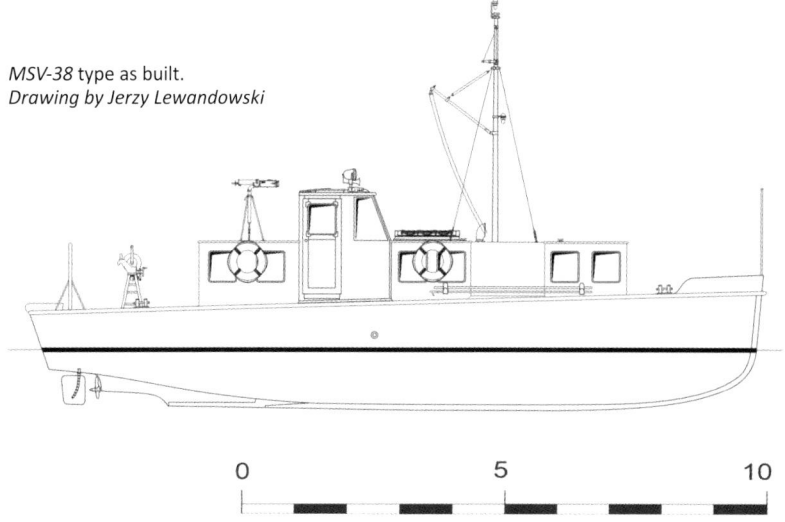

*MSV-38 type as built.
Drawing by Jerzy Lewandowski*

*Kater-tral'shchik № 170.
Vitalij Kostrichenko Collection*

No on Comm	KATShch № 12.11.1943	No 1944	Laid down	Comp	Comm	Fleet	Fate
Builder: MSV, Moskva							
RTShch-13			1940	1941	17.4.1941	Am	Survived the war
RTShch-14			1940	1941	17.4.1941	Am	Survived the war
RTShch-15			1940	1941	17.4.1941	Am	Survived the war
RTShch-16			1940	1941	17.4.1941	Am	Survived the war
RTShch-17			1940	1941	17.4.1941	Am	Survived the war
RTShch-44			1942	1943	14.5.1943	Am	Survived the war
RTShch-45			1942	1943	14.5.1943	Am	Survived the war
RTShch-46			1942	1943	14.5.1943	Am	Survived the war
RTShch-47			1942	1943	14.5.1943	Am	Survived the war
RTShch-48			1942	1943	14.5.1943	Am	Survived the war
RTShch-101			1940	1941	28.4.1941	Da BS	Trfd 21.11.1941 to the Black Sea Fleet. Survived the war
RTShch-102		KEMTShch-102	1940	1941	28.4.1941	Da BS	Trfd 21.11.1941 to the Black Sea Fleet. Survived the war
RTShch-170	№ 170	KT-170	1942	1943	24.6.1943	Vo Dn BS	Trfd 20.2.1944 to the Dnieper Flotilla, trfd 15.7.1944 to the Black Sea Fleet. Conv 31.12.1945 to service craft № 242
RTShch-171	№ 171	KT-171	1942	1943	24.6.1943	Vo Dn BS	Trfd 20.2.1944 to the Dnieper Flotilla, trfd 15.7.1944 to the Black Sea Fleet. Conv 31.12.1945 to service craft № 244
RTShch-172	№ 172	KT-172	1942	1943	24.6.1943	Vo Dn BS	Trfd 20.2.1944 to the Dnieper Flotilla, trfd 15.7.1944 to the Black Sea Fleet. Conv 31.12.1945 to service craft № 241
RTShch-173	№ 173	KT-173	1942	1943	24.6.1943	Vo Dn BS	Trfd 20.2.1944 to the Dnieper Flotilla, trfd 15.7.1944 to the Black Sea Fleet. Conv 31.12.1945 to service craft № 237
RTShch-174	№ 174	KT-174	1942	1943	24.6.1943	Vo Dn BS	Trfd 20.2.1944 to the Dnieper Flotilla, trfd 15.7.1944 to the Black Sea Fleet. Conv 31.12.1945 to service craft № 250
RTShch-212		KEMTShch-212	1943	1944	24.6.1943	Dn BS Da	Trfd 9.4.1944 to the Black Sea Fleet., trfd 13.4.1944 to the Danube Flotilla. Survived the war
RTShch-213		KEMTShch-213	1943	1944	7.3.1944	Dn BS Da	Trfd 9.4.1944 to the Black Sea Fleet., trfd 13.4.1944 to the Danube Flotilla. Survived the war

No on Comm	KATShch № 12.11.1943	No 1944	Laid down	Comp	Comm	Fleet	Fate
RTShch-214		KEMTShch-214	1943	1944	7.3.1944	Dn BS Da	Trfd 9.4.1944 to the Black Sea Fleet, trfd 13.4.1944 to the Danube Flotilla. Sank 15.11.1944 in collision on the Danube off Milanovac
RTShch-215		KEMTShch-215	1943	1944	7.3.1944	Dn BS Da	Trfd 9.4.1944 to the Black Sea Fleet, trfd 13.4.1944 to the Danube Flotilla. Survived the war
RTShch-216		KEMTShch-216	1943	1944	7.3.1944	Dn BS Da	Trfd 9.4.1944 to the Black Sea Fleet, trfd 13.4.1944 to the Danube Flotilla. Survived the war
RTShch-217		KEMTShch-217	1943	1944	7.3.1944	Dn BS Da	Trfd 9.4.1944 to the Black Sea Fleet, trfd 13.4.1944 to the Danube Flotilla. Survived the war
RTShch-218		KEMTShch-218	1943	1944	14.3.1945	Dn BS Da	Trfd 9.4.1944 to the Black Sea Fleet, trfd 13.4.1944 to the Danube Flotilla. Mined 14.3.1945 on the Drina River off Dubravice
RTShch-219		KEMTShch-219	1943	1944	14.3.1945	Dn BS Da	Trfd 9.4.1944 to the Black Sea Fleet, trfd 13.4.1944 to the Danube Flotilla. Survived the war

The effective dates of Pennant Numbers change orders.

Year	Fleet	Date
1944	BS	7.8.1944
	Da	15.11.1944

Design based on the river tugboat type.

RTShch-216.
Vitalij Kostrichenko Collection

Cross reference: Rated as minesweeping boats

KATShch № No	Details	Type	From	To	Fate
EMKATShch-199	*Urme*	Transport	12.11.1943		Survived the war
I-25 – I-26	*KM-2* type	Patrol boat	29.12.1941	14.11.1944	Conv to service craft
I-27	*KM-2* type	Patrol boat	29.12.1941	18.8.1944	Lost
I-28	*KM-2* type	Patrol boat	29.12.1941	25.7.1944	Reverted to patrol boat
I-29	*KM-2* type	Patrol boat	7.9.1941	1.11.1941	Lost
I-31	*KM-4* type	Patrol boat	29.12.1941		Survived the war
I-32	*KM-2* type	Patrol boat	29.12.1941		Survived the war
I-33	*KM-2* type	Patrol boat	29.12.1941	6.10.1944	Conv to service craft
I-43, I-44	*KM-4* type	Patrol boat	3.1.1942		Survived the war
I-45, I-47	*KM-4* type	Patrol boat	29.12.1941		Survived the war
I-48	*KM-2* type	Patrol boat	29.12.1941	13.5.1944	Lost
KATShch-224	*DB* type	Landing craft	18.4.1944		Survived the war
KATShch-225	*DB* type	Landing craft	18.4.1944	21.6.1944	Deleted
KATShch-226	*DB* type	Landing craft	18.4.1944	21.6.1944	Deleted
KATShch-227	*DB* type	Landing craft	18.4.1944	2.5.1944	Lost
KATShch-228 – KATShch-236	*DB* type	Landing craft	18.4.1944		Survived the war
KEMTShch-7	*KM-4* type	Patrol boat	23.2.1943	31.12.1945	Conv to service craft
KEMTShch-8	*KM-4* type	Patrol boat	23.2.1943	31.12.1945	Conv to service craft
KEMTShch-280	*KM-4* type	Patrol boat	4.8.1944	31.12.1945	Conv to service craft
KEMTShch-281	*KM-4* type	Patrol boat	4.8.1944		Survived the war

20.0 Minesweeping boats

Name	Type	Role	Date	Date2	Fate
KEMTShch-282	*KM-4* type	Patrol boat	4.8.1944	31.12.1945	Conv to service craft
KEMTShch-287 – KEMTShch-290	*KM-4* type	Patrol boat	4.8.1944	31.12.1945	Conv to service craft
KTEMShch-511 – KTEMShch-518	*Tender* type	Landing craft	21.6.1944		Survived the war
KEMTShch-581 – KEMTShch-584	*Ia-5* type	Rocket boat	29.7.1944		Survived the war
KEMTShch-586 – KEMTShch-593	*Ia-5* type	Rocket boat	29.7.1944		Survived the war
KEMTShch-594 – KEMTShch-597	*Ia-6* type	Rocket boat	29.7.1944		Survived the war
KEMTShch-660	*R* type	Patrol boat	12.3.1942		Survived the war
KEMTShch-661	*R* type	Patrol boat	12.3.1942		Survived the war
KEMTShch-662	*Ia-5* type	Rocket boat	21.6.1944		Survived the war
KEMTShch-771 – KEMTShch-778	*Ia-5* type	Rocket boat	14.11.1944		Survived the war
KEMTShch-779 – KEMTShch-782	*Ia-6* type	Rocket boat	15.7.1944		Survived the war
KTEMShch-820	*Tender* type	Landing craft	21.6.1944		Survived the war
KT-210	*KM-4* type	Patrol boat	16.2.1945		Survived the war
KT-231	*KM-4* type	Patrol boat	28.6.1945	31.12.1945	Conv to service craft
KT-239	*KM-4* type	Patrol boat	28.6.1945	31.12.1945	Conv to service craft
KT-241 – KT-247	*DB* type	Landing craft	24.5.1944		Survived the war
KT-248 – KT-259	*DMB-100* type	Landing craft	28.1.1944		Survived the war
KT-260 – KT-262	*DB* type	Landing craft	24.5.1944		Survived the war
KT-265	*KM-4* type	Patrol boat	19.8.1944		Survived the war
KT-266	*KM-4* type	Patrol boat	25.11.1945		Survived the war
KT-283	*KM-4* type	Patrol boat	19.12.1944		Survived the war
KT-284	*KM-4* type	Patrol boat	1.9.1945		Survived the war
KT-285	*KM-4* type	Patrol boat	1.9.1945		Survived the war
KT-291	*KM-4* type	Patrol boat	19.8.1944		Survived the war
KT-292	*KM-4* type	Patrol boat	19.8.1944		Survived the war
KT-294	*KM-4* type	Patrol boat	25.11.1945		Survived the war
KT-295	*KM-4* type	Patrol boat	19.8.1944		Survived the war
KT-298	*KM-4* type	Patrol boat	19.12.1944		Survived the war
KT-349 – KT-354	*KM-4* type	Patrol boat	23.6.1944		Survived the war
KT-355	*KM-4* type	Patrol boat	28.6.1944	30.7.1944	Lost
KT-356	*KM-4* type	Patrol boat	23.6.1944		Survived the war
KT-358 – KT-360	*KM-4* type	Patrol boat	23.6.1944		Survived the war
KT-363	*KM-4* type	Patrol boat	2.2.1945		Survived the war
KT-381 – KT-390	*KM-4* type	Patrol boat	21.9.1944		Survived the war
KT-394	*Sukhumi*	Netlayer	3.2.1945		Survived the war
KT-406 – KT-410	*KM-4* type	Patrol boat	21.6.1945		Survived the war
KT-447 – KT-450	*Ia-5* type	Rocket boat	14.11.1944		Survived the war
KT-519	*DB* type	Landing craft	21.6.1944		Survived the war
KT-520	*DMB-100* type	Landing craft	21.6.1944		Survived the war
KT-528 – KT-530	*DMB-100* type	Landing craft	28.1.1944		Survived the war
KT-534 – KT-538	*DMB-100* type	Landing craft	28.1.1944		Survived the war
KT-541 – KT-543	*DMB-100* type	Landing craft	28.1.1944		Survived the war
KT-553 – KT-557	*DMB-100* type	Landing craft	28.1.1944		Survived the war
KT-577 – KT-579	*DMB-100* type	Landing craft	28.1.1944		Survived the war
KT-598 – KT-599	*DMB-100* type	Landing craft	28.1.1944		Survived the war
KT-631 – KT-632	*Ia-5* type	Rocket boat	27.4.1945		Survived the war
KT-643 – KT-651	*DB* type	Landing craft	21.6.1944		Survived the war
KT-653	*DB* type	Landing craft	21.6.1944		Survived the war
KT-653 – KT-657	*Tender* type	Landing craft	21.6.1944		Survived the war
KT-659	*DB* type	Landing craft	21.6.1944		Survived the war
KT-664 – KT-679	*KM-4* type	Patrol boat	21.10.1944		Survived the war
KT-680	*KM-4* type	Patrol boat	21.10.1944	16.11.1944	Lost
KT-681	*KM-4* type	Patrol boat	21.10.1944		Survived the war
KT-682	*KM-4* type	Patrol boat	21.10.1944		Survived the war
KT-717	*R* type	Patrol boat	Aug 1944		Survived the war
KT-805 – KT-806	*DMB-100* type	Landing craft	28.1.1944		Survived the war
KT-816	*Krasnyj Krym*	Patrol boat	21.6.1944		Survived the war
KT-851 – KT-857	*KM-4* type	Patrol boat	16.2.1945		Survived the war
KT-858	*Tender* type	Landing craft	Spr 1945		Survived the war
KT-891 – KT-898	*Tender* type	Landing craft	Spr 1945		Survived the war
KT-952	*KM-4* type	Patrol boat	19.12.1945		Survived the war
KT-954	*KM-4* type	Patrol boat	19.12.1945		Survived the war
KT-955	*KM-4* type	Patrol boat	19.12.1945		Survived the war
KT-958	*KM-4* type	Patrol boat	1.9.1945		Survived the war

KATShch № No	Details	Type	From	To	Fate
KT-960	*KM-4* type	Patrol boat	25.11.1945		Survived the war
KT-962	*KM-4* type	Patrol boat	1.9.1945		Survived the war
KT-965	*KM-4* type	Patrol boat	25.11.1945		Survived the war
KT-966	*KM-4* type	Patrol boat	25.11.1945		Survived the war
KT-967	*KM-4* type	Patrol boat	25.11.1945		Survived the war
KT-968	*KM-4* type	Patrol boat	1.9.1945		Survived the war
KT-972	*KM-4* type	Patrol boat	1.9.1945		Survived the war
KT-973	*KM-4* type	Patrol boat	25.11.1945		Survived the war
KT-974	*KM-4* type	Patrol boat	1.9.1945		Survived the war
KT-975 – KT-979	*KM-4* type	Patrol boat	19.12.1945		Survived the war
MI-8	*KM-4* type	Patrol boat	7.10.1941		Fate unknown
№ 1	*Teplokhod* class	Minelayer	15.7.1941	28.8.1941	Lost
№ 2	*Teplokhod* class	Minelayer	15.7.1941	7.9.1941	Reverted to minelayer
№ 13	*KM-4* type	Patrol boat	30.7.1943		Survived the war
№ 17	*KM-2* type	Patrol boat	18.12.1942		Survived the war
№ 23	*KM-4* type	Patrol boat	21.9.1943		Survived the war
№ 25	*KM-2* type	Patrol boat	7.10.1941		Survived the war
№ 26	*KM-2* type	Patrol boat	3.1.1942	5.6.1944	Deleted
№ 27	*KM-2* type	Patrol boat	3.1.1942	1.9.1942	Lost
№ 27	*KM-2* type	Patrol boat	18.12.1942		Survived the war
№ 28	*KM-2* type	Patrol boat	7.10.1941		Survived the war
№ 29	*KM-2* type	Patrol boat	7.10.1941		Survived the war
№ 30	*KM-2* type	Patrol boat	7.10.1941		Survived the war
№ 31	*KM-2* type	Patrol boat	3.10.1942		Survived the war
№ 33	*KM-4* type	Patrol boat	21.9.1943		Survived the war
№ 37	*KM-2* type	Patrol boat	18.12.1942		Survived the war
№ 43	*KM-4* type	Patrol boat	21.9.1943		Survived the war
№ 44	*R* type	Patrol boat	4.10.1941		Survived the war
№ 47	*KM-2* type	Patrol boat	18.12.1942		Survived the war
№ 47	*A* class	Patrol boat	30.8.1941	26.9.1942	Reverted to patrol boat
№ 49	*A* class	Patrol boat	30.8.1941	26.9.1942	Reverted to patrol boat
№ 53	*KM-4* type	Patrol boat	30.7.1943		Survived the war
№ 53	*Kungas-Kavasaki* type	Patrol boat	7.10.1941	22.10.1942	Conv to patrol boat
№ 54	*Kungas-Kavasaki* type	Patrol boat	7.10.1941	22.10.1942	Conv to patrol boat
№ 57	*KM-2* type	Patrol boat	18.12.1942		Survived the war
№ 63	*KM-4* type	Patrol boat	21.9.1943		Survived the war
№ 67	*KM-4* type	Patrol boat	18.12.1942	28.9.1944	Lost
№ 73	*KM-4* type	Patrol boat	21.9.1943		Survived the war
№ 77	*KM-4* type	Patrol boat	18.12.1942		Survived the war
№ 81	*R* type	Patrol boat	5.7.1941		Survived the war
№ 82	*R* type	Patrol boat	5.7.1941		Survived the war
№ 83	*KM-4* type	Patrol boat	21.9.1943		Survived the war
№ 83 – № 86	*R* type	Patrol boat	5.7.1941		Survived the war
№ 86	*B-2*	Diving tender	1.7.1942	29.9.1942	Reverted to diving tender
№ 87	*KM-4* type	Patrol boat	18.12.1942	4.7.1944	Lost
№ 87	*R* type	Patrol boat	5.7.1941		Survived the war
№ 93	*KM-4* type	Patrol boat	11.9.1942		Survived the war
№ 93	*KM-4* type	Patrol boat	30.7.1943		Survived the war
№ 95	*KM-4* type	Patrol boat	11.9.1942		Survived the war
№ 97	*KM-4* type	Patrol boat	18.12.1942		Survived the war
№ 98	*KM-4* type	Patrol boat	11.9.1942		Survived the war
№ 99	*KM-4* type	Patrol boat	11.9.1942		Survived the war
№ 102	*KM-4* type	Patrol boat	11.9.1942		Survived the war
№ 103	*KM-4* type	Patrol boat	30.7.1943		Survived the war
№ 104	*KM-4* type	Patrol boat	29.1.1944		Survived the war
№ 105	*KM-4* type	Patrol boat	3.1.1942		Survived the war
№ 107	*KM-4* type	Patrol boat	11.9.1942		Survived the war
№ 107	*KM-4* type	Patrol boat	18.12.1942	20.8.1944	Lost
№ 110	*KM-4* type	Patrol boat	16.3.1942		Survived the war
№ 111	*KM-4* type	Patrol boat	29.1.1944		Survived the war
№ 112	*KM-4* type	Patrol boat	11.9.1942		Survived the war
№ 113	*KM-4* type	Patrol boat	21.9.1943		Survived the war

№ 115	KM-4 type	Patrol boat	3.1.1942		Survived the war
№ 118	KM-4 type	Patrol boat	3.1.1942		Survived the war
№ 120	R type	Patrol boat	12.3.1942		Survived the war
№ 121	KM-4 type	Patrol boat	3.1.1942		Survived the war
№ 123	KM-4 type	Patrol boat	30.7.1943		Survived the war
№ 127	R type	Patrol boat	4.9.1941		Survived the war
№ 128	R type	Patrol boat	4.9.1941		Survived the war
№ 129	R type	Patrol boat	12.3.1942		Survived the war
№ 133	KM-4 type	Patrol boat	30.7.1943		Survived the war
№ 143	KM-4 type	Patrol boat	30.7.1943		Survived the war
№ 153	KM-4 type	Patrol boat	30.7.1943		Survived the war
№ 163	KM-4 type	Patrol boat	30.7.1943	9.7.1944	Lost
№ 164 – № 169	Ia-5 type	Rocket boat	24.6.1943		Survived the war
№ 173	KM-4 type	Patrol boat	30.7.1943	30.5.1944	Lost
№ 183	KM-4 type	Patrol boat	30.7.1943		Survived the war
№ 193	KM-4 type	Patrol boat	21.9.1941		Survived the war
№ 203	KM-4 type	Patrol boat	21.9.1941		Survived the war
№ 213	KM-4 type	Patrol boat	21.9.1941		Survived the war
№ 223	KM-4 type	Patrol boat	10.11.1943		Survived the war
№ 233	KM-4 type	Patrol boat	10.11.1943		Survived the war
№ 243	KM-4 type	Patrol boat	10.11.1943		Survived the war
№ 253	KM-4 type	Patrol boat	10.11.1943		Survived the war
№ 263	KM-4 type	Patrol boat	10.11.1943	20.10.1944	Lost
№ 273	KM-4 type	Patrol boat	10.11.1943		Survived the war
№ 283	KM-4 type	Patrol boat	10.11.1943		Survived the war
№ 293	KM-4 type	Patrol boat	10.11.1943		Survived the war
№ 303	KM-4 type	Patrol boat	10.11.1943		Survived the war
№ 313	KM-4 type	Patrol boat	10.11.1943		Survived the war
№ 346	KM-4 type	Patrol boat	30.1.1944		Survived the war
№ 347	KM-4 type	Patrol boat	30.1.1944		Survived the war
№ 348	KM-4 type	Patrol boat	30.1.1944		Survived the war
№ 373	KM-4 type	Patrol boat	10.11.1943	10.10.1944	Lost
№ 383	KM-4 type	Patrol boat	10.11.1943		Survived the war
№ 393	KM-4 type	Patrol boat	10.11.1943		Survived the war
№ 403	KM-4 type	Patrol boat	10.11.1943		Survived the war
№ 407	KM-2 type	Patrol boat	1.10.1943	27.9.1944	Lost
№ 413	KM-4 type	Patrol boat	10.11.1943		Survived the war
№ 423	KM-4 type	Patrol boat	10.11.1943		Survived the war
№ 433	KM-4 type	Patrol boat	10.11.1943		Survived the war
№ 443	KM-4 type	Patrol boat	21.9.1943		Survived the war
№ 453	KM-4 type	Patrol boat	10.11.1943		Survived the war
№ 463	KM-4 type	Patrol boat	10.11.1943		Survived the war
№ 473	KM-4 type	Patrol boat	10.11.1943		Survived the war
№ 483	KM-4 type	Patrol boat	21.9.1943		Survived the war
№ 493	KM-4 type	Patrol boat	10.11.1943		Survived the war
№ 503	KM-4 type	Patrol boat	10.11.1943		Survived the war
№ 602	KM-2 type	Patrol boat	1.6.1942		Survived the war
№ 603	KM-2 type	Patrol boat	29.12.1941	6.10.1944	Returned to Naval Academy
№ 604	KM-2 type	Patrol boat	18.10.1941		Survived the war
№ 605	KM-2 type	Patrol boat	3.1.1942	30.8.1943	Lost
№ 606	KM-2 type	Patrol boat	3.1.1942	28.6.1943	Lost
№ 606	KM-2 type	Patrol boat	30.7.1943		Survived the war
№ 607	KM-2 type	Patrol boat	3.1.1942		Survived the war
№ 614	KM-2 type	Patrol boat	25.7.1941		Survived the war
№ 615	KM-2 type	Patrol boat	25.7.1941		Survived the war
№ 616	KM-2 type	Patrol boat	29.12.1941	25.7.1944	Reverted to patrol boat
№ 617	KM-2 type	Patrol boat	25.7.1941	29.8.1941	Lost
№ 618	KM-2 type	Patrol boat	25.7.1941	29.8.1941	Lost
№ 619	KM-2 type	Patrol boat	25.7.1941	29.8.1941	Lost
№ 620	KM-2 type	Patrol boat	21.10.1942	6.10.1944	Conv to service craft
№ 901	KM-4 type	Patrol boat	7.9.1941	30.7.1943	Conv to patrol boat
№ 906	R type	Patrol boat	25.7.1941	4.8.1944	Lost
№ 911	R type	Patrol boat	25.7.1941		Survived the war
№ 912	R type	Patrol boat	25.7.1941		Survived the war

KATShch № No	Details	Type	From	To	Fate
№ 913	R type	Patrol boat	25.7.1941	16.9.1941	Lost
№ 914	R type	Patrol boat	19.8.1944	5.9.1943	Lost
№ 920	KM-2 type	Patrol boat	21.10.1942	15.3.1943	Conv to patrol boat
№ 921	KM-2 type	Patrol boat	21.10.1942	15.3.1943	Conv to patrol boat
№ 922	KM-2 type	Patrol boat	21.10.1942	15.3.1943	Conv to patrol boat
№ 923	KM-2 type	Patrol boat	21.10.1942	15.3.1943	Conv to patrol boat
№ 924	KM-2 type	Patrol boat	21.10.1942	15.3.1943	Conv to patrol boat
№ 1101 – № 1103	R type	Patrol boat	25.7.1941		Survived the war
№ 1104	R type	Patrol boat	25.7.1941	30.7.1944	Lost
№ 1105	R type	Patrol boat	25.7.1941		Survived the war
№ 1106	R type	Patrol boat	25.7.1941		Survived the war
№ 1107	R type	Patrol boat	24.6.1941	30.7.1944	Lost
№ 1108	R type	Patrol boat	24.6.1941		Survived the war
№ 1109	R type	Patrol boat	25.7.1941		Survived the war
№ 1201 – № 1204	R type	Patrol boat	25.7.1941		Survived the war
№ 1205	R type	Patrol boat	25.7.1941	26.6.1944	Lost
№ 1208	R type	Patrol boat	25.7.1941		Survived the war
№ 1209	R type	Patrol boat	25.7.1941	5.8.1944	Lost
№ 1209	R type	Patrol boat	25.7.1941	1942	Lost
№ 1304	KM-2 type	Patrol boat	25.7.1941	16.9.1941	Lost
№ 1306	KM-2 type	Patrol boat	25.7.1941	16.9.1941	Lost
№ 1307	KM-2 type	Patrol boat	25.7.1941	16.9.1941	Lost
№ 1308	KM-2 type	Patrol boat	25.7.1941	14.9.1941	Lost
№ 1309	KM-2 type	Patrol boat	25.7.1941	16.9.1941	Lost
№ 1310	KM-2 type	Patrol boat	25.7.1941	16.9.1941	Lost
№ 1312	KM-2 type	Patrol boat	25.7.1941	16.9.1941	Lost
№ 1318	KM-2 type	Patrol boat	25.7.1941	16.9.1941	Lost
№ 1401	KM-4 type	Patrol boat	25.7.1941	15.3.1943	Conv to patrol boat
№ 1402	KM-4 type	Patrol boat	25.7.1941	15.3.1943	Conv to patrol boat
№ 1403	KM-4 type	Patrol boat	25.7.1941		Conv to patrol boat
№ 1404	KM-4 type	Patrol boat	25.7.1941	15.3.1943	Lost
№ 1405	KM-4 type	Patrol boat	25.7.1941		Lost
№ 1406	KM-4 type	Patrol boat	25.7.1941	5.8.1944	Deleted
№ 1407	KM-4 type	Patrol boat	25.7.1941		Conv to patrol boat
№ 1408	KM-4 type	Patrol boat	25.7.1941	9.7.1944	Deleted
№ 1409	KM-4 type	Patrol boat	25.7.1941		Conv to patrol boat
№ 1410	KM-4 type	Patrol boat	25.7.1941		Conv to patrol boat
№ 1411	KM-4 type	Patrol boat	25.7.1941		Conv to patrol boat
№ 1412	KM-4 type	Patrol boat	25.7.1941	9.7.1944	Deleted
№ 1413	KM-4 type	Patrol boat	25.7.1941		Conv to patrol boat
№ 1414	KM-4 type	Patrol boat	25.7.1941	24.10.1944	Deleted
№ 1415	KM-4 type	Patrol boat	25.7.1941	26.5.1942	Lost
№ 1416	KM-4 type	Patrol boat	25.7.1941		Conv to patrol boat
№ 1509 – № 1512	R type	Patrol boat	19.08.1941		Survived the war
№ 1513	R type	Patrol boat	19.08.1941	Aug 1941	Lost
№ 1514	R type	Patrol boat	19.08.1941		Survived the war
NORD-VEST	Nord-vest	Patrol boat	6.5.1942	6.11.1943	Decomm
OVR-13	R type	Patrol boat	16.3.1943		Survived the war
PP-1	KM-2 type	Patrol boat	7.10.1941		Survived the war

20.2. War prizes – Bulgaria, 1944

No	Details	Comm	Fleet	Remarks
KT-941 ex-*No 2* (Bul, 1944)	25t; 17.2 x 3.0 x 1.0m; 100hp = 9kts; 1 MG, 8 men	29.9.1944	BS	*MChKs* type Bulgarian motor minesweeper, built 1942. Captured 9.9.1944 at Varna. Returned 2.8.1945
KT-942 ex-*No 3* (Bul, 1944)	25t; 17.2 x 3.0 x 1.0m; 100hp = 9kts; 1 MG, 8 men	29.9.1944	BS	*MChKs* type Bulgarian motor minesweeper, built 1942. Captured 9.9.1944 at Varna. Returned 2.8.1945
KT-943 ex-*No 4* (Bul, 1944)	25t; 17.2 x 3.0 x 1.0m; 100hp = 9kts; 1 MG, 8 men	29.9.1944	BS	*MChKs* type Bulgarian motor minesweeper, built 1942. Captured 9.9.1944 at Varna. Returned 2.8.1945
KT-944 ex-*No 5* (Bul, 1944)	25t; 17.2 x 3.0 x 1.0m; 100hp = 9kts; 1 MG, 8 men	29.9.1944	BS	*MChKs* type Bulgarian motor minesweeper, built 1942. Captured 9.9.1944 at Varna. Returned 2.8.1945
KT-945 ex-*No 6* (Bul, 1944)	25t; 17.2 x 3.0 x 1.0m; 100hp = 9kts; 1 MG, 8 men	29.9.1944	BS	*MChKs* type Bulgarian motor minesweeper, built 1942. Captured 9.9.1944 at Varna. Returned 2.8.1945
KT-946 ex-*Neseb"r* (Bul, 1944)	18t; 16.0 x 3.0 x 0.9m; 60hp = 7.6kts; 1 MG	29.9.1944	BS	Bulgarian motor minesweeper, captured 9.9.1944 at Varna. Returned 2.8.1945
KT-947 ex-*Emona* (Bul, 1944)	18t; 16.0 x 3.0 x 0.9m; 60hp = 7.6kts; 1 MG	29.9.1944	BS	Bulgarian motor minesweeper, captured 9.9.1944 at Varna. Returned 2.8.1945
KT-948 ex-*Balik* (Bul, 1944) ex-*Min'or* (Bul, 1914)	14t; 3.0 x 2.65 x 0.9m; 40hp =9kts; 2MGs; 5 men	29.9.1944	BS	Bulgarian motor minesweeper, captured 9.9.1944 at Varna. Returned 2.8.1945
KT-949 ex-*Ia-5* (Bul, 1945)	•	3.2.1945	BS	Bulgarian motor minesweeper, sunk 1944 by Soviet aircraft at Varna, raised and recomm. Conv 26.9.1945 to service craft *Raz"ezdnoj kater № 233*
KT-950 ex-*T-6* (Bul, 1945)	•	3.2.1945	BS	Bulgarian motor minesweeper, sunk 1944 by Soviet aircraft at Varna, raised and recomm. Conv 26.9.1945 to service craft *Raz"ezdnoj kater № 234*

20.3. Conversions

20.3.1. Naval conversions

D-2, D-4 types *Service craft*

Displacement: 20.3t full load
Dimensions: 16.9 x 3.6 x 1.0m
Machinery: 1-shaft diesel, 75hp = 7.5kts; range 1800nm at 6kts
Armament: 1-0.5in DShK or 1-0.3in Maxim MG, 1 OTSh sweep, 1 KAT sweep
Complement: 11

No on Comm	No 21.10.1944	Name as KT	Comm	Fleet	Remarks
KT-372		IOK-159	6.10.1944	B	Naval engineering service craft conv to minesweeping boat. Survived the war
KT-373		IOK-160	6.10.1944	B	Naval engineering service craft conv to minesweeping boat. Survived the war, conv to service craft *Raz"ezdnoj kater № 321*
KT-374		F-27	6.10.1944	B	Naval service craft conv to minesweeping boat. Survived the war
KT-375		KSK-102	06.10.1944	B	Naval service craft conv to minesweeping boat. Survived the war
OVR-4		LVR-3	16.12.1941	B	Kronshtadt naval service craft conv to minesweeping boat. Mined 15.10.1943 off Namen Island
OVR-5	KT-831	LVR-4	16.12.1941	B	Kronshtadt naval service craft conv to minesweeping boat. Survived the war
OVR-6		LVR-5	16.12.1941	B	Kronshtadt naval service craft conv to minesweeping boat. Sunk 6.8.1942 by mine off Kronshtadt
OVR-7	KT-832		21.10.1941	B	Kronshtadt naval service craft conv to minesweeping boat. Survived the war
OVR-8	KT-833		21.10.1941	B	Kronshtadt naval service craft conv to minesweeping boat. Survived the war
OVR-9	KT-834		21.10.1941	B	Kronshtadt naval service craft conv to minesweeping boat. Mined 6.1.1945 in the East Dvina River estuary
OVR-10	KT-835		21.10.1941	B	Kronshtadt naval service craft conv to minesweeping boat. Sank 7.11.1942 in collision with the minesweeping boat *KATShch № 901* (KM-4 type) off Kronshadt. Raised and recomm in Oct 1944. Survived the war
OVR-11	KT-836		21.10.1941	B	Kronshtadt naval service craft conv to minesweeping boat. Survived the war
OVR-13		OO-1	25.11.1942	B	NKVD service craft conv to minesweeping boat. Reverted 16.3.1943 to service craft
OVR-14	KT-837	UBPL-6	25.11.1942	B	Submarine Brigade service craft conv to minesweeping boat. Survived the war
OVR-15	KT-838	UBPL-4	25.11.1942	B	Submarine Brigade service craft conv to minesweeping boat. Survived the war
OVR-16	KT-839	PL-23	25.11.1942	B	Submarine Brigade service craft conv to minesweeping boat. Survived the war
OVR-17	KT-840	RK № XII-IV	25.11.1942	B	Naval service craft conv to minesweeping boat. Survived the war
OVR-18	KT-841	UO-5	25.11.1942	B	Naval service craft conv to minesweeping boat. Survived the war
OVR-19	KT-842	KVMB-5	25.11.1942	B	Naval service craft conv to minesweeping boat. Survived the war

Apparently wooden construction, service craft of the Baltic Fleet, built at the late 1930s presumably by Yd No 5, Leningrad. Conv to minesweeping boats during the war.

OVR-14 during the war.
Boris Lemachko Collection

OVR-15 and others of this type.
Boris Lemachko Collection

D-2, D-4 type boat on Lake Peipus in 1944. Note the rocket launcher forward.
Boris Lemachko Collection

KLT type
Service craft

Displacement: 10.38t full load
Dimensions: 15.2 x 2.6 x 0.7m
Machinery: 2-shaft diesels, 136hp = 12kts. Range 560nm at 9.5kts
Armament: 1-0.3in Maxim MG, 1-KT? sweep
Complement: 12

KATShch № on Comm	KATShch № 7.9.1941	No 12.11.1944	Name	Laid down	Comp	Comm	Fleet	Remarks
	№ 1210[1] № 713	KT-713	SKA № 2	1939	1940	1940	B	Comp as patrol boat, renumbered № 217 on 1.12.1940, conv 25.7.1941 to minesweeping boat. Survived the war
	№ 1211[1] № 714	KT-714	SKA № 3	1939	1940	1940	B	Comp as patrol boat, renumbered № 218 on 1.12.1940, conv 25.7.1941 to minesweeping boat. Survived the war
№ 1506	№ 715	KT-715	VR-4	1939	1940	25.7.1941	B	Kronshtadt service craft conv to minesweeping boat. Sunk 5.10.1941 by artillery fire, raised and recomm. Survived the war
№ 1504	№ 814	KT-814	VR-2	1939	1940	25.7.1941	B	Kronshtadt service craft conv to minesweeping boat. Survived the war
№ 1505	№ 815	KT-815	VR-3	1939	1940	25.7.1941	B	Kronshtadt service craft conv to minesweeping boat. Survived the war
№ 903		KT-633[4]	PVO-9	1939	1940	16.6.1944	B	Naval AA defence service craft conv 4.6.1944 to minesweeping boat. Survived the war
№ 1503	OVR-12[2]	KT-843[3]	VR-1	1939	1940	25.7.1941	B	Kronshtadt service craft conv to minesweeping boat. Survived the war

Exceptions noted in the main table.

No	Year	Date	Fleet
1	1941	25.7.1941	B
2		29.12.1941	B
3		21.10.1944	B
4		27.4.1945	B

KLT stands for Kater Legkogo Tipa = Light Type Boat. Service craft of the Baltic Fleet conv to minesweepers.

Motorboats

KATShch № No on Comm	No 12.11.1944	Name Motobot No	Details	Comm	Fleet	Remarks
№ 16	KT-57	GE-57	48.5t; 16.2 x 5.0 x 2.4m; 50hp = 6kts; 420nm at 5kts; sweeps; 6 men	16.7.1942	B	Pilot boat. Conv 1.7.1942. Reverted 26.6.1945 to pilot boat *TMB-10*. Survived the war
№ 26	KT-58	GE-58		16.7.1942	B	Pilot boat. Conv 1.7.1942. Survived the war
№ 36		GE-63		16.7.1942	B	Pilot boat. Conv 1.7.1942. Mined 17.6.1942 off Kronshtadt
№ 46	KT-46	GE-65		25.7.1942	B	Pilot boat. Conv 1.7.1942. Survived the war
№ 56	KT-56	GE-66		16.7.1942	B	Pilot boat. Conv 1.7.1942. Survived the war
№ 66	KT-66	GE-69		16.7.1942	B	Pilot boat. Conv 1.7.1942. Reverted 26.6.1945 to pilot boat *PMB-11*
№ 76	KT-76	GE-71		16.7.1942	B	Pilot boat. Conv 1.7.1942. Survived the war
№ 136		№ 85		1.7.1942	B	Transport boat. Reverted 29.9.1942 to service craft
№ 156		•		1.7.1942	B	Transport boat. Reverted 29.9.1942 to service craft
№ 186	KT-186	GE-68		25.10.1942	B	Pilot boat. Conv 24.8.1942. Survived the war
№ 196	KT-196	GE-70		25.10.1942	B	Pilot boat. Conv 24.8.1942. Survived the war
№ 16	KT-40[1]	№ 16	20t; 14.0 x 3.4 x 1.5m; 65hp = 8/3kts; 345nm; 1 MKhT sweep.	11.9.1942	La B	Built 1941. Transport boat, conv Sept 1942. Trfd to the Baltic Fleet 21.10.1944. Survived the war
№ 19	KT-19[1]	LP-19	25t; 14.0 x 3.9 x 1.9m; 65hp = 9kts; 500nm at 8kts; 1 MKhT sweep.	11.9.1942	La B	Built 1941. Transport boat, conv Sept 1942. Trfd to the Baltic Fleet 21.10.1944. Survived the war

KATShch № No on Comm	No 12.11.1944	Name Motobot №	Details	Comm	Fleet	Remarks
№ 20	KT-20[1]	LP-20	25t; 14.0 x 3.9 x 1.9m; 65hp = 9kts; 500nm at 8kts; 1 MKhT sweep.	11.9.1942	La B	Built 1941. Transport boat, conv Sept 1942. Trfd to the Baltic Fleet 21.10.1944. Survived the war
№ 34	KT-34[1]	№ 34	20t; 14.0 x 3.4 x 1.5m; 65hp = 8/3kts; 345nm; 1 MKhT sweep.	11.9.1942	La B	Built 1941. Transport boat, conv Sept 1942. Trfd to the Baltic Fleet 21.10.1944. Survived the war
№ 35	KT-35[1]	№ 35		11.9.1942	La B	Built 1941. Transport boat, conv Sept 1942. Trfd to the Baltic Fleet 21.10.1944. Survived the war
OVR-36	KT-36[2]	OVR-36	30.5t; 4.3 x 3.3 x 0.8 m, 4.5kts, 300nm at 4kts; 2-0.3in MGs, 2 MKhT sweeps, 1 EMT sweep	13.4.1942	Cs	Communication boat, built 1935. Conv 16.2.1942 to minesweeping boat. Conv 20.6.1945 to service craft OK-16
RTShch № 110		RK № 116	•	29.3.1943	BS	Communication boat. Sunk 7.11.1943 by German warships off Eltigen

Exceptions noted in the main table.

No	Year	Date
1	1944	20.10.1944
2		21.10.1944

NKVD sail-motor schooners

KATShch № No on Comm	No 21.6.1944	NKVD No	Details	Comm	Fleet	Remarks
KATShch-604	EMTShch-604	PS-1 ex-*PSh-10* (9.1.1941)	100t; 24.5 x 5.7 x 3.3m; 100hp = 7kts; 1300nm at 6kts; 2-0.3in MGs; 10 men	7.3.1942	BS	Built 1937. Mobilised 22.6.1941, comm 19.7.1941 as service craft. Conv 7.3.1942 to minesweeping boat. Conv 30.4.1944 to magnetic minesweeper. Conv 21.6.1945 to service craft
KATShch-547		PS-2	•	30.4.1942	BS	Mobilised 22.6.1941, comm 19.7.1941 as service craft. Conv 30.4.1942 to minesweeping boat. Sunk 12.5.1942 by aircraft in the Kerch Strait
№ 106	KT-106[1]	KHIURAND ex-*Hiurland* (Est, 1940)	•	25.7.1942	B	Former Estonian?, seized 1940. NKVD naval school boat taken over 1.7.1942. Reverted 30.12.1944

Exceptions noted in the main table.

No	Year	Date
1	1944	12.11.1944

20.3.2. Civilian conversions

20.3.2.1. Passenger, cargo and service motorboats

Taganrog type *Coastal ferry boats*

Displacement: 32.8t
Dimensions: 18.2 x 3.8 x 1.4m
Machinery: 1-shaft, petrol engine, 70hp = 8.5kts. Range 478nm at 7kts
Armament: 1-0.3in MG, 1 KAT sweep
Complement: 8

Pt-No 1941	No on Comm	No 21.6.1944	Kater №	Built	Comm	Fleet	Remarks
Builder: Taganrog Works, Taganrog							
71	T-521		№ 1	1934	30.6.1941	BS	Mobilised 22.6.1941. Sunk 10.9.1943 by artillery fire at Novorossisk
72	T-522	KT-522	№ 2	1934	30.6.1941	BS	Mobilised 22.6.1941. Survived the war

Small passenger coastal ferries.

20.0 Minesweeping boats

Odessa type
Inshore ferry boats

Displacement:	39.5t
Dimensions:	18.3 x 4.3 x 1.4m
Machinery:	2-shaft, petrol engine, 140hp = 8.8kts. Range 478nm at 7kts
Armament:	1-0.3in MG, 1 KAT sweep
Complement:	8

Pt-No 1941	No on Comm	No 21.6.1944	Kater №	Built	Comm	Fleet	Remarks
Builder: Workshops (?) at Odessa							
73	T-523	KT-523	№ 9	1934	30.6.1941	BS	Mobilised 22.6.1941. Survived the war
74	T-524		№ 10	1934	30.6.1941	BS	Mobilised 22.6.1941. Sunk 4.11.1943 by German warships off Eltigen
75	T-525	KT-525	№ 11	1934	30.6.1941	BS	Mobilised 22.6.1941. Survived the war
76	T-526	KT-526	№ 12	1934	30.6.1941	BS	Mobilised 22.6.1941. Survived the war
77	T-527	KT-527	№ 13	1934	30.6.1941	BS	Mobilised 22.6.1941. Survived the war

Rechnoj tramvaj types
River ferry boats

Type:	MSV-•	MSV-7	MSV-•	MSV-•
Power:	30hp	50hp	100hp	120hp
Displacement:	15t	30t		
Dimensions				
Length:	14.5m	21.3m	28.0m	28.0m
Breadth:	3.5m	4.5m	5.0m	4.5m
Draught:	1.0m	0.7m	1.1m	0.8m
Speed:	5.3kts	8.0kts	8.0kts	8.1kts
Machinery:	1-shaft, diesel motor. Oil fuel 0.25m³			
Armament:	1 MG, 1 KAT seep			
Complement:	8–9			

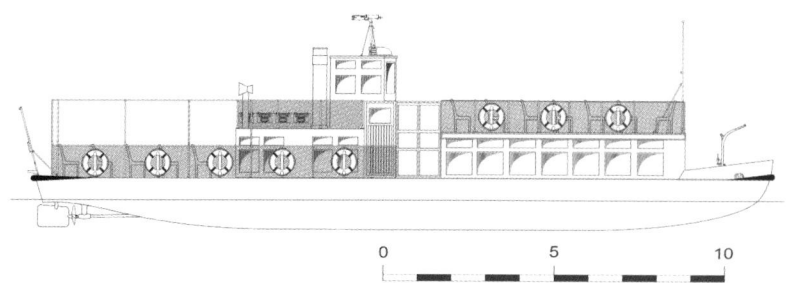

MSV-7 type after minesweeping conversion.
Drawing by Jerzy Lewandowski

KATShch № 4.8.1942 No on Comm	No 9.7.1943	No Red Army	No 31.7.1944	Name Tramvaj №	Built	Comm	Fleet	Remarks
Builder: MSV, Moscow								
120hp MSV type								
№ 311*				PORTOVIK	1933	18.8.1942	Vo	Mobilised 4.8.1942. Conv 5.10.1943 to service craft
№ 312*				RATSIONALIZATOR	1933	18.8.1942	Vo	Mobilised 4.8.1942. Deleted 16.2.1943 for repairs, recomm 8.5.1943. Conv 5.10.1943 to service craft
№ 313*				LIZA CHAJKINA	1933	18.8.1942	Vo	Mobilised 4.8.1942. Conv 5.10.1943 to service craft
№ 314*				15 LET VLKSM	1933	18.8.1942	Vo	Mobilised 4.8.1942. Conv 5.10.1943 to service craft
№ 315*				16-J OKTABR'	1934	18.8.1942	Vo	Built 1934. Mobilised 4.8.1942. Sank 15.9.1942 in collision at Stalingrad
№ 316**				PERVYJ	1934	31.8.1942	Vo	Built 1934. Mobilised 18.8.1942. Sunk 5.10.1942 by artillery fire at Stalingrad
№ 317**				CHETVYORTYJ	1934	31.8.1942	Vo	Built 1934. Mobilised 18.8.1942. Sunk 20.10.1942 by artillery fire at Skudrei
№ 341**	KATShch-341³			VOS'MOJ	1935	31.8.1942	Vo	Built 1935. Mobilised 18.8.1942. Conv 2.6.1944 to service craft
№ 342**				ODINAADTSATYJ	1935	31.8.1942	Vo	Built 1935. Mobilised 18.8.1942. Sunk 18.9.1942 by artillery fire at Stalingrad
№ 343**				CHETYRNADTSATYJ	1935	31.8.1942	Vo	Built 1935. Mobilised 18.8.1942. Sunk 11.10.1942 by artillery fire at Stalingrad
100hp MSV type								
№ 321*				№ 2	1936	18.8.1942	Vo	Built 1936. Mobilised 4.8.1942. Conv 5.10.1943 to service craft
№ 322*				№ 6	1936	18.8.1942	Vo	Built 1936. Mobilised 4.8.1942. Conv 16.2.1943 to service craft

KATShch № 4.8.1942 No on Comm	No 9.7.1943	No Red Army	No 31.7.1944	Name Tramvaj №	Built	Comm	Fleet	Remarks
№ 323*				№ 7	1936	18.8.1942	Vo	Built 1936. Mobilised 4.8.1942. Sunk 15.9.1942 by artillery fire at Stalingrad
№ 324*	KATShch-324[3]			№ 10	1936	18.8.1942	Vo	Built 1936. Mobilised 4.8.1942. Sank Oct 1942 Stalingrad, raised and recomm. Conv 2.6.1944 to service craft
№ 325*				UDARNIK	1934	18.8.1942	Vo	Built 1934. Mobilised 4.8.1942. Conv 5.10.1944 to service craft
№ 326**				PIATYJ	1935	31.8.1942	Vo	Built 1935. Mobilised 18.8.1942. Deleted 11.10.1942. Presumably lost
№ 327**				SHESTOJ	1935	31.8.1942	Vo	Built 1935. Mobilised 18.8.1942. Sunk 20.10.1942 by artillery fire at Skudrei
50hp MSV type				**Kater №**				
№ 351[1]				№ 97	1937	1942	Vo	Built 1937. Mobilised 16.11.1942. Decomm 5.10.1943 to service craft
T-131	KATShch-352	•		№ 87	1934	24.6.1943	Vo	Built 1934. Mobilised 7.6.1943. Sunk 18.9.1942 by artillery fire at Golodnyi Island, raised and recomm. Trfd 7.10.1943 to the Red Army
T-132	KATShch-353	PT-4	T-132	№ 89	1934	24.6.1943	Bo Dn	Built 1934. Mobilised 7.6.1943. Trfd 7.10.1943 to the Red Army, returned 31.7.1944, trfd to the Dnieper Flotilla. Conv 20.8.1944 to service craft
T-133	KATShch-354	•		№ 91	1934	24.6.1943	Vo	Built 1934. Mobilised 7.6.1943. Trfd 7.10.1943 to the Red Army
T-134	KATShch-355	PT-3	T-134	№ 94	1934	24.6.1942	Vo Dn	Built 1934. Mobilised 7.6.1943. Trfd 7.10.1943 to the Red Army, returned 31.7.1944, trfd to the Dnieper Flotilla. Conv 20.8.1944 to service craft
T-135	KATShch-356			№ 108	1934	24.6.1943	Vo	Built 1934. Mobilised 7.6.1943. Conv 6.10.1943 to repair vessel. Conv 19.11.1943 to service craft
T-336	KATShch-383	•		№ 83	1934	24.6.1943	Vo	Built 1934. Mobilised 7.6.1943. Trfd 7.10.1943 to the Red Army
T-337	KATShch-384	•		№ 85	1934	24.6.1943	Vo	Built 1934. Mobilised 20.6.1943. Trfd 7.10.1943 to the Red Army
T-433	KATShch-396[2]	•	T-433[4]	№ 58	1933	24.6.1943	Vo Dn	Mobilised 15.6.1943. Trfd 7.10.1943 to the Red Army, returned 31.7.1944, trfd to the Dnieper Flotilla. Survived the war
T-434	KATShch-388	•	T-434[4]	№ 79	1934	24.6.1943	Vo Dn	Built 1934. Mobilised 7.6.1943. Trfd 7.10.1943 to the Red Army, returned 31.7.1944, trfd to the Dnieper Flotilla. Survived the war
T-435	KATShch-389	•		№ 81	1934	24.6.1943	Vo	Built 1934. Mobilised 7.6.1943. Trfd 7.10.1943 to the Red Army
T-436	KATShch-390	PT-2	T-436	№ 82	1934	24.6.1943	Vo	Built 1934. Mobilised 7.6.1943. Trfd 7.10.1943 to the Red Army, returned 31.7.1944, trfd to the Dnieper Flotilla. Conv 20.8.1944 to service craft
T-437	KATShch-391	•	T-437	№ 84	1934	24.6.1943	Vo	Built 1934. Mobilised 7.6.1943. Trfd 7.10.1943 to the Red Army, returned 31.7.1944, trfd to the Dnieper Flotilla. Conv 20.8.1944 to service craft
T-631	KATShch-434			№ 92	1934	27.6.1943	Vo	Built 1934. Mobilised 23.6.1943. Trfd 7.10.1943 to the Red Army
30hp MSV type				**Passazhirskij tramvaj №**				
T-632	KATShch-433[2]			№ 2	1933	7.7.1943	Vo	Mobilised 29.6.1943. Conv 5.10.1943 to service craft
T-836	KATShch-472[2]			№ 1	1933	13.7.1943	Vo	Mobilised 10.7.1943. Conv 24.4.1943 to service craft

Exceptions noted in the main table.

No	Year	Date
1	1942	16.11.1942
2	1943	31.7.1943
3		18.10.1943
4	1944	5.6.1944

Note on Pennant Numbers
* Pennant RTShch = Rechnoj Tral'shchik (River minesweeper), from 18.8.1942:
KATShch = Kater-tral'shchik (Minesweeping boat)
** Pennant KTShch = Kater-tral'shchik (Minesweeping boat)

Small flat-bottomed passenger river ferries (river trams) built for local short distance connections.

Camouflaged *Rechnoj tramvaj* in left background with *K-15* (*M-17*) type boats in the foreground, on the Volga, 1944. Vitalij Kostrichenko Collection

Miscellaneous

KATShch № No on Comm	No 12.11.1944	Name	Details	Comm	Fleet	Remarks
KMSh-3 EMKATShch-194[2]	KT-194	RODINA	•	12.11.1943	B	Mobilised autumn 1941 service craft, sunk 2.10.1943 by artillery fire at Kronshtadt, raised and recomm, conv Nov 1943 to magnetic minesweeper. Survived the war
KMSh-4 EMKATShch-195[2]	KT-195	VIL'KO	•	12.11.1943	B	Mobilised autumn 1941 service craft, conv Nov 1943 to magnetic minesweeper. Survived the war
№ 22		MOTOBOT № 22	•	Sept 1942	La	Mobilised 11.9.1942. Reverted 16.9.1943 to service craft
№ 166	KT-166	UK-5	48.5t; 16.2 x 5.0 x 2.4m; 50hp = 6kts; 420nm at 5kts; sweeps; 6 men	25.10.1942	B	Mobilised 29.9.1942. Conv 26.6.1945 to pilot boat *PMB-12*
№ 176	KT-176	UK-6		25.10.1942	B	Mobilised 29.9.1942. Survived the war
	KT-267[3]	DEL'FIN	25.5t; 14.8 x 3.8 x 1.9m; 35hp = 6kts; 150nm; 5 men	11.9.1942	B La B	Mobilised autumn 1941, service craft. Conv Sept 1942, returned 21.10.1944
	KT-192[3]	NAVIGATOR	23t; 14.0 x 3.9 x 1.8m; 65hp = 7kts; 400nm; 1 MKhT sweep	Sept 1941	La B	Mobilised 11.9.1942. Trfd to the Baltic Fleet Fleet 21.10.1944. Survived the war
RTShch-60	DZ-1[1] DZ-81[2]	ENTUZIAST	30t; 17.1 x 4.3 x 0.9m; 100hp = 8kts; 1-0.3in MG; 6 men	28.7.1941	Am	Built 1934. Mobilised 25.7.1941, conv to minesweeping boats. Conv 25.7.1942 to smoke screen layers. Survived the war
RTShch-61	DZ-2[1] DZ-82[2]	UDARNIK	30t; 17.1 x 4.3 x 0.9m; 100hp = 8kts; 1-0.3in MG; 6 men	28.7.1941	Am	Built 1934. Mobilised 25.7.1941, conv to minesweeping boats. Conv 25.7.1942 to smoke screen layers. Survived the war
RTShch-62	DZ-3[1] DZ-83[2]	PROIZVODSTVIENNIK	30t; 17.1 x 4.3 x 0.9m; 100hp = 8kts; 1-0.3in MG; 6 men	28.7.1941	Am	Built 1934. Mobilised 25.7.1941, conv to minesweeping boats. Conv 25.7.1942 to smoke screen layers. Survived the war
RTShch-63	DZ-4[1] DZ-84[2]	AKTIVIST	30t; 17.1 x 4.3 x 0.9m; 100hp = 8kts; 1-0.3in MG; 6 men	28.7.1941	Am	Built 1934. Mobilised 25.7.1941, conv to minesweeping boats. Conv 25.7.1942 to smoke screen layers. Survived the war

Exceptions noted in the main table.

No	Year	Date
1	1942	25.7.1942
2	1943	12.11.1943
3	1944	21.10.1944

20.3.2.2. Fishing boats
20.3.2.2.1. Motorboats

Fishing motorboat *PMB-26* (Parusno Motornyj Bot = Sail Motor Boat) in the Arctic
Przemysław Budzbon Collection

Service craft

KATShch № No on Comm	No 12.11.1944	Name Motobot №	Details	Comm	Fleet	Remarks
B-1		VZRYV	30t; 17.0 x 4.5 x 0.9m; 100hp = 8/6kts; 6 men	Aug 1945	Am	Mobilised 15.8.1945, conv to tugs for minesweeping rafts. Survived the war
B-2		OTVAZHNYJ		Aug 1945	Am	
B-3		CHERNINETS		Aug 1945	Am	
B-4		NOVGOROD		Aug 1945	Am	
B-5		VODNIK		Aug 1945	Am	
B-6		SNABZHENIETS-1		Aug 1945	Am	Mobilised 15.8.1945, conv to tug for minesweeping rafts. Conv 16.9.1945 to service craft
B-7		SNABZHENETS-2		Aug 1945	Am	Mobilised 15.8.1945, conv to tug for minesweeping rafts. Survived the war
B-8		GROM		Aug 1945	Am	Mobilised 15.8.1945, conv to tug for minesweeping rafts. Conv 16.9.1945 to service craft
B-9		OSETER		Aug 1945	Am	Mobilised 15.8.1945, conv to tug for minesweeping rafts. Conv 16.9.1945 to service craft
B-10		GEROJ		Aug 1945	Am	Mobilised 15.8.1945, conv to tugs for minesweeping rafts. Survived the war
B-11		BUDYONNYJ		Aug 1945	Am	
KEMTShch-6		PELENG	35t; 16.2 x 3.3 x 1.1m; 35hp = 8.5kts; 1-0.5in, 1 KEMT sweep	11.8.1943	Cs BS	Built 1941. Mobilised 2.8.1943, conv to minesweeping boat. Trfd 27.11.1943 to the Black Sea Fleet. Survived the war
№ 421	KT-421	№ 52	10.1 x 2.4 x 0.7m; 32hp = 6.5kts; 150nm; 1-0.3in, 1 MKhT sweep, 1 OTSH-1 sweep; 8 men	14.10.1941	Wh	Built 1939. Mobilised 30.8.1941. Sunk 14.10.1942 in collision with surveying
№ 422	KT-422	№ 19		14.10.1941	Wh	Built 1939. Mobilised 30.8.1941. Decomm 5.3.1945 to civilian service
№ 425	KT-425	№ 50	12.4t; 11.5 x 2.6 x 0.7m; 52hp = 8kts; 200nm; 1-0.3in, 1 MKhT sweep, 1 OTSH-2 sweep; 8 men	14.10.1941	Wh	Built 1938. Mobilised 30.8.1941. Conv 16.8.1945 to service craft
№ 426	KT-426	№ 90	10.1 x 2.4 x 0.7m; 32hp = 6.5kts; 150nm; 1-0.3in, 1 MKhT sweep, 1 OTSH-1 sweep; 8 men	14.10.1941	Wh	Built 1939. Mobilised 30.8.1941. Decomm 5.3.1945 to civilian service
№ 427	KT-427	№ 91		14.10.1941	Wh	Built 1939. Mobilised 30.8.1941. Conv 16.8.1945 to service craft
№ 428	KT-428	№ 113	12.4t; 11.5 x 2.6 x 0.7m; 52hp = 8kts; 200nm; 1-0.3in, 1 MKhT sweep, 1 OTSH-2 sweep; 8 men	14.10.1941	Wh	Built 1938. Mobilised 30.8.1941. Conv 16.8.1945 to service craft
№ 434	KT-434	SEVTRANZITSPLAV № 24	20.4t; 16.6 x 3.7 x 0.9m; 65hp = 520nm; 3-0.3in, 1 MKhT sweep, 1 OTSH-2 sweep; 7 men	18.8.1942	Wh	Built 1941. Mobilised 18.8.1942. Survived the war
№ 435	KT-435	SEVTRANZITSPLAV № 25		18.8.1942	Wh	Built 1941. Mobilised 18.8.1942. Survived the war

Arctic and Baltic

KATShch № No on Comm	No 12.11.1944	Name	Details	Comm	Fleet	Remarks
	KT-719	KASATKA	45t; 14.0 x 4.7 x 2.1m; 100hp = 10kts; 420nm at 6kts; 1 MKhT; 6 men	14.8.1941	B	Mobilised 6.8.1941. Survived the war
	KT-269[5]	KOMMUNIST	38.8t; 16.9 x 4.7 x 2.1m; 75hp = 7kts; 2000nm at 6kts; 2-0.3in, 1 EMT sweep, 2 MKhT sweeps; 15 men	10.8.1941	La B	Built 1935. Mobilised 2.8.1941. Trfd to the Baltic Fleet 21.10.1944. Survived the war
	KT-268[5]	KOMSOMOLETS	38.8t; 16.9 x 4.7 x 2.1m; 75hp = 7kts; 2000nm at 6kts; 2-0.3in, 1 EMT sweep, 2 MKhT sweeps; 15 men	8.8.1941	La B	Mobilised 1.8.1941. Trfd to the Baltic Fleet 21.10.1944. Survived the war
	KT-720	SIG	208.5t; 29.8 x 7.2 x 3.0m; 300hp = 8/5kts; 340nm; 1 EMT sweep, 1 MKhT sweep; 15 men	8.8.1941	B	Built 1934. Mobilised 1.8.1941. Survived the war
		SKAT	50t; 70hp, 1 MKhT sweep; 6 men	12.8.1941	B	Mobilised 3.8.1941. Stranded 9.8.1941 in a gale in Narva Bay
		SMELYJ	50t; 70hp, 1 MKhT sweep; 6 men	Aug 1941	B	Mobilised 3.8.1941. Stranded 9.8.1941 in a gale in Narva Bay
	KT-718	SVIR'	36.06t; 12.0 x 4.0 x 2.0m; 70hp = 7kts; 740nm at 6kts; 1 MKhT sweep; 16 men	10.8.1941	B	Built 1937. Mobilised 2.8.1941. Survived the war
5M28M1[1]	KT-721	POVODETS	87.4t; 20.3 x 5.6 x 2.7m; 110hp, 6/5kts, 340nm; 1 EMT sweep, 1 MKhT sweeps; 10 men	8.8.1941	B	Built 1937. Mobilised 1.8.1941. Survived the war
5M3		IASTREB	50t; 70hp, 1 MKhT sweep; 6 men	13.8.1941	B	Mobilised 4.8.1941. Mined 24.9.1942 off Kronshtadt
7M15M1[2]		PIKSHA	180t; 250hp = 1 EMT sweep, 1 MKhT sweep; 15 men	8.8.1941	B	Mobilised 1.8.1941. Mined 2.9.1942 at Morskoi Kanal
7M27M1[1]		VORONIN	50t; 70hp, 1 MKhT sweep; 6 men	13.8.1941	B	Mobilised 3.8.1941. Mined 25.6.1942 off Kronshtadt
8M2		VOLKHOV	180t; 250hp = 1 EMT sweep, 1 MKhT sweep; 15 men	12.8.1941	B	Mobilised 3.8.1941. Sunk 16.9.1941 by German aircraft off Saaremaa
EMKATShch-197	KT-197[5]	DVINA	•	3.10.1943	B La B	Mobilised 21.6.1943 service craft, conv Oct 1943 to magnetic minesweeper. Trfd 12.11.1944 to the Baltic Fleet. Conv 13.12.1945 to service craft
EMKATShch-198	KT-198[5]	VOLGA	•	3.10.1943	B La B	Mobilised 21.6.1943 service craft, conv Oct 1943 to magnetic minesweeper. Trfd 12.11.1944 to the Baltic Fleet. Conv 13.12.1945 to service craft
EMKATShch-200	KT-200	LILIIA	•	12.11.1943	B	Mobilised autumn 1941 service craft, conv Nov 1943 to magnetic minesweeper. Survived the war
EMKATShch-201	KT-201	NEVA	•	Nov 1943	B	Mobilised 12.11.1943, conv to magnetic minesweeper. Survived the war
GS-1	KT-722	GAZOKHOD № 1	75t; 20.0 x 4.8 x 2.8m; 120hp = 7kts; 350nm at 5kts, sweeps; 10 men	25.8.1941	B	Wood gas motorboat. Mobilised 12.8.1941. Sank 01.10.1942 in collision with boat № 207, raised and recomm. Survived the war
GS-2	KT-723	GAZOKHOD № 2		29.8.1941	B	Wood gas motorboat. Mobilised 14.8.1941. Survived the war
№ 96		MOTOBOT № 111 PERVENETS	48.5t; 16.2 x 5.0 x 2.4m; 50hp = 6kts; 420nm at 5kts; sweeps; 6 men	1.7.1942	B	Mobilised autumn 1941, service craft. Reverted 29.9.1942
№ 116	KT-116	LEBED'	48.5t; 16.2 x 5.0 x 2.4m; 50hp = 6kts; 420nm at 5kts; sweeps; 6 men	25.7.1942	B	Mobilised 1.7.1942. Conv 30.12.1944 to service craft
№ 126	KT-126	MARTI	48.5t; 16.2 x 5.0 x 2.4m; 50hp = 6kts; 420nm at 5kts; sweeps; 6 men	16.7.1942	B	Mobilised 1.7.1942. Conv 30.12.1944 to service craft

№ 146	KT-146	OPERATIVNYJ	48.5t; 16.2 x 5.0 x 2.4m; 50hp = 6kts; 420nm at 5kts; sweeps; 6 men	17.6.1941	B	Mobilised 1.7.1942. Conv 30.12.1944 to service craft
№ 401	KT-401[4]	IAROSLAVL'	42.3t; 18.0 x 5.1 x 2.2m; 65hp = 6.5kts; 750nm at 4.5kts; 1-45mm/46 21-K, 1-0.5in or 0.3in MG, 1 KEMT-2 sweep, 1 OTSH-2 sweep, 1 KAT sweep; 8 men	29.9.1941	Wh N	Built 1941. Mobilised 25.8.1941. Trfd 17.5.1944 to the Northern Fleet. Survived the war
№ 402	KT-402[4]	PINEGA		29.9.1941	Wh N	Built 1941. Mobilised 25.8.1941. Trfd 17.5.1944 to the Northern Fleet. Decomm 2.3.1945 to civilian service
№ 403	KT-403[4]	MEZEN'		29.9.1941	Wh N	Built 1941. Mobilised 25.8.1941. Trfd 17.5.1944 to the Northern Fleet. Decomm 27.3.1945 to civilian service
№ 404	KT-404[4]	NAR'IAN-MAR		29.9.1941	Wh N	Built 1938. Mobilised 25.8.1941. Sunk 11.5.1943 by aircraft in Motovski Bay, raised and recomm. Trfd 17.5.1944 to the Northern Fleet. Decomm 2.3.1945 to civilian service
№ 405	KT-405[4]	GROMOV	40.2t; 15.1 x 5.0 x 2.4m; 65hp = 5.4kts; 750nm at 4kts; 1-0.5in, 1 KEMT-2 sweep, 1 OTSH-2 sweep, 1 KAT sweep; 8 men	25.8.1941	Wh N	Built 1939. Mobilised 3.8.1941. Rated 10.8.1941 as patrol boat, conv 25.8.1941 to minesweeping boat. Trfd 17.5.1944 to the Northern Fleet. Decomm 2.3.1945 to civilian service
№ 406		CHKALOV		25.8.1941	Wh	Built 1939. Mobilised 3.8.1941. Rated 10.8.1941 as patrol boat, conv 25.8.1941 to minesweeping boat. Decomm 31.3.1945 to civilian service
№ 407		BELOMORSK	56.3t; 19.3 x 5.1 x 2.4m; 50hp = 5kts; 950nm at 4kts; 1-45mm/46 21-K, 1-0.3in, 1 KEMT-2 sweep, 1 OTSH-2 sweep, 1 KAT; 8 men	25.8.1941	Wh N	Built 1940. Mobilised 1.8.1941. Rated 10.8.1941 as patrol boat, conv 25.8.1941 to minesweeping boat. Trfd 17.5.1944 to the Northern Fleet. Conv 8.6.1944 to torpedo recovery tender *MMB-18*
№ 409		RS-2	40.2t; 15.4 x 5.8 x 2.4m; 50hp = 6kts; 950nm at 4kts; 1-45 mm1-0.3in, 1 KAT sweep; 8 men	29.9.1941	Wh	Built 1933. Mobilised 25.8.1941. Decomm 31.12.1943 to civilian service
№ 410		OSIPENKO	40.2t; 15.4 x 5.0 x 2.4m; 65hp = 6kts; 750nm at 4kts; 1-0.3in, 1 KAT sweep; 8 men	29.9.1941	Wh	Built 1939. Mobilised 25.8.1941. Sank 18.12.1943 off Iokanga in collision with the motorboat *IMB-7*. Raised and recomm. Decomm 26.5.1944 to civilian service
№ 411	KT-411[4]	BAJDUKOV	40.2t; 15.4 x 5.0 x 2.4m; 65hp = 6kts; 750nm at 4kts; 1-45mm/46 21-K, 1-0.3in, 1 KAT sweep; 8 men	29.9.1941	N Wh	Built 1939. Mobilised 25.8.1941. Trfd 17.5.1944 to the Northern Fleet. Decomm 2.3.1945 to civilian service
№ 412		STRUIA	45.2t; 15.7 x 5.7 x 2.2m; 50hp = 6kts; 950nm at 4kts; 1-0.3in, 1 OTSH-2 sweep, 1 KEMT-2 sweep, 1 KAT sweep; 8 men	29.9.1941	Wh	Built 1934. Mobilised 25.8.1941. Decomm 26.5.1944 to civilian service
№ 414		TIMANETS			Wh	Built 1934. Mobilised 25.8.1941. Decomm 31.12.1943 to civilian service
№ 413		PELENGATOR	45.2t; 15.7 x 5.7 x 2.2m; 50hp = 6kts; 950nm at 4kts; 1-45mm/46 21-K, 1-0.3in, 1 OTSH-2 sweep, 1 KEMT-2 sweep, 1 KAT sweep; 8 men	29.9.1941	Wh N	Built 1934. Mobilised 25.8.1941. Conv 26.5.1944 to communication vessel *PMB-84*, trfd to the Northern Fleet. Conv 3.11.1945 to service craft
№ 415	KT-415[4]	BABUSHKIN	40.2t; 15.0 x 5.0 x 2.4m; 65hp = 5.5kts; 750nm at 4kts; 1-0.3in, 1 OTSH-2 sweep, 1 KEMT-2 sweep, 1 KAT sweep; 8 men	29.9.1941	Wh	Built 1939. Mobilised 25.8.1941. Trfd 17.5.1944 to the Northern Fleet. Survived the war
№ 423		RS-5	•	14.10.1941	Wh	Mobilised 14.10.1941. Conv 28.5.1942 to guardship *BS-6*
№ 424		MYS VORONOV	•	14.10.1941	Wh	Mobilised 14.10.1941. Conv 28.5.1942 to service craft *AS-6*, *AMB-33* from 23.6.1943

№							
№ 436	KT-436[3]	SETEPOD''EMNIK	41.4t; 14.5 x 5.3 x 2.1m; 50hp = 5kts; 500nm; 3-0.3in, 1 OTSH-2 sweep; 7 men	Aug 1942	Wh	Built 1933. Mobilised 18.8.1942. Decomm 2.3.1945 to civilian service	
№ 438	KT-438[3]	TIULEN'		Aug 1942	Wh	Built 1933. Mobilised 18.8.1942 1942. Lost 6.11.1941 in a gale off Novaya Zemlya	
№ 437	KT-437[3]	GRIZODUBOVA	40.2t; 15.9 x 5.0 x 2.7m; 65hp = 5kts; 320nm; 1-0.5in, 2-0.3in, 1 OTSH-2 sweep; 7 men	Aug 1942	Wh	Built 1937. Mobilised 18.8.1942. Decomm 2.3.1945 to civilian service.	
№ 439	KT-439[3]	NEKRASOV		Aug 1942	Wh	Built 1937. Mobilised 18.8.1942. Decomm 2.3.1945 to civilian service	
№ 610	KT-610	SEJNER № 1	70.5t; 20.3 x 5.2 x 2.4m; 140hp = 7/5kts; 200nm; 1 EMT sweep, 1 MKhT sweep; 10 men	8.10.1942	B	Mobilised 2.10.1942. Survived the war	
№ 611	KT-611	SEJNER № 2		Nov 1942	B	Mobilised 2.10.1942. Survived the war	
№ 612	KT-612	SEJNER № 3		Nov 1942	B	Mobilised 2.10.1942. Survived the war	

Exceptions noted in the main table.

No	Year	Date
1	1941	7.9.1941
2		18.10.1941
3	1944	1.4.1944
4		17.5.1944
5		21.10.1944

Fishing motorboat *Kommunist* following conversion to minesweeping boat.
Przemysław Budzbon Collection

Black Sea and Caspian

No on Comm	No 4.11.1942	EMTShch № No 13.8.1943	Name	Details	Comm	Fleet	Remarks
EMT-01	BTP-51[1] EMTShch-32[2]	EMTShch-314[3] EMTShch-32	SVERDLOV	87t; 22.0 x 6.0 x 1.4m; 35hp = 5kts; 1000nm; 16 men	15.11.1941	Cs	Built 1938. Mobilised 2.7.1941, conv to air warning boat VN-21. Conv 15.11.1941 to magnetic minesweeper EMT-01, conv 20.8.1942 to tug for minesweeping raft BTP-51, conv 24.9.1942 to magnetic minesweeper EMTShch-32. Renumbered EMTShch-314 on 26.5.1943, number reverted 13.8.1943. Conv 3.2.1945 to service craft
EMT-02	BTP-41[1] EMTShch-29[2]	№ 29[7]	IZOTEMICHKA № 10	87t; 22.0 x 6.0 x 1.4m; 35hp = 5kts; 1000nm; 16 men	15.11.1941	Cs Vo	Built 1938. Mobilised, conv to air warning boat VN-23. Conv 15.11.1941 to magnetic minesweeper EMT-02, conv 20.8.1942 to tug for minesweeping raft BTP-41, conv 24.9.1942 to magnetic minesweeper EMTShch-29. Conv 14.7.1943 to charging plant EMTShch № 29, trfd 2.8.1943 to the Volga Flotilla. Conv 2.9.1943 to degaussing station SBR-10. Decomm 29.4.1944 to civilian service.
EMTShch-46			IZOTERMICHKA № 13	80t; 19.4 x 6.1 x 1.6m; 35hp = 7kts; 1800nm at 6kts; 4-0.3in (1x4) MGs; 18 men	28.10.1942	Cs	Built 1938. Mobilised 3.7.1941, conv to air warning boat VN-16. Decomm 12.10.1941 to civilian service, name reverted. Mobilised 20.10.1942, conv 28.10.1942 to magnetic minesweeper EMTShch-46. Decomm 17.1.1943 to civilian service, name reverted. Mobilised 27.5.1943, conv 19.6.1943 to degaussing station SBR-28. Decomm 30.3.1944 to civilian service
EMT-03			IZOTERMICHKA № 7	80t; 19.4 x 6.1 x 1.6m; 35hp = 7kts; 1800nm at 6kts; 4-0.3in (1x4) MGs; 18 men	15.11.1941	Cs	Built 1938. Mobilised 2.7.1941, conv to air warning boat VN-17. Conv 15.11.1941 to magnetic minesweeper EMT-03, conv 6.3.1942 to degaussing station EBR-01. Trfd 26.8.1942 to the Volga Flotilla, renamed SBR-7. Decomm 20.6.1944 to civilian service
EMTShch-45			IZOTERMICHKA № 9	80t; 19.4 x 6.1 x 1.6m; 35hp = 7kts; 1800nm at 6kts; 4-0.3in (1x4) MGs; 18 men	28.10.1942	Cs Vo	Built 1938. Mobilised 2.7.1941, conv to air warning boat VN-18. Decomm 12.10.1941 to civilian service, name reverted. Mobilised 20.10.1942, conv 28.10.1942 to magnetic minesweeper EMTShCh-45. Decomm 17.1.1943 to civilian service, name reverted. Mobilised 27.5.1943, conv 29.5.1943 to degaussing station SBR-27, recomm 19.6.1943. Trfd 30.3.1944 to the Volga Flotilla, renamed SBR-28. Decomm 24.1.1945 to civilian service
EMT-03	EMTShch-15	№ 15[7]	DERBENT	72t; 18.4 x 6.2 x 1.4m; 35hp = 6kts; 1700nm at 5.5kts; 1-0.3in; 8 men	26.8.1942	Cs Vo	Built 1937. Mobilised 18.8.1942, conv to tug for minesweeping raft, rated 4.11.1942 as magnetic minesweeper. Trfd 2.8.1943 to the Volga Flotilla, conv 2.9.1943 to charging station PZS № 52. Decomm 24.4.1944 to civilian service
EMT-04	EMTShch-44	№ 44[7]	NOGAETS	72t; 18.4 x 6.2 x 1.4m; 35hp = 6kts; 1700nm at 5.5kts; 1-0.3in; 8 men	26.8.1942	Cs Vo	Built 1937. Mobilised 18.8.1942, conv to tug for magnetic sweep, rated 4.11.1942 as magnetic minesweeper. Trfd 2.8.1943 to the Volga Flotilla. Conv 30.5.1944 to service craft
EMT-05		№ 05[8] EMTShch-05[9]	FAKEL SOTSIALIZMA	72t; 18.4 x 6.2 x 1.4m; 35hp = 6kts; 1700nm at 5.5kts; 1-0.3in; 8 men	1.11.1942	Cs Vo BS	Built 1937. Mobilised 18.8.1942, conv to tug for magnetic sweep. Trfd to the Volga Flotilla, trfd 30.5.1944 to the Black Sea Fleet.

20.0 Minesweeping boats

Fishing motorboat *Losos'* following conversion to minesweeping boat *EMTShch-06*.
Przemysław Budzbon Collection

EMT-06	№ 06[8] EMTShch-06[9]	LOSOS'	72t; 18.4 x 6.2 x 1.4m; 35hp = 6kts; 1700nm at 5.5kts; 1-0.3in; 8 men	15.11.1942	Cs Vo BS	Built 1937. Mobilised 18.8.1942, conv to tug for magnetic sweep. Trfd to the Volga Trfd 30.5.1944 to the Black Sea Fleet. Conv 31.12.1945 to service craft
EMT-07		TAT	72t; 18.4 x 6.2 x 1.4m; 35hp = 6kts; 1700nm at 5.5kts; 1-0.3in; 8 men	28.8.1942	Cs	Built 1937. Mobilised 18.8.1942, conv to magnetic minesweeper. Conv 11.2.1943 to service craft
EMT-08		FOREL'	72t; 18.4 x 6.2 x 1.4m; 35hp = 6kts; 1700nm at 5.5kts; 1-0.3in; 8 men		Cs	Built 1937. Mobilised 18.8.1942, conv to magnetic minesweeper. Conv 11.2.1943 to service craft
EMT-09		DARGINETS	72t; 18.4 x 6.2 x 1.4m; 35hp = 6kts; 1700nm at 5.5kts; 1-0.3in; 8 men		Cs	Built 1937. Mobilised 18.8.1942, conv to magnetic minesweeper. Conv 11.2.1943 to service craft
EMT-10		KIZLIAR	72t; 18.4 x 6.2 x 1.4m; 35hp = 6kts; 1700nm at 5.5kts; 1-0.3in; 8 men		Cs	Built 1937. Mobilised 18.8.1942, conv to magnetic minesweeper. Conv 11.2.1943 to service craft
EMT-11	MKhTShch-24[5]E MTShch-51	KUMYK	72t; 18.4 x 6.2 x 1.4m; 35hp = 6kts; 1700nm at 5.5kts; 1-0.3in; 8 men	1.11.1942	Cs	Built 1937. Mobilised 18.8.1942. Survived the war
EMTShch-12	№ 12[7]	KIL'KA	72t; 18.4 x 6.2 x 1.4m; 35hp = 6kts; 1700nm at 5.5kts; 1-0.3in; 8 men	1.11.1942	Cs Vo	Built 1937. Mobilised 18.8.1942, conv to tug for magnetic tail sweep. Trfd 2.8.1943 to the Volga Flotilla. Conv 30.5.1944 to service craft
EMTShch-15 EMTShch-04		TARTA	75t; 17.6 x 6.3 x 1.8m; 35hp = 7kts; 2300nm; 4-0.3in (1x4) MGs; 18 men	28.10.1942	Cs	Built 1938. Mobilised 2.7.1941, conv to air warning boat *VN-25*. Decomm 12.10.1941 to civilian service, name reverted. Mobilised 20.10.1942, conv 28.10.1942 to magnetic minesweeper *EMTShch-15*. Conv 4.11.1942 to tug for minesweeping raft *EMTShch-04*. Conv 20.1.1943 to service craft.
EMTShch-16	MKhTShch-23[6] EMTShch-50	FRUNZE	75t; 17.6 x 6.3 x 1.8m; 35hp = 7kts; 2300nm; 4-0.3in (1x4) MGs; 18 men	28.10.1942	Cs	Built 1939. Mobilised 2.7.1941, conv to air warning boat *VN-27*. Decomm 12.10.1941 to civilian service, name reverted. Mobilised 19.10.1942, conv 28.10.1942 magnetic minesweeper *EMTShch-16*. Decmm 17.3.1943 to civilian service, name reverted. Mobilised 24.5.1943, conv 25.6.1943 to tug for magnetic tail sweep *MKhTShch-23*, renumbered *EMTShch-50* on 13.8.1943. Survived the war

No on Comm	No 4.11.1942	EMTShch № No 13.8.1943	Name	Details	Comm	Fleet	Remarks
EMTShch-44	EMTShch-03		SEROV	75t; 17.6 x 6.3 x 1.8m; 35hp = 7kts; 2300nm; 4-0.3in (1x4) MGs; 18 men	28.10.1942	Cs	Built 1937. Mobilised 2.7.1941, conv to air warning boat VN-28. Decomm 12.10.1941 to civilian service, name reverted. Mobilised 20.10.1942, conv 28.10.1942 to magnetic minesweeper EMTShch-44, conv 4.11.1942 to tug for minesweeping raft EMTShch-03. Conv 20.1.1943 to service craft
EMTShch-47		MKhTShch-22[4] EMTShch-49	OPYT	60t; 14.4 x 5.0 x 1.8m; 40hp =6kts; 1100nm; 1-0.3in; 18 men	Dec 1942 6.6.1943	Cs	Built 1931. Mobilised 4.12.1942, conv to magnetic minesweeper, decomm 16.2.1943 to civilian service. Mobilised 25.5.1943, conv to tug for magnetic tail sweep. Conv 12.11.1943 to service craft
EMTShch-93			DAR'IAL	72t; 18.4 x 6.2 x 1.5m; 35hp = 5kts; 1400nm; 2-0.3in (1x2) MGs; 18 men	19.7.1943	Cs	Mobilised 26.5.1943, conv to AA defence boat PVO-110. Conv 19.7.1943 to magnetic minesweeper EMTShch-93. Conv 23.10.1943 to service craft
EMTShch-94			MOTORYBNITSA № 85	72t; 18.4 x 6.2 x 1.5m; 35hp = 5kts; 1400nm; 1-0.3in; 18 men	15.8.1943	Cs	Mobilised 9.7.1943, conv to magnetic minesweeper. Conv 23.10.1943 to service craft
EMTShch-95			SMOLENSK	72t; 18.4 x 6.2 x 1.5m; 35hp = 5kts; 1400nm; 1-0.3in; 18 men	15.8.1943	Cs	Mobilised 15.6.1943, conv to magnetic minesweeper. Conv 23.10.1943 to service craft
KEMTShch-1		KEMTShch-121[3] KEMTShch-1	KATER № 22	35t; 16.2 x 3.3 x 1.1m; 35hp = 8.5kts; 3000nm at 5.5kts; 1-0.5in MG; 1 KEMT-2 sweep; 6 men	18.2.1942	Cs BS	Built 1942. Mobilised 3.9.1942, conv to air warning boat VNOS-10. Renumbered VNOS-11 on 3.10.1942, conv 18.2.1943 to magnetic minesweeping boat KEMTShch-1. Renumbered KEMTShch-121 on 26.5.1943, number reverted on 13.8.1943. Trfd 27.11.1943 to the Black Sea Fleet. Survived the war
KEMTShch-2		KEMTShch-122[3] KEMTShch-2	KATER № 28	35t; 16.2 x 3.3 x 1.1m; 35hp = 8.5kts; 3000nm at 5.5kts; 1-0.5in MG; 1 KEMT-2 sweep, 6 men	18.2.1942	Cs BS Az	Built 1942. Mobilised 3.9.1942, conv to air warning boat VNOS-12. Conv 18.2.1943 to magnetic minesweeping boat KEMTShch-2. Renumbered KEMTShch-122 on 26.5.1943, number reverted on 13.8.1943. Trfd 27.11.1943 to the Black Sea Fleet. Trfd 13.12.1943 to the Azov Flotilla. Deleted 18.4.1944
KEMTShch-3		KEMTShch-123[3] KEMTShch-3	KATER № 38	35t; 16.2 x 3.3 x 1.1m; 35hp = 8.5kts; 3000nm at 5.5kts; 1-0.5in MG; 1 KEMT-2 sweep, 6 men	18.2.1942	Cs BS	Built 1942. Mobilised 3.9.1942, conv to air warning boat VNOS-13. Conv 18.2.1943 to magnetic minesweeping boat KEMTShch-3. Renumbered KEMTShch-123 on 26.5.1943, number reverted on 13.8.1943. Trfd 27.11.1943 to the Black Sea Fleet. Sank 13.11.1943 in a gale off Krotkovo
KEMTShch-4		KEMTShch-124[3] KEMTShch-4	KATER № 44	35t; 16.2 x 3.3 x 1.1m; 35hp = 8.5kts; 3000nm at 5.5kts; 1-0.5in MG; 1 KEMT-2 sweep, 6 men	18.2.1942	Cs BS	Built 1942. Mobilised 3.9.1942, conv to air warning boat VNOS-14. Conv 18.2.1943 to magnetic minesweeping boat KEMTShch-4. Renumbered KEMTShch-124 on 26.5.1943, number reverted on 13.8.1943. Trfd 27.11.1943 to the Black Sea Fleet. Sank 26.11.1943 in a gale off Tuzla spit
KEMTShch-5		KEMTShch-125[3] KEMTShch-5	KATER № 45	35t; 16.2 x 3.3 x 1.1m; 35hp = 8.5kts; 3000nm at 5.5kts; 1-0.5in MG; 1 KEMT-2 sweep, 6 men	18.2.1942	Cs BS	Built 1942. Mobilised 3.9.1942, conv to air warning boat VNOS-15. Conv 18.2.1943 to magnetic minesweeping boat KEMTShch-5. Renumbered KEMTShch-125 on 26.5.1943, number reverted on 13.8.1943. Trfd 27.11.1943 to the Black Sea Fleet. Survived the war

KEMTShch-6			KATER № 46	35t; 16.2 x 3.3 x 1.1m; 35hp = 8.5kts; 3000nm at 5.5kts; 1-0.5in MG; 1 KEMT-2 sweep, 6 men	18.2.1942	Cs	Built 1942. Mobilised Jan 1942, conv to service boat of the Naval Air School. Conv 3.10.1942 to air warning boat *VNOS-16*. Conv 18.2.1943 to magnetic minesweeping boat *KEMTShch-6*, reverted 24.6.1943 to air warning boat, renumbered *VNOS-26*. Conv 29.12.1943 to service craft
MBTShch-111	EMTShch-54		5-e DEKABRIA	50hp	June 1943	Cs	Mobilised 14.6.1943, conv to tug for magnetic sweep. Conv 16.4.1944 to service craft
MBTShch-112	EMTShch-55		TOVARISHCH CHKALOV	•	14.6.1943	Cs	Mobilised 13.5.1943, conv to tug for magnetic sweep. Conv 30.10.1943 to service craft
MBTShch-113	EMTShch-56		CHELIUSKINETS	42hp	29.5.1943	Cs	Mobilised 24.5.1943, conv to tug for magnetic sweep. Conv 25.10.1943 to service craft

Exceptions noted in the main table.

No	Year	Date
1	1942	20.8.1942
2		24.9.1942
3	1943	1.4.1943
4		4.6.1943
5		21.6.1943
6		25.6.1943
7		14.7.1943
8		2.8.1943
9	1944	21.6.1944

20.3.2.2.2. Seiners

Azov and Black Sea

KATSchch № No on Comm	No 26.5.1942	No 21.6.1944	Name	Details	Comm	Fleet	Remarks
KATShch-154		B-154	AKADEMIK ZERNOV •		Sept 1941	BS Az	Pennant number 98. Mobilised 10.9.1941. Rated 30.4.1944 as tug for magnetic sweep. Survived the war
KATShch-155			KIEV	42t	Sept 1941	BS Az	Pennant number 96. Mobilised 4.9.1941. Trfd 8.2.1943 to the Azov Flotilla. Sunk 26.9.1943 by German MTB off Taman
KATShch-156			DNESTR	75t	Sept 1941	BS Az	Pennant number 97. Mobilised 4.9.1941. Trfd 8.2.1943 to the Azov Flotilla. Sunk 31.10.1943 by mines off Cape Panagia
KATShch-165			KIT (SP-226)	80t; 19.1 x 5.0 x 2.4m; 50hp = 5.5kts; 1426nm at 4.5kts; 1-0.3in; 10 men	29.3.1943	BS Az	Built 1938. Mobilised 6.5.1942, comm May 1942 as service craft *SP-226*. Conv 29.3.1943 to minesweeping boat. Mined 1.11.1943 off Cape Panagia
KATShch-166			BOT № 33 (SP-206)	•	27.3.1943	BS	Mobilised 2.3.1943, comm as service craft. Conv 29.3.1943 to minesweeping boat. Deleted 7.5.1943, presumably lost by mine near Yuzhnaya Ozereyevka off Novorossiysk
KATShch-167			GRUZRYBA № 12 (SP-217)	52.5t; 13.8 x 3.8 x 1.4m; 25hp = 6.5kts; 560nm at 5kts; 1-0.3in, 1 MKhT sweep; 10 men	29.3.1943	BS	Built 1933. Mobilised 13.12.1942, comm as service craft *SP-217*. Conv 29.3.1943 to minesweeping boat. Sunk 21.1.1944 by artillery fire off Chushka Spit, raised and recomm. Survived the war
KATShch-170			BOT № 50 KRASNYJ BORETS (SP-221)	22t; 1.5 x 4.5 x 2.0m; 50hp = 6kts; 800nm; 1-0.3in, 1 MKhT sweep; 10 men	27.3.1943	BS	Mobilised 2.3.1943, comm as service craft *SP-221*. Conv 29.3.1943 to minesweeping boat. Sunk 1.6.1943 by aircraft off Cape Tonkii

KATSchch № No on Comm	No 26.5.1942	No 21.6.1944	Name	Details	Comm	Fleet	Remarks
KATShch-171			BOT № 57	55t; 19.3 x 5.0 x 1.8m; 65hp = 7kts; 1-45mm/46 21-K, 1-0.3in, 12 men	27.3.1943	BS	Mobilised 2.3.1943, comm as service craft. Conv 27.3.1943 to minesweeping boat. Mined 13.2.1943 off Gelendzik
KATShch-173			PILAMIDA	55t; 19.3 x 5.0 x 1.8m; 65hp = 7kts; 1-45mm/46 21-K, 1-0.3in, 12 men	25.6.1943	BS	Built 1936. Mobilised 29.3.1943. Sank 24.9.1943 at Taman, raised and recomm. Sunk 8.11.1943 by artillery fire at Eltigen
KATShch-174			PARTIZAN	32t; 15.8 x 4.8 x 1.7m; 35hp = 7kts	31.5.1943	Az	Built 1936. Mobilised 19.3.1943. Sunk 27.4.1943 by aircraft at Achuveska Spit
KATShch-176			SEJNER № 4	•	31.5.1943	Az	Mobilised 19.3.1943. Sunk 9.11.1943 by artillery fire off Kerch
KATShch-177			SEJNER № 5 MK-5	•	31.5.1943	Az	Built 1936. Mobilised 19.3.1943. Stranded 8.1.1944 at gale off Chushka Spit
KATShch-178			SEJNER № 7 MK-7	•	31.5.1943	Az	Mobilised 19.3.1943.. Sunk 25.9.1943 by artillery fire off Galubickaia
KATShch-179		KT-179	NEPTUN	•	25.6.1943	BS	Mobilised 26.4.1943. Conv 21.6.1944 to tug for magnetic sweep. Conv 2.5.1945 to service craft
KATShch-180		EMTShch-180	POLIUS	•	25.6.1943	BS	Mobilised 26.4.1943. Conv 21.6.1944 to magnetic minesweeper. Decomm 4.2.1945 in order to return to civilian service, but recomm 2.7.1945 and conv to service craft
KATShch-183			SEJNER № 6	•	25.6.1943	Az	Mobilised 25.6.1943. Sunk 24.9.1943 by artillery fire off Golubitskaia
KATShch-184			MARAT	•	25.6.1943	Az	Mobilised 25.6.1943. Deleted 31.5.1944
KATShch-190		KT-825	TAGANROG	•	2.10.1943	Az	Captured 2.10.1943 by Soviets at Taganrog, conv to minesweeping boat. Mined 2.11.1943, raised, decomm 6.1.1944 for repairs, recomm 21.6.1944
KATShch-211		KT-211	SEJENER № 6	•	Jan 1944	BS	Mobilised 11.1.1944, comm as service craft. Conv 26.4.1944 to minesweeping boat
KATShch-534			NAKHIMOV	•	30.4.1942	BS	Mobilised 10.9.1941, comm as service craft. Sunk 14.11.1941 by aircraft off Cape Ahilleon, Gelendzhik, raised and recomm. Conv 30.4.1942 to minesweeping boat. Decomm 31.7.1942 for repairs, recomm 21.6.1944. Survived the war
KATShch-538			KODOR	•	30.4.1942	BS	Mobilised 10.9.1941, comm as service craft. Sunk 6.11.1941 by aircraft off Yalta, raised and recomm. Conv 30.4.1942 to minesweeping boat. Decomm 2.3.1943 for repairs, recomm 21.6.1944. Survived the war
KATShch-539		KEMTShch-539	PIONIER	90t	30.4.1942	BS	Mobilised 10.9.1941, service craft. Conv 30.4.1942 to minesweeping boat. Reverted 1.10.1942 to service craft, conv 21.6.1944 to magnetic minesweeping boat. Survived the war
KATShch-540		EMTShch-540	KRASNYJ VODNIK	74.4t; 14.3 x 4.7 x 2.6m; 50hp = 8kts; 656nm at 6kts; 1-0.3in; 13 men	May 1942	BS	Mobilised 30.4.1942. Conv 30.4.1944 to magnetic sweep charger, rated 21.6.1944 as magnetic minesweeper. Survived the war
KATShch-541			SHMIDT	25.6t	May 1942	BS	Mobilised 30.4.1942. Sunk 16.5.1942 by aircraft `off Chushka Spit
KATShch-542			CHERNOMORETS	51.6t	10.9.1941	BS	Mobilised 10.9.1941, comm as service craft. Conv 30.4.1942 to minesweeping boat. Sunk 12.5.1942 by aircraft in Kerch Strait
KATShch-543			VOLGO-DON	50t	May 1942	BS	Mobilised 30.4.1942. Decomm 2.3.1943 for repairs, recomm 21.6.1944. Survived the war
KATShch-544		KT-544	SEJNER № 12	35t	May 1942	BS	Mobilised 30.4.1942, conv to minesweeping boat. Decomm 31.12.1945, laid up
KATShch-552		KT-552	SEJNER № 11	60.1t; 17.5 x 5 x 2.8m; 65hp = 7kts; 380nm at 5.5kts; 1-0.5in, 1 KAT sweep; 13 men	15.5.1942	BS	Built 1939. Mobilised 2.5.1942. Survived the war
KATShch-571			MARS	36t; 14 x 4.0 x 1.4m; 50hp = 7kts	6.6.1942	Az	Mobilised 10.4.1942. Sunk 18.8.1942 by artillery fire in Temryuk Bay

20.0 Minesweeping boats

KATShch-572	KT-572	AKO-2	37.5t; 8.0 x 3.9 x 1.4m; 65hp = 7kts; 550nm at 5 kts; 1-0.3in, sweeps; 12 men	6.6.1942	Az	Built 1939. Mobilised 10.4.1942. Decomm 30.8.1942 for repairs, recomm 14.11.1942
KATShch-573		KHASANOVETS	*	6.6.1942	Az	Mobilised 10.4.1942. Sunk 22.8.1942 by aircraft at Temryuk
KATShch-574		SHTORM	28-36t	6.6.1942	Az	Mobilised 10.4.1942. Sunk 15.8.1942 by German motor minesweepers *R-36*, *R-37* and *R-166* in Temryuk Bay
KATShch-575	KEMTShch-575	ADLER	55t; 19.3 x 5.0 x 1.9m; 65hp = 7kts; 1-45mm/46 21-K, 5-0.3in (1x4, 1x1) MGs; 11 men	4.6.1942	Az	Built 1939. Mobilised 21.5.1942. Decomm 30.8.1942 for repairs, recomm 6.11.1942. Conv 21.6.1944 to magnetic minesweeping boat. Survived the war
KATShch-576	KEMTShch-576	TAJFUN	60t	22.1.1942	Az BS	Mobilised 30.10.1941, trfd to the Black Sea Fleet 7.9.1942. Conv 21.6.1944 to magnetic minesweeping boat. Survived the war
KATShch-577		TSIKLON	60t; 17.0 x 5.0 x 1.2m; 55hp = 7kts;	4.6.1942	Az	Built 1937. Mobilised 21.5.1942. Sunk 20.8.1942 by aircraft off Cape Kamenny
KATShch-578		SHKVAL	•	22.1.1942	Az	Mobilised 30.10.1941. Sunk 20.8.1942 by German motor minesweepers *R-36*, *R-37* and *R-166* off Cape Kamenny
KATShch-579		URAGAN	•	4.6.1942	Az	Mobilised 21.5.1942. Mined 24.8.1942 in Temryuk Bay
KATShch-580	KT-580	POTI	60t; 19.3 x 5.0 x 1.8m; 65hp = 7kts; 1400nm at 5kts; 1-45mm/46 21-K, 1 KAT sweep; 12 men	Nov 1941	Az	Built 1940. Mobilised 30.10.1941. Mined 19.7.1944 in the Kerch Strait
KATShch-581		TUAPSE	63t	4.6.1942	Az	Mobilised 22.6.1941, conv 4.6.1942 to minesweeping boat. Sunk 14.5.1942 by artillery fire at Kerch
KATShch-584		CHAJKA	36t	22.1.1942	Az	Mobilised 30.11.1941. Decomm 30.8.1942 for repairs, recomm 15.1.1943. Sunk 7.3.1943 by artillery fire at Myshanko
KATShch-585	KT-585	TAJFUN № 2	35t; 19.3 x 5.0 x 1.9m; 35hp = 1-45mm/46 21-K, 1-0.3in MG; 18 men	4.6.1942	Az	Mobilised 21.5.1942. Decomm 30.8.1942 for repairs, recomm 6.11.1942. Sunk 26.8.1942 by aircraft off Temryuk. Raised and recomm 13.11.1943. Survived the war
KATShch-586		VENERA	•	22.1.1942	Az	Mobilised 30.11.1941. Sunk 22.8.1942 at Temryuk. Raised and recomm 21.6.1944. Survived the war
KATShch-587		AKULA	•	Dec 1941	BS	Mobilised 30.11.1941. Stranded 26.12.1941 in Kerch Strait. Raised and recomm 21.6.1944. Survived the war
KATShch-605		NOVOROSSIJSK	60t; 19.2 x 5.0 x 1.8m; 65hp = 7kts; 1400nm at 5kts; 1-45mm/46 21-K, 1 KAT sweep; 12 men	24.3.1942	BS	Built 1940. Mobilised 7.3.1942. Mined 1.4.1943 off Gelendzhik
KATShch-606	KT-606	SKUMBRIIA	32t; 18.7 x 4.9 x 1.7m; 35hp = 7kts; 700nm at 6kts; 1-0.3in MG, 1 KAT sweep; 9 men	24.3.1942	BS	Mobilised 22.6.1941, conv 7.3.1942 to minesweeping boat. Survived the war
KATShch-607	EMTShch-607	SPARTAK	37.1t; 18.7 x 4.9 x 1.7m; 35hp = 7kts; 700nm at 6kts; 1-0.3in MG; 8 men	24.3.1942	BS	Built 1939. Mobilised 7.3.1942. Conv 30.4.1944 to magnetic minesweeper. Survived the war
KATShch-608		CHEKHON'	•	24.3.1942	BS	Mobilised 7.3.1942. Mined 14.4.1942 in the Kerch Strait
KATShch-609		SHAMAIA		24.3.1942	BS	Mobilised 7.3.1942. Sunk 11.5.1942 by aircraft in the Kerch Strait
KATShch-610	KT-610	SUDAK	32t; 18.7 x 4.9 x 1.7m; 35hp; 500nm; 1-0.3in MG, 1 KAT sweep; 9 men	24.3.1942	BS	Built 1937. Mobilised 7.3.1942. Survived the war
KATShch-611	KT-611	AZOV	60t; 19.3 x 5.0 x 1.8m; 65hp = 7kts; 1400nm at 5kts; 1-45mm/46 21-K, 1 KAT sweep; 12 men	24.3.1942	BS	Built 1940. Mobilised 7.3.1942. Survived the war

KATSchch № No on Comm	No 26.5.1942	No 21.6.1944	Name	Details	Comm	Fleet	Remarks
KT-546			RO-11	•	17.9.1944	BS	Mobilised 12.5.1944. Conv 31.10.1945 to service craft
KT-547			RO-13	•	17.9.1944	BS	Mobilised 12.5.1944. Conv 31.10.1945 to service craft
		KT-809	PAPANIN	83t; 19.7 x 5.0 x 2.0m; 65hp = 6/5kts; 200nm; 1-0.5in MG, 1 KAT sweep; 10 men	21.6.1944	BS	Mobilised 30.10.1941, conv to submarine hunter. Conv 6.5.1942 to minesweeping boat. Survived the war
№ 38			PRIBOJ	•	Oct 1941	Az	Mobilised 19.7.1941, conv 24.10.1941 to minesweeping boat. Sunk 9.11.1941 by aircraft off Yalta
№ 39	KATShch-582[1]		AZOV	*	Oct 1941	Az	Mobilised 24.10.1941. Sunk 4.2.1942 by aircraft at Kerch Strait. Had number KATShch-582 allocated after loss
№ 40	KATShch-583[1]		TEMRIUK	*	Oct 1941	Az	Mobilised 24.10.1941. Stranded 6.8.1942 at Chushka Spit and destroyed by artillery
№ 121	KATShch-561[1]		AKADEMIK SHMIDT	94t	July 1941	BS	Mobilised 27.7.1941, decomm 15.7.1942 for repairs, recomm 2.2.1943, conv 26.4.1943 to magnetic sweep charger. Conv 22.3.1944 to charging station SBR-3. Survived the war
№ 123	KTShch-563	KT-563	KRYM	75t; 16.2 x 5.1 x 1.2m; 50hp = 4kts; 600nm at 3kts; 3-0.3in	July 1941	BS	Built 1932. Mobilised 27.7.1941, decomm 1.12.1943 for repairs. Recomm 22.4.1944
№ 125 № 126[2]	KTShch-566		KIROV	44t	July 1941	BS	Mobilised 27.7.1941. Sunk 30.6.1942 by artillery at Sevastopol
№ 125	KATShch-565		FRUNZE	35t	Sept 1941	BS	Mobilised 4.9.1941. Sunk 30.6.1942 by artillery at Sevastopol

Exceptions noted in the main table.

No	Year	Date
1	1943	2.6.1943

No on Comm	No 26.5.1943	No 13.8.1943	Name	Details	Comm	Fleet	Remarks
EMTShch-17 ex-BTP-11 (3.10.1942)	EMTShch № 17[5]	EMTShch-17[7]	ARALETS	68t; 17.6 x 6.4 x 1.0m; 35hp = 7kts; 2500nm at kts; 16 men	3.10.1942	Cs Vo BS	Built 1939. Mobilised 20.8.1942 conv to tug for minesweeping raft. Trfd 2.8.1943 to the Volga Flotilla. Trfd 30.5.1944 to the Black Sea Fleet
EMTShch-19			TEMIR	17.5 x 5.0 x 1.6m; 65hp; 2-0.5in MGs	15.1.1943	Cs	Built 1940. Mobilised 20.8.1942, conv to AA defence boat PVO-11. Conv 15.1.1943 to magnetic minesweeper EMTShch-19. Decomm 15.2.1943 to civilian service, name reverted. Mobilised 22.5.1943, conv 26.5.1943 to AA defence boat PVO-102. Conv 25.10.1943 to service craft. Sank 6.12.1943 in a gale off Taman, later raised and repaired
EMTShch-21 ex-BTP-21 (3.10.1942)			SPIRIN	76t; 17.0 x 6.3 x 1.6m; 35hp = 6kts; 1600nm; 16 men	3.10.1942	Cs	Built 1939. Mobilised 20.8.1942, conv to tug for minesweeping raft. Sunk 11.5.1943 by mines in the Verkhne-Solodvikovski shoals
EMTShch-22	EMTShch-312	EMTShch-22	AGITATOR	77t; 18.7 x 6.3 x 1.5m; 35hp = 6kts; 1600nm at kts; 16 men	3.10.1942	Cs	Mobilised 20.8.1942, conv to charging station of magnetic sweep. Conv 13.6.1944 to service craft
EMTShch-18 ex-BTP-12 (3.10.1942)	EMTShch-311	EMTShch-18	IRANETS	87t; 18.5 x 6.5 x 2.4m; 35hp = 7kts, 1400nm at 5kts; 1 MG; 16 men	3.10.1942	Cs	Built 1940. Mobilised 20.8.1942, conv to AA defence boat PVO-12. Conv 3.9.1942 to tug for minesweeping raft BTP-12, renumbered EMTShch-18 on 3.10.1942, renumbered EMTShch-311 on 26.5.1943. Conv 13.8.1943 to magnetic minesweeper, number reverted. Conv 12.6.1944 to service craft

20.0 Minesweeping boats

EMTShch-24		EMTShch-91	KOMAROVETS	87t; 18.5 x 6.5 x 2.4m; 35hp = 7kts, 1400nm at 5kts; 1 MG; 16 men	15.1.1943	Cs	Built 1940. Mobilised 20.8.1942, conv to AA defence boat PVO-21, renumbered PVO-31 on 3.10.1942. Conv 15.1.1943 to magnetic minesweeper EMTShch-24. Decomm 15.2.1943 to civilian service, name reverted. Mobilised 19.6.1943 conv 21.6.1943 to service craft. Conv 15.8.1943 to magnetic minesweeper EMTShch-91. Conv 14.11.1943 to service craft. Sank 10.1.1944 in a gale off Cape Tarhan
EMTShch-27			SAMOSDELETS	87t; 18.5 x 6.5 x 2.4m; 35hp = 7kts, 1400nm at 5kts; 1 MG; 16 men	15.1.1943	Cs	Built 1940. Mobilised 20.8.1942, conv to AA defence boat PVO-22, renumbered PVO-32 on 3.10.1942. Conv 15.1.1943 to magnetic minesweeper EMTShch-27, conv 15.2.1943 to service craft. Sank 21.11.1943 in a gale off Tuzla spit
EMTShch-26 ex-BTP-32 (3.10.1942)			SURKOVETS	87t; 18.5 x 6.5 x 2.4m; 35hp = 7kts, 1400nm at 5kts; 1 MG; 16 men	3.10.1942	Cs	Built 1939. Mobilised 20.8.1942, conv to AA defence boat PVO-32. Conv 3.9.1942 to tug for minesweeping raft BTP-32, conv 3.10.1942 to magnetic minesweeper EMTShch-26. Mined 10.5.1943 off Zaml'iany
EMTShch-30	BTP-315[1]	EMTShch-78	BEKETOVETS	87t; 18.5 x 6.5 x 2.4m; 35hp = 7kts, 1400nm at 5kts; 1 MG; 16 men	15.1.1943	Cs	Built 1940. Mobilised 20.8.1942, conv to AA defence boat PVO-52. Conv 15.1.1943 to magnetic minesweeper EMTShch-30, decomm 5.2.1943 to civilian service, name reverted. Mobilised 31.5.1943, conv 2.6.1943 to tug for minesweeping raft BTP-315. Renumbered EMTShch-78 on 13.8.1943. Conv 13.11.1943 to service craft
EMTShch-31	BTP-317	EMTShch-80	MAIACHNYJ	87t; 18.5 x 6.5 x 2.4m; 35hp = 7kts, 1400nm at 5kts; 1 MG; 16 men	15.1.1943	Cs	Built 1940. Mobilised 20.8.1942, conv to AA defence boat PVO-53. Conv 15.1.1943 to magnetic minesweeper EMTShch-31, decomm 5.2.1943 to civilian service, name reverted. Mobilised 22.5.1943, conv 26.5.1943 to tug for minesweeping raft BTP-317. Renumbered EMTShch-80 on 13.8.1943. Conv 13.11.1943 to service craft
EMTShch-33	BTP-318[2]	EMTShch-81	IL'INETS	87t; 18.5 x 6.5 x 2.4m; 35hp = 7kts, 1400nm at 5kts; 1 MG; 16 men	15.1.1943	Cs	Built 1940. Mobilised 20.8.1942, conv to AA defence boat PVO-54. Conv 15.1.1943 to magnetic minesweeper EMTShch-33, decomm 5.2.1943 to civilian service, name reverted. Mobilised 8.6.1943, conv 9.6.1943 to tug for minesweeping raft BTP-318. Renumbered EMTShch-81 on 13.8.1943. Conv 13.11.1943 to service craft
EMTShch-34	BTP-316[1]	EMTShch-79	BAKHTEMIROVETS	87t; 18.5 x 6.5 x 2.4m; 35hp = 7kts, 1400nm at 5kts; 1 MG; 16 men	15.1.1943	Cs	Built 1940. Mobilised 20.8.1942, conv to AA defence boat PVO-56. Conv 15.1.1943 to magnetic minesweeper EMTShch-34, decomm 5.2.1943 to civilian service, name reverted. Mobilised 31.5.1943, conv 2.6.1943 to tug for minesweeping raft BTP-316. Renumbered EMTShch-79 on 13.8.1943. Conv 13.11.1943 to service craft
EMTShch-25 ex-BTP-31 (3.10.1942)	EMTShch-313	EMTShch-25	GORKI	75t; 17.5 x 6.1 x 1.8m; 35hp = 6kts; 1850nm; 16 men	3.10.1942	Cs	Built 1940. Mobilised 20.8.1942, conv to tug for minesweeping raft. Conv 13.8.1943 to charging station for magnetic sweep. Conv 23.1.1945 to service craft

No on Comm	No 26.5.1943	No 13.8.1943	Name	Details	Comm	Fleet	Remarks
EMTShch-28			EVDOKIIA VINOGRADOVA	68t; 18.2 x 6.4 x 2.3m; 35hp = 7kts, 2000nm at 5.5kts; 2-0.5in DShK MGs, 1 MKhT sweep, 10 men	15.1.1943	Cs	Built 1940. Mobilised 20.8.1942, conv to AA defence boat *PVO-34*. Conv 15.1.1943 to magnetic minesweeper *EMTShch-28*. Conv 15.2.1943 to service craft
EMTShch-90			KHMELEVETS	62t; 18.0 x 6.2 x 2.0m; 35hp = 6.5kts; 2000nm at 6kts; 16 men	15.8.1943	Cs	Mobilised 22.6.1943, conv to magnetic minesweeper. Conv 29.10.1943 to service craft
EMTShch-92			ALGARINETS	62t; 18.0 x 6.2 x 2.0m; 35hp = 6.5kts; 2000nm at 6kts; 16 men	15.8.1943	Cs	Mobilised 9.7.1943, conv to magnetic minesweeper. Conv 29.10.1943 to service craft
EMTShch-93			MYS	62t; 18.0 x 6.2 x 2.0m; 35hp = 6.5kts; 2000nm at 6kts; 16 men	9.7.1943	Cs	Mobilised 1.6.1943, conv to magnetic minesweeper. Conv 19.7.1943 to service craft *A-79*
MKhTShch-24	EMTShch-11[3] EMTShch-51[4]	EMTShch-11[3]	SHTIL'	•	12.6.1943	Cs	Mobilised 10.6.1943, conv to magnetic minesweeper. Conv 23.3.1944 to service craft
MKhTShch-25	EMTShch-52[4]		KRIVOBUZANETS	•	2.8.1943	Cs	Mobilised 24.6.1943, conv to magnetic minesweeper. Conv 15.1.1945 to service craft
MKhTShch-26	EMTShch-53[4]		BATAJSK	•	2.8.1943	Cs	Mobilised 19.6.1943, conv to magnetic minesweeper. Conv 15.1.1945 to service craft
MKhTShch-221		EMTShch-70	DENGIZOVETS	62t; 18.0 x 6.2 x 2.0m; 35hp = 6.5kts; 2000nm at 6kts; 16 men	26.5.1943	Cs	Mobilised 21.5.1943, conv to magnetic minesweeper. Conv 29.10.1943 to service craft
MKhTShch-222		EMTShch-71	IUSHAR	62t; 18.0 x 6.2 x 2.0m; 35hp = 6.5kts; 2000nm at 6kts; 16 men	14.6.1943	Cs	Mobilised 13.6.1943, conv to magnetic minesweeper. Conv 29.10.1943 to service craft
MKhTShch-223		EMTShch-72	KOLGUEV	62t; 18.0 x 6.2 x 2.0m; 35hp = 6.5kts; 2000nm at 6kts; 16 men	23.6.1943	Cs	Mobilised 22.6.1943, conv to magnetic minesweeper. Conv 29.10.1943 to service craft
MKhTShch-224		EMTShch-73	CHASOVOJ	62t; 18.0 x 6.2 x 2.0m; 35hp = 6.5kts; 2000nm at 6kts; 16 men	13.6.1943	Cs	Mobilised 12.6.1943, conv to magnetic minesweeper. Conv 29.10.1943 to service craft
MKhTShch-225		EMTShch-74	TAJMYR	62t; 18.0 x 6.2 x 2.0m; 35hp = 6.5kts; 2000nm at 6kts; 16 men	12.6.1943	Cs	Mobilised 10.6.1943, conv to magnetic minesweeper. Conv 29.10.1943 to service craft
MKhTShch-226		EMTShch-75	IAMAL	62t; 18.0 x 6.2 x 2.0m; 35hp = 6.5kts; 2000nm at 6kts; 16 men	26.6.1943	Cs	Mobilised 25.6.1943, conv to magnetic minesweeper. Conv 29.10.1943 to service craft
MKhTShch-227		EMTShch-76	STALINGRAD	65hp	11.7.1943	Cs	Mobilised 10.7.1943, conv to magnetic minesweeper. Conv 29.10.1943 to service craft

Exceptions noted in the main table.

No	Year	Date
1	1943	2.6.1943
2		9.6.1943
3	1943	21.6.1943
4		30.6.1943
5		14.7.1943
6		21.9.1943
7	1944	21.6.1944

Kater-tral'shchik № 84 (Ki)t at early 1940s
Przemysław Budzbon Collection

Pacific

KATSchch № No on Comm	No 13.9.1944	No 10.8.1945	Name	Details	Comm	Fleet	Remarks
№ 61		KT-61	IUZHNYJ	115t; 22.1 x 4.6 x 2.4m; 150hp = 9.5kts; 1560nm at 8kts; 2-0.3in MGs, 1 OTSh sweep, 1 KAT sweep; 17 men	7.10.1941 10.8.1945	P	Built 1937. Mobilised 22.9.1941. Decomm 5.7.1943 to civilian service, mobilised 1945. Survived the war
№ 62			BYSTRYJ		7.10.1941	P	Built 1937. Mobilised 22.9.1941. Decomm 5.7.1943 to civilian service
№ 63		KT-63	BRAVYJ		7.10.1941 10.8.1945	P	Built 1937. Mobilised 25.9.1941. Decomm 5.7.1943 to civilian service, mobilised 1945
№ 64	KT-64[4]		RESHITEL'NYJ		Oct 1941	P	Built 1937. Mobilised 25.9.1941. Conv 5.10.1945 to training boat
№ 71	KT-71		KHARIUZOV	130t; 23.8 x 5.4 x 2.4m; 150hp = 8.5kts; 2200nm at 6kts; 1-45mm/46 21-K, 5-0.3in (1x4, 1x1) MGs, 1 OTSh sweep, 1 KAT sweep; 17 men	7.10.1941	P	Built 1936. Mobilised 25.9.1941. Survived the war
№ 72		KT-72	ZUBASTYJ		7.10.1941 10.8.1945	P	Built 1936. Mobilised 25.9.1941. Decomm 5.7.1943 to civilian service, mobilised 1945. Survived the war
№ 73	KT-73		SMELYJ		7.10.1941	P	Built 1936. Mobilised 25.9.1941. Survived the war
№ 74	KT-74		OMCHON		7.10.1941 10.8.1945	P	Built 1936. Mobilised 27.9.1941. Decomm 5.7.1943 to civilian service, mobilised 1945. Survived the war
№ 81	KT-81		LAKHTAK		7.10.1941	P	Built 1936 Mobilised 9.7.1941. Survived the war
№ 82	KT-82		MORZH		7.10.1941	P	Built 1936. Mobilised 9.7.1941. Survived the war
№ 83			KASHALOT		7.10.1941	P	Built 1936. Mobilised 2.9.1941. Decomm 5.7.1943 to civilian service
№ 84		KT-84	KIT		7.10.1941 10.8.1945	P	Built 1936. Mobilised 22.9.1941. Decomm 5.7.1943 to civilian service, mobilised 1945. Survived the war
№ 85		KT-85	MCHS-10	68.3t; 19.3 x 5.1 x 2.3m; 65hp, 8kts; 1350nm at 6kts; 1-0.31in MG, 1 KAT sweep; 17 men	7.10.1941 10.8.1945	P	Built 1941. Mobilised 20.8.1941. Decomm 5.7.1943 to civilian service, mobilised 1945. Survived the war
№ 91*	T-91		SEJNER № 11	263t; 28.8 x 6.3 x 3.1m; 270hp = 9kts; 1940nm at 6kts; 1-45mm/46 21-K, 3-0.31in MGs, 1 MTSh sweep, 1 MZT sweep, 1 MKhT sweep; 29 men	Sept 1941	P	Built 1936. Mobilised 18.8.1941.* Rated 8.6.1943 as minesweeper TShch № 91. Survived the war
№ 92*	T-92		SEJNER № 12		Sept 1941	P	Built 1936. Mobilised 18.8.1941.* Rated 8.6.1943 as minesweeper TShch № 92. Survived the war
№ 93*	T-93		SEJNER № 13		Sept 1941	P	Built 1936. Mobilised 18.8.1941.* Rated 8.6.1943 as minesweeper TShch № 93. Survived the war
№ 94*	T-94		SEJNER № 14		Sept 1941	P	Built 1936. Mobilised 18.8.1941.* Rated 8.6.1943 as minesweeper TShch № 94. Survived the war
№ 95		KT-86	MCHS-11	68.3t; 19.3 x 5.1 x 2.3m; 65hp, 8kts; 1350nm at 6kts; 1-0.31in MG, 1 KAT sweep; 17 men	7.10.1941 10.8.1945	P	Built 1941. Mobilised 1.9.1941. Decomm 5.7.1943 to civilian service, mobilised 1945. Survived the war
№ 101		KT-65	RAZVEDCHIK № 12	115t; 22.1 x 4.6 x 2.4m; 150hp = 9.5kts; 1560nm at 8kts; 2-0.3in MGs, 1 OTSh sweep, 1 KAT sweep; 17 men	7.10.1941 10.8.1945	P	Built 1937. Mobilised 2.9.1941. Decomm 5.7.1943 to civilian service, mobilised 1945. Survived the war
№ 121		KT-121	PRIMORETS	124.7t; 25.7 x 5.6 x 2.5m; 150hp = 9.2kts; 1700nm; 1-0.3in MG, 20 mines, 1 OTSh sweep, 1 MKhT sweep; 17 men	7.10.1941	P	Built 1936. Mobilised 9.7.1941. Survived the war
№ 122		KT-122	DEL'FIN		7.10.1941	P	Built 1936. Mobilised 27.7.1941. Survived the war

KATSchch № No on Comm	No 13.9.1944	No 10.8.1945	Name	Details	Comm	Fleet	Remarks
№ 151		KT-151	SATURN	62t; 21.7 x 4.3 x 2.8m; 150hp = 9kts; 700nm at 8kts; 2-0.3in MGs, 4 mines, 1 KAT sweep; 17 men	7.10.1941	P	Built 1936. Mobilised 11.8.1942. Survived the war
№ 152		KT-152	NEPTUN		7.10.1941	P	Built 1936. Mobilised 2.8.1942. Lost 19.8.1945 off Shumshu
№ 153		KT-153	IUPITER		7.10.1941	P	Built 1936. Mobilised 11.8.1942. Survived the war
№ 155	T-155[1]		AVACHA	183t; 28.5 x 6.2 x 3.0m; 150hp = 11.5/10kts; 1-0.3in MGs, 10-12 mines; 1 KAT sweep, 1 OTSh sweep; 20 men	7.10.1941	P	Built 1936. Mobilised 10.9.1941. Rated 8.6.1943 as minesweeper *TShch № 155*. Survived the war
№ 156	T-156[1]		VILIUJ		7.10.1941	P	Built 1936. Mobilised 10.9.1941. Rated 8.6.1943 as minesweeper *TShch № 156*. Survived the war
KT-75			MS-67	68.3t; 19.3 x 5.1 x 2.3m; 65hp, 8kts; 1350nm at 6kts; 1-0.31in MG, 1 KAT sweep; 17 men	10.8.1945	P	Built 1941. Mobilised 1945. Survived the war
KT-78			MS-31				
KT-165			MS-68				
KT-615			MS-11				
KT-616			MS-12				
KT-617			MS-13				
KT-620			MS-29				
KT-634			MS-15				
KT-635			MS-14				
KT-636			MS-16				
KT-638			MS-27				
KT-639			MS-25				
KT-640			MS-30				
KT-641			MS-17				
KT-642			MS-18				

1. Number changed 28.9.1944

20.3.2.2.3. DRIFTERS

KATShch № No on Comm	No 13.9.1944	Name	Details	Comm	Fleet	Remarks
EMTShch-20		DRIFTER № 80	17.5 x 5.0 x 1.6m; 65hp; 2-0.5in MGs	15.1.1943	Cs	Built 1940. Mobilised 20.8.1942, conv to AA defence boat *PVO-14*. Conv 15.1.1943 to magnetic minesweeper *EMTShch-20*. Conv 15.2.1943 to service craft
EMTShch-23		DRIFTER № 79		15.1.1943	Cs	Built 1940. Mobilised 20.8.1942, conv to AA defence boat *PVO-24*. Conv 15.1.1943 to magnetic minesweeper *EMTShch-23*. Conv 15.2.1943 to service craft. Sank 26.11.1943 in a gale off Krotkovo, raised and repaired. Survived the war
EMTShch-36		PUZANOK	•	21.9.1942	Cs	Mobilised 9.9.1942. Conv 9.3.1943 to service craft
EMTShch-37		KOMBAJNER	•	21.9.1942	Cs	Mobilised 10.9.1942, conv to magnetic minesweeper. Lost 1943
EMTShch-38 MKhTShch-21[1]						
EMTShch-48[2]		VOBLA	•	21.9.1942 25.5.1943	Cs	Mobilised 11.9.1942. Decomm 9.2.1943 to civilian service, name reverted. Mobilised 25.5.1943, conv 2.6.1943 to magnetic minesweeper. Conv 12.11.1943 to service craft
EMTShch-39		LENKORANETS	•	3.11.1942	Cs	Mobilised 26.9.1942. Conv 9.2.1943 to service craft

| № 154 | KT-154 | STAKHANOVETS | 131t; 23.8 x 5.3 x 2.7m; 150hp = 9kts; 1-0.3in MG, 1 KAT sweep, 1 OTSh sweep; 17 men | 7.10.1941 | P | Built 1936. Mobilised 10.9.1941. Survived the war |

Exceptions noted in the main table.

No	Year	Date
1	1943	4.6.1943
2		13.8.1943

20.3.2.2.4. Sail-motor schooners

Azov and Black Sea

Pt-No 1941	KATShch № No on Comm	No 21.6.1944	Name	Details	Comm	Fleet	Remarks
91	KATShch-150		KOMSOMOLETS	95t	Sept 1941	BS	Mobilised 4.9.1941. Stranded 28.11.1941 off Dzhubge
94	KATShch-151		BAJDUKOV	75t	Sept 1941	BS Az	Mobilised 4.9.1941. Trfd 8.2.1943 to Azov Flotilla. Sunk 2.11.1943 by artillery fire off Eltigen
95	KATShch-152	EMTShch-152	V. CHKALOV	60.1t; 19.3 x 5 x 2m; 5.5kts; 1000nm at 4.5kts; 2-0.3in; 12 men	Sept 1941	BS Az BS	Mobilised 4.9.1941. Decomm 8.8.1942 for repairs, recomm 2.2.1943. Trfd 8.2.1943 to the Azov Flotilla returned 30.4.1944. Mined 16.8.1944 at Sevastopol
93	KATShch-153		M. GOR'KIJ	87 t.	Sept 1941	BS	Mobilised 4.9.1941. Sunk 24.6.1942 by artillery fire and aircraft at Sevastopol
99	KATShch-157	EMTShch-157	KRYM MRS	90t; 19.9 x 5.3 x 2.5m; 50hp = 6kts; 600nm at 5kts; 12 men	Sept 1941	BS Az BS	Built 1939. Mobilised 4.9.1941. Trfd 8.2.1943 to the Azov Flotilla, returned 30.4.1944. Survived the war
90	KATShch-158		ZHDANOV	28t	Sept 1941	BS	Mobilised 4.9.1941. Sunk 20.6.1942 by aircraft at Sevastopol
92	KATShch-159	EMTShch-159	REVVOYENSOVET	71t	Sept 1941	BS Az	Mobilised 4.9.1941. Decomm 8.8.1942 for repairs, recomm 2.2.1943. Trfd 8.2.1943 to the Azov Flotilla, returned 30.4.1944, conv to charging station for magnetic sweeps
	KATShch-161	EMTShch-161	STALIN	36t	6.5.1942	BS Az BS	Mobilised 31.3.1942, service craft. Conv 6.5.1942 to minesweeping boat. Trfd 8.2.1943 to the Azov Flotilla, returned 30.4.1944, conv to tug for magnetic sweeps, conv 21.6.1944 to magnetic minesweeper
	KATShch-163	B-163	S. KIROV	49t; 16.5 x 4.7 x 1.6m; 65hp = 7kts; 890nm at 5kts; 4-0.3in (1x4) MGs; 9 men	7.12.1941	BS	Built 1935. Mobilised 22.6.1941, service craft. Conv 7.12.1941 to minesweeping boat. Conv 30.4.1944 to conv to tug for magnetic sweep
	KATShch-168[4]		PMSH № 121	•	29.3.1943	BS	Mobilised 13.12.1942, service craft. Conv 9.3.1943 to minesweeping boat, renumbered *KATShch-168* from 30.4.1943. Deleted 5.4.1944
	KATShch-169	KT-169	CHOROKH (SP-233)	64t; 16.9 x 4.7 x 1.8m; 35hp, 6.5kts; 400nm at 5.5kts; 1-0.3in MG, 1 MKhT sweep; 10 men	29.3.1943	BS	Mobilised 13.12.1942, service craft. Conv 29.3.1943 to minesweeping boat. Survived the war
	KATShch-172	KT-172	VEST	•	March 1943	BS	Mobilised 15.3.1943. Survived the war
	KATShch-175	KT-175	MS № 21	74.8t; 30.8 x 5.9 x 2.2m; 90hp = 6kts	March 1943	Az	Mobilised 19.3.1943. Survived the war

KATShch-536		A. SERVOV	•	30.4.1942	BS	Mobilised 10.9.1941, service craft. Sunk 27.10.1941 by aircraft at Kerch. Raised, recomm 30.4.1942 as minesweeping boat. Survived the war
KATShch-537		PUSHKIN	80t	Sept 1941	BS	Mobilised 10.9.1941, service craft. Conv 30.4.1942 to minesweeping boat. Mined 6.5.1942 in Kerch Strait. Raised and recomm 21.6.1944. Survived the war
KATShch-545	KT-545	BRIGADIR	46t; 14 x 4.0 x 2.0m; 35hp = 7.5kts; 690nm at 6kts; 13 men	May 1942	BS	Built 1933. Mobilised 30.4.1942, conv to minesweeping boat. Conv 31.12.1945 to service craft
KATShch-546		ISKRA	•	May 1942	BS	Mobilised 30.4.1942. Deleted 31.7.1942, presumably lost
KATShch-549	EMTShch-549	ISKURIIA	130t; 22.2 x 5.9 x 2.5m; 48hp = 6kts; 800nm at 4kts; 17 men	15.5.1942	BS	Built 1933. Mobilised 2.5.1942. Conv 30.4.1944 to magnetic minesweeper. Survived the war
KATShch-550		ZIUJD-VEST	•	15.5.1942	BS	Mobilised 2.5.1942. Conv 9.6.1943 to service craft. Deleted 20.6.1943
KATShch-551		CHAJ-GRUZIIA	•	15.5.1942	BS	Mobilised 2.5.1942. Sunk 16.7.1942 by aircraft at Poti
KATShch-560		VEGA	110t	26.5.1942	BS	Mobilised 4.9.1941, service craft. Conv 26.5.1942 to minesweeping boat. Damaged 16.7.1942 by aircraft at Poti, constructive total loss
KATShch-601[3]		KRAPIVINTSKIJ	80t	Nov 1941	BS	Mobilised 6.10.1941, conv to tug for magnetic sweep. Conv 7.3.1942 to minesweeping boat numbered KATShch-601. Sank 7.3.1943 in a gale at Myshako
KATShch-602[3]		KIROV	68t	Sept 1941	BS	Mobilised 28.8.1941. Sunk 16.10.1941 by aircraft off Kerch, raised and allegedly recomm. Deleted 22.11.1942. Presumably lost, or the number was allocated to the boat after the loss
KATShch-603		DIMITROV	•	24.3.1942	BS	Mobilised 7.3.1942. Reverted 22.11.1942 to schooner, renumbered ChFMSh-18 on 30.10.1942. Survived the war
KEMTShch-366		DNEPR	•	4.8.1944	BS	Mobilised 26.6.1944. Conv 4.8.1945 to service craft
KEMTShch-367		PROGRESS				
KEMTShch-368		SHMIDT				
KEMTShch-369		20 LET KOMSOMOLA				
KEMTShch-370		3-J VYRISHAL'NYJ				
№ 122 KATShch-562[2]	KT-562	KRASNAIA ARMIIA	115t; 16.9 x 5.2 x 2.5m; 50hp = 6kts; 1400nm at 4kts; 1-45mm; 10 men	Aug 1941	BS	Built 1932. Mobilised 27.7.1941. Survived the war
№ 124		16-IA GODOVSHCHINA OKTIABRIA	•	Aug 1942	BS	Mobilised 27.7.1941. Conv 4.9.1941 to service craft
№ 124 KATShch-564[2]	KEMTShch-564	PIONER	90t	Sept 1941	BS	Mobilised 4.9.1941 Conv 21.6.1944 to magnetic minesweeper. Survived the war
№ 126 № 98[1]		17-J PARTS"EZD	•	Aug 1941	BS	Mobilised 27.7.1941. Conv 10.9.1941 to surveying service craf

Exceptions noted in the main table.

No	Year	Date
1	1941	4.9.1941
2	1942	26.5.1942
3	1943	7.3.1943
4		30.4.1943

20.3.2.3. Tugs

MSV (gazokhod) type
Motor tugs

Displacement: 28t
Dimensions: 21.7 x 4.4 x 0.56m
Machinery: 2-shaft, ChTZ-S-60 diesel engines, 2 gas generators MSV-84; 110hp = 8–9kts. Wood fuel 27m³
Armament: 1- or 2-0.5in (1x1 or 1x2) MG, 1 KAT sweep
Complement: 9

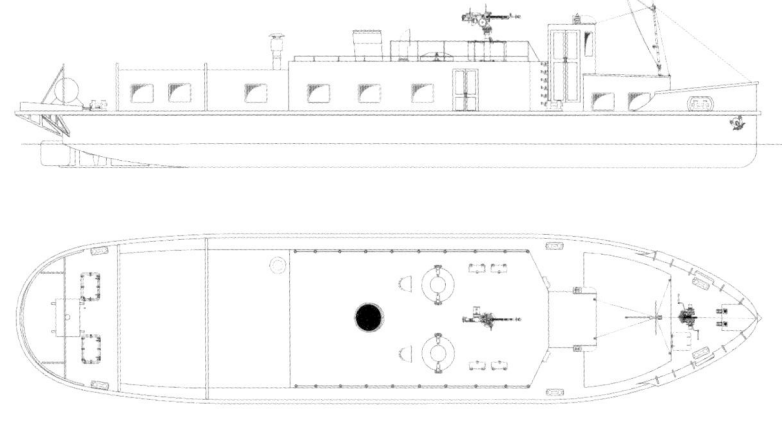

MSV (gazokhod) type before conversion.
Drawing by Jerzy Lewandowski

KATShch № No on Comm	No 9.7.1943	Name Gazokhod №	Built	Comm	Fleet	Remarks
Builder: MSV, Moskva						
№ 06*		PRIPIAT'	1930s	29.7.1941	Pn	Mobilised July 1941, conv to minesweeper. Lost summer 1941
№ 07*		PROGRESS	1930s	29.7.1941	Pn	Mobilised July 1941, conv to minesweeper. Lost summer 1941
№ 08*		KOMSOMOLETS	1930s	29.7.1941	Pn	Mobilised July 1941, conv to minesweeper. Lost summer 1941
№ 09*		NEPEREMOZHNYJ	1930s	29.7.1941	Pn	Mobilised July 1941, conv to minesweeper. Lost summer 1941.
№ 10*		KOMMUNAR	1930s	29.7.1941	Pn	Mobilised July 1941, conv to minesweeper. Lost summer 1941
№ 331**		V-23	1938	18.8.1942	Vo	Mobilised 4.8.1942. Sank 7.9.1942 in collision at Stalingrad
№ 332**	KATShch-332⁵	V-24	1938	18.8.1942	Vo	Built 1938. Mobilised 4.8.1942. Conv 2.6.1944 to service craft
№ 333**		V-26	1936	18.8.1942	Vo	Mobilised 4.8.1942. Conv 5.10.1943 to service craft
№ 334**	KATShch-334⁵	V-38	1936	18.8.1942	Vo	Built 1936. Mobilised 4.8.1942. Conv 2.6.1944 to service craft
№ 335**		V-39	1937	18.8.1942	Vo	Mobilised 4.8.1942. Conv 5.10.1943 to service craft
№ 336		V-3	1936	31.8.1942	Vo	Mobilised 18.8.1942. Sunk 16.9.1942 by artillery fire off Golodnyi Island
№ 337		№ 8	1937	31.8.1942	Vo	Mobilised 18.8.1942. Sunk 19.10.1942 by artillery fire at Stalingrad
№ 344		V-34	1937	Sept 1942	Vo	Mobilised 5.9.1942. Lost, deleted 5.10.1942
№ 345		V-44	1937	Sept 1942	Vo	Mobilised 5.9.1942. Conv 5.10.1943 to service craft
№ 346		V-47	1936	Sept 1942	Vo	Mobilised 5.9.1942. Sunk 10.9.1942 by aircraft off Sapinski Island
№ 347	KATShch-347⁵	V-46	1937	Nov 1942	Vo	Mobilised 16.11.1942. Conv 2.4.1944 to service craft
№ 348		V-42	1937	Nov 1942	Vo	Mobilised 16.11.1942. Conv 5.10.1943 to service craft
T-93 T-925²	KATShch-380²	V-45	1936	7.7.1943	Vo	Mobilised 29.6.1943, conv to minesweeping boat T-93. Renumbered T-925 from 19.7.1943, KATShch-380 from 31.7.1943. Conv 24.4.1944 to service craft
T-94 T-926²	KATShch-381²	V-6	1936	7.7.1943	Vo	Mobilised 29.6.1943, conv to minesweeping boat T-94. Renumbered T-926 from 19.7.1943, KATShch-381 from 31.7.1943. Decomm 5.10.1943 to civilian service
T-331	KATShch-379	V-10	1937	24.6.1943	Vo	Mobilised 20.5.1943, conv to minesweeping boat T-331. Renumbered KATShch-379 from 9.7.1943. Conv 2.6.1944 to service craft
T-332	KATShch-380	№ G-17	1936	24.6.1943	Vo	Mobilised 1.6.1943, conv to minesweeping boat T-332. Renumbered KATShch-380 from 9.7.1943. Conv 5.10.1943 to service craft
T-333	KATShch-381	№ G-22	1937	24.6.1943	Vo	Mobilised 20.5.1943, conv to minesweeping boat T-333. Renumbered KATShch-381 from 9.7.1943. Conv 5.10.1943 to service craft
T-334	KATShch-382	V-36	1937	24.6.1943	Vo	Mobilised 23.5.1943, conv to minesweeping boat T-334. Renumbered KATShch-382 from 9.7.1943. Conv 2.6.1944 to service craft
T-431	KATShch-392	MRG-14	1937	24.6.1943	Vo	Mobilised 6.6.1943, conv to minesweeping boat T-431. Renumbered KATShch-392 from 9.7.1943. Conv 24.6.1944 to service craft
T-432	KATShch-393	V-37	1937	24.6.1943	Vo	Mobilised 23.5.1943, conv to minesweeping boat T-432. Renumbered KATShch-393 from 9.7.1943. Conv 14.12.1944 to service craft
T-531	KATShch-410	№ 22	1937	27.6.1943	Vo	Mobilised 20.5.1943, conv to minesweeping boat T-432. Renumbered KATShch-393 from 9.7.1943. Trdf 7.10.1943 to the Red Army

T-611	KATShch-430	№ G-12	1937	24.6.1943	Vo	Mobilised 18.5.1943, conv to minesweeping boat *T-611*. Renumbered *KATShch-340* from 9.7.1943. Conv 20.6.1944 to service craft
T-641	KATShch-457	№ G-18	1937	7.7.1943	Vo	Mobilised 30.6.1943, conv to minesweeping boat *T-641*. Renumbered *KATShch-457* from 9.7.1943. Conv 20.6.1944 to service craft
T-642	KATShch-443[3]	№ G-27	1937	7.7.1943	Vo	Mobilised 7.7.1943, conv to minesweeping boat *T-642*. Renumbered *KATShch-443* from 31.7.1943. Conv 5.10.1943 to service craft
T-643	KATShch-444[3]	№ 3	1936	7.7.1943	Vo	Mobilised 1.7.1943, conv to minesweeping boat *T-641*. Renumbered *KATShch-444* from 31.7.1943. Conv 24.4.1944 to service craft
T-644	KATShch-445[3]	№ G-8	1937	7.7.1943	Vo	Mobilised 1.7.1943, conv to minesweeping boat *T-644*. Renumbered *KATShch-445* from 31.7.1943. Conv 24.4.1944 to service craft
T-645	KATShch-446[3]	V-16	1937	7.7.1943	Vo	Mobilised 2.7.1943, conv to minesweeping boat *T-645*. Renumbered *KATShch-446* from 31.7.1943. Mined 19.7.1943 off Kerevaevski Island
T-721	KATShch-451	№ 1	1939	24.6.1943	Vo	Mobilised 1.6.1943, conv to minesweeping boat *T-721*. Renumbered *KATShch-451* from 9.7.1943. Conv 5.10.1943 to service craft
T-722	KATShch-452	№ 6	1937	24.6.1943	Vo	Mobilised 19.5.1943, conv to minesweeping boat *T-722*. Renumbered *KATShch-452* from 9.7.1943. Conv 20.6.1944 to service craft
T-723	KATShch-453	№ 6-A	1937	24.6.1943	Vo	Mobilised 1.6.1943, conv to minesweeping boat *T-723*. Renumbered *KATShch-453* from 9.7.1943. Conv 20.6.1944 to service craft
T-724	KATShch-454	V-11	1937	24.6.1943	Vo	Mobilised 5.6.1943, conv to minesweeping boat *T-724*. Renumbered *KATShch-454* from 9.7.1943. Conv 5.10.1943 to service craft
T-725	KATShch-455 T-921[3] KATShch-455[4]	V-14	1937	24.6.1943	Vo	Mobilised 30.5.1943, conv to minesweeping boat *T-725*. Renumbered *KATShch-455* from 9.7.1943, *T-921* from 19.7.1943, number reverted from 23.9.1943. Trfd 7.10.1943 to the Red Army
T-725	KATShch-476	№ G-16	1937	20.7.1943	Vo	Mobilised 1.7.1943, conv to minesweeping boat *T-725*. Renumbered *KATShch-476* from 9.7.1943. Conv 24.4.1944 to service craft
T-726	KATShch-456	V-17	1936	24.6.1943	Vo	Mobilised 20.5.1943, conv to minesweeping boat *T-726*. Renumbered *KATShch-456* from 9.7.1943. Conv 20.6.1944 to service craft
T-727 T-641[1]	KATShch-442[3]	V-18	1938	24.6.1943	Vo	Mobilised 4.6.1943, conv to minesweeping boat *T-727*. Renumbered *T-641* from 7.7.1943, renumbered *KATShch-456* from 31.7.1943. Trfd 7.10.1943 to the Red Army
T-728	KATShch-458	V-27	1937	24.6.1943	Vo	Mobilised 19.5.1943, conv to minesweeping boat *T-728*. Renumbered *KATShch-458* from 9.7.1943. Conv 20.6.1944 to service craft
T-729	KATShch-459	V-51	1937	24.6.1943	Vo	Mobilised 30.5.1943, conv to minesweeping boat *T-729*. Renumbered *KATShch-459* from 9.7.1943. Conv 20.6.1944 to service craft
T-831	KATShch-464 T-922[3] KATShch-464[7]	V-15	1936	24.6.1943	Vo	Mobilised 10.6.1943, conv to minesweeping boat *T-831*. Renumbered *KATShch-464* from 9.7.1943, *T-922* from 19.7.1943, number reverted from from 12.11.1943. Conv 2.6.1944 to service craft
T-832	KATShch-465 T-923[3] KATShch-465[7]	V-48	1937	24.6.1943	Vo	Mobilised 12.6.1943, conv to minesweeping boat *T-832*. Renumbered *KATShch-465* from 9.7.1943, *T-923* from 19.7.1943, number reverted from 12.11.1943. Conv 24.4.1944 to service craft
T-832	KATShch-466[6]	№ G-17	1937	13.7.1943	Vo	Mobilised 6.7.1943, conv to minesweeping boat *T-832*. Renumbered *KATShch-466* from 26.10.1943. Conv 2.6.1944 to service craft
T-833	KATShch-468[6]	V-25	1938	13.7.1943	Vo	Mobilised 9.7.1943, conv to minesweeping boat *T-833*. Renumbered *KATShch-468* from 26.10.1943. Conv 2.6.1944 to service craft
T-834	KATShch-469[6]	G-28	1936	13.7.1943	Vo	Mobilised 8.7.1943, conv to minesweeping boat *T-834*. Renumbered *KATShch-469* from 26.10.1943. Conv 24.4.1944 to service craft
T-837	KATShch-467[4]	G-24	1936	20.7.1943	Vo	Mobilised 8.7.1943, conv to minesweeping boat *T-837*. Renumbered *KATShch-467* from 22.9.1943. Conv 2.6.1944 to service craft

* Rated as minesweepers (TShch). ** Rated as river minesweepers (RTShch) until 18.8.1942.

Exceptions noted in the main table.

No	Year	Date
1.	1943	7.7.1943
2.		19.7.1943
3.		31.7.1943
4.		22.9.1943
		18.10.1943
5.		26.10.1943
6.		12.11.1943

Flat-bottomed river tugboats powered by wood gas generators.

Gazokhod type minesweeping boat on the Volga, 1942. *Przemysław Budzbon Collection*

Dvinosplav type
Motor tugs

Displacement: 18t
Dimensions: 15.0 x 3.1 x 1.1m
Machinery: 104hp = 4.8kts. Range 120 miles
Armament: 1-0.3in MG, 1 KAT sweep
Complement: 7

KATShch № on Comm 1.4.1944	No	Name	Built	Comm	Fleet	Remarks
№ 423	KT-423	KATER № 447	1943	15.10.1943	Wh	Mobilised 1943. Survived the war
№ 424	KT-424	KATER № 448	1943	15.10.1943	Wh	Mobilised 1943. Survived the war
№ 440	KT-440	DVINOSPLAV № 130	1939	Nov 1942	Wh	Mobilised 14.11.1942. Conv 16.8.1945 to service craft
№ 441	KT-441	DVINOSPLAV № 134	1939	Nov 1942	Wh	Mobilised 14.11.1942. Conv 16.8.1945 to service craft
№ 442	KT-442	KOTLASSPLAV № 106	1939	Nov 1942	Wh	Mobilised 14.11.1942. Conv 16.8.1945 to service craft
№ 443	KT-443	KOTLASSPLAV № 132	1939	Nov 1942	Wh	Mobilised 14.11.1942. Conv 16.8.1945 to service craft
№ 444	KT-444	VYCHEGDASPLAV № 5	1939	Nov 1942	Wh	Mobilised 14.11.1942. Conv 16.8.1945 to service craft
№ 445	KT-445	VYCHEGDASPLAV № 25	1939	Nov 1942	Wh	Mobilised 14.11.1942. Conv 16.8.1945 to service craft
№ 446	KT-446	KATER № 446	1943	29.10.1943	Wh	Survived the war

ZhS types
Motor tugs

Displacement: 32–33.5t full load
Dimensions: 17.3 x 3.8 x 1.3–1.5m
Machinery: 1-shaft, ZiS-5 petrol engine, 65hp = 8.5kts. Range 1430nm
Armament: 2-0.3in Maxim MGs, 1 KAT sweep
Complement: 12

Steel-hulled tugboat series developed in 1930s as the *Zh* type; designation changed to *ZhS* and *ZhSL* following introduction of welding from 1931. A total of 200 were built; the ten ordered by the fishing industry in 1941 were taken over by the Navy and completed as minesweeping boats.

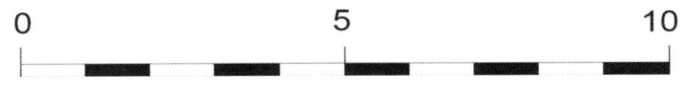

ZhS type as built.
Drawing by Jerzy Lewandowski

KATShch № on Comm 13.9.1944	No	Laid down	Comp	Comm	Fleet	Remarks
Builder: 202, Vladivostok						
№ 53	KT-53	1941	1942	9.10.1942	P	Conv 5.10.1945 to training boat. Survived the war
№ 54	KT-54	1941	1942	9.10.1942	P	Conv 5.10.1945 to training boat. Survived the war
№ 55	KT-55	1941	1942	9.10.1942	P	Conv 5.10.1945 to training boat. Survived the war
№ 56	KT-56	1941	1942	9.10.1942	P	Conv 5.10.1945 to training boat. Survived the war
№ 57	KT-57	1941	1942	9.10.1942	P	Conv 5.10.1945 to training boat. Survived the war
№ 58	KT-58	1941	1942	9.10.1942	P	Conv 5.10.1945 to training boat. Survived the war
№ 150	KT-150	1941	1942	21.1.1943	P	Survived the war
№ 157	KT-157	1941	1942	21.1.1943	P	Survived the war
№ 158	KT-158	1941	1942	21.1.1943	P	Survived the war
№ 159	KT-159	1941	1942	21.1.1943	P	Survived the war

Motor tugs

No on Comm	No 13.8.1943	Name	Details	Comm	Fleet	Remarks
MBTShch-114	EMTShch-57	BOT № 1	70hp	27.6.1943	Cs	Mobilised 26.6.1943, conv 13.8.1943 to tug for magnetic sweep. Conv 27.4.1944 to service craft
MBTShch-116	EMTShch-59	SVOI TRUD	70hp	7.6.1943	Cs	Mobilised 5.6.1943, conv 13.8.1943 to tug for magnetic sweep. Conv 20.10.1943 to service craft
MBTShch-117	EMTShch-60	ELISTA	42hp	5.6.1943	Cs	Mobilised 3.6.1943, conv 13.8.1943 to tug for magnetic sweep. Conv 14.11.1944 to service craft
MBTShch-321	EMTShch-82K EMTShch-82[1]	25-LETNIJ IUBILEJ VKP/B	82hp	26.5.1943	Cs B	Mobilised 20.5.1943, conv 13.8.1943 to tug for magnetic sweep. Trfd 27.11.1943 to the Black Sea Fleet, renumbered KEMTShch-82 from 18.4.1944. Conv 4.2.1945 to service craft
MBTShch-324	EMTShch-85K EMTShch-85[1]	TULA	62hp	29.5.1943	Cs B	Mobilised 28.5.1943, conv 13.8.1943 to tug for magnetic sweep. Trfd 27.11.1943 to the Black Sea Fleet. Conv 4.2.1945 to service craft
MBTShch-325	EMTShch-86	URAL'SK	40hp	29.5.1943	Cs B	Mobilised 28.5.1943, conv 13.8.1943 to tug for magnetic sweep. Trfd 27.11.1943 to the Black Sea Fleet. Mined 4.11.1944 off Enikale
MBTShch-326	EMTShch-87	DUNAJ	50hp	29.5.1943	Cs B	Mobilised 28.5.1943, conv 13.8.1943 to tug for magnetic sweep. Trfd 27.11.1943 to the Black Sea Fleet. Deleted 31.5.1944, presumably lost

Exceptions noted in the main table.

No	Year	Date
1.	1944	18.4.1944

Steam tug

No	Name	Details	Comm	Fleet	Remarks
KT-87	DIOMID	180t; 29.3 x 5.4 x 2.7m; 250hp = 8kts	10.8.1945	P	Mobilised 2.9.1932, conv 1.1.1933 to minesweeper № 13, renumbered № 18 from 1.5.1934. Decomm 9.7.1934 to civilian service. Mobilised summer 1945, conv to minesweeping boat. Survived the war

Tugs

No on Comm	No 21.6.1944	Name	Details	Comm	Fleet	Remarks
KATShch-160	B-160	TIMOFEJ KOPEIKIN ex-Evgenij (1924)	99t; 21.3 x 7.9 x 2.7m; 120hp = 7kts; 480nm at 4.5kts; 1-0.3in MG; 20 men	Sept 1941	BS Az BS	Built 1902. Mobilised 25.6.1941, service craft. Conv 14.9.1941 to magnetic minesweeper, Pt No 900. Trfd 8.2.1943 to the Azov Flotilla, returned 30.4.1944, conv to tug for magnetic sweep. Reverted 30.6.1944 to tug. Survived the war
KATShch-162		ETOR ex-№ 4 (1922) ex-Etor (1920)	125t; 18.6 x 4.8 x 3.0m; 150hp = 9kts; 11 men	28.10.1941	BS Az	Built 1896. Mobilised 28.10.1941, tugboat. Conv 24.6.1942 to minesweeping boat. Trfd 8.2.1943 to th Azov Flotilla. Sank 28.3.1944 in a gale in the Kerch Strait
KATShch-164 ex-SP-44 (29.3.1943)	B-164	TSENTAVR	43t; 16.5 x 4.1 x 1.8m; 50hp, = 8.5kts; 656nm at 5.5kts; 2-0.3in MG, 1 KAT sweep; 10 men	29.3.1943	BS	Built 1935. Mobilised 13.12.1942, service craft. Conv 29.3.1943 to minesweeping boat. Conv 30.4.1944 to tug for magnetic sweep. Survived the war
KATShch-181	KT-181	POMOSHCHNIK	•	June 1943	Az	Mobilised 25.6.1943. Survived the war
KATShch-182	KT-182	SEVRIUGA	•	June 1943	Az	Mobilised 25.6.1943. Survived the war
KATShch-531		VYBORG	•	May 1942	BS	Mobilised 30.4.1942. Mined 2.5.1942 off Kerch

KATShch-532	KT-532	KUBAN'	90t; 19.3 x 5 x 2m; 170hp, = 9.1kts; 1244nm at 8kts; 1-45mm/46 21-K, 1-0.5in; 12 men	May 1942	BS	Built 1941. Mobilised 30.4.1942. Survived the war
KATShch-533		KUTUZOV	78t; 19.3 x 5.1 x 2.3m; 65hp = 6.5kts, 1524nm at 5kts; 1-45mm/46 21-K, 1-0.3in MG; 9 men	May 1942	BS	Built 1941. Mobilised 30.4.1942. Sunk 11.9.1943 by artillery fire off Novorossisk
KATShch-535		STALINETS	•	10.9.1941	BS	Mobilised 10.9.1941, service craft. Conv 30.4.1942 to minesweeping boat. Mined 27.9.1943 off Novorossisk
KATShch-548	KT-548 B-548[1]	TBILISI	115t; 21.4 x 6 x 2.3m; 150hp, 6kts, 800nm at 5kts; 13 men	15.5.1942	BS	Built 1932. Mobilised 2.5.1942. Conv 3.1.1945 to tug for magnetic sweep, renumbered B-548. Survived the war

Exceptions noted in the main table.

No	Year	Date
1.	1945	3.1.1945

Motor tugboats

KATShch № on Comm 13.9.1944	No	Name	Details	Comm	Fleet	Remarks
№ 41	KT-41	BOL'SHEVIK	83t; 20.2 x 4.2 x 2.0m; 150hp = 9kts; 950nm at 7kts; 2-70.21in MGs, 1 KAT sweep; 17 men	7.10.1941	P	Built 1937. Mobilised 3.8.1941. Conv 5.10.1945 to training boat
№ 42	KT-42	OTLICHNIK		7.10.1941	P	Built 1937. Mobilised 27.7.1941. Conv 5.10.1945 to training boat
№ 43	KT-43	AGITATOR		7.10.1941	P	Built 1937. Mobilised 27.7.1941. Conv 5.10.1945 to training boat
№ 44	KT-44	AKTIVIST		7.10.1941	P	Built 1937. Mobilised 27.7.1941. Conv 5.10.1945 to training boat
№ 51	KT-51	ZH-14		7.10.1941	P	Built 1937. Mobilised 27.7.1941. Survived the war
№ 52	KT-52	ZH-17		7.10.1941	P	Built 1937. Mobilised 27.7.1941. Conv 5.10.1945 to training boat
№ 102	KT-102	ZH-19	83t; 20.2 x 4.2 x 2.0m; 150hp = 9kts; 950nm at 7kts; 2-70.21in MGs, 1 KAT sweep; 17 men	7.10.1941	P	Built 1937. Mobilised 29.7.1941. Survived the war
№ 103	KT-103	ZH-20		7.10.1941	P	Built 1937. Mobilised 29.7.1941. Survived the war
№ 104	KT-104	ZH-21		7.10.1941	P	Built 1937. Mobilised 27.8.1941. Survived the war
№ 111	KT-111	AKULA	24.2t; 15.5 x 3.5 x 1.8m; 50hp, 9kts; 600nm at 7kts; 1-0.3in MG, 1 KAT sweep; 6 men	7.10.1941	P	Built 1936. Mobilised 8.8.1941. Survived the war
№ 112	KT-112	RYBAK		7.10.1941	P	Built 1936. Mobilised 14.7.1941. Survived the war
№ 113	KT-113	SPGRT-1		7.10.1941	P	Built 1936. Mobilised 28.7.1941. Survived the war
№ 114	KT-114	SPGRT-3		7.10.1941	P	Built 1936. Mobilised 20.8.1941, conv to minesweeping boat. Numbered KT-114 from 13.9.1944. Survived the war
№ 115	KT-115	SOIUZPROMRYBSNAB		7.10.1941	P	Built 1936. Mobilised 28.7.1941. Survived the war
№ 116	KT-116	B-7		7.10.1941	P	Built 1936. Mobilised 28.7.1941. Survived the war
№ 123	KT-123	TAJMEN'-10		7.10.1941	P	Built 1936. Mobilised 28.7.1941. Survived the war
№ 124	KT-124	OSETR-8		7.10.1941	P	Built 1936. Mobilised 28.7.1941. Survived the war
№ 125	KT-618[1]	SIVUCH		20.10.1941 22.11.1944	P	Built 1936. Mobilised 7.10.1941. Decomm 5.7.1943 to civilian service, recomm 22.11.1944. Survived the war
№ 126	KT-619[1]	KRAB		20.10.1941 22.11.1944	P	Built 1936. Mobilised 7.10.1941. Decomm 5.7.1943 to civilian service, recomm 22.11.1944
	KT-605[2]	PERVENETS	•	10.8.1945	P	Mobilised summer 1945. Survived the war

Exceptions noted in the main table.

No	Year	Date
1.	1944	22.11.1944
2.	1945	10.8.1945

River tugboats

No on Comm	No 25.8.1943	No Red Army	No* 31.7.1944	No* 21.6.1944	Barkas № Name	Details	Comm	Fleet	Remarks
KATShch-477					№ 37	14.5 x 3.4 x 0.5m; 52hp = 5.3kts; 1 MG	12.11.1943	Vo	Mobilised 18.10.1943. Conv 29.4.1944 to service craft
T-141	KATShch-361	T-141	T-141[5]	KT-901[6]	№ 76	14.4 x 3.3 x 0.7m; 65hp = 8kts; 1 MG	16.8.1943	Vo Dn	Built 1939. Mobilised 13.8.1943. Trfd 7.10.1943 to the Red Army, returned 5.6.1944, trfd to the Dnieper Flotilla. Conv Aug 1945 to service craft
T-142	KATShch-362	BARKAS № 020	T-142		№ 114	11.2 x 2.4 x 0.7m; 52hp = 7.6kts; 1 MG	16.8.1943	Vo Dn	Built 1939. Mobilised 13.8.1943. Trfd 7.10.1943 to the Red Army, returned 31.7.1944, trfd to the Dnieper Flotilla. Conv 20.8.1945 to service craft
T-143	KATShch-363				№ 70	11.0 x 2.7 x 0.6m; 30hp = 4.5kts; 1-0.5in MG	16.8.1943	Vo	Built 1934. Mobilised 13.8.1943. Conv 5.10.1943 to service craft
T-144	KATShch-364				№ 82	14.0 x 2.8 x 0.7m; 50hp = 7.5kts; 1-0.5in MG	16.8.1943	Vo BS	Built 1939. Mobilised 13.8.1943. Trfd 6.11.1943 to the Black Sea Feet. Sunk 2.11.1943 by aircraft off Taman.
T-145	KATShch-365				KASPIJ	12.0 x 2.4 x 0.6m; 30hp = 6.5kts; 1 MG	16.8.1943	Vo BS	Built 1933. Mobilised 13.8.1943. Trfd 6.11.1943 to the Black Sea Feet. Deleted 19.11.1943, presumably lost
T-221	KATShch-370[2]				№ 42	13t; 9.5 x 2.4 x 0.5m; 30hp = 8kts; 1-37mm/67.5 70-K, 2-0.5in MGs	27.6.1943	Vo	Built 1932. Mobilised 25.6.1943. Conv 15.9.1943 to service craft
T-222	KATShch-371[2]			KT-371	№ 69	20t; 13.6 x 3.1 x 0.8m; 30hp = 8kts; 1-0.3in MG	27.6.1943	Vo BS	Built 1932. Mobilised 25.6.1943. Trfd 6.11.1943 to the Black Sea Feet. Conv 4.2.1945 to service craft
T-223	KATShch-372[2]	BARKAS № 038	T-223		№ 83	13t; 9.7 x 2.4 x 0.6m; 52hp = 8kts; 1-37mm/67.5 70-K, 2-0.5in MG	27.6.1943	Vo Dn	Built 1938. Mobilised 26.6.1943. Trfd 7.10.1943 to the Red Army, returned 31.7.1944, trfd to the Dnieper Flotilla. Conv 20.8.1944 to service craft
T-224	KATShch-373[2]			KT-373	№ 88	20t; 15.0 x 3.0 x 0.8m; 52hp = 8kts; 1-37mm/67.5 70-K, 2-0.5in MG	27.6.1943	Vo BS	Built 1932. Mobilised 25.6.1943. Trfd 6.11.1943 to the Black Sea Fleet, sank Jan 1944, deleted 9.2.1944, raised and recomm. 17.4.1944. Survived the war
T-433	KATShch-396[4]				№ 48	12t; 12.0 x 2.6 x 0.8m; 30hp = 8kts; 1 MG	20.8.1943	Vo BS	Built 1938. Mobilised 31.7.1943. Shipped by rail 2.10.1943 to Poti, arrived two weeks later. Foundered 29.10.1943, taken by wind off Anapa. Officially listed with the Black Sea Fleet from 6.11.1943
T-438	KATShch-395	T-438	T-438[5]		№ 48	10t; 9.6 x 2.3 x 1.0m; 30hp = 8kts; 1-0.3in MG	24.6.1943	Vo Dn	Mobilised 8.6.1943. Trfd 7.10.1943 to the Red Army, returned 5.6.1944, trfd to the Dnieper Flotilla. Conv 20.8.1944 to service craft
T-439	KATShch-394[1]				MALYSH	10t; 10.0 x 2.5 x 0.6m; 30hp = 9kts; 1-0.3in MG	15.6.1943	Vo	Built 1937. Mobilised 6.6.1943, conv to minesweeping boat *T-439*, renumbered *KATShch-394* from 9.7.1943. Conv 5.10.1943 to service craft
T-441	KATShch-397	T-441			№ 21	12t; 11.8 x 2.6 x 0.8m; 30hp = 4.5kts; 1-0.5in MG	16.8.1943	Vo	Built 1936. Mobilised 4.8.1943. Trfd 7.10.1943 to the Red Army
T-442	KATShch-398				№ 131	16.0 x 3.0 x 0.7m; 52hp = 5.5kts; 1-0.5in MG	16.8.1943	Vo BS	Built 1939. Mobilised 4.8.1943. Shipped by rail 2.10.1943 to Poti, arrived two weeks later. Sunk 5.11.1943 by artillery fire off Eltigen. Officially listed with the Black Sea Fleet from 6.11.1943
T-443	KATShch-399			KT-399	№ 92	20t; 14.0 x 2.8 x 0.7m; 52hp = 6.5kts; 1-0.5in MG	16.8.1943	Vo BS	Built 1939. Mobilised 4.8.1943. Trfd 6.11.1943 to the Black Sea Fleet
T-444	KAThch-400				№ 98	20t; 14.1 x 2.8 x 0.7m; 52hp = 7.5kts; 1-0.5in MG	16.8.1943	Vo BS	Built 1939. Mobilised 6.8.1943. Trfd 6.11.1943 to the Black Sea Fleet. Deleted 28.1.1944, presumably lost
T-445	KATShch-401	T-445 (?)			ALDAN	9.0 x 2.0 x 0.8m; 30hp = 6.5kts; 1 MG	16.8.1943	Vo	Built 1934. Mobilised 3.8.1943. Trfd 7.10.1943 to the Red Army
T-446	KATShch-303[4]				№ 22	10t; 18.0 x 3.2 x 0.7m; 60hp = 8kts; 1-0.3in MG	20.8.1943	Vo BS	Built 1930. Mobilised 26.6.1943. Trfd 6.11.1943 to the Black Sea Fleet. Sank 16.10.1943 in a gale off Gelendzhik
T-447	KATShch-304[4]			KT-304	№ 23	10t; 10.5 x 2.8 x 0.8m; 0hp = 7.5kts; 1 MG	Aug 1943	Vo BS	Built 1930. Mobilised 20.8.1943. Trfd 6.11.1943 to the Black Sea Fleet. Survived the war

20.0 Minesweeping boats

T-448	KATShch-305[4]			№ 41	15t; 13.0 x 2.9 x 0.7m; 52hp = 8kts; 1 MG	Aug 1943	Vo BS	Built 1940. Mobilised 20.8.1943. Trfd 6.11.1943 to the Black Sea Fleet. Sunk 2.11.1943 by aircraft off Taman
T-532	KATShch-415[2]		KT-415	№ 33	20t; 14.1 x 3.1 x 0.9m; 52hp = 8 2; 1-0.3in MG	July 1943	Vo BS	Built 1932. Mobilised 27.6.1943. Trfd 6.11.1943 to the Black Sea Fleet. Sunk 5.11.1943 by artillery fire off Eltigen. Raised and recomm Nov 1943. Conv 31.12.1945 to service craft RK № 266
T-533	KATShch-411[2]	BARKAS № 010 T-533		№ 40	20t; 14.1 x 3.2 x 0.9m; 52hp = 8kts; 1-0.3in MG	27.6.1943	Vo Dn	Built 1932. Mobilised 25.6.1943. Trfd 7.10.1943 to the Red Army, returned 31.7.1944, trfd to the Dnieper Flotilla. Conv 20.8.1944 to service craft
T-534	KATShch-412[2]	T-534 (?)		№ 87	25t; 18.6 x 3.5 x 0.8m; 60hp = 8kts; 1-0.3in MG	27.06.1943	Vo	Built 1939. Mobilised 26.6.1943. Trfd 7.10.1943 to the Red Army
T-535	KATShch-413	BARKAS № 104 T-535	KT-902[6]	№ 92	20t; 15.3 x 3.7 x 0.9m; 52hp = 8kts; 1-0.3in MG	27.6.1943	Vo Dn	Built 1939. Mobilised 26.6.1943. Trfd 7.10.1943 to the Red Army, returned 31.7.1944, trfd to the Dnieper Flotilla. Conv Aug 1945 to service craft
T-536	KATShch-414[2]			№ 104	20t; 15.3 x 3.1 x 0.8m; 52hp = 8kts; 1-0.3in MG	July 1943	Vo BS	Built 1939. Mobilised 27.6.1943. Trfd 6.11.1943 to he Black Sea Fleet. Mined 2.11.1943 off Tulza Spit
T-541	KATShch-419			№ 64	10t; 10.0 x 2.5 x 0.7m; 30hp = 6.5kts; 1 MG	16.8.1943	Vo	Built 1937. Mobilised 4.8.1943. Trfd 6.11.1943 to the Black Sea Fleet. Presumably lost before June 1944
T-542	KATShch-420		KT-420	№ 7	14.0 x 2.8 x 0.7m; 52hp = 6.5kts; 1 MG	16.8.1943	Vo BS	Mobilised 6.8.1943. Trfd 6.11.1943 to the Black Sea Fleet. Conv 31.12.1945 to service craft
T-543	KATShch-421			№ 51	10.6 x 2.8 x 0.8m; 30hp = 6.5kts; 1 MG	16.8.1943	Vo	Built 1937. Mobilised 3.8.1943, conv to minesweeping boat T-543, renumbered KATShch-421 from 25.8.1943. Conv 5.10.1943 to service craft
T-544	KATShch-422		KT-422	№ 107	14.5 x 2.3 x 0.5m; 52hp = 5.5kts; 1-0.5in MG	16.8.1943	Vo BS	Built 1939. Mobilised 5.8.1843. Trfd 6.11.1943 to the Black Sea Fleet, renumbered T-422 from 21.6.1944. Survived the war
T-545	KATShch-423			№ 83	14.5 x 2.4 x 0.5m; 52hp = 5.5kts; 1-0.5in MG	16.8.1943	Vo BS	Built 1938. Mobilised 13.8.1943. Trfd 6.11.1943 to the Black Sea Fleet. Deleted 21.6.1944, presumably lost
T-612	KATShch-431	BARKAS № 037 T-612		IASIEN'	30hp = 1-0.5in MG	9.7.1943	Vo Dn	Built 1932. Mobilised 27.6.1943. Trfd 7.10.1943 to the Red Army, returned 5.6.1944, trfd to the Dnieper Flotilla. Conv 20.8.1944 to service craft
T-613	KATShch-432[1]			PIKHTA	10t; 11.0 x 2.5 x 0.6m; 20hp = 8kts; 1-0.5in MG	26.6.1943	Vo	Built 1933. Mobilised 23.6.1943. Conv 5.10.1943 to service craft
T-614	KATShch-428[1]		KT-428	STAKHA-NOVETS	20t; 15.3 x 3.1 x 0.8m; 65hp = 8kts; 1-0.5in MG	9.7.1943	Vo BS	Built 1940. Mobilised 27.6.1943. Trfd 6.11.1943 to the Black Sea Fleet. Conv 31.12.1945 to service craft
T-615	KATShch-429[1]			IUR'EVETS	25t; 15.2 x 3.5 x 0.8m; 65hp = 8kts; 1-0.5in MG	26.6.1943	Vo	Built 1890. Mobilised 25.6.1943. Conv 29.4.1944 to service craft
T-633	KATShch-435[2]			KRENKEL'	10t; 9.2 x 2.8 x 0.5m; 30hp = 8kts; 1-0.5in MG	14.7.1943	Vo	Built 1927. Mobilised 7.7.1943. Conv 5.10.1943 to service craft
T-634	KATShch-436[2]			URAGAN	10t; 11.8 x 2.8 x 0.6m; 60hp = 8kts; 1-0.3in MG	17.7.1943	Vo	Built 1929. Mobilised 7.7.1943. Conv 5.10.1943 to service craft
T-635	KATShch-437[2]			POGRA-NICHNIK	10t; 11.2 x 2.5 x 0.5m; 30hp = 8kts; 1-0.3in MG	10.7.1943	Vo	Built 1934. Mobilised 7.7.1943. Conv 5.10.1943 to service craft
T-636	KATShch-438[2]			DOZOR	10t; 11.0 x 2.8 x 0.8m; 30hp = 8kts; 1-0.3in MG	8.7.1943	Vo	Built 1934. Mobilised 7.7.1943. Conv 5.10.1943 to service craft
T-637	KATShch-439[2]			CHEPTSA	10t; 11.1 x 2.5 x 0.6m; 30hp = 8kts; 1-0.5in MG	17.7.1943	Vo	Mobilised 7.7.1943. Conv 5.10.1943 to service craft
T-638	KATShch-301[4]		KT-301	№ 6	12t; 14.0 x 2.8 x 0.7m; 60hp = 9kts; 1 MG	Aug 1943	Vo BS	Built 1938. Mobilised 20.8.1943. Trfd 6.11.1943 to the Black Sea Fleet
T-639	KATShch-441[3]	T-639 T-639	KT-903[6]	№ 8	12t; 14.0 x 2.8 x 0.6m; 60hp = 9.1kts; 1 MG	Aug 1943	Vo Dn	Built 1938. Mobilised 20.8.1943. Trfd 7.10.1943 to the Red Army, returned 27.6.1944, trfd to the Dnieper Flotilla. Conv Aug 1945 to service craft
T-646				№ 45	12t; 13.0 x 2.9 x 0.5m; 52hp = 6.2kts; 1 MG	Aug 1943	Vo	Built 1940. Mobilised 20.8.1943, conv to minesweeping boat. Conv 5.10.1943 to service craft
T-647				№ 86	12t; 14.0 x 2.8 x 0.7m; 52hp = 8kts; 1 MG	Aug 1943	Vo	Built 1939. Mobilised 20.8.1943, conv to minesweeping boat. Trfd 7.10.1943 to the Red Army

No on Comm	No 25.8.1943	No Red Army	No 31.7.1944	No 21.6.1944	Barkas № Name	Details	Comm	Fleet	Remarks
T-648		T-648 (?)	T-648	KT-904[6]	№ 136	15t; 15.3 x 3.1 x 0.7m; 65hp = 7.5kts; 1 MG	Aug 1943	Vo Dn	Built 1939. Mobilised 20.8.1943. Trfd 7.10.1943 to the Red Army, returned 27.6.1944, trfd to the Dnieper Flotilla. Conv Aug 1945 to service craft
T-831	KATShch-306[4]				DIANA	15t; 12.2 x 3.1 x 0.6m; 60hp = 9.5kts; 1-0.5in MG	13.7.1943	Vo BS	Built 1898. Mobilised 5.7.1943, conv to minesweeping boat. Trfd 6.11.1943 to the Black Sea Fleet. Laid up 28.1.1944
T-835	KATShch-302[4]			KT-302[6]	№ 8	15t; 14.5 x 3.3 x 0.8m; 60hp = 8kts; 1-0.5in MG	16.7.1943	Vo BS	Built 1937. Mobilised 13.7.1943. Trfd 6.11.1943 to the Black Sea Fleet. Survived the war

Note: No* - number allocated after return from the Red Army.

Exceptions noted in the main table.

No	Year	Date
1.	1943	9.7.1943
2.		31.7.1943
3.		22.9.1943
4.		1.10.1943
5.	1944	5.6.1944
6.		14.9.1944

MSV-34 type
Paddle motor tugboats

Displacement: 90t
Dimensions: 35.0 x 12.4 x 0.5m
Machinery: 2-side wheels, ChTZ-S-60 diesel engines, 2 gas generators MSV-84; 120hp = 9.1kts
Armament: 1-20mm Oerlikon, 1 KAT sweep

No on Comm	No 9.7.1943	Name Gazokhod №	Built	Comm	Fleet	Remarks
Builder: MSV, Moscow						
T-325	B-21	V-68	1937	24.6.1943	Vo	Mobilised 20.5.1943, conv to minesweeper. Reverted 23.9.1943 to tug
T-326	B-22	V-66	1937	24.6.1943	Vo	Mobilised 21.5.1943, conv to minesweeper. Reverted 23.9.1943 to tug
T-335	KATShch-385	MRG-55	1939	24.6.1943	Vo	Mobilised 23.5.1943. Reverted 12.11.1943 to tug
T-711	B-42	MRG-54	1937	24.6.1943	Vo	Mobilised 6.6.1943, conv to minesweeper. Reverted 5.10.1943 to tug
T-712	B-43	№ 72	1937	24.6.1943	Vo	Mobilised 2.6.1943, conv to minesweeper. Reverted 12.11.1943 to tug
T-833	T-924[1] KATShch-379[2]	№ 69	1937	24.6.1943	Vo	Mobilised 10.6.1943. Reverted 28.4.1944 to tug

Exceptions noted in the main table.

No	Year	Date
1	1943	19.7.1943
2		31.7.1943

20.3.3. War prizes – 1944–1945

German B type
Motor tugs

Displacement: 20t
Dimensions: 20.2 x 5.2 x 0.9m
Machinery: diesel motors, wood gas generator, 80–100hp = 7kts
Armament: (from Sept 1944): 1-MG, 1 KAT sweep
Complement: 7

Hamburg *Hafenschuten* type motorboats built from 1943 at Pinsk, fitted with war prize engines and wood gas generators. Captured by the Soviets 14.7.1944 at Pinsk, comm 18.7.1944 with the Dnieper Flotilla as tugboats. Armed with Katyusha launchers and tested from 25.7.1944 as fire support boats. Conv 26.9.1944 to minesweeping boats and renumbered with the pennant *KT*. Laid up 24.12.1944 at Kiev.

20.0 Minesweeping boats

No	Ex-German Name
KT-905	BARBARA
KT-906	BALDUR
KT-907	BERTHOLD
KT-908	BERND
KT-909	BENNO
KT-910	BIANKA
KT-911	BERTHA
KT-912	BETTINA
KT-913	BRIGITTE
KT-914	BERNHARD
KT-915	BRUNHILDE
KT-916	BIANA
KT-917	BRUNO

Nearest boat is *KEMTShch-932*; far right *KEMTShch-937*.
Vitalij Kostrichenko Collection

Miscellaneous

KATShch № on Comm	No 30.10.1944	Details	Comm	Fleet	Remarks
№ 53	KT-921	26.5t; 15.0 x 3.1 x 1.1m; 380hp = 11.5kts; 1-0.5in MG, 1 KAT sweep; 7 men	10.11.1944	Da	Romanian river minesweepers captured Aug 1944 on the Danube, names not known. Had the pennant *KATShch* allocated with double-digit numbers, changed to *KT* pennant with three-digit numbers on 30.10.1944. Survived the war
№ 57	KT-922		10.11.1944	Da	
№ 81	KT-923	40t; 15.6 x 4.0 x 1.3m; 100hp = 6.5kts; 8 men	10.11.1944	Da	
№ 31	KT-924	17t; 15.3 x 3.2 x 1.1m; 180hp = 12kts, 190nm; 1 MZT sweep; 8 men	10.11.1944	Da	
№ 32	KT-925		10.11.1944	Da	
№ 33	KT-926		10.11.1944	Da	
№ 37	KT-927	25t; 11.7 x 3.0 x 1.0m; 100-200hp; 8 men	10.11.1944	Da	
№ 38	KT-928		10.11.1944	Da	
№ 41	KT-929	25t; 15.0 x 3.1 x 1.0m; 65hp; 8 men	10.11.1944	Da	
№ 42	KT-930	185t; 30.7 x 6.3 x 1.3m;	10.11.1944	Da	
	KEMTShch-931	700hp = 11.5kts; 1 EMT sweep; 15 men	10.11.1944	Da	Built 1930 Rutholf. German minesweeping boat *Kehl* captured Sept 1944, comm as magnetic minesweeping boat. Survived the war
	KEMTShch-932	150t; 28.5 x 5.0 x 1.8m; 350hp = 1 EMT sweep; 15 men	10.11.1944	Da	Built 1930 SHIMAG. German minesweeping boat *Kronos VIII* captured Aug 1944. Comm as magnetic minesweeping boat. Survived the war
	KEMTShch-933	147t; 34.5 x 6.2 x 1.2m; 475hp = 15 men; 1-20mm Oerlikon	10.11.1944	Da	German minesweeping boat *Berolina* (?) captured Aug 1944, comm as magnetic minesweeping boat. Survived the war
	KEMTShch-934		10.11.1944	Da	German minesweeping boat *Zeefalke* (?) captured Aug 1944, comm as magnetic minesweeping boat. Survived the war
	KEMTShch-935	60t; 27.4 x 4.0 x 1.4m; 180hp = 16 men	10.11.1944	Da	German minesweeping boat *Hindenburg* (?) captured Aug 1944, comm as magnetic minesweeping boat. Survived the war
	KEMTShch-936	90t; 22.0 x 3.6 x 1.7m; 165hp = 16 men	10.11.1944	Da	German minesweeping boat *Franz* (?) captured Aug 1944, comm as magnetic minesweeping boat. Conv 14.12.1945 to pilot boat *VLB-6*.
	KEMTShch-937	70t; 20.0 x 3.4 x 1.8m; 52hp = 11 men	10.11.1944	Da	Minesweeping boat *Mars* (?) captured Aug 1944, comm as magnetic minesweeping boat. Survived the war
	KEMTShch-938	•	10.11.1944	Da	German minesweeping boat *Arthur* (?) captured Aug 1944, comm as magnetic minesweeping boat. Survived the war
	KT--939	•	1944	BS	Motorboat captured in 1944, numbered *MB-1*, conv 6.10.1945 to magnetic minesweeping boat. Conv 31.12.1945 to service craft *RK № 265*
	KEMTShch-940	•	1944	BS	Motorboat captured in 1944, numbered *№ 1*, conv 6.10.1945 to magnetic minesweeping boat

KATShch № on Comm	No 30.10.1944	Details	Comm	Fleet	Remarks
	KT-860	•	24.5.1945	Da	Motorboat captured in 1945, numbered *AM-9*
	KT-601	25t; 18.9 x 4.0 x 0.6m; 180hp = 7kts	11.5.1945	Da	Built 1930s Korneuburg. German river tug *Hugin* captured spring 1945. Conv 14.12.1945 to diving tender *VRD-803*
	KT-602	•	11.5.1945	Da	German river tugboat *Seestrom-3* (?) captured spring 1945
	KEMTShch-603	55t; 16.15 x 3.8 x 1.5m; 90hp	11.5.1945	Da	Built 1921 Vlaardingen. German river tugboat *Mabi-3* (?) captured spring 1945

KEMTShch-934 rearmed with 20mm Oerlikon gun.
Vitalij Kostrichenko Collection

21. Landing vessels and craft

Десантные суда и плавсредства

21.1. Soviet-built standard types

SB class
Landing ships

Displacement: 720t std
Dimensions: 69.5 x 14.5 x 0.92m
Machinery: 1-shaft diesel, 280hp = 6kts. Range 1900nm
Armament: 2-0.3in MGs, (*SB-4* 1-0.5in DShK MG)
Complement: 18

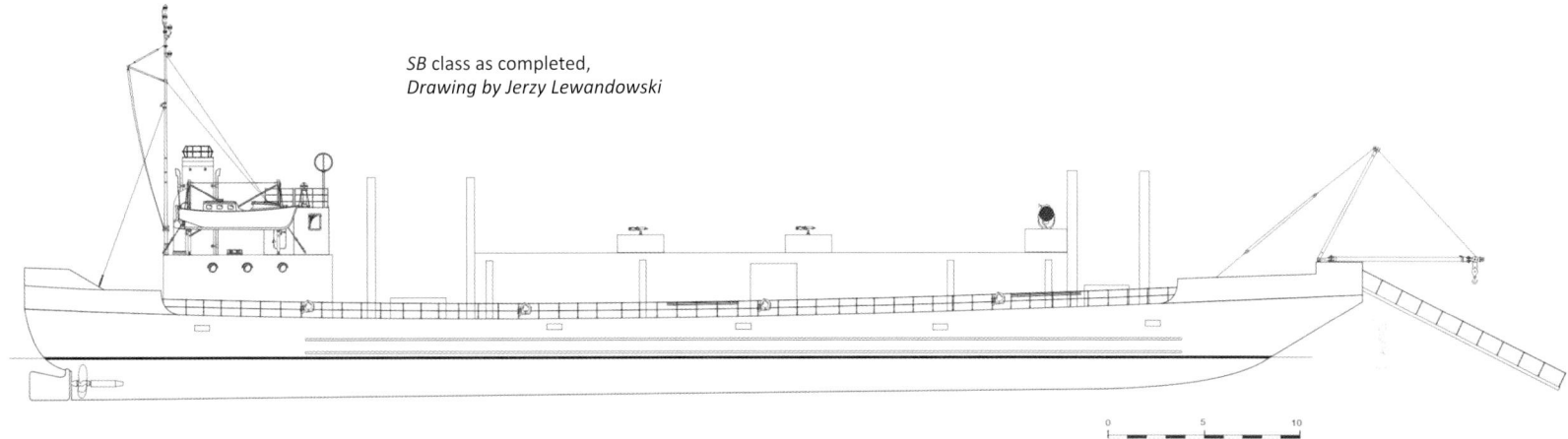

SB class as completed,
Drawing by Jerzy Lewandowski

Built at the naval shiprepair yard (the World War 1 Noblessner Yd) at Tallinn for newly formed marine troops brigade of the Baltic Fleet. Were fitted with platforms in the bow to allow embarkment on a bare shore. Their combat capability was limited due to low speed and lack of seaworthiness. Some sources quoted six ships of this class, with two lost in the Gulf of Viborg.

The wreck of *SB-4* from a wartime Finnish newsreel. Note funnels trunked at sides to allow through access for vehicles. *Przemysław Budzbon Collection*

The wreck of *SB-4* as captured by the Finns. *SA-Kuva 84472*

No	Comp	Comm	Fleet	Remarks
Builder: Naval Shiprepair Yd, Tallinn				
SB-1	1940	28.1.1941	B	Sunk 6.11.1941 by artillery fire in Neva Bay. Raised and recom 1944, conv 28.06.1945 to service craft
SB-2	1940	28.1.1941	B	Decomm 2.2.1942 for repairs, recomm 13.5.1942. Sunk 31.10.1944 by *U-958* off Osmussaasr Island
SB-3	1940	28.1.1941	B	Survived the war
SB-4	1940	28.1.1941	B	Stranded 1.11.1941 off Björkö Island, blown up to avoid capture

Tender types — *Landing craft*

Type	26t	31.5t	39.6t
Displacement (full):	26t	31.5t	39.6t
Length:	10.3m	10.7m	14.3m
Beam:	3.3m	3.6m	3.8m
Draught:	1.1m		
No of holds:	1	2	2
Capacity:	12t or 70 men	15t or 70 men	25t or 90 men
Petrol engine (1-shaft):	ZiS-5		
Total power:	73hp		
Speed (max):	6kts	5kts	
Range:	75nm	80nm	90nm
MGs:	1-0.5in DShK (on some)		
Sweeps (only minesweeping conversions):	1-KT		
Complement:	5		

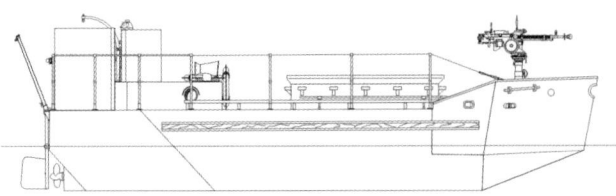
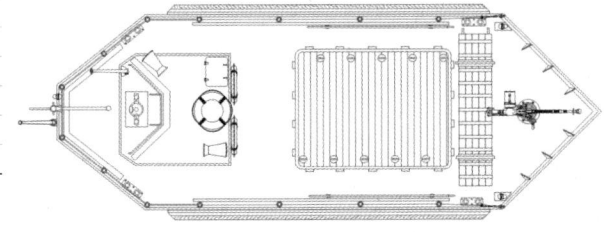

31.5t type.
Drawing by Jerzy Lewandowski

Tender №	No 26.6.1944	No 6.10.1945	Comm	Fleet	Remarks
on Comm					
Builders: 189, 190, 194, 363, 370, Leningrad					
26t type					
№ 11			18.6.1942	La BS	Trfd 6.11.1943 to the Black Sea Fleet. Mined 12.2.1944 in the entrance to Taman Bay
№ 12	KT-653		18.6.1942	La BS	Trfd 28.1.1944 to the Black Sea Fleet. Conv 21.6.1944 to minesweeping boat
№ 13			18.6.1942	La B	Trfd 19.10.1943 to the Baltic Fleet. Conv 22.8.1945 to service craft
№ 14			18.6.1942	B BS	Trfd 6.11.1943 to the Black Sea Fleet. Lost March 1944 off Kerch
№ 15	KEMTShch-511		18.6.1942	B La BS	Trfd to the Ladoga Flotilla. Trfd 6.11.1943 to the Black Sea Fleet. Conv 21.6.1944 to magnetic minesweeping boat. Conv 31.12.1945 to service craft *Raz"ezdnoj kater № 252*
№ 21		KT-894	18.6.1942	B La BS	Trfd to the Ladoga Flotilla, trfd 27.11.1943 to the Black Sea Fleet. Conv spring 1945 to minesweeping boat
№ 22	KT-654		18.6.1942	B La BS	Trfd to the Ladoga Flotilla, trfd 27.1.1944 to the Black Sea Fleet. Conv 21.6.1944 to minesweeping boat
№ 23			18.6.1942	B La B	Trfd to the Ladoga Flotilla, returned 19.10.1943
№ 24			18.6.1942	B La B	Trfd to the Ladoga Flotilla, returned 20.10.1943. Conv 22.8.1945 to service craft
№ 25			18.6.1942	La BS	Trfd 6.11.1943 to the Black Sea Fleet. Mined 8.11.1943 off Kerch
№ 31			18.6.1942	La BS	Trfd 6.11.1943 to the Black Sea Fleet. Sunk 22.1.1944 by artillery fire off Kerch
№ 32	KT-655		18.6.1942	La BS	Trfd 28.11.1943 to the Black Sea Fleet. Conv 21.6.1944 to minesweeping boat
№ 33			18.6.1942	B La B	Trfd to the Ladoga Flotilla, returned 19.10.1943
№ 34			18.6.1942	La BS	Trfd 27.11.1943 to the Black Sea Fleet. Mined 2.1.1944 off Temryuk
№ 35			18.6.1942	La BS	Trfd 6.11.1943 to the Black Sea Fleet. Sunk 10.12.1943 by mine off Kerch

Tender № 23 or 24.
Przemysław Budzbon Collection

№ 41			18.6.1942	La BS	Trfd 6.11.1943 to the Black Sea Fleet. Mined 25.4.1944 off Taman
№ 42			18.6.1942	La BS	Trfd 28.1.1944 to the Black Sea Fleet. Sunk 20.4.1944 by mine off Theodosia
№ 43	KEMTShch-512		18.6.1942	La BS	Trfd 27.11.1943 to the Black Sea Fleet. Conv 21.6.1944 to minesweeping boat. Conv 31.12.1945 to service craft *Raz"ezdnoj kater № 253*
№ 44		KT-895	18.6.1942	La BS	Trfd 27.11.1943 to the Black Sea Fleet. Conv spring 1945 to minesweeping boat
№ 45			18.6.1942	B La B	Trfd to the Ladoga Flotilla, returned 20.10.1943. Conv 22.8.1945 to service craft
№ 51		KT-896	18.6.1942	La BS	Trfd 27.11.1943 to the Black Sea Fleet. Conv spring 1945 to minesweeping boat
№ 52	KEMTShch-513		18.6.1942	La BS	Trfd 27.11.1943 to the Black Sea Fleet. Conv 21.6.1944 to magnetic minesweeping boat. Conv 31.12.1945 to service craft *Raz"ezdnoj kater № 254*
№ 53			18.6.1942	B La B	Trfd to the Ladoga Flotilla, returned 20.10.1943. Conv 22.8.1945 to service craft
№ 54			18.6.1942	B La B	Trfd to the Ladoga Flotilla, returned 20.10.1943
№ 55			18.6.1942	La B	Sunk 30.7.1942 by aircraft at the Lake Ladoga
№ 61			18.6.1942	La B	Trfd to the Ladoga Flotilla, returned 20.10.1943. Conv 26.6.1945 to pilot boat *OST-15*
№ 62	KEMTShch-514		18.6.1942	La BS	Trfd 28.1.1944 to the Black Sea Fleet. Conv 21.6.1944 to magnetic minesweeping boat. Conv 31.12.1945 to service craft *Raz"ezdnoj kater № 255*
№ 63		KT-897	18.6.1942	La BS	Trfd 27.11.1943 to the Black Sea Fleet. Conv spring 1945 to minesweeping boat
№ 64	KEMTShch-515		18.6.1942	La BS	Trfd 28.1.1944 to the Black Sea Fleet. Conv 21.6.1944 to magnetic minesweeping boat. Conv 31.12.1945 to service craft *Raz"ezdnoj kater № 260*
№ 65			18.6.1942	La BS	Trfd 6.11.1943 to the Black Sea Fleet. Sank 7.11.1943 in a gale off Eltigen

Tender № on Comm	No 26.6.1944	No 6.10.1945	Comm	Fleet	Remarks
№ 71			18.6.1942	La	Sunk 30.7.1942 by aircraft on Lake Ladoga
№ 72	KT-656		18.6.1942	La	Trfd 28.1.1944 to the Black Sea Fleet. Conv 21.6.1944 to minesweeping boat
№ 73			18.6.1942	B La B	Trfd to the Ladoga Flotilla, returned 20.10.1943. Conv 22.8.1945 to service craft
№ 74			18.6.1942	B La B	Trfd to the Ladoga Flotilla, returned 20.10.1943. Conv 22.8.1945 to service craft
№ 75			18.6.1942	La	Sunk 30.7.1942 by aircraft on Lake Ladoga
№ 81			18.6.1942	La	Conv Nov 1943 to service craft
№ 82	KEMTShch-516		18.6.1942	La BS	Trfd 28.1.1944 to the Black Sea Fleet. Conv 21.6.1944 to magnetic minesweeping boat. Conv 31.12.1945 to service Raz"ezdnoj kater № 256
№ 83			18.6.1942	La	Sunk 30.7.1942 by aircraft on Lake Ladoga
№ 84			18.6.1942	B La	Trfd to the Ladoga Flotilla, returned 20.10.1943. Conv 22.8.1945 to service craft
№ 85		KT-891	18.6.1942	La BS	Trfd 27.11.1943 to the Black Sea Fleet. Conv spring 1945 to minesweeping boat. Conv 31.12.1945 to service craft Raz"ezdnoj kater № 258
№ 91	KEMTShch-820		18.6.1942	La BS	Trfd 6.11.1943 to the Black Sea Fleet. Conv 21.6.1944 to magnetic minesweeping boat. Conv 31.12.1945 to service craft Raz"ezdnoj kater № 263
№ 92	KT-657		18.6.1942	La BS	Trfd 28.1.1944 to the Black Sea Fleet. Conv 21.6.1944 to minesweeping boat
№ 93			18.6.1942	B La	Trfd to the Ladoga Flotilla, returned 20.10.1943. Conv 22.8.1945 to service craft
№ 94		KT-893	18.6.1942	La BS	Trfd to the Ladoga Flotilla, returned 20.10.1943. Conv Spring 1945 to minesweeping boat
№ 95		KT-858[1]	18.6.1942	La BS	Trfd 27.11.1943 to the Black Sea Fleet. Conv Spring 1945 to minesweeping boat. Conv 31.12.1945 to service craft Raz"ezdnoj kater № 251
№ 101			18.6.1942	B La B	Trfd to the Ladoga Flotilla, returned 19.10.1943. Conv 22.8.1945 to service craft
№ 102	KEMTShch-518		18.6.1942	La BS	Trfd 28.1.1944 to the Black Sea Fleet. Conv 21.6.1944 to minesweeping boat. Conv 31.12.1945 to service craft Raz"ezdnoj kater № 257
№ 103			18.6.1942	La BS	Trfd 6.11.1943 to the Black Sea Fleet. Sank 20.11.1943 at the entry to the Taman Bay

Tender № 73 and the others on Lake Ladoga, 1942. They were vital to keep Leningrad supplied during the siege. *Boris Lemachko Collection*

Two tenders in the Black Sea heading towards shore at Elitgen, 1944. Their awkward shape is evident in this photo. A *Project 1124* AMGB is in the foreground. *Vitalij Kostrichenko Collection*

№ 104		18.6.1942	B La B	Trfd to the Ladoga Flotilla, returned 20.11.1943
№ 105		18.6.1942	La	Sunk 30.7.1942 by aircraft on Lake Ladoga
31.5t type				
№ 16		Sum 1942	La BS	Trfd 6.11.1943 to the Black Sea Fleet. Sank 7.11.1943 in a gale off Eltigen
№ 17		Sum 1942	B La B	Trfd to the Ladoga Flotilla, returned 19.10.1943. Conv 22.8.1945 to service craft
№ 18		Sum 1942	B La B	Trfd to the Ladoga Flotilla, returned 20.5.1943. Conv 22.8.1945 to service craft
№ 26		Sum 1942	La BS	Trfd 6.11.1943 to the Black Sea Fleet. Sank 7.11.1943 in a gale off Eltigen
№ 27		Sum 1942	B La B	Trfd to the Ladoga Flotilla, returned 19.10.1943. Conv 22.8.1945 to service craft
№ 28		Sum 1942	B La B	Trfd to the Ladoga Flotilla, returned 20.5.1943. Conv 22.8.1945 to service craft
№ 36		Sum 1942	La BS	Trfd 6.11.1943 to the Black Sea Fleet. Sank 7.11.1943 in a gale off Eltigen
№ 37		Sum 1942	B La B	Trfd to the Ladoga Flotilla, returned 19.10.1943. Conv 22.8.1945 to service craft
№ 38		end 1942	B La B	Trfd to the Ladoga Flotilla, returned 20.5.1943. Conv 22.8.1945 to service craft
№ 46		Sum 1942	B La B	Trfd to the Ladoga Flotilla, returned 20.11.1943. Conv 22.8.1945 to service craft
№ 47		Sum 1942	B La B	Trfd to the Ladoga Flotilla, returned 19.10.1943. Conv 22.8.1945 to service craft
№ 48		end 1942	B La	Trfd to the Ladoga Flotilla, returned 20.5.1943
№ 56		Sum 1942	La	Sunk 30.7.1942 by aircraft on Lake Ladoga.
№ 57		Sum 1942	B La B	Trfd to the Ladoga Flotilla, returned 19.10.1943. Conv 22.8.1945 to service craft
№ 58		end 1942	B La B	Trfd to the Ladoga Flotilla, returned 20.5.1943. Conv 22.8.1945 to service craft
№ 66		Sum 1942	La BS	Trfd 6.11.1943 to the Black Sea Fleet. Sank 7.11.1943 in a gale off Eltigen.
№ 67		Sum 1942	La	Sunk 30.7.1942 by aircraft on Lake Ladoga
№ 68		end 1942	B La B	Trfd to the Ladoga Flotilla, returned 20.5.1943. Conv 22.8.1945 to service craft
№ 76		Sum 1942	La BS	Trfd 6.11.1943 to the Black Sea Fleet. Deleted 28.1.1944, presumably lost
№ 77		Sum 1942	B La B	Trfd to the Ladoga Flotilla, returned 19.10.1943. Conv 22.8.1945 to service craft
№ 78		end 1942	B La B	Trfd to the Ladoga Flotilla, returned 20.5.1943. Conv 22.8.1945 to service craft
№ 86	KT-892	Sum 1942	La BS	Trfd 6.11.1943 to the Black Sea Fleet. Conv spring 1945 to minesweeping boat. Conv 31.12.1945 to service craft *Raz"ezdnoj kater № 259*
№ 87		Sum 1942	B La B	Trfd to the Ladoga Flotilla, returned 19.10.1943. Conv 22.8.1945 to service craft

Tender № on Comm	No 26.6.1944	No 6.10.1945	Comm	Fleet	Remarks
№ 88			end 1942	B La B	Trfd to the Ladoga Flotilla, returned 20.5.1943. Conv 22.8.1945 to service craft
№ 96			Sum 1942	B La B	Trfd to the Ladoga Flotilla, returned 19.10.1943. Conv 22.8.1945 to service craft
№ 97			Sum 1942	La	Sunk 30.7.1942 by aircraft on Lake Ladoga
№ 98			end 1942	B La B	Trfd to the Ladoga Flotilla, returned 20.5.1943. Conv 22.8.1945 to service craft
№ 106			Sum 1942	La	Sunk 30.7.1942 by aircraft on Lake Ladoga
№ 107			Sum 1942	B La B	Trfd to the Ladoga Flotilla, returned 19.10.1943. Conv 22.8.1945 to service craft
№ 108			end 1942	B La B	Trfd to the Ladoga Flotilla, returned 20.5.1943. Conv 22.8.1945 to service craft
39.6t type					
№ 19			end 1942	B La B	Trfd to the Ladoga Flotilla, returned 19.11.1943. Conv 22.8.1945 to service craft
№ 29			end 1942	La BS	Trfd 27.11.1943 to the Black Sea Fleet. Sank 9.12.1943 in the entrance to Taman Bay
№ 39			end 1942	B La B	Trfd to the Ladoga Flotilla, returned 20.11.1943. Conv 22.8.1945 to service craft
№ 49			end 1942	B La B	Trfd to the Ladoga Flotilla, returned 20.11.1943. Conv 22.8.1945 to service craft
№ 59			end 1942	B La B	Trfd to the Ladoga Flotilla, returned 20.11.1943. Conv 22.8.1945 to service craft
№ 69		KT-898	end 1942	La BS	Trfd 27.11.1943 to the Black Sea Fleet. Conv spring 1945 to minesweeping boat
№ 79			end 1942	B La B	Trfd to the Ladoga Flotilla, returned 20.11.1943. Conv 22.8.1945 to service craft
№ 89			end 1942	B La B	Trfd to the Ladoga Flotilla, returned 20.11.1943. Conv 22.8.1945 to service craft

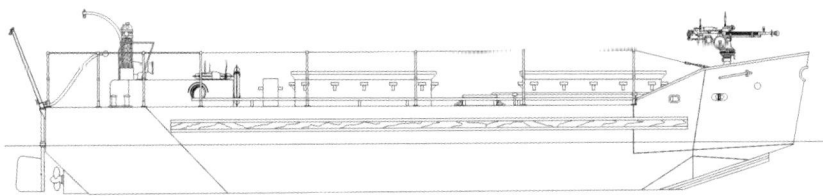

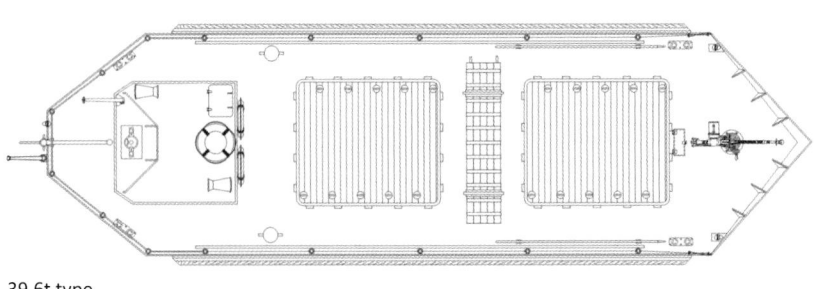

39.6t type.
Drawing by Jerzy Lewandowski

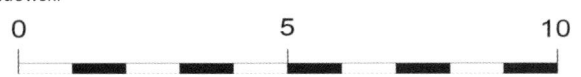

Tender № 911 in Narva Bay on 26 May 1944.
Boris Lemachko Collection

№ 99		end 1942	B La B	Trfd to the Ladoga Flotilla, returned 20.11.1943. Conv 22.8.1945 to service craft
№ 100		end 1942	La BS	Trfd 27.11.1943 to the Black Sea Fleet. Conv 21.6.1945 to service craft
№ 109	KT- •	end 1942	La BS	Trfd 27.11.1943 to the Black Sea Fleet. Conv Spring 1945 to minesweeping boat. Conv 21.6.1945 to service craft
№ 110		end 1942	B La B	Trfd to the Ladoga Flotilla, returned 20.11.1943
№ 111		end 1942	La BS	Trfd 6.11.1943 to the Black Sea Fleet. Deleted 28.1.1944, presumably lost
№ 210		end 1942	B La B	Trfd to the Ladoga Flotilla, returned 20.11.1943. Conv 22.8.1945 to service craft
№ 211		end 1942	B La B	Trfd to the Ladoga Flotilla, returned 19.10.1943. Conv 22.8.1945 to service craft
№ 265		31.7.1942	B	Conv 22.8.1945 to service craft
№ 266		31.7.1942	B	Lost 1944?
№ 267		31.7.1942	B	Conv 22.8.1945 to service craft
№ 268		31.7.1942	B	Conv 22.8.1945 to service craft
№ 269		13.10.1942	B	Conv 22.8.1945 to service craft
№ 276		31.7.1942	B	Conv 22.8.1945 to service craft
№ 280		end 1942	B	Conv 22.8.1945 to service craft
№ 284		end 1942	B	Conv 22.8.1945 to service craft
№ 310		end 1942	B La B	Trfd to the Ladoga Flotilla, returned 19.10.1943. Conv 22.8.1945 to service craft
№ 311		end 1942	B La B	Trfd to the Ladoga Flotilla, returned 19.10.1943. Conv 22.8.1945 to service craft
№ 410		end 1942	B La B	Trfd to the Ladoga Flotilla, returned 19.10.1943. Conv 22.8.1945 to service craft
№ 510		end 1942	B La B	Trfd to the Ladoga Flotilla, returned 19.10.1943. Conv 22.8.1945 to service craft
№ 610		end 1942	B La B	Trfd to the Ladoga Flotilla, returned 19.10.1943. Conv 22.8.1945 to service craft
№ 611		3.7.1943	B	Conv 22.8.1945 to service craft
№ 710		end 1942	B La B	Trfd to the Ladoga Flotilla, returned 19.10.1943. Conv 22.8.1945 to service craft

Fully loaded tender on Lake Ladoga.
Przemysław Budzbon Collection

Tender № 19 on the Gdovka River close to Lake Peipus, 21.8.1944.
Boris Lemachko Collection

Tender № on Comm	No 26.6.1944	No 6.10.1945	Comm	Fleet	Remarks
№ 711			3.7.1943	B	Conv 22.8.1945 to service craft
№ 810			end 1942	B, La, B	Trfd to the Ladoga Flotilla, returned 19.10.1943. Conv 22.8.1945 to service craft
№ 811			3.7.1943	B	Conv 22.8.1945 to service craft
№ 910			end 1942	B, La, B	Trfd to the Ladoga Flotilla, returned 19.10.1943. Conv 22.8.1945 to service craft
№ 911			3.7.1943	B	Conv 22.8.1945 to service craft
№ 1010			end 1942	B	Lost 1944?
№ 1011			3.7.1943	B	Conv 22.8.1945 to service craft
№ 1111			3.7.1943	B	Conv 22.8.1945 to service craft
№ 1211			3.7.1943	B	Conv 22.8.1945 to service craft
№ 1311			3.7.1943	B	Conv 22.8.1945 to service craft
№ 1411			3.7.1943	B	Lost 1944?
№ 1511			3.7.1943	B	Conv 22.8.1945 to service craft

Ordered on 7.5.1942 by the Leningrad Front War Council for transportation of goods across Lake Ladoga and evacuation of people from the besieged city. Of robust construction, they were designed in three series with one or two holds. Steel hulls, welded from flat sections to simplify production. Used at beginning for transportation only, but employed from 1943 as landing craft while 22 were conv to minesweeping boats fitted with one KT type sweep each. Some trfd to the Black Sea.

DB type (*Project 165*) — *Landing motorboats*

Landing motorboats and AA defence boats
Displacement: 15.5t standard, 18.9t full load
Dimensions: 14.6 x 3.6 x 0.9m
Machinery: 2-shaft two GAZ-MM petrol engines, 76hp
 1-shaft GAZ-202 petrol engine, 54hp
 1-shaft ZiS-5 petrol engine, 87hp
Speed: 8.5kts. Range 150nm at 4.5kts
Armament: landing boats: 1-0.5in DShK MG, up to 60 troops
 minesweeping boats: 1-0.5in DShK MG, 1 KT sweep
 AA defence boats: 1-37mm/67.5 70-K, 1-0.5in DShK MG (1-20mm Oerlikon on some)
 armed (rocket) boats: 1-M-8-M 82mm rocket launcher, 1-0.5in DShK MG
Complement: unarmed boats 3, armed boats up to 13

Catamaran (two DB type hulls) floating artillery batteries
Displacement: 33t standard, 18.9t full load
Dimensions: 14.6 x 9.8 x 1.1m
Machinery: two 2-shaft hulls, petrol engines 230hp (*PAB-1220* 152hp, *PAB-1227* 192hp) = 5kts. Range 150nm at 3.5kts
Armament: 1-100mm/56 B-24-BM, 2-0.5in DShK MGs
Complement: 20

DB № No on Comm	No 29.1.1943	No 25.6.1943	No 21.6.1944	YN	Comm	Fleet	Remarks
Builder: 343, Gorokhovets							
№ 1		DB-1		311	20.11.1942	Vo BS	Trfd 31.12.1942 to the Black Sea Fleet. Sunk 12.11.1943 by artillery fire off Taman Peninsula
№ 2		DB-2		316	20.11.1942	Vo BS	Trfd 31.12.1942 to the Black Sea Fleet. Sunk 10.9.1943 by artillery fire off Novorossiysk
№ 3		DB-32[3]		324	20.11.1942	Vo BS	Trfd 31.12.1942 to the Black Sea Fleet. Sunk 10.9.1943 by artillery fire off Tuzla Spit
№ 4		DB-4		317	20.11.1942	Vo BS	Trfd 31.12.1942 to the Black Sea Fleet. Sunk 2.11.1943 by artillery fire off Eltigen
№ 5		DB-5	VRD-73 VRD-216[9]	319	20.11.1942	Vo BS	Trfd 31.12.1942 to the Black Sea Fleet. Conv 21.6.1944 to diving tender.

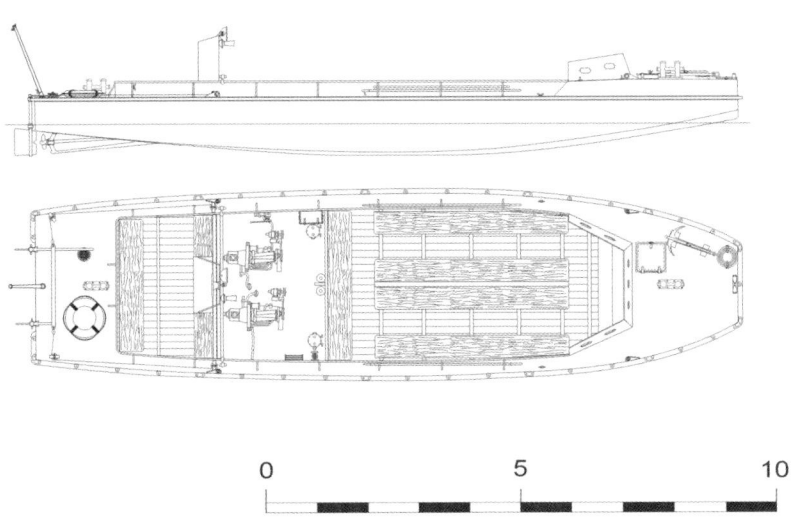

DB type in basic configuration. *Drawing by Jerzy Lewandowski*

DB type after minesweeping conversion. *Drawing by Jerzy Lewandowski*

Close up of landing craft *DB-7*. Gangut

Close up of landing craft *DB-20*. Gangut

№ 6	DB-6		320	20.11.1942	Vo BS	Trfd 31.12.1942 to the Black Sea Fleet. Lost 8.11.1943 off Kerch. Raised and recomm. Conv 5.7.1947 to minesweeping boat *KT-509*. Conv 20.3.1948 to dumb lighter
№ 7	DB-9		321	20.11.1942	Vo BS	Trfd 31.12.1942 to the Black Sea Fleet. Sank 7.11.1943 in a gale off Eltingen
№ 8	DB-10		322	20.11.1942	Vo BS	Trfd 31.12.1942 to the Black Sea Fleet. Sank 7.11.1943 in a gale off Eltingen
№ 9	DB-31[3]		321	20.11.1942	Vo BS	Trfd 31.12.1942 to the Black Sea Fleet. Sunk 25.9.1943 by mine off Anapa
DB-2			366	14.12.1943	BS	Sank 10.1.1944 in a gale off Cape Tarchan
DB-3		KT-643	381	14.12.1943	BS	Conv 21.6.1944 to minesweeping boat. Deleted 17.6.1947 to civilian service
DB-13		KT-644	387	14.12.1943	BS	Conv 21.6.1944 to minesweeping boat. Deleted 17.6.1947 to civilian service
DB-15			318	17.4.1943	BS	Sunk 1.11.1943 by artillery fire off Eltigen
DB-16			325	17.4.1943	BS	Sank 6.11.1943 in a gale south off Taman peninsula
DB-17			326	17.4.1943	BS	Sunk 1.11.1943 by artillery fire off Eltigen
DB-18			327	17.4.1943	BS	Sunk 25.9.1943 in a gale off Cape Utrish
DB-18			503	14.12.1943	BS	Sunk 10.12.1943 by artillery fire off Novorossiysk
DB-19			328	17.4.1943	BS	Sunk 10.9.1943 by artillery fire off Novorossiysk
DB-19			505	14.12.1943	BS	Sunk 10.1.1944 by artillery fire off Cape Tarchan
DB-20		VRD-74 VRD-212[9]	329	17.4.1943	BS	Conv 21.6.1944 to diving tender

No on Comm	No 29.1.1943	No 25.6.1943	No 21.6.1944	YN	Comm	Fleet	Remarks
DB-21				330	17.4.1943	BS	Sank 28.3.1944 in a gale at the entry to the Taman Bay. Raised after the war
DB-22		DB-24	VRD-75 VRD-214[9]	334	11.6.1943	BS	Conv 21.6.1944 to diving tender
DB-22				332	25.6.1943	BS	Sunk 10.9.1943 by artillery fire off Novorossiysk
DB-22			KT-645	506	14.12.1943	BS	Conv 21.6.1944 to minesweeping boat. Conv 20.3.1948 to dumb lighter
DB-23		DB-25		335	11.6.1943	BS	Sunk 2.11.1943 by artillery fire off Eltigen
DB-23				333	25.6.1943	BS	Sunk 10.10.1943 by artillery fire off the Tulza Spit.
DB-23				507	14.12.1943	BS	Sunk 10.1.1944 by artillery fire of Cape Tarchan
DB-24		DB-26		336	11.6.1943	BS	Sunk 6.11.1943 by artillery fire off the Tulza Spit
DB-25		DB-27		337	21.6.1943	BS	Sunk 2.11.1943 by artillery fire off Eltigen
DB-26		DB-28		338	21.6.1943	BS	Sunk 26.9.1943 by mine off Anapa
DB-26				514	14.12.1943	BS	Sank 10.1.1944 in a gale off Cape Tarchan
DB-27		DB-29		329	21.6.1943	BS	Sunk 1.11.1943 by artillery fire off Eltigen
DB-27				515	14.12.1943	BS	Sank 10.1.1944 in a gale off Cape Tarchan
DB-28		DB-30		340	21.6.1943	BS	Sunk 1.11.1943 by artillery fire off Eltigen
DB-28			KT-646	516	14.12.1943	BS	Conv 21.6.1944 to minesweeping boat. Conv 20.3.1948 to dumb lighter
DB-29			KT-651	517	14.12.1943	BS	Conv 21.6.1944 to minesweeping boat. Conv 20.3.1948 to dumb lighter
DB-31			KT-647	518	14.12.1943	BS	Conv 21.6.1944 to minesweeping boat. Conv 20.3.1948 to dumb lighter
DB-32			KT-659	508	14.12.1943	BS	Conv 21.6.1944 to minesweeping boat. Deleted 17.6.1947 to civilian service
DB-33				355	31.8.1943	BS	Sunk 6.10.1943 by artillery fire off the Tuzla Spit
DB-33				519	14.12.1943	BS	Sank 10.1.1944 in a gale off Cape Tarchan
DB-34				358	31.8.1943	BS	Sunk 10.9.1943 by artillery fire off Novorossiysk
DB-34			KT-650	509	14.12.1943	BS	Conv 21.6.1944 to minesweeping boat. Conv 20.3.1948 to dumb lighter
DB-35				359	31.8.1943	BS	Sank 18.11.1943 in a gale off Eltigen
DB-35				510	14.12.1943	BS	Sank 1.12.1943 in a gale off Cape Agriia of Tuapse. Apparently listed afterwards. Deleted 28.1.1944

DB type landing craft in the Black Sea. Note makeshift armament of Maxim MG. The only identified boat is *DB-10* in the middle. *Przemysław Budzbon Collection*

DB-35			520	14.12.1943	BS	Sunk 18.4.1944 by mine off Kerch
DB-36			363	1.8.1943	BS	Sunk 22.8.1943 by *U-24* off Sochi. Apparently listed afterwards. Deleted 1.9.1943
DB-36	DB-37[4]		382	28.9.1943	BS	Sunk 12.11.1943 by artillery fire off the Chushka Spit
DB-37			365	31.8.1943	BS	Sunk 22.8.1943 by *U-24* off Sochi. Apparently listed afterwards. Deleted 1.9.1943
DB-37	DB-39[4]		383	28.9.1943	BS	Sunk 1.12.1943 by artillery fire off the Chushka Spit
DB-38			376	31.8.1943	BS	Sunk 26.9.1943 by artillery fire off Anapa
DB-39	DB-36[4]		360	28.9.1943	BS	Sunk 7.11.1943 by artillery fire off the Chushka Spit
DB-40			384	28.9.1943	BS	Sunk 1.11.1943 by artillery fire off the Chushka Spit
DB-40			513	14.12.1943	BS	Sank 10.1.1944 in a gale off Cape Tarchan
DB-41			385	28.9.1943	BS	Sank 28.10.1943 in a gale near Kuchugury on the Taman Peninsula
DB-42			386	28.9.1943	BS	Sank 28.11.1943 in a gale
DB-43			388	28.9.1943	BS	Deleted 4.6.1944
DB-44			389	28.9.1943	BS	Deleted 4.6.1944
DB-45			390	28.9.1943	BS	Deleted 4.6.1944
DB-46			501	28.9.1943	BS	Sunk 7.11.1943 by artillery fire off the Chushka Spit
DB-47		KT-652	502	28.9.1943	BS	Decomm 14.12.1943, presumably for repairs. Recomm 18.4.1944, conv 21.6.1944 to minesweeping boat. Deleted 19.4.1944, presumably lost
DB-47			511	14.12.1942	BS	Sank 10.1.1944 in a gale off Cape Tarchan
DB-48		KT-519	504	28.9.1943	BS	Sunk 7.11.1943 at the entry to the Taman Bay. Raised, repaired and conv to minesweeping boat, recomm 21.6.1944
DB-48		KT-648	512	14.12.1943	BS	Conv 21.6.1944 to minesweeping boat. Conv 20.3.1948 to dumb lighter
DB-50			331	17.4.1943	BS	Sunk 1.6.1943 by German aircraft off Gelendzhik
DB-111		MK-112[7]		31.10.1944	Dn	Conv 26.12.1944 to armed (rocket) boat. Survived the war
DB-112		MK-113[7]		31.10.1944	Dn	Conv 26.12.1944 to armed (rocket) boat. Survived the war
DB-112				16.6.1945	N	Survived the war
DB-113		MK-114[7]		31.10.1944	Dn	Conv 26.12.1944 to armed (rocket) boat. Survived the war
DB-113				16.6.1945	N	Survived the war
DB-114		MK-115[7]		31.10.1944	Dn	Conv 26.12.1944 to armed (rocket) boat. Survived the war
DB-114				16.6.1944	N	Survived the war
DB-115				16.6.1944	N	Survived the war
DB-116				16.6.1944	N	Survived the war
DB-151				24.8.1945	B	Survived the war
DB-152				24.8.1945	B	Survived the war
DB-153				24.8.1945	B	Survived the war
DB-154				24.8.1945	B	Survived the war
DB-155				24.8.1945	B	Survived the war
DB-156				24.8.1945	B	Survived the war
DB-609				6.12.1945	B	Survived the war
DB-610				6.12.1945	B	Survived the war
DB-611				6.12.1945	B	Survived the war
DB-612				6.12.1945	B	Survived the war
DB-619				6.12.1945	B	Survived the war
DB-620				6.12.1945	B	Survived the war
DMB-01	MB-1 DB-1[1]		301	8.10.1942	Cs BS	Trfd 29.1.1943 to the Black Sea Fleet. Sank 25.2.1943 flooded off Gelendzhik
DMB-02	MB-2 DB-2[1]		302	8.10.1942	Cs BS	Trfd 29.1.1943 to the Black Sea Fleet. Survived the war
DMB-03	MB-3 DB-3[1]		303	8.10.1942	Cs BS	Trfd 29.1.1943 to the Black Sea Fleet. Sunk 10.9.1943 by artillery fire off Novorossiysk
DMB-04	MB-4 DB-4[1]		304	8.10.1942	Cs BS	Trfd 29.1.1943 to the Black Sea Fleet. Survived the war
DMB-05	MB-5 DB-5[1]		305	8.10.1942	Cs BS	Trfd 29.1.1943 to the Black Sea Fleet. Sunk 23.4.1943 by artillery fire off Myschako
DMB-06	MB-6 DB-6[1]		306	8.10.1942	Cs BS	Trfd 29.1.1943 to the Black Sea Fleet. Stranded 23.6.1943 off Myschako, destroyed by heavy seas
DMB-07	MB-7 DB-7[1]		307	8.10.1942	Cs BS	Trfd 29.1.1943 to the Black Sea Fleet. Sank 8.11.1943 in a gale off Eltigen
DMB-08	MB-8 DB-8[1]		308	8.10.1942	Cs BS	Trfd 29.1.1943 to the Black Sea Fleet. Sunk 1.11.1943 by artillery fire off Eltigen
DMB-09	MB-9 DB-9[1]		309	8.10.1942	Cs BS	Trfd 29.1.1943 to the Black Sea Fleet. Deleted 25.6.1943 because of damage
DMB-10	MB-10 DB-10[1]		310	8.10.1942	Cs BS	Trfd 29.1.1943 to the Black Sea Fleet. Sank 6.3.1943 in a gale off Myschako

No on Comm	No 29.1.1943	No 25.6.1943	No 21.6.1944	YN	Comm	Fleet	Remarks
DMB-11	MB-11 DB-11[1]			312	8.10.1942	Cs BS	Trfd 29.1.1943 to the Black Sea Fleet. Sunk 1.11.1943 by mine off the Tuzla Spit
DMB-12	MB-12 DB-12[1]		KT-649	313	8.10.1942	Cs BS	Trfd 29.1.1943 to the Black Sea Fleet. Conv 26.6.1943 to minesweeping boat. Deleted 31.12.1945
DMB-13	MB-13 DB-13[1]			314	8.10.1942	Cs BS	Trfd 29.1.1943 to the Black Sea Fleet. Sunk 26.9.1943 by mine off Anapa
DMB-14	MB-14 DB-14[1]			315	8.10.1942	Cs BS	Trfd 29.1.1943 to the Black Sea Fleet. Sunk 1.11.1943 by artillery fire off Eltigen
AA defence boats							
PVO-10				351	24.6.1943	Vo BS	Trfd 21.10.1943 to the Black Sea Fleet. Sunk 17.11.1943 by mine off Cape Panagia
PVO-11			KATShch-224[5] KT-224	352	24.6.1943	Vo BS	Trfd 21.10.1943 to the Black Sea Fleet. Sank 6.12.1943 in a gale off Taman, raised and recomm. Conv 18.4.1944 to minesweeping boat. Conv 31.12.1945 to service craft *Raz"ezdnoj kater № 261*
PVO-12				353	24.6.1943	Vo BS	Trfd 21.10.1943 to the Black Sea Fleet. Sunk 21.11.1943 by artillery fire off Eltigen
PVO-13			KATShch-225[5]	357	24.6.1943	Vo BS	Trfd 21.10.1943 to the Black Sea Fleet. Conv 18.4.1944 to minesweeping boat. Deleted 21.6.1944, presumably lost
PVO-14			KATShch-226[5]	362	24.6.1943	Vo BS	Trfd 21.10.1943 to the Black Sea Fleet. Conv 18.4.1944 to minesweeping boat. Deleted 21.6.1944, presumably lost
PVO-15			KATShch-227[5]	371	24.6.1943	Vo BS	Trfd 21.10.1943 to the Black Sea Fleet. Conv 18.4.1944 to minesweeping boat. Sunk 2.5.1944 by mine off Kerch

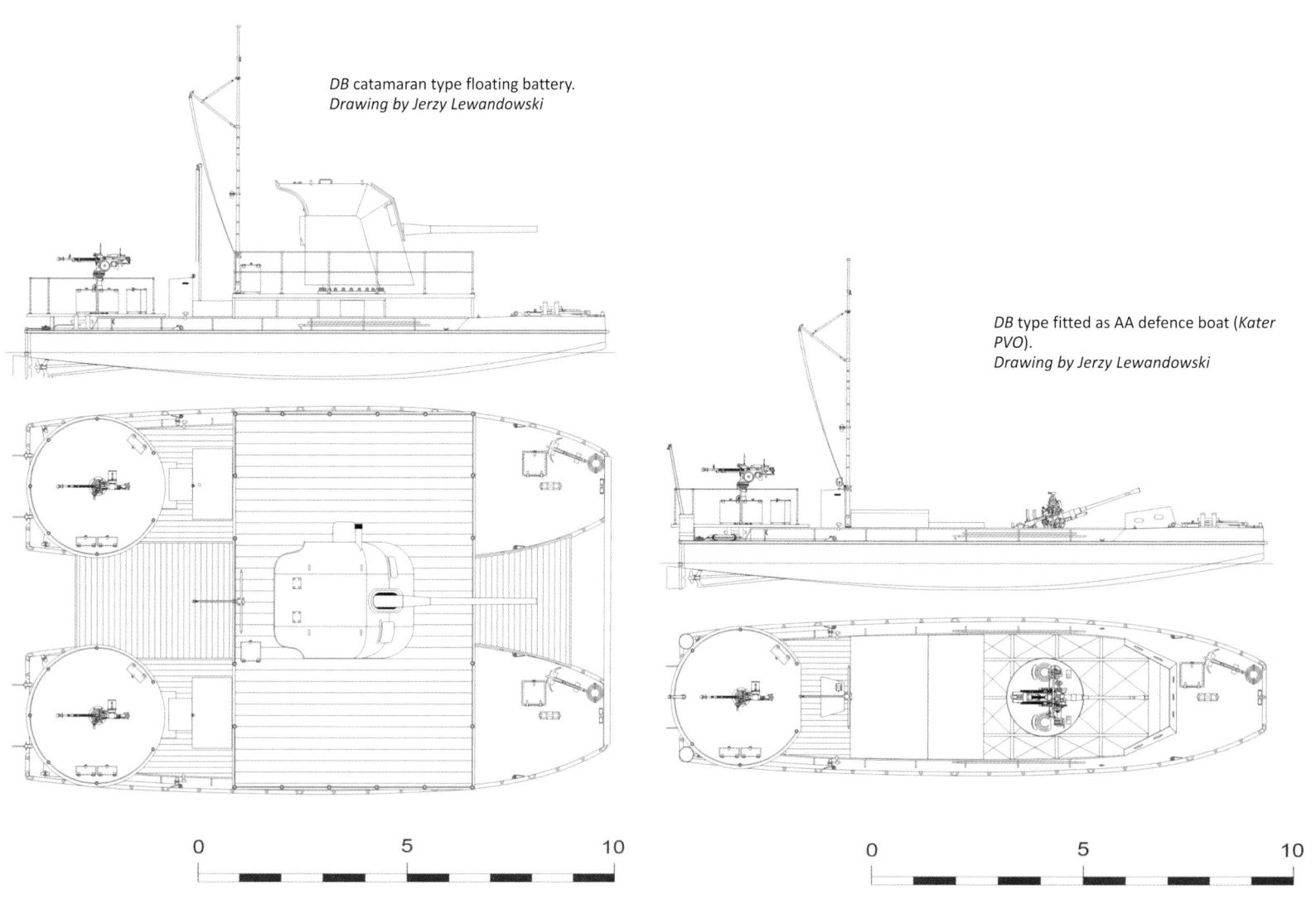

DB catamaran type floating battery.
Drawing by Jerzy Lewandowski

DB type fitted as AA defence boat (*Kater PVO*).
Drawing by Jerzy Lewandowski

PVO-11 AA conversion of the *DB* type landing craft.
Boris Lemachko Collection

PVO-16	KATShch-228[5] KT-228	377	24.6.1943	Vo BS	Trfd 21.10.1943 to the Black Sea Fleet. Conv 18.4.1944 to minesweeping boat. Conv 31.12.1945 to service craft *Raz"ezdnoj kater № 262*
PVO-17	KATShch-229[5] KT229	378	24.6.1943	Vo BS	Trfd 21.10.1943 to the Black Sea Fleet. Conv 18.4.1944 to minesweeping boat. Deleted 17.6.1947
PVO-18	KATShch-230[5] KT-230	379	24.6.1943	Vo BS	Trfd 21.10.1943 to the Black Sea Fleet. Conv 18.4.1944 to minesweeping boat. Deleted 17.6.1947
PVO-19	KATShch-231[5] KT-231	380	24.6.1943	Vo BS	Trfd 21.10.1943 to the Black Sea Fleet. Conv 18.4.1944 to minesweeping boat. Conv 31.12.1945 to service craft *Raz"ezdnoj kater № 248*
PVO-20		354	24.6.1943	Vo Dn BS	Trfd 14.9.1943 to the Dnieper Flotilla. Trfd 21.10.1943 to the Black Sea Fleet. Sunk 21.11.1943 by artillery fire off Eltigen
PVO-21		356	24.6.1943	Vo Dn BS	Trfd 14.9.1943 to the Dnieper Flotilla. Trfd 21.10.1943 to the Black Sea Fleet. Sank 10.1.1944 in a gale of Cape Tarchan
PVO-22		361	24.6.1943	Vo Dn BS	Trfd 14.9.1943 to the Dnieper Flotilla. Trfd 21.10.1943 to the Black Sea Fleet. Sank 21.11.1943 in a gale off the Tulza Spit
PVO-23	KATShch-233[5] KT-233	364	24.6.1943	Vo Dn BS	Trfd 14.9.1943 to the Dnieper Flotilla. Trfd 21.10.1943 to the Black Sea Fleet. Conv 18.4.1944 to minesweeping boat. Conv 20.3.1948 to service craft *Raz"ezdnoj kater № 398*
PVO-24		367	24.6.1943	Vo Dn BS	Trfd 14.9.1943 to the Dnieper Flotilla. Trfd 21.10.1943 to the Black Sea Fleet. Sunk 26.11.1943 rammed by German warship
PVO-25	KATShch-234[5] KT-234	368	24.6.1943	Vo Dn BS	Trfd 14.9.1943 to the Dnieper Flotilla. Trfd 21.10.1943 to the Black Sea Fleet. Sunk 7.12.1943 in a gale, raised and recomm. Conv 18.4.1944 to minesweeping boat. Conv 31.12.1945 to service craft *Raz"ezdnoj kater № 264*
PVO-26		369	24.6.1943	Vo Dn BS	Trfd 14.9.1943 to the Dnieper Flotilla. Trfd 21.10.1943 to the Black Sea Fleet. Sank 15.11.1943 in a gale off the Tuzla Spit
PVO-27		370	24.6.1943	Vo Dn BS	Trfd 14.9.1943 to the Dnieper Flotilla. Trfd 21.10.1943 to the Black Sea Fleet. Sunk 23.11.1943 by German warships in the Kerch Strait
PVO-61			30.6.1944	Dn	Survived the war
PVO-62			30.6.1944	Dn	Survived the war
PVO-63			30.6.1944	Dn	Survived the war
PVO-64			30.6.1944	Dn	Survived the war

No on Comm	No 29.1.1943	No 25.6.1943	No 21.6.1944	YN	Comm	Fleet	Remarks
PVO-65					30.6.1944	Dn	Survived the war
PVO-66					30.6.1944	Dn	Survived the war
PVO-67					30.6.1944	Dn	Survived the war
PVO-68					30.6.1944	Dn	Survived the war
PVO-69			MK-116[8]		30.8.1944	Dn	Conv 17.9.1945 to armed (rocket) boat. Survived the war
PVO-70			MK-117[8]		30.8.1944	Dn	Conv 17.9.1945 to armed (rocket) boat. Survived the war
PVO-71					30.8.1944	Dn	Survived the war
PVO-72					30.8.1944	Dn	Survived the war
PVO-73 – PVO-80					30.8.1944	Dn	Survived the war
Minesweeping boats							
		KT-241 – KT-247			24.5.1944	BS	Survived the war
		KT-260 – KT-262			24.5.1944	BS	Survived the war

Floating AA batteries (PZB)
Floating atrillery batteries (PAB)

PZB № No on Comm	PVO № 2.6.1943	PVO № 24.6.1943	No 21.6.1944	YN	Comm	Fleet	Remarks
№ 1220			PAB-1220[6]		6.7.1943	Vo Dn	Rated as AA battery on completion. Trfd 14.9.1943 to the Dnieper Flotilla. Rated 14.9.1944 as floating artillery battery. Survived the war
№ 1221	№ 1221	PVO-28[2]	KATShch-234[5] KT-234		19.5.1943	Vo Dn BS	Rated as AA battery on completion, rated 2.6.1943 as AA defence boat PVO № 1221. Trfd 14.9.1943 to the Dnieper Flotilla. Trfd 21.10.1943 to the Black Sea Fleet. Conv 18.4.1944 to minesweeping boat. Survived the war
№ 1222	№ 1222	PVO-29[2]			19.5.1943	Vo Dn BS	Rated as AA battery on completion, rated 2.6.1943 as AA defence PVO № 1222. Trfd 14.9.1943 to the Dnieper Flotilla. Trfd 21.10.1943 to the Black Sea Fleet. Sunk 6.12.1943 by artillery fire off Taman, raised and recomm. Survived the war
№ 1223					16.8.1943	Vo On	Rated as AA battery. Trfd 12.4.1944 to the Onega Flotilla. Conv July 1944 to service craft
№ 1224					16.8.1943	Vo On	Rated as AA battery. Trfd 12.4.1944 to the Onega Flotilla. Conv July 1944 to service craft
PAB-1225					1943	Dn	Survived the war
PAB-1226					1943	Dn	Survived the war
PAB-1227					1943	Dn	Survived the war
PAB-1228					1943	Dn	Survived the war

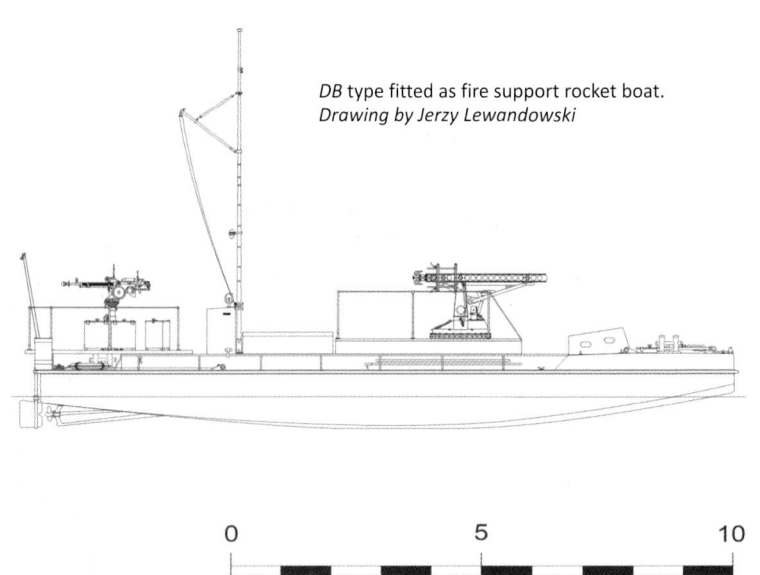

DB type fitted as fire support rocket boat. Drawing by Jerzy Lewandowski

Close up of a *DB* type landing craft AA conversion. Vitalij Kostrichenko Collection

PAB-1229		1943	Dn	Survived the war
PAB-1271		31.10.1944	Dn	Survived the war
PAB-1272		31.10.1944	Dn	Survived the war
PAB-1273		31.10.1944	Dn	Survived the war

Exceptions noted in the main table.

No	Year	Date	Fleet
1	1943	29.3.1943	BS
3		31.8.1943	Vo
4		18.11.1943	BS
5	1944	18.4.1944	BS
6		19.4.1944	Dn
7		26.12.1944	Dn
8	1945	17.9.1945	Dn
9		16.11.1945	BS

Rudimentary steel-hulled utility craft designed in early 1942 to provide disembarking capability on a bare sandy, muddy or rocky shore. Seaworthiness was limited to moderate sea at a distance up to 20 miles from a shoreline. DB stands for Desantnyj bot = Landing boat.

Wartime limited materiel supply enforced use of waste material like 400mm wide steel sheets for the hull or variety of car or truck engines for propulsion, the latter determining the one- or two-shaft arrangement. Following early combat experience with the initial series built in 1942, from autumn 1943 series production added a shield erected around steering wheel and reversible couplings to allow withdrawal astern after beaching.

The following basic configurations were built:

- landing boats without armament or armed with 1-0.5in DShK MG: 99 hulls
- AA defence boats armed with 1-37mm AA gun mounted on the foundation at bottom of the hold: 40 hulls
- artillery batteries of two hulls connected with wooden platform between and stiffened by a beam at bows with a platform for 100mm gun built above the holds: 26 hulls connected in 13 catamaran units.

They underwent several modifications, some of them of purely temporary nature:

- two hulls connected by a wooden platform placed atop and fitted with a ramp up to the bow to allow transportation of large artillery pieces or light tanks – temporary solution
- installation of a winch for the KT type sweep on a deck aft – minesweeper conversion
- installation of the M-8-M rocket launcher on a platform above the hold – rocket boat conversion

Based on the *Project 165* design, a dozen wooden-hulled landing boats were built at the repair workshops of the Black Sea Fleet.

DB type AA conversion as a monument. Note the 20mm Oerlikon gun in the position usually occupied by a DShK MG. Boris Lemachko Collection

DB type floating battery conversions. *Gangut*

DMB-100 type
Landing motorboats

Displacement: 20t full load
Dimensions: 13.6 x 3.85 x 0.4m
Machinery: 1-shaft Continental petrol engine, 105hp = 9kts. Range 180nm at 4kts
Armament: 1 KAT sweep from May 1944
Load: 10.5t, 100 troops
Complement: 4

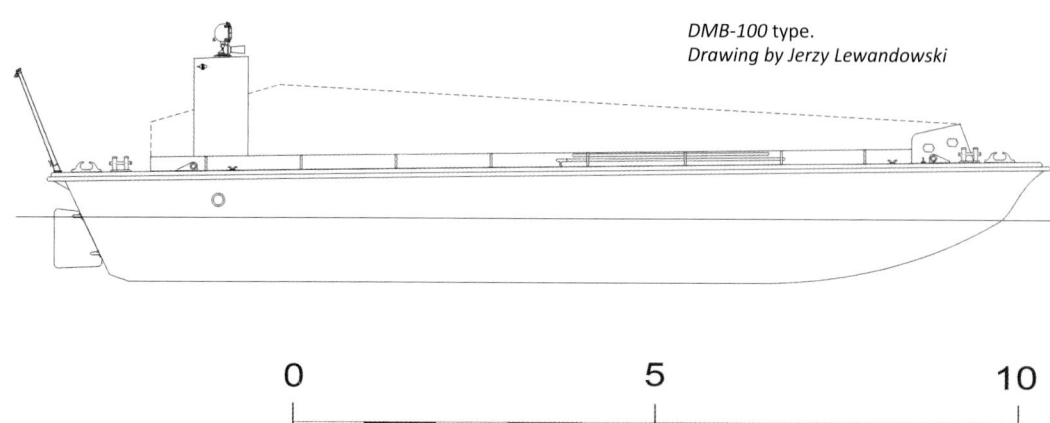

DMB-100 type.
Drawing by Jerzy Lewandowski

No	No	Comm	Fleet	Remarks
		24.5.1944		
Builder: 343, Gorokhovets				
DMB-2 – DMB-13	KT-248 – KT-259	28.1.1944	BS	Survived the war
	KT-520	21.6.1944	BS	Survived the war
	KT-528 – KT-530	21.6.1944	BS	Survived the war
	KT-534 – KT-538	21.6.1944	BS	Survived the war
	KT-541 – KT-543	21.6.1944	BS	Survived the war
	KT-553 – KT-557	21.6.1944	BS	Survived the war
	KT-577 – KT-579	21.6.1944	BS	Survived the war
	KT-598 – KT-599	21.6.1944	BS	Survived the war
	KT-805 – KT-806	21.6.1944	BS	Survived the war

The follow-up design to the *Project 165* landing craft, enlarged to improve seakeeping. DMB stands for Desantnyj Morskoj Bot = Seagoing Landing Craft, 100 for the troop capacity. All were converted to minesweeping boat following cessation of hostilities at the Black Sea.

A and G classes
Dumb landing craft

Class	A	G	G
Type	Landing craft	Landing craft	Floating AA battery
Displacement (full):	1055t	591t	
Length:	68.5m	90.6m	
Beam:	14.5m	15.0m	
Draught:	1.3m	0.5m	
Auxiliary engine:	30hp	30hp	
Armament:	-	-	4-85mm/52 (52-K), 6-37mm/67.5 70-K, 8-0.5in MGs

PZB №	No	Type	Built	Comm	Fleet	Remarks
	DB-61	A	1941	10.12.1941	Am	Survived the war
	DB-62	A	1941	10.12.1941	Am	Survived the war
	DB-63	A	1941	10.12.1941	Am	Survived the war
	DB-64	A	1941	10.12.1941	Am	Survived the war
	DB-65	G	1941	10.12.1941	Am	Survived the war
	DB-67	A	1941	10.12.1941	Am	Survived the war
№ 1230		G	1943	29.8.1941	Am	Survived the war
№ 1231		G	1943	29.8.1941	Am	Survived the war
№ 1233		G	1943	29.8.1941	Am	Survived the war

Non-propelled landing craft; three were completed as AA batteries.

21.2. Lend-lease ships

US LCI(L) type
Landing ships

Displacement: 238t standard, 395t full load
Dimensions: 48.9 x 7.2 x 1.8m (aft)
Machinery: 2-shaft, eight Detroit diesels 6051 quad-71, 1600hp =16kts. Oil fuel 120t, range 6500nm at 11kts (with extra fuel in place of troops and cargo)
Armament: 5-20 mm/70 Oerlikon
Load: 75t of load, 210 troops
Complement: 27

Data according to Russian sources

No	Builder	Comp	Taken over	Comm	Fleet	Remarks
DS-1 ex-*LCI-672* (US, 1945)	Lawley	1944	27.7.1945	28.7.1945	P	Sunk 18.8.1945 by artillery fire at Shumshu Island
DS-2 ex-*LCI-522* (US, 1945)	NJ Ship	1944	27.7.1945	28.7.1945	P	Rated 12.1.1949 as landing ship *DK-104*. Deleted 23.3.1955 returned to the US at Maizuru (Japan)
DS-3 ex-*LCI-523* (US, 1945)	NJ Ship	1944	27.7.1945	28.7.1945	P	Sunk 18.8.1945 by artillery fire at Shumshu Island. Raised and recomm. Rated 12.1.1949 as landing ship *DK-105*. Deleted 23.3.1955 returned to the US at Maizuru (Japan)
DS-4 ex-*LCI-524* (US, 1945)	NJ Ship	1944	27.7.1945	28.7.1945	P	Rated 12.1.1949 as landing ship *DK-106*. Deleted 23.3.1955 returned to the US at Maizuru (Japan)
DS-5 ex-*LCI-525* (US, 1945)	NJ Ship	1944	27.7.1945	28.7.1945	P	Sunk 18.8.1945 by artillery fire at Shumshu Island
DS-6 ex-*LCI-945* (US, 1945)	Consolidated	1944	27.7.1945	28.7.1945	P	Rated 12.1.1949 as landing ship *DK-107*. Deleted 23.3.1955 returned to the US at Maizuru (Japan)
DS-7 ex-*LCI-469* (US, 1945)	NJ Ship	1944	27.7.1945	28.7.1945	P	Rated 12.1.1949 as landing ship *DK-91*. Deleted 23.3.1955 returned to the US at Maizuru (Japan)
DS-8 ex-*LCI-521* (US, 1945)	NJ Ship	1944	27.7.1945	28.7.1945	P	Sunk 18.8.1945 by artillery fire at Shumshu Island. Rated 12.1.1949 as landing ship *DK-92*. Deleted 23.3.1955 returned to the US at Maizuru (Japan)
DS-9 ex-*LCI-554* (US, 1945)	NJ Ship	1944	27.7.1945	28.7.1945	P	Sunk 18.8.1945 by artillery fire at Shumshu Island
DS-10 ex-*LCI-557* (US, 1945)	NJ Ship	1944	27.7.1945	28.7.1945	P	Rated 12.1.1949 as landing ship *DK-93*. Deleted 23.3.1955 returned to the US at Maizuru (Japan)
DS-31 ex-*LCI-593* (US, 1945)	NJ Ship	1944	10.6.1945	27.6.1945	P	Rated 12.1.1949 as landing ship *DK-31*. Laid up 31.7.1954. Deleted 11.7.1956, BU
DS-32 ex-*LCI-950* (US, 1945)	Consolidated	1944	10.6.1945	27.6.1945	P	Rated 12.1.1949 as landing ship *DK-32*. Laid up 31.7.1954. Deleted 11.7.1956, BU
DS-33 ex-*LCI-587* (US, 1945)	NJ Ship	1944	13.6.1945	27.6.1945	P	Rated 12.1.1949 as landing ship *DK-33*. Laid up 1.9.1955. Deleted 11.7.1956, BU
DS-34 ex-*LCI-590* (US, 1945)	NJ Ship	1944	9.6.1945	27.6.1945	P	Rated 12.1.1949 as landing ship *DK-34*. Deleted 23.4.1955 returned to the US at Maizuru (Japan)
DS-35 ex-*LCI-591* (US, 1945)	NJ Ship	1944	9.6.1945	27.6.1945	P	Rated 12.1.1949 as landing ship *DK-35*. Laid up 1.9.1955. Deleted 11.7.1956, BU
DS-36 ex-*LCI-665* (US, 1945)	Lawley	1944	13.6.1945	27.6.1945	P	Rated 12.1.1949 as landing ship *DK-36*. Deleted 26.7.1955 returned to the US at Maizuru (Japan)
DS-37 ex-*LCI-586* (US, 1945)	NJ Ship	1944	13.6.1945	27.6.1945	P	Rated 12.1.1949 as landing ship *DK-37*. Conv 26.11.1953 to accomodation hulk *PKZ-91*. Deleted 11.7.1956, BU
DS-38 ex-*LCI-584* (US, 1945)	NJ Ship	1944	9.6.1945	27.6.1945	P	Rated 12.1.1949 as landing ship *DK-38*. Laid up 1.9.1955. Deleted 11.7.1956, BU
DS-39 ex-*LCI-592* (US, 1945)	NJ Ship	1944	13.6.1945	27.6.1945	P	Rated 12.1.1949 as landing ship *DK-39*. Laid up 1.9.1955. Deleted 11.7.1956, BU
DS-40 ex-*LCI-667* (US, 1945)	Lawley	1944	9.6.1945	27.6.1945	P	Rated 12.1.1949 as landing ship *DK-40*. Deleted 26.7.1955 returned to the US at Maizuru (Japan)
DS-41 ex-*LCI-668* (US, 1945)	Lawley	1944	9.6.1945	27.6.1945	P	Rated 12.1.1949 as landing ship *DK-41*. Laid up 1.9.1955. Deleted 11.7.1956, BU
DS-42 ex-*LCI-675* (US, 1945)	Lawley	1944	9.6.1945	27.6.1945	P	Sunk 18.8.1945 by artillery fire at Shumshu Island. Raised and recomm. Laid up 1.9.1955. Deleted 11.7.1956, BU
DS-43 ex-*LCI-943* (US, 1945)	Consolidated	1944	9.6.1945	22.6.1945	P	Sunk 18.8.1945 by artillery fire at Shumshu Island
DS-44 ex-*LCI-949* (US, 1945)	Consolidated	1944	9.6.1945	22.6.1945	P	Rated 12.1.1949 as landing ship *DK-44*. Deleted 26.7.1955 returned to the US at Maizuru (Japan)

Warships of the Soviet Fleets, 1939–1945

No	Builder	Comp	Taken over	Comm	Fleet	Remarks
DS-45 ex-*LCI-585* (US, 1945)	NJ Ship	1944	9.6.1945	27.6.1945	P	Rated 12.1.1949 as landing ship *DK-45*. Deleted 26.7.1955 returned to the US at Maizuru (Japan)
DS-46 ex-*LCI-526* (US, 1945)	NJ Ship	1944	27.7.1945	28.6.1945	P	Rated 12.1.1949 as landing ship *DK-94*. Laid up 28.11.1953. Deleted 26.7.1955 returned to the US at Maizuru (Japan)
DS-47 ex-*LCI-671* (US, 1945)	Lawley	1944	27.7.1945	28.6.1945	P	Sunk 18.8.1945 by artillery fire at Shumshu Island
DS-48 ex-*LCI-551* (US, 1945)	NJ Ship	1944	27.7.1945	28.6.1945	P	Rated 12.1.1949 as landing ship *DK-95*. Laid up 28.11.1953. Deleted 26.7.1955 returned to the US at Maizuru (Japan)
DS-49 ex-*LCI-946* (US, 1945)	Consolidated	1944	27.7.1945	28.6.1945	P	Rated 12.1.1949 as landing ship *DK-96*. Laid up 28.11.1953. Deleted 26.7.1955 returned to the US at Maizuru (Japan)
DS-50 ex-*LCI-666* (US, 1945)	Lawley	1944	27.7.1945	28.6.1945	P	Rated 12.1.1949 as landing ship *DK-50*. Conv 28.11.1953 to accommodation hulk *PKZ-92*. Deleted 11.7.1956, BU

Thirty trfd to the Soviet Union under Project Hula in anticipation of the Soviets eventually joining the war against Japan, specifically in preparation for planned Soviet invasions of southern Sakhalin and the Kurils. Of them *DS-1–DS-10, DS-43, DS-46* and *DS-48* participated in landing operations in the Kurils, the remaining ones in invasion of Korea.

Above: US and British landing craft in the Naples area prior to a practice landing in Italy, 24.7.1944. *LCI-591* later became Soviet *DS-35*. The landing craft were highly prized during the closing stages of the war. Of those pictured here, four more were also transferred to the Soviet Union in 1945.
Naval History and Heritage Command SC 192675

Right top: *DS-9* (ex-*LCI-554*) wrecked at Shumshu Island with another in the background. Note the US hull number displayed.
Boris Lemachko Collection

Right middle: The LCI *DS-5* (ex-*LCI-525*) wrecked at Shumshu Island. Note the US hull number displayed at the stern.
Boris Lemachko Collection

Right below: A propaganda photo of Soviet *Morskaia pekhota* troops onboard an LCI type craft. Note camouflage painting.
Przemysław Budzbon Collection

US **LCT Mk 6** type *Landing ships*

Displacement: 286t full load
Dimensions: 36.4 x 10.0 x 0.9m (forward)
Machinery: 3-shaft Gray marine diesels, 675hp = 8kts. Range 700nm at 6kts
Armament: 2-20mm Oerlikon
Load: 150t load: 5 *T-34* type tanks or 350 troops with 2 or 3 45mm field guns
Complement: 19

Data according to Russian sources.

Thirteen trfd to the Soviet Union under the Project Hula in anticipation of the Soviets eventually joining the war against Japan, specifically in preparation for planned Soviet invasions of southern Sakhalin and the Kurils. The Pacific Fleet craft took part in the invasion of the Kurils.

LCT-559 (comp 1943) and *LCT-1015* (comp 1944) by Bison reportedly trfd to the Soviet Union, but not mentioned by Russian sources.

No	Builder	Comp	Taken over	Comm	Fleet	Remarks
DS-11 ex-*LCT-1047* (US, 1945)	Bison	1944	15.4.1945	28.7.1945	P	Rated 12.1.1949 as landing ship *DK-97*. Conv 28.11.1953 to dumb lighter *BSN-456311*. Deleted mid-1950s, BU
DS-12 ex-*LCT-561* (US, 1945)	Bison	1944	24.5.1945	28.7.1945	P	Conv 20.6.1947 to surveying vessel *Magnit*. Deleted 11.7.1956, BU
DS-13 ex-*LCT-1438* (US, 1945)	Bison	1944	26.5.1945	28.7.1945	P	Rated 12.1.1949 as landing ship *DK-98*. Laid up 1.9.1955. Deleted 25.6.1956, scuttled in the Strait of Tartary
DS-14 ex-*LCT-1046* (US, 1945)	Bison	1944	24.5.1945	28.7.1945	P	Rated 12.1.1949 as landing ship *DK-99*. Conv 1.9.1955 to dumb lighter *BSN-48120*. Deleted late 1950s, BU
DS-15 ex-*LCT-1442* (US, 1945)	Bison	1944	24.5.1945	28.7.1945	P	Rated 12.1.1949 as landing ship *DK-102*. Laid up 2.11.1953. Deleted 25.6.1956, scuttled in the Strait of Tartary
DS-16 ex-*LCT-1445* (US, 1945)	Bison	1944	24.5.1945	28.7.1945	P	Rated 12.1.1949 as landing ship *DK-103*. Laid up 2.11.1953. Deleted 11.7.1956, BU
DS-17 ex-*LCT-1434* (US, 1945)	Bison	1944	26.5.1945	28.7.1945	P	Rated 12.1.1949 as landing ship *DK-108*. Conv 1.2.1954 to transport barge *BSS-68263*. Conv 3.12.1955 to landing stage, deleted 4.7.1956, BU
DS-18 ex-*LCT-1435* (US, 1945)	Bison	1944	26.5.1945	28.7.1945	P	Rated 12.1.1949 as landing ship *DK-109*. Conv 1.2.1954 to transport barge *BSS-69263*. Deleted 25.6.1956, scuttled in the Strait of Tartary
DS-19 ex-*LCT-1436* (US, 1945)	Bison	1944	26.5.1945	28.7.1945	P	Rated 12.1.1949 as landing ship *DK-110*. Conv 1.2.1954 to transport barge *BSS-70263*. Deleted 25.6.1956, scuttled in the Strait of Tartary
DS-20 ex-*LCT-1437* (US, 1945)	Bison	1944	26.5.1945	28.7.1945	P	Rated 12.1.1949 as landing ship *DK-111*. Conv 1.2.1954 to transport barge *BSS-71263*. Laid up 3.12.1955. Deleted 25.6.1956, scuttled in the Strait of Tartary
DS-101 ex-*LCT-563?* (US, 1945)	Bison	1944	24.5.1945	27.11.1945	BS	Rated 12.1.1949 as landing ship *DK-81*, rated 12.2.1954 as tank transport *TDS-138*. Laid up 11.7.1956. Conv 12.1.1957 to ammunition barge *BAMT-81140*. Deleted 20.3.1959, BU
DT-1 ex-*LCT-1163* (US, 1945)	Bison	1944	20.8.1945	14.6.1945	N	Rated 12.1.1949 as landing ship *DK-351*. Laid up 28.2.1948, conv 28.3.1953 to dumb lighter *BSN-444100*. Deleted mid-1950s, BU
DT-2 ex-*LCT-1176* (US, 1945)	Bison	1944	20.8.1945	14.6.1945	N	Rated 12.1.1949 as landing ship *DK-352*. Laid up 28.2.1948, conv 28.3.1953 to dumb lighter *BSN-445100*. Deleted mid-1950s, BU

LCM / LCV / LCP types *Landing craft*

Type	LCM Mk1	LCV(P)	LCP(L)
Displacement (full):	19t	11t	12t
Length:	13.7m	11.0m	11.2m
Beam:	4.3m	3.3m	3.2m
Draught:	1.4m	0.9m	1.1m
Shafts	2	1	1
Total power:	120hp	250hp	450hp
Seed (max):	8.5kts	9kts	11kts
MGs:	2-0.303in Lewis	-	1 or 2-0.303in

No	Inventory No on delivery	Type	Comm	Fleet	Remarks
DB-201	29301	LCM	6.5.1945	N	Rated 12.1.1949 as landing boat *KD-201*. Converted 11.4.1952 to service craft. Deleted mid-1950s
DB-202	29309	LCM	6.5.1945	N	Deleted 28.8.1948 to civilian service
DB-203	42116	LCV	6.5.1945	N	Rated 12.1.1949 as landing boat *KD-203*. Converted 11.4.1952 to service craft. Deleted mid-1950s
DB-204	42737	LCV	6.5.1945	N	Rated 12.1.1949 as landing boat *KD-204*. Converted 11.4.1952 to service craft. Deleted mid-1950s
SK-301	7653	LPC	31.5.1945	N	Laid up 18.11.1947. Deleted 10.6.1955
SK-302	51393	LPC	31.5.1945	N	Laid up 18.11.1947. Deleted 10.6.1955

21.3. War prizes 1943-1945

No	Details	Comm	Fleet	Remarks
BDB-1 ex-*F-328* (Ger, 1944)	250t; 51.3 x 6.5 x 1.2m; 396hp = 10kts; 700nm at 7kts; 1-3in, 1-45mm/ 46 21-K, 3-0.5in MGs; 32 men	4.2.1944	BS	German *MFP* A type. Sunk 27.5.1943 by Soviet aircraft on Lake Solyonoe. Raised autumn 1943, repaired. Training ship from 12.9.1945, decomm 6.10.1945 to civilian service. Conv to cargo barge, renamed *Krymskaia* on 13.2.1953. Discarded late 1950s
BDB-2 ex-*F-406* (Ger, 1944)		20.10.1944	BS	German *MFP* C type. Scuttled 14.9.1944 by the Germans off Ochakov, captured and comm. Detached 3.1.1945 to civilian service, returned 31.2.1945. Conv 20.4.1945 to transport barge *ChF-118150*, renumbered *BSS-30150* on 16.5.1949. Deleted 20.6.1961
BDB-3 ex-*F-848* (Ger, 1944)		20.10.1944	BS	German *MFP* D type. Stranded 28.5.1944 off Varna, captured Sept 1945, raised and comm. Rated 12.1.1949 as landing ship *DK-82*, conv 4.12.1956 to ammunition barge *BAMT-47110*. Deleted early 1960
BDB-4 ex-• (Bul, 1944) ex-*F-851* (Ger, 1944)		20.10.1944	BS	German *MFP* D type. Trfd 28.8.1944 by the Germans to Bulgaria at Varna, captured 9.9.1944. Rated 12.1.1949 as landing ship *DK-4*, rated 9.11.1956 as landing craft *BSS-113110*. Deleted early 1960
BDB-5 ex-*F-852* (Ger, 1944)		20.10.1944	BS	German *MFP* D type. Trfd 28.8.1944 by the Germans to Bulgaria at Varna, captured 9.9.1944. Rated 12.1.1949 as landing ship *DK-83*. Conv 18.8.1956 to service craft, conv 4.12.1956 to experimental vessel *OS-17*. Deleted 12.2.1960.
BDB-6 ex-*F-900* (Ger, 1944)		20.10.1944	BS	German *MFP* D type. Trfd 28.8.1944 by the Germans to Bulgaria at Varna, captured 9.9.1944. Rated 12.1.1949 as landing ship *DK-84*, conv 4.12.1956 to ammunition barge *BAMT-46110*. Deleted 5.9.1957, trfd to the air force.
BDB-7 ex-*F-901* (Ger, 1944)		20.10.1944	BS	German *MFP* D type. Trfd 28.8.1944 by the Germans to Bulgaria at Varna, captured 9.9.1944. Rated 12.1.1949 as landing ship *DK-7*. Conv 24.5.1957 to experimental vessel *OS-22*. Deleted 29.11.1958, to civilian service
BDB-8 ex-*F-312* (Ger, 1944)		20.10.1944	BS	German *MFP* A type. Sunk 28.8.1944 by Soviet aircraft at Varna. Captured Sept 1944, repaired and recomm. Detached 14.11.1944 to civilian service, returned 27.3.1945. Conv 24.4.1945 to transport barge *ChF-119150*. Deleted 11.10.1947
BDB-9 ex-*F-325* (Ger, 1944)		20.10.1944	BS	German *MFP* A type. Sunk 28.8.1944 by Soviet aircraft at Varna. Captured Sept 1944, repaired and recomm. Detached 14.11.1944 to civilian service, returned 27.3.1945. Deleted 26.7.1945 to civilian service.
BDB-10 ex-*SM-242* (Ger, 1944) ex-*F-405* (Ger, 1944)		20.10.1944	BS	German *MFP* C type. Captured Sept 1944 at Varna. Detached 14.11.1944 to civilian service, returned 27.3.1945. Deleted 26.7.1945 to civilian service
BDB-11 ex-*F-495* (?) (Ger, 1944)		20.10.1944	BS	German *MFP* C2 type. Captured Sept 1944 at Varna. Detached 30.11.1944 to civilian service, returned 27.3.1945. Conv 24.4.1945 to transport barge *ChF-120150*. Deleted 2.6.1945 to civilian service
BDB-12 ex-*F-128* (Ger, 1944)		20.10.1944	BS	German *MFP* A type. Captured Sept 1944. Detached 30.11.1944 to civilian service, renamed *Tamanskaia* on 26.2.1946. Discarded 1950s
BDB-13 ex-*F-176* (Ger, 1944)		20.10.1944	BS	German *MFP* A type. Sunk 26.2.1943 by Soviet aircraft in the Kerch Strait, wreck raised June 1944 by the Soviets. Temporarily detached to civilian service from 30.11.1944. Conv 24.4.1945 to transport barge *ChF-121150*, conv 23.5.1947 to degaussing station *SBR-4*. Deleted 30.9.1959
BDB-14 ex-• (Ger, 1944)		20.10.1944	BS	German *MFP* type. Captured Sept 1944. Conv 3.1.1945 to service craft
BDB-15 ex-• (Ger, 1944)		20.10.1944	BS	German *MFP* type. Captured Sept 1944. Conv 3.1.1945 to service craft
BDB-16 ex-• (Ger, 1944)		20.10.1944	BS	German *MFP* type. Captured Sept 1944. Conv 3.1.1945 to service craft
BDB-20 ex-*F-575* (Ger, 1944)		30.10.1944	Da	German *MFP* C2 type. Captured 29.8.1944 at the Danube off Sistov. Deleted 28.8.1948 to civilian service. Discarded 1950s
BDB-21 ex-*F-471* (Ger, 1944)		30.10.1944	Da	German *MFP* C type. Sunk 31.8.1944 by Soviet artillery fire at the Danube off Calafat. Raised Sept 1944, comm. Trfd 7.4.1947 to the Black Sea Fleet, deleted 27.11.1948 to civilian service
BDB-25 ex-• (Ger, 1944)		11.5.1945	Da	German *MFP* type. Captured 13.4.1945 at Lintz. Laid up 9.1.1946, recomm and trfd 25.11.1946 to the Black Sea Fleet. Deleted 27.11.1948 to civilian service.
BDB-26 ex-• (Ger, 1944)		11.5.1945	Da	German *MFP* type. Captured 13.4.1945 at Lintz. Laid up 9.1.1946, recomm and trfd 25.11.1946 to the Black Sea Fleet. Rated 12.1.1949 as landing ship *DK-430*. Deleted 31.1.1958.
BDB-27 ex-*F-1023* (Ger, 1944)		11.5.1945	Da	German *MFP* D type. Captured incomplete 13.4.1945 at Lintz, completed by the Soviets. Laid up 10.1.1946, recomm and trfd 25.11.1946 to the Black Sea Fleet.

21.0 Landing vessels and craft

Name	Specs	Date	Fleet	Notes
				Rated 12.1.1949 as landing ship *DK-27*. Conv 4.12.1956 to ammunition barge *BAMT-48110*. Deleted 8.8.1960
BDB-28 ex-*F-1024* (Ger, 1944)		11.5.1945	Da	German *MFP* D type. Captured incomplete 13.4.1945 at Lintz, completed by the Soviets. Laid up 10.1.1946, recomm and trfd 25.11.1946 to the Black Sea Fleet. Rated 12.1.1949 as landing ship *DK-28*. Conv 11.3.1958 to transport barge *BSS-167110*, trfd to the Danube Flotilla. Deleted 10.9.1960
BDB-29 ex-*F-894* (Ger, 1944)		25.6.1945	BS	German *MFP* D type. Scuttled 29.8.1944 off Varna. Raised spring 1945 and comm. Rated 12.1.1949 as landing ship *DK-29*. Conv 24.5.1957 to target ship *Tsl-11*. Deleted 28.1.1958
DB-49 ex-*V-31* (?) (Ger, 1944)		18.12.1944	B	German *MFP* type. Captured 1944 in the Bay of Vyborg
DB-50 ex-*V-1* (?) (Ger, 1944)		18.12.1944	B	German *MFP* type. Captured 1944 in the Bay of Vyborg
DB-51	143t; 68.9 x 14.9 x 2.1m; 640hp = 7.5kts, 350nm; 1-40mm, 2-20mm	5.8.1943	B	German *Siebelfähre*. Captured 22.10.1942 off Suko Island in Lake Ladoga. Trfd 23.9.1944 to the Baltic Fleet
DB-51	29t; 15.0 x 4.65 x 0.7m; 84–90hp = 7.5–8kts; 350nm; 20t load or 100 troops; 6 men	30.10.1944	Dn	German *Labo* types *Pionierlandungsboote*. Captured Sept 1944 on the Danube
DB-52		30.10.1944	Dn	
DB-53		30.10.1944	Dn	
DB-54	50t; 19.0 x 5.9 x 0.75m; 136–180hp = 8–9kts; 415nm; 40t load or 150 troops; 6 men	30.10.1944	Dn	
DB-71	20t; 14.5 x 3.4 x 0.75m; 60hp–150hp = 8kts	13.9.1945	P	Japanese *Daihatsu* types. Captured 22.8.1945 at Port Arthur
DB-72		13.9.1945	P	
DB-73		13.9.1945	P	
DB-74		13.9.1945	P	
DB-75		13.9.1945	P	
DB-76		13.9.1945	P	
DB-77		13.9.1945	P	
DB-78		13.9.1945	P	
DB-137 ex-*No 101* (Fin)	65t; 18.9 x 5.9 x 0.9m; 180hp; 6 men	20.8.1945	B	Finnish landing craft. Trfd from Finland as reparation
DB-138 ex-*No 102* (Fin)		20.8.1945	B	
DB-139 ex-*No 103* (Fin)		20.8.1945	B	
DB-140 ex-*No 104* (Fin)		20.8.1945	B	

BDB stands for Bystrokhodnaia Desantnaia Barzha = Fast Landing Craft

The landing craft *DB-51*, a captured German *Siebelfähre* on Lake Ladoga. Note the mixed armament of German 20mm *Vierling* quadruple guns and the Soviet 37mm 70-K gun abaft the bridge.
Boris Lemachko Collection

Warships of the Soviet Fleets, 1939–1945

Cross reference: Rated as landing ships

No	Name	Details	Type	From	To	Fate
T-451	IVAN BORISOV	*Vladimir Polukhin* class	Minesweepers	13.12.1943	31.8.1949	Comp as minesweeper
T-452	SERGEJ SHUVALOV	*Vladimir Polukhin* class	Minesweepers	13.12.1943	30.8.1949	Comp as minesweeper

Considering the number of amphibious operations undertaken by the Soviet Navy – almost 400,000 troops were disembarked during the war – purpose-built landing ships were far too few to meet the demand. Therefore, most landings were carried out from small combat craft like MTBs, AMGBs or patrol boats and civilian craft of various origins. The photograph at left was taken in Sept 1944 in the Baltic, apparently in the Gulf of Finland. The one at bottom probably in the Arctic.
Boris Lemachko Collection

Index of names in the ship data tables*

1-e Maia 217
3-j vyrishal'nyj 264
5-e dekabria 255
10 let Sovetskoj Turkmenii 151
15 let VLKSM 245
16-ia godovshchina Oktiabria 264
16-j Oktiabr' 245
17-j parts"ezd 264
18-j parts"ezd VKP(b) 217
20 let komsomola 264
20 let Oktiabria 134
25-letnij iubilej VKP(b) 268
A. Rasskin 171
A. Serov 264
Adler 257
Agitator (Minesweeper), 258
Agitator (Minesweeping boat), 269
Ajsberg 28
Akademik Shmidt 258
Akademik Zernov 255
AKO-2 257
Aktivist (Minesweeping boat), 269
Aktivist (River minesweeper), 247
Akula (KATShch-587), 257
Akula (KT-111), 269
Akula (Patrol boat), 125
Akustik 41
Al'batros 16
Aldan 270
Aleksandr Petrov 167
Algarinets 260
Anakriia 130
Anastas Mikoian 217
Andrian Zasimov 167
Antikajnen 203
Ara (Minesweeper), 200
Ara (Patrol boat), 135
Aralets 258
Arkhangel'sk 195
Artillerist 40
Ashkadar 220
Askol'd 35
Astrakhan' (AA defence ship), 149
Astrakhan' (Escort ship), 29
Astrakhan' (Minelayer), 158
Atarbekov 36
Avacha 262
Avangard 136
Aviator 152
Avrora 146
Azov (KATShch-582), 258
Azov (KATShch-611), 257
B-30 – 31 207
B-7 269
Babushkin (Minesweeper), 213
Babushkin (Minesweeping boat), 250
Bajdukov (KATShch-151), 263
Bajdukov (KT-411), 250
Bajdukov (Minesweeper), 213

Bajkal 212
Baken 220
Bakhtemirovets 259
Baklan 195
Balakhna 151
Balmashev 216
Baltvod 218
Barbius 210
Barkas
 № 6 – 7 271
 № 8 (KATShch-302), 272
 № 8 (KATShch-441), 271
 № 21 – 23 270
 № 33 271
 № 37 270
 № 40 – 41 271
 № 42 270
 № 45 271
 № 48 (KATShch-395), 270
 № 48 (KATShch-396), 270
 № 51 271
 № 64 271
 № 69 – 70 270
 № 76 270
 № 82 270
 № 83 (KATShch-372), 270
 № 83 (KATShch-423), 271
 № 86 – 87 271
 № 88 270
 № 92 (KATShch-399), 270
 № 92 (KATShch-413), 271
 № 98 270
 № 104 271
 № 107 271
 № 114 270
 № 131 270
 № 136 272
Batajsk 260
Batumi 29
BDB-1 – 27 294
BDB-28 – 29 295
Beketovets 259
Belek 133
Beliakov (Minesweeper), 210
Beliakov (River minesweeper), 213
Beloberezh'e 225
Belomorets 30
Belomorsk (Minesweeper), 218
Belomorsk (Minesweeping boat), 250
Beluga (Minesweeper), 215
Beluga (Patrol boat), 136
Berkut 16
Bidzhan 162
Bira 162
BK № 8 137
BK-1 – 2 123
BK-4 134
BO-51 – 54 50
BO-147 – 153 44

BO-171 44
BO-172 – 180 46
BO-201 – 220 47
BO-221 – 231 48
BO-232 – 246 49
BO-270 44
BO-301 – 316 49
BO-317 – 329 50
BO-331 – 332 50
BO-335 50
Bodryj 132
Boevoj (AA defence boat), 148
Boevoj (Minesweeper), 215
Boevoj (Patrol boat), 132
Bol'shevik (Escort ship), 38
Bol'shevik (Minesweeper), 195
Bol'shevik (Minesweeping boat), 269
Borets za kommunu 218
Boris Zhemchuzhin 167
Bot
 № 1 268
 № 33 255
 № 50 255
 № 57 256
Botsman 41
BPL-1 201
BPL-36 202
Bravyj 261
Brigadir (Minesweeper), 218
Brigadir (Minesweeping boat), 264
Brilliant 19
Briz (RT-49), 33
Briz (RT-58), 28
Budyonnyj 248
Buek 215
Bugel' 171
Buj 170
Bujrep 165
Buksirnyj parokhod
 № 1 – 2 201
 № 5 (A-35), 203
 № 5 (Osinovets), 201
 № 20 202
 № 21 – 23 203
 № 25 – 27 204
 № 29 – 30 204
 № 31 – 35 205
 № 37 – 38 205
 № 39 206
 № 53 202
 № 63 – 65 206
 № 66 207
 № 69 207
 № 71 207
 № 75 207
 № 81 – 83 202
 № 85 202
 № 582 210
 № 584 210

Buran 33
Burevestnik 134
Bureviestnik 16
Buria 11
Buriat 151
Burun (Escort ship), 11
Burun (Tug), 206
Bystryj 261
Chaj-Gruziia 264
Chajka 257
Chapaev (Minesweeper), 211
Chapaev (Tug), 202
Chasovoj 260
Cheboksary 219
Cheka 170
Chekhon' 257
Cheliabinsk 151
Cheliuskinets 255
Cheliuskinets Pavlov 28
Cheptsa 271
Cherninets 248
Chernomorets 256
Chernyshevskij 216
Chervonyj kazak 224
Chetvyortyj 245
Chetyrnadtsatyj 245
Chicherin 149
Chkalov (AA defence ship), 150
Chkalov (EMTShch-63), 217
Chkalov (Minesweeping boat), 250
Chkalov (River minesweeper), 213
Chkalov (TShch № 132), 210
Chorokh 263
ChTZ-17 151
D-11 223
D-15 223
Dagestanets 150
Dal'nomershchik 41
Danilin 213
Dar'ial 254
Darginets 253
DB-2 – 3 283
DB-13 283
DB-15 – 17 283
DB-18 (YN 326), 283
DB-18 (YN 503), 283
DB-19 (YN 328), 283
DB-19 (YN 505), 283
DB-20 283
DB-21 284
DB-22 (YN 506), 284
DB-22 (YN 332), 284
DB-22 (YN 334), 284
DB-23 (YN 333), 284
DB-23 (YN 355), 284
DB-23 (YN 507), 284
DB-24 – 25 284
DB-26 (YN 338), 284
DB-26 (YN 514), 284

DB-27 (YN 329), 284
DB-27 (YN 515), 284
DB-28 (YN 340), 284
DB-28 (YN 516), 284
DB-29 284
DB-31 – 32 284
DB-33 (YN 355), 284
DB-33 (YN 519), 284
DB-34 (YN 358), 284
DB-34 (YN 509), 284
DB-35 (YN 359), 284
DB-35 (YN 510), 284
DB-35 (YN 520), 285
DB-36 (YN 363), 285
DB-36 (YN 382), 285
DB-37 (YN 365), 285
DB-37 (YN 383), 285
DB-38 – 39 285
DB-40 (YN 384), 285
DB-40 (YN 513), 285
DB-41 – 46 285
DB-47 (YN 502), 285
DB-47 (YN 511), 285
DB-48 (YN 504), 285
DB-48 (YN 512), 285
DB-49 295
DB-50 (ex-*V-1*), 295
DB-50 (Project 165), 285
DB-51 (*Labo* type), 295
DB-51 (*Siebenfähre* type), 295
DB-52 – 54 295
DB-61 – 65 290
DB-67 290
DB-71 – 78 295
DB-111 285
DB-112 (Dn), 285
DB-112 (N), 285
DB-113 (Dn), 285
DB-113 (N), 285
DB-114 (Dn), 285
DB-114 (N), 285
DB-115 – 116 285
DB-137 – 140 295
DB-151 – 156 285
DB-201 – 204 293
DB-609 – 612 285
DB-619 – 620 285
Del'fin (*KT-122*), 261
Del'fin (*KT-267*), 247
Del'fin (Patrol boat), 125
Dengizovets 260
Derbent 252
Desantnyj bot № 1 – 5 282
Desantnyj bot № 6 – 9 283
Dezhnyov 26
Diana 272
Dimitrov (AA defence ship), 150
Dimitrov (Minesweeping boat), 264
Diomid 268
DMB-01 – 09 285
DMB-2 – 9 290
DMB-10 (*DB* type), 286
DMB-10 (*DMB* type), 290
DMB-11 (*DB* type), 286
DMB-11 (*DMB* type), 290

DMB-12 (*DB* type), 286
DMB-12 (*DMB* type), 290
DMB-13 (*DB* type), 286
DMB-13 (*DMB* type), 290
DMB-14 285
Dmitriev 151
Dmitrij Lysov 171
Dnepr 264
Dnestr 255
Dolban 151
Don 218
Doob 160
Doroteia 224
Dozor 271
Drifter
  № 1 – 2 225
  № 111 135
  № 112 – 113 136
  № 276 – 277 135
  № 79 – 80 262
DS-1 – 10 291
DS-11 – 20 293
DS-31 – 44 291
DS-45 – 50 292
DS-101 293
DT-1 – 2 293
Dunaj 268
Dvina (Minesweeper), 199
Dvina (Minesweeping boat), 249
Dvinosplav № 130 267
Dvinosplav № 134 267
DZ-211 – 212 113
DZ-213 – 214 114
DZ-215 – 219 113
DZ-220 114
DZ-221 – 222 113
Dzerzhinskij (*EMTShch-69*), 217
Dzerzhinskij (Patrol ship), 20
Dzerzhinskij (*T-34*), 209
Dzhalita 222
Egurcha 226
Ejna 135
EK-1 – 30 23
Eksportles № 18 – 19 209
Ekvator 145
Elektrik 43
Elista 268
Emel'ian Pugachyov 215
EMTShch-70 – 73 211
EMTShch-631 227
EMTShch-648 227
EMTShch-656 – 657 227
EMTShch-659 227
EMTShch-660 (ex-*Constanța*), 227
EMTShch-660 (ex-*Jacques Vuccino*), 227
EMTShch-661 – 664 227
Energichnyj 218
Entuziast 247
Etor 268
Evdokiia Vinogradova 260
F. Engel's 38
Fakel sotsializma 252
Fedorov 132
Feliks Dzerzhinskij 194
Feodosiia 217

Finval 198
Fioletov 150
Forel' (Minesweeper), 193
Forel' (Minesweeping boat), 253
Fregat 16
Frunze (*KATShch-565*), 258
Frunze (Minesweeper), 253
Frunze (Minesweeping boat), 213
Fugas 170
Furmanov 203
FY.1724 187
Fyodor Litke 25
Fyodor Mitrofanov 167
G-24 266
G-28 266
G. Chernenko 213
Gafel' 171
Gagara type 196
Gak 171
Garibal'di 165
Garpun 171
Gazokhod
  № 1 (*KT-722*), 249
  № 1 (*T-721*), 266
  № 2 249
  № 22 265
  № 3 266
  № 6 266
  № 6-a 266
  № 69 272
  № 72 272
  № 8 265
  № G-12 266
  № G-16 266
  № G-17 (*T-332*), 265
  № G-17 (*T-832*), 266
  № G-18 266
  № G-22 265
  № G-27 266
  № G-8 266
GE-57 – 58 243
GE-63 243
GE-65 – 66 243
GE-68 – 71 243
Gelendzhik 212
Geroj 248
Geroj Chkalov 151
Gidroakustik 42
Gidrograf 154
Gol'fstrim 29
Golets 135
Gordyj 132
Gorki 259
Gorniak 217
Gornostaj 35
GP-4 210
Grad (*RT-55*), 33
Grad (*RT-82*), 28
Grif 16
Grif 16
Grizodubova 251
Grom (Escort ship), 11
Grom (Minesweeping boat), 248
Gromkij 152
Gromoboj 151

Gromov (Minesweeping boat), 250
Gromov (Patrol boat), 132
Groza (Escort ship), 11
Groza (Minesweeper), 210
Groznyj 28
Gruz 170
Gruzryba № 12 255
I. Papanin 30
Iaguar 16
Iakor' 171
Iamal 260
Iaroslavl' 250
Iasen' 271
Iastreb (Escort ship), 16
Iastreb (Minesweeping boat), 249
Il'inets 259
Imanta 190
Indiga 30
Inzhener (Minesweeper), 221
Inzhener (Submarine hunter), 43
Inzhener Begam 220
Iokoganshchik 218
Iranets 258
Iset' 163
Iskatel' 170
Iskra 264
Iskuriia 264
Iumashev 213
Iupiter 262
Iur'evets 271
Iushar (Minelayer), 159
Iushar (Minesweeper), 260
Iuzhnyj 261
Iva 151
Ivan Borisov 167
Ivan Sladkov 167
Izhorets № 8 – 9 201
Izhorets-3 201
Izhorets-87 202
Izhorets-88 203
Izhorets-92 203
Izotermichka № 7 252
Izotermichka № 9 – 10 252
Izotermichka № 13 252
K-1 – 4 103
K-12 103
K-14 – 16 103
K-18 103
K-25 – 28 103
K-35 103
K-37 103
K-38 103
K-43 103
K-47 103
K-67 – 73 103
K-83 – 84 103
K-92 103
K-99 103
K-107 103
K-112 – 114 103
K-161 – 163 101
K-164 – 165 119
K-166 – 168 101
K-186 – 187 106
K-188 – 190 101

K-191 106
K-192 122
K-193 – 196 93
K-197 119
K-198 123
K-206 – 208 93
K-209 123
K-210 122
K-211 106
K-212 101
K-213 – 218 102
K-219 119
K-220 93
K-221 – 226 102
K-227 106
K-228 102
K-229 93
K-230 120
K-231 – 234 122
K-235 106
K-236 – 238 102
K-239 123
K-240 120
K-241 – 243 102
K-244 120
K-271 – 272 119
K-273 – 274 122
K-276 138
K-277 – 284 102
K-285 (KM-2 type), 102
K-285 (KM-4 type), 106
K-286 – 289 102
K-291 – K-296 102
K-297 – 298 103
K-316 – 318 103
K-319 – 324 106
K-325 – 326 93
K-327 – 331 94
K-332 – 334 119
K-335 122
K-336 – 338 103
K-340 103
K-356 – 357 103
K-358 – 359 106
K-360 103
K-371 – 374 103
K-386 119
K-387 103
K-388 – 389 106
K-390 119
K-391 – 395 121
K-396 – 397 119
K-406 106
K-407 103
K-411 – 413 106
K-421 – 424 106
K-425 – 428 120
K. Marks 38
Kaganovich (AA defence ship), 151
Kaganovich (Patrol boat), 132
Kakhovka 212
Kamynin 151
Kanin 160
Kapitan Voronin 28
Kapsiul' 171

Kareliia 151
Karl Marks 149
Karl Zedin 167
Kasatka (Escort ship), 37
Kasatka (Minesweeping boat), 249
Kashalot 261
Kaspij 270
Kater
  № 1 244
  № 2 244
  № 9 245
  № 10 – 13 245
  № 22 254
  № 28 254
  № 38 254
  № 44 – 45 254
  № 46 255
  № 58 246
  № 79 246
  № 81 246
  № 82 – 85 246
  № 87 246
  № 89 246
  № 91 – 92 246
  № 94 246
  № 97 246
  № 108 246
  № 446 – 448 267
Kater-tral'shchik
  № 13 109
  № 17 105
  № 23 109
  № 25 105
  № 27 – 30 105
  № 31 – 32 273
  № 33 (ex-Rom), 273
  № 33 (KM-4 type), 109
  № 37 (ex-Rom), 273
  № 37 (KM-2 type), 105
  № 38 273
  № 41 – 42 273
  № 43 109
  № 44 98
  № 47 (A class), 114
  № 47 (KM-2 type), 105
  № 49 114
  № 53 (ex-Rom), 273
  № 53 (KM-4 type), 109
  № 53 (Zh type), 267
  № 54 – 56 267
  № 57 (ex-Rom), 273
  № 57 (KM-2 type), 105
  № 57 (Zh type), 267
  № 58 267
  № 60 105
  № 63 109
  № 67 109
  № 73 109
  № 77 109
  № 81 (ex-Rom), 273
  № 81 (R type), 98
  № 82 98
  № 83 (KM-4 type), 109
  № 83 (R type), 98
  № 84 – 86 98

  № 87 (KM-4 type), 109
  № 87 (R type), 98
  № 93 109
  № 97 109
  № 103 – 105 109
  № 107 109
  № 111 109
  № 113 109
  № 115 109
  № 118 109
  № 120 98
  № 121 109
  № 123 109
  № 127 – 129 98
  № 133 109
  № 143 109
  № 150 267
  № 153 109
  № 155 – 156 228
  № 157 (K-15 (M-17) type), 228
  № 157 (ZhS type), 267
  № 158 (K-15 (M-17) type), 228
  № 158 (ZhS type), 267
  № 159 (K-15 (M-17) type), 228
  № 159 (ZhS type), 267
  № 160 – 162 228
  № 163 (K-15 (M-17) type), 228
  № 163 (KATShch № 316), 109
  № 173 109
  № 183 109
  № 193 109
  № 203 110
  № 213 110
  № 223 110
  № 233 110
  № 243 110
  № 253 110
  № 263 110
  № 273 110
  № 283 110
  № 293 110
  № 303 110
  № 311 – 312 229
  № 313 (K-15 (M-17) type), 229
  № 313 (KM-4 type), 110
  № 314 – 315 228
  № 316 229
  № 321 – 326 229
  № 346 – 348 110
  № 373 110
  № 383 110
  № 393 110
  № 403 110
  № 413 110
  № 423 110
  № 433 110
  № 443 110
  № 453 110
  № 463 110
  № 473 110
  № 483 110
  № 493 110
  № 503 110
  № 606 105
  № 620 105

  № 901 110
  № 920 105
  № 921 – 924 105
  № 1103 98
  № 1105 – 1108 98
  № 1304 101
  № 1308 101
  № 1312 101
  № 1401 – 1410 110
  № 1411 – 1416 111
  № 5385 98
  № 6684 – 6685 98
KEMTShch-280 113
KEMTShch-281 – 282 113
KEMTShch-287 – 290 113
KEMTShch-603 274
KEMTShch-931 – 938 273
KEMTShch-940 273
Keri 154
Khadzhibej 225
Khar'kov 213
Khariuzov 261
Kharlov 135
Khasanovets 257
Khenkin 212
Khimik 43
Khiurland 244
Khmelevets 260
Khosta 224
Kiev 255
Kil'ka (Minesweeping boat), 253
Kil'ka (Patrol boat), 132
Kirov (KATShch-566), 258
Kirov (KATShch-602), 264
Kirov (Minesweeper), 199
Kirov (Patrol ship), 20
Kirovets 42
Kit (KT-84), 261
Kit (Minesweeper), 198
Kit (SP-226), 255
Kizil-Su 151
Kiziltash 225
Kizliar 253
KL-13 202
Kliuz 166
Knekht 171
Knipovich 135
Kochegar 43
Kodor 256
Kokkinaki 134
Kolguev 260
Kolguevets 29
Kolkhoznik (Escort ship), 28
Kolkhoznik (Minelayer), 160
Kolomna 29
Komarovets 259
Kombajner 262
Komintern 134
Kommuna 218
Kommunar 265
Kommunist 249
Komsomolets (AA defence ship), 149
Komsomolets (KATShch-150), 263
Komsomolets (KT-268), 249
Komsomolets (Minesweeper), 265

299

Komsomolets (Patrol boat), 136
Komsomolka 136
Kondor 16
Konka 226
Kontr-admiral Iurkovskij 171
Kontr-admiral Khoroshkhin 171
Korall 40
Korall 189
Korshun 16
Kosa 152
Kostroma 210
Kotlassplav № 106 267
Kotlassplav № 132 267
KP-11 119
KP-19 – KP-22 207
KP-42 201
KP-52 202
KP-110 – 111 143
Krab (Escort ship), 198
Krab (Minesweeper), 212
Krab (Minesweeping boat), 269
Krambol 171
Krapivintskij 264
Krasnaia Armiia 264
Krasnoarmeets 198
Krasnoflotets 217
Krasnoznamenets 152
Krasnyj Krym 134
Krasnyj onezhanin 29
Krasnyj rybak 132
Krasnyj vodnik 256
Krenkel' (Minesweeper), 217
Krenkel' (Minesweeping boat), 271
Krenkel' (Patrol boat), 132
Krivobuzanets 260
Krym 258
Krym MRS 263
KT-210 112
KT-231 112
KT-239 112
KT-241 – 247 288
KT-260 – 262 288
KT-265 – 266 112
KT-283 – 285 112
KT-291 – 292 112
KT-294 – 295 112
KT-298 112
KT-349 – 356 112
KT-358 – 360 112
KT-363 112
KT-372 – 375 241
KT-381 – 390 112
KT-520 290
KT-528 – 530 290
KT-534 – 538 290
KT-541 – 543 290
KT-553 – 557 290
KT-577 – 579 290
KT-598 – 599 290
KT-601 – 602 274
KT-664 – 682 112
KT-693 – 700 233
KT-717 98
KT-729 – 733 233
KT-734 – 745 234

KT-805 – 806 290
KT-851 – 855 112
KT-856 – 857 113
KT-860 274
KT-905 – 917 273
KT-939 273
KT-941 – 950 241
KT-952 113
KT-954 – 955 113
KT-958 113
KT-960 113
KT-962 113
KT-965 – 968 113
KT-972 – 979 113
Kuban' 269
Kuguar 16
Kujbyshev 28
Kumyk 253
Kurortnik 223
Kursk 218
Kutuzov 269
Kuznetsk 213
Lajne 37
Lakhtak 261
Lastochka 132
Lastola 133
Lebed' 249
Lebedin 133
Lebedka 197
Lejtenant Shmidt 152
Lenin 198
Leninets (Escort ship), 35
Leninets (Minesweeper), 217
Leningrad (Escort ship), 29
Leningrad (Minesweeper), 213
Lenkoranets 262
Lenvodput' № 12 – 13 201
Lenvodput' № 15 – 16 201
Lenvodput' № 17 202
Leopard 16
LF-150 201
Liapidevskij 215
Liliia 249
Limenda 214
Linek 132
Liubimets 132
Liza Chajkina 245
LK-2 207
LK-13 207
Lomonosov 218
Losos' (Minesweeper), 199
Losos' (Minesweeping boat), 253
LP-19 243
LP-20 244
Luka Pankov 167
Lukomskij 160
Lyotchik 43
M-11 60
M-12 (MO-112), 60
M-12 (SKA № 045), 60
M-13 (SKA № 0155), 60
M-13 (SKA № 0212), 60
M-14 – M-15 60
M. Gor'kij (Minesweeper), 195
M. Gor'kij (Minesweeping boat), 263

Maiachnyj 259
Maiakovskij 220
Majkop 224
Malyj okhotnik
 № 1 56
 № 12 – 29 56
 № 106 – 108 56
 № 113 (MO-4 type), 56
 № 113 (MO-5), 79
 № 114 – 115 56
 № 131 (MO № 123 N), 56
 № 131 (MO № 301 B), 56
 № 131 (MO № 311 B), 56
 № 132 (MO-302), 56
 № 132 (MO-423), 56
 № 132 (MO № 312 B), 56
 № 133 (MO-103), 56
 № 133 (MO-303), 56
 № 133 (MO № 121 N), 56
 № 141 (MO-104), 56
 № 141 (MO-313), 56
 № 141 (MO № 124 N), 56
 № 142 (MO-314), 56
 № 142 (MO-426), 56
 № 142 (MO № 105), 56
 № 143 (MO-4 type B), 56
 № 143 (MO-424), 56
 № 143 (MO № 313 B), 56
 № 153 56
 № 161 – 162 56
 № 163 58
 № 204 58
 № 208 58
 № 209 – 210 58
 № 213 (MO-199), 58
 № 213 (MO-223), 58
 № 214 (MO-214), 58
 № 214 (MO № 208 B), 58
 № 215 – 216 58
 № 227 – 228 58
 № 307 – 310 58
 № 311 (MO-4 type B), 58
 № 311 (VR-21), 58
 № 312 – 313 58
 № 321 – 323 58
 № 351 – 357 91
 № 411 58
 № 504 – 510 60
 zav. № 150 81
Malysh 270
Manych 225
Marat 256
Mariupol' 39
Marksist 130
Mars 256
Marsovyj 41
Marti (Minelayer), 156
Marti (Minesweeping boat), 249
Mary 150
Mashinist 43
Mazuruk 213
MChS-10 – 11 261
Meduza 131
Mekhanik 42
Menzhinskij 209

Meridian 145
Metel' 11
Mezen' (Minesweeper), 218
Mezen' (Minesweeping boat), 250
Mezen' (Netlayer), 163
Mgla 35
MI-8 111
Mikhail Martynov 167
Mikoian 198
Mina 170
Miner 40
Minrep 170
Minsk 218
MO-1 – 6 60
MO-11 – 17 60
MO-18 62
MO-32 – 34 62
MO-114 62
MO-211 81
MO-216 – 221 81
MO-224 – 226 81
MO-229 82
MO-230 (MO-1 class), 116
MO-230 (OD-200 type), 82
MO-231 (MO-1 class), 116
MO-231 (OD-200 type), 82
MO-232 (MO-1 class), 116
MO-232 (OD-200 type), 82
MO-233 (MO-1 class), 116
MO-233 (OD-200 type), 82
MO-234 (MO-1 class), 116
MO-234 (OD-200 type), 82
MO-235 (MO-1 class), 116
MO-235 (OD-200 type), 82
MO-236 (MO-1 class), 116
MO-236 (OD-200 type), 82
MO-237 (MO-1 class), 116
MO-237 (OD-200 type), 82
MO-238 (MO-1 class), 116
MO-238 (OD-200 type), 82
MO-239 (MO-1 class), 116
MO-239 (OD-200 type), 82
MO-240 (MO-1 class), 116
MO-240 (OD-200 type), 82
MO-241 (MO-1 class), 116
MO-241 (OD-200 type), 82
MO-242 (MO-1 class), 116
MO-242 (OD-200 type), 82
MO-243 (MO-1 class), 116
MO-243 (OD-200 type), 82
MO-244 (MO-1 class), 116
MO-244 (OD-200 type), 82
MO-245 (MO-1 class), 116
MO-245 (OD-200 type), 82
MO-246 (MO-1 class), 116
MO-246 (OD-200 type), 82
MO-247 (MO-1 class), 116
MO-247 (OD-200 type), 82
MO-248 (MO-1 class), 116
MO-248 (OD-200 type), 82
MO-249 (MO-1 class), 116
MO-249 (OD-200 type), 83
MO-250 83
MO-321 – 329 83
MO-357 – 359 83

MO-360 84
MO-362 84
MO-368 – 371 84
MO-376 – 379 84
MO-435 – 444 116
MO-445 – 458 117
MO-461 – 462 84
MO-533 – 541 86
MO-543 – 546 87
MO-547 – 548 84
MO-549 – 556 85
MO-558 – 559 85
MO-563 – 567 85
MO-621 – 638 87
Mogilevich 132
Mogilevskij 35
Moguchij 214
Molniia 11
Mologa 163
Molot 150
Molotov (Escort ship), 28
Molotov (Minesweeper), 214
Moriak № 1 215
Moriana 130
Moroz 225
Morzh 261
Moskva (AA defence ship), 149
Moskva (Minesweeper), 214
Motobot
 № 16 243
 № 19 248
 № 22 247
 № 34 – 35 244
 № 50 248
 № 52 248
 № 8 133
 № 85 243
 № 90 248
 № 91 248
 № 111 249
 № 113 248
Motorist 43
Motorybnitsa № 85 254
MRG-14 265
MRG-54 – 55 272
MS № 21 263
MS-11 – 18 262
MS-25 262
MS-27 262
MS-29 262
MS-30 – 31 262
MS-38 – 39 217
MS-67 – 68 262
Mud'iuzhanin 29
Musson (RT-54), 24
Musson (ex-*Sborul*), 33
Mys 260
Mys Voronov 250
MZ-1 207
N. Shchors 137
Nakhimov 256
Nalim 193
Nar'ian-Mar 250
Natsflot 214
Navigator 247

Navodchik 41
Nekrasov 251
Nenets 29
Neperemozhnyj 265
Neptun (Escort ship), 27
Neptun (KT-152), 262
Neptun (KT-179), 256
Neva (Minesweeping boat), 249
Neva (T-845), 220
Neva (T-905), 199
Nikolaj Markin 167
Nikołaj Pozharov 167
NK-1 – 2 131
Nogaets 252
Nokuev 135
Nord 222
Nord-vest 136
Norek 215
Novator 218
Novgorod 248
Novorossijsk 257
Obdorsk 218
Oborona 214
Ochakovskij kanal 212
Odesskij Gorsovet 28
Odinnadtsatyj 245
Ognemetchik 41
Olonka 214
Omchon 261
Onega 163
Operativnyj 250
OPS-1 125
Opyt 254
Orden 135
Ordzhonikidze 209
Orlan 16
Oryol (Escort ship), 16
Oryol (Patrol boat), 132
Oseter 248
Osetr-8 269
OShK-26 111
OShK-28 111
Osipenko 250
Osoaviakhim 29
Ost (Escort ship), 37
Ost (Minesweeper), 222
Ost (Patrol boat), 134
Osyotr 215
Otlichnik 269
Otvazhnyj 248
OV-45 – 46 127
OV-51 – 55 127
OV-61 – 65 127
OV-71 – 75 127
OV-81 – 85 127
OV-91 – 95 127
OV-101 – 107 127
OV-111 – 116 134
OV-121 – 126 127
OV-131 – 136 127
OV-141 – 142 127
OV-143 – 149 128
OV-152 – 156 128
OV-161 – 165 104
OV-211 – 214 108

OV-311 – 316 108
OVR-4 – 11 241
OVR-13 (D-2 type), 241
OVR-13 (R type), 98
OVR-14 – 19 241
OVR-36 244
Ozernoj 214
P-11 146
PAB-1225 – 1228 288
PAB-1229 289
PAB-1271 – 1273 289
Pamiati Kuznetsova 218
Pantera 16
Papanin (KT-809), 258
Papanin (RTShch-55), 213
Paravan 171
Parizhskaia kommuna 38
Partizan 256
Passat (RT-102), 29
Passat (RT-52), 33
Passazhirskij tramvaj № 1 246
Passazhirskij tramvaj № 2 246
Patrokl 212
Patron (Minesweeper), 170
Patron (Netlayer), 165
Pavel Golovin 167
Pavel Khokhriakov 167
Pavel Vinogradov 167
Pavlik Morozov 124
PB-1 – 3 147
Pechorets 30
Peleng 248
Pelengas 131
Pelengator 250
Pelikan 200
Pervenets 269
Pervyj 245
Peshkov 34
Petrash 37
Petrozavodsk 216
PG-1 (Am), 142
PG-1 (Vo), 141
PG-2 (Am), 142
PG-2 (Vo), 141
PG-3 (Am), 142
PG-3 (Vo), 141
PG-4 (Am), 142
PG-4 (Vo), 141
PG-5 (Am), 142
PG-5 (BS), 141
PG-5 (Vo), 141
PG-6 – 7 141
PG-8 (Da), 142
PG-8 (Vo), 141
PG-9 (Da), 142
PG-9 (Vo), 141
PG-10 – 19 141
PG-20 (BS), 141
PG-20 (Vo), 141
PG-21 – 32 141
PG-33 (BS), 141
PG-33 (Da), 142
PG-33 (Vo), 141
PG-34 (BS), 141
PG-34 (Da), 142

PG-34 (Vo), 141
PG-35 (BS), 141
PG-35 (Vo), 141
PG-36 (BS), 141
PG-36 (Da), 142
PG-36 (Vo), 141
PG-37 (BS), 141
PG-37 (Da), 142
PG-37 (Vo), 141
PG-38 (BS), 141
PG-38 (Vo), 141
PG-39 (BS), 141
PG-39 (Da), 142
PG-39 (Vo), 141
PG-40 (BS), 141
PG-40 (Vo), 141
PG-41 (BS), 141
PG-41 (Da), 142
PG-41 (Vo), 141
PG-42 (BS), 141
PG-42 (Da), 142
PG-42 (Vo), 141
PG-43 (BS), 141
PG-43 (Vo), 141
PG-44 (BS), 141
PG-44 (Da), 142
PG-44 (Vo), 141
PG-50 (BS), 141
PG-50 (Da), 142
PG-50 (Dn), 141
PG-51 (BS), 141
PG-51 (Da), 142
PG-51 (Dn), 141
PG-52 (BS), 141
PG-52 (Da), 142
PG-52 (Dn), 141
PG-53 (BS), 141
PG-53 (Da), 142
PG-53 (Dn), 141
PG-54 (BS), 141
PG-54 (Da), 142
PG-54 (Dn), 141
PG-55 (BS), 141
PG-55 (Da), 142
PG-55 (Dn), 141
PG-56 (BS), 141
PG-56 (Da), 142
PG-56 (Dn), 141
PG-57 (BS), 141
PG-57 (Da), 142
PG-57 (Dn), 141
PG-58 (BS), 141
PG-58 (Da), 142
PG-58 (Dn), 141
PG-59 (BS), 141
PG-59 (Da), 142
PG-59 (Dn), 141
PG-60 (BS), 141
PG-60 (Da), 142
PG-60 (Dn), 141
PG-61 (BS), 141
PG-61 (Da), 142
PG-62 – 63 141
PG-65 – 67 141
PG-81 (BS), 141

PG-81 (Da), 142
PG-82 (BS), 141
PG-82 (Da), 142
PG-83 (BS), 141
PG-83 (Da), 142
PG-84 (BS), 141
PG-84 (Da), 142
PG-85 (BS), 141
PG-85 (Da), 142
PG-86 – 90 141
PG-91 (BS), 141
PG-91 (Da), 142
PG-92 (BS), 141
PG-92 (Da), 142
PG-110 141
PG-200 141
PG-201 – 211 142
PG-385 141
PG-427 141
PG-432 141
PG-437 141
PG-587/10 141
PG-1088 141
Piatyj 246
Pikhta 271
Piksha 249
Pilamida 256
Pilot 43
Pina 155
Pinega 250
Pinsk 219
Pioner (EMTShch-61), 217
Pioner (KATShch № 124), 264
Pioner (KATShch-539), 256
PK-3 66
PK-5 66
PK-7 – 13 78
PK-16 – 19 78
PK-23 – 24 78
PK-25 – 27 66
PK-28 – 30 78
PK-33 – 36 78
PK-37 66
PK-38 – 42 78
PK-61 – 66 78
PK-73 – 76 55
PK-77 – 78 66
PK-91 – 102 66
PK-115 52
PK-116 66
PK-117 52
PK-118 – 123 66
PK-124 52
PK-125 66
PK-126 – 128 52
PK-129 – 130 66
PK-131 – 138 68
PK-139 51
PK-140 52
PK-141 – 148 68
PK-171 – 177 52
PK-200 – 215 68
PK-216 52
PK-217 53
PK-218 – 219 68

PK-220 – 221 70
PK-224 92
PK-225 – 231 53
PK-232 70
PK-233 – 235 78
PK-236 – 237 53
PK-238 – 239 70
PK-251 – 252 70
PK-261 – 262 53
Plastun 194
Plavuchaia artillerijskaia batereia
 № 4 144
 № 97 – 100 144
Plavuchaia zenitnaia batereia
 № 3 147
 № 588 146
 № 614 – 615 146
 № 616 – 618 147
 № 1220 – 1224 288
 № 1230 – 1231 290
 № 1232 146
 № 1233 290
Plekhanov 214
PMSh № 121 263
Podsekatel' 170
Podtyolkov 219
Pogranichnik 271
Polianka 137
Poliarnik 210
Poliarnyj 28
Polius (AA battery), 145
Polius (Minesweeping boat), 256
Polius (Patrol boat), 132
Poltoratsk 149
Poluglisser
 № 1 – 2 141
 № 18 – 23 142
 № 62 – 87 142
 № 101 – 132 142
 № 668 141
Pomoshchnik 268
Portovik 245
Postavshchik 219
Poti 257
Povodets 249
PP-1 105
Priboj 258
Primorets (Minesweeping boat), 261
Primorets (Patrol boat), 133
Pripiat' 265
Profintern (EMTShch-88), 217
Profintern (T-902), 198
Profsoiuz 165
Progregss 264
Progress 265
Proizvodstvennik 247
Provodnik 170
Prozhektorist 41
PS-1 (EMTShch-604), 244
PS-1 (ex-PSh-13), 126
PS-1 (SK-601), 124
PS-1 (SK-77), 126
PS-2 (ex-Fin), 138
PS-2 (ex-PSh-14), 126
PS-2 (KATShch-547), 244

PS-2 (SK-602), 125
PS-3 (ex-Fin), 138
PS-3 (ex-PSh-8), 126
PS-3 (SK-603), 125
PS-4 (BS), 126
PS-4 (PS-230), 126
PS-4 (SK-604), 125
PS-5 (Cs), 130
PS-5 (ex-K-50), 126
PS-5 (N), 125
PS-6 (Cs), 130
PS-6 (ex-K-10), 126
PT-2 124
PT-4 – 10 124
PT-12 124
Purga (Escort ship), 11
Purga (NKVD Patrol ship), 22
Pushkin (Escort ship), 38
Pushkin (Minesweeping boat), 264
Puzanok (Minesweeping boat), 262
Puzanok (Patrol boat), 132
PVO-9 243
PVO-10 – 15 286
PVO-16 – 27 287
PVO-41 98
PVO-61 – 64 287
PVO-65 – 80 288
PVO-1270 146
Rabochij 28
Radist 41
Raskova 133
Ratsionalizator 245
Raz"ezdnoj kater
 № 0115 – 0116 143
 № 0215 – 0216 143
 № 0306 143
 № 0309 143
 № 0315 – 0316 143
 № 0415 – 0416 143
 № 0515 – 0516 143
 № 0615 – 0616 143
 № 0715 – 0716 143
 № 0815 – 0816 143
 № 0915 – 0916 143
 № 7 143
 № 116 244
 № 1015 – 1016 143
 № 1115 – 1116 143
 № 1215 – 1216 143
 № 1315 – 1316 143
 № 1415 – 1416 143
Razvedchik № 12 261
Reka 39
Rekord 151
Reshitel'nyj 261
Revoliutsiia (Minesweeper), 217
Revoliutsiia (Trawler), 28
Revvoensovet 263
Rif 132
Ristna 161
RK-1 135
RO-11 258
RO-13 258
Rodina 247
Rolik 197

Rot-Front 130
RS-1 133
RS-2 250
RS-5 250
RS-6 133
RSK-1 – 5 143
RSK-7 – 10 143
RTShch-7 – 8 229
RTShch-9 – 12 230
RTShch-13 – 17 235
RTShch-18 – 43 230
RTShch-44 – 48 235
RTShch-101 – 102 235
RTShch-103 – 112 230
RTShch-113 231
RTShch-118 231
RTShch-119 – 120 230
RTShch-133 230
RTShch-134 – 145 231
RTShch-146 – 152 232
RTShch-153 (KT-151), 232
RTShch-153 (KT-153), 232
RTShch-154 232
RTShch-170 – 174 235
RTShch-187 – 191 232
RTShch-205 – 206 234
RTShch-212 – 213 235
RTShch-214 – 219 236
RTShch-220 – 223 234
RTShch-491 – 500 234
Rubin 19
Rulevoj 39
Rybak 269
Rybets 199
Rym 171
Rynda 135
Rys' 16
S. A. Levanevskij 26
S. Kirov 263
S. Ordzhonikidze 159
Sakko 210
Samosdelets 259
Sapfir 19
Saratov 28
Sary-Kamyshi 226
Saturn 262
SB-1 – 4 275
SB-58 165
Sejner
 № 1 – 3 251
 № 4 256
 № 5 (Minesweeping boat), 256
 № 5 (Patrol boat), 134
 № 6 (KATShch-183), 256
 № 6 (KATShch-211), 256
 № 6 (Patrol boat), 134
 № 7 256
 № 11 (KATShch № 91), 261
 № 11 (KT-552), 256
 № 12 (KATShch № 92), 261
 № 12 (KT-544), 256
 № 13 – 14 261
 № 83 152
Sel'd' 134
Semyon Pelikhov 167

Semyon Roshal' 167
Sergej Kirov (BTShch-11), 216
Sergej Kirov (Mine hulk), 158
Sergej Kirov (TShch № 74), 209
Sergej Kostrikov 220
Sergej Shuvalov 167
Sergo Ordzhonikidze 30
Serov 254
Setepod"emnik 251
Sevastopol' 27
Sever 210
Severnyj (Minesweeper), 29
Severnyj (Patrol boat), 135
Sevgosrybtrest 33
Sevriuga 268
Sevtranzitsplav № 24 248
Sevtranzitsplav № 25 248
Sh-1 – 2 141
Shamaia 257
Shaumian 149
Shchit 170
Shchors (Escort ship), 202
Shchors (Minesweeper), 211
Shestoj 246
Ship 132
Shkiv 171
Shkval (Escort ship), 11
Shkval (Minesweeping boat), 257
Shkval (Tug), 206
Shmidt (KATShch-541), 256
Shmidt (KEMTShch-368), 264
Shpil' 171
Shtag 171
Shtil' (Escort ship), 25
Shtil' (Minesweeping boat), 260
Shtil' (Patrol boat), 125
Shtil' (Trawler), 33
Shtorm (Escort ship), 11
Shtorm (Miesweeping boat), 257
Shturman (Escort ship), 39
Shturman (Submarine hunter), 42
Shturval 132
Shturval'nyj 219
Shuia 214
Sig 249
Signal'shchik 41
Sigovets 216
Sil'nyj 157
Sivash 225
Sivuch 269
SK-105 137
SK-109 137
SK-117 – 118 128
SK-127 – 128 128
SK-210 119
SK-237 – 239 128
SK-250 – 258 117
SK-265 – 270 140
SK-301 – 302 293
SK-318 86
SK-418 86
SK-501 – 520 86
SK-521 (B), 86
SK-521 (N), 117
SK-522 (B), 86

SK-522 (N), 117
SK-523 (B), 86
SK-523 (N), 117
SK-524 (B), 86
SK-524 (N), 117
SK-525 (B), 86
SK-525 (N), 117
SK-526 (B), 86
SK-526 (N), 117
SK-527 (B), 86
SK-527 (N), 117
SK-528 – 532 86
SK-533 – 542 86
SK-752 – 758 139
SK-761 – 793 128
SK-794 – 809 129
SK-812 – 840 129
SK-841 130
SK-848 – 855 130
SKA-1 – 3 139
Skat 249
Skumbriia (Minesweeping boat), 257
Skumbriia (Patrol boat), 136
Smelyj (KT-73), 261
Smelyj (Minesweeping boat B), 249
Smena 29
Smerch 11
Smolensk 254
Snabzhenets-1 248
Snabzhenets-2 248
Sneg 11
Sobol' 35
Soiuzpromrybsnab 269
Sokol (Minesweeper), 196
Sokol (Patrol boat), 132
Sokol' 16
Som (T-83), 207
Som (TShch № 122), 215
Sosnovets 160
Sovetskaia Rossiia 224
Sovkombajn 219
SP-48 – 49 143
SP-54 143
Spartak (AA defence ship), 148
Spartak (Minesweeping boat), 257
SPGRT-1 269
SPGRT-3 269
Spirin 258
Stakhanov 152
Stakhanovets (KATShch-428), 271
Stakhanovets (KT-154), 263
Stalin 263
Stalinets 269
Stalingrad (Minesweeper), 213
Stalingrad (Minesweeping boat B), 260
Staritsa 218
Stepan Gradushko 167
Stepan Razin 216
Steregushchij 218
Storozhevoj kater
  № 013 – 014 64
  № 017 – 022 64
  № 023 (SKA № 0131), 64
  № 023 (SKA № 094), 64
  № 024 (MO-36), 64

№ 024 (SKA № 051), 64
№ 025 – 028 64
№ 031 64
№ 033 64
№ 034 79
№ 043 64
№ 052 – 053 64
№ 054 79
№ 058 64
№ 061 79
№ 062 – 063 64
№ 071 64
№ 091 64
№ 095 64
№ 099 – 0101 64
№ 0111 64
№ 0121 – 0122 64
№ 0132 64
№ 0165 64
№ 0175 64
№ 0317 81
№ 0336 81
№ 0340 81
№ 0354 – 0356 81
№ 0361 80
№ 0367 81
№ 0375 80
№ 0380 81
№ 0385 81
№ 0389 80
№ 0393 81
№ 0398 80
№ 0512 79
№ 1 123
№ 102 108
№ 107 – 108 108
№ 110 108
№ 112 108
№ 12 104
№ 14 (A class), 113
№ 14 (KM-2 type), 104
№ 15 104
№ 16 108
№ 18 104
№ 2 (BKM-70 type), 123
№ 2 (KLT type), 243
№ 3 (BKM-70 type), 123
№ 3 (KLT type), 243
№ 4 – 5 123
№ 21 – 23 104
№ 25 104
№ 26 (KM-2 type), 104
№ 26 (KM-4 type), 108
№ 27 – 28 104
№ 31 – 32 108
№ 38 104
№ 48 104
№ 58 108
№ 68 108
№ 78 108
№ 88 108
№ 93 – 95 108
№ 98 (KT-98), 108
№ 98 (SK-98), 108
№ 99 108

№ 311 – 317 96
№ 321 – 322 96
№ 323 (KATShch № 1208), 96
№ 323 (ex-MU-57), 96
№ 324 (KATShch № 1209), 96
№ 324 (NS-5), 96
№ 325 – 327 96
№ 361 – 367 96
№ 411 – 416 96
№ 417– 427 98
№ 602 – 607 105
№ 617 – 618 138
№ 619 – 626 125
№ 661 – 667 114
№ 1012 64
№ 1112 64
№ 1212 64
№ 1312 64
№ 1412 64
№ 1812 64
№ 1512 64
№ 1612 64
№ 1712 64
Stratostat 152
Strela 170
Strelok 43
Stroevoi 43
Stroitel' 152
Struia 250
Sudak 257
Sukhona 163
Sukhumi (AA defence ship), 130
Sukhumi (Netlayer), 165
Sulev 24
Surkovets 259
Surop 161
Suvorov 134
Sverdlov 252
Sviazist 41
Svir' 249
Svoj trud 268
Syomga 198
T-11 – 13 141
T-21 – 23 141
T-31 – 33 141
T-41 – 43 141
T-51 – 53 141
T-61 – 63 141
T-71 – 73 141
T-83 – 85 141
T-101 – 107 187
T-108 – 110 188
T-111 – 120 182
T-121 – 122 188
T-181 – 192 185
T-215 – 216 171
T-218 171
T-220 171
T-222 (Fugas class), 171
T-222 (Project 253-L), 179
T-223 (Fugas class), 171
T-223 (Project 253-L), 179
T-224 – 249 179
T-271 – 285 182
T-331 – 336 182

T-337 – 339 183	№ *81 – 85* 278	*Triumnyj* 43	*Visliana* 220
T-351 – 364 178	№ *86 – 87* 279	*Tros* 170	*Vladimir Polukhin* 167
T-365 – 369 179	№ *88* 280	*Tsentavr* 268	*Vladimir Trefolev* 167
T-370 – 377 178	№ *89* 280	*Tsiklon* (Escort ship), 11	*Vobla* 262
T-378 – 385 179	№ *91 – 95* 278	*Tsiklon* (Minesweeping boat), 257	*Vodnik* 248
T-386 – 389 178	№ *96 – 98* 279	*Tuapse* 257	*Vodop'ianov* 38
T-390 – 391 180	№ *99 – 100* 281	*Tucha* (Escort ship), 11	*Vojkov* 39
T-413 – 415 171	№ *101 – 103* 278	*Tucha* (Minesweeper), 210	*Volga* 249
T-434 – 435 180	№ *104 – 105* 279	*Tula* 268	*Volgo-Don* 256
T-439 – 441 180	№ *106 – 108* 280	*Tura* 163	*Volkhov* 249
T-459 – 470 180	№ *109 – 111* 281	*Turbinist* 43	*Volodarskij* 145
T-472 – 479 180	№ *210 – 211* 281	*Turist* 223	*Voron* 16
T-521 – 527 184	№ *265 – 269* 281	*Udarnik* (AA defence ship), 152	*Voron* 16
T-588 – 604 184	№ *276* 281	*Udarnik* (Minesweeper, B), 166	*Voronin* 249
T-605 – 607 185	№ *280* 281	*Udarnik* (Minesweeping boat), 246	*Voroshilov* 38
T-608 184	№ *284* 281	*Udarnik* (*RTShch-61*), 247	*Voroshilovsk* 157
T-609 – 611 185	№ *310 – 311* 281	*Udarnik* (*T-136*), 210	*Vos'moj* 245
T-651 – 655 191	№ *410* 281	*UK-5 – 6* 247	*Voskhod* 151
T-666 – 669 191	№ *510* 281	*UK-100* 215	*Vozhak* 132
T-670 227	№ *610 – 611* 281	*Ul'ianov* 216	*VR-1 – 4* 243
T-671 – 679 191	№ *710* 281	*Uragan* (Escort ship), 11	*Vtoroj* 218
T-680 (ex-Ger), 227	№ *711* 282	*Uragan* (*KATShch-436*), 271	*VVS-65* 207
T-680 (ex-*KFK-582*), 191	№ *810 – 811* 282	*Uragan* (*KATShch-579*), 257	*Vyborg* 268
T-685 – 694 192	№ *910 – 911* 282	*Ural* 28	*Vychegda* 163
Taganrog 256	№ *1010 – 1011* 282	*Ural'sk* 268	*Vychegdasplav* № *5* 267
Tajfun (Escort ship), 11	№ *1111* 282	*Uran* 37	*Vychegdasplav* № *25* 267
Tajfun (Minesweeping boat), 257	№ *1211* 282	*V-3* 265	*Vyksa* 220
Tajfun (Patrol boat), 135	№ *1311* 282	*V-6* 265	*Vzryv* (*B-1*), 248
Tajfun № *2* 257	№ *1411* 282	*V-10* 265	*Vzryv* (*T-410*), 171
Tajmen'-10 269	№ *1511* 282	*V-11* 266	*Vzryvatel'* 170
Tajmyr 260	*Teodor Nette* 158	*V-14 – 18* 266	*Zapal* 166
Talovets 152	*Terek* 194	*V-23 – 24* 265	*Zaria* (AA battery), 145
Tarta 253	*Tigr* 16	*V-25* 266	*Zaria* (Escort ship), 34
Tat 253	*Timanets* 250	*V-26* 265	*Zaria* (Minelayer), 160
Tatarin 151	*Timiriazev* 151	*V-27* 266	*Zariad* 170
Tbilisi (Escort ship), 29	*Timofej Kopejkin* 268	*V-34* 265	*Zarnitsa* 11
Tbilisi (Minesweeping boat), 269	*Timofej Uliantsev* 167	*V-36 – 39* 265	*Zashchitnik* 170
Tekhnik (Escort ship), 38	*Tiulen'* (Minesweeper), 215	*V-42* 265	*Zasol'shchik* 198
Tekhnik (Submarine hunter), 43	*Tiulen'* (Minesweeping boat), 251	*V-44 – 47* 265	*Zenit* 146
Tel'man 148	*Tobol'sk* 158	*V-48* 266	*Zenitchik* 40
Telegrafist 41	*Tomsk* 158	*V-51* 266	*Zh-14* 269
Temir 258	*Topaz* 40	*V-66* 272	*Zh-17* 269
Temriuk 258	*Toros* 24	*V-68* 272	*Zh-19 – 21* 269
Tender	*Torpedist* 40	*V. Chkalov* 263	*Zhdanov* (Minesweeper), 30
№ *11 – 15* 276	*Tovarishch* 124	*V'iuga* 11	*Zhdanov* (Minesweeping boat), 263
№ *16 – 18* 279	*Tovarishch Chapaev* 217	*V'iun* 132	*Zheliabov* 217
№ *19* 280	*Tovarishch Chkalov* 255	*Vaer* 197	*Zhemchug* 19
№ *21 – 25* 276	*Tral* (Minesweeper), 170	*Vajndlo* 154	*Zhuravlyov* 213
№ *26 – 28* 279	*Tral* (Trawler), 197	*Vantsetti* 210	*Ziujd-Vest* 264
№ *29* 280	*Tral'shchik*	*Vasilij Gromov* 167	*ZM-11* 161
№ *31 – 35* 276	№ *01 – 05* 221	*Vecherkovich* 219	*ZM-12 – 17* 130
№ *36 – 38* 279	№ *1 – 2* 189	*Vega* 264	*ZM-21* 161
№ *39* 280	№ *3 – 5* 188	*Vekha* 170	*ZM-22 – 27* 130
№ *41 – 45* 277	№ *18 – 19* 212	*Velikan* 132	*ZM-31* 161
№ *46 – 48* 279	*Tralbarzha*	*Venera* (Minesweeping boat), 257	*ZM-32 – 37* 130
№ *49* 280	№ *201 – 203* 218	*Venera* (Patrol boat), 132	*ZM-41* 161
№ *51 – 55* 277	№ *344 – 346* 218	*Verp* 171	*ZM-42 – 47* 130
№ *56 – 58* 279	№ *398 – 410* 218	*Vest* 263	*Zmej* 221
№ *59* 280	*Tralmejster* 198	*Veter* 25	*Zubastyj* 261
№ *61 – 65* 277	*Tramvaj*	*Viatka* 163	*Zubr* 219
№ *66 – 68* 279	№ *2* 245	*Vidlitsa* 214	
№ *69* 280	№ *6* 245	*Viesturs* 190	* The full Index including ex-names,
№ *71 – 75* 278	№ *7* 246	*Vikhr'* 11	renamings, cross-indexes, names in ship
№ *76 – 78* 279	№ *10* 246	*Viliuj* 262	histories will be found in Vol III.
№ *79* 280	*Transport* 220	*Virsajtis* 189	

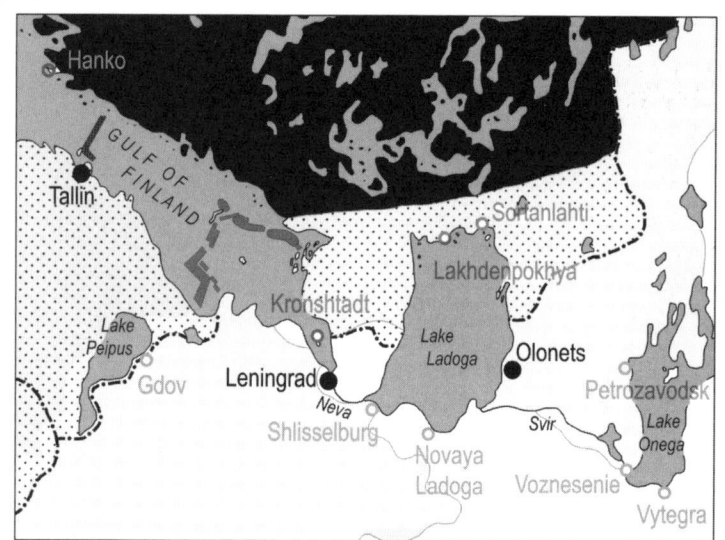

BALTIC and adjoining areas

Location	Facility
Leningrad (Baltic)	Admiralty / A. Marti Works (№ 194)
	Baltijskij Works / Ordzonikidze (№ 189)
	Izhora Yd (№ 363)
	Kanonerski Works
	New Admiralty / Sudomekh (№ 196)
	NKVD Yard (№ 5)
	Petrozavod (№ 370)
	Severnaia Yard / Zdanov Works (№ 190)
Olonets (Lake Ladoga)	Lodejnopl'ska Yard
Tallinn (Baltic)	Naval Shiprepair Yard

ARCTIC

Location	Facility
Kotlas (river Dvina)	Limendskaya Yard
Molotovsk (White Sea)	Severnoe Plant (№ 402)
Murmansk (Barents Sea)	Murmansk Yard
Syktyvkar (river Vychegda)	Vychegda Yard

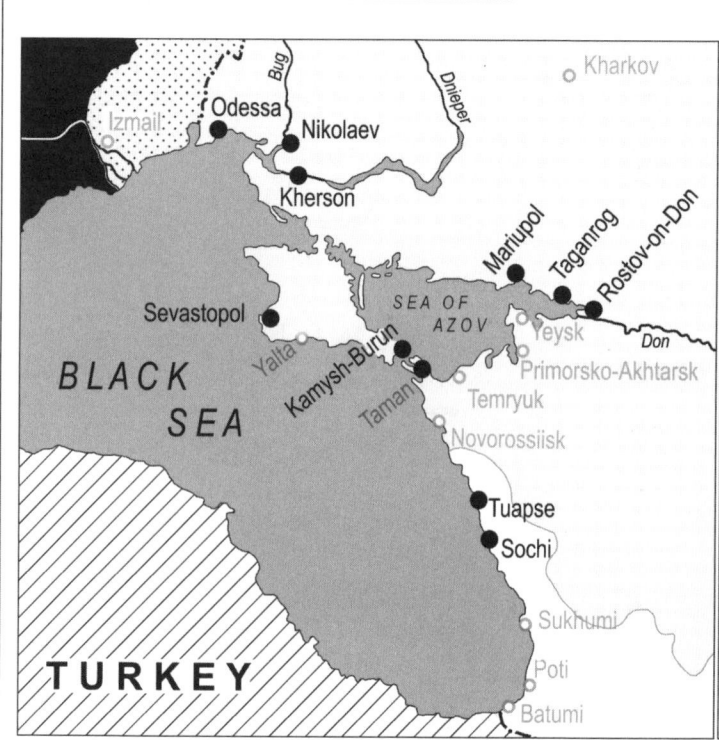

MOSCOW area

Khimki	Chkalov Works (№ 84)
Moscow	MSV (Moskovskaia Yd)
Tushino	№ 445 Works

river DNIEPER

Location	Facility
Kiev	Iuzhnorski Works
	Sukhomlina Yd / Leninskaia kuznitsa (№ 300, later № 302)

BLACK SEA and adjoining areas

Location	Facility
Kamysh-Burun (Sea of Azov)	Kamysh-Burun Works (№ 532)
Kherson (river Dnieper)	Dokstroj (№ 70)
	Kherson Yard
	Komintern Yard (№ 144)
Mariupol (Sea of Azov)	Mariupol Works
Nikolaev (Black Sea)	Naval / A. Marti Works (№ 198, later № 444)
	Russud / 61 Kommunara Works (№ 200, later № 445)
Odessa (Black Sea)	A. Marti Works
Rostov-on-Don (river Don)	Krasnyj Flot
Sevastopol (Black Sea)	Admiralty / Ordzhonikidze Works (№ 201, later № 497)
Sochi (Black Sea)	Lazarevska Yard
Taganrog (Sea of Azov)	Taganrog Works
Tuapse (Black Sea)	Dzerzhinski Works